The Four Gospels

A Guide to Their Historical Background, Characteristic Differences, and Timeless Significance

William S. Stob

THE FOUR GOSPELS ::

A Guide to Their Historical Background, Characteristic
Differences, and Timeless Significance

AMBASSADOR INTERNATIONAL
GREENVILLE, SOUTH CAROLINA & BELFAST, NORTHERN IRELAND

THE FOUR GOSPELS

The publisher has acknowledged copyright holders for various quotations within this book. These quotations comply with the copyright principle of fair comment or fair usage.

All Scripture references are from the King James Version of the Bible with the exception of those that might appear within a quoted source or otherwise noted.

ISBN: 978-1-932307-75-7

Cover Design & Page Layout by
David Siglin of A&E Media

Published by the Ambassador Group

Ambassador International
427 Wade Hampton Blvd.
Greenville, SC 29609, USA
www.emeraldhouse.com

Ambassador Productions Ltd.
Providence House
Ardenlee Street
Belfast
BT6 8QJ
Northern Ireland
www.ambassador_productions.com

The colophon is a trademark of Ambassador

This book is dedicated to

Pastor Donald E. Weiss,

friend and role model, whose life is characterized by devotion to Christ, obedience to Scripture, and faithfulness in service.

Contents at a Glance

Table of Contents

List of Illustrations

INTRODUCTION

THE PURPOSE FROM THE BEGINNING

For there is hope of a tree, if it be cut down,
that it will sprout again, and that the
tender branch thereof will not cease.

JOB 14:7

It entered into the purpose of God from the beginning, to give the divine religion of the Christian revelation to all mankind. The great commission sent the Apostles to preach the Gospel to every creature. In its fulfillment it required just so many and just such Gospels to meet the wants of the world of the apostolic age in commending Jesus to all men as the Savior from sin.[1]

-D. S. Gregory, *Why Four Gospels?*

The four canonical Gospels are the greatest books in the world. Perhaps we realize this most easily if we imagine ourselves deprived of them. Suppose that these four had shared the fate of the "many" known to St. Luke, and that every copy of them had perished. Eagerly we should scrutinize the remaining New Testament books, in the vain hope of deducing from them the work, the words, the character of Jesus Christ. We should learn, indeed, that He was betrayed, instituted the eucharist on the night of betrayal, was crucified, rose from the dead, was seen of many witnesses. Beyond these bare statements we should know practically nothing. Of the Ascension alone we should possess an account, supplied by a few sentences in the Acts. That our Lord had brought a new super-natural power into the world would be evident from the amazing growth of the Church. But our guesses concerning the nature of that power, and of the way in which it became operative, must have gone hopelessly astray. Lacking the Gospels, who could have imagined such deeds and such teaching as are described in their pages? Whether or no we count ourselves Christians, we cannot escape the influence of the Gospel ideal upon thought and conduct. And, as Christians, while we might still have without the Gospels a Lord to reverence, we should not have a Friend to love. The four little books can be given us in perhaps a hundred and fifty pages of print. They can be read from start to finish in a few hours. Yet they have shaped history to a degree almost impossible to exaggerate. As the Bible is incomparably the greatest collection of writings, so are the Gospels the supreme treasure of the Bible.[2]

-Anthony C. Deane, *How to Understand the Gospels*

---

[1] D. S. Gregory, *Why Four Gospels? Or, the Gospel for All the World* (New York: Funk & Wagnalls, Publishers, 1890), 343.

[2] Anthony C. Deane, *How to Understand the Gospels* (New York: Harper & Brothers Publishers, 1929), 1-2.

Figure 0-1. Holman Hunt: The Light of the World

The Synoptic Gospels portray Jesus Christ in His three-fold office of Prophet (Mark), Priest (Luke), and King (Matthew). The Gospel of John, by contrast, presents the Lord as *"the true Light, which lighteth every man that cometh into the world"* (1:9). These four unique aspects of Christ's ministry are represented in this masterpiece by Holman Hunt (1827-1910).

Jesus is portrayed at the door of the human heart, dressed as Prophet (the white robe), Priest (the breastplate), and King (the crown of gold with the thorns). He had approached in the night-time, and brings a two-fold light: the light from Christ's face (which reveals the hope of salvation), and the lantern (representing the light of conscience). The light falls on the door with the rusty hinges, the weeds, and an apple—all of which symbolize the sin of man.

CHAPTER ONE

The Question: Why Four Gospels?

As the children of Israel were nearing the end of their forty-year ordeal in the wilderness, Moses brought them to Moab, where the twelve tribes were to receive instructions for the partitioning of the Promised Land of Canaan. Before arriving on the Plains of Moab, however, the Israelites stopped at Kadesh-Barnea, where in addition to the report of the spies and the rebellion of Korah, there was this startling announcement to the tribe of Levi:

> *And the Lord spake unto Aaron, Thou shalt have no inheritance in their land, neither shalt thou have any part among them: I am thy part and thine inheritance among the children of Israel.* NUM. 18:20

Whereas some members of the priestly tribe of Levi might have felt that they were being short-changed, so to speak, God had, in fact, by those words made them richer than all their brethren, "richer than all the kings and rajas who have ever lived in the world. And there is a spiritual principle here, a principle still valid for every priest of the Most High God."[1] Dr. A. W. Tozer explained this principle as follows:

> The man who has God for his treasure has all things in One. Many ordinary treasures may be denied him, or if he is allowed to have them, the enjoyment of them will be so tempered that they will never be necessary to his happiness. Or if he sees them go, one by one, he will scarcely feel a sense of loss, for having the Source of all things he has in One all satisfaction, all pleasure, all delight. Whatever he may lose he has actually lost nothing, for he now has it all in One, and he has it purely, legitimately, and forever.[2]

Unfortunately, many of God's children do not appreciate the treasure they have inherited through Christ. "Tragically, many Christians today have set their affections on the temporal things of this world, exchanging their great privilege of knowing God better for that which is mundane."[3] But God Himself rebukes that kind of attitude:

> *Thus saith the Lord, Let not the wise man glory in his wisdom, neither let the mighty man glory in his might, let not the rich man glory in his riches: But let him that glorieth glory in this, that he understandeth and knoweth me. . . .* JER. 9:23-24A

The Importance of the Life of Christ

A study of the life of Jesus Christ, *"who is the image of the invisible God"* (Col. 1:15a), should be the desire of every born-again believer, since "knowing God is the essence of being a Christian."[4] Recording the high-priestly prayer of our Lord, the Apostle John wrote: *"And this is life eternal, that they might know thee the only true God, and Jesus Christ, whom thou hast sent"* (John 17:3). The Apostle Paul said, *"I count all things but loss for the excellency of the knowledge of Christ Jesus my Lord"* (Phil. 3:8a).

Not only sincere believers, but secular writers as well have recognized and acknowledged the monumental importance of the life of Christ. French historian, philosopher, and prolific writer, Ernest Renan (1823-1892), stated:

> The principal event in the history of the world is the revolution by which the noblest portions of humanity have forsaken the ancient religions, which are

classed together under the vague name of Paganism, for a religion founded on the Divine Unity, the Trinity, and the Incarnation of the Son of God. Nearly a thousand years were required to achieve this conversion. The new religion itself took at least three hundred years in its formation. But the origin of the revolution in question is a historical event which happened in the reigns of Augustus and Tiberius. At that time there lived a man of supreme personality, who, by his bold originality, and by the love which he was able to inspire, became the object, and the settled direction, of the future faith of mankind.[5]

Comparing the life of Socrates to that of Jesus Christ, the famous French philosopher and social theorist, Jean Jacques Rousseau (1712-1778), admitted:

What an infinite disproportion there is between them! Socrates, dying without pain or ignominy, easily supported his character to the last; and, if this easy death had not crowned his life, it might have been doubted whether Socrates, with all his wisdom, was anything more than a mere sophist. He invented, it is said, the theory of ethics. Others, however, had before put them into practice: he had only to say, therefore, what they had done, and to reduce their examples to precepts. Aristides had been just before Socrates defined justice. Leonides had given up his life for his country before Socrates declared patriotism to be a duty. The Spartans were a sober people before Socrates recommended sobriety. Before he had even defined virtue, Greece abounded in virtuous men. But where could Jesus learn, among his contemporaries, that pure and sublime morality of which he only has given us both precept and example? The greatest wisdom was made known among the most bigoted fanaticism; and the simplicity of the most heroic virtues did honour to the vilest people on earth. The death of Socrates, peacefully philosophizing among friends, appears the most agreeable that one could wish: that of Jesus, expiring in agonies, abused, insulted, and accused by a whole nation, is the most horrible that one could fear. Socrates, indeed, in receiving the cup of poison, blessed the weeping executioner who administered it; but Jesus, amidst excruciating tortures, prayed for his merciless tormentors. "Yes, if the life and death of Socrates were those of a sage, the life and death of Jesus are those of a God."[6]

Commenting on the life of Christ, the great military genius, Napoleon Bonaparte (1769-1821), said:

Everything in him astonishes me. His spirit overawes me, and his will confounds me. Between him and whoever else in the world there is no possible term of comparison. He is truly a being by himself. His ideas and his sentiments, the truth which he announces, his manner of convincing, are not explained either by human organization or by the nature of things.

His birth, and the history of his life; the profundity of his doctrine, which grapples the mightiest difficulties, and which is of those difficulties the most admirable solution; his gospel, his apparition, his empire, his march across the ages and the realms—everything is for me a prodigy, a mystery insoluble, which plunges me into reveries which I cannot escape; a mystery which is there before my eyes; a mystery which I can neither deny nor explain. . . .

His religion is a revelation from an intelligence which certainly is not that of man. There is there a profound originality which has created a series of words and of maxims before unknown. Jesus borrowed nothing from our science. One can absolutely find nowhere, but in him alone, the imitation of the example of his life. He is not a philosopher, since he advances by miracles; and, from the commencement, his disciples worshipped him. He persuaded them far more by an appeal to the heart than by any display of method and of logic. Neither did he impose upon them any preliminary studies, or any knowledge of letters. All his religion consists in believing.

In fact, the sciences and philosophy avail nothing for salvation; and Jesus came into the world to reveal the mysteries of heaven and the laws of the spirit. Also he has nothing to do but with the soul; and to that alone he brings his gospel. The soul is sufficient for him, as he is sufficient for the soul. Before him, the soul was nothing. Matter and time were masters of the world. At his voice, everything returns to order. Science and philosophy become secondary. The soul has reconquered its sovereignty. All scholastic scaffolding falls as an edifice ruined, before one single word—faith.[7]

Although never a religious man, the celebrated British philosopher and author, John Stuart Mill (1806-1873), wrote:

> Above all, the most valuable part of the effect on the character which Christianity has produced by holding up in a Divine Person a standard of excellence and a model for imitation, is available even to the absolute unbeliever, and can never more be lost to humanity. For it is Christ, rather than God, whom Christianity has held up to believers as the pattern of perfection for humanity. It is the God incarnate, more than the God of the Jews or nature, who being idealized has taken so great and salutary a hold on the modern mind. And whatever else may be taken away from us by rational criticism, Christ is still left; a unique figure, not more unlike all his precursors than all his followers, even those who had direct benefit of his personal teaching.[8]

Irish historian, William Edward Hartpole Lecky (1838-1903), who won international recognition with his *History of European Morals from Augustus to Charlemagne* (1869), noted:

> If Christianity was remarkable for its appeals to the selfish or interested side of our nature, it was far more remarkable for the empire it attained over disinterested enthusiasm. The Platonist exhorted men to imitate God; the Stoic, to follow reason; the Christian, to the love of Christ. The later Stoics had often united their notions of excellence in an ideal sage, and Epictetus had even urged his disciples to set before them some man of surpassing excellence, and to imagine him continually near them; but the utmost the Stoic ideal could become was a model for imitation, and the admiration it inspired could never deepen into affection.
>
> It was reserved for Christianity to present to the world an ideal character, which through all the changes of eighteen centuries has inspired the hearts of men with an impassioned love, has shown itself capable of acting on all ages, nations, temperaments, and conditions, has been not only the highest pattern of virtue, but the strongest incentive to its practice, and has exercised so deep an influence that it may be truly said that the simple record of three short

years of active life has done more to regenerate and to soften mankind than all the disquisitions of philosophers and all the exhortations of moralists.[9]

Another nineteenth-century scholar, F. V. N. Painter, who wrote *A History of Education* (1886), admitted:

> The life of Christ, apart from its religious significance in the world's redemption, is well worth a careful study. It is now . . . nineteen centuries since his birth. During this vast period, the world has moved forward in its gigantic process of development. The sum of human knowledge has been immeasurably increased, new arts and sciences have arisen, yet the life of Christ stands forth in unapproachable beauty. The greatest minds of modern times, with the docility of the Galilean fishermen, have paid him the tribute of reverent admiration.[10]

One of the great minds of modern times was the highly revered poet and playwright, Johann Wolfgang von Goethe (1749-1832). He was to Germany what Shakespeare was to England—the country's greatest literary genius. The crowning achievement of Goethe's long life was the dramatic masterpiece, *Faust* (first part, 1808; second, 1832). In this drama Goethe's Faust makes a compact with the devil because he genuinely desires to extend the boundaries of his knowledge; yet eleven day before his own death, Goethe confessed:

> No matter how much the human mind may progress in intellectual culture, in the science of nature, in breadth and depth: it will never be able to rise above the elevation and moral culture of Christianity as it shines in the Gospels.[11]

The Accounts of the Life of Christ

The life and teachings of Jesus Christ are recorded in the Gospels, and, as such, deserve our ever-renewed and attentive study.

> The four Gospels form in some respects the most important portion of the Bible. Their value partly arises out of their relation to other portions of it. All its earlier revelations flow into them. All its later revelations flow out of them. They are, as it were, the heart through which, like life's blood, all its revelations circulate. But it is in their relation to Christ that their value pre-eminently consists. "In other parts of Scripture we hear Christ by the hearing of the ear, but here our eye seeth Him. Elsewhere we see Him through a glass darkly, but here face to face." On this account they claim the most affectionate as well as reverent perusal of the Church.[12]

Nevertheless, in spite of their supreme importance and extensive familiarity, many Christians still cannot answer the question: Why Four Gospels?

> It seems strange that such a question needs to be asked at this late date. The New Testament has now been in the hands of the Lord's people for almost two thousand years, and yet, comparatively few seem to grasp the character and scope of its first four books. No part of the Scriptures has been studied more widely than have the four Gospels: innumerable sermons have been preached from them, scores of commentaries have been written upon them, and every two or three years sections from one of the Gospels is assigned as the course for study in our Sunday Schools. Yet the fact remains, that the peculiar design and character of Matthew, Mark, Luke, and John, is rarely perceived even by those most familiar with their contents.

Why four Gospels? It does not seem to have occurred to the minds of many to ask such a question. That we have four Gospels which treat of the earthly ministry of Christ is universally accepted, but as to why we have them, as to what they are severally designed to teach, as to their peculiar characteristics, as to their distinctive beauties—these are little discerned and even less appreciated.[13]

Why Four Gospels? In order to answer the question, we need to discern the significance of the number four, and we turn our attention now to the first reference of this numeral in Scripture. In the second chapter of Genesis we read:

And the Lord God planted a garden eastward in Eden; and there he put the man whom he had formed. And out of the ground made the Lord God to grow every tree that is pleasant to the sight, and good for food; the tree of life also in the midst of the garden, and the tree of knowledge of good and evil. And a river went out of Eden to water the garden; and from thence it was parted, and became into four heads. GEN. 2:8-10

Note carefully the words "from thence." In Eden itself "the river" was one, but "from thence" it "was parted" and became into four heads. There must be some deeply hidden meaning to this, for why tell us how many "heads" this river had? The mere historical fact is without interest or value for us, and that the Holy Spirit has condescended to record this detail prepares us to look beneath the surface and seek for some mystical meaning. And surely that is not far to seek. "Eden" suggests to us the Paradise above: the "river" which "watered" it tells of Christ who is the Light and Joy of Heaven. Interpreting this mystic figure, then, we learn that in Heaven Christ was seen in one character only—"The Lord of Glory"—but just as when the "river" left Eden it was parted and became "four heads" and as such watered the earth, so too, the earthly ministry of the Lord Jesus has been, by the Holy Spirit, "parted into four heads" in the Four Gospels.[14]

Another Old Testament passage, which anticipated a four-fold division of Christ's ministry, is found in the book of Exodus. In the twenty-sixth chapter we read:

And thou shalt rear up the tabernacle according to the fashion thereof which was shewed thee in the mount. And thou shalt make a veil of blue, and purple, and scarlet, and fine twined linen of cunning work: with cherubims shall it be made: And thou shalt hang it upon four pillars of shittim wood overlaid with gold: their hooks shall be of gold, upon the four sockets of silver. EXOD. 26:30-32

From Hebrews 10:19-20 we learn that the "veil" foreshadowed the Incarnation, God manifest in flesh—"through the veil, that is to say, His flesh." It is surely significant that this "veil" was hung upon "four pillars of shittim wood overlaid with gold:" the wood, again, speaking of His humanity, and the gold of His deity. Just as these "four pillars" served to display the beautiful veil, so in the four Gospels we have made manifest the perfections of the only-begotten of the Father tabernacling among men.[15]

The opening verses of the fourth Gospel, in fact, introduce Jesus Christ as the only-begotten of the Father tabernacling among men. John wrote:

In the beginning was the Word, and the Word was with God, and the Word was God. The same was in the beginning with God. . . . And the Word was made flesh, and dwelt among us, (and we beheld his glory, the glory as of the only begotten of the Father,) full of grace and truth. JOHN 1:1-2, 14

It will be noticed in this passage that the first three uses of the Word are in relationship to God and His eternal existence, but the fourth reference to the Word is linked to Jesus' incarnation and earthly existence—"*The Word was made flesh, and dwelt among us.*"

Yet, even though the fourth Gospel is markedly different from the three synoptic Gospels—much as the fourth soil is very different from the other three in the Parable of the Four Soils—all the Gospels, nevertheless, present the only-begotten of the Father tabernacling among men on earth. Why Four Gospels? Because they deal with the earthly ministry of Jesus Christ. Four is the number of the earth.

> There are four points to earth's compass—north, east, south, and west. There are four seasons to earth's year—spring, summer, autumn, and winter. There are four elements connected with our world—earth, air, fire, and water. There have been four, and only four, great world empires—the Babylonian, the Medo-Persian, the Grecian, and the Roman. Scripture divides earth's inhabitants into four classes—"kindred, and tongue, and people, and nation" (Rev. 5:9 etc.). In the Parable of the Sower, our Lord divided the field into four kinds of soil, and later He said, "the field is the world." The fourth commandment has to do with rest from all earth's labors. The fourth clause in what is known as the Lord's prayer is, "Thy will be done on earth." And so we might go on. Four is thus the earth number. How fitting, then, that the Holy Spirit should have given us four Gospels in which to set forth the earthly ministry of the Heavenly One.[16]

As mentioned above, Scripture divides earth's inhabitants into four classes, and these were represented in the first century by the Jew, the Roman, the Greek, and the Christian. These groups personified four different outlooks on life—four kinds of ambitions and expectations—that still exist today. Why Four Gospels? Because the earth was, and still is, inhabited by four classes of people.

> The theory presented explains the fitness of the Gospels for the world in all ages. Those classes were representative classes for all time. There are the same needs among men today—one man needing, for conviction of the truth of Christianity, to hear an authoritative word of God in type or prophecy, in the Scriptures, and to be assured of its fulfillment as proclaiming the divine mission of Jesus; a second needing to see him as the divine power in his living activity, confirming his own claims; a third requiring a manifestation of God addressed to reason, through the perfect manhood of Jesus; a fourth demanding only the spiritual presence and teachings of Jesus to recognize in him the light and life. The Gospels appeal respectively to the instincts which lead men to bow to divine authority, power, perfection, and spirituality, and may thus be shown to exhaust the sides of man's nature from which he may best be reached and led to submission to the Savior, and to completeness in him. The four Gospels given to men in the apostolic times are therefore the complete Gospel of God for the world in all ages.[17]

Unfortunately, much of the beauty, structure, and meaning of the Gospels is lost to the modern reader because of a lack of understanding of the historical setting in which the four narratives originated. Furthermore, many of us have read about the events in the life of our Savior "from our childhood up, until the familiarity with the language in which they are written often causes us to overlook its sublime and inspired import."[18] This book is an attempt to remedy this condition in order for the reader to see more clearly the unalterable design and unfading significance of the four Gospels, as well as to know and treasure more fully the Savior whose life, death, and resurrection are therein recorded.

In addition to the unique way Christ is portrayed in each Gospel, there are certain themes and distinctive features that are entirely lost to the reader, who has little or no knowledge of the passions and perspectives of the ancient peoples to whom the Gospels were originally addressed. To this end numerous authorities of various disciplines and persuasions, both past and present, will be quoted throughout the book, in order to provide a qualified analysis and description of the nature of the times, the character of the people, and the influence of the culture at the beginning of the Christian era. Some of the most notable literary works of permanent value—which are, unfortunately, out of print and not readily accessible—will be cited in an attempt to fix the attention and excite the interest of those who cannot behold with indifference the life and ministry of Jesus Christ, as well as the historical background against which the events of His life unfolded.

> No revolutionary movement can be understood apart from its historical background. The primary background of Jesus, early Christianity, and the New Testament is first-century Judaism. Judaism is, of course, one of the world's major religions, as it was in the first Christian century. A remarkable continuity or similarity exists between the Judaism of today and that of the first century, despite the changes that the centuries have wrought. This continuity is in itself a clue to the character of that ancient faith. Both Judaism and Christianity are historical religions. This means more than that they have histories or even a common history. They share a faith in a God who deals with men, individually and collectively, in such a way that his will can be discerned in history. Crucial to both religions is the idea that God reveals Himself in history.[19]

This concept will be developed more fully as we look at the Gospel of Matthew and the Importance of the Past. And in like manner, as we cannot understand the Gospel of Matthew apart from its relationship with Judaism, so too, we cannot fully appreciate the other Gospels apart from a knowledge of the Greek, Roman, and Oriental forces that shaped the Hellenistic world. For example, "when we turn to Greece to view the general trend and history of her civilization we face a totally different kind of people."[20]

> The Israelites are Orientals but the Greeks are Occidentals. That explains much in the outlook of each. But especially important is the fact that the particular achievement of Israel lay in the field of special grace. This fact has been stated by Bavinck in these words: "Israel was the people of the Sabbath, the pagans are the people of the week. In art, science, political science, in all that belongs to the realm of culture, Israel stood far behind many heathen peoples." The achievement of Greece lay in the field of common grace. Of course Israel too enjoyed the fruits of common grace. Life in an organized society is not possible without it. But the point here is that what was distinctive of each was the result of common grace in the one, and of special grace in the other.[21]

Why Four Gospels? Because this number—no more and no less—is needed to meet the needs of people in all ages. Each Gospel is specifically written to appeal to a unique segment of the world's population. Understanding how this is accomplished, much narrative that initially appears to be confusing and irrelevant becomes lucid and useful. With certain background information, which this book is intended to convey, the reader will, hopefully, be encouraged to get to know Christ better. In fact, equipped with sufficient knowledge of (1) the purpose of the author, (2) the intended audience, (3) the way Christ is presented, and (4) the major themes of a particular Gospel, one can not only appreciate, but also in large measure anticipate, what events and circumstances are to be included or omitted in any Gospel account. Matthew addressed his Gospels to the Jews, and only he, for example, "records the rending of the veil of the Temple, the earthquake and the signs that followed it, which, at the time, could hardly have had any special significance except for the Jews (Matt. 27:51-53)."[22] Luke by contrast wrote for a Gentile audience, so only in his Gospel are we told that *"Jerusalem shall be trodden down of the Gentiles, until the times of the Gentiles be fulfilled"* (Luke 21:24).

Regarding omissions, we note that Matthew does not record the ascension of Christ, Mark gives no account of His birth or genealogy, Luke omits the ministry of the angels to Christ after His temptation, and John makes no mention of the Transfiguration. Why? Because these omissions are to be expected in view of how the four Gospels portray Christ in His various roles and relationships to a holy God and a sinful people. Matthew, presenting Christ as King with the offer of an earthly kingdom, concludes his narrative with Christ still on earth. Mark omits Christ's genealogy and the story of His birth, because these are not essential references for One who is introduced as a Servant. Luke makes no mention of ministering angels, because he portrays Christ in His role as Priest, emphasizing His intercession on behalf of man toward God—earth toward heaven, not heaven toward earth. John, stressing the deity of Christ, omits the Transfiguration, because this event highlighted His perfect humanity.

The synoptic Gospels—Matthew, Mark, and Luke—do, however, share much material in common and recount many of the same events. Nevertheless, there are both subtle and significant differences in how these particulars are described. For example, the first Gospel relates Christ's announcement to His disciples of His coming transfiguration as follows: *"Verily I say unto you, There be some standing here, which shall not taste of death, till they see the Son of man coming in his kingdom"* (Matt. 16:28). By contrast Mark's version of Christ's announcement reads: *"Verily I say unto you, That there be some of them that stand here, which shall not taste of death, till they have seen the kingdom of God come with power"* (Mark 9:1). The reason for the different choice of words in these parallel accounts lies in the fact that Matthew presents Christ as King and heir to a kingdom (cf. Matt. 1:1; 2:2), whereas Mark portrays Christ as the Servant of God (cf. Mark 10:45). Consequently, Matthew anticipates Christ coming in His kingdom, but Mark sees Him in relationship to the kingdom of God.

Briefly comparing a few other statements from the Synoptic Gospels, we find that Matthew poses the question of the townspeople as: *"Is not this the carpenter's son?"* (Matt. 13:55), whereas Mark's account reads, *"Is not this the carpenter?"* (Mark 6:3). Matthew, recording the Sermon on the Mount, says, *"Be ye therefore perfect, even as your Father which is in heaven is perfect"* (Matt. 5:48). Luke's account, by contrast, reads, *"Be ye therefore merciful, as your Father also is merciful"* (Luke 6:36). Comparing versions of the Lord's Prayer, we have Matthew saying, *"And forgive us our debts, as we forgive our debtors"*

(Matt. 6:12), whereas Luke records, *"and forgive us our sins"* (Luke 11:4). In relating the Parable of the Great Supper Matthew begins by saying, *"The kingdom of heaven is like unto a certain king, which made a marriage for his son, and sent forth his servants to call them that were bidden to the wedding"* (Matt. 22:2-3). Luke's version, on the other hand, begins, *"A certain man made a great supper, and bade many: and sent his servant at supper time to say to them that were bidden, Come; for all things are now ready"* (Luke 14:16-17).

The rationale for these variations—and countless others that could be cited—will not now be explained, but left to the investigation and contemplation of the reader. Nevertheless, it needs to be stressed that the very language of these inspired Gospels, including every jot and tittle (cf. Matt. 5:18), is the consequence of a specific plan and thereby suited for special people.

The Four Gospels have characteristic differences (see Appendices A and B) that will make sense to the reader somewhat in proportion to his knowledge of the Hellenistic age in which the New Testament originated. Details that may have been obvious to the casual reader of the first century are all but obliterated to the contemporary student of the Bible after nearly twenty centuries. Nevertheless, this book is intended to be neither an exhaustive commentary on the Gospels, nor a compendium of miscellaneous facts. Rather, the work is designed to be an instructional Guide—an illustrated, authoritative reference work, equally suited as a tool for personal study or as assigned reading in a formal classroom situation. Additionally, a two-part test on the Gospels is found in Appendix C and may be photocopied.

Although this study guide does contain original material, much of the main text incorporates selected excerpts from some of the great literary works of the past, which relate in one way or another to the subject at hand. In gathering up and sifting through this material, which has been harvested from the labors of others, we are reminded of the Apostle Paul's words to young Timothy: *"And the things that thou hast heard of me among many witnesses, the same commit thou to faithful men, who shall be able to teach others also"* (2 Tim. 2:2). Nevertheless, the works of certain writers, whose theology may be unacceptable to some, are cited because of their historical value and insight. The reference to any particular author should not be construed as an endorsement of either his doctrinal position or ecclesiastical associations. Be that as it may, an exposure to a wide variety of literary sources should enable the student of God's Word to better understand and more fully appreciate the historical background, characteristic differences, and timeless significance of the Four Gospels.

It is exciting to discover new truths from the life of Christ and gain further insight into how God reached out to a lost world in commending to all men the *"Savior, which is Christ the Lord"* (Luke 2:11).

> *For mine eyes have seen thy salvation, Which thou hast prepared before the face of all people;*
> *A light to lighten the Gentiles, and the glory of thy people Israel.* LUKE 2:30-32

It is with the desire that the followers of Christ will value more highly the treasure they have in Him and His Word, that this work is offered for the curiosity and candor of its readers.

Chapter One Notes

[1] A. W. Tozer, *The Pursuit of God* (Wheaton, Ill.: Tyndale House Publishers, n.d.), 19.

[2] Ibid., 20.

[3] John MacArthur, Jr., *God: Coming Face to Face with His Majesty* (Wheaton, Ill.: Victor Books, 1993), 11.

[4] Ibid., 10.

[5] William G. Hutchison, translator, *Renan's Life of Jesus* (London: Walter Scott Publishing Co., Ltd., n.d.), 1.

[6] Philip Schaff, *The Person of Christ: The Perfection of His Humanity Viewed as a Proof of His Divinity. With a Collection of Impartial Testimonies to the Character of Jesus*, 12th ed. (New York: American Tract Society, 1882), 216-18.

[7] *Ibid.*, 238-39.

[8] *Ibid.*, 280.

[9] *Ibid.*, 294-95.

[10] F. V. N. Painter, *A History of Education* (New York: D. Appleton and Co., 1886), 82.

[11] Schaff, *op. cit.*, 256.

[12] Edward A. Thomson, *The Four Evangelists; with the Distinctive Characteristics of Their Gospels* (Edinburgh: T. & T. Clark, 38 George Street, 1868), 1.

[13] Arthur W. Pink, *Why Four Gospels?* (Swengel, Penn.: Bible Truth Depot, 1921), 9.

[14] *Ibid.*, 17-18.

[15] *Ibid.*, 18.

[16] *Ibid.*, 22-23.

[17] D. S. Gregory, *Why Four Gospels? Or, the Gospel for All the World* (New York: Funk & Wagnalls, Publishers, 1890), 82-83.

[18] John Fleetwood, *The Life of Our Blessed Lord and Savior Jesus Christ: and the Lives and Sufferings of His Holy Evangelists and Apostles* (Philadelphia: J. W. Bradley, 48 North Fourth St., 1858), 7.

[19] Robert A. Spivey and D. Moody Smith, Jr., *Anatomy of the New Testament: A Guide to its Structure and Meaning*, 2nd ed. (New York: Macmillan Publishing Co., Inc., 1974), 7.

[20] Ralph Stob, *Christianity and Classical Civilization* (Grand Rapids, Mich.: Wm. B. Eerdmans Publishing Company, 1950), 43.

[21] *Ibid.*, 43-44.

[22] Charles John Ellicott, *The Gospel According to St. Matthew, with commentary by E. H. Plumptre* (London: Cassell & Company, Limited, n.d.), x.

PERSPECTIVE

The General State of the World by Thomas Gisborne

The general state of the world, at the time when Christianity was promulgated, was confessedly such as to render a farther revelation of the will of God highly desirable to mankind. The Heathen nations, Greeks, Romans, Barbarians, were immersed in the grossest idolatry. It was not merely that they worshipped stocks and stones. Their supposed deities were usually represented of characters so detestably flagitious, that we should rather have expected them to have been singled out as objects of abhorrence than of adoration. We know with how much greater proneness and facility men imitate a pattern of vice than of virtue. . . . We might therefore form, by speculative reasoning, a just opinion of the state of morals likely to be prevalent among nations who worshipped Jupiter and Bacchus, and Mercury, and their associates in the Heathen Pantheon. Turn to history, and you find the display of depravity, which your imagination had pictured, delineated in still more glaring colours. The scattered examples of eminent virtue recorded in the annuls of Greece and Rome, examples the brighter on account of their scarcity and of the gloomy contrast with which they are surrounded, militate not against the truth of this general representation. . . . Such being the general conditions of mankind, in consequence of their having rendered thus inefficacious, by their own frailty and perverseness, the invitations and motives to righteousness which their merciful Creator had for so many ages set before them, partly by the light of natural conscience, and partly by special revelation: it perhaps was not wholly unreasonable humbly to hope, that He who had already done so much of his own free-will for his undeserving and sinful creatures, might yet in his infinite mercy do somewhat more.[1]

---

[1] Thomas Gisborne, *A Familiar Survey of the Christian Religion, and of History As Connected with the Introduction of Christianity, and with Its Progress to the Present Time*, 6th ed. (London: Printed for T. Cadell and W. Davies, in the Strand, 1816), 237-40.

PART I

THE FULLNESS OF TIME

The voice of him that crieth in the wilderness,
Prepare ye the way of the Lord,
make straight in the desert a highway for our God.
Every valley shall be exalted,
and every mountain and hill shall be made low:
and the crooked shall be made straight,
and the rough places plain:
And the glory of the Lord shall be revealed,
and all flesh shall see it together:
for the mouth of the Lord hath spoken it.

ISAIAH 40:3-5

From the whole that history presents us, we deduce conclusions that have an important bearing on human happiness and virtue. This we consider as the most signal benefit derivable from the record of past ages. It gives us, in connexion with revelation, which furnishes a most interesting portion of the world's history, a correct estimate of life and of human nature in all its variety. It shows us how man has acted according to his own pleasure, whether uprightly or wickedly, and at the same time, how God has conducted the train of events to bring about the purposes of His wisdom and grace.[1]

-Rev. Royal Robbins, *The World Displayed, in Its History and Geography*

There were in the world at that time three outstanding nations who dwelt along the shores of the Mediterranean. At least they were outstanding from the point of view of their influence upon the course of history in Western Europe. These three peoples are the Jews, the Greeks and the Romans. The remarkable thing is that the influence of each of these is traceable to the limits of each of the other two. Or rather, these civilizations lived side by side, each acquainted with and influenced by both of the others. Our purpose is to seek to get at the genius of each people, its major characteristics and achievements, to evaluate that, and to point out its significance in relation to the Advent. Too frequently the idea of the fullness of time has been restricted to external and physical conditions. The preparation for and the contributions to the Advent are then limited to the universal language of the Greeks, the Pax Romana and the good roads and safe travel on land and sea of the Romans. These are very significant elements, but the whole realm of the spirit of the peoples and that in relation to Christianity is passed by. Yet that is surely the more important phase since Christianity is first of all a thing of the spirit. It need hardly be said that just as that is the more significant, it is too immeasurably more difficult. It is no easy task to get at and describe the genius of one's own people. Here we have more than one, existing centuries ago, and in addition to the description we are compelled to give an evaluation. For God did send his Son in the fullness of time.[2]

-Ralph Stob, *Christianity and Classical Civilization*

---

[1] Royal Robbins, *The World Displayed, in Its History and Geography; Embracing A History of the World, from the Creation to the Present Day* (New York: Published by H. Savage, 1833), 7.

[2] Ralph Stob, *Christianity and Classical Civilization* (Grand Rapids, Mich.: William B. Eerdmans Publishing Company, 1950), 39.

Figure I-1. Antonio Ciseri: "Ecce Homo"

For centuries prior to the birth of Jesus Christ, God had been preparing the world for the reception of the Messiah and the rapid spread of Christianity in the Greco-Roman world. The fullness of time had come, but the vast majority of the Jewish nation rejected their Messiah when He appeared. *"He came unto his own, and his own received him not"* (John 1:11).

In this picture, *"Ecce Homo"* ("Behold the Man"), we see that "a nation's fate is hanging in the balance. But clamor and hatred are tipping the beam, with direst consequences. The nation that rejects its heavenly King in favor of an earthly will ere long reject the earthly also, the white wonder of this Temple will dissolve in Titus' fervent heat, and forever they who would not have this Man to rule over them shall be a People of Dispersion, kingless, and homeless, because they knew not the time of their visitation. This is the insight Ciseri gives us—the Jewish nation is sealing its own doom."[3]

<hr />

[3] Cynthia Pearl Maus, *Christ and the Fine Arts* (New York: Harper & Row, Publishers, 1959), 357.

Chapter Two

The Work of God: World Preparation

The death of Malachi not only silenced the voice of the prophet, but it ushered in a period lasting over four centuries, during which God Himself no longer spoke to His people. Israel's prophetic era had come to an end with the passing of Malachi.

> In most Bibles the period between the Old and the New Testaments is represented by a single blank page which, perhaps, has symbolic significance. 'From Malachi to Matthew' has for long remained vague and unfamiliar to many readers of the Scriptures.[1]

Many people assume that because God did not speak during this time, that He also did not act in any significant, historical way. It would be a gross mistake, however, to suppose that God's purposeful activity ended with the death of Malachi, and did not resume again until John the Baptist made his appearance in the wilderness. The truth is, that for centuries, both before and during the Intertestamental Period, God had been preparing the world for the advent of His Son. Without ever being aware of it, nations moved on and off the stage of history, fulfilling the roles that were assigned to them (cf. Acts 17:24-26). In fact, some of the most important preparations of the world were taking place in the 400 years between the Old and New Testaments.

Cultural and Political Preparations

The man God used more than any other single individual during this time to prepare the world for the advent of Christ is referred to several times in the Book of Daniel. One of these references is in Chapter Eleven, where we read:

> *And a mighty king shall stand up, that shall rule with great dominion, and do according to his will. And when he shall stand up, his kingdom shall be broken, and shall be divided toward the four winds of heaven; and not to his posterity, nor according to his dominion which he ruled: for his kingdom shall be plucked up, even for others beside those.* DANIEL 11:3-4

The mighty king was Alexander the Great, who ascended to the throne at the age of 20 years, when his father—King Philip II of Macedonia—was assassinated in the summer of 336 B.C. by a captain of his guards.

At the time of his death, Philip had already subjected Greece to the dominion of Macedonia, and was designing the conquest of Persia.

> The young monarch determined to follow the glorious path marked out by his father; and having quelled an insurrection, which the fiery eloquence of Demosthenes had aroused against him among the Greeks, and destroyed the noble city of Thebes, he convoked a General Council of the States at Corinth; renewed the proposal of invading and conquering Persia, and was appointed, as his father had been, generalissimo of the Greeks.
> Having assembled an army of 30,000 foot and 5000 horse, Alexander, with provisions only for a single month, crossed the Hellespont, and with these slender means commenced the conquest of the Persian empire.[2]

Alexander had crossed the Hellespont (modern Dardanelles) in the spring of 334 B.C. and during the next few years revealed to the world why he is considered one of the greatest military geniuses of all time.

More than two centuries of Persian domination came to an end late in the fourth century before Christ, when Alexander of Macedon and his armies moved east, sweeping everything before them. Alexander overran the Jewish homeland, and over the years he and his successors attempted to introduce Greek culture and customs there, as was their practice in all conquered territories. . . .

Although Alexander did not succeed in establishing a Macedonian empire that would survive his death, his efforts to spread Greek language and culture and to embed them in the life of the East proved highly successful, especially in the cities. He left as his heritage a string of Greek cities across the area of his conquest, outposts of Greek language and culture. Probably the largest and most successful of these was the great Egyptian center of Alexandria, which appropriately bore his name. It was here that a large colony of Jews settled and that the first and most important translation of the Hebrew scriptures into Greek was made.[3]

The world that Alexander the Great left behind was "one world" in a sense that it had never been before. Previously, there had been great empires, such as those of Egypt, Assyria, Babylon, and Medo-Persia. And certainly various peoples and cultures had interacted, but never before had there been such a concerted effort to create a common world civilization as was actually brought about by Alexander and his successors.

It was Alexander who first projected the plan of opening a communication between Europe and India, through the Nile, the Red Sea, and the Indian Ocean. But he, whose will never bowed to man, could not resist the messenger of God, sent to call him to his final account. After having been the means of death to so many of his fellow-beings, he sickened with a fever, occasioned by his excesses, and died in the thirty-third year of his age.[4]

In retrospect it appears that "Alexander was as much a missionary of Greek culture as a conquering general."[5] In fact, his success in this area may be even more remarkable than his military feats.

Without necessarily subscribing to the theory that history is made by great men alone, one can and must grant the singular and outstanding historical importance of Alexander in giving a particular form and character to the world into which Christianity was born. Nothing is more important for human history and culture than language, and nothing promotes communication and understanding like a common language. Among other things, Alexander bequeathed to the Mediterranean world a common language, Greek. It was not the Greek of Plato or Sophocles, but another newer and somewhat simpler dialect known as koine, or common, Greek. This Greek became the lingua franca of the ancient world 300 years before the time of Christ.[6]

Although Greece had lost its political significance by the first century A.D., the koine language had, nevertheless, spread through all areas of Greek influence. As people from distant countries and divergent backgrounds came together, they could talk to each other in Greek. Perhaps they could not diagram complex sentences, nor speak with perfect diction, but they could make themselves understood. Needless to say, this gift of common speech was of great importance in encouraging commerce and other sorts of interchange throughout the Greco-Roman world. In the centers of Greek culture established by Alexander the Great, conscious attempts were made to promote and spread the manners and customs, the arts and architecture, the literature and science, and even the athletic games of Hellenic civilization.

> The importance of this universal civilization for Judaism and its stepchild Christianity can scarcely be overestimated. For Judaism it was at once a threat and a benefit—a threat in that it tended to eliminate just those distinguishing features of life which characterized the Jewish community as such, but a benefit in that it made possible greater extension of the scope and influence of Judaism, especially Greek-speaking Judaism. For Christianity it was an immense boon. Without Alexander the rapid spread of Christianity through the Greco-Roman world might never have taken place.[7]

Certainly, the Christian message can stand on its own feet, and its foothold cannot be attributed to favorable cultural factors alone. "Nevertheless, it is a striking fact that the spread of Christianity in the first centuries occurred principally in those areas which fell under the sway of Alexander's, or at least of Greek, influence."[8] The great city of Ephesus, for example, which was settled by Ionian Greeks and located about halfway between Jerusalem and Rome, was the approximate geographic center of the Roman Empire, as well as the chief commercial center of Asia. And not by mere coincidence, Ephesus had also become by the end of the first century "the approximate geographic and numerical center of the Christian population of the world,"[9] even though the Christian Church was born in Jerusalem less than 60 years earlier.

> When the Roman empire achieved supremacy, it is fortunate, or we prefer to say, providential, that there was no spirit of pan-Romanism. No effort seems to have been made to overthrow the Hellenistic ideals, to replace the Greek language with the Latin, or to develop an indigenous Roman culture. To expect the world to adopt a second universal language so soon would be to expect the impossible. Greek continued to be the language of the empire for several centuries. Moreover, the Romans were imitators rather than originators. Their art is largely Greek art, and other elements of their culture owe much to the Greeks who preceded them. Rome made a different type of contribution to the culture of the world; perhaps we could say it was more practical. Hellenism was an ideal. *Pax Romana* [Roman Peace] and *Lex Romana* [Roman Law] were not ideals, they were realities; and because they were realities, the Hellenistic ideal was able to take even firmer root than it had, and the unity of which Alexander dreamed was realized in the Roman empire.[10]

Alexander the Great had created a world, but he did not live long enough to govern it. "To anyone who reads his life with care it is evident that Alexander started with an equipment of training and ideas of unprecedented value. As he got beyond the wisdom of his upbringing he began to blunder and misbehave—sometimes with a dreadful folly. The defects of his character had triumphed over his upbringing long before he died."[11] Nevertheless, Alexander, who was idolized by his men and hailed as divine in the lands he won, passed into the legends of three continents. In time, however, the task of governing Alexander's world was finally performed by the Romans—the heirs to both his empire and ambitions. Caesar Augustus, emperor "*when the fullness of the time was come*" (Gal. 4:4a), not only emulated his deeds, but wore the image of "Alexander's head on a signet ring."[12]

The Roman Empire, in contrast to the empire of Alexander, was different in both origin and scope. In Daniel's vision of the four beasts that came up from the sea, the prophet has this to say in regards to the empire of Rome:

After this I saw in the night visions, and behold a fourth beast, dreadful and terrible, and strong exceedingly; and it had great iron teeth: it devoured and brake in pieces, and stamped the residue with the feet of it: and it was diverse from all the beasts that were before it, and it had ten horns. Daniel 7:7

Whereas Alexander's empire was short-lived, Rome succeeded in maintaining for some centuries an empire even greater than that achieved by the conquests of Alexander the Great. Furthermore, it needs to be emphasized that this fourth beast was diverse from all the empires that preceded it. English novelist and secular historian, H. G. Wells, wrote:

> But this new empire was, as we shall try to make clear, a political structure differing very profoundly in its nature from any of the great Oriental empires that had preceded it. Great changes in the texture of human society and in the conditions of social interrelationships had been going on for some centuries. The flexibility and transferability of money was becoming a power and, like all powers in inexpert hands, a danger in human affairs. It was altering the relations of rich men to the state and to their poorer fellow citizens. This new empire, the Roman empire, unlike all the preceding empires, was not the creation of a great conqueror. No Sargon, . . . no Nebuchadnezzar, no Cyrus nor Alexander . . . was its fountainhead. It was made by a republic. It grew by a kind of necessity through new concentrating and unifying forces that were steadily gathering power in human affairs.[13]

It is, of course, true that the limits of Alexander's world extended farther to the east, whereas the empire of Rome stretched far beyond Italy to the North and West. Yet in a very real sense the world of Alexandrian Hellenism and the world of Rome were one and the same world.

> Through her own conquest of Greece and wholesale appropriation of Greek culture in the second century B.C., Rome fell heir to the legacy of Greece just when she was emerging as the dominant military force and political power of the Western world. For a half-century before Christ and nearly half a millennium after, the Roman Empire gave to the Mediterranean world a political unity and stability, which, though not unbroken, was about as continuous and dependable as anything so large and varied a segment of the world has known before or since. The marvel is not that the Roman Empire fell—crumbled is the better word—but that it stood so long. At the time of its greatest extent and vitality—that is, during the New Testament period—the Roman Empire stretched from Syria and Palestine to the British Isles. Of western Europe, only Germany and the Scandinavian countries remained outside the Roman orbit, and only Scandinavia completely outside. The southern and western-most parts of Germany came under Roman domination, as did Austria as far north as the Danube.[14]

The Roman Empire—stretching some 3000 miles East to West and about 2000 miles North to South—consisted of 43 distinct provinces, which were managed under the principle of colonial home rule: allowing the inhabitants considerable freedom as long as they paid their taxes and obeyed Roman laws. Local law enforcement and administration, such as collection of taxes, were left in the hands of local officials. Where local law enforcement broke down, such as in Judea at the time of Christ, the Romans intervened to make sure that anarchy did not reign. To be sure, Roman officials were not universally good; Pontius Pilate, for example, left a great deal to be desired. Yet the Romans, themselves, removed Pilate from office.

The Romans had in some way at least learned to balance local autonomy and central authority; that is, the rights of individuals and the rights of the state. For the most part the Romans administered the empire with firmness, but with a certain sensitivity for the varieties of people and customs within their boundaries. Furthermore, the Roman practice of colonial home rule added a sense of personal dignity and individual value.

"But a sense of human value can cause trouble,"[15] especially in an empire that is under-girded by the institution of slavery. When slaves realize that they also have human dignity, this can result in strife for those who want to be masters. History often appears to be a struggle between the oppressed and the more favored classes, and like the great empires that preceded it, Rome experienced major problems because of slavery.

> In the particular case of Rome it cannot be doubted that it largely contributed to the impurities which disgraced private life, as seen in the pages of Juvenal, Martial, and Petronius. It is shocking to observe the tone in which Horace, so characterized by geniality and bonhomie, speaks of the subjection of slaves to the brutal passions of their masters. . . . The hardening effect of the system appears perhaps most strikingly in the barbarous spectacles of the amphitheatre, in which even women took pleasure and joined in condemning the gladiator who did not by his desperate courage satisfy the demands of a sanguinary mob. It led further, to a contempt for industry, even agriculture being no longer held in esteem. . . . The existence of slavery, degrading free labour while competing with freemen for urban employment, multiplied the idle and worthless population of Rome, who sought only "panem et circenses." These had to be supported by public distributions, which the emperors found they could not discontinue, and by the bounty of patrons, and . . . formed a dangerous class, purchasable by selfish ambitions and ready to aid in civil disturbances.[16]

Life was expendable. Nearly one-half of the population of Rome were slaves, and every year thousands of these individuals were sent into the arena, where they were slaughtered for the sake of entertainment. Immorality was prevalent. Roman writers, such as Seutonius, have left detailed and disgusting accounts of life in their day.[17] Others, however, were recoiling against such depravity. Cicero's orations against Cataline in 63 B.C., once known by every high school Latin student, are a classic example. In the first of a series of speeches before the Roman senate, statesman and man of letters, Marcus Tullius Cicero, declared:

> For what is there, O Cataline, that can now afford you any pleasure in this city? For there is no one in it, except that band of profligate conspirators of yours, who does not fear you—no one who does not hate you. What brand of domestic baseness is not stamped upon your life? What disgraceful circumstance is wanting to your infamy in your private affairs? From what licentiousness have your eyes, from what atrocity have your hands, from what iniquity has your whole body ever abstained? Is there one youth, when you have once entangled him in the temptations of your corruption, to whom you have not held out a sword for audacious crime, or a torch for licentious wickedness?
> What? When lately by the death of your former wife you had made your house

empty and ready for a new bridal, did you not even add another incredible wickedness to this wickedness? But I pass that over, and willingly allow it to be buried in silence, that so horrible a crime may not be seen to have existed in this city, and not to have been chastised. I pass over the ruin of your fortune, which you know is hanging over you against the Ides of the very next month; I come to those things which relate not to the infamy of your private vices, not to your domestic difficulties and baseness, but to the welfare of the republic and to the lives and safety of us all.[18]

As it was in the days of Noah, so it seemed to be once again that *"the wickedness of man was great in the earth"* (Genesis 6:5). Be that as it may, however, "there is a nobler side, even in fallen man, for which we ought to thank God. Men were grappling with serious matters."[19] The Greek philosophers, Roman statesmen, and other ancient sages and writers, may not have come up with the right answers to some of the more perplexing problems of their day—much less understand why some people are given *"over to a reprobate mind, to do those things which are not convenient; being filled with all unrighteousness"* (Romans 1:28b-29a)—but one fact stands out very clearly: "when God was ready to send His Gospel into the world, there were men who were ready to give it serious consideration."[20]

Greek philosophy and literature, marred as they were in some of their conceptions of the universe and of human life, rendered a notable service in preparing the human mind to think in the larger terms of the Christian religion. The increased stimulus given to travel and intercourse under the Roman sway made the people generally acquainted with the rich treasures of Greek learning; this immensely enriched the minds of the people, and also created a bond of intellectual and moral sympathy. The literary and artistic genius of the Greeks became generally recognized, and their achievements in philosophy, literature, science, and art were esteemed and appropriated by the many nationalities that commingled in the Roman Empire. Thus the intellectual range was immensely extended, the spirit of inquiry was greatly quickened, and the mind was made more hospitable to new adventures into the wide realms of thought.[21]

God was preparing the world. The fullness of time was coming!

Physical Preparations

Not only had "early Christianity benefited considerably from the peaceful and lawful conditions of Roman rule which accompanied its beginnings,"[22] but it also profited from the fine network of roads and sea transportation that the Romans had developed and maintained largely for military purposes. Again, policing of the roads was left to the various local authorities as long as they could do the job; but when they couldn't, the Roman military marched in "to keep roads open for travel and free of bandits and other potential harassments."[23]

It would certainly be wrong to imagine that travel in ancient times was as easy and comfortable as it is today. Nevertheless, travel between virtually all parts of the empire—from any one country to another—was possible. In fact, it was decidedly easier to go from Jerusalem to Rome in Paul's day, than it was to travel the Oregon Trail from Independence, Missouri, to the Pacific Northwest in the 1840's.

Long journeys by sea and land, such as Paul undertook, were in his day nothing out of the ordinary. "By the end of the Punic Wars seven great roads led from, or to, Rome; together with their many branches and connecting roads they formed a comprehensive network, giving rise to the expression 'all roads lead to Rome.'"[24] An ancient inscription on the tombstone of a Phrygian merchant—in the heart of what is now Turkey—"proudly proclaims that in his lifetime he made seventy-two journeys to Rome alone."[25]

The busy, well maintained imperial roads were equipped with halts for changing chariots and horses. Inns and hostelries provided rest and refreshment for travelers. "Among the outstanding features of Roman roads were their straightness, solid foundations, cambered surfaces, and systematic arrangement."[26] They were in their way the finest network for land transportation that Western Europe knew until the railways began to be built in the 19th century. In fact, an article published early in the 20th century still claimed that in "solidity of construction they have never been excelled, and many of them still remain, often forming the foundation of a more modern road, and in some instances constituting the road surface now used."[27]

The Romans were the greatest road builders of ancient times. "At the height of the empire . . . the Roman highway system consisted of more than 50,000 mi. of first-class roads. . . . Solidly built, Roman roads took the direct line wherever possible, using piles and embankments over marshy ground and cuts and even tunnels in hilly or mountainous country. In addition, a network of lesser roads, amounting to perhaps 200,000 mi., linked the smaller towns and rural areas with the main highways."[28]

> Thus favorable conditions of language and culture as well as an orderly government and a workable transportation system favored the spread of the Christian gospel in the Greco-Roman world. They help explain the rapid growth of the church and the ways in which the gospel found expression—not the least of which is the New Testament itself, a collection of books written in Greek, and in many cases written from one Christian or group of Christians to or for another. These documents attest not only a lively faith but also a sense of tangible relationship between one Christian church and another, which was made possible by the conditions of the time. Moreover, they display a concrete sense of mission concerning something called "the world" . . . , a concept not previously unknown, but given particular point and form by the vision and work of Alexander the Great and the political reality of the Roman Empire.[29]

God was preparing the world. The fullness of time was coming!

Religious Preparations

The four and a half centuries between the close of the Old Testament and the birth of Christ were years of life-changing experience for the Jewish people. Back in the sixth century B.C., they had been carried off into captivity in Babylon. Years later Cyrus the Great, who conquered Babylon, had granted the Jews permission to return to their land. But many Jews never returned to Judah. In fact as many as 90 percent remained in exile and made a new home for themselves. That home was the world. Most Jews, by the time of Christ, did not live in Palestine, but in other parts of the world. In fact, there were probably more Jews in the city of Alexandria alone, than in all of Palestine. The Jews who were dispersed to the four corners of the world were called the "Diaspora," or the Jews of the Dispersion.

Attempts at numbering ancient populations are of necessity educated guesses. The total number of Jews in the world at the time of Christ cannot be accurately computed. "Perhaps four to four and a half million, or roughly seven percent of the total population of the Roman world, is a fair guess. In line with the early and fairly probable statements (cf. Philo) that there were a million Jews in Egypt alone, rather more in Syria, probably at least ten thousand in Rome at the time of Tiberius, this figure does not seem excessive. Of this total probably not more than seven hundred thousand were to be found in Palestine."[30]

From available sources it seems reasonable that not more than fifteen percent of world Jewry lived in their ancient homeland. "Furthermore, many Jews who resided in Palestine were actually as much in the dispersion as their brethren in Alexandria or Antioch. The seacoast towns, except Joppa and Jamnia, were prevailingly Gentile; the tetrarchy of Philip almost completely so. To be sure, Galilee and part of the Perea were nominally Jewish, but the population was far from pure."[31]

> Several things happened to the Jewish people in the Dispersion. For one thing, they developed a world view. Too long had they associated their God merely with the land of Palestine. By the rivers of Babylon they had wept because they had thought they could not sing the Lord's song in a foreign land (see Psalm 137:1-4). But now they had come to realize that the world was the Lord's. They not only could sing the Lord's song in foreign lands—they could even translate the song into foreign languages! In Babylon and the Mesopotamian region, as well as in the land of Egypt to which the Jews had migrated in the time of Jeremiah and possibly earlier, Aramaic became the language of the Jewish people. Jews gradually spread to other parts of the world, and began to speak the Greek language. As their knowledge of the original Hebrew language decreased, it became increasingly necessary to have an explanation of the meaning of the Scriptures. Interpretations in Aramaic were at first preserved in oral form only, known as Targums, but later these were standardized in written form. Likewise Greek translations of the Old Testament Scriptures were made, which were far more significant for the New Testament period than were the Aramaic Targums.[32]

The reason why the Greek translations were far more significant can be explained by the fact that the Jewish people were undergoing a process of Hellenization. Consciously or unconsciously, they were accommodating to Greek culture. Although the Jews succeeded in maintaining their ethnic identity and a certain separateness in their way of living, they were, nevertheless, and inevitably, influenced by the Gentile world around them.

> If they were not all participating in the games in the stadium—some indeed going so far as to have the visible signs of circumcision removed by an operation—at least their vocabulary was being expanded with Greek ideas. When the Hebrew Old Testament was translated into Greek, Hebrew words that had narrow meanings were often translated by Greek words that had broader meanings. Key theological terms had to be translated by words that had various nuances and connotations not present in the original. It could not possibly be otherwise. Our words are integrally part of our culture. When two cultures merge, the language has to become richer.[33]

The Greek language was by far the richest one in existence, and the best instrument to convey the details of the life and ministry of Jesus Christ.

Of all ancient languages, the Greek language was the best medium for accuracy of expression. And in New Testament times it was better in this respect than it is now. It had eight cases which, with the use of prepositions, facilitated stating truth unambiguously. And its tense system exceeded that of all other ancient languages in making unmistakably clear what a writer had in mind. . . . Not only through its complex and adequate verb system, but also because of its extensive philosophical, ethical and religious vocabulary, the Greek language was the best vehicle for the record of God's glorious revelation in Christ given in the New Testament.[34]

By the time of Christ the Jewish people had entered the mainstream of Hellenistic culture. And the most outstanding benefit of Greek culture for the Jews was the Greek language. Having been exposed to it now for over three centuries, they became a bilingual people. "Judaism in the Greco-Roman world was largely Greek-speaking."[35]

The old wineskins had become stretched. The new wine, therefore, required new wineskins! "The Old Testament was written in Hebrew, the language of ancient Israel, the New Testament in Greek, the language of the Hellenistic world."[36] The New Testament Scriptures, as found in our Bibles today, were written to a Church that had grown up in the midst of the Hellenistic culture of the Roman Empire. The old garment was worn thin. *"No man putteth a new cloth into an old garment . . ."* (Matt. 9:16a). "It is highly doubtful that Paul could have preached his gospel in the Gentile world if he had been limited to the concepts of the Hebrew Old Testament, and certainly impossible if he had been limited to the Hebrew language."[37]

In addition to the Greek language, the Jewish Synagogue was a vital ingredient in the religious preparation of the world in the first century.

Another feature of the Dispersion was the development of the synagogue to serve as a partial substitute for, and later to take the place of, the temple at Jerusalem. While Jews lived in the land of Palestine, it was possible to fulfill literally the law requiring attendance at the annual feasts. When, because of distance, this could no longer be fulfilled, the synagogue provided a means of religious expression. It also provided a means of community, so that the Jews of the Dispersion continued to use the Scriptures of the Old Testament, and to a lesser and modified extent they preserved the elements of worship. It does not need to be argued that the preachers of the gospel found their first steppingstones into the Gentile world in the synagogues scattered throughout the world.[38]

The Greek-speaking Jews of the Dispersion—with their "world view" and widely scattered synagogues—prepared the way for the universal emphasis of the Christian Gospel.

In fact, the existence of this kind of Judaism helps explain how an historically exclusive community such as Judaism could have produced a missionary religion like Christianity. The Hellenistic synagogue itself did not disdain the missionary enterprise. There is some evidence of a sustained and serious effort to convert Gentiles to Judaism. And not a few Gentiles were attracted by the antiquity and moral seriousness of the Jewish religion.[39]

Another attraction of the Jewish religion for a literate Gentile audience was the Messianic expectation of the Jewish people. "A whole literature was being produced centering largely about this theme. False messiahs had arisen and would continue to arise for another century."[40] Nevertheless, the Jewish hope that the day of deliverance was at hand was burning brightly.

> Nor was this sense of expectation limited to the Jews. There was in the Gentile world a sense of dissatisfaction with existing religions, and alongside this an expectation of something better. The Greeks had climbed Mount Olympus and found no gods there. ... All over the Gentile world many were becoming proselytes to Judaism, and it seems reasonable to suppose that it was the Messianic hope rather than the Mosaic law that was appealing to them.[41]

According to the Book of Acts, the Apostle Paul began his famous speech on Mars Hill by saying, *"Men of Athens, I see that in every way you are very religious"* (17:22, N.I.V.). What Paul observed was not only true of Athens, but of the entire Mediterranean world. Christianity did not originate during a time of religious indifference.

Whatever may have been the general state of culture and morality in the first century, religion did not lack vitality and variety. "This too is represented in Paul's speech, for he mentions the objects of their worship, among which is an altar inscribed to an unknown God, as if the Athenians were taking no chances on omitting, and therefore offending, any deity."[42]

This toleration and syncretism of many gods does not mean that most people did not take religion seriously.

> If anything, just the opposite was the case. Only from the Christian or Jewish point of view could this toleration of, and participation in, a multiplicity of religious cults be taken as an indication of frivolity. The exclusivism of Judaism and Christianity was itself regarded as odd and even impious in ancient times, and the refusal of Christians and Jews to worship any god other than their own led their neighbors to brand them as atheists. This persistence in worshiping only one God was perhaps the factor that most clearly distinguished Christians and Jews in the ancient world, and it may have had something to do with the fact that of the religions of that civilization only Christianity and Judaism survive today.[43]

As a result of Greek culture in general, and the writings of Homer in particular, the old gods were, nevertheless, and for all practical purposes, already "dead" by the time of Christ. Although they were still worshipped, they offered little hope. With the beginning of the *Pax Romana* under Caesar Augustus "many people began looking upon the city of Rome and the Roman emperor as a new kind of god, as a kind of savior of the world. But the new 'gods,' of course, offered nothing beyond this life. If Rome and its emperor were the only hope, there was little hope. But Rome and its emperor were not the only hope. Unawares they had made final preparations for Christ."[44]

The fullness of time had come. God had prepared His world. Politically, it was at peace under a stable Roman government, with a vast network for good transportation, both by land and sea. Culturally, it was united in the Greek language and the Hellenistic ideal with a sense of mission concerning something called "the world." Additionally, the hearts and minds of the Gentile world had been prepared to give the Gospel serious consideration. "And the Jews, the people of God, scattered throughout the world, had at last come to the threshold and were ready to enter in to fulfill the promise made to Abraham," [45] that through him *"shall all families of the earth be blessed"* (Gen. 12:3).

Chapter Two Notes

[1] D. S. Russel, *Between the Testaments* (Philadelphia: Fortress Press, 1975), 11.

[2] Perce C. Grace, *Outlines of History* (New York: Edward Dunigan and Brother, 1851), 50-51.

[3] Robert A. Spivey and D. Moody Smith, Jr., *Anatomy of the New Testament: A Guide to Its Structure and Meaning*, 2nd ed. (New York: Macmillan Publishing Co., Inc., 1974), 10, 29.

[4] Emma Willard, *Universal History in Perspective: Divided into Three Parts, Ancient, Middle, and Modern*, Rev. ed. (New York: A. S. Barnes & Company, 1855), 88.

[5] Spivey, *op. cit.*, 10.

[6] *Ibid.*, 30.

[7] *Ibid.*

[8] *Ibid.*

[9] Henry H. Halley, *Halley's Bible Handbook*, 24th ed. (Grand Rapids, Mich.: Zondervan Publishing House, 1965), 701.

[10] William Sanford LaSor, *Great Personalities of the New Testament: Their Lives and Times* (Westwood, N.J.: Fleming H. Revell Company, 1961), 18.

[11] H. G. Wells, *The Outline of History*, 4th ed., vol. 2 (New York: P.F. Collier & Son Company, 1925), 377.

[12] National Geographic Society, *Greece and Rome: Builders of Our World* (Washington, D.C.: National Geographic Society, 1968), 243.

[13] Wells, *op. cit.*, 457.

[14] Spivey, *op. cit.*, 31-32.

[15] LaSor, *op. cit.*, 19.

[16] "Slavery," *Encyclopaedia Britannica* (1903), XXII:133.

[17] Seutonius, *The Twelve Caesars*, trans. by Robert Graves (Harmondsworth, Middlesex, England: Penguin Books, Ltd., 1978).

[18] Lewis Copeland, editor, *The World's Great Speeches* (New York: The Book League of America, 1942), 39-40.

[19] LaSor, *op. cit.*, 19.

[20] *Ibid.*

[21] George M. Gibson, *A History of New Testament Times* (Nashville, Tenn.: Cokesbury Press, 1926), 78-79.

[22] Spivey, *op. cit.*, 33.

[23] *Ibid.*, 34.

[24] Rondo Cameron, "Roads and Highways," *Encyclopaedia Britannica* (1970), 19:367.

[25] Werner Keller, *The Bible as History*, 2nd rev. ed., trans. by William Neil (New York: Bantam Books, 1980), 399.

[26] Cameron, *op. cit.*

[27] Thomas Cadrington, "Roads and Streets," *Encyclopaedia Britannica* (1903), XX:582.

[28] Cameron, *op. cit.*, 368.

[29] Spivey, *op. cit.*, 34.

[30] Morton Scott Enslin, *Christian Beginnings: Parts I and II* (New York: Harper & Row, Publishers, 1956), 78-79.

[31] *Ibid.*, 78.

[32] LaSor, *op. cit.*, 20.

[33] *Ibid.*, 20-21.

[34] Julius Robert Mantey, "New Testament Backgrounds," *The Biblical Expositor*, ed. Carl F. H. Henry (Philadelphia: A. J. Holman Company, 1973), 788-89.

[35] Spivey, *op. cit.*, 46.

[36] *Ibid.*, 6.

[37] LaSor, *op. cit.*, 21.

[38] *Ibid.*

[39] Spivey, *op. cit.*, 47.

[40] LaSor, *op. cit.*

[41] *Ibid.*, 21-22.

[42] Spivey, *op. cit.*, 34.

[43] *Ibid.*, 34-35.

[44] Jerry H. Combee, *The History of the World in Christian Perspective*, vol. I (Pensacola, Fla.: A Beka Book Publications, 1979), 261.

[45] LaSor, *op. cit.*, 22.

PERSPECTIVE

Remarks on the Gospel History by William Nast

With the incarnation of the Son of God commences, and on it rests, the fullness of time (Gal. 4:4). It is the end of the old world, and the beginning of the new, which is dated from his birth. The entire development of humanity, especially of the religious ideas of all nations, before the birth of Christ, must be viewed as an introduction to this great event. The preparation for it began indeed with the very creation of man, who was made in the image of God, and destined for communion with him through the eternal Son, and with the promise of deliverance by the seed of the woman, some vague memories of which promise survived in the heathen religions. With the call of Abraham, some two thousand years before the birth of Christ, the religious development of humanity separates into two independent and antagonistic lines, Judaism and heathenism. In the former the development was influenced and directed by a continuous course of Divine cooperation; in the latter it was left to the unaided powers and capacities of man. These two parallel lines continued side by side with each other till, in the fullness of time, they merged in Christianity, which they were mutually to serve by their appropriate fruits, and results, and respectively-peculiar developments; but with which, also, the ungodly elements of both would enter into a deadly conflict. As Christianity is the reconciliation and union of God and man in and through Jesus Christ, the God-man and Savior, it must have been preceded by a twofold process of preparation—an approach of God to man, and an approach of man to God. In Judaism the preparation is direct and positive, proceeding from above downward, and ending with the birth of the Messiah. In heathenism it is indirect, and mainly, though not entirely, negative, proceeding from below upward, and ending with a helpless cry of mankind for redemption. . . . In Judaism the true religion was prepared for mankind, and in heathenism mankind was prepared for its reception. . . .

The flower of paganism appears in the two great nations of classic antiquity, Greece and Rome. With the language, morality, literature, and religion of these nations Christianity came directly into contact. These, together with the Jews, were the chosen nations of the ancient world, and shared the earth among them. While the Jews were chosen for things eternal, to keep the sanctuary of the true religion, the Greeks prepared the elements of natural culture, of science and art for the use of the Church, and the Romans developed the idea of law, and organized the civilized world in a universal empire, ready to serve the spiritual universality of the Gospel. On the one hand God endowed the Greeks and Romans with the richest natural gifts, that they might reach the highest civilization possible without the aid of Christianity, and thus both provide the instruments of human science, art, and law for the use of the Christian Church, and yet at the same time show the utter impotence of these alone to bless and save the world. On the other hand, the universal empire of Rome was a positive groundwork for the universal empire of the Gospel. It served as a crucible, in which all contradictory and irreconcilable peculiarities of the ancient nations and religions were dissolved into the chaos of the new creation. The Roman legions razed the partition-walls among the ancient nations, brought the extremes of the civilized world together in free intercourse, and united North and South, and East and West in the bonds of a common language and culture, of common laws and customs. Thus they evidently, though unconsciously, opened the way for the rapid and general spread of that religion which unites all nations in one family of God by the spiritual bond of faith and love. . . .

Thus was the way for Christianity prepared on every side, positively and negatively, directly and indirectly, in theory and practice, by truth and by error, by false belief and by unbelief, by Jewish religion, by Grecian culture, and by Roman conquest; by the vainly-attempted amalgamation of Jewish and heathen thought, by the exposed impotence of natural civilization, philosophy, art, and political power, by the decay of the old religions, by the universal distraction and hopeless misery of the age, and by the yearnings of all earnest and noble souls for the unknown God.

In the fullness of time, when the fairest flowers of science and art had withered, and the world was on the verge of despair, the Virgin's Son was born to heal the infirmities of mankind. Christ entered a dying world as the author of a new and imperishable life.[1]

---

[1] William Nast, *The Gospel Records: Their Genuineness, Authenticity, Historic Verity, and Inspiration, with Some Preliminary Remarks on the Gospel History* (Cincinnati: Cranston and Stowe, 1866), 350-52, 361-62.

PART II

THE IMPORTANCE OF THE PAST

Behold, the days come, saith the Lord,
that I will raise unto David a righteous Branch,
and a King shall reign and prosper,
and shall execute judgment and justice in the earth.

Jeremiah 23:5

The Apostles had to unfold and declare the significance of the Past. They had to point out the substance of Christianity as shadowed forth in the earlier dispensation. They had to make known the mighty Lawgiver of a new covenant, the divine King of a spiritual Israel, the Prophet of a universal Church. They had to connect Christianity with Judaism.[1]

-Brooke Foss Westcott, *An Introduction to the Study of the Gospels*

To the Christian, no chapter in the history of mankind can be more instructive or important, than that which contains the rise, progress, and downfall of his religious ancestors.[2]

-H. H. Milman, *The History of the Jews*

It follows, as a matter of course, that in receiving St. Matthew's Gospel the Church commits herself to a definite and very exalted view of Jewish history and prophecy. To this view, indeed, she is committed with her very life, because her Master is so committed. Whatever theories may be formed of possible limitations of His human knowledge, to suppose Him ignorant of a matter so directly bearing upon the purpose of His mission, is to suppose Him fatally incompetent for the execution of the very work which he came to perform. The Church will follow the course of all true criticism of the Hebrew Scriptures with a deep and reverent interest, without panic and without perturbation, with fearless patience and with perfect impartiality. All that is proved she will accept, and find her vision enlarged. All that is conjectural, however exquisitely ingenious, she will let pass with a sigh or with a smile. The spirit of the first Gospel will help her to discriminate in Judaism that which is accidental and merely part of the equipment of preparation from that which is living and eternal. The first of these elements of Judaism is like the rusted anchor which lies upon the shore, or like the torn and sodden nest in the wood. The second is like the vessel which the anchor once held, now moving far away upon the sea; or like the bird, once helpless in the nest, now exulting in its liberty. More and more the Church will be guided, not so much to learn Christ from the Old Testament as to learn the Old Testament from Christ; not so much to learn the New Testament through the Old, as to learn the Old Testament through the New.[3]

-William Alexander, *The Leading Ideas of the Gospels*

---

[1] Brook Foss Westcott, *An Introduction to the Study of the Gospels* (London: Macmillan & Co., 1875), 219.

[2] H.H. Milman, *The History of the Jews from the Earliest Period to the Present Time* (New York: Harper & Brothers, Cliff St., 1837),7.

[3] William Alexander, *The Leading Ideas of the Gospels* (London: Macmillan and Co., 1892), 46-47.

Figure II-1. Leonardo da Vinci: The Last Supper

This wonderful painting, with Raphael's *Madonna di San Sisto* and Michelangelo's *Last Judgment*, "is the third most celebrated picture of the world. It was painted, twenty years the earliest of the three, on the refectory wall of the convent of Santa Maria della Grazie at Milan, where its defaced remains are still an object of pilgrimage and wonder."[4]

The only curved line in the entire architectural framework of the composition is over the central opening, and "is the focal point of all lines in the composition."[5] Our attention is immediately focused on the rejected Christ, who has, presumably, just spoken the fateful words, "*One of you shall betray me*" (Matt. 26:21). In response to this statement the disciples "*were exceedingly sorrowful, and began every one of them to say unto him, Lord, is it I?*" (Matt. 26:22).

Matthew emphasizes the rejection of the King, and The Last Supper depicts the very moment when Christ predicts His betrayal. His "unexpected words have fallen upon the group like an electric shock; they have broken the company into four distinct groups, each distinguished by its peculiar psychological state, and exhibiting in the several faces every emotion of which the situation is capable."[6]

---

[4] *Enclyclopaedia Britannica* (1903), XIV:458.

[5] Helen Gardner, *Art Through the Ages*, 4th ed., Edited by Sumner McK. Crosby (New York: Harcourt Brace & World, Inc., 1959), 329.

[6] Albert Edward Bailey, *The Gospel in Art* (Boston: The Pilgrim Press, 1946), 302.

Chapter Three

The Gospel of Matthew: Righteousness Through Obedience

The Gospel of Matthew, which stands at the beginning of the New Testament, "was probably not the earliest Gospel to be written, but there is no book of the New Testament which could so fittingly occupy this introductory position. For Matthew's first chapter begins with a genealogical tree whose roots go down deep into Old Testament history, showing how Jesus is the descendent of Abraham and the heir to King David's throne."[1] Quoting more Old Testament Scriptures than Mark, Luke, and John combined, Matthew's narrative is the most logical of the four Gospels to link the Old and New Testaments. In discussing its transitional nature, the late Dr. James M. Gray wrote:

> Keep in mind that Matthew is writing for Jewish people, and is seeking, under the inspiration of the Holy Spirit, to present Jesus to them as the One who fulfills the Old Testament features of the Messiah.[2]

Israel's Perspective of the Past

The Gospel of Matthew not only reveals the importance of the past, as it relates the fulfillment of Old Testament prophecies (cf. 1:22; 2:15, 17, 23; 4:14; 8:17; 12:17; 13:14, 35; 21:4; 26:54, 56; 27:9, 35), but it was addressed to an audience that had a greater sense of history—and its significance—than did any other people in the ancient world. In fact, one will search in vain to find another culture that had the same perspective of the past as the Jewish nation. Matthew wrote his Gospel to a people that have no parallel in the annals of history. Contrasting the meaning in history as understood by the Hebrews and their contemporaries can show this.

> According to most classical philosophies and religions ultimate reality is disclosed when man, either by rational contemplation or mystic ascent, goes beyond the flow of events which we call "history." The goal is the apprehension of an order of reality unaffected by the fleeting days or by the unpredictable fortunes of mankind. In Hinduism, for instance, the world of sense experience is regarded as maya, illusion; the religious man, therefore, seeks release from the wheel of life in order that his individuality may fade out into the World-Soul, Brahma. Or, Greek philosophers looked upon the world as a natural process which, like the rotation of the seasons, always follows the same rational scheme. The philosopher, however, could soar above the recurring cycles of history by fixing his mind upon the unchanging absolutes which belong to the eternal order. Both of these views are vastly different from the Biblical claim that God is found within the limitations of the world of change and struggle, and especially that he reveals himself in events which are unique, particular, and unrepeatable. For the Bible, history is neither maya nor a circular process of nature; it is the arena of God's purposive activity.[3]

The Jewish people had an insight into history's significance, which was never shared by their polytheistic contemporaries.

For India, man's destination is beyond history altogether. The world in which he currently lives is . . . "middle world;" it will always contain approximately the same amount of good and evil, pleasure and pain, right and wrong. This being its inherent and intended condition, all thought of cleaning it up, of changing it appreciably, is in principle misguided. The nature religions of Egypt, Mesopotamia, and other Mediterranean folk reached the same conclusion by a different route. For these, man's destination was not beyond history; it was in history all right but in history as it was currently manifesting itself, not in history as amenable to improvement. We can see why not. If one's attention is on nature, as the nature polytheist's always was, one does not look beyond nature for fulfillment. But neither—and this is the point—does one look for improvement in the natural order. The idea of an improved nature scarcely suggests itself to man, for the matter seems completely out of his hands. The Egyptians no more asked whether the sun god Ra was shining as he should than the modern astronomer asks whether sunlight travels at a proper speed. In nature the emphasis is on what is rather than what ought to be.[4]

Israel's historical outlook was much different from any of her polytheistic neighbors because she had a different perspective of God.

The nature polytheisms that surrounded Judaism all buttressed the status quo. Conditions might not be all the heart would wish, but what impressed the polytheist was that they might be a great deal worse. For if the powers of nature reside in many gods—in Mesopotamia their number was in the thousands— there was always the danger that these gods might fall out among themselves and universal chaos result. As a consequence, religion's attention was directed toward keeping things as they were. Egyptian religion, for example, repeatedly contrasted the "passionate man" to the "silent man," exalting the latter because he never disturbs the established order.[5]

It should come as no surprise, then, to learn that no nature polytheism has ever produced a major social revolution that was initiated by a concept of social justice. In any nation dominated by polytheism, the existing social order is not likely to be changed.

In Judaism, by contrast, history is in tension between its divine potentialities and its present frustrations. There is a profound disharmony between God's will and the existing social order. As a consequence, more than any other religion of the time Judaism laid the groundwork for social protest. As things are not as they should be, revolution in some form is to be expected. The idea bore fruit. It is in the countries that have been affected by the Jewish perspective on history, which was taken over by Christianity and to some extent by Islam, that the most intensive movements for social reform have occurred.[6]

Whereas people who were under the influence of polytheistic cultures might look at history with indifference, the Jewish estimate of the Past was the exact opposite of this attitude.

To the Jews history was of towering significance. It was important, first, because they were convinced that the context in which life is lived affects that life in every way, setting up its problems, delineating its opportunities, conditioning its fulfillment. . . .

Second, if contexts are crucial for life so is group action—social action as we usually call it—for there are times when it takes group action to change contexts to the needed extent. The destiny of the individual Hebrew slave in bondage in Egypt is not depicted as depending on the extent to which he "rose above" his slavery by praising God with his spirit while his body was in chains; he had to rise with his people and break for the desert.

Third, history was important for the Jews because they saw it, always, as a field of opportunity. God was the ruler of history; nothing, therefore, happened by accident. His hand was at work in every event—in Eden, the Flood, the Tower of Babel, the years in the wilderness—shaping each sequence into a teaching experience for those who had the wit to learn.

Finally, history was important because its opportunities did not stream forth on an even plateau. Events, all of them important, were nevertheless not of equal importance. It was not the case that anyone, anywhere, at any time could turn to history and find awaiting him an opportunity equivalent to any other. Each opportunity was unique but some were decisive. . . . One must, therefore, attend to history carefully, for when opportunities pass they are gone.[7]

In the eleventh chapter of the Letter to the Hebrews, we find a long list of Old Testament characters who responded in obedience to God through circumstances, which involved His direct intervention in history at certain critical points. For example, we read:

By faith Noah, being warned of God of things not seen as yet, moved with fear, prepared an ark to the saving of his house; by the which he condemned the world, and became heir of the righteousness which is by faith. HEB. 11:7

The Hebrew mind understood that it is impossible to talk about Biblical characters apart from the particular circumstances that surrounded them and from which their lives took shape. In the case of Noah, he is revered as a man of faith because he obeyed God and built the ark, when common sense and peer pressure would have led him to do otherwise.

By faith Abraham, when he was called to go out into a place which he should after receive for an inheritance, obeyed; and he went out, not knowing whither he went. HEB. 11:8

From the pagan culture of Sumeria "God calls Abraham. He is to go forth into a new land to establish a new people. The moment is decisive. Because Abraham seizes it, he ceases to be anonymous. He becomes the first Hebrew, the first of 'the chosen people.'"[8]

By faith Moses, when he was born, was hid three months of his parents, because they saw he was a proper child; and they were not afraid of the king's commandment. HEB. 11:23

Moses' parents, likewise, made the right decision at a very decisive moment in history!

By faith Moses, when he was come to years, refused to be called the son of Pharaoh's daughter; Choosing rather to suffer affliction with the people of God, than to enjoy the pleasures of sin for a season; Esteeming the reproach of Christ greater riches than the treasures in Egypt: for he had respect unto the recompence of the reward. By faith he forsook Egypt, not fearing the wrath of the king: for he endured, as seeing him who is invisible. Through faith he kept the Passover,

and the sprinkling of blood, lest he that destroyed the firstborn should touch them. By faith they
passed through the Red Sea as by dry land: which the Egyptians assaying to do were drowned.
HEB. 11:24-29

The Importance of the Exodus

The Exodus was a decisive moment in history. The Jews—individually and collectively—had to respond in obedience, as God Himself personally intervened in the
affairs of men at a critical point in time. In fact, the Exodus "was not only the event
which launched the Jews as a nation. It was also the first clear act by which God made
known to the Jews the fullness of His nature."[9]

And why did God choose to make known the fullness of His character through
His actions? Because "action alone can adequately express character; and it is character in God that men most need to know, and he most wishes to express."[10] God
primarily revealed Himself and His nature to the Jewish people, not in writing, but in
actual life—in living history! Nineteenth-century theologian, William Newton Clarke,
asserted that God's revelation to man was made less by what He said than by what He
did. He wrote:

> So when God showed himself to Abraham, we hear of no written revelation,
> of some spoken revelation, and of much acted revelation; for it was in what
> he did to the man who trusted him that God became known for what he was.
> Revelation to Israel through Moses was not made in writing; it was made in
> small part by speech, but mainly by action,—for Israel was taught to know
> God and his will mainly in what he did among them. To Israel throughout
> its history God revealed himself not mainly in words, and still less in writ-
> ing, but in action. The prophets did indeed speak of him as a God manifest
> in his doings,—a God present and acting, and known by his acts. God was
> revealed in Israel by his providential care, his great deliverances, his historical
> judgments; by his appointed institutions and his spiritual influences, inspiring
> piety, penitence, and hope; by his influence upon prophets, awakening them
> to utter his truth, and by his persistent purpose to train the nation for himself.
> He revealed himself by entering into the life of Israel and acting there. The
> truth that he would practically teach he expressed in living history.
> Thus it was not in writing that God revealed himself. The revelation that we
> find in the Book of Exodus was not made in the Book of Exodus, but in the
> events that the book records,—not, for example, in the fourteenth chapter,
> but in the deliverance from Egypt. So throughout the Old Testament: God
> showed himself in the life of men; and the story of his self-showing, with the
> substance of what men learned from it, was written afterward.[11]

The Exodus, however, was the watershed event in the history of the Jewish people.

> It is true that Genesis describes a number of occasions on which God disclosed
> himself before the Exodus, but these accounts were all written later in the light
> of this decisive experience. That God was a direct party to their escape from
> Pharaoh the Jews had no doubt. "By every known sociological law," writes Carl
> Mayer, "the Jews should have perished long ago." The Biblical writers would
> have placed the emphasis differently: by every known sociological law the Jews

should never have begun to exist at all. Yet here was the fact: a tiny, loosely-related group of people who had no real collective life of their own and who were in servitude to the great power of the day had succeeded in making their get-away and in eluding the chariots of the pursuers. Knowing their own weakness as vividly as Egypt's strength, it seemed to the Jews flatly impossible that the liberation was of their own doing. It was a clear miracle. . . .

Having been made vividly aware of God's saving power in the Exodus, the Jews proceeded to review their earlier history in the light of this revealing experience. As their liberation had obviously been engineered by God, what of the sequence leading up to it? Had this been mere chance? Looking back it seemed to the Jews that God's initiative had been involved in every decisive step of their corporate existence. No vagabond impulse had prompted Abraham to leave his home in Ur and assume the long, uncharted trek toward Canaan. Yahweh had called him to father a people to destiny. So it had been throughout: Isaac and Jacob had been kept providentially and Joseph exalted in Egypt for the express purpose of preserving his people from famine. From the perspective of the Exodus everything fell into place: from the very beginning God had been leading, protecting, and shaping his people for this climactic event which gave birth to their nation.

The Exodus, we are saying, was more than an historical divide which turned a people into a nation. It was an episode in which this people became overwhelmingly aware of God and for the first time perceived his character clearly.[12]

And just what was the true nature of God that the Hebrew people saw revealed in the Exodus? First of all, He was a God of infinite power—"power enough to outdo the mightiest empire, Egypt, with whatever gods might be backing it."[13]

Secondly, He was a God of marvelous goodness and love. "Had the Jews done anything to deserve this miraculous release? Not as far as they could see. Freedom had come to them as an act of sheer, spontaneous, unmerited grace, a clear instance of Yahweh's unanticipated and astonishing love."[14]

Finally, He was a God who was intensely concerned with man and his activities.

Whereas the gods of the other people of the region were primarily nature gods, deifying the numinous awe men felt for the natural powers of the universe, Israel's God had revealed himself not primarily in sun or storm or fertility but in an historical event. The difference this made to Jewish religion cannot be exaggerated. Disclosing to them as it did a God who cared enough about man's historical situation to intervene directly in it, it turned Judaism from the prevailing preoccupation of the surrounding religions—which was to keep the forces of nature operating beneficially—and directed its primary concern toward achieving God's will in the affairs of men.[15]

Given these three basic aspects of God's character that were revealed in the Exodus, "the Jews' other insights into his nature followed readily enough. If God is himself good, there can be little question concerning his will for men: he will want them to be good as well. Hence Sinai. It was no accident that the Ten Commandments, as the Jews' understanding of God's will for his people, followed the Exodus immediately. God's goodness calls for an answering goodness from men."[16]

At Sinai God made a covenant with the Jews, which involved special blessings contingent on their obedience to Him. Speaking from the mountain, God instructed Moses what to tell the children of Israel:

> *Ye have seen what I did unto the Egyptians, and how I bare you on eagles' wings, and brought you unto myself. Now therefore, if ye will obey my voice indeed, and keep my covenant, then ye shall be a peculiar treasure unto me above all people: for all the earth is mine: And ye shall be unto me a kingdom of priests, and an holy nation. These are the words which thou shalt speak unto the children of Israel.* EXOD. 19:4-6

Not surprisingly, then, we would expect a Gospel written to the Jewish people to place a special emphasis on obedience and righteousness. And the truth is, from one end of Matthew's account to the other—from the narrative of Christ's birth to His last words to the disciples—the theme of obedience recurs (cf. 5:17-20; 7:15-27; 21:28-32; 28:20). Furthermore, the importance of making the right decision at the right time is stressed in Matthew, as illustrated in the parable of the ten virgins, of whom *"five of them were wise, and five were foolish"* (25:2).

Throughout the Gospel of Matthew there is portrayed the contrast between those who make the right decisions, and those who do not. In the Sermon on the Mount Jesus said:

> *Enter ye in at the strait gate: for wide is the gate, and broad is the way, that leadeth to destruction, and many there be which go in thereat: Because strait is the gate, and narrow is the way, which leadeth unto life, and few there be that find it.* MATT. 7:13-14

In Matthew's account we see the disparity between the righteous and the unrighteous; the obedient and the disobedient; the good and the evil. Specifically, we note the contrast between the wheat and the tares (13:25); the pearls and the swine (7:6); the good tree with the good fruit and the corrupt tree with the evil fruit (7:17); the wise man with the house upon the rock and the foolish man with the house on the sand (7:24-27); the devils that are either cast out by Beelzebub or by the Spirit of God (12:27-28); the good man with the good treasure and the evil man with the evil treasure (12:35); ears that are dull of hearing and ears that hear (13:15-16); eyes that are closed and eyes that see (13:15-16); hearts that are waxed gross and hearts that understand (13:15); seed in the stony places among thorns and seed in the good ground (13:20-23); the children of the kingdom and the children of the wicked one (13:38); the good that is put into a vessel and the bad that is cast away (13:48); the wicked that are severed from the just (13:49); the disciples that transgress the traditions of the elders and the elders that transgress the commandments of God (15:2-3); fair weather and foul weather (16:2-3); those who would save their life but lose it and those who will lose their life but find it (16:25); the rebuked devil and the cured child (17:18); the compassionate lord and the wicked servant (18:27, 32); the first that shall be last and the last that shall be first (19:30); the many called and the few chosen (20:16, 22:14); the house of prayer and the den of thieves (21:13); the son who said I will not but did and the son who said I will but did not (21:28-30); the elders who believed not and the harlots who believed (21:32); the exalted that shall be abased and the humble that shall be exalted (23:12); the one taken from the field and the other that was left (24:40); the woman taken at the mill and the other left grinding (24:41); the good, faithful servant and the wicked, slothful servant (25:21, 26); the sheep on the right hand and the goats on the left (25:33); those who go into everlasting punishment and those who enter into life eternal (25:46).

God's Will Accomplished in History

The narrative material in the opening chapters of Matthew's account, which are unique to the first Gospel, demonstrates how God accomplishes His will in history through the lives and decisions of various individuals. As we see the dilemmas faced by (1) Joseph at Mary's conception, (2) the wise men at Jerusalem and Bethlehem, (3) John the Baptist at Jesus' baptism, and (4) Christ at the Temptation, we get a glimpse of their characters as expressed in their actions. Their obedience to God's will, as evidenced in their conduct, sets the tone for the discourses of Christ which follow.

Approximately three-fourths of Matthew's Gospel is composed of the teachings of Christ, which stress the need for righteousness and obedience. An overview of these five discourses will be given in the next chapter, but for now it is sufficient to remind the reader of Christ's injunction to *"seek ye first the kingdom of God, and his righteousness"* (6:33). Standing in contrast to Joseph, John the Baptist, the wise men, and Christ—who seek God's righteousness in their lives—are those in Matthew's Gospel who are indifferent and/or resistant to God's will. Nevertheless, God accomplishes His purposes and fulfills Old Testament prophecies in spite of their opposition. We see, furthermore, the weakness of character revealed in the lives of such unrighteous men as Herod Antipas, Judas Iscariot, Pontius Pilate, and of course the nameless but numerous scribes and Pharisees.

Herod Antipas, for example, had John the Baptist beheaded. Although he was sorry about it, he nevertheless ordered the execution because of a foolish oath he had made (14:1-11). Judas, when he saw that Christ was condemned, admitted his guilt by saying, *"I have sinned in that I have betrayed the innocent blood"* (27:4). Nevertheless, instead of seeking true forgiveness, he *"went and hanged himself"* (27:5). Pontius Pilate, being warned by his wife about Christ and knowing *"that for envy they had delivered him"* (27:18), nevertheless *"delivered him to be crucified"* (27:26). Acting contrary to his own convictions, *"he took water and washed his hands before the multitude, saying, I am innocent of the blood of this just person: see ye to it"* (27:24).

History is the theater of God's purposive activity, and through the lives of both good and evil people, God was staging events in fulfillment of Old Testament prophecies. Throughout the Gospel of Matthew—from being called out of Egypt to purchasing the potter's field; from the weeping in Rama to the parting of Christ's garments—we read that all was done *"that it might be fulfilled which was spoken of the Lord by the prophet"* (cf. 1:22; 2:15, 17, 23; 4:14; 8:17; 12:17; 13:14, 35; 21:4; 26:54, 56; 27:9, 35).

The Story of Jesus' Birth

The first Old Testament prophecy recorded by Matthew as being fulfilled, was that spoken of Isaiah; namely, that *"a virgin shall conceive, and bear a son, and shall call his name Immanuel"* (Isa. 7:14). Before we examine this event, we should note that the genealogy of Christ in the opening verses of Matthew's Gospel (1:1-17) sets the stage for understanding the drama surrounding His birth (1:18-25). For any Jewish reader with even a rudimentary knowledge of Hebrew history, the genealogy reminds one that nothing in history happens by accident and God's hand was at work in every event. Remember, all events in history may be important, but not all are of equal importance. The genealogy of Christ, however, cites names and places that are associated with events that were very important. For example:

(1) The pair of names in the opening verse are linked with two of the great covenants that God made in the Old Testament; namely, the Abrahamic covenant that Christ was to fulfill (cf. Gen. 12:3), and the Davidic throne that He was to occupy (cf. II Sam. 7:8-13).

(2) The mention of the Babylonian captivity brings to mind the miraculous events of that period—the interpretation of dreams and visions, the protection of Daniel in the lion's den, and the preservation of his three friends in the fiery furnace—when God worked supernaturally to carry out His program.

(3) The inclusion of women in a Hebrew genealogy, which was most unusual, brings to mind the important decisions that each faced within the context of their own historical circumstances. "According to Raymond E. Brown in his work *The Birth of the Messiah* (Doubleday), each of these women 'showed initiative . . . and so, came to be considered the instrument of God's providence' in bringing forth the Messiah."[17] Furthermore, it is of interest to note that "there was something unusual about each woman's relationship to her husband—a narrative element that was irregular, even scandalous, but necessary to perpetuate the Messianic line. Thus did these women foreshadow Mary, who responded in humble but anxious faith to the angel's announcement of her miraculous but unusual pregnancy, and who possibly endured malicious rumors concerning the birth of her first son."[18]

The Jews viewed history as a field of opportunity, where God was shaping each sequence of events "into a teaching experience for those who had the wit to learn."[19] Within this setting, then, we can now begin to look at the events surrounding the advent of Christ and the dawning of the age of fulfillment.

Lessons from the Life of Joseph

Only Matthew and Luke record the story of Jesus' birth. Where Luke, however, emphasizes the wonder of it all from the perception of the virgin Mary, Matthew's account clearly focuses on Joseph's response to the pregnancy of his espoused wife. Though Matthew explicitly mentions the virgin birth (cf. 1:18, 20, 23, 25), his emphasis is "rather on how Joseph will react to the dilemma posed by the question of whether she is pregnant from unfaithfulness or the power of God. Not only is the question posed within the birth story itself but also by the preceding section. Inclusion of the women in Matthew's genealogy raises the question of how God works to achieve his purposes, and at the culmination of the birth story Joseph must decide whether Mary's pregnancy is God's action."[20]

When Joseph discovered that Mary *"was found with child"* (1:18), he must have been deeply hurt and offended. Although Scripture doesn't tell us how Joseph felt, it does say this about him:

> And Joseph her husband, being a righteous man, and not wanting to disgrace her, desired to put her away secretly. 1:19, NASB

"According to Jewish law, a man could do one of two things. He could bring his betrothed to public trial where conviction of infidelity might carry the penalty of death by stoning, or he could divorce his betrothed privately. Engagement, like marriage, could only be severed by divorce. Joseph generously opts for the latter course."[21] Considering these circumstances, Joseph had the intention—and every right—to disengage himself from such a compromised entanglement.

> *But while he thought on these things, behold the angel of the Lord appeared unto him in a dream, saying, Joseph, thou son of David, fear not to take unto thee Mary thy wife: for that which is conceived in her is of the Holy Ghost. And she shall bring forth a son, and thou shalt call his name JESUS: for he shall save his people from their sins.* 1:20-21

It was a decisive moment in history. There was no other living man on earth at the time through which Jesus could have been given the legal right to the throne of David. On the other hand, Joseph had every right to disannul his association with Mary, and spare himself any further humiliation from a continued relationship with her. But the heart of this story is Joseph's response to the dilemma:

> *Then Joseph being raised from sleep did as the angel of the Lord had bidden him, and took unto him his wife: And knew her not till she had brought forth her firstborn son: and he called his name JESUS.* 1:24-25

"Joseph accepts the presence of God, when it draws near to him in a dream. The text simply states that when he 'woke from sleep, he did as the angel of the Lord commanded him.' . . . Joseph obeyed; he practiced a higher righteousness."[22] He took Mary as his wife, yet refrained from any intimate relationship with her until she gave birth to her firstborn Son. Joseph also called His name Jesus, as the angel had instructed him in the dream.

It is of interest to compare Matthew's Joseph with the Joseph of the Old Testament. "In what are called the Elohist sections of the Pentateuch, God makes His will known pre-eminently in dreams, and Joseph 'the dreamer of dreams' is one who is particularly favored by God with this form of revelation. It is possible that the Old Testament Joseph is in this respect regarded as the precursor of the New Testament Joseph."[23] The credibility of the dreams of Matthew's Joseph—if he was at all attentive to history—may have to some degree been conditioned by their genuineness in the life of the patriarch Joseph. Because both Josephs were obedient and righteous men, they could trust that their dreams were from God.

Their righteousness was evidenced in their obedience. In Genesis 37:12-14, for example, we find that the elder Joseph "loved and honoured his father, and would have gladly gone anywhere to please and serve him."[24]

> Joseph was ever ready to comply with his father's wishes, as soon as they were intimated to him. Jacob, deeply concerned for the welfare of all his children, although he entertained a peculiar regard to the best of his sons, sends Joseph to Shechem, to bring him intelligence whether all his brethren were safe and well. As soon as Joseph was called by his father, he said, Here am I. Our Lord, in a parable, speaks of two sons commanded by their father to go and labour in the vineyard, one of whom said to his father, I go, sir, but went not; the other said, I go not, but went. The last was, without question, the best of the two; but Joseph was better than either. He said, I go; and he went.[25]

Joseph obeyed. Joseph always obeyed. His entire life as recorded in Scripture was marked by a consistent obedience to God's will!

In the second chapter of Matthew, we find that the younger Joseph, who has earlier been described as a righteous man (cf. 1:19), also acts in obedience—immediately—whenever the angel of the Lord reveals God's will to him.

> *And . . . behold, the angel of the Lord appeareth to Joseph in a dream, saying, Arise, and take the young child and his mother, and flee into Egypt, and be thou there until I bring thee word: for Herod will seek the young child to destroy him. When he arose, he took the young child and his mother by night, and departed into Egypt: And was there until the death of Herod: that it might be fulfilled which was spoken of the Lord by the prophet, saying, Out of Egypt have I called my son. . . . But when Herod was dead, behold, and angel of the Lord appeared in a dream to Joseph in Egypt, Saying, Arise, and take the young child and his mother, and go into the land of Israel: for they are dead which sought the young child's life.*
>
> *And he arose, and took the young child and his mother, and came into the land of Israel. But when he heard that Archelaus did reign in Judaea in the room of his father Herod, he was afraid to go thither: notwithstanding, being warned of God in a dream, he turned aside into the parts of Galilee: And he came and dwelt in a city called Nazareth: that it might be fulfilled which was spoken by the prophets, He shall be called a Nazarene.* 2:13-15, 19-23

Both Josephs ended up in Egypt due to circumstances beyond their own control, yet both had confidence that their families would not remain there forever. The elder Joseph, even though he spent most of his life in Egypt, knew he was not there "for the sake of the honours and pleasures which the court of Egypt could afford him, but because it was the will of God that he should dwell there, to be a father to Pharaoh, and to be the shepherd of Israel."[26] Both Josephs were sent to Egypt in order to be the shepherd and protector of their respective families.

As the patriarch Joseph—still in Egypt—approached the end of his life, he had this to say to his family:

> *And Joseph said unto his brethren, I die: and God will surely visit you, and bring you out of this land unto the land which he sware to Abraham, to Isaac, and to Jacob. And Joseph took an oath of the children of Israel, saying, God will surely visit you, and ye shall carry up my bones from hence.* GEN. 50:24-25

Joseph had lived but a short time in Canaan. He had received great favours from the King and people of Egypt. He had spent the greatest part of his life in that country, enjoying all the pleasures which it could afford, and receiving all the honour which a higher-minded man than Joseph would have wished. Yet he never considered Egypt but Canaan as his home; he desired that his bones should lie, not with the dust of the princes of Egypt, but in the land which God sware to Abraham, Isaac, and Jacob. By that faith by which he was persuaded of the truth of the promise, and of its goodness, he gave commandment concerning his bones.[27]

> *So Joseph died, being an hundred and ten years old: and they embalmed him, and he was put in a coffin in Egypt.* GEN. 50:26

Joseph lived by faith in spite of the fact that he died before he saw the realization of the promise, that his people would be redeemed from the land of Egypt and brought to the Promised Land. The same can be said of his namesake. Matthew's Joseph also lived by faith in spite of the fact that he died before he saw the realization of the promise made to him by the angel—that Jesus would *"save his people from their sins"* (Matt. 1:21).

Joseph may have wondered how God could bring the promised Messiah-King into the world at this time in history. Except for a brief period of independence under the rule of the Hasmonaeans, the nation of Israel had been under foreign domination for centuries. Although he himself was a direct descendent of the kings of Judah, he was not royalty, but a peasant. Furthermore, the wickedness of some of the later kings listed in the genealogy, finally climaxed with the following curse put on Jechonias (cf. Matt. 1:11), who was referred to as Coniah by the prophet Jeremiah:

> *As I live, saith the Lord, though Coniah the son of Jehoiakim king of Judah were the signet upon my right hand, yet would I pluck thee thence; . . . Is this man Coniah a despised broken idol? Is he a vessel wherein is no pleasure? Wherefore are they cast out, he and his seed, and are cast into a land which they know not? . . . Thus saith the Lord, Write ye this man childless, a man that shall not prosper in his days: for no man of his seed shall prosper, sitting upon the throne of David, and ruling any more in Judah.* JER. 22:24, 28, 30

In view of the dismal situation brought about by the follies of his own ancestors and the political realities of Roman domination, Joseph may have considered the fulfillment of the Davidic covenant a lost cause. Nevertheless, he acted in obedience to the instructions of the angel of the Lord, even though it may not have seemed reasonable to do so in light of the prevailing circumstances. Yet if he knew anything at all about the Joseph of the Old Testament, he knew that God was able to accomplish His purposes in spite of insurmountable obstacles and insoluble complications. Two lessons from history—from the life of the patriarch Joseph—are noteworthy.

First of all, when Joseph's brethren tried to deceive their father Jacob about Joseph's fate, they brought him the many-colored coat, which had been dipped in blood. When Jacob saw the familiar garment, he said:

> "It is my son's coat; some evil beast hath devoured him; Joseph is without doubt rent in pieces." Nothing could be more like to truth than this conjecture. There appeared to be no reason for calling it in question. It would have been a flagrant breach of charity to suspect the truth, while there was no evidence of it. You see that sometimes the things which are so probable as to appear morally certain, are untrue, and that things may be true that have scarcely the most distant appearance of truth. We ought, therefore, in matters of importance, to examine well before we fix our judgment. "The simple believeth every word; but the prudent man looketh well to his goings."[28]

The second lesson from the life of Joseph was that God had superintended the events in history so as to reverse Joseph's misfortunes. Born as a peasant and sold as a slave, Joseph was, nevertheless, exalted to the second highest official position in the Egyptian Empire, which at that time was the most powerful kingdom on earth!

Fortunately—or we should say providentially—the Joseph of Matthew's Gospel was also a prudent and God-fearing man. He may not have understood how the Messiah could succeed upon the throne of David, especially since the throne was gone and a curse was on David's descendents to boot, but he acted in obedience, nevertheless. Joseph did not live to see the Son give His life as a Sacrifice to fulfill the Abrahamic covenant, or ascend to the throne as King to fulfill the Davidic covenant. But he had the promises of God that *"a virgin would conceive and bare a son"* (Isa. 7:14) and also that *"there shall come forth a rod out of the stem of Jesse, and a Branch shall grow out of his roots"* (Isa. 11:1). The kingly branch had been cut out of the genealogical tree, but Joseph knew that the day would come when *"there shall be a root of Jesse, which shall stand for an ensign of the people; to it shall the Gentiles seek: and his rest shall be glorious"* (Isa. 11:10).

Wise Gentiles Seek the Promised Ensign

In the second chapter of Matthew we find that the Gentiles did, indeed, seek the promised Ensign.

>Whereas Joseph showed the reaction of a loyal, just Jew to the birth of Jesus, now we see the response of wise Gentiles (28:19). They have come to worship him as they would a king or a god (2:2, 8, 11; cf. 14:33; 28:17). Their reaction to Jesus' birth contrasts with that of Herod, the political king, who can think of Jesus only as a threat to his rule. And with some reason, for the unusual star's appearance serves as a sign of a crucial event: the old age, typified by Herod's kingdom, yields to the new, manifested in the birth of Jesus.[29]

The appearance of Gentile magi in search of the Jewish Messiah is both interesting and instructive. Matthew records the scenario as follows:

>*Now when Jesus was born in Bethlehem of Judaea in the days of Herod the king, behold, there came wise men from the east to Jerusalem. Saying, Where is he that is born King of the Jews? For we have seen his star in the east, and are come to worship him. When Herod the king had heard these things, he was troubled, and all Jerusalem with him. And when he had gathered all the chief priests and scribes of the people together, he demanded of them where Christ should be born. And they said unto him, In Bethlehem of Judaea: for thus it is written by the prophet, And thou Bethlehem, in the land of Juda, art not the least among the princes of Juda: for out of thee shall come a Governor, that shall rule my people Israel. Then Herod, when he had privily called the wise men, enquired of them diligently what time the star appeared. And he sent them to Bethlehem, and said, Go and search diligently for the young child; and when ye have found him, bring me word again, that I may come and worship him also. When they had heard the king, they departed; and, lo, the star, which they saw in the east, went before them, till it came and stood over where the young child was. When they saw the star, they rejoiced with exceeding great joy. And when they were come into the house, they saw the young child with Mary his mother, and fell down, and worshipped him: and when they had opened their treasures, they presented unto him gifts; gold, and frankincense, and myrrh. And being warned of God in a dream that they should not return to Herod, they departed into their own country another way.* 2:1-12

Into which country did they return? Who were these wise men and how did they learn about those things for which they sought? An aura of mystery and confusion surrounds these Gentiles and their journey of faith. The well-known Christmas carol, for example, reads:

>*We three kings of Orient are:*
>*Bearing gifts we traverse afar—*
>*Field and fountain, moor and mountain—*
>*Following yonder star.*[30]

Several misconceptions about the wise men are revealed in the opening line of the above verse.

>First, the number of wise men who made the trip to Bethlehem is unknown. Tradition placed their number at three probably because of the three gifts of gold, frankincense, and myrrh—the assumption being one gift, one giver. Second, they were not kings. When the early church father, Tertullian, said, "The East considers magi almost as kings," he was not saying that they were actually

monarchs. Rather, their powerful standing in court made them "almost" like kings. . . . Finally, they did not come from as far away as the "Orient"—that is, the Far East. "The East" is identified variously as any country from Arabia to Media and Persia.[31]

Babylon, which was mentioned by Matthew in the context of Christ's genealogical record, is the logical vicinity from which the wise men peregrinated. Centuries earlier, the priestly caste of the magi came into contact with God's Word through the testimony of a young Jewish captive, who was taken to Babylon by Nebuchadnezzar around 605 B.C. Through the providence and sovereignty of God, Daniel not only saved the lives of the wise men of his day (cf. Dan. 2:24), but was made *ruler over the whole province of Babylon, and chief of the governors over all the wise men of Babylon*" (Dan. 2:48). "Because Daniel held a prominent position among the wise men of his day, the magi likely would have studied his writings through the centuries."[32]

The Hebrew Scriptures, of which Daniel's writings are a part, are divided into three groups known as Torah (Law), Nebi'im (Prophets), and Kethubim (Writings). "These consist of twenty-four books which, by different division, appear in the Authorized Version as thirty-nine."[33] It is of interest, furthermore, to note "the influence that each of the three divisions of the Hebrew Old Testament . . . had on the magi to aid them on their quest."[34]

From the Kethubim (Writings) the wise men learned about the prophecy of the "seventy weeks" as recorded in Daniel 9:24-27. "For the magi, this portion of Daniel's prophecy provided a timetable for the Messiah's arrival."[35]

From the section of the Hebrew Bible called the Torah (Law) the wise men learned about the prophecy of Balaam: *"I shall see him, but not now: I shall behold him, but not nigh: there shall come a star out of Jacob, and a scepter shall rise out of Israel"* (Num. 24:17).

> Unknown to the magi, the extraordinary star that they saw may have been the manifestation of the shining glory of God. This glory is referred to in Hebrew as the *Shekinah*. God may have chosen to overrule the evil of astrology and, on this occasion, to direct these wise men to the place where the Messiah could be found by a method that suited their habit of star-gazing and their understanding of astronomy for the sole purpose of giving homage. "The heavens declare the glory of God, and the firmament showeth his handiwork" (Ps. 19:1). If the star was a manifestation of the Shekinah glory, it also helps to explain its movement in Matthew 2:9. Such movement could be difficult to comprehend if it was a physical star in the sky.
>
> Interestingly, these Gentile magi did a better job of interpreting the prophecy of Numbers 24:17 than the Jewish leaders did.[36]

Upon their arrival in Jerusalem and subsequent interview at the court of Herod the Great, the wise men were directed to Bethlehem. This information was derived from the section of the Hebrew Scriptures known as the Nebi'im (Prophets). The chief priests and scribes informed Herod about the prophecy of Micah: *"But thou, Bethlehem Ephratah, though thou be little among the thousands of Judah, yet out of thee shall he come forth unto me that is to be ruler in Israel; whose goings forth have been from old, from everlasting"* (Micah 5:2).

> The entire canon of Old Testament Scripture contributed to the steps of faith taken by these wise men from the East. From the Torah they read the predic-

tion about a star, but this was only the beginning. By itself it was insufficient. From the Writings came the insight from Daniel's prophecy concerning the timing of the Messiah's coming. But still more revelation was needed. Then from the Prophets came Micah 5:2, telling where He was to be born. The culmination of their journey was God's gift to them—Jesus.[37]

How the Jewish Leaders Reacted to the Birth of Jesus

Standing about midway between Herod the Great on one side, and the wise men on the other, were the religious leaders of Judaism. Although they did not yet display the hatred of the former (cf. 2:12-13), neither did they render the homage of the latter (cf. 2:11). "One would wonder why the presence of foreigners asking about a Jewish King did not capture the attention of the religious leaders. They knew of Herod's cruelty."[38] To eliminate any threat to his own power, Herod had over the years massacred priests and nobles, decimated the Sanhedrin, had three of his own sons executed, and even ordered the strangulation of the favorite of his ten wives—the beautiful Hasmonean princess, Marianne. In addition to these, an assortment of in-laws and expendable friends fell victim to Herod's sanguinary and suspicious nature. His reign "was so cruel that, in the energetic language of the Jewish ambassadors to the Emperor Augustus, 'the survivors during his lifetime were even more miserable than the sufferers.'"[39]

By the time Christ was born, Herod the Great had reigned as King of Judea for over 30 years. To be fair, it should be acknowledged that he was a very capable and excellent ruler. To his subjects, "he was generous to a fault; in times of famine he relieved the resulting distress, at one time buying eight hundred thousand measures of corn which he distributed free. He is said to have clothed whole villages in winter. On at least two occasions he made drastic reductions in the taxes: thirty-three percent in 20 B.C., twenty-five percent in 14 B.C. Following the lead of Augustus, his building activity was carried on with a lavish scale—temples, gymnasiums, cloisters, amphitheatres, and aqueducts."[40]

But to his opponents, or anyone whom Herod viewed with suspicion, his legacy was red with the blood of murder. Herod the Great had been around long enough for the religious leaders of Judaism to know all about his character and past conduct.

> It would not have been difficult to figure out that Herod's diligent inquiry to determine the earliest appearance of the star might have been to synchronize that information with the arrival of the magi and thereby estimate the time of the child's birth. Then he could have the newborn king killed. Still the religious leaders did nothing to protect their long-awaited Messiah. Their indifference to the things of God was already present before their hatred for Jesus was ever formed.[41]

Jesus and John the Baptist

Moving from the second chapter of Matthew to the third, we find that a period of about 30 years is eclipsed. Jesus is now a grown man and we discover that His "first act in the Gospel of Matthew occurs in connection with his baptism. In Mark, Jesus did not really act at the baptism; rather he was acted upon by John the Baptist. Consequently, Jesus' first action in Mark was the calling of the disciples. Matthew, however, shows Jesus acting during this baptism by John."[42] We read:

> *Then cometh Jesus from Galilee to Jordan unto John, to be baptized of him. But John forbad him, saying, I have need to be baptized of thee, and comest thou to me? And Jesus answering said unto him, Suffer it to be so now: for thus it becometh us to fulfill all righteousness. Then he suffered him. And Jesus, when he was baptized, went up straightway out of the water: and, lo, the heavens were opened unto him, and he saw the Spirit of God descending like a dove, and lighting upon him: And lo a voice from heaven, saying, This is my beloved Son, in whom I am well pleased.* 3:13-17

It can be observed from the above passage, moreover, that "Matthew's Jesus, unlike Mark's, decides to leave Galilee in order to be baptized by John (vs. 13). What seemingly just happened to Jesus in Mark (1:9) occurs in Matthew because of Jesus' decision and action (cf. vs. 14)."[43]

Another point to be noted from the above Scripture passage is the decision that John the Baptist had to wrestle with:

> John's protest about the inappropriateness of his baptizing Jesus is answered by the first words of Jesus in Matthew, "Let it be so now; for thus it is fitting for us to fulfill all righteousness" (vs. 15). This answer, appearing only in Matthew, explains why the sinless Jesus needed a baptism for repentance. . . .
>
> The unexpected plural in Jesus' answer to John, "thus it is fitting for us to fulfill all righteousness," must in this context refer to Jesus and John the Baptist. John the Baptist also is obedient ("he consented"—vs. 15). Jesus obeyed in his decision to come from Galilee to be baptized and John the Baptist acted to complete Jesus' obedience. With their fulfillment of all righteousness, the Spirit of God appears visually to Jesus and aurally to John the Baptist (in Mark 1:11 the voice spoke to Jesus).
>
> This interpretation of the story of Jesus' baptism is supported by the following temptation story (4:1-11). The beloved Son of God, announced in the baptism, now acts as the Son in response to each temptation. "If you are the Son of God" (vss. 3, 6) does not really imply that Jesus might not be the Son of God. The baptism (3:17) left no doubt that Jesus was the Son of God. The only doubt concerns the nature of the Sonship, whether Jesus will act in obedience to God or on his own authority. Just as obedience characterized his baptism, so the temptations show the Son of God acting in accordance with the will of God (vss. 4, 7, 10).[44]

Jesus acted in obedience to the will of God, not only to fulfill all righteousness (cf. Matt. 3:15), but also to fulfill the Old Testament law and the words of the prophets. In the Sermon on the Mount, Jesus said:

> *Think not that I am come to destroy the law, or the prophets: I am not come to destroy, but to fulfil. For verily I say unto you, Till heaven and earth pass, one jot or one tittle shall in no wise pass from the law, till all be fulfilled. Whosoever therefore shall break one of these least commandments, and shall teach men so, he shall be called the least in the kingdom of heaven: but whosoever shall do and teach them, the same shall be called great in the kingdom of heaven. For I say unto you, That except your righteousness shall exceed the righteousness of the scribes and Pharisees, ye shall in no case enter into the kingdom of heaven.* 5:17-20

The "Righteousness" of the Scribes and Pharisees

In the last verse quoted above we find that the righteousness involved in fulfilling the law needs to *"exceed the righteousness of the scribes and Pharisees."* This is noteworthy because "in the time of Jesus they were the groups most likely to show obedience."[45] The scribes and the Pharisees were of all the people considered the most righteous, yet Jesus taught that a higher righteousness was required.

The scribes and the Pharisees may have kept the letter of the law, but they missed the whole intent of it. They focused on their external behavior to such an extent that they overlooked the proper motivation for obeying the law in the first place. Jesus' attitude toward the scribes and the Pharisees is revealed in the 23rd chapter of Matthew, where we find the Lord castigating them with a series of statements beginning with *"Woe unto you scribes and Pharisees, hypocrites!"* (23:13, 14, 15, 23, 25, 27, 29). The following verses fairly well summarize this particular discourse:

> *Woe unto you, scribes and Pharisees, hypocrites! For ye are like unto whited sepulchers, which indeed appear beautiful outward, but are within full of dead men's bones, and of all uncleanness. Even so ye also outwardly appear righteous unto men, but within ye are full of hypocrisy and iniquity.* 23:27-28

In the preceding chapter Matthew records the discussion that took place between Jesus and the Pharisees, which led up to the eight *"Woe unto you"* statements. Matthew describes the incident as follows:

> *But when the Pharisees had heard that he had put the Sadducees to silence, they were gathered together. Then one of them, which was a lawyer, asked him a question, tempting him, and saying, Master, which is the great commandment in the law? Jesus said unto him, Thou shalt love the Lord thy God with all thy heart, and with all thy soul, and with all thy mind. This is the first and great commandment. And the second is like unto it, Thou shalt love thy neighbour as thyself. On these two commandments hang all the law and the prophets.* 22:34-40

In summarizing the law and the prophets, Jesus says the first and great commandment is love of God and the second is love of neighbor. Note that all the law and the prophets depend on these two commandments (v. 40). This conclusion, which appears only in Matthew, suggests that the righteousness that the law required "consists of a primary relation with God and a secondary relation with other men."[46] This view of a righteousness that must *"exceed the righteousness of the scribes and Pharisees,"* as Jesus taught in the Sermon on the Mount (5:20), helps explain the condemnation of these prominent religious groups. "As we noted, they are chastised because they do not observe the law and are hypocrites. Yet by any 'normal' measure the scribes and Pharisees were the most observant group within Israel, during both the time of Jesus and of Matthew. Only by the extraordinary norm of the love of God and the love of man, which nevertheless is derived from the law and the prophets, could they be denounced."[47]

Certainly there were God-fearing and righteous people in Jesus' time. Furthermore, many of these people, such as Joseph and Mary, probably did not belong to any of the major parties within Judaism, but were euphemistically referred to as the *Ame Ha-ares*, or "people of the land." Scripture calls them "the multitude." For many of the *Ame Ha-ares*, however, their religion was only an outward shadow of what it had once been; it was form without substance. Notice the reaction of John the Baptist to some of these people who came out to be baptized by him. Both Matthew and Luke record his reaction. Luke portrays the scene as follows:

> *Then said he to the multitude that came forth to be baptized of him, O generation of vipers, who hath warned you to flee from the wrath to come? Bring forth therefore fruits worthy of repentance, and begin not to say within yourselves, We have Abraham to our father: for I say unto you, That God is able of these stones to raise up children unto Abraham. And now also the axe is laid unto the root of the trees: every tree therefore which bringeth not forth good fruit is hewn down, and cast into the fire.* LUKE 3:7-9

Now look at the same scene as pictured by Matthew:

> *But when he saw many of the Pharisees and Sadducees come to his baptism, he said unto them, O generation of vipers, who hath warned you to flee from the wrath to come? Bring forth therefore fruits meet for repentance: And think not to say within yourselves, We have Abraham to our father: for I say unto you, that God is able of these stones to raise up children unto Abraham. And now also the axe is laid unto the root of the trees: therefore every tree which bringeth not forth good fruit is hewn down, and cast into the fire.* MATT. 3:7-10

According to Luke, who is addressing a Gentile audience, John's scathing remarks are directed against the multitude because they are not bearing "*fruits worthy of repentance.*" Matthew, however, has John the Baptist reproving "*many of the Pharisees and Sadducees,*" even though "in the time of Jesus they were the groups most likely to show obedience. Thus through his presentation of the incident, Matthew stresses that even the Pharisees are not bearing good fruit. Therefore, they are liable to judgment, and their claim to descent from Abraham will be of no avail against final judgment (vss. 9 f.). A higher righteousness is demanded."[48]

The Hebrew Nation: On Trial and Awaiting Judgment

In the Gospel of Matthew the Hebrew nation is on trial and awaiting judgment! "*And now also the axe is laid unto the root of the trees: therefore every tree which bringeth not forth good fruit is hewn down, and cast into the fire*" (7:10). It is of interest to note that of the 66 books in the canon of Scripture, the Gospel of Matthew is number 40—a number always used in the Bible in reference to trials and testing. For example, (1) it rained 40 days and 40 nights at the time of the Flood; (2) Moses fled to the desert for 40 years; (3) the nation of Israel wandered in the wilderness for 40 years; and (4) Jesus was tempted by the devil for 40 days. Matthew addressed his Gospel to the Jewish people, and they are being tested and tried with the Messiah in their midst and the promised kingdom within their reach.

> *In those days came John the Baptist, preaching in the wilderness of Judaea, And saying, Repent ye: for the kingdom of heaven is at hand. For this is he that was spoken of by the prophet Esaias, saying, The voice of one crying in the wilderness, Prepare ye the way of the Lord, make his paths straight. And the same John had his raiment of camel's hair, and a leathern girdle about his loins; and his meat was locusts and wild honey.* 3:1-4

The diet of John the Baptist is symbolic of the two-pronged nature of his message; namely, the offer of salvation and blessing, and the threat of judgment (cf. 3:11-12). Honey is associated in Scripture with God's blessing (cf. Exod. 3:8; Deut. 6:3; Prov. 24:13; Ezek. 3:3), while locusts are agents of destruction and judgment (cf. Exod. 10:4; Ps. 105:34-35; Isa. 33:4).

For the most part Judaism of the first century was not producing fruit worthy of repentance, because it was a religion that had gone to seed. The whole tenor of Matthew's Gospel, although stressing righteousness and obedience, nevertheless concedes the preponderance of unrighteousness and disobedience within the Jewish community. Consequently, the following analysis of Matthew's Gospel, written about a century ago, admits:

> Matthew finds less space than Luke for the parables which point to the inclusion of the Gentiles, and more for those which point to the exclusion of the workers of lawlessness and of the unworthy Jews. He alone among the evangelists has the saying, "many are called but few chosen." . . . Matthew, more than the rest of the evangelists, seems to move in evil days, and amid a race of backsliders, among dogs and swine who are unworthy of the pearls of truth, among the tares sown by the enemy, among fishermen who have to cast back again many of the fish caught in the net of the gospel; the broad way is ever in his mind, and the multitude of those that go thereby, and the guest without the wedding garment, and the foolish virgins, and the goats as well as the sheep, and those who even "cast out devils" in the name of the Lord, and yet are rejected by Him because they "work lawlessness." Where Luke speaks exultantly of "joy in heaven" over one repentant sinner, Matthew in more negative and sober phrases declares that it is not the will of the Father that one of the little ones should perish; and as a reason for not being distracted about the future it is alleged that "sufficient for the day is the evil thereof."[49]

The Jewish nation had been waiting centuries for the Messiah to come; yet when He did, they had Him crucified. How could a people who held history and prophecy in such high regard, commit such a blunder? The answer lies partly in the fact that Jesus Christ was "not the kind of Messiah looked for by either the Jews or the disciples. They were looking for a ruling king; but He has come to be the suffering Savior. Furthermore, Judaism had never understood, nor had the Old Testament revealed, that the Messiah would be the incarnate Son of God."[50]

The Jews were looking for a Messiah-King who would forcibly remove the iron heel of Rome, which had been crushing them since Pompey captured Palestine in 63 B.C. Maybe they were anticipating a miracle or two of the magnitude of those in the days of the Exodus, when God destroyed Pharaoh's army and *"overthrew the Egyptians in the midst of the sea"* (Exod. 14:27). However, neither the Jewish nation in general, nor the disciples in particular, understood that Christ had to first crush the head of the serpent (cf. Gen. 3:15) before He could extricate the heel of the Roman. As the Son of David Christ would eventually reign as King, but as the Son of Abraham He would first have to die as the Sacrifice.

The Trial of Jesus

Immediately after Peter's confession at Caesarea Philippi, where he said, *"Thou art the Christ, the Son of the living God"* (16:16), Matthew tells us:

> *From that time forth began Jesus to shew unto his disciples, how that he must go unto Jerusalem, and suffer many things of the elders and chief priests and scribes, and be killed, and be raised again the third day.* 16:21

Commenting on the timing of this disclosure by Christ, Dr. J. Vernon McGee wrote:

For the first time the Lord Jesus announces to His disciples His death and resurrection. The time was approximately six months before He was actually crucified. Why did He wait so long to make such an important announcement? Obviously, His disciples were not prepared for it, even at this time, judging from their reaction. He repeated five times the fact that He was going to Jerusalem to die (17:12; 17:22, 23; 20:18, 19; 20:28). In spite of this intensive instruction, the disciples failed to grasp the significance of it all until after His resurrection.[51]

Then Peter took him, and began to rebuke him, saying, Be it far from thee, Lord: this shall not be unto thee. 16:21-22

In essence Peter said, "You are the Messiah; You are the Son of God. You must not, You cannot go to the cross!" The cross was not in the thinking of the apostles at all, as you can see.[52]

For this reason the Lord rebuked Peter, saying, *"Get thee behind me, Satan: thou art an offence unto me: for thou savourest not the things that be of God, but those that be of men"* (16:23). Scripture confirms that it was by *"the determinate counsel and foreknowledge of God"* (Acts 2:23) that Jesus Christ was destined to be the *"Lamb slain from the foundation of the world"* (Rev. 13:8). Yet in order to accomplish the will of the Father, the Son needed to obey. And it was not a casual decision, as reflected in Matthew's narrative of the events leading up to His betrayal:

Then cometh Jesus with them unto a place called Gethsemane, and saith unto the disciples, Sit ye here, while I go and pray yonder. And he took with him Peter and the two sons of Zebedee, and began to be sorrowful and very heavy. Then saith he unto them, My soul is exceeding sorrowful, even unto death: tarry ye here, and watch with me. And he went a little farther, and fell on his face, and prayed, saying, O my Father, if it be possible, let this cup pass from me: nevertheless not as I will, but as thou wilt. And he cometh unto the disciples, and findeth them asleep, and saith unto Peter, What, could ye not watch with me one hour? Watch and pray, that ye enter not into temptation: the spirit indeed is willing, but the flesh is weak. He went away again the second time, and prayed, saying, O my Father, if this cup may not pass away from me, except I drink it, thy will be done. And he came and found them asleep again: for their eyes were heavy. And he left them, and went away again, and prayed the third time, saying the same words. Then cometh he to his disciples, and saith unto them, Sleep on now, and take your rest: behold, the hour is at hand, and the Son of man is betrayed into the hands of sinners. 26:36-45

In the hours that followed Jesus was indeed betrayed, arrested, abused, and even forsaken! After being shuffled from one official to another, he was sent to Pontius Pilate, the current Roman Procurator of Judea.

Pilate also had a decision to make regarding Christ. Knowing that it was *"for envy that they had delivered him"* (27:18), he tried to find some way out of the dilemma. Only Matthew tells us that Pilate's wife tried to influence his decision:

When he was set down on the judgment seat, his wife sent unto him, saying, Have thou nothing to do with that just man: for I have suffered many things this day in a dream because of him. 27:19

Pilate hoped to release Jesus by giving the multitude a choice between Him and *"a notable prisoner, called Barabbas"* (27:16).

But the chief priests and elders persuaded the multitude that they should ask Barabbas, and destroy Jesus. The governor answered and said unto them, Whether of the twain will ye that I release unto you? They said, Barabbas. Pilate saith unto them, What shall I do then with Jesus which is called Christ? They all say unto him, Let him be crucified. And the governor said, Why, what evil hath he done? But they cried out the more, saying, Let him be crucified. When Pilate saw that he could prevail nothing, but that rather a tumult was made, he took water, and washed his hands before the multitude, saying, I am innocent of the blood of this just person: see ye to it. Then answered all the people, and said, His blood be on us, and our children. Then released he Barabbas unto them: and when he had scourged Jesus, he delivered him to be crucified. 27:20-26

Although Pilate *"washed his hands"* in protest of the whole affair, he nevertheless has the dubious distinction of being the only person named in any major church creed to be implicated in the crucifixion of Christ. The Apostle's Creed, which is recited weekly in certain Protestant churches, states in part that Jesus Christ "was conceived by the Holy Spirit, born of the virgin Mary; suffered under Pontius Pilate; was crucified, dead, and buried. . . ." Pilate's character was revealed in his conduct.

Of the four Gospels only Matthew records the fact that Pilate *"washed his hands before the multitude"* (27:24), while all the people shouted, *"His blood be on us, and on our children"* (27:25).

The decisions made that day by the religious leaders and the multitude brought upon themselves and their descendents consequences that were unimaginable and sufferings that were indescribable. No people in the history of the world have suffered more than the Jews.

The trial of Jesus Christ was a decisive moment in the history of the Jewish nation. The people had the opportunity to make the right decision at a critical point in time. They had a choice between obedience and blessing, or disobedience and punishment. They could select a diet of honey or one of locusts! Unfortunately, they choose the latter. Lamenting over the eventual fate that would befall the Jewish nation, Jesus said:

That upon you may come all the righteous blood shed upon the earth, from the blood of righteous Abel unto the blood of Zacharias son of Barachias, whom ye slew between the temple and the altar. Verily I say unto you, All these things shall come upon this generation. O Jerusalem, Jerusalem, thou that killest the prophets, and stonest them which are sent unto thee, how often would I have gathered thy children together, even as a hen gathereth her chickens under her wings, and ye would not! Behold, your house is left unto you desolate. 23:35-39

Their house was left desolate when the holy city and magnificent Temple were destroyed during the Jewish Revolt against Rome between 66-70 A.D. According to the Jewish historian, Josephus, approximately 1,100,000 Jews lost their lives and another 97,000 were sold as slaves.[53] But the suffering did not end then and there. Their words at the trial of Jesus were prophetic:

Then answered all the people, and said, His blood be on us, **and on our children.**
EMPHASIS ADDED 27:25

The Sufferings of the Jewish People

Decisions have consequences. The context in which the Jewish people lived their lives delineated its opportunities and conditioned its fulfillment. Taking no precautions at His birth, the Jews were not likely to defend Christ at His trial. As a result the children of Israel have endured continual discrimination and incredible persecution as the flames of anti-Semitism have swept the globe, reaching out and touching them wherever they have fled! The following account is but a sampling of what they have endured over the centuries:

> In 135 A.D., the Emperor Hadrian took over Jerusalem and persecuted the Jews. He posted edicts against the practice of Judaism, and any infringement brought the death penalty. Jews were barred from Jerusalem; those trying to enter the city were killed. During the first crusade in 1096, Jews were branded as the enemies of Christendom, and 12,000 were killed along the Rhine River in Germany. In 1181, King Phillip of France banished the Jews from his country, stripping them of their land and houses. In 1189, at the coronation of Richard the Lionhearted, persecution of the Jews broke out resulting in most Jewish houses in London being burned, people killed, and their possessions claimed by the Crown. In 1348, Jews were blamed for the Black Plague of Europe. Jews were killed in Strausberg (2,000), Maintz (6,000), and Erfut (3,000). In 1478, the Spanish Inquisition broke out, and in 1492, 300,000 Jews were banished from the country and many more killed. In 1520, Jews were banished from Naples, Genoa, and Venice, Italy. In 1794, Jews were restricted in Russia, and Jewish men were forced to serve 25 years in the Russian army. By 1903, renewed restrictions were levied against Jews, and frequent pogroms (massacres) broke out as the Russians destroyed many Jewish villages. The worst holocaust to come upon the Jews took place between 1933 and 1945 when 6,000,000 died at the hands of Hitler's Germany as he systematically ordered the destruction of European Jewry.[54]

Precisely as Christ predicted (23:38) their house was left desolate with "the destruction of Jerusalem because the holy city had rejected its Messiah. However, this rejection is not final and ultimate; the day will come when Israel will say, 'Blessed be he who comes in the name of the Lord' (vv. 37-39). The Kingdom of God is not taken from the Jews that they might be forever abandoned; 'all Israel' is yet to be saved and brought within the redemptive purpose of God."[55]   Another day of opportunity is coming!

The Hebrew nation saw God's love, power, and concern for man revealed in the supernatural act of the Exodus. But can they see God's love in their suffering? It seems "paradoxical that the nation chosen for exaltation and selected to be a special means of divine revelation should also be destined for suffering which would exceed that of any other nation of the world."[56] Nevertheless, if the Jews attend to history carefully, they can see that God does indeed love them. Dr. John F. Walvoord explains the relationship between Israel's suffering and God's love as follows:

> The trials of Israel stem from the basic conflict between divine purpose and satanic opposition. The very fact that God selected Israel as a special means of divine revelation makes the nation the object of special satanic attack. Satanic hatred of the seed of Abraham is manifested from the beginning of God's dealings with Abraham and continues through the entire course of human history. . . . Undoubtedly one of the principal causes for Israel's suffering has been the unending opposition of Satan to the fulfillment of God's purpose in the nation.
>
> Coupled with Israel's failures as recorded in the Scriptures is the fact of divine discipline exercised on the nation. Israel was not only to be the channel

of divine revelation of God, but also the example of God's faithfulness to a sinning people who are the objects of His love and grace. Accordingly, many pages of the Old Testament are dedicated to giving the sacred records of God's dealings with His wandering people. The studies of Israel's sufferings will illustrate this basic reason for the sufferings inflicted on the nation.

The sufferings of Israel, while revealing God's discipline and righteousness, are also demonstrations of His love. Joined to every righteous judgment upon Israel are many manifestations of divine grace in preserving a godly remnant, in giving them that which is far greater than they deserved and fulfilling His divine purpose in and through them in spite of their own failure and Satan's efforts to hinder the purpose of God. There is a majestic drama in the whole sequence of events that relate to Israel's history, and they epitomize to some extent the conflict between good and evil which is the basic Christian philosophy of history. The sufferings of Israel, therefore, should be seen in the context of satanic persecution, of divine discipline for sin, and of divine faithfulness to His chosen people.[57]

Conclusion

In the next chapter we will examine the various groups within the chosen nation of Israel, and note the importance that each gave to both the written Word of God and their own traditions. As we conclude this chapter, however, we need to remember that when God revealed Himself to the Jewish nation in the Old Testament, it was primarily through History—in life and action. "In the Scriptures the name 'Word of God' is rarely if ever applied to writings. It always denotes the living communication of God to human beings."[58] Likewise, when God revealed Himself in the New Testament era, as recorded in the Gospels, the method was the same. It was a living communication within the context of an historical setting. God showed Himself in the life of a man.

> When God revealed himself in Christ, the method was . . . historical revealing—done in life, and not in writing. We have so long associated the Christian revelation with the New Testament that we may almost think it was made when the New Testament was written. Not so: it was made in the person, mission, and work of Christ. God showed himself in what Christ actually was, said, and did. "Thus was the Lord, thus said the Lord, thus did the Lord," in Christ. When Christ had finished his course, this greatest chapter in revelation was finished; for they who knew him had seen the Father. The Gospels partially narrate the life and acts in which God was revealed; but the revelation was made before the Gospels were written, and they could never have been written if it had not been made already.[59]

God revealed Himself in this manner in order to demonstrate those aspects of His character that might not be comprehended in any other way; namely, His goodness, love, and mercy. "If God desired to make himself thoroughly known to men in character, his only course was to come near to them, within their range of personal knowledge, and live a life among them, in which they might see him as he is. This he did in Christ; and the life and death of Christ showed men what manner of God they had to deal with."[60] As such, men's lives must display a corresponding goodness, as evidenced in their obedience to Him, and their righteousness must *"exceed the righteousness of the scribes and Pharisees"* (Matt. 5:20).

Chapter Three Notes

[1] F. F. Bruce, "The Gospels," *The Biblical Expositor*, ed. Carl F. H. Henry (Philadelphia: A. J. Holman Company, 1973), 803-04.

[2] James M. Gray, *Christian Workers' Commentary on the Whole Bible* (Old Tappan, N.J.: Fleming H. Revell Company, 1973), 386.

[3] Bernhard Anderson, *Rediscovering the Bible* (New York: Haddam House, 1954), 27-28.

[4] Huston Smith, *The Religions of Man* (New York: Harper & Row, Publishers, 1989), 364-65.

[5] *Ibid.*, 365-66.

[6] *Ibid.*, 366.

[7] *Ibid.*, 362-63.

[8] *Ibid.*, 364.

[9] *Ibid.*, 389.

[10] William Newton Clarke, *An Outline of Christian Theology* (New York: Charles Scribner's Sons, 1898), 14.

[11] *Ibid.*, 13-14.

[12] Smith, *op. cit.*, 389-90.

[13] *Ibid.*, 391.

[14] *Ibid.*

[15] *Ibid.*, 391-92.

[16] *Ibid.*, 392.

[17] Douglas Bookman, "The Genealogies of Jesus," *Israel My Glory* (June/July, 2000), 58:17.

[18] *Ibid.*

[19] Smith, *op. cit.*, 363.

[20] Spivey, *op. cit.*, 118.

[21] *Ibid.*, 118-19.

[22] *Ibid.*, 119.

[23] H. D. A. Major, et. al., *The Mission and Message of Jesus*, (New York: E. P. Dutton and Co., Inc., 1951), 231.

[24] George Lawson, *The Life of Joseph* (1807; reprint, Southampton, Great Britain: The Camelot Press, 1988), 11.

[25] *Ibid.*

[26] *Ibid.*, 464.

[27] *Ibid.*, 474.

[28] *Ibid.*, 23.

[29] Spivey, *op. cit.*, 120.

[30] John H. Hopkins, Jr., *We Three Kings.*

[31] Peter Colon, "The Wise Men: Gentiles on a Journey of Faith," *Israel My Glory* (Dec./Jan., 1996-97), 54:16.

[32] *Ibid.*, 18.

[33] D. S. Russell, *Between the Testaments* (Philadelphia: Fortress Press, 1975), 59.

[34] Colon, *op. cit.*, 16.

[35] *Ibid.*, 18.

[36] *Ibid.*, 17.

[37] *Ibid.*, 18.

[38] *Ibid.*

[39] G. F. Maclear, "History of Herod, King of the Jews," *Introduction to The Holy Bible* (Philadelphia: A. J. Holman & Co., n.d.), n.p.

[40] Morton Scott Enslin, *Christian Beginnings: Parts I and II* (Harper & Row, Publishers, 1956), 53.

[41] Colon, *op. cit.*

[42] Spivey, *op. cit.*, 123.

[43] *Ibid.*, 124.

[44] *Ibid.*, 124-25.

[45] *Ibid.*, 123.

[46] *Ibid.*, 127.

[47] *Ibid.*

[48] *Ibid.*, 123.

[49] "Gospels," *Enclyclopaedia Britannica* (1903), X:804.

[50] George Eldon Ladd, "Matthew," *The Biblical Expositor*, ed. Carl F. H. Henry (Philadelphia: A. J. Holman Company, 1973), 835.

[51] J. Vernon McGee, *Matthew, Vol. II* (Pasadena, Calif.: Thru the Bible Books, 1980), 41-42.

[52] *Ibid.*, 42.

[53] William Whiston, trans., *The Life and Works of Flavius Josephus* (Philadelphia: The John C. Winston Company, n.d.), 832.

[54] David Levy, "Israel: The Nation of Destiny," *Israel My Glory* (Jun./Jul., 1990), 48:26.

[55] Ladd, *op. cit.*, 847.

[56] John F. Walvoord, *Israel in Prophecy* (Grand Rapids, Mich.: Zondervan Publishing House, 1980), 101.

[57] *Ibid.*, 101-03.

[58] Clarke, *op. cit.*, 14.

[59] *Ibid.*

[60] *Ibid.*, 14-15.

Chapter Four

The Hebrews: Chosen and Zealous

In the previous chapter we noted that the Exodus was the great watershed experience in the stormy history of the Jewish people. It was not only the event that launched the Jews as a nation, but the Exodus "was also the first clear act by which God made known to the Jews the fullness of his nature."[1]

> The Exodus, we are saying, was more than an historical divide which turned a people into a nation. It was an episode in which this people became overwhelmingly aware of God and for the first time perceived his character clearly. But to put it this way—to say that the Jews perceived God—is to put the matter quite backward from the way they saw it. As the initiative had obviously come from God, he should be the subject of the assertion, not its object. Strictly speaking, the Jews had not perceived God; God had disclosed himself to them, inescapably and overwhelmingly.[2]

A Chosen People

Why had God disclosed Himself so uniquely to the Jewish people? Had they done anything special to merit their miraculous release from Egypt? Probably not, as far as they or anyone else could see! "Freedom had come to them as an act of sheer, spontaneous, unmerited grace, a clear instance of Yahweh's unanticipated and astonishing love."[3]

For the Hebrew people, history is—and always has been—of utmost importance. More than any of their polytheistic neighbors, the Jews derived meaning from the events of the Past. "Meaning is here, it is true, but from the Jewish perspective it was not gotten because the Jews sought it with exceptional diligence. It was revealed to them; by which we do not mean that it was told to them but that it was shown to them through decisive events. . . . But why was this disclosure made to the Jews? Their answer has been: because we were chosen."[4] As Moses had told his fellow Jews:

> *The Lord thy God hath chosen thee to be a special people unto himself, above all people that are upon the face of the earth. The Lord did not set his love upon you, nor choose you, because ye were more in number than any people; for ye were the fewest of all people: But because the Lord loved you, and because he would keep the oath which he had sworn unto your fathers, hath the Lord brought you out with a mighty hand, and redeemed you out of the house of bondmen, from the hand of Pharaoh king of Egypt.* DEUT. 7:6B-8

Whereas in the minds of some critics the idea of God choosing one nation over another "outrages the principles of impartiality and fair play,"[5] it needs to be stressed "that the heart of the doctrine is not the issue of favoritism. In the realm of theory, Judaism expressly affirms that the righteous of every nation shall have a part in the world to come."[6] Granted, it has been argued that within Judaism "the number of proselytes was never much superior to that of apostates."[7] But it is equally true—and probably more noteworthy—that "in the realm of historical fact no people have suffered as much as the Jews. The central claim of the election is not that God objectively favored the Jews above all other people but that he revealed himself most clearly through them."[8]

God chose the Jewish people to be a nation separate unto Himself for a specific reason and purpose. There are aspects of God's nature that can only be revealed to the Jews—as well as to the rest of the world—through the process of divine election.

> Nothing can register on man's attention unless it stands in some contrast to the rest of the world. Carry this point into theology and what do we have? God doubtless blesses us through the air we breathe as much as through anything, but if piety had had to wait for man to infer God's goodness from the availability of oxygen, it would have been long in coming. Air is too common to provoke a vivid sense of wonder and gratitude. The same holds for history. If God had freed every little people from their oppressors, the Jews would have taken their liberation for granted; the incident would have been routine. Chalk it to man's obtuseness if you will, the fact remains that God's favors could surround man like the sea surrounds fish; if they were standard they would be regarded as commonplace. This being so, is it possible that the only medium through which God could have disclosed himself vividly at the start was the particular, the unique, the individual?[9]

The Value of Tradition

> Returning to where we left off in Moses' injunction to his fellow Jews, we read:
> *Know therefore that the Lord thy God, he is God, the faithful God, which keepeth covenant and mercy with them that love him and keep his commandments to a thousand generations.*
> DEUT. 7:9

Maybe the more intractable question for the Jews to answer is not why they were chosen, but how are they to continue to love God and "keep his commandments to a thousand generations"? Their answer? Through tradition!

> Without attention, man's sense of wonder and the holy will stir occasionally, but to become a steady flame it must be deliberately fed. One of the best means of doing this is to be steeped in a history that cries aloud of God's superb acts of providence and mercy in every generation. Against those who would throw the past away with both hands that they may grasp the present more readily, Judaism accounts the memory of the past a priceless treasure. Most historically minded of all the religions, it finds holiness and history inseparable. In sinking the roots of his life deep in the past, the Jew draws nourishment from events in which God's acts were clearly visible and in doing so keeps the deadly prosaicness of the God-eclipsed perspective at bay. The Sabbath eve with its candles and cup of sanctification, the Passover feast with its many symbols, the austere solemnity of the Day of Atonement, the ram's horn sounding the New Year, the scroll of the Torah adorned with breastplate and crown—the Jew finds nothing less than the meaning of life in these things, a meaning which spans the centuries in affirming God's great goodness to man. Even when he recalls the tragedy of his people and the price of their survival he is made vividly aware of God's sustaining hand.[10]

The Various Groups Within Judaism

Today, there is a noticeable disparity among Jewish people with regard to tradition and ritual observances. In fact, Jews can be anything from extreme fundamentalists on one side of the religious spectrum to ultra-liberals on the other. Although the Jews are a very distinct people, it should be noted that their shared identity is not the result of common doctrine.

> There is nothing one has to believe in order to be a Jew. Jews run the entire gamut from those who are convinced that every syllable of the Torah was dictated by God to those who do not believe in God at all. Indeed, it is impossible to name any one thing which of itself suffices to make a person a Jew. Judaism is a complex. It is like a circle: a whole, yet divisible into sections all of which converge toward a common center. There is no law or authority which says that a Jew must incarnate all of these areas—or any of them—or face excommunication from this people. At the same time, the more a Jew does embody these features, the more completely will he be a Jew.[11]

Contemporary Judaism consists of the Orthodox Jews on the right hand, the Reform Jews on the left, with the Conservative Jews about midway between the other two groups. All of these, however, are basically an outgrowth of the party known in the Gospels as the Pharisees. The explanation being that of all the major parties that comprised Judaism in the first century, the Pharisees were the only group to survive the fall of Jerusalem, the destruction of the Temple, and the ensuing deportations. The other parties, for all intent and purpose, exited the stage of history.

The major reason that the Pharisees survived the Jewish Revolt of 66-70 A.D., whereas the other parties passed out of existence, has nothing to do with their zeal of the Law. Regardless of party affiliation, or lack of it, all within the Hebrew community considered themselves Jews, and from their own perspectives, most loyal Jews. "The Torah was the very ground-work of Judaism and the foundation of their nationhood. This is not to say, however, that all the parties agreed on the significance of the Torah or on its interpretation. In point of fact there were greatly divergent opinions on this very matter so that, whereas their loyalty to the Torah was a bond of union, their conception of it was a constant cause of division among them."[12]

The reason, then, why the Pharisees outlived the destruction of Jerusalem is found in their ability to adapt to the culture of the times. Whereas all the Jewish parties were steeped in the things of the past, they were divided as to their outlook toward the future. "Obedience to the Torah is, and has been, the paramount obligation of the Jew; it is the way to true righteousness. Because of its central position, practically every major religious group within Judaism can be categorized according to its attitude to the law."[13]

Comparing the Pharisees, Sadducees, and the Essenes—that ultra-strict group that "far out-Phariseed the Pharisees"[14]—one historian wrote:

> Actually, the point of cleavage between Pharisee, Sadducee, and Essene appears . . . to lie in their capacity for change. The bulk of the law came from the past when life was simple and uncomplicated. The years had brought their changes; the old law just would not fit. This the Sadducee simply denied; by closing his eyes to the changes he saw no need for alteration. The Essenes,

on the contrary, recognized the changes, and sought to turn life back to the simpler days. By retiring from civilization they cut the Gordian knot. The Pharisees sought by their interpretations to make the law fit the new environs, believing as they did that God had provided for every circumstance that could arise.[15]

The Pharisees were probably the most influential and significant religious group within the Jewish community of the first century. This should not be construed, however, to assume that most of the Jews of the New Testament were Pharisees. "It has been calculated that Pharisees, Sadducees and Essenes together would number only 30,000-35,000 out of a total of 500,000-600,000 in the time of Jesus. The Pharisees would number about five per cent of the total population and the Sadducees and Essenes together about two per cent."[16]

The history of the Pharisees as a major force within Judaism is somewhat obscure. Even the origin of their name is uncertain, although reasonable suggestions have been made.

> The word Pharisee seems to be derived from a Hebrew verb meaning "to separate." If so, it would appropriately designate the Pharisees as those separated or chosen by God for full obedience to the law. Pharisaism was fundamentally a lay movement. Not surprisingly, therefore, Pharisees emphasized the necessity of obeying the laws of purity outside the temple precincts, particularly in their own homes and around their tables. Because they understood Judaism primarily as interpretation of and obedience to the law, rather than in terms of nationalistic hopes or temple worship, the Pharisees were well situated to reconstitute and redefine Judaism in the aftermath of the destruction of the temple in the Roman War.[17]

Closely linked with the Pharisees in the Gospel narratives are the scribes. But whereas the former were primarily a lay group, the latter were the professional teachers and learned men—the Ph.D.'s of their time. The scribes are also referred to in the Gospels as lawyers, and they were the authoritative custodians and interpreters of the law. "Their verdict on the law, when ratified by the Sanhedrin—to which body some of the scribes apparently belonged—itself became law."[18]

As we encounter the phrase "*scribes and Pharisees*" in the Gospel of Matthew, keep in mind that, although they are closely allied, they are not identical groups. Some scribes were indeed Pharisees (cf. Mark 2:16), but not all Pharisees were scribes. The scribes existed long before the Pharisees ever appeared as a distinct group.

> Yet it does not surprise us that the historic task of the scribes was taken up by the Pharisees, whose consuming interest was the interpretation and application of the law to every sphere of life. They continued and expanded the traditional interpretations of the law, the fruition of which is to be found in the so-called rabbinic literature, a large body of interpretive material from the earlier centuries of our era dealing with every phase of the law and with almost every aspect of religious and secular life.[19]

The other major group within first-century Judaism, second only to the Pharisees, were the Sadducees. "The Sadducees seem to have stood in something of the same relation to the priests as the Pharisees to the scribes."[20] In Acts 4:1, for example, we find the Sadducees associated with the priests and the captain of the Temple. Likewise, in Acts 5:17 the Sadducees are in the company of the high priests. "Whatever the history of the name and of the group, by New Testament times the Sadducees were the priestly aristocracy."[21]

Whereas the Pharisees focused their attention upon the authoritative interpretation of the law, the Sadducees centered their attention on activities related to Temple worship. "Pharisees and Sadducees were thus religious brotherhoods centering upon the authoritative interpretation of the law and the temple worship, respectively. As such they represented the chief foci of Jewish faith as it existed prior to A.D. 70. Although the temple and its service of worship had declined in practical importance as the majority of Jews came to live outside the land of Israel, it was nevertheless the symbolic center of Judaism."[22]

> In theory Judaism was a religion of sacrifice; the temple in Jerusalem was the sole place where sacrifices could be offered. Accordingly a surrogate for the temple became imperative if Judaism were to survive. This was found in the synagogue. In the days of the New Testament synagogues were to be found not only in Palestine and Egypt, but in all the lands of the dispersion. They had become the rallying-points of Judaism. . . .
>
> Yet, while the synagogues, which were to be found in every Jewish community at home and abroad, provided the means of worship in lieu of the distant temple, their chief function, as all the early Jewish writers reveal, was instruction. They were, as Philo calls them, houses of instruction. Judaism was, as we shall see, a religion where knowledge was imperative. God had revealed his will to men; they in turn must know it to do it. . . .
>
> Thus study of the law, even though many of its requirements could not be carried out away from Jerusalem, was not only at once the duty and privilege of every Jew wherever he might find himself; it was also one of the most powerful factors in keeping ever before his eye the fact that he was one of the children of Zion. It was the sacred responsibility of parents to teach their children God's law. The very fact of dwelling in an alien land amid surroundings that tended to make law observance difficult must often have tended to make this responsibility the more keenly felt.[23]

The Importance of the Torah

While Judaism as a whole was rooted deeply in the past, each of its branches—although blowing in different directions with regard to the future—were, nevertheless, striving to obey the law of God in the present. If anything was typical of New Testament Judaism, it was devotion to the Law—known in their language as the Torah. "Notwithstanding its human mediation through Moses, the Jew regarded the law as divine revelation. . . . Strictly speaking, the law consists of the five books of Moses—the Pentateuch—which stand at the beginning of the Bible. Obedience to the Torah is, and has been, the paramount obligation of the Jew; it is the way to true righteousness."[24]

Keeping the Law of Moses was for first-century Judaism synonymous with morality and religion. Consequently, the Jewish people strove with all their might to learn God's will and obey it.

> Judaism was a revealed religion and took itself seriously as such. Failure to grasp this central fact has led to all sorts of misconceptions about Jewish law

and its fancied burden to Israel. God was the center of the Jew's life and thought. He it was who had revealed a religion through the fathers and Moses which was destined to become the universal religion of mankind. God had revealed his whole will; everything that men were to do, he had revealed to them. Moral conduct, the way men were to worship him and regard him, even their attitudes of mind and will—all these things had been revealed and were man's for the learning. The law—the Jew called it Torah—was thus God's great gift to his children.[25]

Considering the towering significance the Jews attached to the sacred Torah, it is little wonder that Matthew structured his Gospel narrative around five major discourses of Christ, reminiscent of the five books of Moses. Each of these discourses, furthermore, focuses on a particular aspect of the Kingdom of Heaven, which was the central theme of Christ's teaching. They can be described as follows:

1. The Foundation of the Kingdom (5:1-7:29)
2. The Feasibility of the Kingdom (10:1-42)
3. The Form of the Kingdom (13:1-58)
4. The Fellowship of the Kingdom (18:1-35)
5. The Future of the Kingdom (24:1-25:46)

The narrative material that separates these five discourses "is arranged in such a way that each block of narrative leads up naturally to the subject of the discourse which follows it. Consequently, it is usually rather easy to remember exactly where in Matthew's Gospel a given passage is to be found."[26] Conversely, the transition from discourse to narrative is easy to recognize, as each discourse ends with a similar formula (cf. 7:28; 11:1; 13:53; 19:1; 26:1).

Ever zealous for keeping the Law and their traditions, the Jews in general and the disciples in particular needed, nevertheless, to have some things put into proper perspective. As such, these discourses reveal some of the major issues that the Lord wanted to address in order to challenge their attitudes or correct their thinking. With this in mind we will examine these several discourses, and perhaps understand a little better what was deficient within first-century Judaism—and in need of the Lord's admonition and instruction. The Law of Moses was of supreme importance to the Jews, yet here we have the Words of One who *"was counted worthy of more glory than Moses"* (Heb. 3:3).

Discourse One: The Foundation of the Kingdom (5:1-7:29)

One does not read very far into Matthew's Gospel before the similarities between the lives of Moses and Christ become apparent. Not only were both men born while their nation was under Gentile oppression, but their own lives were threatened by an official edict to destroy newborn Hebrew children (cf. Exod. 1:16 and Matt. 2:16). Both were to be prophets from God and Savior to their people (cf. Exod. 3:10 and Matt. 1:21). Yet both were rejected at their first appearance to save the Jews (cf. Exod. 2:11-14 and John 1:11) and, consequently, departed to take a Gentile bride (cf. Exod. 2:15-21 and Acts 2:47). Fortunately, Moses was accepted at his second coming and the same will be true for Christ (cf. Exod. 3:18 and Matt. 23:39).

Moses is a type of Christ. Noble by character and great by mission, his life properly coincides with Israel's creative period of Old Testament revelation, much like Christ's life and teaching constitutes the creative period of New Testament revelation. As Moses fasted 40 days in the wilderness of Sinai (Exod. 24:18) prior to bringing the old Law down from the mountain (Exod. 31:18), so Christ fasted 40 days in the wilderness (Matt. 4:1-2) before delivering the new Law in what is referred to as the Sermon on the Mount (Matt. 5:3-7:27). And as Moses faced growing rebellion against his authority in the wilderness, so too Matthew traces the developing rift between those who accept and those who oppose Christ's teaching. From the first nugget of truth that Christ threw into the still waters of Jewish society, as it were, we see the rippling and widening circles of effect (cf. 8:19-22; 22:46; 26:3-4).

The Sermon on the Mount, as taught by Christ and arranged by Matthew, establishes the foundational truths upon which the Kingdom of Heaven is built. The central pillar is True Righteousness, and in this first discourse Jesus discusses its nature as applied to the moral, religious, social, and economic life of man. The key verse is found in Chapter Five, where Jesus declared: *"For I say unto you, that except your righteousness shall exceed the righteousness of the scribes and Pharisees, ye shall in no case enter into the kingdom of heaven"* (5:20).

Although the scribes and Pharisees were men of high profession, the Savior held them in low esteem. From Christ's first mention of them here in the Sermon on the Mount (5:20), and throughout the entire Gospel of Matthew, the scribes and Pharisees are singled out for their hypocrisy and false pretenses. The climax comes in Chapter 23, however, where the Lord pronounces a startling series of woes upon them.

> He accuses them of living a life that belies their teaching; of being enemies to that kingdom of heaven of which they speak with reverence and hope, refusing it for themselves and forbidding it to others; of eagerly making proselytes to the law, whom they immediately initiate deep into their own wickedness; of seldom trifling with oaths, deliberately minimizing the claims of the divine sanctity; of extreme punctiliousness about the minutiae of the law, while they ignore the great moral duties to which it bears witness; of laying great stress upon a fair exterior, while they make a reputable life a cover for hidden iniquity; of vain boasting of their superiority to their fathers who killed the prophets, when they are about to kill the Christ.[27]

It should be obvious to even a casual reader of the Gospels, that whereas Luke has more space for parables, which point to the inclusion of the Gentiles, Matthew gives more attention to those things which point to the exclusion of the workers of lawlessness and of the unworthy Jews. To this end the picture of hypocrisy is illustrated and charged home upon the scribes and Pharisees. (Note Christ's teachings regarding almsgiving, prayer and fasting in Chapter Six, as well as His instructions regarding judging in 7:1-5).

> A hypocrite is an actor, and hypocrisy is playing a part. Perhaps it might have been better if the words had been thus translated. In Jesus' usage here, hypocrisy consists in doing something that ought to have a serious meaning, not only without that meaning, but with some other instead. It is doing religious acts with a motive that is something else than religious. For such conduct hypocrisy, or acting, was a good name, and still is. The acts are religious, but the ethical insincerity nullifies the religion.[28]

Hypocrites may perform religious acts toward God, but their motive is to be seen by men. "Their desire is that men may admire their piety, and so they plan to perform these acts openly and elaborately. They address them professedly to God, but really to the spectators for effect."[29] For this play-acting, they will have their reward (cf. 6:2, 5, 16), but it will not be access to the Kingdom of Heaven (cf. 5:20)!

Who, then, will have access to the Kingdom? The Beatitudes (5:3-12) and the analogies of salt and light, which immediately follow (5:13-16) in the opening section of the Sermon on the Mount, relate the personal qualifications one needs in order to enter into the Kingdom of Heaven. These requirements, furthermore, are unlike those for citizenship in any other kingdom, as noted by nineteenth-century professor, Richard G. Moulton:

> The shock of the opening text makes us feel how by the doctrine of Jesus the center of gravity of human life and character is wholly shifted. It is to the 'poor in spirit' that the exaltation of the new kingdom comes; and this phrase of the text gathers fullness with its sevenfold expansion—the mourners are blessed, and not the gay; the meek, and not the mighty; those who hunger after a righteousness they have not attained, and not the satisfied Pharisee; the merciful, and not the oppressor; the pure and not the worldly; the peacemaker, and not the conqueror; the persecutor is beneath his victim. Again, in contrast with the received ideal of a personal righteousness that would outshine that of others, the second and third maxims, with their images of the salt and the lamp, put forward an exaltation that is exalted only so long as it exerts its purifying and illuminating force upon others. The central article of the discourse brings out that the gospel is no relaxation of the law, but its intensification; the exposition of this thought is the paradox that the new righteousness must exceed the righteousness of Scribes and Pharisees, and its final word is perfection.[30]

Christ's instructions regarding almsgiving, prayer and fasting in the central portion of the discourse (chapter 6), focus on religious acts, which should denote loyalty to God, and the performing of them should be an unspoken acknowledgement of Him. What is wanted is not outward play-acting, but an inward reality!

> Let almsgiving be secret, let prayer be with God alone, let fasting be unprofessed and invisible. The one to be considered is the Father who is in secret and sees in secret. He knows the service for exactly what it is, and has power to recompense it with divine acknowledgment. This is obviously right: what is done unto God, unto God let it be done. Then things will be what they seem, and this is the ideal way: prayer will not be pretence, nor almsgiving ostentation, nor fasting an empty show. It is necessary, and it is enough, that he who sees in secret should find there the same thing that is done in public.[31]

Unfortunately, not all that heard the Lord's teachings would possess a worthy character with a genuine heart toward God. Christ concluded the Sermon on the Mount by saying:

> *Not every one that saith unto me, Lord, Lord, shall enter into the kingdom of heaven; but he that doeth the will of my Father which is in heaven. Many will say to me in that day, Lord, have we not prophesied in they name? And in thy name have cast out devils? And in thy name done many wonderful works? And then will I profess unto them, I never knew you: depart from me, ye that work iniquity. Therefore whosoever heareth these sayings of mine,*

and doeth them, I will liken him unto a wise man, which built his house upon a rock: And the rain descended, and the floods came, and the winds blew, and beat upon that house; and it fell not: for it was founded upon a rock. And every one that heareth these sayings of mine, and doeth them not, shall be likened unto a foolish man, which built his house upon the sand: And the rain descended, and the floods came, and the winds blew, and beat upon that house; and it fell: and great was the fall of it. 7:21-27

Then Matthew adds:

And it came to pass, when Jesus had ended these sayings, the people were astonished at his doctrine: For he taught them as one having authority, and not as the scribes. 7:28-29

Discourse Two: The Feasibility of the Kingdom (10:1-42)

Both John the Baptist and Jesus Christ had preached the same basic message; namely, *"Repent: for the kingdom of heaven is at hand"* (cf. 3:2 and 4:17). Repentance is a change of mind that is evidenced in a changed life (cf. 3:8). The Kingdom of Heaven was at hand, but its inauguration was contingent on the repentance of its people. The time had come to determine the feasibility of establishing the literal Kingdom of Heaven on earth. Were the foundational truths upon which the Kingdom would be instituted—the higher righteousness as taught in the Sermon on the Mount—evident in the lives of the Jewish people? To this end Jesus sent forth the twelve disciples, saying:

Go not into the way of the Gentiles, and into any city of the Samaritans enter ye not: But go rather to the lost sheep of the house of Israel. And as ye go, preach, saying, the kingdom of heaven is at hand. 10:5B-7

This second major discourse in Matthew's Gospel, as found in Chapter 10, involves Christ's instructions to the disciples regarding this special mission. Matthew is the teaching Gospel, and only in the Gospels and Acts are the twelve apostles called "disciples," which means learners. A disciple is one who is taught by another. During the Gospel period the disciples were taught by the Master, and in the book of Acts the word "disciple" is used as a synonym for believer. It is noteworthy that the term does not appear anywhere else in the New Testament. The rest of the Scriptures refer to the disciples as apostles—a term that denotes those who are chosen and sent forth with a special commission from the sender.

Here, for the first time, the twelve disciples are to be sent out as apostles—the authorized representatives of their sender, Jesus Christ. As such, they can expect the same reception as would be given their Master (cf. 10:24-25). Furthermore, the instructions recorded in this chapter not only would apply to their present task, but to their future ministry as well. Comparing verses 5 and 18 we see that the immediate mission of the twelve was limited to *"the lost sheep of the house of Israel,"* whereas in the future they would *"be brought before governors and kings . . . for a testimony against them and the Gentiles."*

Christ also warned the disciples about the strife, persecution, and even death that could result from their mission (vv. 34-37). The reference to a cross (v. 38) did not refer to coping with a little unpleasantness now and then. Rather, taking up one's cross was synonymous with martyrdom, for in the very next verse Jesus said, *"He that findeth his life shall lose it: and he that loseth his life for my sake shall find it"* (v. 39).

The Jews, scattered across the Roman Empire, needed no explanation about what a cross signified. They had over the centuries of Roman rule witnessed thousands of

crucifixions. After the Revolt of the Gladiators was finally put down in 71 B.C., for example, crosses were erected along the Appian Way for some 30 miles as 6000 captured
gladiators were crucified. Rome established the *Pax Romana*—the Roman Peace—but
it was a frightful peace! So Christ forewarned His disciples, when He said, *"And he that
taketh not his cross, and followeth after me, is not worthy of me"* (v. 38).

Matthew terminates this second discourse by saying, *"And it came to pass, when Jesus
had made an end of commanding his twelve disciples, he departed thence to teach and to preach in
their cities"* (11:1).

Discourse Three: The Form of the Kingdom (13:1-58)

The narrative material between the second and third major discourses in Matthew—as well as even a scant knowledge of world history—clearly indicates that the
conditions for establishing the literal, earthly kingdom were not met at Christ's first
coming. When certain scribes and Pharisees approached Christ, as recorded in Chapter 12, and asked for a sign from Him, Jesus answered them by saying:

> *An evil and adulterous generation seeketh after a sign; and there shall no sign be given to it,
> but the sign of the prophet Jonas: For as Jonas was three days and three nights in the whale's
> belly; so shall the Son of man be three days and three nights in the heart of the earth. The
> men of Nineveh shall rise in judgment with this generation, and shall condemn it: because
> they repented at the preaching of Jonas; and, behold, a greater than Jonas is here. The queen
> of the south shall rise up in the judgment with this generation, and shall condemn it: for she
> came from the uttermost parts of the earth to hear the wisdom of Solomon; and, behold,
> a greater than Solomon is here. When the unclean spirit is gone out of a man, he walketh
> through dry places, seeking rest, and findeth none. Then he saith, I will return into my house
> from whence I came out; and when he is come, he findeth it empty, swept, and garnished.
> Then goeth he, and taketh with himself seven other spirits more wicked than himself, and
> they enter in and dwell there: and the last state of that man is worse than the first. Even so
> shall it be also unto this wicked generation.*   12:39-45

The third discourse in Matthew's Gospel explains the nature or form that the
Kingdom of Heaven will assume during the interval of time between Christ's first
and second advents. The great truths found in this 13th chapter were addressed to a
great multitude (v. 2), spoken through parables (v. 3), and revealed as mysteries (v. 11).
When the disciples asked Christ why He spoke to the people in this manner, the Lord
answered them by saying:

> *Because it is given unto you to know the mysteries of the kingdom of heaven, but to them it
> is not given. For whosoever hath, to him shall be given, and he shall have more abundance:
> but whosoever hath not, from him shall be taken away even that he hath. Therefore speak I
> to them in parables: because they seeing see not; and hearing they hear not, neither do they
> understand. And in them is fulfilled the prophecy of Esaias, which saith, By hearing ye
> shall hear, and shall not understand; and seeing ye shall see, and shall not perceive: For this
> people's heart is waxed gross, and their ears are dull of hearing, and their eyes they have
> closed; lest at any time they should see with their eyes, and hear with their ears, and should
> understand with their heart, and should be converted, and I should heal them. But blessed
> are your eyes, for they see: and your ears, for they hear.*
> 13:11B-16

Because the Jewish people had rejected their Messiah, God's program for them would be set aside until that day when they will say, *"Blessed is he that cometh in the name of the Lord"* (23:39). The mystery form of the Kingdom would remove the Jewish nation from their place of blessing and deal primarily with those Gentiles, who would have eyes to see and ears to hear. This is intimated in the opening verse, which reads: *"The same day went Jesus out of the house, and sat by the sea side"* (13:1). In Scripture the term "house" is associated with the nation of Israel (cf. Ezek. 24:3, 21), whereas the "sea" is symbolic of Gentile peoples (cf. Dan. 7:3; Rev. 13:1).

The mystery form of the Kingdom lives in the lives of true believers, and is evidenced collectively through the Church—the Body of Christ. As such, the mystery parables reveal the nature of the Church as reflected throughout its course of history. Not surprisingly, then, we would expect to discover a similarity between the seven parables of Matthew 13 and the letters to the seven churches as found in the book of Revelation.

1. THE PARABLE OF THE SOWER (MATT. 13:1-23) AND THE LETTER TO THE CHURCH OF EPHESUS (REV. 2:1-7). The mystery form of the Kingdom begins by sowing the seed of the Gospel into the world. The seed doesn't take root everywhere, as represented by the four soils (four = the number of the earth). Nevertheless, the Gospel does go to the whole world (cf. Matt. 13:38; Rom. 1:5; Col. 1:5-6). The seed of the Gospel found good soil in the first century, *"and brought forth fruit, some an hundredfold, some sixtyfold, some thirtyfold"* (Matt. 13:8). This is "greatly desired," which is the meaning of the name Ephesus, and the city became the numerical center of the Christian world by the end of the first century.

2. THE PARABLE OF THE WHEAT AND TARES (MATT. 13:24-30, 34-43) AND THE LETTER TO THE CHURCH IN SMYRNA (REV. 2:8-11). As expected, Satan would attempt to thwart the spread of the Gospel, and persecution of true believers became his primary offensive weapon in the Smyrna period of church history. Satan sowed tares amidst the wheat, as it were, and certain religious Jews were trying to choke out the followers of Christ (cf. Acts 17:5-8, 13). One characteristic of the church age is that there will be false believers in the professing Body of Christ, which will be difficult to get rid of, *"lest while ye gather up the tares, ye root up also the wheat with them"* (Matt. 13:29).

3. THE PARABLE OF THE MUSTARD SEED (MATT. 13:31-32) AND THE LETTER TO THE CHURCH IN PERGAMOS (REV. 2:12-17). Pergamos means "thoroughly married" and the Church in the Pergamum period of church history eventually married the state. The persecution of Christians ceased with the Edict of Milan in 313 A.D., and by the end of the fourth century Christianity became the official religion of the Roman Empire. As a result, the Church experienced unnatural growth, as taught in the Parable of the Mustard Seed. The plant grew into a tree, which was large enough to accommodate the birds. In the first parable the birds were removing the good seed from the soil, and here, also, they are up to no good. The Parable of the Mustard Seed predicted that the Church would realize false growth, and it has for over 1500 years, as much of the organized Church was yoked with the ruling political powers of Asia and Europe.

4. THE PARABLE OF THE LEAVEN (MATT. 13:33) AND THE LETTER TO THE CHURCH IN THYATIRA (REV. 2:18-29). The Church in Thyatira represents the mystery form of the Kingdom during the Dark Ages, when learning and civilization regressed rather than progressed. Immoral leadership, religious idolatry, and superstitious ceremony characterized the recognized Church of this period. The Parable of the Leaven teaches that the Medieval Church would be characterized by false doctrine, as pictured by the woman who hid leaven (evil) in three measures of meal (product of the seed). As Jezebel (Rev. 2:20) brought idolatry into Israel, so Thyatira introduced idolatry and pagan practices into the Medieval Church.

5. THE PARABLE OF THE HID TREASURE (MATT. 13:44) AND THE LETTER TO THE CHURCH IN SARDIS (REV. 3:1-6). The Church in Sardis (which means "those escaping") represents the Reformation period in the history of Christendom. Describing the situation in Sardis at the time, John said there were a few *"which have not defiled their garments; and they shall walk with me in white: for they are worthy"* (Rev. 3:4). Fortunately, not all church leaders were blotted out of the Book of Life by the 16th century, but were, as the parable teaches, hid in a field. Men, such as Martin Luther, and others who followed in his footsteps, eventually escaped from the organized Church after Luther nailed 95 theses to the door of the Castle Church in Wittenberg and started the Protestant Reformation on October 31, 1517.

6. THE PARABLE OF THE PEARL OF GREAT PRICE (MATT. 13:45-46) AND THE LETTER TO THE CHURCH IN PHILADELPHIA (REV. 3:7-13). The Church in Philadelphia (which means "brotherly love") represents the true Body of Christ in the end times. *"And this commandment have we from him, that he who loveth God loveth his brother also"* (I John 4:21; cf. John 13:34; 15:12; Heb. 13:1). To this Church was given the promise of the rapture before the Great Tribulation: *"Because thou hast kept the word of my patience, I also will keep thee from the hour of temptation, which shall come upon all the world, to try them that dwell upon the earth"* (Rev. 3:10).

The Lord set before this Church *"an open door"* (Rev. 3:8), and the Philadelphia age of church history saw the great revivals and missionary movements of the 18th and 19th centuries. In 1732 a Dutch ship left Copenhagen headed for St. Thomas Island in the West Indies with two Moravian missionaries on board, and the modern missionary movement was born. The First Great Awakening also occurred in the 1700's in England and America with the preaching of John Wesley and George Whitefield. The latter, who could speak to 20,000 people without a loudspeaker, became the best-known man in the American colonies. The Second Great Awakening began in the early 1820's with the preaching of Charles Finney.

Although the Philadelphia Church was promised *"an open door, and no man can shut it"* (Rev. 3:8), Satan nevertheless attempted to counter-attack the work of God by raising up several cults and false philosophies in the 19th century. Consequently, the doors of opportunity may not always be as wide open as we would like, yet we have this additional promise from the Lord: *"Behold, I will make them of the synagogue of Satan, which say they are Jews, and are not, but do lie; behold, I will make them to come and worship before thy feet, and to know that I have loved thee"* (Rev. 3:9).

The Pearl of Great Price also represents the true Church of Jesus Christ. A pearl is not a stone like a diamond—it cannot be cut like other gems, but is formed instead by a living organism. A grain of sand or other foreign object lodges in the shell of an oyster, and the small sea creature creates the beautiful pearl around this intrusion. Likewise, Christ bore our sins in His own body, was made sin for us (Isa. 53:5), and covers us with His own righteousness (Eph. 2:10). Christ left heaven's glory, *"sold all that he had"* (Matt. 13:46), as it were, and bought us with the price of His own life.

7. THE PARABLE OF THE DRAGNET (Matt. 13:47-50) AND THE LETTER TO THE CHURCH OF THE LAODICEANS (Rev. 3:14-22). Whereas the letters to the previous six Churches in the Book of Revelation are addressed to the Angel of the Church in—or of—a particular city (cf. 2:1, 8, 12, 18; 3:1, 7), the message in consideration here is given to *"the angel of the church of the Laodiceans"* (14:1). This is the apostate church of the end times, and is addressed as such not to a Church of Jesus Christ in the city of Laodicea, but to the church of the Laodiceans, themselves. The tems "Laodicea" means "people ruling," and it is a fitting label for this humanistic church. The leaven that was put into the meal during the Middle Ages (cf. Matt. 13:33; Rev. 2:18-25) has done its work, *"till the whole was leavened"* (Matt. 13:33).

Christ is seen outside the Laodicean Church, and knocking to get in (Rev. 3:20). Although there are some true believers in Laodicean-type churches today, they will be translated before the Great Tribulation, whereas the main body of the membership—being *"neither cold not hot"* (Rev. 3:15)—will enter that *"hour of temptation, which shall come upon all the world, to try them that dwell upon the earth"* (Rev. 3:10). The Lord Jesus Christ had warned this Church, saying, *"Because thou art lukewarm, and neither cold nor hot, I will spue thee out of my mouth"* (Rev. 3:16).

This is not a picture of a true Church here, as the Lord would not spew out true believers. Furthermore, the persecutions that await the followers of Christ in the end times would not leave them lukewarm, but would either ignite the flame or put it out altogether!

For the most part the Laodicean Church represents the apostate church that enters the Tribulation period. Although they may say, *"I am rich, and increased with goods, and have need of nothing,"* they are, nevertheless, *"wretched, and miserable, and poor, and blind, and naked"* (Rev. 3:17).

What awaits this apostate church is the final Judgment of Christ, as pictured in the Parable of the Dragnet:

> *Again, the kingdom of heaven is like unto a net, that was cast into the sea, and gathered of every kind: Which, when it was full, they drew to shore, and sat down, and gathered the good into vessels, but cast the bad away. So shall it be at the end of the world: the angels shall come forth, and sever the wicked from among the just, And shall cast them into the furnace of fire: there shall be wailing and gnashing of teeth.* MATT. 13:47-50

We have observed a relationship between the mystery parables of Matthew Thirteen and the messages to the Churches in the Book of Revelation. Although it can be argued that "the mystery form of the kingdom is not synonymous with the visible church, yet, since the time period is essentially the same in the two passages, we may reasonably expect that there would be a parallelism of development. . . . It is not intended to infer that there is an identity in the revelation of the two passages, rather, that there is a similarity in the progress of the course of the age as revealed in the two portions."[32]

Matthew terminates Christ's teaching on the mystery form of the Kingdom by saying, *"And it came to pass, that when Jesus had finished these parables, he departed thence"* (13:53).

Discourse Four: The Fellowship of the Kingdom (18:1-35)

Early in the history of the Hebrew nation, the administrative basis of Jewish society was organized around twelve separate tribes—that well-known division, which can be traced back to Jacob's blessing of his twelve sons (cf. Gen. 49:1-27). By the first century, however, great changes had taken place in the social and political structure of Israel, especially as they related to the traditional organization of the twelve tribes. One historian noted:

> These traditional concepts had had scarcely any importance left by the time of Christ: they had almost faded out of existence. The house was still used as an expression showing illustrious descent, however, and the evangelist does not fail to point out that Jesus belonged to the house of David. Families preserved genealogies which went very far back, sometimes even as far as Abraham. As for the tribe to which a man belonged, this only had a meaning for those who belonged to the tribe of Levi, for they had the privilege of providing the Temple with its servants, the Levites. Yet people also took a certain pride in claiming to belong to Judah or Benjamin, those tribes which had repopulated the Holy Land with true followers of God after the exile. Apart from these cases, however, when "the people of the twelve tribes" were spoken of, it was either a reference to history or to the end of time, to that day of glory when, as Saint Paul told King Agrippa, "the promise should be attained" (Acts 26:6), and when, according to the Apocalypse, there would be the great counting of the chosen, while the seven trumpets gave their terrifying blast.[33]

By the time of Christ a man's social standing was not based primarily according to the tribe from which he descended. "When the horizontal separation disappeared it was replaced by a series of vertical distinctions, a social stratification or differentiation by class."[34] In the Greco-Roman world social status was generally achieved through one of two primary ways.

One method of moving up the social ladder, so to speak, was the result of performing some great service for the benefit of society as a whole. A foreign recruit who entered military service, for example, might be granted Roman citizenship after 20 years of faithful service. In the distant past one did not experience this kind of social mobility in a tribal society, where people were "theoretically linked by blood and historically bound to one another by more or less legendary traditions; mystically bound by ceremonies, commensal feasts and intermarriage; militarily and administratively bound by obedience to a single chief."[35]

In a society where one is recognized for his or her contributions or merit, a sense of pride in one's accomplishments is, unfortunately, inevitable. To the Greeks, humility was a weakness and therefore despised, yet Christ taught His disciples in this fourth discourse recorded by Matthew, that humility is one of the great virtues that characterizes the fellowship within the Kingdom of God. It was an attribute of Moses, who *"was a very humble man, more humble than anyone else on the face of the earth"* (Num. 12:3,

NIV). When the disciples, however, came to Jesus asking, *"Who is the greatest in the king-dom of heaven?"* (18:1), they were assuming His answer would reveal the name of the individual who had performed the greatest service in the opinion of the Master! The disciples must have been shocked when Jesus called a little child unto Him, set him before them, and said:

> *Verily I say unto you, Except ye be converted, and become as little children, ye shall not enter into the kingdom of heaven. Whosoever therefore shall humble himself as this little child, the same is greatest in the kingdom of heaven. And whoso shall receive one such little child in my name receiveth me. But whoso shall offend one of these little ones which believe in me, it were better for him that a millstone were hanged about his neck, and that he were drowned in the depth of the sea.* 18:3-6

The other way of attaining social status in the Roman world—besides rendering some great service—was through the possession of money. Whereas the *humiliores* were "the humble people without any real, visible capital,"[36] the *honestiores*, or tradesmen, were "made respectable by the possession of five thousand sesterces; the members of the noble orders also owed their position to their fortunes, since those of the equestrian order had to have four hundred thousand sesterces, and the senators, those splendid people who supplied the legates and proconsuls of wealthy provinces and the commanders of legions, no less than a million."[37]

Describing the influence of money on the fabric of Roman society, British historian, H. G. Wells, wrote:

> But this new empire was, as we shall try to make clear, a political structure differing very profoundly in its nature from any of the great Oriental empires that had preceded it. Great changes in the texture of human society and in the conditions of social interrelations had been going on for some centuries, The flexibility and transferability of money was becoming a power and, like all powers in inexpert hands, a danger in human affairs. It was altering the relations of rich men to the state and to their poorer fellow citizens.[38]

It is of interest to note how the New Testament writers addressed the social in-equalities of the ancient world. One historian declared:

> It is a striking fact that nowhere in the New Testament is there a reference to a distinction as between what we would call gentle and simple, or nobles and commoners; but on the other hand one continually finds rich and poor. How many of Christ's parables have to do with status based upon wealth, that distinction which our modern society knows so well. The ruling class (unlike that of the West at the height of the Middle Ages) asserted itself not because of the services that it gave but because of the wealth it possessed and of the political connections that its wealth provided.[39]

In this fourth discourse recorded by Matthew, Christ taught that forgiveness is another virtue—besides humility—that must be evident in the Kingdom of God. Since "the transferability of money was becoming a power . . . in inexpert hands" as well as "a danger in human affairs," as noted above, the occurrence of offenses and resentments would be inevitable. Our Lord insisted, however, that forgiveness is a duty, and the extent of it He illustrated by the Parable of the King and the Debtor:

> *Therefore is the kingdom of heaven likened unto a certain king, which would take account of his servants. And when he had begun to reckon, one was brought unto him, which owed*

him ten thousand talents. But forasmuch as he had not to pay, his lord commanded him to be sold, and his wife, and children, and all that he had, and payment to be made. The servant therefore fell down, and worshipped him, saying, Lord, have patience with me, and I will pay thee all. Then the lord of that servant was moved with compassion, and loosed him, and forgave him the debt. But the same servant went out, and found one of his fellowservants, which owed him an hundred pence: and he laid hands on him, and took him by the throat, saying, Pay me that thou owest. And his fellowservant fell down at his feet, and besought him, saying, Have patience with me, and I will pay thee all. And he would not: but went and cast him into prison, till he should pay the debt. So when his fellowservants saw what was done, they were very sorry, and came and told unto their lord all that was done. Then his lord, after that he had called him, said unto him, O thou wicked servant, I forgave thee all that debt, because thou desiredst me: Shouldest not thou also have had compassion on they fellowservant, even as I had pity on thee? And his lord was wroth, and delivered him to the tormentors, till he should pay all that was due unto him. So likewise shall my heavenly Father do also unto you, if ye from your hearts forgive not every one his brother their trespasses. 18:23-35

Does this parable teach that God may rescind His forgiveness? One theologian answers this question by saying:

This is a parable; and its details cannot be pressed to embody any teaching about whether God will first forgive sins and then retract His forgiveness. The parable embodies a simple and clear truth: When a man professes to have been forgiven an incalculable debt of sin, but is utterly unwilling in turn to forgive the minor offense of another, his profession is a mockery and void of reality. God's forgiveness precedes and provides the basis for the forgiveness of brother with brother, and it is such forgiveness that must characterize Christian fellowship.[40]

Matthew concludes the fourth discourse in his Gospel by noting, *"And when it came to pass, that when Jesus had finished these sayings, he departed from Galilee, and came into the coasts of Judaea beyond Jordan"* (19:1).

Discourse Five: The Future of the Kingdom (24:1-25:46)

The fifth and final discourse of Jesus Christ as recorded by Matthew was occasioned by three questions posed by the disciples. Matthew sets the stage for this discourse as follows:

And Jesus went out, and departed from the temple: and his disciples came to him for to shew him the buildings of the temple. And Jesus said unto them, See ye not all these things? Verily I say unto you, There shall not be left here one stone upon another, that shall not be thrown down. And as he sat upon the mount of Olives, the disciples came unto him privately, saying, Tell us, when shall these things be? And what shall be the sign of they coming, and of the end of the world? 24:1-3

In response to Jesus' prediction of the destruction of the buildings of the Temple, the first and most important question of the disciples was, *"When shall these things be?"* It is of interest to note that they did not ask why—or by whom—the Temple would be destroyed, for the prophet Daniel, more than five centuries earlier, had written:

Seventy weeks are determined upon thy people and upon thy holy city, to finish the transgression, and to make an end of sins, and to make reconciliation for iniquity, and to bring in everlasting

righteousness, and to seal up the vision and prophecy, and to anoint the most Holy.
Know therefore and understand, that from the going forth of the commandment to restore and to build Jerusalem unto the Messiah the Prince shall be seven weeks, and threescore and two weeks: the street shall be built again, and the wall, even in troublous times. And after threescore and two weeks shall Messiah be cut off, but not for himself: and the people of the prince that shall come shall destroy the city and the sanctuary; and the end thereof shall be with a flood, and unto the end of the war desolations are determined. And he shall confirm the covenant with many for one week: and in the midst of the week he shall cause the sacrifice and the oblation to cease, and for the overspreading of abominations he shall make it desolate, even until the consummation, and that determined shall be poured upon the desolate. DAN. 9:24-27

Daniel had predicted that not only would the Temple (sanctuary) be destroyed, but the entire city of Jerusalem as well. The disciples wanted to know when these things would happen. Daniel had said they would take place after the 69th week (heptad) of his prophecy, yet not during the 70th week. Between these last two weeks is a parenthesis period of time that is known as the Church Age. When the Bride of Christ is called out at the rapture, God will resume His dealings with the nation of Israel (cf. Rom. 11), and the time of Jacob's trouble will begin (cf. Jer. 30:7). As the destruction of the Temple took place during the Church age, Matthew does not record any response that Jesus may have given regarding the disciples' initial question. Nevertheless, considering the magnificence and grandeur of this second Temple—known as Herod's Temple—it is no wonder that the disciples would be curious about when the words of the Lord would be fulfilled; namely, that *"there shall not be left here one stone upon another, that shall not be thrown down"* (24:2).

"The rebuilt second Temple was regarded as one of the marvels of the ancient world. Josephus tells us that the Temple was made of marble overlaid with gold, and appeared from a distance as a mountain of snow glistening in the sun."[41] At the beginning of Christ's public ministry it had been under construction for 46 years (cf. John 2:20) and would not be completely finished until a few years before its ultimate destruction in 70 A.D. At the time it was probably the largest and most beautiful enclosed structure on the face of the earth. Personally designed by Herod the Great, who was an architect without equal in his day, the Temple buildings and surrounding courtyards covered an area of over 35 acres. By comparison the Louisiana Superdome in New Orleans, which is the largest arena in the history of mankind, covers 13 acres of ground. Herod's Temple complex would also dwarf Rockefeller Center in New York City, which extends from 5th Ave. to the Avenue of the Americas between 48th and 52nd streets, and has 19 buildings occupying approximately 22 acres.

The Temple of Herod was actually the last in a series of temples on Mount Moriah—the history of which had spanned a thousand years. The first temple was constructed by Solomon and had stood almost 400 years, but the apostasy of the Jews and the conquest of the Babylonians brought it to an end. After Babylon fell to the Persians, about 50,000 Jews returned to Jerusalem in 538 B.C. and a second temple was constructed under the direction of Zerubbabel.

Some confusion arises at this point, since both Zerubbabel's and Herod's Temples are referred to collectively as the Second Temple. This is because Herod's work was actually a reconstruction rather than an entirely new venture. His new Temple, however, was such an enlargement and embellishment of the Zerubbabel structure that it was practically a brand new building.

Herod envisioned a greatly enlarged Temple area with an enormous courtyard. This was a very difficult goal to achieve, since the Temple sat atop the pinnacle of Mount Moriah. To accommodate his plans, his engineers built huge retaining walls more than 150 feet high from bedrock west of the Temple and on the slopes up from the Kidron valley to the east. With thousands of tons of back fill material, his workmen flattened the top of the mount. The lower stone courses of those walls can be seen today on the three sides of the Temple mount and have been further exposed by archeologists.[42]

One of the most exciting archeological discoveries of recent years involves the Western Wall Tunnel Project, which is explained as follows:

The Western Wall, known to Jews as Ha-Kotel ("the Wall"), and popularly as the "Wailing Wall" has been the subject of hundreds of books. It is the Temple's only remnant and monument to Israel's glorious past that has survived the thousands of years. . . .

But the relatively small above-ground section of the Wall, originally part of a retaining wall of the vast platform that supported the Temple and palace complex built by Herod, is not the only remnant that has survived the millennia.

Since 1867 when Charles Warren discovered an ancient entrance gate to the Temple Mount north of Wilson's Arch, it has been known that the entire length of the Western Wall is in existence. Because of the presence of a long hall running alongside the Wall, thought to have been used by Temple priests, the excavated remains have been popularly called the Rabbinic Tunnel. The Recovery of the entire Western Wall, and of four entrances to the Temple, has been sponsored by Israel's Ministry of Religious Affairs and is now directed by the Western Wall Heritage Foundation. Under the oversight of archaeologist Dan Bahat, a team of workmen finished unearthing the wall in 1986, and the site was opened for tourism in July 1991. Until then, few visitors to the long-exposed 200-foot vestige of this wall, the Wailing Wall, had any idea that the full length of the wall continued another 1,000 feet underground. . . .

If you were a visitor, upon entering this ancient Western Wall concourse you would pass through an immense subterranean hall that dates from the time of the second Temple. Serving today as an exhibition hall, the area contains a large-scale model of Herod's Temple, designed by Bahat to conform to new evidence unearthed in the Western Wall tunnel excavation.

As you move through the entrance to the tunnel itself, a huge stone section of the Western Wall is visible. This section of wall, named by scholars the Master Course, contains one of the largest building stones ever discovered in Israel. . . . Of Herodian origin, it is 40 feet long, ten feet in height and depth, and weighs approximately 458 tons. By comparison, the largest stone in the Great Pyramid of Cheops in Giza weighs only 20 tons.[43]

The enormity of the Temple complex cannot be overstated. The Sears Tower in Chicago, at 1454 feet in height, would if laid on its side, fit on the Temple Mount with room to spare! That the Temple complex would be totally destroyed, must have seemed almost incomprehensible to the disciples at the time. Yet it is not recorded that they questioned why or how such devastation would occur. Whereas "the engineering necessary to construct the walls surrounding and supporting the Temple complex and the Temple itself was nothing short of genius,"[44] dismantling it would be no small task either. Yet it was totally demolished as the Lord had predicted.

The excavations of the Temple Mount not only draw one's attention to its past glory, but also to its future prospect, as a third Temple will someday be constructed on this site. And it is this future Temple to which the Lord made reference in the fifth and final discourse of Matthew's Gospel.

The first question that Jesus answered for the disciples on the Mount of Olives had to do with the signs of the end of the age (24:4-28). A comparison of Revelation 6:1-11 with Matthew 24:4-8 seems to indicate that the Lord is describing the first half of the Tribulation in this section of His discourse. The parallelism between the Seal Judgments and Christ's predictions are described as follows:

> The first seal was opened revealing a man on a white horse, who had a bow, who went forth to conquer. The Lord Jesus shall come on a white horse, but this is not He, but a false Christ, who establishes a temporary peace. What is the first prediction of Matthew twenty-four. "Many shall come in My name, saying, I am Christ" (vs. 5). The second seal was opened revealing a man on a red horse, who should take peace from the earth. The second prediction of Matthew twenty-four is found in verses six and seven: "Wars and rumors of wars . . . nation shall rise against nation." The third seal was opened revealing a man on a black horse, who had balances in his hand; and "a voice in the midst of the four beasts" indicated famine. The third prediction of Matthew twenty-four is: "There shall be famines" (vs. 7). The fourth seal was opened revealing one on a pale horse, whose name was Death, and the fourth prophecy of Matthew twenty-four tells of pestilences and earthquakes. The fifth seal has to do with those who were slain for the Word of God, who, under the altar, cry, "How long, O Lord, holy and true, dost Thou not judge and avenge our blood on them that dwell on the earth?" What is the fifth prophecy of Matthew twenty-four? "Then shall they deliver you up to be afflicted, and shall kill you" (vs. 9).[45]

Whereas verses 4-8 outline the first half of the Tribulation, verses 9-28 describe the events of the last half. The word "then" in verse nine introduces the terrible persecutions against Israel that are described in Revelation 12:12-17, and foretold by the Apostle John to last for the entire second half of the Tribulation period (Rev. 12:14). Furthermore, the mention of the *"abomination of desolation spoken of by Daniel the prophet"* (Matt. 24:15) is clearly stated to occur in the middle of the Tribulation (Dan. 9:27).

> The Lord's outline of the events of the tribulation period can thus be determined. In the first half of the week Israel will experience the chastisements of the events of verses 4-8 (the seals of Rev. 6), although they will dwell in relative safety under the false covenant (Dan. 9:27). In the middle of the week great persecution will break out (v. 9; Rev. 12:12-17) because of the Desolator (v. 15; 2 Thess. 2; Rev. 13:1-10), who will cause Israel to flee from the land (vs. 16-20). Unbelieving Israel will be deceived by the false prophet (v. 11; Rev. 13:11-18) and go into apostasy (v. 12; 2 Thess. 2:11). Believing Israel will be a witnessing people, carrying the good news that these events

herald the approach of the Messiah (v. 14). This period will be terminated by the second advent of the Messiah (v. 27). Such seems to be the Lord's summary of the chronology of the tribulation period.[46]

Following the description of the Tribulation period (24:4-28), the Lord now answers another question posed by the disciples in 24:3; namely, *"What shall be the sign of thy coming?"* He set forth a chronology of events in verses 29-31 that can be summarized as follows:

(1) It will take place "immediately after the tribulation of those days" (v. 29). The events of the tribulation age continue until the second advent of Messiah, whose coming terminates it. (2) It will be preceded by signs (v. 30). What these signs are is not revealed. Many signs have preceded this one, as described in verses 4-26, but this is a unique sign which will herald Messiah's advent. (3) This coming will be sudden (v. 27), and (4) it will be evident (v. 30), at which time His power and glory will be manifested throughout the earth. . . .

Verse 31 suggests that the event to follow the second advent will be the regathering of Israel. They had been scattered because of the anger of Satan (Rev. 12:12) and the desolation of the Beast (Matt. 24:15), but, according to promise, they will be regathered to the land (Deut. 30:3-4; Ezek. 20:37-38; 37:1-14). This regathering is through special angelic ministries. The "elect" of verse 31 must have reference to the saints of that program with which God is then dealing, that is, Israel (Dan. 7:18, 22, 27).[47]

The remainder of chapter 24 (vv. 32-51) contains instructions that will be of special importance to those who will witness these end-time events. Whereas the Parable of the Fig Tree (vv. 32-35) was given to show the certainty of Christ's second coming, the reference to the days of Noah (vv. 36-39) dramatizes the uncertainty of the time of His coming. That people will be unprepared for this event is further illustrated by the two in the field and the two at the mill (vv. 40-41), as well as by the faithful and faithless servants (vv. 45-51). "In each of the three illustrations that show the unexpectedness of the event the individuals concerned were occupied with the usual round of life without any thought of Messiah's return. The lesson to be drawn is in the words 'watch' (v. 42), 'be ye also ready' (v. 44) and 'in such an hour as ye think not the Son of Man cometh' (v. 44, also 50)."[48]

The material in chapter 25, which concludes the Olivet Discourse, is unique to Matthew's Gospel. The Parable of the Ten Virgins (vv. 1-13), as well as The Parable of the Talents (vv. 14-30), not only further illustrates the meaning of watchfulness, but actually resumes the chronology of prophesied events. By introducing these parables with the word "then" in verse one, "the Lord is indicating that, following the regathering of Israel (Matt. 24:31), the next event will be the judging of living Israel on earth to determine who will go into the Kingdom. This has been anticipated in Matthew 24:28, where unbelieving Israel is likened unto a lifeless corpse which is consigned to the vultures, a picture of judgment."[49]

The final event described by the Lord in this fifth discourse of Matthew's Gospel is the judgment of the Gentile nations. It is "a dramatic picture illustrating the single great truth of what the coming of the Son of Man will mean in terms of the ultimate separation of men. . . . Eternal punishment on the one hand and eternal life on the other are the final issue of this judgment (25:46)."[50]

Following the same formula for terminating the other major discourses, Matthew ends this final teaching section by noting:

> *And it came to pass, when Jesus had finished all these sayings, he said unto his disciples,*
> *Ye know that after two days is the feast of the Passover, and the Son of man is betrayed to*
> *be crucified.* 26:1-2

Conclusion

The cross of Calvary—upon which Christ was crucified—marks the spot in the spiritual journey of men that separates the narrow road from the broad way. We have seen in the discourses recorded by Matthew that these alternate paths are always in view.

> The broad way is ever in his mind, and the multitude of those that go thereby, and the guest without the wedding garment, and the foolish virgins, and the goats as well as the sheep, and those who even "cast out devils" in the name of the Lord, and yet are rejected by Him because they "work lawlessness." . . .
> The condition of the Jews, their increasing hostility to the Christians, and the wavering or retrogression of many Jewish converts when the hostility became intensified shortly before and during the siege of Jerusalem—this may well explain one side of Matthew's Gospel; and the other side (the condemnation of "lawlessness") might find an explanation in a reference to Hellenizing Jews, who (like some of the Corinthians) considered that the new law set them free from all restraint, and who, in casting aside every vestige of nationality, wished to cast aside morality as well. Viewed in light of the approaching fall of Jerusalem, and the wavering or retrogression of great masses of the nation, the introduction into the Lord's Prayer of the words, "Deliver us from the evil," and the prediction (xxiv. 12) that "by reason of the multiplying of lawlessness the love of many shall wax cold," will seem not only appropriate, but typical of the character of the whole of the First Gospel.[51]

Chapter Four Notes

[1] Huston Smith, *The Religions of Man* (New York: Harper & Row, Publishers, 1989), 389.

[2] *Ibid.*, 390-91.

[3] *Ibid.*, 391.

[4] *Ibid.*, 393-94.

[5] *Ibid.*, 399.

[6] *Ibid.*

[7] Hugh R. Trevor-Roper, *Introduction to The Decline and Fall of the Roman Empire*, by Edward Gibbon (New York: Twayne Publishers, Inc., 1963), 89.

[8] Smith, *op. cit.*, 399.

[9] *Ibid.*, 399-400.

[10] *Ibid.*, 387.

[11] *Ibid.*, 403.

[12] D. S. Russel, *Between the Testaments* (Philadelphia: Fortress Press, 1975), 49.

[13] Robert A. Spivey and D. Moody Smith, Jr., *Anatomy of the New Testament: A Guide to Its*

Structure and Meaning, 2nd ed. (New York: Macmillan Publishing Co., Inc., 1974), 16.

[14] Morton Scott Enslin, *Christian Beginnings: Parts I and II* (New York: Harper & Row, Publishers, 1956), 122.

[15] *Ibid.*, 115.

[16] Russell, *op. cit.*, 48.

[17] Spivey, *op. cit.*, 16-17.

[18] Enslin, *op. cit.*, 119.

[19] Spivey, *op. cit.*, 18.

[20] *Ibid.*

[21] *Ibid.*

[22] *Ibid.*

[23] Enslin, *op. cit.*, 92-93.

[24] Spivey, *op. cit.*, 15-16.

[25] Enslin, *op. cit.*, 99.

[26] F. F. Bruce, "The Gospels," *The Biblical Expositor*, ed., Carl F. H. Henry (Philadelphia: A. J. Holman Company, 1973), 804.

[27] William Newton Clarke, *The Ideal of Jesus* (New York: Charles Scribner's Sons, 1911), 113.

[28] *Ibid.*, 110-11.

[29] *Ibid.*, 111.

[30] Richard G. Moulton, *Introduction to St. Matthew, St. Mark and the General Epistles* (New York: The Macmillan Company, 1898), xiv-xv.

[31] Clarke, *op. cit.*, 111-12.

[32] J. Dwight Pentecost, *Things to Come: A Study in Biblical Eschatology* (Grand Rapids, Mich.: Zondervan Publishing House, 1964), 153.

[33] Henri Daniel-Rops, *Daily Life in the Time of Jesus*, trans. by Patrick O'Brian (New York: Hawthorn Books, Inc., 1962), 160-61.

[34] *Ibid.*, 161.

[35] *Ibid.*, 160.

[36] *Ibid.*, 161.

[37] *Ibid.*

[38] H. G. Wells, *The Outline of History*, 4th ed. (New York: P. F. Collier & Son Company, 1925), II:457.

[39] Daniel-Rops, *op. cit.*, 162.

[40] George Eldon Ladd, "Matthew," *The Biblical Expositor*, ed. Carl F. H. Henry (Philadelphia: A. J. Holman Company, 1973), 807-56.

[41] Thomas Ice and Randall Price, *Ready to Rebuild: The Imminent Plan to Rebuild the Last Days Temple* (Eugene, Oreg.: Harvest House Publishers, 1992), 67-68.

[42] William C. Varner, "The Temple in the First Century," *Israel My Glory* (Dec./Jan., 1997-98), 55:9.

[43] Ice and Price, *op. cit.*, 139-40.

[44] Varner, *op. cit.*, 9.

[45] E. Schuyler English, *Studies in the Gospel According to Matthew* (New York: Our Hope, 1943), 173-74.

[46] Pentecost, *op. cit.*, 279-80.

[47] *Ibid.*, 280.

[48] *Ibid.*, 281-82.
[49] *Ibid.*, 282.
[50] Ladd, *op. cit.*, 849-50.
[51] "Gospels," *Encyclopaedia Britannica* (1903), X:804.

Chapter Five

The Son of David: Rightful King

In the second chapter of the book of Ezra we find that an account has been preserved in writing of the families that returned from the Babylonian captivity, as well as the numbers of each family involved. Recorded with accuracy, but pronounced with difficulty, are the names of those who returned to Jerusalem under the leadership of Zerubbabel. Commenting on this chapter, Matthew Henry explains the reasons for this record as follows:

> This was done for their honour, as part of their recompense for their faith and courage, and their affection to their own land, and to stir up others to follow their good example. . . . The account that was kept of the families that came up from the captivity was intended also for the benefit of posterity, that they might know from whom they descended, and to whom they were allied.[1]

Unfortunately, there were some families who could not prove from whom they descended and to whom they were allied. Of the sad fate of some of these individuals, we are told:

> And these were they which went up from Tel-melah, Tel-harsa, Cherub, Addan, and Immer: but they could not shew their father's house, and their seed, whether they were of Israel: The children of Delaiah, the children of Tobiah, the children of Nekoda, six hundred fifty and two. And the children of the priests: the children of Habaiah, the children of Koz, the children of Barzillai; which took a wife of the daughters of Barzillai the Gileadite, and was called after their name: These sought their register among those that were reckoned by genealogy, but they were not found: therefore were they, as polluted, put from the priesthood.
> Ezra 2:59-62

The Jewish people attached a great deal of importance to their genealogical records, as evidenced in the books of Genesis and First Chronicles. In fact, the Gospel of Matthew begins with a genealogy, whose introduction is almost verbatim to the one recorded in Genesis 5:1. Matthew presents the genealogy of Christ in the opening verses of his narrative, for this above all else must be substantiated first, if Jesus is to be recognized by the Jews as the promised Messiah. If Jesus is ever to be regarded as the King of the Jews, it is essential to prove that He is the Son of David.

Names Associated with the Messiah

In addition to providing evidence of Jesus' royal descent, Matthew records in the first two chapters of his narrative three names that are associated with the promised Messiah. One name applied to this Person who was to appear is mentioned by the angel of the Lord in a dream, saying:

> Joseph, thou son of David, fear not to take unto thee Mary thy wife: for that which is conceived in her is of the Holy Ghost. And she shall bring forth a son, and thou shalt call his name JESUS: for he shall save his people from their sins. 1:20-21

Matthew then introduces another name associated with the Messiah, when he says:

> Now all this was done, that it might be fulfilled which was spoken of the Lord by the

prophet, saying, Behold a virgin shall be with child, and shall bring forth a son, and they shall call his name Emmanuel, which being interpreted is, God with us. 1:22-23

A third name applied to the Messiah is found in Herod's interrogation of the chief priests and scribes after the wise men came and asked, *"Where is he that is born King of the Jews? For we have seen his star in the east, and are come to worship him"* (2:2). Matthew tells us:

> *When Herod the king had heard these things, he was troubled, and all Jerusalem with him. And when he had gathered all the chief priests and scribes of the people together, he demanded of them where Christ should be born.* 2:3-4

The term "Christ" is derived from the Greek word "Christos," which is the equivalent of the Hebrew word "Messiah." Both terms mean "the anointed one." The name "Jesus," however, means "Savior," and was explained as such by the angel of the Lord to Joseph.

The opening words of Matthew's Gospel, then, are very significant. The word "generation," furthermore, is a translation of the Greek word "genesis." As such, the first verse of this Gospel could be rendered, "The book of the genesis of Jesus the Messiah, the Son of David, the Son of Abraham." This verse not only forms an introduction to the genealogy of Christ recorded in the first chapter, but could also be used as the title of the entire Gospel, as it is the record of the beginning of the program of the Messiah, the King of the Jews. Furthermore, the preface of Matthew's narrative is a most fitting link that connects the New Testament Gospels with the chain of thought traced through the lives of Abraham and David, and developed in the two great covenants of the Old Testament, which are associated with their respective names.

> The preface (chaps. 1 and 2) reveals part of the purpose of the whole Gospel, in tracing the genealogy of Jesus, not from David merely, who was under the law, but from Abraham, who was the receiver of the promise (Gal. 3:16) and the father of the faithful (Gal. 3:7). Such a genealogy is the fitting preface of a book which aims at exhibiting the law, not as trampled upon but as fulfilled and developed into a higher law of promise, in which all the families of the world were to be blessed (Gen. 12:3). But by this time also the Church required some distinct affirmation concerning the divine origin of Jesus. The gap left in the opening of Mark's Gospel needed to be filled up. The mere earthly pedigree from Abraham was insufficient; nor did it suffice that Jesus should be declared to be spiritually the Son of God. It was necessary that the verity of the spiritual birth of Jesus from the Father should be embodied in a narrative so expressed as to be intelligible to all.[2]

The Manifestation of the Messiah

Only Matthew tells us that Jesus Christ was *"born King of the Jews"* (2:2). Whereas many a prince became king at an early age, it is very unusual to be born King. This was especially true for the Jewish nation at the time, in view of the fact that they were under foreign domination and had not had a legitimate Jewish king on the throne for centuries. No wonder Matthew tells us, *"When Herod the king had heard these things, he was troubled, and all Jerusalem with him"* (2:3).

Although Jesus was descended from the royal line, He was born of peasant stock.

This helps explain the ancient prophecy of Isaiah, which claimed:

> *And there shall come forth a rod out of the stem of Jesse, and a Branch shall grow out of his roots: And the spirit of the Lord shall rest upon him, the spirit of wisdom and understanding, the spirit of counsel and might, the spirit of knowledge and of the fear of the Lord. . . . And in that day there shall be a root of Jesse, which shall stand for an ensign of the people; to it shall the Gentiles seek: and his rest shall be glorious.* ISAIAH 11:1-2, 10

The royal branch had been pruned out of the family tree, so to speak, and Christ grew as a rod out of the stem of Jesse. Rather than being groomed in the palace of a mighty king, Jesus Christ was reared in the home of a lowly carpenter. Joseph descended from the royal line of David, but he was reduced to the social class of Jesse. He passes off the pages of history with no notice, pomp or ceremony. The fact that we read nothing about Joseph during the period of Christ's public ministry, strongly suggests that he had passed away by this time. It might be, however, that out of respect for Joseph, who had the legal—if not viable—right to the throne, that Jesus did not present Himself as King until after his demise.

Strangers and Sojourners

Although Matthew presents Christ as the King of the Jews, he also informs us that Jesus was forced into exile (cf. Matt. 12:14-15). Furthermore, Matthew quotes Jesus as saying, *"The foxes have holes, and the birds of the air have nests; but the Son of man hath not where to lay his head"* (8:20). At first glance these circumstances do not seem to be fitting of a King. But Christ is no ordinary King—He is King of the Jews. Upon further examination, however, we see that such conditions are to be expected for One who is not only the representative of the Jewish nation, but also *"the Son of David, the Son of Abraham"* (1:1).

Both Abraham and David not only lived for a time in exile (cf. Gen. 12:9-20; I Sam. 19 ff.), but each admitted to being a stranger and a sojourner in the lands wherein they dwelt (cf. Gen. 23:4; Ps. 39:12). In fact, since very remote times this has been the typical experience for most of the Jewish people. "It is a curious fact that, for more than three-quarters of their existence as a race, a majority of Jews have always lived outside the land they call their own. They do so today."[3]

While Abraham was dwelling in the land of Canaan, the Lord promised to give this land to him and his seed forever. In Genesis 13 we read:

> *And the Lord said unto Abram, after that Lot was separated from him, Lift up now thine eyes, and look from the place where thou art northward, and southward, and eastward, and westward: For all the land which thou seest, to thee will I give it, and to thy seed for ever.*
> GEN. 13:14-15

Although Abraham was promised all of Canaan, the only land he ever owned was a burial site located 19 miles southwest of Jerusalem and approximately 3,000 feet above sea level in a shallow valley in the Judean hills. Hebron is one of the oldest cities in the world, and it is here that Abraham and Sarah are buried in the cave of Machpelah. When Abraham purchased the field of Machpelah from the Hittites, he made the statement that was to portend the experience of the Jewish people for the next 4,000 years. Historian Paul Johnson explains the significance of the event for the

Jewish people as follows:

> Hebron is the site of their first recorded acquisition of land. Chapter 23 of the
> Book of Genesis describes how Abraham, after the death of his wife Sarah,
> decided to purchase the Cave of Machpelah and the lands which surrounded
> it, as a burying-place for her and ultimately for himself. The passage is among
> the most important in the entire Bible, embodying one of the most ancient
> and tenaciously held Jewish traditions, evidently very dear and critical to
> them. It is perhaps the first passage in the Bible which records an actual event,
> witnessed and described through a long chain of oral recitation and so pre-
> serving authentic details. The negotiation and ceremony of purchase are
> elaborately described. Abraham was what might now be termed an alien,
> though a resident of long standing in Hebron. To own freehold land in the
> place he required not merely the power of purchase but the public consent
> of the community. The land was owned by a dignitary called Ephron the
> Hittite. . . . Abraham had first to secure the formal agreement of the com-
> munity . . . to make the transaction; then to bargain with Ephron about the
> price, 400 shekels (i.e. pieces) of silver; then to have the coins . . . weighed
> out and handed over before the communal elders.
>
> This was a memorable event in a small community, involving not merely
> transfer of ownership but change of status: the ritualistic bowings, the dis-
> simulations and false courtesies, the hardness and haggling, are all brilliant-
> ly conveyed by the Bible narrative. But what strikes the reader most, what
> lingers in the mind, are the poignant words with which Abraham begins
> the transaction: "I am a stranger and a sojourner with you;" then, when
> it was concluded, the repeated stress that the land "was made sure unto
> Abraham for a possession" by the local people (Genesis 23:20). In this first
> true episode in Jewish history, the ambiguities and the anxieties of the race
> are strikingly presented.[4]

The fact that the Jews would be pilgrims and sojourners on the earth is not
inconsistent with God's justice, but commensurate to it.

> The Old Testament, it is important to grasp, is not primarily about justice as
> an abstract concept. It is about God's justice, which manifests itself by God's
> acts of choice. In Genesis we have various examples of the "just man," even
> the only just man . . . in the story of Noah and the Flood . . . , for example.
> Abraham is a just man too, but there is no suggestion that God chose him
> because he was the only one, or in any sense because of his merits. The Bible
> is not a work of reason, it is a work of history, dealing with what are to us
> mysterious and even inexplicable events. It is concerned with the momentous
> choices which it pleased God to make. It is essential to the understanding
> of Jewish history to grasp the importance the Jews have always attached to
> God's unrestricted ownership of creation. Many Jewish beliefs are designed
> to dramatize this central fact. The notion of an elect people was part of God's
> purpose to stress his possession of all created things. Abraham was a crucial
> figure in this demonstration. The Jewish sages . . . believed that God gave
> generously of his creation, but retained (as it were) the freehold of everything
> and a special, possessive relationship with selected elements.[5]

Thus we find in the Midrash—Jewish literature that interprets Scripture—
the following:

> The Holy One, blessed by He, created days, and took to Himself the Sabbath;
> He created the months, and took to Himself the festivals; He created the years,
> and chose for Himself the Sabbatical Year; He created the Sabbatical years,
> and chose for Himself the Jubilee Year; He created the nations, and chose for
> Himself Israel. . . . He created the lands, and took to Himself the land of Israel
> as a heave-offering from all other lands, as it is written: "the earth is the Lord's,
> and the fullness thereof." MIDRASH TEHILLIM 24:3

In a sense the nation of Israel and the territory promised to her are a tithe of the
people and lands of the world that rightfully belong to God.

> The election of Abraham and his descendants for a special role in God's provi-
> dence, and the donation of the land, are inseparable in the Biblical presentation
> of history. Moreover, both gifts are leasehold, not freehold: the Jews are chosen,
> the land is theirs, by grace and favour, always revocable. Abraham is both a real
> example and a perpetual symbol of a certain fragility and anxiety in Jewish
> possession. He is a "stranger and sojourner" and remains one even after God's
> election, even after he has elaborately purchased the Cave of Machpelah. This
> uncertainty of ownership is transferred to all his descendents, as the Bible
> repeatedly reminds us. Thus God tells the Israelites: "And the land is not to be
> sold in perpetuity, for all land is Mine, because you are strangers and sojourners
> before me;" or again, the people confess: "For we are strangers before you, and
> sojourners like all our forefathers;" and the Psalms have David the King say: "I
> am a stranger with thee, and a sojourner, as all my fathers were."[6]

As a descendent of Abraham and David, Jesus could identify with the people who
confessed, *"For we are strangers before thee, and sojourners, as were all our fathers"* (I Chron.
29:15). Although He was the rightful King of the Jews, the Lord lived a life of hardship
as a sojourner, even amidst His own people. When a certain scribe came to the Lord
and said, *"Master, I will follow thee whithersoever thou goest"* (8:19), it was then that Jesus
said, *"The foxes have holes, and the birds of the air have nests; but the Son of man hath not where
to lay his head"* (8:20).

Jesus Christ was born King of the Jews, but He did not proclaim the truths of the
Kingdom of God from a palace. Instead, He lived as a pilgrim without even a place to
call His home. He experienced the uncertainty of ownership that has been transferred
to all of Abraham's descendents. As such, the Lord could relate to the common people,
and He was moved with compassion for them. We read:

> *And Jesus went about all the cities and villages, teaching in their synagogues, and preaching
> the gospel of the kingdom, and healing every sickness and every disease among the people.
> But when he saw the multitudes, he was moved with compassion on them, because they
> fainted, and were scattered abroad, as sheep having no shepherd.* MATT. 9:35-36

Abraham remained a stranger and sojourner even after God's election; so too the
twelve men chosen by the Lord would share the same experience. Since *"the disciple is
not above his master, nor the servant above his lord"* (10:24), Christ informed His followers
that they, also, would live as strangers and sojourners. Notice how Matthew records the
Lord's instructions to the disciples as He sends them out to proclaim that the Kingdom
of Heaven is at hand:

Provide neither gold, nor silver, nor brass in your purses, Nor scrip for your journey, neither two coats, neither shoes, nor yet staves: for the workman is worthy of his meat. And into whatsoever city or town ye shall enter, enquire who in it is worthy; and there abide till ye go thence. And when ye come into an house, salute it. And if the house be worthy, let your peace come upon it: but if it be not worthy, let your peace return to you. And whosoever shall not receive you, nor hear your words, when ye depart out of that house or city, shake off the dust of your feet. . . . Behold, I send you forth as sheep in the midst of wolves: be ye therefore wise as serpents, and harmless as doves. But beware of men: for they will deliver you up to the councils, and they will scourge you in their synagogues; And ye shall be brought before governors and kings for my sake, for a testimony against them and the Gentiles. . . . But when they persecute you in this city, flee ye into another: for verily I say unto you, Ye shall not have gone over the cities of Israel, till the Son of man be come. 10:9-14, 16-18, 23*

Matthew continues to stress in the following chapters the fact that Jesus Christ was a stranger and sojourner, as were all the Jewish forefathers. Commenting on chapters 10 through 12, one nineteenth-century writer noted:

From the Apostles the narrative turns . . . to the world, and brings out the growing isolation of Jesus in his ministry: he gradually draws apart from the imperfect ministry of his forerunner; from the Pharisaic doctrine of the Sabbath, the great outward mark of the Hebrew nation; other opposition of the Pharisees is pronounced a blasphemy against the Spirit of Holiness; from the wisdom and might of the great cities he turns to the simplicity of babes, to those who labour and are heavy laden; a final touch is found in the separation of Jesus from his very mother and brethren.[7]

Confrontations and Conspiracies

The Gospel of Matthew portrays Jesus Christ as the rightful King of the Jewish nation. The estrangement and isolation experienced by Christ, rather than negating His claims to be King, are actually circumstances that could be expected of One who was *"the son of David, the son of Abraham"* (1:1). Furthermore, the rebellion against His principles, the plots against His life, and even the betrayal of a friend, are all part of the drama that surrounds the life of a king.

Only Matthew records the fact that Herod the Great *"slew all the children that were in Bethlehem, and in all the coasts thereof, from two years old and under, according to the time which he had diligently enquired of the wise men"* (2:16). From the time of Jesus' birth to His eventual crucifixion, the enemies of Christ continually plotted to prevent His being recognized and accepted as King of the Jews.

Whereas John does not record the Temptation of Christ, and Mark merely notes that *"he was in the wilderness forty days tempted of Satan"* (Mark 1:13), Matthew (as well as Luke) elaborates on the specific nature of their confrontation. For example, Matthew wrote:

Again, the devil taketh him up into an exceeding high mountain, and sheweth him all the kingdoms of the world, and the glory of them; And saith unto him, All these things will I give thee, if thou wilt fall down and worship me. Then saith Jesus unto him, Get thee hence, Satan: for it is written, Thou shalt worship the Lord thy God, and him only shalt thou serve. 4:8-10*

A king needs a kingdom, and Satan offered Christ *"all the kingdoms of the world and the glory of them"* (4:8). It is of interest to note that Matthew emphasizes the grandeur of the kingdoms, which would be of interest to a king. By contrast Luke, written from the perspective of a man of science, notes rather that the devil *"shewed unto him all the kingdoms of the world in a moment of time"* (4:5). At any rate Jesus Christ, as King of the Jews and Son of God, refused Satan's offer, because He was introducing and representing the Kingdom of Heaven.

Later, in Chapter Twelve, we find the Lord being confronted by the Pharisees regarding certain activities on the Sabbath day. As a result of this controversy, Matthew notes:

> *Then the Pharisees went out, and held a council against him, how they might destroy him. But when Jesus knew it, he withdrew himself from thence.* 12:14-15A

In Chapter 21 Matthew records the following parable of Jesus, which was addressed to the religious leaders of the Jewish nation:

> *There was a certain householder, which planted a vineyard, and hedged it round about, and digged a winepress in it, and built a tower, and let it out to husbandmen, and went into a far country: And when the time of the fruit drew near, he sent his servants to the husbandmen, that they might receive the fruits of it. And the husbandmen took his servants, and beat one, and killed another, and stoned another. Again he sent other servants more than the first: and they did unto them likewise. But last of all he sent unto them his son, saying, They will reverence my son. But when the husbandmen saw the son, they said among themselves, This is the heir; come, let us kill him, and let us seize on his inheritance. And they caught him, and cast him out of the vineyard, and slew him. When the lord therefore of the vineyard cometh, what will he do unto those husbandmen?* 21:33B-40

How did the audience respond to this parable? Matthew tells us:

> *And when the chief priests and Pharisees had heard his parables, they perceived that he spake of them. But when they sought to lay hands on him, they feared the multitude, because they took him for a prophet.* 21:45-46

Nevertheless, the die was cast, so to speak, and the conspiracy against the Lord was taking on a definite form. Jesus forewarned his disciples about the outcome of this conspiracy, by saying:

> *Ye know that after two days is the feast of the Passover, and the Son of man is betrayed to be crucified.* 26:2

To which Matthew adds:

> *Then assembled together the chief priest, and the scribes, and the elders of the people, unto the palace of the high priest, who was called Caiaphas, And consulted that they might take Jesus by subtilty, and kill him. But they said, Not on the feast day, lest there be an uproar among the people.* 26:3-5

Nevertheless, Jesus would die during the time of the Passover. As the Son of David, the Messiah would eventually reign as righteous King, but as the Son of Abraham, He would first become the perfect Sacrifice.

> *Now when Jesus was in Bethany, in the house of Simon the leper, There came unto him a woman having an alabaster box of very precious ointment, and poured it on his head, as he sat at meat. But when his disciples saw it, they had indignation, saying, To what purpose is this waste? For this ointment might have been sold for much, and given to the poor. When Jesus understood it, he said unto them, Why trouble ye the woman? For she hath wrought a*

good work upon me. For ye have the poor always with you; but me ye have not always. For in that she hath poured this ointment on my body, she did it for my burial. Verily I say unto you, Wheresoever this gospel shall be preached in the whole world, there shall also this, that this woman hath done, be told for a memorial of her. Then one of the twelve, called Judas Iscariot, went unto the chief priest, And said unto them, What will ye give me, and I will deliver him unto you? And they covenanted with him for thirty pieces of silver. And from that time he sought opportunity to betray him. 26:6-16

Judas' opportunity to betray Jesus came soon enough, and Christ "suffered under Pontius Pilate; was crucified, dead, and buried."[8] Yet the conspiracy against the King did not end here. Matthew notes:

Now the next day, that followed the day of the preparation, the chief priests and Pharisees came together unto Pilate, Saying, Sir, we remember that that deceiver said, while he was yet alive, After three days I will rise again. Command therefore that the sepulcher be made sure until the third day, lest his disciples come by night, and steal him away, and say unto the people, He is risen from the dead: so the last error shall be worse than the first. Pilate said unto them, Ye have a watch: go your way, make it as sure as ye can. So they went, and made the sepulcher sure, sealing the stone, and setting a watch. 27:62-66

But after three days Jesus Christ did rise again! Matthew wrote:

In the end of the Sabbath, as it began to dawn toward the first day of the week, came Mary Magdalene and the other Mary to see the sepulcher. And, behold, there was a great earthquake: for the angel of the Lord descended from heaven, and came and rolled back the stone from the door, and sat upon it. His countenance was like lightning, and his raiment white as snow: And for fear of him the keepers did shake, and became as dead men. And the angel answered and said unto the women, Fear not ye: for I know that ye seek Jesus, which was crucified. He is not here: for he is risen, as he said. Come, see the place where the Lord lay. And go quickly, and tell his disciples that he is risen from the dead; and, behold, he goeth before you into Galilee; there shall ye see him: lo, I have told you. And they departed quickly from the sepulcher with fear and great joy; and did run to bring his disciples word. And as they went to tell his disciples, behold, Jesus met them, saying, All hail. And they came and held him by the feet, and worshipped him. Then said Jesus unto them, Be not afraid: go tell my brethren that they go into Galilee, and there shall they see me. 28:1-10

At this point Matthew adds more details regarding the conspiracy. He noted:

Now when they were going, behold, some of the watch came into the city, and shewed unto the chief priests all things that were done. And when they were assembled with the elders, and had taken counsel, they gave large money unto the soldiers, Saying, Say ye, His disciples came by night, and stole him away while we slept. And if this come to the governor's ears, we will persuade him, and secure you. So they took the money, and did as they were taught: and this saying is commonly reported among the Jews until this day. 28:11-15

Only Matthew relates this plot to explain the empty tomb. His narrative portrays Jesus Christ as King, and conspiracies are part of the drama that surrounds the life and death of a king. On the other hand, the loyalties of His followers, the obedience to His commands, the submission to His authority, and even the homage of strangers, which are all evident in Matthew's Gospel, give credence to the accusation that was "set up over his head" and placed on His cross:

THIS IS JESUS THE KING OF THE JEWS. 27:37

Proof of Jesus' Claim to be the Messiah

In spite of any and all circumstantial evidence that could be accumulated, this would still not be sufficient to convince the Jews. For them, the real proof of Jesus' claim to be the promised Messiah/King needed to be substantiated from the Old Testament Scriptures. To this end Matthew "presents one continual comparison of Jesus of Nazareth with the Messiah of the Prophets, a comparison which could not fail to have marvelous convincing power with any candid Jew."[9]

> The Gospel takes the life of Jesus as it was lived on earth, and his character as it actually appeared, and places them alongside the life and character of the Messiah as sketched in the Prophets, the historic by the side of the prophetic, that the two may appear in their marvelous unity and in their perfect identity. The greatness of the Prophet like unto Moses is seen in the Nazarene, as he speaks for God the fundamental truths of the kingdom of heaven and fore-tells its future. The grandeur of the suffering Servant of Jehovah, "despised and rejected of men," "wounded for our transgressions," shines through all his words and acts that culminate in his vicarious death on Calvary. The sub-limity of the King of whom Jehovah said, "I have set my King on my holy hill of Zion," appears in the Son of David, as he forms and gives law to a world-wide spiritual society, an everlasting state, the kingdom of heaven. Jesus and the Messiah are demonstrated to be in all respects one and the same.
> All this was just what was needed to commend him as a Savior to the Jews.[10]

The Jewish people were not looking simply for the Son of God, who was "wielding almighty power in establishing a universal empire."[11] This approach would appeal to the readers of Mark's Gospel, but not to the Jews, who "had been holding out for ages . . . against the material power of all the great nations of the world, and who ever bowed to Scriptures and prophecy, but never to mere power."[12]

> Equally vain would it have been to bring him forward as Luke does—as the divine-man, coming down from God out of heaven, passing through a perfect human development, entering into sympathy with all suffering and sorrowing humanity—for the Jew was not looking for the perfect man, the son of Adam, the son of God, but for a son of Abraham, a king descended from David by the royal line.
> Still more fruitless would it have been to exhibit him as John does—as the eternal Word, the very God, the light and life of the world—for the veil was before the eyes of the Jew, and he could not discern the spiritual God as manifested in the Word. The light shone into the darkness and the darkness comprehended it not.
> For the Jew the credentials of Jesus must be drawn from Moses and the Prophets. In his origin, human and divine, in the capital facts of his life, in his character private and official, in short, in his work and in his kingdom, he must be shown to meet the requirements of the Messianic Scriptures. Jesus must be set over against the prophetic Messiah, so that they shall both be seen to be one and the same. This work properly done, no Jew could escape the conclusion: Jesus of Nazareth is the Messiah.[13]

Chapter Five Notes

[1] Matthew Henry, *Commentary on the Whole Bible*, One volume edition, Edited by Dr. Leslie F. Church (Grand Rapids, Mich.: Zondervan Publishing House, 1961), 482.

[2] "Gospels," *Encyclopaedia Britannica* (1903), X:803.

[3] Paul Johnson, *A History of the Jews* (New York: Harper & Row, Publishers, 1987), 4.

[4] *Ibid.*, 4-5.

[5] *Ibid.*, 18.

[6] *Ibid.*, 19.

[7] Richard G. Moulton, *Introduction to St. Matthew, St. Mark and the General Epistles* (New York: The Macmillan Company, 1898), xvi-xvii.

[8] Apostles' Creed, Article IV.

[9] D. S. Gregory, *Why Four Gospels? Or, the Gospel for All the World* (New York: Funk & Wagnalls, Publishers, 1890), 128.

[10] *Ibid.*, 129.

[11] *Ibid.*, 103.

[12] *Ibid.*

[13] *Ibid.*, 104.

PERSPECTIVE

The Rejected Messiah by Charles Erdman

Matthew is the Gospel of the Messiah. The appearance of this princely figure has been predicted by the Hebrew prophets. In fact, every important event in his career has been explicitly foretold; his birth of a virgin in the town of Bethlehem; his residence in Egypt, in Nazareth, and in Capernaum; his healing of the sick; his speaking in parables; his royal entry into Jerusalem; his desertion by his followers; his triumphant spirit in death. Allusions are made to sixty-five Old Testament passages, forty-three are verbally quoted, a number equal to that of all the other Gospels combined. Thus Matthew is the Gospel of fulfillment. It faces the Old Testament; it properly begins the New. The scenes are colored by Jewish customs; Jewish symbols and types abound. The Law, the Prophets, and the Psalms, all are shown to have pointed forward to Jesus of Nazareth. In him are found their significance, their meaning, and their goal; he is the expected Son of David, the son of Abraham; he is the predicted Messiah; he is the Christ of God. With all propriety Matthew is placed as the first Gospel, showing how the ancient Scriptures are linked with the good news of salvation in Jesus Christ.

Matthew is further the Gospel of rejection. Of course the fact is essential to all the Gospels; but here it is presented continually. It colors all the teaching, it forms the background of every scene; its shadow is never lifted. Before Jesus is born, his mother is in danger of being repudiated by Joseph; at his birth Jerusalem is troubled and Herod seeks to take his life; on the plains of Bethlehem no angel choir sings, but mothers are weeping in anguish over their slaughtered babes; Jesus is hurried away to Egypt and hidden for thirty years in Nazareth; his forerunner is imprisoned, and beheaded in a dungeon. As Jesus points men to "the narrow way" he declares that few will find it. To the many he is to say as he sits in judgment "I never knew you: depart from me;" men marvel at his miracles and offer to follow him, but he declares that the "Son of man hath not where to lay his head;" he warns his messengers that they, too, are to be rejected. His parables indicate that his kingdom will not be realized on earth until the present age ends; as soon as his disciples understand that he is the Messiah, he begins to express and iterate the truth of his cruel sufferings and death; he relates to the people his "parables of rejection;" he pronounces his most solemn woes on the rulers of the people; he predicts the destruction of the city and the anguish of the nation; in the hour of his death is heard that desolate cry, "My God, my God, why hast thou forsaken me?" No penitent thief is praying, no word of human sympathy is spoken; those who pass by revile, the chief priests and elders mock him; even after his death they set a seal and a watch; even after his resurrection they hire soldiers to hide his glory with their lie. In no Gospel is the attack of his enemies so bitter; in no other is the King more definitely offered to the nation, and in none is his rejection so cruel and so complete.[1]

---

[1] Charles R. Erdman, *The Gospel of Matthew* (Philadelphia: The Westminster Press, 1948) 10-11.

PART III

THE MEANING OF THE PRESENT

*Hear now, . . . for, behold, I will bring forth
my servant the Branch.*
ZECHARIAH 3:8

Yet more: they had to vindicate the claims of the Present. They had to set forth the activity and energy of the Lord's life apart from the traditions of Moriah and Sinai; to exhibit the Gospel as a simple revelation from heaven; to follow the details of its announcement as they were apprehended in their living power by those who followed most closely on the steps of Christ. They had to connect Christianity with history.[1]

-Brooke Foss Westcott, *An Introduction to the Study of the Gospels*

It entered into the design of the evangelist, not only to describe our Lord's success, but the malignant opposition of his enemies. He now presents the dark side of the picture, and enables us to trace the growth of this malignant opposition from its earliest appearance in a series of charges brought against him as a violator of the law; by claiming power to forgive sins; by holding intercourse with publicans and sinners, and even calling a publican to be one of his apostles; by his free and simple mode of life, involving the neglect (as they supposed) of all ascetic duties; and lastly by his frequent violation of the Sabbath.

But in spite of this increasing opposition, his fame and popularity were growing still more rapidly; and when they had attained their height, . . . he refuses to be checked in his labours, either by the well-meant but mistaken interference of his friends, or by the growing rancour of his enemies, who now accuse him of collusion with the Evil One; but solemnly repels both forms of opposition, by warning men against the unpardonable sin, and by asserting his own independence of all natural relations, when in conflict with the claims of his great spiritual family.[2]

-J. A. Alexander, *The Gospel According to Mark*

Mark had no thought of writing to meet the needs of posterity. He wrote to steady the faith of the average Roman Christian in a persecution situation. He undertook to present to the Christian community at Rome such a sketch of Jesus' life and death as would justify their faith, refute the calumnies of the enemies, make the suffering of Christ intelligible, and dignify their own by showing it was the technique of saviorhood.[3]

-Albert E. Barnett, *The New Testament: Its Making and Meaning*

---

[1] Brooke Foss Westcott, *An Introduction to the Study of the Gospels* (London: Macmillan & Co., 1875), 219.

[2] Joseph Addison Alexander, *The Gospel According to Mark* (London: The Banner of Truth Trust, 1960), xvii.

[3] Albert E. Barnett, *The New Testament: Its Making and Meaning* (New York: Abingdon Press, 1946), 140.

Figure III-1. Bartolome' Esteban Murillo: Feeding the Five Thousand

The strenuous activity of Jesus Christ is highlighted by His deeds of divine power, and this is the emphasis of the second Gospel. Mark is the Gospel of miracles, and one of the most important—the only one recorded by all four evangelists—is the Feeding of the Five Thousand. *"And when he had taken the five loaves and the two fishes, he looked up to heaven, and blessed, and brake the loaves, and gave them to his disciples to set before them; and the two fishes divided he among them all. And they did all eat, and were filled"* (Mark 6:41-42).

The breaking of the loaves and the feeding of the five thousand is an exemplification of the fact that *"the Son of Man came not to be ministered unto, but to minister, and to give his life a ransom for many"* (Mark 10:45). This is the message that has been beautifully captured on canvas by the seventeenth-century painter, Bartolome' Esteban Murillo.

Chapter Six

The Gospel of Mark: Victory Through Suffering

In his Gospel Matthew set forth Jesus Christ as one who was not only *"born King of the Jews"* (Matt. 2:2), but who also fulfilled all the Old Testament requirements of the promised Messiah. As a former publican, Matthew was an official in a vast kingdom, and presented Christ as the heir to an even greater Kingdom (cf. Matt. 1:1).

The Gospel of Mark, however, stresses neither the kingly office of Christ, nor the fulfillment of ancient prophecies. In his narrative we find, for example, no genealogy of Jesus, no miraculous birth, no reference to Bethlehem, no adoration of wise men, no Sermon on the Mount, no arraignment of the Hebrew nation, no sentence passed on Jerusalem, no reference to the Lord's right to summon angels in the garden, and no promise of a kingdom to the thief on the cross. In fact, the omissions in Mark's Gospel are essentially Jewish in character, for he was addressing an audience for whom such information was not necessary.

A Source of Conflict

As a young man John Mark accompanied his cousin Barnabas (cf. Col. 4:10) and the Apostle Paul as they set out for Cyprus on the First Missionary Journey to Asia Minor. Before the team reached the cities of Galatia, however, we find: *"Now when Paul and his company loosed from Paphos, they came to Perga in Pamphylia: and John departing from them returned to Jerusalem"* (Acts 13:13). Discouraged but not deterred, Paul and Barnabas continued their missionary endeavors without the aid of Mark, but eventually they, also, returned safely to Jerusalem. Soon, however, another journey was planned. We read:

> And some days after Paul said unto Barnabas, Let us go again and visit our brethren in every city where we have preached the word of the Lord, and see how they do. And Barnabas determined to take with them John, whose surname was Mark. But Paul thought not good to take him with them, who departed from them from Pamphylia, and went not with them to the work. And the contention was so sharp between them, that they departed asunder one from the other: and so Barnabas took Mark, and sailed unto Cyprus; And Paul chose Silas, and departed, being recommended by the brethren unto the grace of God. ACTS 15:36-40

The book of Acts does not explain why Mark abandoned the missionary journey at Perga and returned home. Consequently, this decision, together with the serious breach it caused between Paul and Barnabas, has puzzled Bible commentators and brought into question the true character and real convictions of John Mark during this earlier period of his life.

Various suggestions have been given concerning the cause of Mark's defection. Some think he had experienced a great deal of sickness; it is entirely possible in that part of the world. Some think he was worrying about his mother; that too is possible, and many men have had to give up work they would like to do for the sake of the parents they love. Some think he was afraid; I am inclined to doubt that reason. It seems to me that the "sharp contention"

between Paul and Barnabas, however, requires a much more significant reason than any of these expressed. The only reason that would have sufficient
magnitude would be one arising from the Judaizer problem. Paul seemed
to be able to tolerate almost anything else; but when anyone suggested that
anything should be added to the gospel of grace, Paul could find no point of
compromise. On this issue he was willing to censure Peter, yes, even Barnabas
(Galatians 2:11-14). As I reconstruct the situation, Mark had found Paul's
work with Gentiles contrary to his own view of the Law. When it became
obvious that they were going to move into territory where Gentiles would
predominate, Mark drew the line. He went home.[1]

John Mark became a source of conflict between Paul and Barnabas, but this un-
fortunate experience and the lessons learned from it would eventually be superintended by the Holy Spirit as Mark would select and organize the material from the life of
Christ, which would be used in the Gospel that would bear his name. One of the major
themes in Mark's narrative is how Christ handled conflict, and taught His disciples the
true meaning of suffering.

A History of Conflict

There were two great Gentile peoples in the first century—the Romans and the
Greeks—and Mark wrote for the first-named. The theme of Mark's Gospel would be
of special interest to the Romans, who built the greatest empire the world has ever
seen, through a process of conflict and confrontation. The entire history of the Roman Republic—from the sixth century B.C. until the formation of the Empire under
Caesar Augustus shortly before the birth of Christ—can be outlined and described as
a series of conflicts:

(1). The internal conflict between patricians and plebeians (509-367 B.C.).
After winning the right to run for consul and even be senators, the plebs won
the right for their assembly to make laws for all citizens, patrician or plebeian.
With this change, the final say in Roman government passed to the plebs. The
Roman aristocratic republic became a democratic republic. . . . The patricians
had claimed the right to rule because of their religious position, but the plebs'
claim had no such basis. The plebs' victory established the principle that the
greater force would rule Rome.[2]

Nevertheless, "this period closed with the fusion of the old classes into a united
people."[3]

(2). The external conflict of this united Rome with her neighbors (367-266 B.C.) and
Carthage (264-146 B.C.), which resulted, respectively, in the expansion of her territories
over Italy and the Mediterranean coasts.

(3). The new internal conflict (146-30 B.C.). This period can be further sub-divided,
as an older textbook on ancient history suggests, into "a threefold conflict: in Rome,
between rich and poor; in Italy, between Rome and her 'Allies'; in the empire at large,
between Italy and the provinces."[4]

During this final period in the history of the old republic, Rome found itself in a series of civil wars between rival generals and their armies. Here we could tell of the conflicts between Marius and Sulla, Pompey and Caesar, or Antony and Octavian. But growing in popularity were also the horrible gladiatorial contests; and suffice it to say that "the Roman government itself now resembled the deadly circuses. Political disagreements could be resolved only by force and violence."[5]

The leadership within the Senate had "carried Rome triumphantly through her great wars, but it had failed to devise a plan of government fit for the conquests outside Italy. It knew how to conquer, but not how to rule. There followed a century of gross misgovernment abroad. This corrupted the citizens and lowered the moral tone at home, until the Republic was no longer fit to rule even Italy or herself."[6] As a result, "most people now accepted one man rule as inevitable."[7]

> From 49 to 44 B.C. Caesar controlled Rome and therefore much of the world. Romans called him father and supreme ruler. He had himself made dictator for life and held absolute power. Caesar turned the Senate into a political joke. Increasing the number of members, Caesar filled the Senate with men prepared to follow his orders with no questions asked.
>
> Caesar's rule, for all practical purposes, marked the end of the Roman Republic and the beginning of the Roman Empire and one-man rule.[8]

During the five years that he held power, Julius Caesar took additional measures to secure his position. He could agree in principle with the statement, *"No man can enter into a strong man's house, and spoil his goods, except he will first bind the strong man, and then he will spoil his house"* (Mark 3:27). For Caesar the strong man was the Senate, and in addition to spoiling his house, "he freely pardoned many old enemies and won admiration as a man of generosity. He proved himself a friend of the poor by reducing debts and providing employment on construction projects."[9]

> Caesar had many grand visions for Rome. He hoped to rebuild the city with beautiful new public buildings and an altered course for the Tiber River. He planned many new roads, and even a sea canal in Greece. Caesar also looked forward to vast new lands being added to the empire in the west and the east.
>
> By this time Caesar also had a grand vision of himself. His rise to power had been the result of force and violence. He recognized that more than the benefits he was offering would be required to secure his rule. Caesar would have to be considered more than a man.
>
> Caesar was moving toward making himself a god.[10]

However, not all Romans, including some of his friends, were willing to submit to the rule of Julius Caesar, whatever his qualifications and pretensions! He was, after all, only a man.

> And Rome was still the city that, according to legend, had begun with murder of brother by brother. Force and violence once again had their way in Rome on March 15, 44 B.C. when Caesar was stabbed to death in the Senate.
>
> Caesar's murderers had hoped to restore the Senate to power and reestablish the old republic, but their hopes were in vain.
>
> They had to flee Rome for their lives.[11]

Within 15 years, after more conflicts were resolved by force and violence, Caesar's grandnephew, Octavian, became the undisputed ruler of the Roman Empire, and assumed the title of "Caesar Augustus." The days of the Republic were officially over, and the monarchic government—although not an ideal situation—was certainly preferred over anarchy.

> Moreover, to say that monarchic government was the happiest solution possible for Rome is not to call it an unmixed good. No perfectly happy outcome was possible to that Roman world, destitute of representative institutions and based on slavery. But a despotism can get along on less virtue and intelligence than a free government can. The evils that were finally to overthrow the Empire five centuries later had all appeared in the last century of the Republic. Ruin seemed imminent. The change to the imperial system restored prosperity and staved off the final collapse for a time as long as separates us from Luther or Columbus.
>
> The interval was precious; for in it, under Roman protection, priceless work was to be done for humanity. But finally the medicine of despotism exhausted its good effect; its own poison was added to the older evils; and the collapse, threatened in the first century B.C., came in the fifth century A.D.[12]

How Christ Handled Conflict

Mark addressed his Gospel to a Roman audience, and explained the priceless work that was done for humanity. He presents One who is greater than any Caesar; not One who would become a god, but *"Jesus Christ, the Son of God"* (Mark 1:1).

The ancient Romans responded to conflict through force and violence—by shedding the blood of their enemies. Jesus Christ, however, dealt with conflict differently. He achieved victory through suffering—by shedding His own blood for those who were His enemies (cf. Rom. 5:10).

The introduction of Mark's Gospel (1:1-13) suggests that *"the gospel of Jesus Christ"* (1:1) "concerns a victory (the Spirit over Satan) to be won only through conflict (the wilderness) and obedience (the baptism of Jesus). The rest of Mark's Gospel narrates the triumph in conflict, which Jesus effects through his exorcisms, debates, and suffering."[13]

Whereas the ancient Romans faced many potential and actual conflicts, and "in the process received constant practice in war,"[14] we also experience conflict and suffering of one sort or another on a regular basis. It is the common problem of the present hour, no matter what or where our situation in life. Furthermore, for the followers of Jesus Christ, there is an ever-present spiritual battle that we are engaged in. The apostle Paul said, *"For we wrestle not against flesh and blood, but against principalities, against powers, against the rulers of the darkness of this world, against spiritual wickedness in high places"* (Eph. 6:12).

The Gospel of Mark gives insight to our present circumstances, by showing how Jesus Christ handled conflict and taught His disciples the true meaning of suffering.

> In the first half of the Gospel of Mark (1:16-8:21), opposition to Jesus comes in the main from two camps—the demons and the Pharisees. Jesus faces the opposition of the demons with exorcism and that of the Pharisees with debate. Thus this first half of Mark centers upon Jesus' miracles and teachings. Indeed, as we shall see, miracles and teachings are mingled within individual units of tradition because both are means of opposing his

enemies. The two forms of meeting opposition differ in that the demons recognize Jesus yet do battle against him, whereas the Pharisees, though also utterly antagonistic to Jesus, do not recognize his true identity.[15]

The following miracle, which is the first recorded by Mark, sets the tone for his narrative and underscores the nature of the opposition to Christ. "The very man who has come to Jesus with an evident desire for relief, cries out against him in hatred and dread."[16]

> *And there was in their synagogue a man with an unclean spirit; and he cried out, Saying, Let us alone; what have we to do with thee, thou Jesus of Nazareth? Art thou come to destroy us? I know thee who thou art, the Holy One of God. And Jesus rebuked him, saying, Hold thy peace, and come out of him. And when the unclean spirit had torn him, and cried with a loud voice, he came out of him. And they were all amazed, insomuch that they questioned among themselves, saying, What thing is this? For with authority commandeth he even the unclean spirits, and they do obey him. 1:23-27*

Regarding the importance of this miracle, Professor Charles R. Erdman wrote:

> There is something specially significant in the fact that the one first recorded reveals superhuman forces of evil, by which men are oppressed, but which are powerless in the presence of Christ. Miracles of the same nature are specially prominent in the Gospel of Mark; and the mention of this particular miracle as the story opens, serves to illustrate the strength of the opposition to Christ, the need of his work, and his invincible power to save.[17]

The miracles of Jesus dominate this first half of Mark's Gospel. We find nature miracles, such as calming the storm (4:35-41), walking on water (6:45-52), and feeding the multitudes (6:30-44; 8:1-9); numerous miracles of healing (1:29-31, 40-45; 2:3-12; 3:1-6; 7:31-37), including the raising of Jairus' daughter from the dead (5:35-43); and miracles of exorcism—the driving out of demons (1:21-28; 5:1-13; 7:24-30). In addition to these specific miracles, which are described in detail, Mark refers to innumerable miracles of healing and exorcism in general. When Jesus was in the region of Gennesaret, for example, we read:

> *And whithersoever he entered into villages, or cities, or country, they laid the sick in the streets, and besought him that they might touch if it were but the border of his garment: and as many as touched him were made whole. 6:56*

Yet it is most interesting to note that when Mark summarized the Galilean ministry of Christ, he wrote, *"And he preached in their synagogues throughout all Galilee, and cast out devils"* (1:39). "Evidently, for Mark, miracles are understood through exorcisms. They do not constitute a separate class of acts or events."[18]

An important question in regard to these exorcisms—one that may not have been answered from Mark's brief report of the Temptation experience—was whether Christ performs miracles by the power of Satan or by God. Mark tells us:

> *And the scribes which came down from Jerusalem said, He hath Beelzebub, and by the prince of the devils casteth he out devils. And he called them unto him, and said unto them in parables, How can Satan cast out Satan? And if a kingdom be divided against itself, that kingdom cannot stand. And if a house be divided against itself, that house cannot stand. And if Satan rise up against himself, and be divided, he cannot stand, but hath an end. No man can enter into a strong man's house, and spoil his goods, except he will first bind the strong man; and then he will spoil his house. Verily I say unto you, All sins shall be forgiven unto the sons*

of men, and blasphemies wherewith soever they shall blaspheme: But he that shall blaspheme against the Holy Ghost hath never forgiveness, but is in danger of eternal damnation: Because they said, He hath an unclean spirit. 3:22-30

Naturally, in Mark Jesus performs exorcisms with the help of God; anyone who denies this source of Jesus' power (cf. 3:30) must be on the side of Satan. Now that the strong man, Satan, has been bound by the Spirit, Jesus is to plunder the house, to rid the world of demons (3:27). In demon exorcism we are to recognize a transcendent battle taking place in the life of Jesus and his contemporaries. Demons inhabit human beings; they are part of human history. Yet their power comes from beyond, from Satan. Similarly, Jesus exorcises demons from men and teaches men, but claims a power from beyond; for in Mark he is the Son of God, the one upon whom the Spirit descends.[19]

On the transcendent level Jesus confronts demons. On the human level the conflict is primarily with the scribes and Pharisees. In the beginning section of his Gospel Mark gives several examples to show the degree to which the Lord was criticized and oppressed by His enemies. "With the second chapter begins a record of conflict. The people still throng about him; but the rulers are offended by his claims, they are shocked by his reception of sinners, they are angered by his teaching in reference to fasting and to Sabbath observance."[20]

The chapter opens (2:1-12) with the incident of the paralytic, who was let down through the roof by his four friends. After Jesus told the sick of the palsy, *"Son, thy sins be forgiven thee"* (2:5), Mark says:

> *But there were certain of the scribes sitting there, and reasoning in their hearts, Why doth this man thus speak blasphemies? Who can forgive sins but God only? And immediately when Jesus perceived in his spirit that they so reasoned within themselves, he said unto them, Why reason ye these things in your hearts? Whether is it easier to say to the sick of the palsy, Thy sins be forgiven thee; or to say, Arise, and take up thy bed, and walk? But that ye may know that the Son of man hath power in earth to forgive sins, (he saith to the sick of the palsy,) I say unto thee, Arise, and take up thy bed, and go thy way into thine house. And immediately he arose, took up the bed, and went forth before them all; insomuch that they were all amazed, and glorified God, saying, We never saw it on this fashion.* 2:6-12

The next scene (2:13-14) is by the seaside, and involves the call of Levi, who was a publican, or tax gatherer, for the despised Roman government. "That one from this degraded class should have been called by Jesus to become an intimate companion was a challenge to the prejudices of the times and a particular offense to the proud and self-righteous Pharisees."[21]

The next incident (2:15-17) takes place in the home of Levi, or Matthew, where Jesus *"sat at meat"* with *"many publicans and sinners"* (v. 15). "The presence of Jesus at the feast of Levi is a still clearer expression of his attitude toward sinners, and a further aggravation of his offense against the Pharisees."[22]

> *And when the scribes and Pharisees saw him eat with publicans and sinners, they said unto his disciples, How is it that he eateth and drinketh with publicans and sinners? When Jesus heard it, he saith unto them, They that are whole have no need of the physician, but they that are sick: I came not to call the righteous, but sinners to repentance.* 2:16-17

In the next several verses (2:18-22) Mark relates the confrontation Jesus had with *"the disciples of John and of the Pharisees"* (v. 18a):

> *And they come and say unto him, Why do the disciples of John and of the Pharisees fast, but thy disciples fast not? And Jesus said unto them, Can the children of the bride chamber fast, while the bridegroom is with them? As long as they have the bridegroom with them, they cannot fast. But the days will come, when the bridegroom shall be taken away from them, and then shall they fast in those days.* 2:18ʙ-20

In the first part of his reply Jesus suggests that fasting, like all religious rites, may be fitting if it is a true expression of religious feeling; but if it is a matter of rule, or requirement, or a supposed ground of merit, it is an absurdity and an impertinence. . . .

In the second part of his reply, Jesus teaches that even the most expressive rites and the most significant ceremonies have but a small place in religion as established and interpreted by himself. He had not come to regulate or to require the Jewish ritual, nor could its forms rightfully express the new spirit of truth he embodied and proclaimed. Such is the general meaning of the two brief parables which form the conclusion to his answer.[23]

> *No man also seweth a piece of new cloth on an old garment: else the new piece that filled it up taketh away from the old, and the rent is made worse. And no man putteth new wine into old bottles: else the new wine doth burst the bottles, and the wine is spilled, and the bottles will be marred: but new wine must be put into new bottles.* 2:21-22

In the very next section (2:23-28) we find that the Pharisees again confront the Lord. Mark wrote:

> *And it came to pass, that he went through the corn fields on the Sabbath day; and his disciples began, as they went, to pluck the ears of corn. And the Pharisees said unto him, Behold, why do they on the Sabbath day that which is not lawful? And he said unto them, Have ye never read what David did, when he had need, and was an hungered, he, and they that were with him? How he went into the house of God in the days of Abiathar the high priest, and did eat the shewbread, which is not lawful to eat but for the priests, and gave also to them which were with him? And he said unto them, the Sabbath was made for man, and not man for the Sabbath.* 2:23-28

> Jesus had aroused the enmity of the Pharisees by his disregard of the burdensome rules their rabbis had made in reference to fasting; he now stirs this enmity into murderous hate by his rebuke of their interpretation of the Sabbath law, and of their absurd scruples about Sabbath observance.[24]

Chapter Three opens with the episode in the synagogue, where Jesus is once again in conflict with His enemies. Mark notes:

> *And he entered again into the synagogue; and there was a man there which had a withered hand. And they watched him, whether he would heal him on the Sabbath day; that they might accuse him. And he saith unto the man which had the withered hand, Stand forth. And he saith unto them, is it lawful to do good on the Sabbath days, or to do evil? To save life, or to kill? But they held their peace. And when he looked round about on them with anger, being grieved for the hardness of their hearts, he saith unto the man, Stretch forth thine hand. And he stretched it out: and his hand was restored whole as the other.* 3:1-5

The occasion for which the Pharisees had been hoping has finally come. *"And they watched him, whether he would heal him on the Sabbath day; that they might accuse him"* (v. 2). The Pharisees were not concerned about the man with the withered hand. Therefore, after sternly rebuking the former, Jesus miraculously cured the latter, but did so without breaking any Sabbath law.

Jesus had done no work; he had not touched the man; that act might have been construed as labor. He had not told the man to work; to hold out a hand could not be called labor. Yet the man was cured, and Jesus had done nothing which, upon even the most technical grounds, could be called a breach of the Sabbath law. His enemies were defeated; he had merely looked on them with anger at their ignorance and blind unbelief; they now regarded him with the most malignant and deadly hate.[25]

And the Pharisees went forth, and straightway took counsel with the Herodians against him, how they might destroy him. 3:6

Jesus lived under a lot of stress, not only from the conflicts created by His enemies, but also from the demands pressed on Him by the multitudes. No wonder Mark says:

And the multitude cometh together again, so that they could not so much as eat bread. And when his friends heard of it, they went out to lay hold on him: for they said, He is beside himself. 3:20-21

But yet, after the scribes and Pharisees were rebuked, and many other miracles were performed in the presence of the disciples, "the task of making true disciples still remained,"[26] Mark concludes the first half of his narrative by saying:

Now the disciples had forgotten to take bread, neither had they in the ship with them more than one loaf. And he charged them, saying, Take heed, beware of the leaven of the Pharisees, and of the leaven of Herod. And they reasoned among themselves, saying, It is because we have no bread. And when Jesus knew it, he saith unto them, Why reason ye, because ye have no bread? Perceive ye not yet, neither understand? Have ye your heart yet hardened? Having eyes, see ye not? And having ears, hear ye not? And do ye not remember? When I brake the five loaves among five thousand, how many baskets full of fragments took ye up? They say unto him, Twelve. And when the seven among four thousand, how many baskets full of fragments took ye up? And they said, Seven. And he said unto them, How is it that ye do not understand? 8:14-21

Making True Disciples

The twelve men that the Lord had chosen were apparently disciples, but essentially they were not. Still to come was one of the greatest miracles the Lord was to perform—that of making true disciples

In the second half of Mark (8:22-15:47) the major opposition that Jesus faced was not that of enemies but rather of friends, his disciples. To be sure, the disciples did not put Jesus to death; the chief priests and scribes, along with the Roman authorities, were responsible for his crucifixion. Still, the disciples did oppose Jesus because they failed to understand why he had to suffer and die. Unless we keep in mind the disciples' misunderstand-ing opposition, the full meaning of Jesus' actions and teachings against the demons and the Pharisees will be missed. The Gospel of Mark shows that the opposition of enemies was met by direct action through exorcisms and debates; however, the opposition of friends required indirect persuasion, even apparent defeat in death.

This preference for persuading rather than compelling the disciples elucidates a major problem in the first half of Mark. After several disclosures of divine healing power, Jesus curiously asks to keep these miracles secret (1:43f.; 3:12; 5:43). The reader wonders why such deeds should be kept secret until he realizes that Jesus' power had to be a hidden power. He won disciples not simply by naked, brute force, either of deeds or of arguments. Stark power did not convince, did not make a believer, did not get rid of fear. When demons had been exorcized and silenced in debate, the task of making true disciples still remained.[27]

Mark begins the second half of his narrative with the Lord's arrival in Bethsaida. We read:

> And he cometh to Bethsaida: and they bring a blind man unto him, and besought him to touch him. And he took the blind man by the hand, and led him out of the town; and when he had spit on his eyes, and put his hands upon him, he asked him if he saw ought. And he looked up, and said, I see men as trees, walking. After that he put his hands again upon his eyes, and made him look up: and he was restored, and saw every man clearly. And he sent him away to his house, saying, Neither go into the town, nor tell it to any in the town. 8:22-26

Only Mark records this miracle. It is the only two-stage healing in the Gospels.

When Jesus first heals, the man sees only dimly and men look like trees walking; then Jesus heals again and the blind man sees everything clearly. The unique manner of this healing seems to prefigure the "seeing" of the disciple Peter in the next episode. Peter sees that Jesus is the Christ; however, he does not yet understand the suffering nature of Jesus' messiahship (vs. 32). Peter, like the other disciples, must go through a second stage of "healing" before he can become a true disciple (cf. 8:34ff.).[28]

Immediately after Peter confessed to the Lord, "*Thou are the Christ*" (8:29), Mark notes:

> And he charged them that they should tell no man of him. And he began to teach them, that the Son of man must suffer many things, and be rejected of the elders, and of the chief priests, and scribes, and be killed, and after three days rise again. And he spake that saying openly. And Peter took him, and began to rebuke him. But when he had turned about and looked on his disciples, he rebuked Peter, saying, Get thee behind me, Satan: for thou savourest not the things that be of God, but the things that be of men. 8:30-33

In the subsequent section Jesus elaborates on the nature of true discipleship. We read:

> And when he had called the people unto him with his disciples also, he said unto them, Whosoever will come after me, let him deny himself, and take up his cross, and follow me. For whosoever will save his life shall lose it; but whosoever shall lose his life for my sake and the gospel's, the same shall save it. For what shall it profit a man, if he shall gain the whole world, and lose his own soul? Or what shall a man give in exchange for his soul? Whosoever therefore shall be ashamed of me and of my words in this adulterous and sinful generation; of him also shall the Son of man be ashamed when he cometh in the glory of his Father with the holy angels. And he said unto them, Verily I say unto you, That there be some of them that stand here, which shall not taste of death, till they have seen the kingdom of God come with power. 8:34-9:1

The account of the transfiguration of Jesus Christ, which begins the next section (9:2-10), is the second of three occasions in Mark when the Lord takes Peter, James and John aside from the other disciples and gives them special instruction.

The names of Peter, James and John are associated on more than one occasion, and the fact certainly must have significance. Very many reasons have been suggested for the fact that the Master took these men to certain places to which the other disciples were not taken. Without discussing those theories, one reason may be considered. To discover this it will be helpful to call to mind the occasions upon which it happened. They are three in number. These men were taken to the house of Jairus, to the mount of transfiguration, to the garden of Gethsemane. In each case they were brought into the presence of death, and in that fact lies a partial solution to the problem.[29]

Peter's attitude toward death was revealed in the incident at Caesarea Philippi, which was referred to earlier. Although he recognized that Jesus was the Messiah (8:29), Peter rebuked the Lord (8:32) after being told *"the Son of man must suffer many things . . . and be killed"* (8:31). "Thus it will be seen that he had followed Jesus to the point of death, and then halted. This distinctly proves that Peter had no true conception of his Master's attitude toward death."[30]

"Mark gives the account of the coming of James and John to Jesus, and their asking that when He should come into His kingdom they might sit one on His right hand and one on His left."[31] We read:

And James and John, the sons of Zebedee, come unto him, saying, Master, we would that thou shouldest do for us whatsoever we shall desire. And he said unto them, What would ye that I should do for you? They said unto him, Grant unto us that we may sit, one on thy right hand, and the other on thy left hand, in thy glory. But Jesus said unto them, Ye know not what ye ask: can ye drink of the cup that I drink of? And be baptized with the baptism that I am baptized with? And they said unto him, We can. And Jesus said unto them, Ye shall indeed drink of the cup that I drink of; and with the baptism that I am baptized withal shall ye be baptized: But to sit on my right hand and on my left hand is not mine to give; but it shall be given to them for whom it is prepared. And when the ten heard it, they began to be much displeased with James and John. But Jesus called them to him, and saith unto them, Ye know that they which are accounted to rule over the Gentiles exercise lordship over them; and their great ones exercise authority upon them. But so shall it not be among you: but whosoever will be great among you, shall be your minister: And whosoever of you will be the chiefest, shall be servant of all. For even the Son of man came not to be ministered unto, but to minister, and to give his life a ransom for many. 10:35-45

That James and John would confront the Lord with their desire at this time is all the more incredible, considering that *"they were in the way going up to Jerusalem"* and Jesus had once again *"began to tell them what things should happen unto him"* (10:32). Nevertheless, in spite of the horrible ordeal that was before Him and on His mind (cf. 10:33-34), the Lord was attentive to their request.

In great pity and love the Master had looked at them and said: "Ye know not what ye ask. Are ye able to drink the cup that I drink? Or to be baptized with the baptism that I am baptized with?" They answered, "We are able." Feeling that there was no cup that He should drink that they were not able to share with Him, and no baptism through which He should pass in which they were unable to have fellowship with Him. They were "sons of thunder" and what could make them afraid? If He could pass through baptism, so also could they. If He were able to drink some strange cup, so also were they. James and

John had followed Jesus to the point of death, and dared all results. Peter was afraid. James and John were blindly courageous. Both attitudes were wrong. None of these men understood the death towards which the Master moved, nor the triumph that awaited Him through death. They must be taught, and the teaching began before their speech revealed their attitude, and was continued after the experience of the holy mount. The sequence of the teaching is most clearly revealed in the Gospel of Mark.[32]

First, there is the visit to the house of Jairus. Note, incidentally, the opposition the Lord faced as Mark recorded the incident:

> And he suffered no man to follow him, save Peter, and James, and John the brother of James. And he cometh to the house of the ruler of the synagogue, and seeth the tumult, and them that wept and wailed greatly. And when he was come in, he saith unto them, Why make ye this ado, and weep? The damsel is not dead, but sleepeth. And they laughed him to scorn. But when he had put them all out, he taketh the father and the mother of the damsel, and them that were with him, and entereth in where the damsel was lying. And he took the damsel by the hand, and said unto her, Tali-tha cumi; which is, being interpreted, Damsel, I say unto thee, arise. And straightway the damsel arose, and walked; for she was of the age of twelve years. And they were astonished with a great astonishment. And he charged them straitly that no man should know it; and commanded that something should be given her to eat. 5:37-43

Next, we go to the mount of transfiguration. Mark wrote:

> And after six days Jesus taketh with him Peter, and James, and John, and leadeth them up into an high mountain apart by themselves: and he was transfigured before them. And his raiment became shining, exceeding white as snow; so as no fuller on earth can white them. And there appeared unto them Elias with Moses: and they were talking with Jesus. And Peter answered and said to Jesus, Master, it is good for us to be here: and let us make three tabernacles; one for thee, and one for Moses, and one for Elias. For he wist not what to say; for they were sore afraid. And there was a cloud that overshadowed them: and a voice came out of the cloud, saying, This is my beloved Son: hear him. And suddenly, when they had looked round about, they saw no man any more, save Jesus only with themselves. And as they came down from the mountain, he charged them that they should tell no man what things they had seen, till the Son of man were risen from the dead. And they kept that saying with themselves, questioning one with another what the rising from the dead should mean. 9:2-10

Finally, we come to the garden of Gethsemane. Mark notes:

> And they came to a place which was named Gethsemane: and he saith to his disciples, Sit ye here, while I shall pray. And he taketh with him Peter and James and John, and began to be sore amazed, and to be very heavy; And saith unto them, My soul is exceeding sorrowful unto death: tarry ye here, and watch. And he went forward a little, and fell on the ground, and prayed that, if it were possible, the hour might pass from him. And he said, Abba Father, all things are possible unto thee; take away this cup from me: nevertheless not what I will, but what thou wilt. And he cometh, and findeth them sleeping, and saith unto Peter, Simon, sleepest thou? Couldest not thou watch one hour? Watch ye and pray, lest ye enter into temptation. The spirit truly is ready, but the flesh is weak. And again he went away, and prayed, and spake the same words. And when he returned, he found them asleep again, (for their eyes were heavy,) neither wist they what to answer him. And he cometh the third time, and saith unto them, Sleep on now, and take your rest: it is enough, the hour is come;

behold, the Son of man is betrayed into the hands of sinners. Rise up, let us go; lo, he that betrayeth me is at hand. 14:32-42

Thus it is at once seen that each time He took these men aside, He conducted them into the presence of death, and He revealed His threefold attitude towards death. In the house of Jairus He was Master of death. On the mount of transfiguration He stood superior to death, transfigured, and yet conversing of death to be accomplished. In Gethsemane He bowed and yielded Himself to death—a strange progression. These men, of whom one was afraid, and the other two imagined there was nothing to fear, were led through this private and special ministry of infinite patience, that they might see the Master's connection with death.[33]

In the days to come this private and special ministry they had been led through by the Lord would prove invaluable. At the moment, however, Peter, James and John, along with the other disciples, understood neither the necessity of Christ's death, nor the nature of true discipleship. On three separate occasions the Lord had taught the disciples *"that the Son of man must suffer many things, and be rejected of the elders, and of the chief priests, and scribes, and be killed, and after three days rise again"* (8:31; also 9:30-32 and 10:32-34). "The disciples' continuing misunderstanding or inability to accept this prediction becomes clear in the garden of Gethsemane. . . . They could not watch and pray."[34] Furthermore, after Jesus' arrest *"they all forsook him, and fled"* (14:50). "Indeed, even the closest disciple, Peter, denied Jesus not once, but three times (14:66-72)."[35]

The disciples' denial and flight occur because of their unwillingness to acknowledge that their own discipleship must share the same quality as Jesus' suffering. Mark's Gospel speaks not only about the nature of Jesus' messiahship, but also about the nature of discipleship, and the second half implies that there is no victory except through suffering and conflict.[36]

In the Garden of Gethsemane, just prior to His arrest, trial and crucifixion, Jesus struggled with the conflict between His own feelings and the will of His Father. Even though His soul was *"exceeding sorrowful unto death"* (14:34), and *"prayed that, if it were possible, the hour might pass from him"* (14:35), nevertheless, the Lord could say to the Father, *"not what I will, but what thou wilt"* (14:36). He had told others about doing *"the will of God"* (3:35) and honoring one's father (cf. 7:10 and 10:19), and now He would do the same. After all, He had come *"not to be ministered unto, but to minister, and to give his life a ransom for many"* (10:45).

Through His own suffering and death, Jesus Christ revealed the true nature of God and the depths of His love. The apostle Paul would later write that Christ *"is the image of the invisible God"* (Col. 1:15) and Jesus Himself said, *"he that hath seen me hath seen the Father"* (John 14:9). "If that be true, then what fell on Jesus, fell on God, what he bore, God bore; his cross was God's cross. Then this outward cross that was lifted up in history is a sign of that inward cross that lies upon the heart of God. We who are bounded by our senses could not see this inward cross upon God's heart unless and until it was lifted up before our senses."[37] And we, like the Lord's disciples, cannot become true followers of Jesus Christ, unless we can begin to understand the love of God, the necessity of the cross, and the true meaning of suffering.

Jesus Christ accepted the way of the cross with all its pain and suffering, because it was the only way to reveal both the holiness and love of God, as it came into contact with the sinfulness of man. In the words of one author, "the cross, then, is God's heartbreak."[38]

That heartbreak is inevitable in a world like this. In a human home where love meets sin in the loved one, at the junction of that love and that sin a cross of pain is set up. A pure love suffers when it comes into contact with sin in the loved one, and the purer the love the more poignant the pain. When the pure and holy love of God comes into contact with sin in us, his loved ones, then at that junction of that sin and that love a cross is set up. It is inevitable. It is inherent in the nature of things. . . . For love cannot be love, and remain apart and aloof. If it be love, it will insinuate itself into the sins and sorrows of others and make them its own. . . . Love cannot be love and refuse the burdens of love. In a world like this God cannot refuse the cross and remain a God of love.[39]

In the Garden of Gethsemane Jesus accepted the will of God and the way of the cross, not as a passive bystander, but as an active participant. After returning from prayer the third time and finding the disciples asleep once again, He said, *"the hour is come; behold, the Son of man is betrayed into the hands of sinners. Rise up, let us go; lo, he that betrayeth me is at hand"* (14:41b-42). *"Rise up, let us go"*—Let us go "to meet the betrayal, the rejection, the accusations, the spittle, the cross. The will of God was to be done by taking hold of the whole miserable business and turning it into a triumph of the love of God. That was what it meant by the will of God being done—that will was active, redemptive, breaking through in love to men in spite of their cruelty and hate."[40]

The Lord's command, *"Rise up, let us go,"* is the key to understanding the words, *"not what I will, but what thou wilt"* (14:36). "We can see Jesus in Gethsemane no longer the Victim of the will of God, but the Victor through that will."[41]

Not only in Mark's narrative, but in the other Gospels as well, we find:

> From that moment on he assumed command of every situation. He healed the ear of the man who came to arrest him. He pronounced the doom of every kingdom, founded on blood and fear, in the words, "They that take the sword shall perish with the sword." By the terror of his silence he made Pilate tremble on his throne—the Accused judged the judge and with him his whole empire. He would not accept the tears of the weeping multitude—he told them to weep for themselves and for their children. He dispensed paradise to a dying thief on a near-by cross, and commended his murderers to the mercy and forgiveness of God. At the end he cried, "It is finished"—the will of God had been done—done in spite of the hate of men, yes, through it, and that will was redemptive love.[42]

From the very beginning of His public ministry, Jesus ran afoul of the Pharisees, who sought to destroy Him (cf. 2:13-3:6). But at the same time He attracted *"a great multitude"* (3:7), *"ordained twelve, that they should be with him"* (3:14), and proclaimed that *"whosoever shall do the will of God, the same is my brother"* (3:35). Nevertheless, throughout Mark's Gospel it seems questionable whether the followers of Jesus would ever become true disciples.

> Mark . . . continually stresses the ease with which Jesus' central message can be misconstrued. Neither Jesus' family, nor his disciples, nor the world at large comprehend what it means to be God's Messiah, any more than they can grasp the essential nature of God's Kingdom. Only in two climactic moments does

awareness break through: at Caesarea Philippi, when Peter confesses, "Thou are the Christ" (Mk 8:29); and when a Roman centurion at Jesus' crucifixion declares, "Truly this man was the Son of God" (Mk 15:39). Between these events, Jesus' ministry is a constant struggle to make himself understood.[43]

Even the disciples who were closest to Jesus were for the most part like the blind man of Bethsaida after the first stage of healing. They see somewhat, but not clearly. They recognize that Jesus is the Messiah, yet do not have a vision for following Him in suffering for all people. The second stage of healing would only take place for the disciples after Christ's crucifixion and resurrection. They still had to learn the lesson of victory through suffering.

The Suffering of Christ

Mark stresses the pain and suffering that Christ endured, as He was *"to give his life a ransom for many"* (10:45). Only he and Matthew, for example, relate the abuse Jesus suffered at the hands of the soldiers. Mark wrote:

> *And the soldiers led him away into the hall, called Praetorium; and they call together the whole band. And they clothed him with purple, and platted a crown of thorns, and put it about his head, And began to salute him, Hail, King of the Jews! And they smote him on the head with a reed, and did spit upon him, and bowing their knees worshipped him. And when they had mocked him, they took off the purple from him, and put his own clothes on him, and led him out to crucify him.* 15:16-20

From the cross upon which He was crucified, the Lord uttered seven separate statements that reveal, to some extent at least, the mystery of His passion and the depth of His pain. Of these seven last words, Mark records only one. He wrote:

> *And when the sixth hour was come, there was darkness over the whole land until the ninth hour. And at the ninth hour Jesus cried with a loud voice, saying, Eloi, Eloi, lama sabachthani? Which is being interpreted, My God, My God, why hast thou forsaken me?* 15:33-34

That Mark would mention only this one utterance is significant. For it is in these words that we hear "the cry of One who has fathomed the deepest depth of sorrow. . . . In this hour when Jesus was made sin, and was therefore God-forsaken, He knew as none had ever known, the profundity of pain."[44] But yet, "these words may be a cry of victory, for they duplicate the opening words of Psalm 22, which begins in despair but ends on a note of triumph."[45] The Psalmist wrote:

> *All the ends of the world shall remember and turn unto the Lord: and all the kindreds of the nations shall worship before thee. For the kingdom is the Lord's: and he is the governor among the nations.* PSALM 22:27-28

By way of the cross and apparent defeat, the ultimate defeat of His enemies was assured and the winning of true disciples was accomplished. Through His suffering the Lord Jesus Christ effected triumph.

The Marks of True Discipleship

Mark reports three responses to Jesus' death, each of which reveals an aspect of what true discipleship involves. The actions of the Roman centurion (15:39), Joseph of

Arimathaea (15:42-46), and the women (15:40-41, 47; 16:1-8), each stand in contrast to the behavior—at least at this time—of the chosen disciples of Christ.

Mark introduced Jesus Christ as *"the Son of God"* (1:1). At both His baptism and transfiguration, a voice from heaven confirmed it (cf. 1:11; 9:7). Now, at Jesus' death a Gentile confesses it. Based primarily on the manner in which Jesus faced death and endured suffering, the centurion declared, *"Truly this man was the Son of God"* (15:39). Unlike Peter, this Gentile recognized the suffering aspect of Jesus' messiahship. One cannot be a true disciple of Jesus Christ until this truth is understood.

Furthermore, in contrast to the "real" disciples of Christ, who out of fear *"forsook him and fled"* (14:50), we find that Joseph of Arimathaea *"came, and went boldly unto Pilate"* (15:43) in order to secure Jesus' body for burial. Being *"an honourable counselor"* (15:43) and member of the official body that sanctioned the Lord's execution, this action would likely bring certain repercussions. Nevertheless, in Joseph of Arimathaea we see that true discipleship is not believing in spite of evidence, but following in spite of consequences. Additionally, we are told that this Joseph *"also waited for the kingdom of God"* (15:43). Whereas the disciples appear to be seeking their own welfare (cf. 10:35-45), Joseph of Arimathaea seeks the kingdom of God!

The third response to the death of Christ, in addition to that of the centurion and Joseph of Arimathaea, is that of the women. While Christ was still alive, we are told that they *"followed him, and ministered unto him"* (15:41).

> Of course, "following" is another way of saying discipleship (cf. esp. 1:17), and their "ministering" picks up Jesus' emphasis upon "service" (the same Greed word): "For the Son of man also came not to be served but to serve, and to give his life as a ransom of many" (10:45). Furthermore, Jesus charged his disciples, "If anyone would be first, he must be last of all and servant of all" (9:35). These women are the first followers of Jesus to see his death, witness his burial, and hear the resurrection report.[46]

Upon the death of Christ, we find that the women are still available for service. Whereas the disciples are nowhere to be found, we find: *"And when the Sabbath was past, Mary Magdalene, and Mary the Mother of James, and Salome, had brought sweet spices, that they might come and anoint him"* (16:1). The actions of the women reveal that true discipleship is *"not to be ministered unto, but to minister"* (10:45); not to be served, but to serve.

In contrast to the disciples, who were preoccupied and consoling one another *"as they mourned and wept"* (16:10), the women, in spite of their grief and need for solace, were more concerned about their service to the crucified Lord.

> And very early in the morning the first day of the week, they came unto the sepulchre at the rising of the sun. And they said among themselves, Who shall roll us away the stone from the door of the sepulchre? And when they looked, they saw that the stone was rolled away: for it was very great. And entering into the sepulchre, they saw a young man sitting on the right side, clothed in a long white garment; and they were affrighted. And he saith unto them, Be not affrighted: Ye seek Jesus of Nazareth, which was crucified: he is risen; he is not here: behold the place where they laid him. But go your way, tell his disciples and Peter that he goeth before you into Galilee: there shall ye see him, as he said unto you. And they went out quickly, and fled from the sepulchre; for they trembled and were amazed: neither said they any thing to any man; for they were afraid. 16:2-8

The women, disciples, and Peter are promised that something more will occur. Jesus will go before them into Galilee (16:7). Of course, they have no guarantee other than the angel's word (cf. 14:28) that he will appear in Galilee. The precise reason for the choice of Galilee is not certain. Perhaps the disciples are to meet Jesus in Galilee, rather than Jerusalem, in order to gather forces for the Gentile mission. The precise meaning of the promise is also unclear. Perhaps the disciples are to await the second coming of Christ, the parousia, when God's kingdom will fully come (cf. chap. 13). More likely, they will await a resurrection appearance of Jesus ("there you will see him"; cf. 14:28). Whatever the exact meaning, the promise stresses the future. Everything has not yet happened; a future victory awaits. The Markan story of Jesus does not promise to deliver the church from persecution, even though in Jesus' life and death a first victory has been won. Satan was bound, demons were exorcized, opponents were defeated in debate, disciples were gathered. Moreover, the future promises a second complete victory. But the future can still only be assured through faith. In the present the church faces strife and persecution.[47]

In two of the oldest, extant manuscripts of the New Testament, the Gospel of Mark ends with the eighth verse of the sixteenth chapter, as cited above. Whether from problems within the Church or from persecution from without, Mark may have been interrupted in his writing, and finished the Gospel at a later time. Whatever the case, if Mark's narrative originally terminated at this point, it would be of special interest, especially in view of the theme we have suggested regarding victory through conflict and suffering. The concluding words—*"for they were afraid"* (16:8)—fit this interpretation. "In the present the church faces strife and persecution."[48]

> The women are left with fear, the normal and ever-present fear of a church undergoing persecution. . . . Of course, Mark wishes to encourage endurance, faith, and prayer in spite of fear, but the Gospel does not command faith at the last instance. Instead, Mark's whole Gospel implies the need for faith in a final victory, because an initial triumph through suffering has occurred in Jesus. Mark is realistic enough to acknowledge fear and Christian enough to proclaim the breaking of fear's power through faith in a future victory promised by the suffering and resurrected Jesus.[49]

That future victory promised by the resurrected Jesus is yet to come. But for the present, the Church is still in the midst of conflict. As the hymn-writer noted:

Though with a scornful wonder
    Men see her sore oppressed,
By schisms rent asunder,
    By heresies distressed,
Yet saints their watch are keeping,
    Their cry goes up, "How long?"
And soon the night of weeping
    Shall be the morn of song.
'Mid toil and tribulation
    And tumult of her war,
She waits the consummation
    Of peace forevermore,

Till with the vision glorious
       Her longing eyes are blest,
And the great Church victorious
       Shall be the Church at rest.[50]

Peter and the other disciples (with the exception of Judas Iscariot, of course), while not the first true disciples, were certainly amongst the foremost followers of Jesus Christ. After the Lord appeared to them, as recorded in Mark 16:9-18, we find that *"they went forth, and preached everywhere, the Lord working with them, and confirming the word with signs following"* (16:20). And what were these signs? Before His ascension (cf. 16:19) the Lord told the disciples, *"And these signs shall follow them that believe; In my name shall they cast out devils"* (16:17). Because the initial victory had been won by the crucified and risen Christ, the house of the strong man—Satan—can be spoiled (cf. 3:27), as the disciples cast out devils and *"preach the gospel to every creature"* (16:15).

Almost all of the eleven originally chosen disciples of Jesus Christ were martyred for their faith. Where once *"they all forsook him, and fled"* (14:50), eventually they would remain loyal, even in the face of death. How could such a transformation take place? The answer lies in the revelation of the nature and love of God that was seen by way of the cross. The disciples saw what we need to see if we are ever to become true disciples:

> If the revelation of what we see in the cross is true, then we can trust what lies back of it. If the Heart that is back of the universe is like this gentle, strong Heart that broke upon the cross, then he can have my heart, and that without reservation.[51]

The Lesson of True Happiness

The disciples learned the lesson of true happiness; and that lesson is this:

> The really happy are those who deliberately take on themselves pain for the sake of others; and the unhappy are those who center on themselves and refuse to do anything for others at cost to themselves. . . . The God who would sit apart from the tragedy and pain and misery of the world would be a God self-centered, therefore unhappy. But the God who would know the joy of a cross would be a God who would know the deepest joy of this universe—the joy of serving others at cost to oneself. The God who would have the highest thing in the world, namely, love, absent from his nature would be a God who would be imperfect, and therefore not God. The Psalmist asks: "He that planted the ear, shall he not hear? He that formed the eye, shall he not see?" And Browning adds, "He that made love, shall he not love?" And we might add, "He that put the impulse to sacrifice self in the heart of the highest men, shall he not sacrifice himself?"[52]

Jesus Christ sacrificed Himself, and He put that impulse into the heart of His disciples. For Peter, James, and John, especially, the special ministry through which the Lord took them was part of the perfect plan for their lives.

Thus the presence of these men on the mount was part of a perfect scheme. These were experiences which the Master was storing for them, which should have their explanation in days that were yet to come. Presently, when the work of the cross was accomplished, and the Paraclete had been poured upon them, these men would begin to understand what happened in the house of Jairus, upon the holy mount, and most wonderful of all, how that when His soul was sorrowful unto death, they had beheld the Master of death bowing to death, in order that He might slay death. After that, Peter writing a letter, and speaking of his own death, did not so name it, but borrowing the word he heard upon the mount, wrote, "After my exodus" (2 Pet. 1:15). Thus death was transfigured for these men through the patient process of a special training which the Master gave them.[53]

The disciples came to understand that the purpose of God and the destiny of man were fulfilled by Christ, because of *"the suffering of death"* (Heb. 2:9). Furthermore, as the writer to the Hebrews noted:

Though he were a Son, yet learned he obedience by the things which he suffered; And being made perfect, he became the author of eternal salvation unto all them that obey him. HEB. 5:8-9

Yes, Christ, though He was Son, and therefore endowed with right of access for Himself to the Father, being of one essence with the Father, for man's sake, as man, won the right of access to the throne of God for perfected humanity. He learnt obedience, not as if the lesson were forced upon Him by stern necessity, but by choosing, through insight into the Father's will, that self-surrender even to the death upon the Cross which was required for the complete reconciliation of man with God. And so the absolute union of human nature, in its fullest maturity, with the Divine in the one Person of our Creator and Redeemer, was wrought out in the very school of life in which we are trained.

When once we grasp this truth the records of the Evangelists are filled with a new light. Every work of Christ is seen to be a sacrifice and a victory. The long years of obscure silence, the short season of conflict, are found to be alike a commentary on the Lord's words, "For their sakes I sanctify myself." And we come to understand how His deeds of power were deeds of sovereign sympathy; how the words in which Isaiah spoke of the Servant of the Lord, as "taking our infirmities and bearing our sicknesses," were indeed fulfilled when the Son of man healed the sick who came to Him, healed them not be dispensing from His opulence a blessing which cost Him nothing, but by making His own the ill which He removed.

Dimly, feebly, imperfectly we can see in this way how it became God to make the Author of our salvation perfect through sufferings; how every pain which answered to the Father's will, became to Him the occasion of a triumph, the disciplining of some human power which needed to be brought into God's service, the advance one degree farther towards the Divine likeness to gain which man was made; how, in the actual condition of the world, His love and His righteousness were displayed in tenderer grace and grander authority through the gainsaying of enemies; how, in this sense, even within the range of our imagination, He saw of the travail of His soul and was satisfied.

Dimly, feebly, imperfectly we can see also how Christ, Himself perfected through suffering, has made known to us once for all the meaning, and the value of suffering; how He has interpreted it as a Divine discipline, the provision of a Father's love; how He has enabled us to perceive that at each step in the progress of life it is an opportunity; how He has left to us to realize "in him" little by little the virtue of His work; to fill up on our part, in the language of St. Paul, that which is lacking of the afflictions of Christ in our own sufferings, not as if His work were incomplete or our efforts meritorious, but as being living members of His body through which He is pleased to manifest that which He has wrought for men.

For we shall observe that it was because He brought many sons to glory, that it became God to make perfect through sufferings the Author of their salvation. The fitness lay in the correspondence between the outward circumstances of His life and of their lives. The way of the Lord is the way of His servants. He enlightened the path which they must tread, and shewed its end. And so it is that whenever the example of Christ is offered to us in Scripture for our imitation, it is His example in suffering. So far, in His strength, we can follow Him, learning obedience as He learned it, bringing our wills into conformity with the Father's will, and thereby attaining to a wider view of His counsel in which we can find rest and joy.[54]

The disciples had learned the reality of Victory through Suffering, and this is the solemn fact that we, too, must dare to face. Life can be discouraging, especially during times of trial and conflict, but we—like the disciples of old—can experience the joys and blessings of following Jesus Christ.

So, amid the conflict, whether great or small,
Do not be discouraged, God is over all;
Count your many blessings, angels will attend,
Help and comfort give you to your journey's end.[55]

Chapter Six Notes

[1] William Sanford LaSor, *Great Personalities of the New Testament: Their Lives and Times* (Westwood, NJ: Fleming H. Revell Company, 1961), 125-26.

[2] Jerry H. Combee, *The History of the World in Christian Perspective, Vol. I* (Pensacola, Fla.: A Beka Book Publications, 1979), 224.

[3] Willis Mason West, *The Ancient World from the Earliest Times to 800 A.D.* (Boston: Allyn and Bacon, 1904), 350.

[4] *Ibid.*, 350-51.

[5] Combee, *op. cit.*, 235.

[6] West, *op. cit.*, 350.

[7] Combee, *op. cit.*, 243.

[8] *Ibid.*, 242-43.

[9] *Ibid.*, 243.

[10] *Ibid.*

[11] *Ibid.*

[12] West, *op. cit.*, 389.

[13] Robert A. Spivey and D. Moody Smith, Jr., *Anatomy of the New Testament: A Guide to Its Structure and Meaning*, 2nd ed. (New York: Macmillan Publishing Co., 1974), 88.

[14] Combee, *op. cit.*, 225.

[15] Spivey, *op. cit.*

[16] Charles R. Erdman, *The Gospel of Mark* (Philadelphia: The Westminster Press, 1945), 35.

[17] *Ibid.*, 34-35.

[18] Spivey, *op. cit.*, 90.

[19] *Ibid.*

[20] Erdman, *op. cit.*, 44.

[21] *Ibid.*, 47.

[22] *Ibid.*, 49.

[23] *Ibid.*, 52.

[24] *Ibid.*, 54.

[25] *Ibid.*, 59.

[26] Spivey, *op. cit.*, 89.

[27] *Ibid.*, 88-89.

[28] *Ibid.*, 99.

[29] G. Campbell Morgan, *The Crises of the Christ* (Old Tappan, N.J.: Fleming H. Revell Company, 1936), 247.

[30] *Ibid.*

[31] *Ibid.*

[32] *Ibid.*, 247-48.

[33] *Ibid.*, 249.

[34] Spivey, *op. cit.*, 98.

[35] *Ibid.*

[36] *Ibid.*

[37] E. Stanley Jones, *Christ and Human Suffering* (New York: The Abingdon Press, 1933), 150-51.

[38] *Ibid.*, 151.

[39] *Ibid.*, 151-52.

[40] *Ibid.*, 112.

[41] *Ibid.*, 112-13.

[42] *Ibid.*, 113.

[43] *Reader's Digest Family Guide to the Bible: A Concordance and Reference Companion to the King James Version* (Pleasantville, N.Y.: The Reader's Digest Association, Inc., 1984), 30.

[44] Morgan, *op. cit.*, 297, 300.

[45] Spivey, *op. cit.*, 107.

[46] *Ibid.* 109.

[47] *Ibid.*, 110-11.

[48] *Ibid.*, 111.

[49] *Ibid.*

[50] Samuel J. Stone, *The Church's One Foundation* (1866).

[51] Jones, *op. cit.*, 154.

[52] *Ibid.*, 154-55.

[53] Morgan, *op. cit.*, 250.

[54] Brook Foss Westcott, *Christus Consummator: Some Aspects of the Work and Person of Christ in Relation to Modern Thought* (London: Macmillan and Co., 1890), 25-28.

[55] Johnson Oatman, Jr., *Count Your Blessings* (1897).

Chapter Seven

The Romans: Practical and Powerful

The greatest authority on the Romans, the people to whom Mark addressed his Gospel, was, perhaps, the eighteenth-century historian, Edward Gibbon. As one of the outstanding writers of the Enlightenment, he is possibly "the only one of them who is still read not only as a stylist, but also as a historian. . . . Gibbon is the first great historian of a remote past whom the work of later centuries has not driven from the field."[1]

The product of his life's ambition, almost a million and a quarter words of historical documentation, is *The History of the Decline and Fall of the Roman Empire*. Gibbon began this monumental work by noting:

> In the second century of the Christian Era, the empire of Rome comprehended the fairest part of the earth, and the most civilized portion of mankind. The frontiers of that extensive monarchy were guarded by ancient renown and disciplined valor. The gentle, but powerful influence of laws and manners had gradually cemented the union of the provinces. Their peaceful inhabitants enjoyed and abused the advantages of wealth and luxury. The image of a free constitution was preserved with decent reverence. The Roman Senate appeared to possess the sovereign authority, and devolved on the emperors all the executive powers of government.[2]

A silent but visible witness of the extent to which the Roman Empire encompassed the ancient world can be seen in the Wall of Hadrian, portions of which still stand in the northern regions of Britain near the Scottish border. Emperor Hadrian had ordered the construction of this immense fortification—"a massive stonework that stretched for 73 miles, linking 14 forts and fortified at one-mile intervals with 100-man garrisons. . . . Standing about 20 feet high and eight feet thick, the wall faced a wild, barbarian land, and marked off one geographical extreme of an empire which was won by force and held by strength."[3]

The Concept of Power

Centuries before Rome was ever a world power, the prophet Daniel predicted that this kingdom would be *"strong as iron"* (2:40), *"exceedingly dreadful"* (7:19), and would *"devour the whole earth"* (7:23). Rome brought a form of peace to the ancient world, but it was a dreadful peace!

> Law, and duty, or obedience to law, were ideas common to both Jew and Roman. But the Jew taught the world law in its statical, divine, and eternal relations. With him it was a divine precept revealed from heaven, pointing out the only way of blessedness and perfection for man here and hereafter, waiting patiently for man to come up to its requirements. . . . The Romans, on the contrary, gave the world law in its dynamic, governmental, and temporal aspects. With him it was not a precept waiting for man to fall in with, but the expression of a present force, the organized and martial might of Rome, demanding submission and remorselessly crushing men and nations into its iron moulds.[4]

By the time Christ was born, most of the known world was under one government, and two centuries of this peace had begun with the reign of Caesar Augustus, the first and greatest of the Roman emperors. Whereas the centuries of the former Republic were marked by strife and conflict, the advent of the *Pax Romana* is remembered, at least by comparison, as a time of peace and prosperity. Noting this transition, Gibbon wrote:

> The principal conquests of the Romans were achieved under the republic; and the emperors, for the most part, were satisfied with preserving those dominions which had been acquired by the policy of the senate, the active emulation of the consuls, and the martial enthusiasm of the people. The seven first centuries were filled with a rapid succession of triumphs; but it was reserved for Augustus, to relinquish the ambitious design of subduing the whole earth, and to introduce a spirit of moderation into the public councils. Inclined to peace by his temper and situation, it was easy for him to discover, that Rome, in her present exalted situation, had much less to hope than to fear from the chance of arms; and that, in the prosecution of remote wars, the undertaking became every day more difficult, the event more doubtful, and the possession more precarious, and less beneficial.[5]

"The *Pax Romana* seemed such a great improvement in conditions during the centuries after the break-up of Alexander the Great's empire that many people began to look upon the city of Rome and the Roman emperor as a kind of savior of the world."[6] Whereas the Jews had one God and the Greeks had many gods, the Romans outgrew them all, as it were, and recognized only the power of the state, and eventually reverenced the person of the emperor. Nineteenth-century scholar, Dr. D. S. Gregory, wrote:

> Certain characteristics clearly distinguish the Romans from the other great historic races of the age of Christ. They represented the idea of active human power in the ancient world. They embodied that idea in the state or empire as the repository of law and justice. They came in process of time to deify the state as the grandest concrete manifestation of power. With the consciousness of being born to rule the world, they pushed the idea of national power to universal empire.
>
> . . . The Roman, as such, cared little for distinctively supernatural and spiritual power such as moved the Jew; he cared as little for the logical and aesthetic power of the Greek; his was the power of the will, his the beauty of action, his the logic of deeds. He became, accordingly, the mighty worker of the world, casting up highways across empires, and leaving behind him public improvements in every form and of a grandeur fitted to astonish the race to the remotest ages.
>
> The Romans embodied their peculiar idea of power in the state. . . . The will of the individual was lost in the will of the state, the Roman lost in Rome. Rome regarded the race as being in a condition of anarchy, so to speak, out of which it was her mission to bring it. Her power was power ordered and organized, taking the form of law and government, directing and controlling.[7]

"Rome thus became to the Roman at once the kingdom of god and god."[8]

Contrary to the view held by the ancient Romans, the Scriptures teach that the human race is in a state of anarchy against God (cf. Rom. 3:23), out of which it was the mission of Jesus Christ to bring it. The Romans brought justice and established peace through the use of force and violence, and by building fortified walls to keep out their enemies. Jesus Christ, on the other hand, accomplished His mission by shedding His own blood, rather than that of His enemies, *"and the veil of the temple was rent in twain"* (Mark 15:38), in order that those who would be reconciled might have access to God. Whereas the Romans thought the Pax Romana was good news, the Gospel of Mark proclaims that the good news had a different source and focus. Mark's introduction reads, *"The beginning of the gospel of Jesus Christ, the Son of God"* (1:1). The good news—the meaning of "gospel"—begins here!

> The central idea of the Gospel according to Mark is found in the opening verse. . . . The Evangelist, accordingly, presents Jesus, not as the fulfillment of a past divine revelation, as does Matthew; . . . but as the personal embodiment of the Son of God, in the fullness of his present, living energy, demonstrating himself the Son of God by his divine working. Everything, from the opening with the mission of the Baptist to the closing vision of Jesus exalted to the throne of God, is so shaped as to deepen the impression of his almighty power.
>
> This Gospel represents him as proclaiming and establishing a kingdom, but it is a kingdom of power, and not of prophecy.[9]

The Gospel of Mark emphasizes the fact that Jesus Christ came to establish a kingdom of power. Six days before He was transfigured in the presence of His disciples, the Lord said unto them:

> *Verily I say unto you, That there be some of them that stand here, which shall not taste of death, till they have seen the kingdom of God come with power.* MARK 9:1

Compare this with Matthew's account, which reads:

> *Verily I say unto you, There be some standing here, which shall not taste of death, till they see the Son of man coming in his kingdom.* MATT. 16:28

In Luke's version of this incident, the Lord says:

> *But I tell you of a truth, there be some standing here, which shall not taste of death, till they see the kingdom of God.* LUKE 9:27

Only Mark tells us that the kingdom comes with power. He did so because he addressed his Gospel to the Romans, and the idea of power would be of special interest to them. Dr. Gregory noted:

> The Romans represented the idea of active human power in the ancient world. The liberty is taken here of assuming that, under Providence, the history of each nation is, either consciously or unconsciously, the embodiment and working out of some grand idea. That idea once seized upon furnishes the key to the nation's character, conduct, and mission, and shows what is needed, humanly speaking, in order to commend Jesus Christ to that nation as the divine deliverer of men.
>
> This key to the character, career, and wants of the Romans is found in the idea of power.[10]

The Apostle Paul also drafted a letter to the Romans, and he, too, recognized this idea of power. He wrote, *"For I am not ashamed of the gospel of Christ: for it is the power of God to every one that believeth . . ."* (Rom. 1:16). Additionally, in commending Jesus Christ to his readers, Paul said He was *"declared to be the Son of God with power, according to the spirit of holiness, by the resurrection from the dead"* (Rom. 1:4).

As predicted by Scripture (cf. Dan. 7:7) and realized in history, the Romans did indeed embody the idea of active human power in the ancient world. Consequently, a Gospel written for them would necessarily be molded by this impression.

> Scripture and prophecy, so potent with the Jew, would count for little with the Roman; he was ignorant of both. Reason and philosophy, so convincing to the Greek, would be scoffed at by the Roman; he had no appreciation of either. Before the beginning of faith he was blind to the grand doctrines so precious to the Christian. The Gospel for him must present the character and career of Jesus from the Roman side, or point of view, as answering to the idea of divine power, work, law, conquest, and universal sway. It must exhibit Jesus as adapted, in his power and mercy, in his mission and work, to the wants of the Roman nature and world. To the Roman these are the credentials of Jesus, no less essential than prophecy to the Jew, or philosophy to the Greek. Without them there could not even be a reasonable hope of arresting his attention.[11]

The mission and work of Jesus Christ, as the mighty Prophet and compassionate Servant of God, will be addressed and developed in the following chapter. For now, however, it should be noted that Mark's narrative extends Christ's power and mercy to that of forgiving sins. This was a power the Romans seldom, if ever, exercised. Whereas they certainly gave the world law and justice, they most assuredly did not extend mercy. In this regard, the following incident recorded by Mark is extremely significant. Recounting Jesus' activity in the region of Galilee in the opening section of his narrative, Mark wrote:

> And again he entered into Capernaum after some days; and it was noised that he was in the house. And straightway many were gathered together, insomuch that there was no room to receive them, no, not so much as about the door: and he preached the word unto them. And they come unto him, bringing one sick of the palsy, which was borne of four. And when they could not come nigh unto him for the press, they uncovered the roof where he was: and when they had broken it up, they let down the bed wherein the sick of the palsy lay. When Jesus saw their faith, he said unto the sick of the palsy, Son, thy sins be forgiven thee. But there were certain of the scribes sitting there, and reasoning in their hearts, Why doth this man thus speak blasphemies? Who can forgive sins but God only? And immediately when Jesus perceived in his spirit that they so reasoned within themselves, he said unto them, Why reason ye these things in your hearts? Whether is it easier to say to the sick of the palsy, Thy sins be forgiven thee; or to say, Arise, and take up thy bed, and walk? But that ye may know that the Son of man hath power on earth to forgive sins, (he saith to the sick of the palsy,) I say unto thee, Arise, and take up thy bed, and go thy way into thine house. And immediately he arose, took up the bed, and went forth before them all; insomuch that they were all amazed, and glorified God, saying, We never saw it on this fashion. 2:1-12

Whereas the scribes at least recognized that only God could forgive sins, the attitude of the Romans was that—if God did exist—He needn't bother. From past experience and by natural inclination, the Romans were prone to put lawlessness and opposition under their iron heel and *"tread it down, and break it in pieces"* (Dan. 7:23).

The Romans believed in brute physical power to maintain law and order. Martial might, fortified walls, wooden crosses, and iron bars, were some of the means by which the Roman Peace was enforced. They knew nothing of the kind of power that would hold men in prison when *"all the doors were opened, and every one's bands were loosed"* (Acts 16:26).

The Romans were realists and used their power to break and subdue *"all things"* (Dan. 2:40) in order to establish peace and maintain law and order. In the midst of all their activity, they promised protection to the people who were oppressed, and brought justice to the provinces, even in the most remote regions of the empire. The Romans were men of action and purpose, and as far as they were concerned, they went about doing good.

Speaking to a Roman centurion, the Apostle Peter noted that Jesus Christ also went about doing good, but He had a different source of power. Peter recounted:

> *How God anointed Jesus of Nazareth with the Holy Ghost and with power: who went about doing good, and healing all that were oppressed of the devil; for God was with him. And we are witnesses of all things which he did both in the land of the Jews, and in Jerusalem; whom they slew and hanged on a tree: Him God raised up the third day, and shewed him openly; Not to all the people, but unto witnesses chosen before of God, even to us, who did eat and drink with him after he rose from the dead. And he commanded us to preach unto the people, and to testify that it is he which was ordained of God to be the judge of quick and dead. To him give all the prophets witness, that through his name whosoever believeth in him shall receive remission of sins.* ACTS 10:38-43

In the account of the healing of the paralytic, cited earlier and recorded by Mark, we find that Jesus confirmed His power to remit sins, not by arguing from Scripture or quoting Old Testament prophecies, but by His actions—by active divine/human power! We are told:

> *But that ye may know that the Son of man hath power on earth to forgive sins, (he saith to the sick of the palsy,) I say unto thee, Arise, and take up thy bed, and go thy way into thine house.* MARK 2:10-11

A Practical People

Mark's account of this incident is also significant for another reason; it appeals to the practical bent of the Roman character. The method, by which the four bearers of the paralytic secured Jesus' attention, would also attract the notice of Mark's readers. He wrote:

> *And when they could not come nigh unto him for the press, they uncovered the roof where he was: and when they had broken it up, they let down the bed wherein the sick of the palsy lay.* 2:4

The typical Roman would appreciate the ingenuity of the friends of the paralytic. As one historian noted:

> The . . . Roman source of satisfaction was really derived from the nature of his genius, which was in all things essentially practical. In the practical management of men and things the Roman displayed his specific character and took peculiar pleasure.[12]

Elaborating on his management of things, the same author wrote:

> The Roman loved his country, and he loved to possess land and to take up the challenge which it offered. He took from it the joy of ownership and the satisfaction of making it produce. . . .

It is the soil which offers a worthy livelihood, which sustains son and grandson, and gives increase of crop and beast and vine; here is real family life, and traditions of goodness, and innocent gaiety. This was the manner of life in which were bred the Romans of old, and through it Rome was made the most glorious thing in the world.[13]

The Gospel of Mark, written for a people of action rather than meditation, omits many of the teaching parables of the Lord. Yet it should be observed that the few, which are recorded, would be of special interest to the Roman. The parables of The Sower (4:1-20), The Seed Growing Secretly (4:26-29), and The Mustard Seed (4:30-34), are all tied to the soil and the land, the love of which "exercised a strong pull"[14] for the Roman. "The earliest Romans were farmers in a hostile land, and no matter how urbanized Rome later became, Roman roots remained firmly fixed in the soil."[15]

The forceful but practical disposition of the ancient Romans is also revealed in their massive construction projects. "In addition to their justly famous highways, they built bridges and aqueducts making use of the arch. They also developed a new technique by using concrete. . . . Its utilization enabled them to erect giant amphitheaters, public baths, and the high-rise tenement buildings that housed Rome's exploding population in the late second and first centuries B.C."[16]

Although the Greeks may have been the greatest architects of ancient times—if not all times—the Romans were the greatest builders. There is a difference. Greek architecture exceeded that of the Roman in beauty and style, yet it did not compare in sheer enormity and grandeur. Furthermore, whereas the best examples of the former were temples dedicated to non-existent gods or goddesses, the strongest and most substantial structures of the latter were the aqueducts, designed for a very useful purpose, and "which still in their ruins excite our astonishment."[17] Edward Gibbon noted that "the boldness of the enterprise, the solidity of the execution, and the uses to which they were subservient, rank the aqueducts among the noblest monuments of Roman genius and power."[18]

> Fourteen aqueducts, of a total length of 265 miles, met the needs of the city of Rome, delivering perhaps fifty gallons each day per head of the population. In many regions of the provinces the water supply was better in Roman times than today; and some of the Roman aqueducts are still in use. The well-known Pont du Gard near Nimes carries across the valley of the Gard the water which up to that point is enclosed in subterranean channels; it is composed of three tiers of arches one above another, and its greatest height is 160 feet. The aqueduct, still standing, which supplied Carthage was 95 miles in length, partly tunneled, partly carried on gigantic arches; that at Tarragona in Spain was 22 miles, and at Lyons 11 miles. . . .
> The same massive grandeur is a mark of everything which the Romans constructed; they built for use and for permanence. Roman roads are the supreme example. Originally their purpose was military and administrative; they grew according to need, and in time they served every need of war and peace, trade and communication.[19]

Over the course of several centuries, the Romans scientifically planned and "created what was actually a transcontinental system of highways, greater than anything the world had ever seen."[20] Hundreds of cities in three continents were linked by thousands of miles of good roads, and helped to unite "the subjects of the most distant provinces by an easy and familiar intercourse."[21] In the first volume of his book, published in 1776, Gibbon wrote:

> All these cities were connected with each other, and with the capital by the public highways, which issuing from the Forum of Rome, traversed Italy, pervaded the provinces, and were terminated only by the frontiers of the empire. If we carefully trace the distance from the wall of Antoninus to Rome, and from thence to Jerusalem, it will be found that the great chain of communication, from the north-west to the south-east point of the empire, was drawn out to the length of four thousand and eighty Roman miles. The public roads were accurately divided by mile-stones, and ran in a direct line from one city to another, with very little respect for the obstacles either of nature or private property. Mountains were perforated, and bold arches thrown over the broadest and most rapid streams. The middle part of the road was raised into a terrace which commanded the adjacent country, consisted of several strata of sand, gravel, and cement, and was paved with large stones, or in some places, near the capital, with granite. Such was the solid construction of the Roman highways, whose firmness has not entirely yielded to the effort of fifteen centuries.[22]

If the great highways of the Roman Empire seemed built to defy time, they were also designed to defy nature. One authority claims:

> Unlike the Greeks, who hated to disturb nature, the Romans did not hesitate to overpower nature whenever it got in the way of their road building. The Romans liked their roads straight. . . . One gets the impression from aerial photographs of old Roman road routes that once the Romans decided to build a road from one point to another, they built it. And they built it level and direct—regardless of what nature had put in the way. . . .
> There is one theory that the Romans, in surmounting formidable obstacles to keep their roads straight, were expressing their dominance over the land as well as the people. Possibly this is true in part.[23]

As cited earlier, it was in the practical management of men and things that "the Roman displayed his specific character and took peculiar pleasure."[24] And it was because of the construction and management of his roads that the Roman was able to pave the way toward his management of men. The remarkable road system was a powerful reminder and extensive proof of the fact that the iron heel of Rome had been put down upon the greater part of the civilized world. Gibbon noted that the primary purpose of the Roman roads was to "facilitate the marches of the legions" and that no country was considered "completely subdued, till it had been rendered, in all its parts, pervious to the arms and authority of the conqueror."[25] To a certain extent, at least, the road system of the ancient Roman civilization "symbolized not only the growth but also the ambitions of the empire,"[26] and it is a foreboding of things to come (cf. Dan. 2:42-45) that the foundations of the former have survived the collapse of the latter.

During the years of Rome's rise to power, however, men and nations were crushed into its iron molds. In the same year (146 B.C.) that Rome totally destroyed Carthage and became master of the western Mediterranean, the city of Corinth met the same fate as Carthage. When the former, as leader of the Achaean League, became involved in a fatal conflict with Rome, the city was destroyed in order to teach the surviving Greeks a lesson. For a century Corinth lay in ruins until Julius Caesar had it rebuilt in even greater splendor. By the first century A.D. Corinth had become a leading center of commerce, and was the administrative capital of Achaea. As the fourth largest city in the empire, it had been rebuilt on a grand scale, typical of what would be expected from the genius of Roman engineering. Describing the monuments of Roman architecture, Gibbon wrote, "All the . . . quarters of the capital, and all the provinces of the empire, were embellished by the same liberal spirit of public magnificence, and were filled with amphitheatres, theatres, temples, porticos, triumphal arches, baths, and aqueducts, all variously conducive to the health, the devotion, and the pleasures of the meanest citizen."[27]

Corinth was no exception to the above description, yet it was to this city, which had been rebuilt from the ground up, that the Apostle Paul sent a letter, wherein he stated: *"No man can lay a foundation other than the one which is laid, which is Jesus Christ"* (I Cor. 3:11, NASB).

A Sure Foundation

The Romans were experts at designing and laying elaborate foundations. They laid enough roads to cover a distance equal to ten times the circumference of the earth at the equator. Moreover, "a good Roman road turned on end would have put to shame many a castle wall by its massiveness."[28] Yet in spite of all their skill at laying stones, the Romans never found the right Stone, firmly placed, upon which to build their lives. Speaking through the prophet Isaiah, whom Mark alluded to in his introduction, the Lord God said:

> *Behold, I am laying in Zion a stone, a tested stone, a costly cornerstone for the foundation, firmly placed. He who believes in it will not be disturbed. And I will make justice the measuring line, and righteousness the level.* ISAIAH 28:16-17, NASB

Mark introduced to his Roman readers *"the stone which the builders rejected"* (12:10). Jesus Christ is the tested stone and foundation stone, as evidenced in His temptation and passion, respectively, and is the costly cornerstone in His relationship to those who believe on Him (cf. Ps. 118:22; I Pet. 2:6-10). This is the good news that Mark's readers needed to hear (cf. 1:1). The Romans brought peace to a troubled world, but offered nothing for the disturbed soul. They skillfully used the measuring line and the level, yet knew nothing of true righteousness. They built solid roads that were straight and direct, yet they were like the wicked, who *"walk on every side, when the vilest men are exalted"* (Ps. 12:8).

The Romans were out of step with God, and Mark addressed his Gospel to them, in order to put them on the right path. Mark commends Jesus Christ to his Roman readers, but first introduces His forerunner, as prophesied in the Old Testament. He wrote:

> *As it is written in the prophets, Behold, I send my messenger before thy face, which shall prepare thy way before thee. The voice of one crying in the wilderness, Prepare ye the way of the Lord, make his paths straight.* 1:2-3

The Prophecies of Isaiah

These ancient prophecies are the only direct quotes that Mark takes from the Old Testament. The reference about making His paths straight, is taken from the 40th chapter of Isaiah, and would certainly catch the attention of any reader who ever ventured out on a Roman road. Furthermore, it is of interest to note that the book of Isaiah is strikingly similar to the entire Bible in its structure, and is symbolic, at least, in its application to the Roman world of the first century.

The book of Isaiah (like the Bible itself) has 66 chapters (books), divided into two main sections. The first part (chapters 1-39) deals with law and judgment, while the last 27 chapters (40-66) promise grace and salvation.

> The Old Testament opens with God's case against man because of his sins. Isaiah opens the same way (Isa. 1:18). The first section closes with the prophecy of the coming King of Righteousness and the redemption of Israel (34-35), just as the prophets close the Old Testament with the prediction of His coming Kingdom. The second part of Isaiah (chapter 40) opens with the voice of him that crieth in the wilderness (John the Baptist), and is concerned with the person and work of Jesus Christ. The New Testament opens in exact accord with this. John the Baptist, the forerunner of Jesus, is announced. . . . Isaiah ends with the vision of new heavens and a new earth wherein dwelleth righteousness. The New Testament closes with this same view in Revelation. This striking similarity between Isaiah and the whole Bible is unforgettable when once mastered.[29]

There is a time gap of several centuries between the closing of the Old Testament with the 39th book of the Bible and the opening of the New Testament. Likewise, there is a period of several hundred years between the incident in the 39th chapter of Isaiah and the fulfillment of Isaiah's prophecy in the 40th chapter. The 39th chapter concludes with the following words, which Isaiah spoke to king Hezekiah:

> *Behold, the days come, that all that is in thine house, and that which thy fathers have laid up in store until this day, shall be carried to Babylon: nothing shall be left, saith the Lord. And of thy sons that shall issue from thee, which thou shalt beget, shall they take away; and they shall be eunuchs in the palace of the king of Babylon. Then said Hezekiah to Isaiah, Good is the word of the Lord which thou hast spoken. He said moreover, For there shall be peace and truth in my days.* ISAIAH 39:6-8

The 39th chapter of Isaiah, which terminates the first major section of the book, concludes with the statement, *"For there shall be peace and truth in my days"* (v. 8). In the years between the closing of the Old Testament and the opening of the New, a time of Peace was ushered in by the power of Rome, and the incarnation of Truth was manifested by the person of Jesus Christ.

The 40th chapter of Isaiah introduces the second and final section of the book. The prophet describes the appearance of John the Baptist, which is recorded in the synoptic Gospels, as follows:

> *The voice of him that crieth in the wilderness, Prepare ye the way of the Lord, make straight in the desert a highway for our God. Every valley shall be exalted, and every mountain and hill shall be made low: and the crooked shall be made straight, and the rough places plain: And the glory of the Lord shall be revealed, and all flesh shall see it together: for the mouth of the Lord hath spoken it.* ISAIAH 40:3-5

The glory of the Lord was revealed in the person of Jesus Christ, and the Gospel of Mark clearly presents Him to the Romans as foretold by the prophet. Isaiah predicted:

> Behold, the Lord God will come with strong hand, and his arm shall rule for him: behold, his reward is with him, and his work before him. He shall feed his flock like a shepherd: he shall gather the lambs with his arms. . . . Who hath measured the waters in the hollow of his hand, and meted out heaven with the span, and comprehended the dust of the earth in a measure, and weighed the mountains in scales, and the hills in a balance? Who hath directed the spirit of the Lord, or being his counselor hath taught him? With whom took he counsel, and who instructed him, and taught him in the path of judgment, and taught him knowledge, and shewed to him the way of understanding? . . . Have ye not known? have ye not heard? Hath it not been told you from the beginning? Have ye not understood from the foundations of the earth? It is he that sitteth upon the circle of the earth, and the inhabitants thereof are as grasshoppers; that stretcheth out the heavens as a curtain, and spreadeth them out as a tent to dwell in: That bringeth the princes to nothing; he maketh the judges of the earth as vanity. . . . . Lift up your eyes on high, and behold who hath created these things, that bringeth out their host by number: he calleth them all by names by the greatness of his might, for that he is strong in power. . . . He giveth power to the faint; and to them that have no might he increaseth strength. Even the youths shall faint and be weary, and the young men shall utterly fall: But they that wait upon the Lord shall renew their strength; they shall mount up with wings as eagles; they shall run, and not be weary; and they shall walk, and not faint.
> ISAIAH 40:10-14, 21-23, 26, 29-31

The Romans may not have known the Old Testament Scriptures, but it is important to realize that Christ is, nevertheless, presented to them in fulfillment of these prophecies. He is the mighty prophet and servant, the great builder and architect—the one whose miracles proved that no obstacle in nature or power in the universe was too great to overcome. *"We heard him say, I will destroy this temple that is made with hands, and within three days I will build another made without hands"* (Mark 14:58). To the Romans, especially, Jesus is portrayed as the Man of strength and power, in His mission and work, both in life and death.

The Verdict on the Romans

As noted above, the Lord Jesus Christ used His power to give strength to the faint. *"He shall feed his flock like a shepherd: he shall gather the lambs with his arm, and carry them in his bosom, and shall gently lead those that are with young. . . . And to them that have no might he increaseth strength"* (Isaiah 40:11, 29b). The Romans, by contrast, used their power to *"devour the whole earth, and . . . tread it down, and break it in pieces"* (Dan. 7:23).

The Roman Empire was built upon a foundation of force and violence, not love and compassion. It set up a judicial system that extended to the ends of the civilized world, yet none—from prominent citizen to impoverished slave—could hope for leniency. It established a world of peace, yet it aggravated—rather than relieved—the disturbed soul. Citizen and subject, alike, were guaranteed justice, but longed for mercy. Dr. Gregory noted:

> In carrying out his mission of power the Roman was . . . the representative of natural justice in the world. It was doubtless some alleviation that the moulds

into which the Roman power so remorselessly crushed men and nations were moulds of justice; yet in proportion as the world was a wicked world was the justice a terrible justice. Rome is aptly described by the prophet Daniel as the iron kingdom: "The fourth kingdom shall be strong as iron, forasmuch as iron breaketh in pieces and subdueth all things, and as iron that breaketh all these shall it break in pieces and bruise;" and again, as the ferocious beast, "dreadful and terrible, and strong exceedingly, with great iron teeth, which devoured and brake in pieces, and stamped the residue with the feet of it." It was justice practically omnipotent and omnipresent, and so neither to be resisted nor escaped—justice which never dreamed of mercy until the work of conquest and consolidation was done. It made men long for mercy, because it demonstrated to them that there was no hope for them in righteous law.[30]

It has been rightly stated, "The Roman legacy has penetrated regions that Romans never ruled and continents they never dreamed of reaching."[31] And their most notable legacy and greatest achievement, "whether we consider it on its own intrinsic merits or in its influence on the history of the world, is without doubt their law."[32] It provided "a historical basis for the widespread modern belief that fairness in law demands that it be in written form."[33] And from 450 B.C., when the Law of the Twelve Tables was engraved on bronze tablets, the ancient Romans kept the letter and enlarged the spirit of the law until Justinian I, ruler of the Byzantine Empire, finally codified its successive accumulation in 533 A.D. "These tables and their Roman successors, including the Justinian Code, led to civil-law codes that provide the main source of law in much of modern Europe, South America, and elsewhere."[34]

It has been universally recognized that "the Romans were a law-inspired nation, but the law was of their making and they imposed it on themselves."[35] Furthermore, it needs to be realized that whatever praise or "harangues we make upon the Justice, Temperance, and other celebrated Virtues of the old Romans, they at last . . . debased the noble and generous Spirit of their Ancestors; and this Corruption was, without doubt, the only cause of the Declension and Ruin of the Empire."[36] In spite of almost a thousand years in developing a legal system that was their greatest intellectual bequest to the world, it is doubtful after all was said and done whether they ever kept the two greatest commandments of all! In a conversation with one of the scribes, the Lord summarized the Law of God for him by stating:

> And thou shalt love the Lord thy God with all thy heart, and with all they soul, and with all thy strength: this is the first commandment. And the second is like, namely this, Thou shalt love thy neighbour as thyself. There is none other commandment greater than these. MARK 12:30-31

On these two counts the Roman was guilty. The strong man did not love God with all his strength, nor his neighbor as himself.

> As it is written, There is none righteous, no not one: There is none that understandeth, there is none that seeketh after God. They are all gone out of the way, they are together become unprofitable; there is none that doeth good, no not one. . . .
> Destruction and misery are in their ways:
> And the way of peace have they not known:
> There is no fear of God before their eyes.
> Now we know that what things soever the law saith, it saith to them who are under the law:

that every mouth may be stopped, and all the world may become guilty before God. Therefore by the deeds of the law there shall no flesh be justified in his sight: for by the law is the knowledge of sin. ROM. 3:10-12, 16-20

Before the tribunal of God the Roman was guilty as charged. Nothing he has done—or could do in his own strength—would aid his defense or help his case. "God, as the Scriptures witness, is the creator of heaven and earth. He is thus Lord of the universe. His jurisdiction knows no bounds, and his authority is absolute. Because he is God he is the very standard of justice and equity, to his judgments all men are obliged to conform, and from his decisions there is no appeal."[37]

But yet, there is "good news" (cf. Mark 1:1) and it is found in the person and work of Jesus Christ. Blind Bartimaeus, who *"sat by the highway side begging"* (Mark 10:46), recognized this; and the Roman needed to realize that he, too, if not in the same predicament, was nevertheless under the same pronouncement of sin. Standing before the presence of God the Roman did not want to demand justice, but needed to make the same plea as did blind Bartimaeus. Mark reports:

And when he heard that it was Jesus of Nazareth, he began to cry out, and say, Jesus, thou son of David, have mercy on me. And many charged him that he should hold his peace: but he crieth the more a great deal, Thou son of David, have mercy on me. 10:47-48

The Roman had *"become guilty before God"* (Rom. 3:19); and although he knew justice, he needed mercy!

Chapter Seven Notes

[1] Hugh R. Trevor-Roper, *Introduction to The Decline and Fall of the Roman Empire by Edward Gibbon* (New York: Twayne Publishers, Inc., 1963), vii.

[2] Edward Gibbon, *The History of the Decline and Fall of the Roman Empire*, Edited by David Womersley, 3 vols. (London: Penguin Books, Ltd., 1995), I:31.

[3] Moses Hadas and the editors of Time-Life Books, *Imperial Rome* (New York: Time Incorporated, 1965), 32-33.

[4] D. S. Gregory, *Why Four Gospels? Or, the Gospel for All the World* (New York: Funk & Wagnalls, Publishers, 1890), `158-59.

[5] Gibbon, *op. cit.*

[6] Jerry H. Combee, *The History of the World in Christian Perspective, Vol. I* (Pensacola, Fla.: A Beka Book Publications, 1979), 247.

[7] Gregory, *op. cit.*, 157-58.

[8] *Ibid.*, 160.

[9] *Ibid.*, 176.

[10] *Ibid.*, 157-58.

[11] *Ibid.*, 161-62.

[12] R. H. Barrow, *The Romans* (Baltimore: Penguin Books, 1961), 130.

[13] *Ibid.*, 130-32.

[14] *Ibid.*, 132.

[15] Hadas, *op. cit.*, 12.

[16] Jackson J. Spielvogel, *Western Civilization*, vol. I, 2nd ed. (Minneapolis/St. Paul: West Publishing Company, 1994), 151.

[17] "Aqueduct," *Encyclopaedia Britannica* (1903), II:219.

[18] Gibbon, *op. cit.*, I:74.

[19] Barrow, *op. cit.*, 135-36.

[20] Edwin Hoag, *The Roads of Man* (New York: G. P. Putnam's Sons, 1967), 58-59.

[21] Gibbon, *op. cit.*, I:77.

[22] *Ibid.*

[23] Hoag, *op. cit.*, 62-63.

[24] Barrow, *op. cit.*, 130.

[25] Gibbon, *op. cit.*

[26] Hoag, *op. cit.*, 60.

[27] Gibbon, *op. cit.*, I:74.

[28] Hoag, *op. cit.*, 64.

[29] Henrietta C. Mears, *What the Bible Is All About* (Glendale, Calif.: Regal Books Division, Gospel Light Publications, 1966), 211.

[30] Gregory, *op. cit.*, 54.

[31] Hadas, *op. cit.*, 166.

[32] Barrow, *op. cit.*, 209.

[33] "Law," *Funk & Wagnalls New Encyclopedia* (1990), 16:8.

[34] *Ibid.*

[35] Barrow, *op. cit.*, 218.

[36] Basil Kennett, *The Antiquities of Rome* (Dublin: Printed for J. Exshaw and H. Bradley, in Dame-Street, 1767). 62.

[37] Henry Stob, *Ethical Reflections: Essays on Moral Themes* (Grand Rapids, Mich.: William B. Eerdmans Publishing Company, 1978), 240.

Chapter Eight

The Servant of God: Mighty Prophet

Some of the most remarkable men in the annals of world history were the Hebrew prophets. Without obvious credentials or human endorsements, they nevertheless spoke with such authority that even kings submitted to their demands for justice. Two episodes from the Old Testament Scriptures make this unmistakably clear. "One is the story of Naboth who, because he refused to turn over his family vineyard to King Ahab, was framed on false charges of blasphemy and subversion and stoned."[1]

> *And it came to pass, when Jezebel heard that Naboth was stoned, and was dead, that Jezebel said to Ahab, Arise, take possession of the vineyard of Naboth the Jezreelite, which he refused to give thee for money: for Naboth is not alive, but dead. And it came to pass, when Ahab heard that Naboth was dead, that Ahab rose up to go down to the vineyard of Naboth the Jezreelite, to take possession of it. And the word of the Lord came to Elijah the Tishbite, saying, Arise, go down to meet Ahab king of Israel, which is in Samaria: behold, he is in the vineyard of Naboth, whither he is gone down to possess it. And thou shalt speak unto him, saying, Thus saith the Lord, Hast thou killed, and also taken possession? And thou shalt speak unto him, saying, Thus saith the Lord, In the place where dogs licked the blood of Naboth shall dogs lick thy blood, even thine. And Ahab said to Elijah, Hast thou found me, O mine enemy? And he answered, I have found thee; because thou hast sold thyself to work evil in the sight of the Lord. Behold, I will bring evil upon thee, and will take away thy posterity.* I KINGS 21:15-21A

The story carries revolutionary significance for human history for it is the story of how a man without official position of any sort took the side of a wronged man and denounced a king to his very face on grounds of injustice. One will search in vain in the literature of other religions of the time to find its parallel. Elijah is not a priest. He had no formal authority for the terrible judgment he delivered. The normal pattern of the times would have called for him to be struck down by the king's guard on the spot. But the fact that he was "speaking for" an authority not himself is so transparent that the king accepted this verdict of the moral conscience as divine and hence ultimate.

The same striking sequence recurred in the incident of David and Bathsheba. From the top of his roof David glimpsed Bathsheba bathing and wanted her for his wife. One obstacle stood in the way; she was already married. To the royalty of those days, however, this was a small matter. David simply ordered Uriah to the front lines with instructions to his commanding officer that he be placed in the thick of the fighting and support withdrawn so he would be killed. Everything went as planned, indeed the entire procedure seemed routine, until Nathan the prophet got wind of it.[2]

> *And the Lord sent Nathan unto David. And he came unto him, and said unto him, . . . Wherefore hast thou despised the commandment of the Lord, to do evil in his sight? Thou hast killed Uriah the Hittite with the sword, and hast taken his wife to be thy wife, and hast slain him with the sword of the children of Ammon. Now therefore the sword shall never depart from thine house; because thou hast despised me, and hast taken the wife of Uriah the Hittite to be thy wife. Thus saith the Lord, Behold, I will raise up evil against thee*

out of thine own house, and I will take thy wives before thine eyes, and give them unto thy neighbour, and he shall lie with thy wives in the sight of this sun. For thou didst it secretly: but I will do this thing before all Israel, and before the sun. II SAM. 12:1A, 9-12

The surprising point in each of these accounts is not what the kings do; for they were merely exercising the universally accepted prerogatives of royalty in their day. The revolutionary and unprecedented fact is the way the prophets challenged their behavior.[3]

Elijah and Nathan were able to successfully challenge the behavior of the kings, because they proclaimed the very words of God Himself. Other ancient peoples may have had their prophets, but the Hebrew prophets were in a class by themselves.

The Biblical prophet must be distinguished from the *prophetes* of the Greeks. The latter really acted as an interpreter for the muses and the oracles. The prophets, however, were not interpreters. They uttered the actual words which God had given to them, without any modification or interpretation upon their part. The Bible itself gives an accurate description of the function of the true prophet, ". . . and will put my words in his mouth; and he shall speak unto them all that I shall command him" (Deut. 18:18b). The words are placed in the prophets mouth by God, i.e., they are revealed to the prophet, and then the prophet speaks unto the nation precisely what God has commanded him. . . .

In ancient Greece we have the god, the oracle, the prophet, and the people. The same seems to have been the case in the Mesopotamian countries also. In Israel, however, there was only one intermediary between God and the people, namely, the prophet. This arrangement was truly unique. One who heard the words of the prophet heard the very words of God Himself, and these words required implicit obedience.[4]

As spokesmen for the only true God, the prophets of Israel and Judah "spoke words the world has been unable to forget,"[5] and have been recognized as some of the most influential men who have ever lived. One writer even claims: "These men were greater than kings, for you cannot select, say four Israelite kings so influential upon the world as were Amos, Hosea, Isaiah, and Jeremiah."[6] Another noted:

The prophets came upon the stage of history like a strange, elemental, explosive force. They live in a vaster world than those about them, a world in which pomp and ceremony, wealth and splendor count for nothing, where kings seem small and the power of the mighty is as nothing compared with purity, justice and mercy. So it is that whenever men and women have gone to history for encouragement and inspiration in the age-long struggle for justice they have found it, more than anywhere else in the prophets.[7]

Although the Hebrew prophets are some of the most amazing individuals to be found anywhere, yet, strangely enough, very little is known about them or their background. Of some, such as Nathan or Obadiah, we know nothing at all. Most made their appearance at the eleventh hour, so to speak, at a time of national crisis, political conflict, or some other disturbing event.

Isaiah, for example, was called to be a prophet to the southern kingdom of Judah about the time that king Uzziah died, and the clouds on the horizon were ominous with impending catastrophe, because of the threat of Assyrian imperialism.

Hosea made his appearance in the northern kingdom of Israel, and delivered

God's message of judgment and disaster a few years before the nation would be carried away to captivity in Assyria.

Joel appeared at a time of devastation by locusts. The calamity was so great that it is described as an invading army (Joel 2:5)—a harbinger of future events in *"the day of the Lord"* (cf. 1:15, 2:1, 11).

Amos traveled to the northern kingdom *"two years before the earthquake"* (Amos 1:1) in order to deliver an urgent call to repentance as the only escape from the inevitable consequences of divine judgment.

These, and many of the other prophets, seem to suddenly appear on the stage of history at times of conflict, turmoil, and confusion. And their message, whether or not it included predictive prophecy of future events, was always given to influence a particular people's attitudes and behavior in the present. Amidst the various crises of the prophets' day, therefore, we can begin to grasp the necessity of their calling and the nature of their message.

I Will Raise Them Up a Prophet (Deut. 18:18a)

The Old Testament prophets foreshadowed the One predicted by Moses—"a prophet whose word on all questions would be final."[8] In his written legacy to the Jewish nation, known as the Pentateuch, Moses wrote:

> *The Lord thy God will raise up unto thee a Prophet from the midst of thee, of thy brethren, like unto me; unto him ye shall hearken; According to all that thou desiredst of the Lord thy God in Horeb in the day of the assembly, saying, Let me not hear again the voice of the Lord my God, neither let me see this great fire any more, that I die not. And the Lord said unto me, They have well spoken that which they have spoken. I will raise them up a Prophet from among their brethren, like unto thee, and will put my words in his mouth; and he shall speak unto them all that I shall command him. And it shall come to pass, that whosoever will not hearken unto my words which he shall speak in my name, I will require it of him.*
> Deut. 18:15-19

Jesus Christ ultimately fulfilled this prophetic role, and the Gospel of Mark portrays Him in this capacity. As such, it is of interest to note—but of no surprise to learn—that Mark begins the public ministry of Christ during a time of crisis. He wrote:

> *Now after that John was put in prison, Jesus came into Galilee, preaching the gospel of the kingdom of God. And saying, The time is fulfilled, and the kingdom of God is at hand: repent ye, and believe the gospel.* 1:14-15

> The plan and method of Mark are indicated by the very phrase of time and place by which he announces the beginning of the ministry of Jesus: "Now after John was delivered up, Jesus came into Galilee." The many events which occurred in Judea, after the temptation of Jesus and before the imprisonment of John, are passed in silence. Mark is to be concerned with the Galilean ministry of Jesus; he therefore omits all mention of the preceding incidents, which are recorded in the Gospel of John, including the visit to Jerusalem, the cleansing of the Temple, and the conversation with Nicodemus. He mentions only the event which made it necessary for Jesus to withdraw into Galilee. However, he does not state this necessity. The other Gospels intimate that because of the crisis produced by the arrest of John, and because of the jealous hatred of the rulers, Jesus left Judea. Mark merely suggests that, when the

work of John had been ended, the ministry of Jesus began.[9]

The primary nature of a prophet's ministry is "forth telling," and Jesus appears in Galilee, "not first of all as a worker of miracles, but as the Bearer of a message."[10] Furthermore, this message is from God: *"The time is fulfilled, and the kingdom of God is at hand: repent ye, and believe the gospel"* (1:15).

Galilee, the most northern of the three provinces of Palestine, was the region of the Lord's upbringing and the home of His kinfolk. Yet Mark makes no mention of this, nor any other information, regarding the background and personal history of Jesus Christ. In his Gospel there is no record of the angel Gabriel appearing to the virgin Mary with the news that she would bring forth One who *"shall be great, and shall be called the Son of the Highest"* (Luke 1:32). There is no mention of Mary's espousal to Joseph, nor the latter's reaction when the former was found with child of the Holy Ghost. There is no record of a Roman census that brought Joseph and Mary from Nazareth to Bethlehem, the city of David. There is no reference to any genealogy, indicating that Jesus' parents were of the house and lineage of David. There is no mention that Mary *"brought forth her firstborn son, and wrapped him in swaddling clothes, and laid him in a manger; because there was no room for them in the inn"* (Luke 2:7). There is no indication that Jesus' birth was announced to shepherds, who were *"abiding in the field, keeping watch over their flock by night"* (Luke 2:8). There is no record of wise men from the east, coming to visit the newborn King, and bearing gifts of *"gold, and frankincense, and myrrh"* (Matt. 2:11). There is no mention that Jesus was taken to Egypt to escape the wrath of Herod, and only returned to Nazareth after the angel told Joseph: *"They are dead which sought the young child's life"* (Matt. 2:20). There is no information relating to the fact that *"the child grew, and waxed strong in spirit, filled with wisdom"* (Luke 2:40). There is no record of Jesus' visit to Jerusalem during the Feast of Passover, when the twelve year old—lost by his parents on their return home—was after three days found *"in the temple, sitting in the midst of the doctors, both hearing them, and asking them questions. And all that heard him were astonished at his understanding and answers"* (Luke 2:46-47).

In Mark's Gospel the details of the early life and background of Jesus are conspicuous by their absence. The Hebrew prophets made their appearance on the stage of history and the pages of Scripture with little or no introduction, and this is the format used in the second Gospel. Mark leaves the first three decades of Christ's life shrouded in obscurity, and presents Him at the onset of His ministry already girded for action. He introduces the Lord with these words: *"The beginning of the gospel of Jesus Christ, the Son of God"* (1:1).

It is of interest to find that many of the Old Testament prophets were introduced in a strikingly similar way. For the most part, the only information given regarding the prophet was the identity of his father. Note, for example, the following introductions:

The vision of Isaiah the son of Amoz . . . ISA. 1:1

The words of Jeremiah the son of Hilkiah . . . JER. 1:1

The word of the Lord came expressly unto Ezekial the priest, the son of Buzi . . . EZEK. 1:3

The word of the Lord that came unto Hosea, the son of Beeri . . . HOSEA 1:1

The word of the Lord that came to Joel the son of Pethuel . . . JOEL 1:1

Now the word of the Lord came unto Jonah the son of Amittai . . . JONAH 1:1

The word of the Lord which came unto Zephaniah the son of Cushi . . . ZEPH. 1:1

In the eighth month, in the second year of Darius, came the word of the Lord unto Zechariah, the son of Berechiah . . . ZECH. 1:1

The Hebrew prophets had different fathers, but they were all servants of the same God. In order to be the prophet of God, they had to be His servant. The author of the Second Book of the Kings—attributed by Jewish tradition to the prophet Jeremiah—wrote:

> Yet the Lord testified against Israel, and against Judah, by all the prophets, and by all the seers, saying, Turn ye from your evil ways, and keep my commandments and my statutes, according to all the law which I commanded your fathers, and which I sent to you by my servants the prophets. 2 KINGS 17:13

Behold, My Servant (Isaiah 52:13)

As the rightful King, Jesus had to be the Son of David; but as the true Prophet, He had to be the Servant of Jehovah. This latter aspect of Christ's work is what is highlighted in the Gospel of Mark.

> The Gospel of the Son of God would as a matter of course be the Gospel of the Servant of Jehovah. Sonship and service always are joined in the Scriptures. In Exodus we read, "Israel is my son, even my first-born; let my son go, that he may serve me . . ." (Exod. 4:22-23). Paul exhorts all the sons of God to present their bodies holy, acceptable unto God, which is their spiritual service (Rom. 12:1-2). The incarnate Son of God, the First-Born, did that. He took upon him the form of a servant (Phil. 2:7). His life was a life of devoted and incessant service. The Pentecostal church called the Lord by that title, "Thy holy Servant Jesus, whom thou didst anoint" (Acts 4:27). They said, "God . . . hath glorified his Servant Jesus" (Acts 3:13). Matthew presented the King; Mark presents the Servant. . . . This is . . . the Gospel of the ministering Christ, the One who came not to be ministered unto but to minister.[11]

Unlike a king or a priest, God's servant the prophet lived more intimately amongst the people he ministered unto, and was in a position to be more watchful and attentive to their needs. Whether to correct their errors, combat their prejudices, or cure their diseases, Mark portrayed Jesus Christ as One who *"looked round about"* in His role as God's Servant (cf. 3:5, 34; 5:32; 12:41)—highlighting the fact that He *"came not to be ministered unto, but to minister"* (10:45). Note Mark's description of the watchful Servant in the following three incidents, and compare his accounts with those recorded by Matthew and Luke:

(1). The Lord's response when the disciples rebuked those who brought little children to Him (cf. Mark 10:13-14 with Matt. 19:13-14 and Luke 18:15-16);

(2). The Lord's encounter with the rich young ruler (cf. Mark 10:17-25 with Matt. 19:16-24 and Luke 18:18-25);

(3). Jesus' entrance into the Temple after His triumphal entry (cf. Mark 11:11, 15-19 with Matt. 21:12-17 and Luke 19:45-46).

In addition to a watchful eye, other attributes of a good servant are the strength of his arms and the use of his hands. In Mark's Gospel these features are prominent, portraying the actions of God's Servant. When Jesus healed Peter's mother-in-law, He *"took her by the hand, and lifted her up"* (1:31). When He was approached by a leper, Jesus *"put forth his hand, and touched him"* (1:41). In the process of raising the dead daughter of Jairus, *"he took the damsel by the hand"* (5:41). When Jesus returned to His hometown of Nazareth, *"he laid his hands upon a few sick folk, and healed them"* (6:5). When Jesus healed the deaf mute, *"he took him aside from the multitude, and put his fingers into his ears, and he spit, and touched his tongue"* (7:33). At Bethany *"he took the blind man by the hand"* and afterwards *"put his hands upon him"* (8:23, 25). When He cured the demonic boy, *"Jesus took him by the hand, and lifted him up"* (9:27). When the disciples rebuked those who *"brought young children to him, that he should touch them"* (10:13), Jesus said, *"Suffer the little children to come unto me, . . . and he took them up in his arms, put his hands upon them, and blessed them"* (10:14, 16).

At Capernaum *"he took a child, and set him in the midst of them: and when he had taken him in his arms"* (9:36), Jesus explained to the quarreling disciples the nature of true greatness in the Kingdom of God. *"If any man desire to be first, the same shall be last of all, and servant of all"* (9:35).

In Mark's Gospel Jesus is portrayed as the Servant of all, and this role is especially prominent in the opening chapters. The evangelist records a typical day in the life of Christ as follows:

> *And they went into Capernaum; and straightway on the Sabbath day he entered into the synagogue, and taught. And they were astonished at his doctrine: for he taught them as one that had authority, and not as the scribes. And there was in their synagogue a man with an unclean spirit; and he cried out, Saying, Let us alone; what have we to do with thee, thou Jesus of Nazareth? Art thou come to destroy us? I know thee who thou art, the Holy One of God. And Jesus rebuked him, saying, Hold thy peace, and come out of him. And when the unclean spirit had torn him, and cried with a loud voice, he came out of him. And they were all amazed, insomuch that they questioned among themselves, saying, What thing is this? What new doctrine is this? For with authority commandeth he even the unclean spirits, and they do obey him. And immediately his fame spread abroad throughout all the region round about Galilee. And forthwith, when they were come out of the synagogue, they entered into the house of Simon and Andrew, with James and John. But Simon's wife's mother lay sick of a fever, and anon they tell him of her. And he came and took her by the hand, and lifted her up; and immediately the fever left her, and she ministered unto them.* 1:21-31

It was a busy day, but yet there was no time to relax when evening came. Mark continues:

> *And at even, when the sun did set, they brought unto him all that were diseased, and them that were possessed with devils. And all the city was gathered together at the door. And he healed many that were sick of divers diseases, and cast out many devils; and suffered not the devils to speak, because they knew him.* 1:32-34

It would have been nice to sleep in the next morning, but such was not the privilege for the Servant of God. Mark notes:

> *And in the morning, rising up a great while before day, he went out, and departed into a solitary place, and there prayed. And Simon and they that were with him followed after him. And when they had found him, they said unto him, All men seek for thee. And he said unto them, Let us go into the next towns, that I may preach there also: for therefore came I forth. And he preached in their synagogues throughout all Galilee, and cast out devils.* 1:35-39

The ceaseless activity of God's Servant is stressed by the conjunction "and," which begins almost three out of four verses in the entire Gospel account. Furthermore, the Greek word *eutheos*—which is translated "forthwith," "straightway," or "immediately"— occurs no less than 40 times in this Gospel, and adds to the urgency of the work that needed to be accomplished. "There is only one way to read this gospel, and that is at a sitting, and it leaves one tense and exhausted."[12]

Some of the other special literary characteristics of Mark's narrative, which help to make it the Gospel of intense activity, have been identified as follows:

(1). Mark usually prefers the present tense, and he represents the action as taking place before us. Matthew in the parallel accounts changes the tenses again and again from the present into the past. Compare 1:40 with Matt. 8:2, and 14:43 with Matt. 26:47. There are one hundred and fifty-one historic presents in Mark, and of these Matthew retains only twenty-one.

(2). Mark has the imperfect tense [the Greek tense which denotes continued action in past time] two hundred and eighteen times, and Matthew avoids this tense in his parallels by omission and by paraphrase one hundred and eighty-seven times, and thirty-one times he changes it outright into the aorist [the simple past tense in Greek].

(3). Mark delights to note the beginning of an action and he uses the verb . . . [Greek for "began"] . . . twenty-six times: he began to teach, he began to preach, he began to speak, he began to rebuke, he began to cry aloud, and so on (1:45; 4:1; 10:28; 10:41; 10:47). The disciples began to make a way through the field when the Pharisees objected (2:23). In only six of these cases does Matthew retain the verb to begin.[13]

We have spoken of the acts and looks of God's Servant, but a few references to some of his words of ministry, which are peculiar to Mark's Gospel, might also be instructive.

One example we find in the raising of the daughter of Jairus. The scene is common to three Evangelists, but here only do we get some particulars full of marked tenderness. Thus St. Mark alone relates, that when some said, Thy daughter is dead, "Jesus, as soon as He heard the word that was spoken, (as if to save the father a moment's anguish and unbelief,) said, Be not afraid;" brief words, but full of grace, revealing the Servant's heart, who, even while He healed, watched to aid the spiritual progress of those He came to comfort. In the same spirit of mindful affection is Peter specially named here, when after the resurrection a message is sent by the women to the disciples. In St. Matthew the angels say, "Go and tell His disciples:" here only, "Tell His disciples, and Peter, that He goeth before you into Galilee." For Peter more than the rest needed a special word, and so above the rest he is remembered. The good Shepherd, who loves all, has peculiar pity towards the wounded sheep. Thus did this Servant of servants speak a word in season: "He spake," as St. Mark tells us, (and the words are peculiar to this Gospel,) "as they were able to bear it;" with milk for babes, and meat for the strong, distributing His words, even as His acts, in special pity to the feeble, shewing more abundant grace to that which lacked.[14]

A few additional details, which are peculiar to Mark's Gospel, reveal that true servant-hood is no slight service. Dr. Andrew Jukes noted:

Here only do we read that "He sighed," and again, that "He sighed deeply" (7:34 and 8:12); for in His service He did not offer to God that which cost Him nothing; teaching us too that if we would serve as He did, there must be many "sighs," the fruit first of sympathy with the pain around us, and then of rejected kindnesses. Then again, here only are we told, when He was led out to suffer, that "They bear Him." First we read, "They led Him out that they might crucify Him:" but He seems to have failed under the burden, for soon "They compel another to bear His cross;" and then St. Mark tells us "They bear Him" (15:20, 22), as if actually supporting Him, "to the place called Golgotha." A fit end to such an unsparing labor. He was worn out, and needed to be borne, and long before the thieves crucified with Him were dead, He had resigned His spirit. For indeed service is sacrifice throughout, and "the ox strong to labor" is also the chosen victim for the Lord's altar.[15]

In addition to those particulars already described, Jesus' role as the Servant of God is also evidenced in Mark's narrative in a number of other ways, several of which are noted below:

(1). Whereas Matthew records 14 parables of the Lord, Mark recounts only four; namely, The Sower (4:1-20), The Seed Growing Secretly (4:26-29), The Mustard Seed (4:30-32), and The Vineyard (12:1-12). Not only is there omission in number, but also in type. The parables in Mark's account are limited to those activities and settings in which a servant would by expectation be found and by experience be familiar.

(2). Whereas the solitude of a king is more likely to be respected, the privacy of a servant is apt to be intruded upon, and this is exactly what we find in the second Gospel. Only Mark tells us that Jesus' time was so demanded of by the multitudes that He "could not so much as eat bread" (3:20). In fact, "When his friends heard of it, they went out to lay hold on him: for they said, He is beside himself" (3:21). Later "the same day, when the even was come" (4:35), Mark added:

> And when they had sent away the multitude, they took him even as he was in the ship. And there were also with him other little ships. And there arose a great storm of wind, and the waves beat into the ship, so that it was now full. And he was in the hinder part of the ship, asleep on a pillow: and they awake him, and say unto him, Master, carest thou not that we perish? 4:36-38

It is of interest to note, furthermore, that the question posed by the disciples reveals their concern that Jesus was remise in His sense of duty and attention to service. None of the other evangelists, who record this incident, make any such implication. In Matthew's version the disciples "awoke him, saying, Lord, save us: we perish" (Matt. 8:25). Luke wrote, "And they . . . awoke him, saying, Master, Master, we perish" (Luke 8:24). Mark, by contrast, gives us a glimpse into the stress and frustration that the busy Servant of God must have experienced in the exercise of His duties and the fulfillment of His calling. "Master, carest thou not that we perish?"

(3). Whereas a king might wield universal sway, a servant is more limited in his scope of influence. "The second Gospel tells us that Jesus wished for certain things which he did not obtain, and found that there were certain things which he could not do; and Matthew either omits these statements altogether or so modifies them"[16] as to veil the restrictions to His ability and the resistance to His authority. For example, after Jesus healed the man with leprosy, Mark noted:

> And he straitly charged him, and forthwith sent him away; And saith unto him, See thou say nothing to any man: but go thy way, shew thyself to the priest, and offer for thy cleansing those things which Moses commanded, for a testimony unto them. But he went out, and

> *began to publish it much, and to blaze abroad the matter, insomuch that Jesus could no more openly enter into the city, but was without in desert places: and they came to him from every quarter.* 1:43-45

By comparison, Matthew wrote:

> *And, behold, there came a leper and worshipped him, saying, Lord, if thou wilt, thou canst make me clean. And Jesus put forth his hand, and touched him, saying, I will; be thou clean. And immediately his leprosy was cleansed. And Jesus saith unto him, See thou tell no man; but go thy way, shew thyself to the priest, and offer the gift that Moses commanded, for a testimony unto them.* MATT. 8:2-4

When Jesus *"came into his own country"* (Mark 6:1) and was met by unbelief, Mark tells us: *"And he could there do no mighty work, save that he laid his hands upon a few sick folk, and healed them"* (6:5). Matthew changes this statement to read: *"And he did not many mighty works there because of their unbelief"* (13:58).

"The following statements as to the desires of Jesus, found in Mark, are omitted altogether in Matthew:"[17]

> *And from thence he arose, and went into the borders of Tyre and Sidon, and entered into an house, and would have no man know it, but he could not be hid.* 7:24
>
> *And he charged them that they should tell no man: but the more he charged them, so much the more a great deal they published it.* 7:36

(4). Whereas a king is expected to give commands (cf. Matt. 8:18 with Mark 4:35), a servant is more likely to ask questions. "Mark represents Jesus as asking questions for information continually. Matthew for the most part leaves these questions out of his narrative. For example, the questions asked by Jesus, recorded in Mark 5:9; 5:30; 6:38; 8:12; 8:23; 9:12; 9:16; 9:21; 9:33; 10:3; 14:14 are all omitted by Matthew."[18]

(5). When contrasted with the other Gospel records, the omissions in Mark's narrative are most suggestive.

(a) He has no royal genealogy, no story of a supernatural conception, no worship by Wise men come from afar to offer their gifts to a new-born King, as Matthew had. (b) He does not begin with any reference to preexistent and ever existent glory, as John does. (c) Mark has no Sermon on the Mount, laying down the laws for a new kingdom, for here we have the servant and not the king. (d) Here we find no national manifesto and arraignment and judgment, such as the other Gospels have. (e) Here there is no reference to his right to summon twelve legions of angels to his help. (f) Here there is no promise of paradise to the thief on the cross. These things belong to the prerogatives of a king. (g) It has even been suggested that the Gospel closed abruptly at 12:8 as it begins abruptly with the active ministry, because this is the Gospel of Jesus as the Servant. "A servant comes, fulfills his task, and departs—we do not ask about his lineage, nor follow his subsequent history."[19]

His Name Shall Be Called Wonderful (Isaiah 9:6)

What is not omitted from Mark's account is the attention given to the miracles of Jesus Christ. In fact, "Mark's gospel devotes proportionately more space to Christ's miracles than the other gospels."[20] Whereas Luke's account, for example, cites 20 miracles in 91 pages of Greek text, Mark includes 18 miracles in only 53 pages of the same text.

The miracles of Jesus occupy a prominent place in Mark's narrative, as they emphasize both the activity of God's Servant and the authenticity of His Prophet. They are "the manifestation of the presence and power of God,"[21] and it would be strange, indeed, if those wonderful phenomena were absent from the record of One who is introduced as *"the Son of God"* (Mark 1:1). As distinguished churchman and celebrated author, Richard Chenevix Trench, noted:

> We shall greatly miss them, if they did not appear, . . . if we could not point to them there; for they belong to the very idea of a Redeemer, which would remain most incomplete without them. We could not ourselves, without having that idea infinitely weakened and impoverished, conceive of Him as not doing such works; and those to whom we presented Him as a Lord and a Savior might very well answer, "Strange, that one should come to deliver men from the bondage of nature which was crushing them, and yet Himself have been subject to its heaviest laws—Himself wonderful, and yet his appearance accompanied by no analogous wonders in nature—claiming to be the Life, and yet Himself helpless in the encounter with death; however much he promised in deed; giving nothing in hand, no first fruits of power, no pledges of greater things to come." They would have a right to ask, "Why did He give no signs that He came to connect the visible with the invisible world? Why did He nothing to break the yoke of custom and experience, nothing to show men that the constitution which He pretended to reveal has a true foundation?"[22]

The unprecedented miracles, recorded by Mark and described in detail, not only revealed "the mighty power of God which was inherent in Christ Himself,"[23] but effected great astonishment in those in whose presence they were performed. This wonder and awe, while not designed to be an end in itself, did, nevertheless, claim the special attention of the multitudes, and helps explain in part Mark's emphasis upon the privacy that Christ sought and the withdrawals that He required. As one nineteenth-century author noted:

> Especially prominent is the constant crowding of the multitudes roused by the works of wonder, which drive Jesus into desert places to seek privacy, which, if he enters a house, the whole city is gathered at the door.[24]

The miraculous powers of Christ, and the effects it would produce on those in whose sight they were observed, was foretold in the Old Testament Scriptures. Several centuries before the birth of the Messiah, the prophet Isaiah wrote:

> *For unto us a child is born, unto us a son is given: and the government shall be upon his shoulder: and his name shall be called Wonderful, Counsellor, The mighty God, The everlasting Father, The Prince of Peace.* 9:6

Jesus would be called *"Wonderful,"* because He would produce *"Wonders"*—one of the most frequently used words in Scripture for what we commonly call miracles. The term "indicates the state of mind produced on the eyewitnesses by the sight of miracles."[25]

Although it can be argued that God's created, natural processes are miraculous wonders in themselves, those miraculous phenomena generally referred to as wonders (*terasin*), signs (*semeiois*), or works of power (*dunamesin*) (cf. Acts 2:22), form a unique medium by which God's Prophet brings near the presence of God and delivers a special message with proof of its genuineness. However, whereas the laws of the former are observable by all mankind, the significance of the latter is only revealed to certain individuals. As Archbishop Trench observed:

> All is wonder; to make a man is at least as great a marvel as to raise a man from the dead, The seed that multiplies in the furrow is as marvelous as the bread that multiplied in Christ's hands. The miracle is not a greater manifestation of God's power than those ordinary and ever-repeated processes; but it is a different manifestation. By those other God is speaking at all times and to all the world; they are a vast revelation of Him. "The invisible things of Him are clearly seen, being understood by the things that are made, even his eternal power and Godhead" (Rom. 1:20). Yet from the very circumstances that nature is thus speaking evermore to all, that this speaking is diffused over all time, addressed unto all men, that its sound is gone out into all lands, from the very vastness and universality of this language, it may miss its aim. It cannot be said to stand in nearer relation to one man than to another, to confirm one man's word more than that of others, to address one man's conscience more than that of every other man. However it may sometimes have, it must often lack, a peculiar and personal significance. But in the miracle, wrought in the sight of some certain men, and claiming their special attention, there is a speaking to them in particular. There is then a voice in nature which addresses itself directly to them, a singling of them out from the crowd. It is plain that God has now a peculiar word which they are to give heed to, a message to which He is bidding them to listen.[26]

Of all the specific miracles of Jesus Christ, selected for inclusion in the four Gospels, only two are unique to Mark's account. One is the two-stage healing of the blind man at Bethsaida (Mark 8:22-26), the significance of which was explained in Chapter Six. The other is the healing of the deaf mute in Decapolis, the details of which are as follows:

> *And again, departing from the coasts of Tyre and Sidon, he came unto the sea of Galilee, through the midst of the coasts of Decapolis. And they bring unto him one that was deaf, and had an impediment in his speech; and they beseech him to put his hand upon him. And he took him aside from the multitude, and put his fingers into his ears, and he spit, and touched his tongue; And looking up to heaven, he sighed, and saith unto him, Ephphatha, that is, Be opened. And straightway his ears were opened, and the string of his tongue was loosed, and he spake plain. And he charged them that they should tell no man: but the more he charged them, so much the more a great deal they published it; And were beyond measure astonished, saying, He hath done all things well: he maketh both the deaf to hear, and the dumb to speak.* 7:31-37

> What a picture is here presented of the sinner's moral and spiritual condition as the fruit of the Fall! God lost man's ear in the garden, and since that fatal day he will listen to anyone else rather than God. "Oh, that my people had hearkened unto me" (Psalm 81:13; Hebrews 3:2). The tongue of the unsaved person is as estranged from God as his ear. Even the most cultured and educated sinner betrays an impediment in his speech as soon as spiritual truths are introduced.[27]

This miracle is of special importance, as it reveals both the love of God and the labor of His Prophet. Note, first of all, that after Jesus put His hand upon the deaf mute, *"He took him aside from the multitude"* (v. 33). There would be in this miracle, "wrought in the sight of some certain men, and claiming their special attention, . . . a speaking to them in particular."[28] Then, after *"looking up to heaven"* (v. 34), the direction from which the Prophet's authority and power has come, Christ commanded, *"Ephphata, that is, Be opened"* (v. 34), and immediately the man could hear. A prophet comes with a message from God—"a peculiar word which they are to give heed to, a message to which He is bidding them to listen."[29] But the ability to hear the Prophet's words is only the first step. One also needs to respond to it; so Jesus loosened the tongue of the dumb man *"and he spake plain"* (v. 35).

> The order of the cure is . . . significant—right speech returned directly when the ear was opened. . . . This is the order of nature. "The receiving of articulate sounds by the ear and their action in the brain and mind awakens and educates functions of speech. It is only when we consider this relation between sound and speech in the mechanism of the senses and the brain that we can appreciate the truly stupendous nature of the miracle. The entire process of establishing communication between the centers of hearing and speech was bridged in a moment." In the spiritual realm it is the same, for the ear must be opened to receive divine instruction before the tongue is able to speak forth God's praise. "We believe, and therefore we speak" (Romans 10:17; 2 Corinthians 4:13). Receiving by way of the ear the Gospel of redeeming love and grace into the heart, we delight to speak of the marvels of divine grace to all around.[30]

After Jesus healed the man of his infirmities, Mark tells us:

> *And he charged them that they should tell no man: but the more he charged them, so much the more a great deal they published it; And were beyond measure astonished, saying, He hath done all things well: he maketh both the deaf to hear, and the dumb to speak.* 7:36-37

Why would Jesus perform such a miracle, and then order those who witnessed the event to remain silent about it? The answer, at least in part, is found in knowing the location wherein the incident occurred, and Jesus' reason for being there. Dr. Erdman explains:

> Only once in the earthly career of our Lord does he leave his own land; but from the time he crosses "into the borders of Tyre and Sidon" until he departs for Jerusalem and the cross, he is either in Gentile territory or in the lonely regions of northern Galilee. It is a season of retirement. Jesus has been rejected by the nation. The multitudes who still throng about him have failed to appreciate the spiritual nature of his message or to recognize him as the Messiah; his townsmen in Nazareth have refused to accept him, and the religious leaders are leagued against him in deadly hate. Jesus therefore seeks places of seclusion where he can instruct his disciples in anticipation of his coming death and resurrection. He is not making missionary journeys, his ministry is not for the multitudes; nevertheless he cannot escape from the crowds, and he never fails to respond to the appeal of distress and of faith. The great Teacher is seeking to be alone with his disciples, but Mark still pictures him as the mighty Servant, the wonder-working Son of God.[31]

Initially, upon Jesus' withdrawal to northern Galilee, Mark notes:

> *And . . . he . . . went into the borders of Tyre and Sidon, and entered into an house, and would have no man know it, but he could not be hid. For a certain woman, whose young*

daughter had an unclean spirit, heard of him, and came and fell at his feet: The woman was
a Greek, a Syrophenician by nation; and she besought him that he would cast forth the devil
out of her daughter. But Jesus said unto her, Let the children first be filled: for it is not meet
to take the children's bread, and to cast it unto the dogs. 7:24-27

Of course, Jesus means to say that his work, for the present, is for Jews and
not for Gentiles; that in the brief space of his earthly ministry he must lay
foundations among people already prepared, in order that later his salvation
may be offered to all nations. Nevertheless his words appear harsh, almost
cruel, unless we see veiled beneath them the meaning and sympathy upon
which the wit and the faith of the woman at once lay hold. She was perfectly
familiar with the proud scorn of the Jews and their claim of superior rights,
and she must have detected the gentle irony in the tone of Jesus as he refers to
his people who have just rejected him. He seems to be saying, "My ministry
must be among the Jews, and you know that they regard you Gentiles as dogs,
and themselves as the special favorites of God." Then, too, he uses the word
"little dogs," from which she might conclude that they could have some place
in the household; and he begins by saying, "Let the children first be filled," indicating that a time might come when Gentiles also might be saved. Upon all
these suggestions the woman at once seizes. She does not "entrap him in his
words," she does not defeat him in his argument, but she sees the hidden truth
in his utterance, and in his apparent refusal she finds a promise of help.[32]

And she answered and said unto him, Yes, Lord: yet the dogs under the table eat of the
children's crumbs. 7:28

She admits that she is a Gentile, she makes no claim upon him whose ministry
lies among the Jews, but she suggests that while he is on Gentile territory, it
will not be interfering with his work, it will not be robbing his own people, it
will be but letting a crumb fall from the table, in case he makes this exception, and grants her request. It was not mere humility or wit which her words
expressed, but rather, a triumphant faith. His answer did seem to contain a
refusal, even a reproach; but she believed in the love and kindness which his
words almost concealed; she trusted his power and his grace. The reply of
Jesus had been a severe test of her faith; but it had distinguished the people
of the living God from the unbelieving world; and it had made clear to the
woman, and to all who heard, the relation in which Jesus stood to her and to
all Gentiles; and it made it possible for him to grant her petition when her
faith had stood the test.[33]

And he said unto her, For this saying go thy way; the devil is gone out of they daughter. 7:29

As "she went away unto her house, and found the child laid upon the bed,
and the demon gone out," a promise was given, virtually, to the whole Gentile
world of salvation through Christ to everyone that believes. Quite as definite
is the message, for every follower of Christ, to keep on with prayer, even in the
darkest hour, to believe that behind the cloud of apparent refusal our Lord is
concealing his purpose of love. However, let us ask, not as a matter of merit
or desert, but only as supplicants, making our conscious unworthiness the
very ground of our appeal to his grace.[34]

If the healing of the daughter of the Syrophenician woman was an inconspicuous promise of blessing to the Gentiles, the feeding of the 4,000, which occurred shortly thereafter, was a more obvious and tangible guarantee of this fact. Only Matthew and Mark record this miracle. Mark's version reads:

> In those days the multitude being very great, and having nothing to eat, Jesus called his disciples unto him, and saith unto them, I have compassion on the multitude, because they have now been with me three days, and have nothing to eat: And if I send them away fasting to their own houses, they will faint by the way: for divers of them came from far. And his disciples answered him, From whence can a man satisfy these men with bread here in the wilderness? And he asked them, How many loaves have ye? And they said, Seven. And he commanded the people to sit down on the ground: and he took the seven loaves, and gave thanks, and brake, and gave to his disciples to set before them; and they did set them before the people. And they had a few small fishes: and he blessed, and commanded to set them also before them. So they did eat, and were filled: and they took up of the broken meat that was left seven baskets. And they that had eaten were about four thousand: and he sent them away. 8:1-9

The wide excitement produced by the reported healing of the deaf man has led to the sudden gathering of great multitudes who throng about the Master eager to hear his word; and when they have continued with him for three days and are in want of food Jesus proceeds, as on a former occasion, to supply the needs of the people by the miraculous multiplication of a few loaves and fishes. While the number of men, of loaves, and of baskets of fragments, and other circumstances, are so different as to make certain that this is not merely a second account of the identical miracle, yet the main features and the obvious teachings are much the same.[35]

In both cases the patient compassion of Jesus is contrasted to the unbelief of His disciples. After previously witnessing the miraculous feeding of the 5,000 (cf. Matt. 14:14-21; Mark 6:34-44; Luke 9:12-17; John 6:5-13), it seems almost unbelievable that the disciples would on this occasion ask, *"From whence can a man satisfy these men with bread here in the wilderness?"* (8:4). "Some commentators insist that such stupidity is incredible and that this portion of the story must have been borrowed by the writer from the former narrative."[36] Yet nothing could be further from the truth, for the two miracles—while similar as to certain features—are different as to final purpose.

> In both miracles we note the abundant supply for the multitudes, and remember the message of supreme importance which Jesus intended to convey, namely, that he is himself the true Bread for the soul, and that they who trust in him shall have eternal life. It is in relation to this symbolic interpretation that the two similar miracles contain slightly different suggestions. The five thousand who were miraculously fed by Christ were all Jews, the four thousand were probably Gentiles. The first miracle in this period [the healing of the daughter of the Syrophenician woman] intimated that crumbs of bread might fall from the table for the needy Gentiles; here there may be an intimation that Jesus, rejected by his own people, is to give his life for the world, and is to be the living Bread for all nations.[37]

Centuries before the arrival of the Promised Messiah, the Old Testament Scriptures outlined the tasks to which the Servant of God was commissioned to perform. The prophet Isaiah, for example, wrote:

And now, saith the Lord that formed me from the womb to be his servant, to bring Jacob again to him, Though Israel be not gathered, yet shall I be glorious in the eyes of the Lord, and my God shall be my strength. And he said, It is a light thing that thou shouldest be my servant to raise up the tribes of Jacob, and to restore the preserved of Israel: I will also give thee for a light to the Gentiles, that thou mayest be my salvation unto the ends of the earth.
ISAIAH 49:5-6

Each of the miracles that Christ performed were important, not merely as wonders, but as "signs and pledges of something more than and beyond themselves."[38] This is especially evident in the last miracle recorded by Mark, as it conveys the Prophet's final message to the chosen people to whom He was sent.

> The miracle which stands last in this gospel of miracles is more important than it may seem. It is the more significant because the last; for it is a parable as well as a miracle, and it has a definite reference to the guilty nation which was about to reject and kill its King.
>
> If it were not that the purpose of Jesus was to teach a solemn and important lesson, his act would have been unreasonable, petulant, wanton. His divine power was usually employed only to bless and to heal; but here the withering of a tree is employed to prophesy the coming judgment upon an unrepentant and profitless people.[39]
>
> *And on the morrow, when they were come from Bethany, he was hungry: And seeing a fig tree afar off having leaves, he came, if happily he might find any thing thereon: and when he came to it, he found nothing but leaves; for the time of figs was not yet. And Jesus answered and said unto it, No man eat fruit of thee hereafter for ever. And his disciples heard it. . . . And in the morning, as they passed by, they saw the fig tree dried up from the roots. And Peter calling to remembrance saith unto him, Master, behold, the fig tree which thou cursedst is withered away.* 11:12-14, 20-21
>
> The tree evidently had been planted in an advantageous position, sheltered from the wind, favored by moisture and sunlight; and as Jesus sees its great wealth of leaves he looks for fruit, even though the season for figs has not come; but when he finds nothing but leaves, he declares that henceforth the tree never shall bear fruit. What a mysterious union of the human and divine, in the person of Jesus, is here revealed; hungry on his morning journey, disappointed in his expectation of food, yet able by a single word to render a tree forever fruitless, and predicting, with divine foreknowledge, the doom of a nation! What a picture, also, the pretentious foliage presents of the pride and hypocrisy and faithlessness of Israel! God had placed his chosen people advantageously among the nations of the world, he had bestowed upon them peculiar spiritual opportunities and religious advantages; and when the Son of God visited his people he found them making great professions of holiness, boasting their superior goodness, and maintaining a form of godliness; but beneath all the hypocrisy and pretense he could find no fruit of righteousness. The ministry of Jesus was just concluding; he was about to be rejected by the people who had been especially prepared for his coming, and he caused the fig tree to wither as a prophecy of the approaching judgment of God upon the fruitless, unfaithful nation.[40]

Concern has been voiced by some, and objection has been raised by others, that Jesus would at this season curse a fig tree for not bearing figs, since Mark clearly states, *"the time of figs was not yet"* (11:13). Nevertheless, this added information provided by Mark, rather than confusing the matter, was intended to highlight the significance of Jesus' actions. Archbishop Trench noted:

> At that early period of the year, March or April, neither leaves nor fruit were naturally to be looked for on a fig tree; . . . nor in ordinary circumstances would any one have sought them there. But that tree, by putting forth leaves, made pretension to be something more than others, to have fruit upon it, seeing that in the fig tree the fruit appears before the leaves. This tree, so to speak, vaunted itself to be in advance of all the other trees, challenged the passer-by that he should come and refresh himself with its fruit. Yet when the Lord accepted its challenge, and drew near, it proved to be but as the others, without fruit as they; for indeed, as the Evangelist observes, the time of figs had not yet arrived—its fault, if one may use the word, lying in its pretension, in its making a shew to run before the rest, when it did not so indeed. It was condemned, not so much for having no fruit, as for this, that not having fruit, it clothed itself abundantly with leaves, with the foliage which, being there, did, according to the natural order of the tree's development, give pledge and promise that fruit should be found on it, if sought.
>
> And this will then exactly answer to the sin of Israel, which under this tree was symbolized—that sin being not so much that they were without fruit, as that they boasted of so much. Their true fruit, the true fruit of any people before the Incarnation, would have been to own that they had no fruit, that without Christ, without the incarnate Son of God, they could do nothing; to have presented themselves before God, bare and naked and empty altogether. But this was exactly what Israel refused to do. Other nations might have nothing to boast of, but they by their own showing had much. And yet on closer inspection, the reality of righteousness was as much wanting on their part as anywhere among the nations (Rom. 2).
>
> And how should it have been otherwise? "For the time of figs was not yet"—the time for the bare stock and stem of humanity to array itself in bud and blossom, with leaf and fruit, had not come, till its engrafting on the nobler stock of the true Man. All which anticipated this, which would say that it could be anything or do anything otherwise than in Him and by Him, was deceptive and premature. The other trees had nothing, but they did not pretend to have anything; this tree had nothing, but it gave out that it had much. So was it severally with Gentile and with Jew. The Gentiles were empty of all fruits of righteousness, but they owned it; the Jews were empty, but they vaunted that they were full. The Gentiles were sinners, but they hypocrites and pretenders to boot, and by so much farther from the kingdom of God, and more nigh unto a curse. Their guilt was not that they had not the perfect fruits of faith, for the time of such was not yet; but that, not having, they so boastfully gave out that they had: their condemnation was, not that they were not healed, but that, being unhealed, they counted themselves whole. The law would have done its work, the very work for which God ordained it, if it had stripped them of these boastful leaves, or rather had hindered them from ever putting them forth.

Here then, according to this explanation, there is no difficulty either in the Lord's going to the tree at that unseasonable time—He would not have gone, but for those deceitful leaves which announced that fruit was there—nor in the (symbolic) punishment of the unfruitful tree at a season of the year, when, according to the natural order, it could not have had any. It was punished not for being without fruit, but for proclaiming by the voice of those leaves that it had such; not for being barren, but for being false. And this was the guilt of Israel, a guilt so much deeper than the guilt of the nations.[41]

He Was Numbered with the Transgressors (Isaiah 53:12; Mark 15:28)

Although some may boast of their own righteousness, the Scriptures declare, *"There is none that doeth good, no, not one"* (Psalm 14:3b). "It is not a little remarkable that it was with the fig leaves that in Paradise Adam attempted to deny his nakedness, and to present himself as other than a sinner before God."[42] Nevertheless, as the Apostle Paul told his Roman readers, *"We have before proved both Jews and Gentiles, that they are all under sin"* (Rom. 3:9). He added:

> *Now we know that what things soever the law saith, it saith to them who are under the law: that every mouth may be stopped, and all the world may become guilty before God.* Rom. 3:19

In the courtroom of the Supreme Judge of the universe, every defense is insufficient and every voice is silenced. All are guilty before God. Yet by His mercy and in His providence, God sent His Son to be *"numbered with the transgressors"* (Isa. 53:12; Mark 15:28), to die a substitutionary death, and *"to be a propitiation"* (Rom. 3:25) for the sins of all mankind.

Seven centuries before the Messiah appeared, the prophet Isaiah described not only the ultimate triumph of God's Servant, but His agonizing death as well. In what is generally regarded as one of the most treasured and important passages in the Old Testament, we are told of the rejection the Messiah could expect and the suffering He would experience. Isaiah wrote:

> *Behold, my servant shall deal prudently, he shall be exalted and extolled, and be very high. As many were astonied at thee; his visage was so marred more than any man, and his form more than the sons of men: So shall he sprinkle many nations; the kings shall shut their mouths at him: for that which had not been told them shall they see; and that which they had not heard shall they consider. Who hath believed our report? And to whom is the arm of the Lord revealed? For he shall grow up before him as a tender plant, and as a root out of dry ground: he hath no form nor comeliness; and when we shall see him, there is no beauty that we should desire him. He is despised and rejected of men; a man of sorrows, and acquainted with grief: and we hid as it were our faces from him; he was despised, and we esteemed him not. Surely he hath borne our griefs, and carried our sorrows: yet we did esteem him stricken, smitten of God, and afflicted. But he was wounded for our transgressions, he was bruised for our iniquities: the chastisement of our peace was upon him; and with his stripes we are healed. All we like sheep have gone astray; we have turned every one to his own way; and the Lord hath laid on him the iniquity of us all. He was oppressed, and he was afflicted, yet he opened not his mouth: he is brought as a lamb to the slaughter, and as a sheep before her shearers is dumb, so he openeth not his mouth. He was taken from prison and from judg-*

ment: and who shall declare his generation? For he was cut off out of the land of the living: for the transgression of my people was he stricken. And he made his grave with the wicked, and with the rich in his death; because he had done no violence, neither was any deceit in his mouth. Yet it pleased the Lord to bruise him; he hath put him to grief: when thou shalt make his soul an offering for sin, he shall see his seed, he shall prolong his days, and the pleasure of the Lord shall prosper in his hand. He shall see of the travail of his soul, and shall be satisfied: by his knowledge shall my righteous servant justify many; for he shall bear their iniquities. Therefore will I divide him a portion with the great, and he shall divide the spoil with the strong; because he hath poured out his soul unto death: and he was numbered with the transgressors; and he bare the sin of many, and made intercession for the transgressors. Isaiah 52:13-53:12

Jesus Christ *"became obedient unto death"* (Phil. 2:8) and shared the same fate as many of God's faithful servants and true prophets, who suffered martyrdom at the hands of wicked men. In compiling his list of those heroes of faith, the author of the Letter to the Hebrews wrote:

And what shall I more say? For the time would fail me to tell of Gideon, and of Barak, and of Samson, and of Jephthah; of David also, and Samuel, and of the prophets:
Who through faith subdued kingdoms, wrought promises, stopped the mouths of lions,
Quenched the violence of fire, escaped the edge of the sword, out of weakness were made strong, waxed valiant in fight, turned to flight the armies of the aliens. Women received their dead raised to life again: and others were tortured, not accepting deliverance; that they might obtain a better resurrection: And others had trial of cruel mockings and scourgings, yea, moreover of bonds and imprisonment: They were stoned, they were sawn asunder, were tempted, were slain with the sword: they wandered about in sheepskins and goatskins; being destitute, afflicted, tormented; (Of whom the world was not worthy:) they wandered in deserts, and in mountains, and in dens and caves of the earth. And these all, having obtained a good report through faith, received not the promise: God having provided some better thing for us, that they without us should not be made perfect. Hebrews 11:32-40

All these died before the final unfolding of God's promise and the coming of his Messiah into the world. It was as if God had so arranged things that the full blaze of his glory should not be revealed until we and they can enjoy it together.[43]

The Lord Working with Them, . . . with Signs Following (Mark 16:20)

The Old Testament saints died, beholding more the shadow than the substance of God's promises, yet they looked forward to the day when God would raise them up and establish His kingdom here on earth. As of today those promises have not yet been fulfilled, because God is still patiently calling people out of this world, and adding *"to the church daily such as should be saved"* (Acts 2:47).

While it is acknowledged that the Church in her visible existence is not what it should be in her true essence, yet over the centuries millions of lives have been transformed, as repentant sinners have come to a saving knowledge of Jesus Christ. From the earliest years of the Church's history, the Body of Christ has been plagued by heresy and torn by strife, but a sizable remnant has always been faithful to its Head and relevant to its world. The reason for the continued existence and steady growth

of the true Church of Jesus Christ—that invisible body of the Just made perfect by
the finished work of the resurrected Savior—is found in the closing verse of Mark's
account:

> *And they went forth, and preached every where, the Lord working with them, and confirming*
> *the word with signs following.* 16:20

The Lord Jesus Christ is working in the midst of His followers in the process
of building His Church. Even secular historians acknowledge that this supernatural
character of Christianity is the only explanation for its prolonged survival and powerful influence in a world that was opposed to its birth and hostile to its growth. One
authority noted:

> The history of the world presents no phenomenon so striking as the rise and
> early progress of Christianity. Originating in a country not remarkable for
> any political, commercial, or literary influence, emanating from One who
> occupied a humble sphere in the community amidst which He appeared, and
> announced in the first instance by men of mean extraction, of no literary
> culture, and not endowed with any surpassing gifts of intellect,—it neverthe-
> less spread so rapidly that in an incredibly short period of time it had been
> diffused throughout the whole civilized world, and in the fourth century of
> its existence became the recognized and established religion of the Roman
> empire. When it is remembered that this result was achieved not only without
> the aid of any worldly influence, but in the face of the keenest opposition on
> the part of all the learning, wealth, wit, and power of the most enlightened
> and mightiest nations of the earth, the conclusion is strongly forced upon us
> that a power beyond that of man was concerned in its success, and that its
> early and unexampled triumphs afford an incontestable proof of its inherent
> truth and its divine origin. Nor has the rapid advance of Christianity been
> confined to its earlier years. "After a revolution of fourteen or fifteen centuries
> that religion is still professed by the nations of Europe, the most distinguished
> portion of human kind in art and learning as well as in arms. By the industry
> and zeal of Europeans, it has been widely diffused to the most distant shores
> of Asia and Africa, and by means of their colonies has been firmly established
> from Canada to Chili in a land unknown to the ancients." And when we
> turn to the results of modern missionary enterprise we find a success no less
> remarkable.[44]

All the great world empires have come and gone, but the Church triumphant is in
the process of fulfilling the Lord's prediction, *"I will build my church; and the gates of hell
shall not prevail against it"* (Matt. 16:18). As one of our nineteenth-century hymn writers
so beautifully stated:

O where are kings and empires now
Of old that went and came?
But, Lord, Thy Church is praying yet,
A thousand years the same.

We mark her goodly battlements
And her foundations strong;

We hear within the solemn voice
Of her unending song.

For not like kingdoms of the world
Thy holy Church, O God;
Tho earthquake shocks are threat'ning her,
And tempests are abroad:

Unshaken as eternal hills,
Immovable she stands,
A mountain that shall fill the earth,
A house not made with hands.[45]

The Romans spent five centuries in completing a road system to every corner of an empire that no longer exists. Their roads, which "eventually covered a distance equal to ten times the circumference of the earth at the equator,"[46] were laid down wherever their authority extended; yet today they have no authority.

The ancient city of Rome—"showplace of the Empire" and "the archetype of all the great metropolises of Europe in later centuries"[47]—was in times past adorned by some of the most magnificent examples of architecture to be found anywhere. "Roman architects and builders seized on ancient concepts and coupled them with a new building material—concrete—that enabled them to overcome all ancient limits of height and weight."[48] Today, however, most of the great architecture of Rome lies in ruins—a spectacle of the expired glory "of the most extraordinary dominion which has ever invaded and oppressed the world."[49]

> As time passed, the great architecture of Rome fell into decay. The city's wealth and population dwindled after the Fourth Century, and building maintenance fell off. Nature and the heedlessness of man hastened the process of disintegration. A series of earthquakes in the Middle Ages toppled part of the Colosseum; the ruins were later used as a stone quarry. The Forum Romanum was similarly cannibalized. Many of its buildings were broken up, and supplied construction materials for churches and other buildings; the marble in them was burned to obtain lime. By the 15th century the once-handsome Forum was in complete disrepair. In 1431 a Renaissance writer observed: "The Roman Forum, the most celebrated place in the city, . . . and the nearby Comitium, where magistrates were chosen, are now deserted through the malignance of Fortune. The one is given over to swine and cattle; the other is enclosed as a vegetable garden."[50]

It is of interest to note that during a tour of Italy, Edward Gibbon visited the ruins of the Capitol in Rome, "and it was while there that the idea of composing a history of the decline and fall of the Roman Empire first came to him."[51] He wrote:

> It was at Rome, on the 15 October 1764, as I sat musing amidst the ruins of the Capitol, while the bare-footed friars were singing vespers in the Temple of Jupiter, that the idea of writing the decline and fall of the city first started on my mind.[52]

Twelve years elapsed, however, before the first volume of his six-volume work was published (1776). "The second and third volumes of *Decline and Fall* were published in 1781 and these bring the history through to the end of the Empire in the West. The final three volumes were completed in 1787 and published in 1788."[53] In the final chapters of this monumental work, Gibbon summarized the principal causes that continue to bring further disintegration to the ruins of Rome. He began this section by noting:

> The art of man is able to construct monuments far more permanent than the narrow span of his own existence: yet these monuments, like himself, are perishable and frail; and in the boundless annals of time, his life and his labors must equally be measured as a fleeting moment.[54]

The immense empire of Rome, "erected on the ruins of so many kingdoms, republics, and states both barbarous and civilized,"[55] has likewise disintegrated, and her own monuments, too, are now in ruins. The Romans bequeathed to the Western world a system of just laws, yet their Empire collapsed under the weight of its own injustices. They invested centuries constructing great works of architecture, yet the decay and destruction of the same is a constant reminder that the lives and labors of those who inspired these monuments must equally be measured as a fleeting moment.

In contrast to the monuments of Rome, the Church of Jesus Christ, both visible and invisible, is proof of the enduring nature of Her Founder and Redeemer. And while the former (the visible Church), as mentioned before, may not be synonymous with the latter (the invisible Church), yet both provide evidence that the life and labor of Jesus—in spite of the narrow span of His own ministry—has a presence and power in the world that transcends the boundless annals of time.

Death and the grave were not powerful enough to hold the Lord Jesus Christ, and after His resurrection He gave the following instructions to His disciples:

> *And he said unto them, Go ye into all the world, and preach the gospel to every creature. He that believeth and is baptized shall be saved; but he that believeth not shall be damned. And these signs shall follow them that believe; In my name shall they cast out devils; they shall speak with new tongues; They shall take up serpents; and if hey drink any deadly thing, it shall not hurt them; they shall lay hands on the sick, and they shall recover. So then after the Lord had spoken unto them, he was received up into heaven, and sat on the right hand of God. And they went forth, and preached every where, the Lord working with them, and confirming the word with signs following.* 16:15-20

During the Apostolic period of Church history, miraculous signs (as noted in verses 17 and 18) confirmed the preaching of the Word. When these signs passed away, however, the Lord did not stop working with and through His followers. The transformed lives of the invisible Church, the fellowships for worship that have been formed, and the places of meeting that have been built by the visible Church, are all signs and ways in which the common life of Jesus and His people can be seen and known throughout the world. While it is understood that no New Testament reference to the Church is ever associated with a building where believers are gathered for worship, yet the sanctuaries that have been constructed down through the ages, and continue to be built today, are visible signs and tangible evidence of the significance of Christ's life, the value of His death, and the reality of His resurrection.

The persistent presence of New Testament churches—from the great cathedrals of Europe to the thatched-roof structures in Africa; from big metropolitan Tabernacles to small rural chapels—is evidence that the Lord's instructions are being carried out, and the Gospel is being preached to every creature. In spite of any inaccuracies of belief or inconsistencies in behavior of any worshipper assembled within its walls, the visible church stands as confirmation that God's Servant is still at work in the world. And when this world as we know it passes away—and we see *"a new heaven and a new earth: for the first heaven and the first earth were passed away"* (Rev. 21:1)—the redeemed of every age will be assembled in that celestial tabernacle, in order to worship the One, whose love will become more precious and whose labor more priceless, as we move beyond the boundless annals of time. Until then, and in anticipation of that joyous time, we can sing what the Psalmist and songwriter so long ago wrote:

O Lord of host, how lovely Thy Tabernacles are;
For them my heart is yearning In banishment afar.
My soul is longing, fainting, Thy sacred courts to see;
My heart and flesh are crying, O living God, for Thee.

Beneath Thy care the sparrow Finds place for peaceful rest;
To keep her young in safety The swallow finds a nest;
Then, Lord, my King Almighty, Thy love will shelter me;
Beside Thy holy altar My dwelling-place shall be.[56]

Chapter Eight Notes

[1] Huston Smith, *The Religions of Man* (New York: Harper & Row, Publishers, 1989), 372.
[2] *Ibid.*, 372-73.
[3] *Ibid.*, 373-74.
[4] "Prophets," *The Living Bible Encyclopedia in Story and Pictures* (1968), 13:1661.
[5] Smith, *op. cit.*, 376.
[6] Kenneth J. Grider, "The Prophetic Books," *The Biblical Expositor*, Ed. Carl F. H. Henry (Philadelphia: A. J. Holman Company, 1973), 498.
[7] Smith, *op. cit.*, 377.
[8] H. A. Ironside, *Mark*, Rev. Ed. (Neptune, N.J.: Loizeaux Brothers, Inc., 1994), 13.
[9] Charles R. Erdman, *The Gospel of Mark* (Philadelphia: The Westminster Press, 1945), 29.
[10] *Ibid.*, 30.
[11] D. A. Hayes, *The Synoptic Gospels and the Book of Acts* (New York: The Methodist Book Concern, 1919), 150-51.
[12] Morton Scott Enslin, *The Literature of the Christian Movement* (New York: Harper & Brothers, 1956), 375.
[13] Hayes, *op. cit.*, 136.
[14] Andrew Jukes, *The Characteristic Differences of the Four Gospels* (New York: Fleming H. Revell Company, n.d.), 76-77.
[15] *Ibid.*, 83-84.
[16] Hayes, *op. cit.*, 161.
[17] *Ibid.*
[18] *Ibid.*
[19] *Ibid.*, 151.

[20] D. Edmond Hiebert, *An Introduction to the New Testament, Volume I: The Gospels and Acts* (Winona Lake, Ind.: BMH Books, 1993), 98.

[21] Richard Chenevix Trench, *Notes on the Miracles of Our Lord*, 6th ed. (London: John W. Parker and Son, West Strand, 1858), 11.

[22] *Ibid.*, 94.

[23] Herbert Lockyer, *All the Miracles of the Bible* (Grand Rapids, Mich.: Zondervan Publishing House, 1965), 16.

[24] Richard G. Moulton, *Introduction to St. Matthew, St. Mark and the General Epistles* (New York: The Macmillan Company, 1898), xix.

[25] Lockyer, *op. cit.*, 15.

[26] Trench, *op. cit.*, 11-12.

[27] Lockyer, *op. cit.*, 207-08.

[28] Trench, *op. cit.*, 11.

[29] *Ibid.*, 12.

[30] Lockyer, *op. cit.*, 209.

[31] Erdman, *op. cit.*, 110-11.

[32] *Ibid.*, 111.

[33] *Ibid.*, 112.

[34] *Ibid.*

[35] *Ibid.*, 115.

[36] *Ibid.*

[37] *Ibid.*, 115-16.

[38] Trench, *op. cit.*, 3.

[39] Erdman, *op. cit.*, 157.

[40] *Ibid.*, 157-58.

[41] Trench, *op. cit.*, 441-44.

[42] *Ibid.*, 442.

[43] William Barclay, *The Letter to the Hebrews*, Rev. ed. (Philadelphia: The Westminster Press, 1977), 171.

[44] "Christianity," *Encyclopaedia Britannica* (1903), V:695-96.

[45] A. Cleveland Coxe, *O Where Are Kings and Empires Now*.

[46] Moses Hadas and the editors of Time-Life Books, *Imperial Rome* (New York: Time Incorporated, 1965), 163.

[47] *Ibid.*, 162.

[48] *Ibid.*

[49] H. H. Milman, ed., *Introduction and Notes to The History of the Decline and Fall of the Roman Empire by Edward Gibbon, in six volumes* (Boston: Phillips, Sampson, and Company, 1856), iv.

[50] Hadas, *op. cit.*, 162-63.

[51] Rosemary Williams, ed., *Gibbon's Decline and Fall of the Roman Empire, Abridged and Illustrated* (Chicago: Rand McNally & Company, 1979), 9.

[52] *Ibid.*

[53] *Ibid.*

[54] Edward Gibbon, *The History of the Decline and Fall of the Roman Empire*, Edited by David Womersley, in 3 volumes (London: Penguin Books, Ltd., 1995), III:1065.

[55] Milman, *op. cit.*

[56] Justin H. Knecht (1799) and Edward Husband (1871), *O Lord of Hosts, How Lovely* (Psalm 84).

PERSPECTIVE

The Opposition to the Servant by Arthur W. Pink

Here we shall take a rapid review of Mark's reference to this feature of his theme, instead of commenting on each passage, though a remark here and there will, perhaps, not be out of place.

"But there were certain of the scribes sitting there, and reasoning in their hearts (there are usually a few such in most congregations), Why does this man thus speak blasphemies?" (2:6-7). "And when the scribes and Pharisees saw Him eat with publicans and sinners, they said unto His disciples, How is it that He eateth and drinketh with publicans and sinners?" (2:16). "And the Pharisees said unto Him, behold, why do they on the Sabbath day that which is not lawful?" (2:24). The servant of God must expect to be misunderstood and encounter criticism and opposition. "And they watched Him whether He would heal him on the Sabbath day" (3:2). And the servant of God is still watched by unfriendly eyes! "And the Pharisees went forth, and straightway took counsel with the Herodians against Him, how they might destroy Him" (3:6). Every faction of the people was "against" Him. "And the scribes which came down from Jerusalem said, He hath Beelzebub, and by the prince of the demons casteth He out demons" (3:22). The servant may expect to be called hard names. "And they began to pray Him to depart out of their coasts" (5:17). Christ was not wanted. His testimony condemned His hearers. So will it be now with every servant of God that is faithful. "And they laughed Him to scorn" (5:40). To be sneered and jeered at, then, is nothing new: sufficient for the disciple to suffer what his Master did before him. "And they were offended at Him" (6:3). The Christ of God did not suit everybody; far from it. But let us see to it that we give none other occasion for "offence" than He did! "And He could there do no mighty work, save that He laid His hands upon a few sick folk, and healed them" (6:5). The servant of God will come to some places which are unfavorable for effective ministry, and where the unbelief of the professing people of the Lord will hinder the Spirit of God. "Then came together unto Him the Pharisees, and certain of the scribes, which came from Jerusalem. And when they saw some of His disciples eat bread with defiled, that is to say, with unwashen hands, they found fault" (7:1-2). Nevertheless, the Lord Jesus declined to respect their "traditions," refusing to allow His disciples to be brought into bondage thus. Well for God's servants now if they disregard the "touch not, taste not, handle not" of men, yet must they be prepared to be "found fault" with as the result. "And the Pharisees came forth, and began to question with Him, seeking of Him a sign from heaven, tempting Him" (8:11). So, too, will the emissaries of the Enemy seek now to entangle and ensnare the servants of God. Compare Mark 10:2. "And the scribes and chief priests heard it, and sought how they might destroy Him: for they feared Him, because all the people was astonished at His doctrine" (11:18). They were jealous of His influence. And human nature has not changed since then! "And they come again to Jerusalem: and as He was walking in the temple, there came to Him the chief priests and the scribes, and the elders. And say unto Him, By what authority dost Thou these things? And who gave Thee this authority?" (11:27-28). How history repeats itself! From what College have you graduated? And in which Seminary were you trained? are the modern form of this query. "And they sent unto Him certain of the Pharisees, and of the Herodians, to catch Him in His words" (12:13). And some of their descendants still survive, and woe be to the man who fails to pronounce their shibboleths! What a list this is! And we have by no means exhausted it; see further 12:18; 12:28; 14:1 etc. All the way through, the perfect Servant of God was dogged by His enemies; at every step He encountered opposition and persecution in some form. And these things are all recorded for our instruction. The Enemy is not dead. God's servants today are called to tread a similar path.[1]

[1] Arthur W. Pink, *Why Four Gospels?* (Swengel, Penn.: Bible Truth Depot, 1921), 79-81.

PART IV

THE NEEDS OF THE FUTURE

And speak unto him, saying,
Thus speaketh the Lord of hosts, saying,
Behold the man whose name is The Branch;
and he shall grow up out of his place,
and he shall build the temple of the Lord.

ZECHARIAH 6:12

From another point of view they had to proclaim the hopefulness of the Future. They had to show that the Gospel fully satisfies the inmost wants of a man's nature; that not only removes the leprosy of castes and the blindness of pagan sensuality, but gives help and strength to the hopeless sufferer who has no one to put him in the healing waters, while it confers pardon on the returning prodigal and happiness on the believing robber. They had to connect Christianity with Man.[1]

-Brooke Foss Westcott, *An Introduction to the Study of the Gospels*

If ... St. Matthew presents to us our Redeemer more especially as the Messiah, the Son of Abraham and the Son of David; if St. Mark more especially presents Him to us as the incarnate and wonder-working Son of God, assuredly St. Luke presents Him to us in the most wide and universal aspects as the God-man, the Friend and Redeemer of fallen humanity, yea, even as his own genealogy declares it, not merely the Son of David and the Son of Abraham, but the Son of Adam and the Son of God.[2]

-C. J. Ellicott, *Historical Lectures on the Life of Our Lord Jesus Christ*

St. Luke ... wrote in Greece, for the bright, clever, affable Greek world. Hence his Gospel is in its language the most accurate, in its order the most historical and artistic. It is the first volume of a great narrative, tracing the victorious advance of Christianity from Galilee to Jerusalem, from Jerusalem to Antioch, from Antioch on its westward course to Rome. It reflects the tone of mind which was prevalent in the school of St. Paul. It is the universal Gospel of the Gentile convert. It does not deal with the yearnings of the past, or with the glory of the present, but with the aspirations of the future. It paints Christ's Gospel not as the fulfillment of Prophecy, or as "the Kingdom of the Age," but as the satisfaction of our moral cravings; it describes Jesus to us, not as the Jewish Messiah, or the Universal Lord, but as the Savior of sinners. One of its keynotes is "My spirit hath rejoiced in God my Savior." It is a Gospel, not national, but universal; not regal, but human. It is the Gospel, "cleansed from the leprosy of castes," and the blindness of limitations. It is the Gospel for sinners, for Samaritans, for Gentiles. It is "the revelation of divine mercy;" it is "the manifestation of divine philanthropy." It is Christianity for man.[3]

-F. W. Farrar, *The Messages of the Books*

---

[1] Brooke Foss Westcott, *An Introduction to the Study of the Gospels* (London: Macmillan & Co., 1875), 219-20.

[2] C. J. Ellicott, *Historical Lectures on the Life of Our Lord Jesus Christ, Being the Hulsean Lectures for the Year 1859. With Notes, Critical, Historical, and Explanatory* (Boston: Gould and Lincoln, 1867), 42-43.

[3] F. W. Farrar, *The Messages of the Books Being Discourses and Notes on the Books of the New Testament* (New York: E. P. Dutton & Co., 1885), 17.

Figure IV-1. Mihaly Munkacsy: Christ Before Pilate

Luke was, indeed, the first true historian of the life and work of Jesus Christ, yet "what he wrote was to serve not only as a history of the Christian religion but a defense of it. Both the Gospel and Acts are planned to refute the allegation that Christianity is a merely Jewish creed, and that from the first it was condemned by the officials of Rome. . . . Luke does this most effectively by showing that our Lord addressed His message to Jew and Gentile alike, that it was a Jewish crowd which clamored for His death,"[4] and a Roman procurator who affirmed His innocence. Not once, but three times Luke tells us that Pilate found no fault in Christ (cf. Luke 23:4, 14, 22).

While the ministry of Christ and the program of the Church may have at times appeared to be hindered by secular powers and other annoying circumstances, it needs to be remembered that the success of Christianity is independent of earthly conditions. Regardless of the outcome of Christ's trial before Pilate, the purposes of God would be realized. In fact, it was not Christ's fate that was determined before that Roman Tribunal; rather, the accusers and judges of the Lord sealed their own destinies on that day.

"Christ stands in the center of composition. . . . His searching glance in reality reverses the relations that he and Pilate sustain. . . . He is in reality Judge, and Pilate is on trial. Pilate is measuring himself against a great ideal of Law, which in spite of their faults the Romans had established throughout the circle of the lands; he is being weighed in the balances and found wanting. And the Roman governor, like the traitor Judas, will be written "Guilty" on the judgment-rolls of eternity."[5]

---

[4] Anthony C. Deane, *How to Understand the Gospels* (New York: Harper & Brothers Publishers, 1929), 140-41.

[5] Albert Edward Bailey, *The Gospel in Art* (Boston: The Pilgrim Press, 1946), 339.

Chapter Nine

The Gospel of Luke: Evidence Through Witnesses

In the first four verses of his narrative Luke revealed his intentions in writing yet another account of the life and ministry of Jesus Christ. Using a literary device not found in the other Gospels, he wrote:

Forasmuch as many have taken in hand to set forth in order a declaration of those things which are most surely believed among us, Even as they delivered them unto us, which from the beginning were eyewitnesses, and ministers of the word; It seemed good to me also, having had perfect understanding of all things from the very first, to write unto thee in order, most excellent Theophilus, That thou mightest know the certainty of those things, wherein thou hast been instructed. 1:1-4

The style of Luke's preface followed the literary convention of his day. This can be seen by comparing it with the writings of the well-known historian, Flavius Josephus. His *Against Apion*, Book I, begins:

I suppose that by my books of the Antiquity of the Jews, most excellent Epaphroditus, I have made it evident to those who peruse them, that our Jewish nation is of very great antiquity, and had a distinct subsistence of its own originally; as also, I have therein declared how we came to inhabit this country wherein we now live. Those Antiquities contain the history of five thousand years, and are taken out of our sacred books, but are translated by me into the Greek tongue. However, since I observe a considerable number of people giving ear to the reproaches that are laid against us by those who bear ill-will to us, and will not believe what I have written concerning the antiquity of our nation, . . . I therefore have thought myself under an obligation to write somewhat briefly about these subjects, in order to convict those that reproach us of spite and voluntary falsehood, and to correct the ignorance of others, and withal to instruct all those who are desirous of knowing the truth of what great antiquity we really are. As for the witnesses whom I shall produce for the proof of what I say, they shall be such as are esteemed to be of the greatest reputation for truth, and the most skillful in the knowledge of all antiquity by the Greeks themselves.[1]

Josephus wrote in a style that would render his work "acceptable to the learned and accomplished of all nations"[2] and in this he succeeded. Although he was descended from Jewish nobility, Josephus designed his writing for Gentile readers, and became recognized as one of the great historians of his day.

Josephus . . . was esteemed in the first ages of Christianity as an author deserving a high degree of respect for research and integrity. Pious and learned men of later ages have continued to view him in the same light. The care bestowed upon numerous editions of his works in the original Greek proves that they have been deemed worthy of the attention of the most erudite of modern scholars.[3]

It has been suggested that "the works of Josephus may be placed, at least, on a level with the most esteemed monuments of ancient learning"[4] and the same can be said for the Gospel of Luke. Furthermore, the very fact that Luke, like Josephus, "followed the prevailing literary fashion of his day indicates part of his purpose—to make his Gospel acceptable to the literate man."[5] Using the best Greek of any of the evangelists, Luke fashioned his narrative for the representatives of reason, culture, and learning in the ancient world.

Yet the preface suggests an intent more definite and a more wide-ranging purpose.

With the admission that many others have undertaken to compile a narrative about the things that he will relate, Luke obviously gives up any claim to originality. Nor does he claim a divine revelation superseding all other previous accounts. Yet the opening verses unmistakably give the impression that he means to set things right in this Gospel. Though there have been other compilers and eyewitnesses and ministers of the word, Luke purposes to write a better . . . Gospel than anything yet presented.[6]

Luke's intention to write an accurate, historical account *"of those things which are most surely believed among us"* (1:1), based on eyewitness testimony as well as his own *"perfect understanding of all things from the very first"* (1:3), would be of special interest to the Greeks, who knew a thing or two about the subject of history. One author explains:

History as we know it, as the systematic analysis of past events, was a Greek creation. Herodotus (c. 484-425 B.C.), an Ionian Greek from Asia Minor, has rightly been called the "father of history" since his *History of the Persian Wars* is usually regarded as the first real history in Western civilization. It is indeed the earliest lengthy Greek prose work to have survived intact.[7]

The Greek word *historia* from which we obviously derive our word "history," actually means "research," and it is translated this way in *The Histories* of Herodotus. Furthermore, it is in the opening line of this great work that we find the first recorded use of the word:

These are the researches of Herodotus of Harlicarnassus, which he publishes, in the hope of thereby preserving from decay the remembrance of what men have done, and of preventing the great and wonderful actions of the Greeks and the Barbarians from losing their due meed of glory; and withal to put on record what were their grounds of feud.[8]

As a result of their overseas trade and travel, especially under the Persian Empire, the Ionian Greeks developed what has been called "an ethnographical literature. Thus they were able to measure their traditions against the antiquity of the east and to recognize the importance of first-hand inquiry, which is the root meaning of 'history'. Writers in this style, the 'logographers,' used literary prose, and their work reached its height in the 5th century B.C."[9] The Greeks were not only the inventors, but "remain the unsurpassed masters of the artistic form of history."[10] As one authority noted:

That extraordinary insight into the true conditions of harmony, proportion, and grace which guided them in other departments of literature and art did not forsake them in this. As in the drama a few tentative and experimental essays soon led to the master works of Aeschylus, Sophocles, and Aristophanes, so a few precursors were sufficient to direct Herodotus to the main outlines of historical composition. By one of those mysterious accidents, not to be accounted for, which produce genius, Herodotus was closely followed by the greatest mind that ever applied itself to history. Thucydides remains the unsurpassed ideal of artistic history. As the famous statue of Polycletus, called the Doryphorus, represented the proportions of the human body in such complete beauty "that it was regarded by the ancient artists as a canon of the rules on this point," so the history of the Peloponnesian War may serve, as its author seemed to know it would, as a model which all may copy, but none may equal.[11]

Shortly after Herodotus wrote his famous account of the Persian Wars, Thucy-dides began his classic study of the Peloponnesian War between Athens and Sparta. "These men recorded contemporary or near-contemporary events in prose narra-tives of striking style, depending as much as possible on eyewitness or other reliable testimony for evidence."[12]

The works of Herodotus and Thucydides are extremely significant in view of the fact that "until modern times, history was regarded primarily as a special kind of literature that shared many techniques and effects with fictional narrative. Historians were committed to factual materials and personal truthfulness, but like writers of fiction they wrote detailed narratives of events and vivid character sketches with great attention to language and style,"[13] Writing at the very beginning of the twen-tieth century, one scholar noted:

> History never deviated from the lines laid down by the Greeks till the advent of the modern school towards the end of the last and the beginning of this century. Between Thucydides and Gibbon there is no change of the ideal plan on which history should be written, though of course there is every degree of success and failure in striving after its realization.[14]

The ideal historian would combine rigorous truthfulness with a gift of developed expression, and Luke was such an historian. His account of the life and ministry of Jesus Christ is marked by beauty of style and noted for accuracy of detail. Not only is the third Gospel the most comprehensive of the four, but "many of the most beautiful acts, parables and sayings of Jesus known to us today appear only in Luke's narrative."[15]

History has been defined as "the prose narrative of past events, as probably true as the fallibility of human testimony will allow."[16] Because of the infallibility of divine inspiration, however, Luke's record is absolutely true! Over the years numerous attempts have been made to disprove some of the statements in his Gospel, yet all have been unsuccessful. For example, "Sir William Ramsay, who had few peers in classical studies and none in the historical geography of Asia Minor, could find no flaw in Luke's produc-tion."[17] He wrote:

> You may press the words of Luke in a degree beyond any other historian's, and they stand the keenest scrutiny and the hardest treatment, provided always that the critic knows his subject and does not go beyond the limits of science and justice.[18]

Very few historians can write history that is truthful in every respect and free of personal bias. This stress on truthfulness was one of the factors, which gave the works of Herodotus and Thucydides an authority that influenced succeeding historians; yet Luke's work is superior to that of the Greeks or their successors.

Will and Ariel Durant spent four decades writing *The Story of Civilization*. Designed to accompany these ten monumental volumes, they also put together *The Lessons of His-tory*, wherein they confessed:

To begin with, do we really know what the past was, what actually happened, or is history "a fable" not quite "agreed upon"? Our knowledge of any past event is always incomplete, probably inaccurate, beclouded by ambivalent evidence and biased historians, and perhaps distorted by our own patriotic or religious partisanship. "Most history is guessing, and the rest is prejudice."[19]

The Durants went on to say that the writing of history could not be considered a science.

It can only be an industry, an art, and a philosophy—an industry by ferreting out the facts, an art by establishing a meaningful order in the chaos of materials, a philosophy by seeking perspective and enlightenment.[20]

If this were the case, Dr. Luke was—in addition to whatever industrious disposition he possessed—a master artist and a wise philosopher. His writing of history was an art by beautifully setting forth *"in order a declaration of those things which are most surely believed among us"* (1:1). It was also a philosophy by seeking perspective and enlightenment that we might *"know the certainty to those things"* (1:4) wherein we have been instructed.

Luke stresses that he is going to write an "orderly account" (vs. 3). This cannot mean he is going to arrange his account differently, for Luke generally follows Mark's order. Probably Luke refers to his general scheme for placing Jesus within the history of the Church. He emerges as an author who is quite aware of what he is doing. . . . He seeks to write a Gospel of Jesus which will serve as the foundation of the Church. Luke understands himself as living at a time in which true remembering needs to take place, and wishes to recover and reformulate the roots of Christian faith so that the certainty and continuity of Christian faith from the beginning up to the present can be established: from Israel through Jesus to the Church. Implied within this positive purpose is Luke's intention that his reader be guarded from error or heresy—which is another way of saying the reader must hear the whole Christian tradition, not just part of it.[21]

In order to accomplish his purpose and insure the truthfulness of his account, Luke emphasizes the twofold nature of witness. In his opening chapter, for example, we find the following:

The birth of Jesus is coupled with the birth of John. A revelation occurs to Mary, the mother of Jesus; a revelation is also given to Zechariah, husband of Elizabeth, mother of John the Baptist. Both Simeon (2:22 ff.) and the prophetess Anna (2:36 ff.) testify to Jesus.[22]

Throughout his Gospel Luke affirms "the necessity for accurate and continuous witness."[23] This emphasis "consists of accurate observation (eyewitnesses) and truthful testifying (ministers of the word). Apostles, disciples, and women accompanied Jesus throughout his ministry; they in turn became, or were followed by, preachers who declared Jesus' own themes of repentance and forgiveness (Luke 15; 24:47; Acts 2:38)."[24]

The Introduction (1:1-2:52)

In the opening chapters of his account, Luke records the birth stories of both John the Baptist and Jesus of Nazareth. The degree to which these events are described is noteworthy, as the ministry of the former was to bear witness to that of the latter (cf. John 1:6-8). Next Luke records the twofold witness of Simeon and Anna in the Temple (2:22-40), followed by the incident in the same location when Jesus was twelve years old, whereupon it was noted that *"Jesus increased in wisdom and stature, and in favor"* by the twofold witness of *"God and man"* (2:52).

Selecting the Witnesses (3:1-9:50)

The first major section in Luke's Gospel narrates Jesus' gathering of witnesses in Galilee.

> Many people flock to him (4:15, 42; 5:1, 15); Some are in opposition (5:30; 6:2) and remain only in the crowd (6:17; 7:11); but he gathers the disciples (5:1-1). Indeed, from the disciples, he calls the twelve together whom he "named apostles" (6:13; cf. Mark 3:14). Here in Jesus' own territory there is the gathering of those who will be witnesses to carry on his work after his death. (At Jesus' ascension, two men address the disciples as "men of Galilee"—Acts 1:11.) The continuing importance of women is shown by their inclusion alongside the twelve as part of Jesus' retinue (8:2 f.). Later, they too, along with the twelve, will be witnesses. "The women who had come with him from Galilee followed, and saw the tomb, and how his body was laid; then they returned, and prepared spices and ointments" (23:55 f.; see 23:49). Luke seeks to establish certainty of witness: someone had accompanied Jesus all the time, from his baptism until the day when he was taken up (see Acts 1:21 f.).[25]

This certainty of witness that Luke seeks to establish would be an essential requirement for the success of the Church in the days ahead. Addressing the disciples just prior to His ascension, the Lord said:

> *But ye shall receive power, after that the Holy Ghost is come upon you: and ye shall be witnesses unto me both in Jerusalem, and in all Judaea, and in Samaria, and unto the uttermost part of the earth.* ACTS 1:8

Other Scriptures declare: *"It is also written in your law, that the testimony of two men is true"* (John 8:17).

The testimony of true witnesses would be necessary to meet the needs of the future, and Luke records this evidence for posterity. "Gathering sure disciples in Galilee assures the faithful continuation of the word of God into the time of the Church,"[26] and the Gospel of Luke documents this witness for the Church in every age.

> The conclusion of the first part of Luke, "the gathering of witnesses in Galilee," begins a discussion of Jesus' identity, and especially of the necessity of his suffering (9:21-27, 43b-45). At the close of this first major section instead of Mark's "he that is not against us is for us" (Mark 9:40), Luke's Jesus says, "he that is not against you is for you" (9:50 RSV). These are clearly instructions for the early church. Luke anticipates the separation of Jesus from his disciples in the post resurrection period after Jesus has ascended into heaven (cf. Acts 1:9-11).[27]

Instructing the Witnesses (9:51-19:27)

"The Galilean witnesses gathered by Jesus must journey with him to Jerusalem. Luke's second major section, which narrates the journey, seems much longer than the short distance (about sixty miles) and the brief time (about three days) that it would take to travel from Galilee to Jerusalem."[28] Luke's reason for such an extensive account of the trip, however, is not geographic, but didactic. In this portion of Scripture we find Jesus instructing the witnesses as to the meaning of those things, which they would eventually observe and proclaim.

The opening verse is a key for this section, "when the days drew near for him to be received up, he set his face to go up to Jerusalem" (9:51; only in Luke). Jesus goes to Jerusalem because, "I must go on my way today and tomorrow and the day following; for it cannot be that a prophet should perish away from Jerusalem" (13:33; only in Luke). As prophet to Israel, Jesus goes to Jerusalem, the capitol of Israel. The journey turns out to be instruction in the purpose and meaning of Jesus' death. . . .

Luke stresses a theme of witness throughout this section in two senses: (1) a witness observes something; (2) a witness testifies to something. These senses correspond to his distinction between "eyewitnesses and ministers of the word" (1:2). The first two episodes (9:51-56 and 9:57-62; mainly special Lukan material) indicate the necessity of following Jesus closely— that is, of observing. The mission of the seventy (10:1-17) implies that the twelve remained with Jesus even during the sending out of the seventy (10:1; note "other"); moreover, the disciples are singled out, "Then turning to the disciples he said privately, "Blessed are the eyes which see what you see!'" (10:23; cf. Matt. 13:16). Other passages point out that disciples are always with Jesus so that his journey has been faithfully observed (11:1; 12:1, 22, 41; 16:1; 17:1, 5, 22). By the end of this section the emphasis includes not only faithful observation but also faithful testifying to what has been observed (cf. 19:11-27).[29]

The journey motif that Luke set in motion in his Gospel is further developed in his account of the Acts of the Apostles.

A comparison of the structure of Luke's Gospel with that of the Acts of the Apostles reveals a striking similarity that helps to illuminate the reason for the journey. In Acts the order is: first, the Spirit's appearance in Jerusalem; second, journeys of missionaries, especially Paul; third, Paul's arrest and trial ending in Rome. In Luke the order is: first, gathering of witnesses in Galilee; second, the journey to Jerusalem accompanied by preaching the word; third, Jesus' arrest, trial, crucifixion, and resurrection in Jerusalem. Together Luke-Acts shows a continuity of witness stretching from Galilee to Rome; the journey motif emphasizes an orderly, gradual development of the new faith.[30]

Hearing the Witnesses (19:28-24:53)

In the third and final section of his Gospel, Luke relates the passion and resurrection of Jesus Christ. A major motif of this portion of Scripture is the trial and death of the innocent Jesus.

A special Lukan detail illustrates this emphasis: at Jesus' trial before Pilate, the elders of the people accuse Jesus of having forbidden the giving of tribute to Caesar (23:1-5; cf. Mark 15:1-5), but an earlier debate about Jesus' authority absolutely established the falsity of this charge (20:19-26). In Mark, Pilate, the Roman procurator, finds Jesus not guilty on only one occasion (15:14), but in Luke this verdict of innocence occurs three times (cf. 23:4, 14-16, 22). Luke alone records the incident of Herod's declaring Jesus innocent (23:6 ff.). Furthermore, in Luke the centurion at the cross says, "Certainly, this man was innocent" (23:47); whereas in Mark he said, "Truly this man was the Son of God" (15:39; cf. Matt. 27:54). The subtle way in which Luke opposes Jesus to Barabbas suggests that Jesus was not an insurrectionist like Barabbas (cf. Luke 23:19, 25 with Mark 15:7). Jesus' climactic word from the cross establishes his innocence, "Father, forgive them for they know not what they do" (23:34; only in Luke). Luke further underlines Jesus' innocence as one of the thieves from the cross says, "We are receiving the due reward of our deeds; but this man has done nothing wrong" (23:41; only in Luke). This major theme receives further and unqualified substantiation in Acts, "This Jesus . . . you crucified and killed by the hands of lawless men" (Acts 2:23; cf. Acts 8:32 ff. and 17:30).[31]

The Lord was falsely accused, shamefully tried, and cruelly executed, although witnesses testified to His innocence. Yet Luke does not focus on the victimization of Christ, or the official misconduct of His executioners.

Instead of concentrating upon the guilt of those responsible for this miscarriage of justice, Luke focuses upon Jesus' triumph even under adversity. At the cross Jesus' general word of forgiveness (23:34) and his forgiveness of the repentant thief (23:39-43) show that guilt need not be overwhelming. Finally, this passion is the working out of God's plan ("This Jesus, delivered up according to the definite plan and foreknowledge of God"—Acts 2:23; cf. 3:18 and Luke 22:22). Jesus dies a martyr's death prefiguring the martyrdom of others in the early church, especially Stephen and James (cf. Acts 7:54-8:3; 9:1; 12:1 ff.). But through all these events God's word of "repentance and forgiveness of sins" is being preached to all nations (24:47), and his plan thus fulfilled.[32]

The fulfillment of God's plan required that Jesus Christ be resurrected from the dead, and the accurate and continuous witness found in Luke's Gospel guarantees the authenticity of this crucial event. His account of the empty tomb, the initial reaction of the disciples, and the incident on the road to Emmaus, all reveal the importance of corroborating, eyewitness testimony. Whereas Mark's Gospel has the women entering the sepulcher greeted by *"a young man"* (Mark 16:5), Luke tells us *"two men stood by them in shining garments"* (Luke 24:4).

Moreover, Luke's story of the empty tomb points ahead to the confirmatory appearances to the disciples, for when the apostles hear the report from the women, "these words seemed to them an idle tale, and they did not believe them" (24:11). Luke's stress upon both continuity and certainty required more than an account by excited women. Full recognition of the resurrected Jesus occurs only when his followers meet him on the road to Emmaus (24:13

ff.). That this meeting takes place "on the road" is in keeping with the journey motif of Luke; and this encounter will prepare the disciples for their preaching throughout the Roman world. Furthermore, we hear twice in this episode about "the things that have happened" (24:14, 18); indeed, Jesus asks, "What things?" (24:19). These lines recall the Gospel's introduction, for this was to be a narrative about "the things which have been accomplished among us" (1:1; cf. 1:4).[33]

The puzzling aspect of this encounter on the Emmaus Road is that the two witnesses did not immediately recognize Jesus. Nevertheless, God must have willed it so, for Luke says, *"But their eyes were holden that they should not know him"* (24:16).

At this point the Lord uses the opportunity to have the two disciples review the events of the last few days and instruct them regarding their proper significance.

> *And he said unto them, What manner of communications are these that ye have one to another, as ye walk, and are sad? And the one of them, whose name was Cleopas, answering said unto him, Art thou only a stranger in Jerusalem, and hast not known the things which are come to pass there in these days? And he said unto them, What things? And they said unto him, Concerning Jesus of Nazareth, which was a prophet mighty in deed and word before God and all the people: And how the chief priests and our rulers delivered him to be condemned to death, and have crucified him. But we trusted that it had been he which should have redeemed Israel: and beside all this, to day is the third day since these things were done. Yea, and certain women also of our company made us astonished, which were early at the sepulcher; And when they found not his body, they came, saying, that they had also seen a vision of angels, which said that he was alive. And certain of them which were with us went to the sepulcher, and found it even so as the women had said: but him they saw not. Then he said unto them, O fools, and slow of heart to believe all that the prophets have spoken: Ought not Christ to have suffered these things, and to enter into his glory? And beginning at Moses and all the prophets, he expounded unto them in all the scriptures the things concerning himself. And they drew nigh unto the village, whither they went: and he made as though he would have gone further. But they constrained him, saying, Abide with us: for it is toward evening, and the day is far spent. And he went in to tarry with them. And it came to pass, as he sat at meat with them, he took bread, and blessed it, and brake, and gave to them. And their eyes were opened, and they knew him; and he vanished out of their sight.* 24:17-31

"The crucial moment of recognition comes during the meal. . . . Later their report confirms that the decisive act was 'the breaking of bread'"[34] Luke notes:

> *And they rose up the same hour, and returned to Jerusalem, and found the eleven gathered together, and them that were with them, Saying, The Lord is risen indeed, and hath appeared to Simon. And they told what things were done in the way, and how he was known of them in breaking of bread.* 24:33-35

There are at least two immediate possibilities for understanding the significance of the "breaking of bread": (1) Jesus performed a familiar act which they had often observed; therefore, they recognized him; (2) the "breaking of bread" was a sacramental communal act of worship in the early church (Acts 2:42, 46), and Luke thereby implies that the believer knows the resurrected Jesus primarily in the sacrament of the church. Neither view is wholly satisfying. The first ignores the fact that Jesus must have done other familiar things on the way, and the second presupposes a strong sacramental emphasis not otherwise present in Luke.

A different interpretation takes its cue from the act of eating. In the following story (24:36-43), even though Jesus appears directly to the disciples and tells them to look at his hands and feet, they still "disbelieved for joy" (vs. 41). Only after he has eaten does he speak his farewell address. Again, eating seems to be crucial for full recognition. The closest previous reference to eating was during the last supper with the apostles (22:14-19), at which Jesus said, "I have earnestly desired to eat this Passover with you before I suffer; for I tell you I shall not eat it until it is fulfilled in the kingdom of God" (vss. 15 f.; only in Luke). Evidently, Jesus will not eat until suffering is accomplished. That he now eats with the disciples indicates that his suffering has been completed and that he is now raised to glory. Therefore, in Luke the scripture interpretation emphasizes the necessity for suffering (24:26 f.), and the eating with the disciples (24:30, 35, 42 f.) emphasizes that the suffering is accomplished and the glory of Jesus has begun. With that sure foundation, the church can now receive its charge from the risen Christ.[35]

Summary and Conclusion

The purpose of the Gospel of Luke is to provide evidence through witnesses, in order that all future generations might *"know the certainty of those things"* wherein they have been instructed (cf. 1:4). As one commentator noted:

Of all the Gospel writers Luke is the most consciously interested in preserving the truth about the life of Jesus. But for him, as for most so-called "historians" in the first century, truth is not simply equated with historical data. Luke intended for his reader to see the life of Jesus through a proper perspective, that of the third generation. He wrote so that careful observation and a comprehensive outlook would be available to the church of his day.[36]

The writings of Luke are distinctive, and reveal his insight into the needs of the future.

Only Luke follows his Gospel on Jesus with a second volume on the early church. In itself this structure indicates Luke's interest not only in Jesus, but also in the church which he originated. A long-range perspective on the life of Jesus is also suggested by the preface, where Luke writes of three stages of the tradition: eyewitnesses, ministers of the word, and writing of the Gospel.

In Luke's introduction Simeon, a man of Israel who has long awaited salvation, is finally rewarded by Jesus' appearance to him in the temple. Toward the close of his life Jesus frequents the temple and, in effect, triumphs in this central religious institution of Israel. After Jesus' death and resurrection the disciples return to the temple in order to wait for the coming of the Spirit, which will empower their preaching of repentance and forgiveness to all people. Their testimony to Jesus' message is certain because they have observed its beginning from Galilee to Jerusalem.[37]

Together, the books of Luke and Acts "show how the old is incorporated into the new. Israel is on a journey through the Old Testament culminating in the life of Jesus and moving into the early church. Luke's structure is devised to insure that the journey has been closely recorded and presented in the correct order."[38]

At the end of the Gospel the disciples are in the temple blessing God and waiting for the Spirit's coming with power for the mission. At the end of Acts of the Apostles Paul is preaching in Rome and things will turn out well. Luke idealizes the story, perhaps, but he thereby testifies to the faith and history of Jesus and the early church. What was founded by Jesus, observed by the apostles, and proclaimed by them will continue without faltering until all [who are chosen] have come into the kingdom of God and the fellowship of the Lord Jesus Christ "quite openly and unhindered" (Acts 28:31).[39]

The book of Acts seems to end rather abruptly, but the last words recorded are actually a fitting culmination of an argument implicit in both volumes of Luke's two-part work. The concluding statement reveals that Luke wanted to do more than provide us with an invaluable record of the life of Christ and of early Christianity. "What he wrote was to serve not only as a history of the Christian religion but a defense of it."[40]

It is quite obvious . . . that Luke's historical motivation was not the only purpose for writing. For one thing, he was anxious to answer charges of sedition by proving that Jesus was not a political revolutionary intent on overturning the Roman government. Persecutions arose as soon as it became clear that Christianity was not simply a Jewish sect but a separate movement whose founder had been duly examined and condemned by a Roman court. This was sufficient proof that he was politically dangerous, for Roman justice could not be challenged. In the Gospels of Mark and Matthew there is an obvious attempt on the part of Christian apologists to show that the Jews, and the Jews only, were responsible for the execution of Jesus. His death was strictly a religious matter and had nothing to do with politics. Luke carries this apologetic interest farther, going out of his way to stress the moral and religious nature of Jesus' ministry and teaching. In Luke's account of the trial of Jesus, Pilate asserts no less than three times that he found no evidence for a criminal charge.[41]

And the whole multitude of them arose, and led him unto Pilate. And they began to accuse him, saying, We found this fellow perverting the nation, and forbidding to give tribute to Caesar, saying that he himself is Christ a King. And Pilate asked him, saying, Art thou the King of the Jews? And he answered him and said, Thou sayest it. Then said Pilate to the chief priests and to the people, I find no fault in this man. And they were the more fierce, saying, He stirreth up the people, teaching throughout all Jewry, beginning from Galilee to this place. . . . And Pilate . . . said unto them, Ye have brought this man unto me, as one that perverteth the people: and, behold, I, having examined him before you, have found no fault in this man touching those things whereof ye accuse him: No, nor yet Herod: for I sent you to him; and, lo, nothing worthy of death is done unto him. I will therefore chastise him, and release him. (For of necessity he must release one unto them at the feast.) And they cried out all at once, saying, Away with this man, and release unto us Barabbas: (Who for a certain sedition made in the city, and for murder, was cast into prison.) Pilate therefore, willing to release Jesus, spake again to them. But they cried, saying, Crucify him, crucify him. And he said unto them the third time, Why, what evil hath he done? I have found no cause of death in him: I will therefore chastise him, and let him go. And they were instant with loud voices, requiring that he might be crucified. And the voices of them and of the chief priests prevailed.

> *And Pilate gave sentence that it should be as they required. And he released unto them him that for sedition and murder was cast into prison, whom they had desired; but he delivered Jesus to their will* 23:1-5, 13-25

Herod Antipas had agreed with Pilate that Jesus was innocent of anything worthy of death (cf. 23:6-12). As such, "the blame is laid entirely on the Jews in contrast to the Romans, whose view is represented by the centurion at the foot of the cross."[42]

> *Now when the centurion saw what was done, he glorified God, saying, Certainly this was a righteous man.* 23:47

Then the reader should notice with what skill St. Luke carries out the same purpose in his second volume. He shows how the attacks on St. Paul came not from Rome, but from the Jews, how one Roman court after another—of Gallio, of Felix, of Festus—found him innocent; how well-disposed to him were various Roman officials, from Sergius Paulus onwards; how his transshipment to Rome came not from any condemnation by a Roman tribunal but from his own action: "This man might have been set at liberty if he had not appealed to Caesar." And at the end, with this clue to his purpose, we shall see that the last words of the book are no tame casual sentence, but a triumphant climax. If this Christian teacher had been regarded as a dangerous traitor by the authorities at Rome, what would have happened upon his arrival there? He would have been allowed to utter no word of his mischievous doctrine. He would have been flung into prison. His trial and execution would have followed swiftly. Such must have been the sequel if this theory were true that in the first days Rome condemned Christianity as treasonable. But what, in point of fact, did happen?[43]

> *And Paul dwelt two whole years in his own hired house, and received all that came in unto him, Preaching the kingdom of God, and teaching those things which concern the Lord Jesus Christ, with all confidence, no man forbidding him.* ACTS 28:30-31

> *Be it known therefore unto you, that the salvation of God is sent unto the Gentiles, and that they will hear it.* ACTS 28:28

Chapter Nine Notes

[1] William Whiston, Trans., *The Life and Works of Flavius Josephus* (Philadelphia: The John C. Winston Company, n.d.), 858.

[2] Henry Stebbing, Introduction to *The Life and Works of Flavius Josephus*, trans. by William Whiston, (Philadelphia: The John C. Winston Company, n.d.), vi.

[3] *Ibid.*, xiv.

[4] *Ibid.*, v.

[5] Robert A. Spivey and D. Moody Smith, *Anatomy of the New Testament: A Guide to Its Structure and Meaning*, 2nd ed. (New York: Macmillan Publishing Co., Inc., 1974), 152.

[6] *Ibid.*, 152-53.

[7] Jackson J. Spielvogel, *Western Civilization*, Vol. I: To 1715, 2nd ed. (Minneapolis/St. Paul: West Publishing Company, 1994), 85.

[8] Herodotus, *The Histories*, trans. by George Rawlinson, with introduction by Rosalind Thomas (New York: Alfred A. Knopf, Inc., 1997), 5.

[9] "History," *Encyclopaedia Britannica* (1970), 11:530.

[10] "History," *Encyclopaedia Britannica* (1903), XII:19.

[11] *Ibid.*, 19-20.

[12] "History and Historiography," *Funk & Wagnalls New Encyclopedia* (1990), 13:127.

[13] Ibid.

[14] "History," *Encyclopaedia Britannica* (1903), XII:20.

[15] J. Norval Geldenhuys, "Luke," *The Biblical Expositor*, ed., Carl F. H. Henry (Philadelphia: A. J. Holman Company, 1973), 890.

[16] "History," *Encyclopaedia Britannica* (1903), XII:19.

[17] William Sanford LaSor, *Great Personalities of the New Testament: Their Lives and Times* (Westwood, N.J.: Fleming H. Revell Company, 1961), 134.

[18] Sir William Ramsay, *The Bearing of Recent Discoveries on the Truthfulness of the New Testament*, 4th ed. (London: Hodder & Stoughton, Ltd., 1920), 89.

[19] Will and Ariel Durant, *The Lessons of History* (New York: Simon and Schuster, 1968), 11-12.

[20] *Ibid.*, 12.

[21] Spivey, *op. cit.*, 154.

[22] *Ibid.*, 155.

[23] *Ibid.*, 179.

[24] *Ibid.*

[25] *Ibid.*, 161.

[26] *Ibid.*, 166.

[27] *Ibid.*

[28] *Ibid.*

[29] *Ibid.*, 167.

[30] *Ibid.*

[31] *Ibid.*, 172-73.

[32] *Ibid.*, 173.

[33] *Ibid.*, 176.

[34] *Ibid.*

[35] *Ibid.*, 176-77.

[36] *Ibid.*, 178.

[37] *Ibid.*

[38] *Ibid.*

[39] *Ibid.*, 180.

[40] Anthony C. Deane, *How to Understand the Gospels* (New York: Harper & Brothers Publishers, 1929), 132.

[41] Edward W. Bauman, *An Introduction to the New Testament* (Philadelphia: The Westminster Press, 1961), 121-22.

[42] *Ibid.*, 122.

[43] Deane, *op. cit.*, 133-34.

Chapter Ten

The Greeks: Cultured and Idealistic

Oliver Goldsmith (1728-1774) remains one of the foremost names in the field of English literature, which he enriched with such enduring works as *The Vicar of Wakefield* (1766), *The Deserted Village* (1770), and *She Stoops to Conquer* (1773). He was a gifted writer with a most pleasant style, but in practical matters Goldsmith's abilities were a different story.

By the time his fame and familiarity in London's literary circles had grown, he might also have been considered a prosperous man. Yet his extravagance and openhandedness toward needy friends found him spending far more than he was earning. As a result of increasing debts, Goldsmith contracted to produce popular books in order to supplement his already substantial income.

> He compiled for the use of schools a History of Rome, by which he made £300; a History of England, by which he made £600; a History of Greece, for which he received £250; a Natural History, for which the booksellers covenanted to pay him 800 guineas. These works he produced without any elaborate research, by merely selecting, abridging, and translating into his own clear, pure, and flowing language, what he found in books well known to the world, but too bulky or too dry for boys and girls.[1]

These contracted works produced by Goldsmith are very readable, if not replete. "Yet . . . few writers have done more to make the first steps in the laborious road to knowledge easy and pleasant. His compilations are widely distinguished from the compilations of ordinary bookmakers. He was a great, perhaps an unequaled, master of the art of selection and condensation. In these respects his histories . . . , even when most concise, are always amusing, and to read them is considered by intelligent children not as a task but as a pleasure."[2]

The histories of Goldsmith were read and enjoyed by generations of students in the English-speaking world, but are now generally out of circulation, if not cognizance as well. Yet they provide valuable insights into the structure and cultures of these earlier societies, and it is toward one of these histories that we now turn in order to better understand the people to whom Luke addressed his Gospel.

The History of Greece

In *Pinnock's Improved Edition of Dr. Goldsmith's History of Greece*, published in Philadelphia in 1838 as the first American edition of this work, we are introduced in Chapter One to the geographical character of Greece. It begins:

> A glance at the map of the world, as known to the ancients, will be sufficient to convince us, that no country derived more advantages from its natural position, than that which we, in imitation of the Romans, denominate Greece. It was in the center of the most cultivated portions of the three continents; a short passage by sea divided it from Italy; and the voyage to Egypt, Asia Minor, and Phoenicia, though somewhat longer, seemed scarcely more dangerous. Its extensive coasts, indented with bays, landing-places, and natural

harbors, compensated for the absence of large rivers, and pointed it out in the earliest ages as the country best situated for commerce; and though Phoenicia was the parent of navigation, that art is indebted to Greece for its most material improvements.

The nature of the country afforded the inhabitants other advantages equally striking; watered in every direction by an infinite number of small streams, intersected by ranges of lofty hills alternating with fertile plains, and enjoying a warmer climate than any other part of Europe, the Greeks were enabled to pay equal attention to the different branches of cultivation, and to pursue a diversity of occupations.[3]

After thirty more paragraphs of description of the natural and political geography of Greece, the chapter closes with these summary statements:

This survey of Greece, considered merely in its geographical character, enables us to deduce certain inferences which may throw light on the history of the nation. And first, it appears that Greece was naturally cut up into certain divisions, of which one could not easily control the other. Thessaly could not without difficulty retain dominion over the nations south of Mount Oeta; still less could Hellas exercise supremacy over the Peloponnesus, or the Peloponnesus over Hellas. There were limits provided by nature for those who desired and could enjoy freedom, within which liberty was secured against all attacks of neighboring states. It was easy to defend Thermopylae and the Corinthian isthmus. Even a foreign conqueror could effect little, so long as the nation refused to forge its own chains.

Secondly, there never was a country of the same extent as Greece, in which nature had done so much for the different branches of industry. It was not merely an agricultural, pastoral, or commercial country, but it was all three in conjunction. This variety of pursuits in active life, led to the acquisition of various kinds of knowledge, and prevented the narrowness of thought which arises from attention to a single object.

Finally, as we have already stated, no country afforded such facilities to navigation, while the art was as yet imperfect. On the way to Asia Minor and Phoenicia, one island almost touched another; it was not difficult to reach Italy; and the coasts of Egypt were not far distant from Crete. Thus does Greece appear, in the dispensation of Providence, to have been marked out as the country by which the blessings of civilization should be brought from the eastern into the western world.[4]

Nevertheless, geography alone could scarcely account for the unique qualities of the ancient Greeks. In another chapter Oliver Goldsmith describes the religion of Greece, contrasts it with the prevailing religions of the East, and explains its effects on the national character. He wrote:

Instead of enumerating the names and attributes of the deities, which may be found in any pantheon, we shall endeavor rather to discover what was the nature of the Grecian religion, in its effect on the character of the people, and contrast it with the superstitions of Asia. The great struggle between the eastern and western world is the most prominent feature in the ensuing history; any light that can be thrown on the character of the combatants will not only make us more interested in their fortunes, but also greatly assist us in understanding the nature of the contest.

Every inquiry that has been made into the superstitions that prevailed in Asia has contributed to prove, that the divinities of the East were purely elementary, or in other words, founded on some power or object of nature, and that the attribute which they principally contemplated in the object of their worship, was resistless power. The sun, the moon, the starry host, the earth, the river that watered the country, the storms and whirlwinds that laid waste the fields, these and similar objects mingled with rude ideas of a creating, preserving, and destroying power, formed the ground-work of the different religious systems that prevailed in the East. They did, indeed, sometimes represent their deities in the human form, because men naturally associate ideas of excellence with their own shape; but they did not from thence deduce that the deities were actuated by human feelings. The form was always a secondary consideration, and they did not hesitate to disfigure it by the most unnatural combinations, in order to convey more forcibly their ideas of divine power. The Hindoo represents his god with fifty arms, the Egyptians gave to their deities the heads and limbs of animals. In all these cases the statue was looked on as a symbol rather than a representation.

Beings possessed of boundless power, whom men had no reason to hope would sympathize in their condition, naturally inspired terror; hence the Asiatics adopted a religion of fear, and worshipped their gods rather to avert evil, than procure good. This naturally led to cruel sacrifices; human beings were and still continue to be offered up in the East, for mercy and love form no part of the attributes with which their deities are invested. The influence of such a belief on the mind must have been injurious in the highest degree; it predisposed men to slavery, because they were naturally ready to acknowledge in the government of their country, those principles by which they believed the whole world to be directed. Despotism in its worst form they looked upon as the great principle that ruled the natural world, their gods were to be conciliated, not by rectitude and piety, but by cruel sufferings, severe austerities, and inhuman sacrifices. We find that these same principles pervaded all the Asiatic forms of government; let us now see what practical effect they were likely to produce.

The Asiatics could have no idea of political rights or justice; their patriotism must have consisted in simple attachment to the soil, their only connection with the government was blind submission to the ruler's will. Hence, when a war broke out, they might fight for pay or plunder, through love of their leader, or attachment to their sovereign, but never from a desire to serve their country, or secure its independence. This simplified the business of conquest in the East; when an army was beaten the country was subdued, the general body of the people no more dreamed of resisting a victor, than they would attempt to struggle against an earthquake, or a whirlwind. Sesostris, Cyrus, Alexander, and many others, overran the East with forces scarcely sufficient to garrison one of its provinces.

From the same habit of looking on their individual leader as every thing and themselves as nothing, the success of an Asiatic army depended altogether on the character of its general. There was no emulation between the different bodies of the army, no soldier dared to think for himself, he fought indeed where he was commanded, but if his leader fell, or was made prisoner, he fought no longer; when the general fled, his army ran away; the Asiatics were habituated to act as mere machines, and consequently became useless when the moving power was destroyed. This was the fatal secret on which the fortune of Persia depended, the celebrated expedition of the ten thousand revealed it to the Greeks, and Alexander, by availing himself of the knowledge, decided the fate of the eastern world at Issus and Arbela.

The religion of the Greeks was one of the most extraordinary phenomena that the world ever witnessed; it was formed by the poets, and upheld by the fine arts. To use the expressive words of an old philosopher, its gods were immortal men, and its men were mortal gods. Instead of the single attribute of brute force, the divinities of Greece were supposed to possess all the passions and affections of human nature, joined indeed with the possession of supreme power, but power subjected to the control of wisdom and justice. Though many absurdities flowed from thus attributing human characters to the gods, it gave a warmth and affection to their worship, which produced salutary effects. The Greeks honored his deity as his friend, he presented the same gifts at the altar as he would have offered to a fellow-mortal whose favor he wished to conciliate, he celebrated the sacred festivals with songs and dances, because such things delighted himself, and gratified all his acquaintance. . . .

The most striking consequence of their religion was, the ardor with which the Greeks cultivated the fine arts. The gods were supposed to possess a human form, but the beauty and sublimity of their appearance was far superior to that of ordinary mortals. The poets labored to describe the majesty of the deities by the most lively images. The painter and statuary endeavored to embody these conceptions on the canvas, and in the marble. This was the origin of ideal beauty, or the discovery of the highest degree of perfection which the human form can be conceived to attain. Thus with its religion was associated all that makes the name of Greece honored by posterity; epic poetry celebrated the wars of gods, and heroes descended from them; the lyric writers composed hymns in their praise, and the dramatic writers labored strenuously to produce pieces worthy of being represented at their festivals; poetry, painting, sculpture, music, were cultivated, not so much for their own excellence, as for their connection with the service of deities, who were loved as friends, while they were worshipped as rulers.

All these circumstances combined to accelerate the progress of civilization in Greece. Athens had arrived at a pitch of refinement higher than Rome ever attained, when the entire west of Europe remained sunk in barbarism. But perhaps this very refinement may have been the chief cause of its ruin, by introducing a lavish expenditure in matters merely ornamental, and exhausting those treasures on which the nation relied for its defense, in splendid buildings, and pompous processions.[5]

By the beginning of the fifth century, B.C., most of the ancient world was dominated by one great empire. Founding the most powerful of all oriental kingdoms, the Medo-Persian alliance conquered, "one by one, all the ancient lands of the Middle East, spreading to the Mediterranean, and only prevented from occupying Europe by the courage, intelligence, and cunning of a relatively small number of Greeks, determined to be free."[6]

On the other side of the Aegean Sea, however, "the Ionian Greek cities in western Asia Minor had already fallen subject to the Persian Empire by the mid-sixth century B.C."[7]

> For a time the Ionians submitted to the Persian regime, even though they did not take kindly to it. But in 490 B.C., they revolted. This time Athens sent 20 shiploads of soldiers to help, and Eretria, on the island of Euboea, sent five. The Ionians began promisingly enough by advancing inland to the city of Sardis and burning it. After this initial sally, however, the Athenian and Eretrian allies went home, and the Ionians were left to their own resources. For a while they stubbornly struggled on alone, but ultimately the revolt collapsed.[8]

With the Ionian revolt crushed and the rebels punished, Darius the Great, the Persian monarch, decided to expand his empire westward, and at the same time chastise the European Greeks for giving aid to his rebellious subjects. To this end Darius began vast preparations for the invasion of Greece.

> A great army was gathered at the Hellespont under Mardonius, son-in-law of the king; and a large fleet was made ready to accompany the army with supplies. In 492, these forces set out, advancing along the shores of the Aegean. But the army suffered from the constant attacks by the savage Thracian Tribes, and finally, as the fleet was rounding the rocky promontory of Mount Athos, a terrible storm dashed it to pieces. With it were wrecked all hopes of success. Mardonius had no choice but to retreat into Asia as best he could.[9]

Although 300 ships had been lost and the army never did reach the Greek peninsula, Darius was undismayed by this disaster. He issued orders for the raising and equipping of a larger and stronger expeditionary force, displaced his son-in-law with two elder and abler generals, and sent them away "to what he considered as a certain conquest."[10] Goldsmith wrote:

> They were furnished with a fleet of six hundred ships, and an army of a hundred and twenty thousand men (of these ten thousand were cavalry); and their instructions were to give up Athens and Eretria to be plundered, to burn all the houses and temples, and to lead the inhabitants into captivity. The country was to be laid desolate, and the army was provided with a sufficient number of chains for binding the prisoners.[11]

In 490 B.C. the Persians sailed across the Aegean Sea, captured Eretria on the island of Euboea, and moved their army to the plain of Marathon, only 26 miles from Athens. "To oppose this formidable invasion," according to Goldsmith, "the Athenians had only about ten thousand men, but all of them animated with that invincible spirit which the love of liberty ever inspires."[12]

The Athenians seemed hopelessly outnumbered at Marathon, yet it was there that they determined to hold their ground. Goldsmith tells us:

There the Athenians resolved to oppose them; but not thinking themselves singly equal to such an undertaking, they sent first to the Spartans for assistance, and would certainly have obtained it, had it not been for a foolish superstition, which would not allow them to begin a march before the full moon.

They then applied to the other states of Greece; but these, except the Plataeans, who sent one thousand soldiers, were too much intimidated by the power of Persia to venture to move in their defense.

Obliged, therefore, to depend upon their own courage alone, they collected all their forces, to the number of eleven thousand freemen, with probably an equal number of armed slaves, and entrusted the command of them to ten generals, of whom Miltiades was the chief; and each of these was to have the direction of the troops for one day in regular succession.

But this arrangement was soon found to be so very inconvenient, that, by the advice of Aristeides, the chief command was vested in Miltiades alone, as the ablest and most experienced of all the generals.

At the same time it was resolved in a council of war, though only by a majority of one vote, to meet the enemy in the open field, instead of waiting for them within the walls of the city.

Miltiades, sensible of the inferiority of his numbers when compared to those of the enemy, endeavored to make up for this defect by taking possession of an advantageous ground. He therefore drew up his army at the foot of a mountain, so that the enemy should not be able to surround him, or charge him in the rear, At the same time he fortified his flanks with a number of large trees that were cut down for the purpose, and strewed the ground in his front with branches, piles of stones, and other obstacles, to impede the Persian cavalry, which in consequence seem to have been rendered useless in the engagement.

Datis [one of the Medo-Persian generals] saw the advantage which the Athenians must derive from this masterly disposition; but relying on the superiority of his numbers, and unwilling to wait till the Spartan succors should arrive, he resolved to begin the engagement.

The signal for battle, however, was no sooner given, than the Athenians, instead of waiting for the onset of the enemy, rushed in upon them, according to their usual custom, with irresistible fury.

The Persians regarded this as the result of madness and despair, rather than of deliberate courage; but they were soon convinced of their mistake, when they found that the Athenians maintained the charge with the same spirit with which they had begun it.

Miltiades had purposely and judiciously made his wings much stronger than his center, where the slaves were posted under the command of Themistocles and Aristeides.

The Persians, availing themselves of this circumstance, attacked the center with great bravery, and were just upon the point of making it give way, when the two wings, having now become victorious, suddenly wheeled about, and falling upon the enemy on both flanks at once, threw them into disorder.

The Persians fought with swords and battle-axes; the Greeks used the spear.

When their dense line of lances fell upon the hostile flanks, the shock was irresistible; the rout became universal, and the enemy fled to their ships with great precipitation. The Athenians pursued them as far as the beach, and even set several of their ships on fire. . . .

Seven of the enemy's ships were taken, and above six thousand men left dead upon the field of battle, not to mention those who were drowned as they were endeavoring to escape, or were consumed in the ships that were set on fire.

Of the Greeks there fell not above two hundred; and among these was Callimachus, who gave the casting vote for fighting the enemy in the field. . . .

Such was the famous battle of Marathon, one of the most important that is to be found in history, as it first taught the Greeks to despise the power of the Persian monarch, bravely to maintain their independence, and to go on cultivating those arts and sciences which had so evident a tendency to polish and refine their own manners, and which have since diffused their benign influence over all the rest of Europe.[13]

After some time the Persians would mount a third invasion of Europe under Xerxes—the son and successor of Darius—who "was bent on revenge and expansion."[14] Ten years after the Battle of Marathon, Xerxes crossed the Hellespont with one of the largest armies ever assembled in the ancient world. The Greeks were defeated at Thermopylae, and Athens, being abandoned, was sacked and burned. Meanwhile, the Persian navy—mostly Phoenician and Ionian vessels—pursued the Greek fleet to Salamis, an island in what is now known as the Saronic Gulf. It was here in 480 B.C. that one of the greatest naval battles in ancient history was fought. Goldsmith described it as follows:

As the Persians now fought under the eye of their sovereign, who beheld the action from a neighboring promontory, they exerted themselves for some time with great spirit; but their courage abated when they came to a closer engagement.

The numerous disadvantages of circumstances and situation then began to appear. The wind blew directly in their faces; the height and heaviness of their vessels rendered them unwieldy and almost useless; and even the number of their ships only served to embarrass and perplex them in that narrow sea.

The Ionians, mindful of their Hellenic descent, were far from being anxious for a victory that would have enslaved the land of their fathers; in the very first onset many of them fled, while others deserted to the Greeks. The Phoenician galleys being thus disordered, and their flanks exposed, dashed against each other, and crowded into a confused mass, deprived of all power of action. The Athenians, with consummate skill, increased the confusion by forcing fresh hostile ships into the narrow space in which the Phoenicians were entangled. And thus, as the poet Aeschylus, who personally shared in the battle, declares, the whole Persian fleet "was caught and destroyed like fish in a net."

In the general consternation which thus occasioned, Artemisia, queen of Halicarnassus, who had come to the assistance of Xerxes with five ships, exerted herself with so much spirit, that the monarch was heard to say, his soldiers behaved like women in the conflict, and the women like soldiers. Her glory, however, is sullied by the unjustifiable means which she made use of to escape from the fatal strait. The Athenian captain Ameinias, the brother of the poet Aeschylus, had distinguished himself above all his compeer, by superior skill in the management of his vessel, and by the havoc which he made in the hostile fleet. As he bore down against the galley of Artemisia, the queen, aware that resistance would be useless, ordered her pilot to run her ship against the galley of a Lycian prince, with whom she had been at variance. The Lycian vessel was run down, and all on board perished; Ameinias, conjecturing from this that the queen's ship was one of those that had deserted to the Greeks, gave over the pursuit, and Artemisia was enabled to continue her flight in safety.

Nothing, however, could repair the disorder that had now taken place in the Persian fleet. They fled on all sides; some of them were sunk, and more taken; above two hundred were burnt, and all the rest entirely dispersed.

Such was the issue of the battle of Salamis, in which the Persians received a more severe blow than any they had hitherto experienced from Greece.

Themistocles is said to have been so elated with this victory, that he proposed breaking down the bridge over the Hellespont, and thus cutting off the retreat of the enemy; but from this he was dissuaded by Aristeides, who represented the danger of reducing so powerful an army to despair.

Xerxes, however, seems to have been so apprehensive of this step being taken, that after leaving about three hundred thousand of his best troops behind him under Mardonius, not so much with a view of conquering Greece as in order to prevent a pursuit, he hastened back with the rest to the Hellespont, where, finding the bridge broken down with the violence of the waves, he was obliged to pass over in a small boat; and this manner of leaving Europe, when compared with his ostentatious entry, rendered his disgrace the more poignant and afflicting.[15]

In the following year, 479 B.C., The remainder of the Persian army and navy were defeated at the Battles of Plataea and Mycale, respectively. "On the very evening of the day which the victory at Plataea was won, another, equally glorious, was obtained at Mycale, on the coast of Ionia."[16]

After the defeat of Salamis, the remains of the Persian fleet retired to Samos; but the Greeks lost no time in pursuing them. . . .

The Persians were no sooner informed of their approach, than, conscious of their own inferiority by sea, they drew up their ships upon dry land at Mycale, and fortified them with a wall and deep trench, while they at the same time protected them with an army of sixty thousand men, under the command of Tigranes.

But nothing could secure them from the fury of the Grecians, who, immediately coming on shore, and dividing themselves into two bodies, the Athenians and Corinthians advanced directly on the plain, while the Lacedaemonians fetched a compass over hills and precipices, in order to take possession of a rising ground.

But before these last arrived, the former had entirely put the enemy to flight, and, on being joined by the Spartans, soon set all their ships on fire; so that nothing could be more complete than the victory now obtained. Tigranes, the Persian general, with forty thousand of his men, lay dead on the field of battle; the fleet was destroyed; and of the great army which Xerxes brought into Europe, scarcely a single man remained to carry back the news of its defeat.[17]

Never again would the Persian Empire advance into Europe. "The Greeks had won the war decisively and were now free to pursue their own destiny."[18] And Athens, although it needed to be rebuilt, would as a result of its brilliant leadership in the Persian Wars become the most influential and splendid city in Greece.

The Periclean Age

The Golden Age of Athens under the leadership of Pericles immediately followed the Persian Wars, and was in large measure a product of it. Describing its impact on the people in general and the poets in particular, Goldsmith noted:

> The Persian invasion roused all the energies of the Grecian nation, and called forth a display of talent, courage, and patriotism, that has never been paralleled. It is at such a time, when the minds of men are filled with sublime feelings, from the contemplation of heroic deeds, that the lofty outpourings of genius are most frequently displayed. Aeschylus had witnessed that brilliant series of events, which terminated in the destruction of the Persian invaders; and came to his task of perfecting the drama with a mind filled up with ideas of grandeur and honor.
>
> The overthrow of potent dynasties, by means, apparently insignificant, the mysterious struggle between human agency and the powers of destiny, the wildest vicissitudes of fortune, are the poet's favorite themes; they appear the most suitable to his gigantic imagination, and they were naturally suggested by the wondrous events which he had witnessed, and the scenes in which he had acted a distinguished part. How far the drama had been improved by Thespis it is impossible to discover, but to Aeschylus it indisputably owes its perfection. He is in every sense the first of Greek tragedians, and even in the closet his works leave an impression on the mind which cannot be effaced.[19]

Since the beginning of time, there has never been such a display of genius as occurred in the fifth century B.C. Within the span of only three generations the Greeks produced such tragic poets as Aeschylus, Sophocles, and Euripedes; lyric poets such as Simonides and Pindar, and the comic poet, Aristophanes; philosophers such as Anaxagorus, Socrates, and Plato; statesmen such as Miltiades, Aristeides, Themistocles, and of course, Pericles; architects such as Ictinus and Callicrates, who together designed the Parthenon; sculptors and painters such as Phidias and Polygnotus, respectively; historians such as Herodotus, Thucydides, and Xenophon; scientists such as Democritus, who developed the atomic theory, and the greatest physician of antiquity, Hippocrates.

Every one of these men lived during the same century, and the great majority were from Athens. Yet "these were only the most distinguished. There were many others who, in a less brilliant age, would have shone as brightly as Marlow, Ford and Jonson might have done had they not lived in the age of William Shakespeare."[20] In the fifth century B.C. the city of Athens alone produced more great men "than all the world besides has produced in any period of equal length."[21]

The Greeks were markedly different from any ancient civilization that preceded them, as both secular historians and Biblical expositors have recognized. Dr. G. Campbell Morgan, for example, in his commentary, *The Gospel According to Luke*, wrote:

> The master passion of Greek idealism and Greek philosophy was that of the perfection of personality. The thinking, in those about three centuries of virile thought in Greek history, was not particularly concerned with human inter-relationships, but with personality and the question of the perfecting of personality. Take the old-fashioned illustration, for it has been used very many times. Compare China with Greece. The history of China stretches back over millenniums. The history of Greece was virile for about three centuries only. In those three centuries, Greece flung up more outstanding personalities than China has in all the millenniums of her history. I am not speaking disrespectfully of China. I am comparing two great, but entirely different outlooks on life. China has stood through all the centuries and millenniums of her history for the solidarity of the race, the worship of ancestors has proved it, and reinforced it; her passion has not been that of perfecting of individuals, but that of maintaining racial relationships. Greece was not so concerned; she sought for the perfecting of the individual; and she wrought her ideal out into marble, and until this day, the canon and criterion of all accuracy in presentation and beauty in sculpture is that of Greece.[22]

With the possible exception of the Hebrew nation, the marks of every oriental civilization that existed prior to the Periclean Age "were uniformity, extravagance, depotism, submissive thought; the corresponding marks of European civilization were to be diversity, moderation, freedom, and originality. These new elements were first seen among the Greeks."[23]

The structure of Greek society was different from the cultures that both preceded and followed it, yet this does not imply that the ancient Greeks were not greatly indebted to oriental peoples. In fact, "the Greeks were the principal channel through which the achievements of those earlier civilizations have flowed down to us."[24] One historian, writing in the 1950's, noted:

> If we try to concentrate on the broader picture, ignoring the details, and looking only for the continuing threads which link our own culture with that of the ancient world, we have to recognize that from this point onwards for a thousand years the peoples of western Asia—with one exception—had little further direct influence on Western civilization. Their indirect contributions were very great—far, far more than was recognized before the development of scientific archaeology during the past century. Until about one hundred years ago it was assumed that our intellectual and material culture rested mainly on foundations laid by the Greeks. The Greeks themselves admitted owing a great debt to the oriental peoples, especially the Egyptians, but it has been left mainly to archaeologists and philologists to discover just how great that debt was—in science (especially mathematics), art, and craftsmanship. But by 450 B.C., and even earlier, the Greeks were already in possession of most of this knowledge and skill, and with their agile, free-thinking minds,

had adapted and reused it to shape their own distinctive culture pattern. . . . From now on, therefore, we have to focus our attention mainly on them.[25]

Although the Hebrew nation, through their sacred Scriptures and promised Messiah, would eventually have a more powerful influence on the growth of Western civilization than all the oriental empires put together, it should be noted that in the fifth century B.C., when Athens would reach the peak of her glory, a Greek visitor to Judea at the time would probably see nothing there to interest him.

> Jerusalem was an unimportant little town on a hill with a ruined palace and a rebuilt temple (to which he would not be admitted), and the country itself was the home of herdsmen and small farmers, living a simple existence in the hills, along the Jordan valley, and around Lake Galilee. No fine roads and high-towered temples, as in Babylon; no pyramids, tombs, and obelisks, as in Egypt. The Jewish heritage resided in two things, both invisible to the Greek visitor. One was the blood and genius of the Jewish race, which would one day be carried to the ends of the earth. The other lay hidden in the archives of the Temple. For there, jealously guarded by the priesthood, were the texts, from Moses to . . . Isaiah; the Mosaic Law, the chronicles of Judges and Kings, the Psalms of David, the teachings of the Prophets, the songs of Deborah, of Miriam, of Solomon; epic poems of war not inferior to the battle-pieces of Homer; passionate love poetry; books of history, wisdom and prophecy; but no philosophy which the Greek would have recognized as such. For whereas the Hellenic thinkers reasoned their way to the idea of "the one god," the Hebrew prophets, scorning reason, claimed direct divine inspiration. . . .
>
> But for centuries to come this treasure house of literature and moral wisdom was locked from the rest of the world.[26]

Eventually, those Jewish Scriptures and the Gospels that followed would be put into the Greek language as an eternal legacy to mankind, but before that would happen the Greeks "bequeathed to the world the grandest models of beauty and of thought that the unaided human mind has ever produced."[27]

As "the representatives of reason and humanity in the ancient world," the Greeks "looked upon themselves as having the mission of perfecting men."[28] And all their endeavors—from architecture to athletics, from music to medicine, from painting to philosophy, from literature to sculpture—were intended to accomplish this mission.

Of all their intellectual pursuits and creative achievements, however, the Greeks reached their zenith in their art forms. In his excellent textbook, *A History of Greece from the Earliest Times to the Roman Conquest*—published in 1855 and "beyond all question, the best summary in our language of the ancient history of that country,"[29] Dr. William Smith noted:

> The perfection of Greek art is still more wonderful than the perfection of Greek literature. In poetry, history, and oratory, other languages have produced works which may stand comparison with the masterpieces of Greek literature; but in architecture and sculpture the preeminence of the Hellenic race is acknowledged by the whole civilized world, and the most successful artist of modern times only hopes to approach, and dreams not of surpassing, the glorious creations of Grecian art. The art of a people is not only a most interesting branch of its antiquities, but also an important part of its history.

It forms one of the most durable evidences of a nation's growth in civilization and social progress. The remains of the Parthenon alone would have borne the most unerring testimony to the intellectual and social greatness of Athens, if the history of Greece had been a blank, and the names of Pericles and Pheidias unknown.[30]

Whereas much of the modern art that characterized the later half of the 20th century seems to be the result of an experiment to shock rather than civilize the thoughts and emotions of the viewer, Greek art was never this way.

Classical Greek art did not aim at experimentation for experiment's sake, but was concerned with expressing eternally true ideals. Its subject matter was basically the human being, but expressed harmoniously as an object of great beauty. The classic style, based on the ideals of reason, moderation, symmetry, balance, and harmony in all things, was meant to civilize the emotions.[31]

The Greeks were looking for the perfect man, and their art is a visual representation and lasting tribute to their ambitions. A comparison of their art with that of other cultures, furthermore, reveals the degree to which the ancient Greeks succeeded in their efforts.

Egyptian art, especially as it portrayed the human form, never varied for thousands of years. An examination of Figure 10-1 reveals the conventional method of treating the human figure throughout the entire course of Egyptian art. Describing the bas-relief from the great Temple of Abydos in Upper Egypt, as seen in this illustration, noted 19th century professor of classical archaeology, Dr. F. B. Tarbell, wrote:

King Seti I of the Nineteenth Dynasty stands in an attitude of homage before a seated divinity, of whom almost nothing appears in the illustration. On the palm of his right hand he holds a figure of Maat, goddess of truth. In front of him is a libation-standard, on which rests a bunch of lotus flowers, buds, and leaves. . . . As regards the treatment of the human figure, we have here the stereotyped Egyptian conventions. The head, except the eye, is in profile, the shoulders in front view, the abdomen in three-quarters view, the legs again in profile. As a result of the distortion of the body, the arms are badly attached at the shoulders. Furthermore, the hands, besides being badly drawn, have in this instance the appearance of being mismated with the arms, while both feet look like right feet. The dress consists of the usual loin-cloth and of a thin, transparent over-garment, indicated only by a line in front and below. Now surely no one will maintain that these methods and others of like sort which there is no opportunity here to illustrate are the most artistic ever devised. Nevertheless serious technical faults and shortcomings may coexist with great merits of composition and expression. So it is in this relief of Seti. The design is stamped with unusual refinement and grace. The theme is hackneyed enough, but its treatment here raises it above the level of commonplace.[32]

Turning our attention from Egyptian to Greek bas-relief, we see an example of one of exceptional beauty in the so-called Orpheus relief, as found in Figure 10-2. The figures, representing—from left to right—Hermes, Eurydice, and Orpheus, are far more realistic, and convey more feeling and emotion than anything ever done by Egyptian artists. The story, as set forth in the illustration, is one of the most touching in Greek mythology, and is described by Dr. Tarbell as follows:

Orpheus, the Thracian singer, has descended into Hades in quest of his dead wife, Eurydice, and has so charmed by his music the stern Persephone that she has suffered him to lead back his wife to the upper air, provided only he will not look upon her on the way. But love has overcome him. He has turned and looked, and the doom of an irrevocable parting is sealed. In no unseemly paroxysm of grief, but tenderly, sadly, they look their last at one another, while Hermes, guide of departed spirits, makes gentle signal for the wife's return. In the chastened pathos of this scene we have the quintessence of the temper of Greek art in dealing with the fact of death.[33]

In his excellent book, *Why Four Gospels? Or the Gospel for All the World*, Dr. Gregory says the Greeks "made their gods in the likeness of men, in their own likeness,"[34] and as such it is often difficult for the average person to distinguish an immortal god from a mortal human as represented in their art forms. In the next two illustrations (Figures 10-3 and 10-4) one features a god and the other a man. But can you tell which is which? The truth is the clothed man (Figure 10-3) is a representation of the great tragic poet, Sophocles, whereas the naked individual (Figure 10-4) is Apollo, who in Greek mythology was the son of Zeus and "primarily a god of prophecy."[35]

He was also a master archer and a fleet-footed athlete, credited with having been the first victor in the Olympic games. . . . Perhaps because of his beauty and perfect physique, Apollo was represented in ancient art more frequently than any other deity.[36]

Although it may seem strange to us—if not irreverent—to portray gods as naked beings it should be noted that "Greek sculpture had a strongly idealizing bent. Gods and goddesses were conceived in the likeness of human beings, but human beings freed from every blemish made august and beautiful by the artistic imagination."[37]

In his classic work, *The History of Greek Art*, Dr. Tarbell elaborates on this subject. He wrote:

It may be proper here to say a word in explanation of that frank and innocent nudity which is so characteristic a trait of the best Greek art. The Greeks admiration for the masculine body and the willingness to display it were closely bound up with the extraordinary importance in Greece of gymnastic exercises and contests and with the habits which these engendered. As early as the seventh century, if not earlier, the competitors in the foot race at Olympia dispensed with the loin-cloth, which had previously been the sole covering worn. In other Olympic contests the example thus set was not followed till some later, but in the gymnastic exercises of every-day life the same custom must have early prevailed. Thus in contrast to primitive Greek feeling and to the feeling of "barbarians" generally, the exhibition by men among men of the naked body came to be regarded as something altogether honorable. There could not be better evidence of this than the fact that the archer-god, Apollo, the purest god in the Greek pantheon, does not deign in Greek art to veil the glory of his form.[38]

"The striking rapidity with which Greek sculptural technique evolved may be taken as evidence for the claim that sculpture is the art most expressive of the Greek genius." [39] Furthermore, "most of the generally acknowledged masterpieces of Greek sculpture were created in the fifth and fourth centuries."[40] And one of the finest examples of this period, and the most famous *kouros* (nude male) statue of that time was the *Doryphorus* (Spear Bearer) by Polyclitus. Unfortunately, this fifth-century bronze statue has been lost, and is only known to us today from Roman marble copies, which convey little of the beauty of the original. Nevertheless, the *Doryphorus* was according to one authority "renowned as the standard embodiment of the classical ideal of human beauty."[41] Another stated:

> This statue was known as the Canon or Model, because it embodied Polyclitus' view of what ideal human proportions should be. And indeed the sculptor himself wrote a book called the Canon, showing that the Doryphorus was a deliberate proclamation and illustration of this very ideal. Beauty, to him, was a matter of ratio and proportion (*symmetria*), and the figure demonstrated the corporeal proportions which he regarded as perfect.[42]

Whereas the ancient Greek and Roman artists could portray the human figure very realistically, this artistic skill was lost in the centuries to come, as evidenced by the painting in Figure 10-5. This picture was painted on a church altar in Italy during the Middle Ages, and the main figure, St. Francis of Assisi (1182-1226), seems to be standing on his toes rather than firmly on his feet.

> Most paintings during the Middle Ages were flat. They lacked a sense of depth or perspective (picturing objects the way they appear to the eye in relation to one another). People and things did not appear real and natural in the way God created them.
>
> If men do not see God right, they will not see themselves right. The distorted Christianity of the Middle Ages inevitably distorted art.[43]

Eventually, the desire to recover the culture of antiquity from the dust and neglect of a millennium ushered in that well-known but somewhat indefinite period of time called the Age of the Renaissance.

The Renaissance

In describing the transition from classical antiquity to the Middle Age, one authority emphasized the rise of Islam as marking the real separation between the two eras. He wrote:

> No comparable event sets off the Middle Ages from the Renaissance. The fifteenth and sixteenth centuries to be sure, witnessed far-reaching developments: the fall of Constantinople and the Turkish conquest of southeastern Europe; the journeys of exploration that led to the founding of overseas empires in the New World, in Africa and Asia, with the subsequent rivalry of Spain and England as the foremost colonial powers; the deep spiritual crisis of Reformation and Counter Reformation. But none of these events, however vast their effects, can be said to have produced the new era. By the time they happened, the Renaissance was well under way. Thus it is hardly surprising that the causes, the extent, and the significance of the Renaissance have long been a favorite subject of debate among historians, and that their opinions vary like those of the proverbial blind men trying to describe an elephant. Even if we disregard the minority of scholars who would deny the existence of the animal altogether, we are left with an extraordinary diversity of views on the Renaissance. Every

branch of historic study has tended to develop its own image of the period. While these images overlap, they do not coincide, so that our concept of the Renaissance may vary as we focus on its fine arts, music, literature, philosophy, politics, economics, or science. Perhaps the only essential point on which most experts agree is that the Renaissance had begun when people realized they were no longer living in the Middle Ages.

This statement is not as simple-minded as it sounds; it brings out the undeniable fact that the Renaissance was the first period in history to be aware of its own existence and to coin a label for itself. . . . Medieval man did not think he belonged to an age distinct from classical antiquity; the past, to him, consisted simply of "B.C." and "A.D.," the era "under the Law" (that is, of the Old Testament) and the era "of Grace" (that is, after the birth of Christ). From his point of view, then, history was made in Heaven rather than on earth. The Renaissance, by contrast, divided the past not according to the Divine plan of salvation, but on the basis of human achievements. It saw classical antiquity as the era when man had reached the peak of his creative powers, an era brought to a sudden end by the barbarian invasions that destroyed the Roman Empire. During the thousand-year interval of "darkness" which followed, little was accomplished, but now, at last, this "time in-between" or "Middle Age" had been superseded by a revival of all those arts and sciences which flourished in classical antiquity. The present, the "New Age," could thus be fittingly labeled a "rebirth"—*rinascita* in Italian (from the Latin *renasci*, to be reborn), *renaissance* in French and, by adoption, in English. The origin of this revolutionary view of history can be traced back to the 1330s in the writings of the Italian poet Petrarch, the first of the great men who made the Renaissance. Petrarch, however, thought of the new era mainly as a "revival of the classics," that is, limited to the restoration of Latin and Greek to their former purity and the return to the original texts of ancient authors. During the next two centuries, this concept of the rebirth of antiquity grew to embrace almost the entire range of cultural endeavor, including the visual arts. The latter, in fact, came to play a particularly important part in shaping the Renaissance, for reasons that we shall have to explore later.

That the new historic orientation—to which, let us remember, we owe our concepts of the Renaissance, the Middle Ages and classical antiquity—should have had its start in the mind of one man is itself a telling comment on the new era. Petrarch's plea for a revival of antiquity is extraordinary not for his veneration of the ancients—classical revivals, we recall, had been far from unknown in the Middle Ages—but, rather, for the outlook, strangely modern for his time, that underlies his plea, revealing him to be both an individualist and a humanist. Individualism—a new self-awareness and self-assurance—enabled him to proclaim, against all established authority, his own conviction that the "age of faith" was actually an era of darkness, while the "benighted pagans" of antiquity really represented the most enlightened stage of history. Such readiness to question traditional beliefs and practices was to become profoundly characteristic of the Renaissance as a whole. Humanism, to Petrarch, meant a belief in the importance of what we still call "the humanities" or "humane letters" (rather than Divine letters, or the study of Scripture); that is, the pursuit of learning in languages, literature, history, and philosophy for its own end, in a secular rather than a religious framework. Here again he set a pattern that proved to be most important, for the humanists, the new breed of scholar who followed him, became the intellectual leaders of the Renaissance.[44]

Although the literary production of Petrarch (1304-1374) as poet, historical moralist, and outstanding representative of the new culture was enormous, the modern concept of the Renaissance has been shaped largely by the writings of the 19th century Swiss historian and art critic, Jacob Burckhardt (1818-1897). In his celebrated work, *The Civilization of the Renaissance in Italy*, published in 1860, Burckhardt "established the basic terms in which all serious analysis of the Italian Renaissance has been conducted ever since."[45] His work has become "one of the rare, certifiable historical classics,"[46] and in it "he traced the cultural patterns of transition from the medieval period to the awakening of the modern spirit and creativity of the Renaissance."[47] Burckhardt "portrayed Italy in the fourteenth and fifteenth centuries as the birthplace of the modern world . . . and saw the revival of antiquity, the 'perfecting of the individual,' and secularism . . . as its distinguishing features."[48]

The task of "perfecting the individual," which the ancient Greeks sought to accomplish, was carried on with even greater success—at least visually—by the three greatest artists of the Italian Renaissance. Leonardo da Vinci, Michelangelo, and Raphael integrated the humanistic ideals of ancient Greece in their most celebrated works of art, many of which had been commissioned by the established church of their day. These artists, and their masterpieces, have been held in high esteem—if not reverential awe—by all subsequent generations. Nevertheless, their works have compromised biblical truth with pagan philosophy, and are, therefore, worthy of our consideration and evaluation. These gifted men and their magnificent works have shaped the Church's perspective—and influenced the world's perception—of Christianity even now in the 21st century. The impact of Greek idealism, channeled through the Renaissance, has had a lasting influence upon Christendom, as thousands of people still visit the famous sites and view the impressive scenes of High Renaissance art.

Leonardo da Vinci (1452-1519)

According to one historian, "Leonardo da Vinci was the impetus behind the High Renaissance concern for the idealization of nature, moving from a realistic portrayal of the human figure to an idealized form."[49] Another wrote:

> In Florence, at the turn of the 16th century, painters and sculptors were not so interested in . . . unequivocal realism of detail. An artist as renowned as Leonardo da Vinci . . . was seldom willing to paint a portrait and, when he did, it seems to have been because his sitter could be made to represent an ideal rather than a particular human being.[50]

The most famous portrait painted by his hand is that of the wife of the Florentine silk merchant, Francesco del Giocondo. In this masterpiece, known as the *Mona Lisa* (Figure 10-6), both the figure and the landscape are idealized. Furthermore, "the ideal which the *Mona Lisa* represents, no matter how illusive it is, is certainly a matter of inner life rather than physical externals; it radiates through her flesh and skin."[51]

Many people on seeing this picture for the first time at the Louvre in Paris have expressed surprise that so homely a woman should have become so famous; but nobody in his senses would for one moment maintain that this picture should be admired because it presents a type of feminine beauty. Dozens of artists have painted far more attractive women. In none of Leonardo's paintings is there any sexual appeal, because his outlook is wholly intellectual. *Mona Lisa* is world-famous not because it represents a particular woman but because it typifies Everywoman. It is a final and complete statement of the eternal enigma of womanhood, a confession that men never can understand women, and an unforgettable revelation of what women really think about men, of their pride in their ancient wisdom, of their secret sense of superiority, of their amused tolerance for the antics of the creature who think themselves men but whom women know to be mere children. All this and more is expressed by Leonardo in his *Mona Lisa*; and is not this an infinitely greater achievement than painting the face of a pretty girl?[52]

The enigmatic expression and confident bearing of Leonardo's subject appears to be heightened because of the mysterious—if not fantastic—background scene, which seems more related to the world of imagination rather than fact. The stark contrast between the appearance of the lady and the nature of the landscape highlights the Renaissance spirit of self-awareness. The resolute countenance of the former, set against the malevolent appearance of the latter, suggests "that century's optimistic belief in the power of man's mind to comprehend the world around him."[53]

Leonardo da Vinci may not have claimed to be a student of the Greeks, but he perfectly applied the principles and ideals of classical antiquity to what has since become one of the world's most famous paintings.

Michelangelo (1475-1564)

Michelangelo—sculptor, architect, painter, and poet—was another giant of the High Renaissance in Italy, and arguably one of the most gifted creators in the history of art.

Fiercely driven by his desire to create, he worked with great passion and energy on a remarkable number of projects. Michelangelo was influenced by Neoplatonism, especially evident in his figures on the ceiling of the Sistine Chapel in Rome. These muscular figures reveal an ideal type of human being with perfect proportions. In good Neoplatonic fashion, their beauty is meant to be a reflection of divine beauty; the more beautiful the body, the more god-like the figure.[54]

Commissioned for the colossal Sistine Chapel project by Pope Julius II, Michelangelo "devised an intricate system of decoration that included nine scenes from the Book of Genesis, beginning with *God Separating Light from Darkness*, and including the *Creation of Adam*, the *Creation of Eve*, the *Temptation and Fall of Adam and Eve*, and the *Flood*."[55]

"Working high above the chapel floor, lying on his back on scaffolding, Michelangelo painted between 1508 and 1512 some of the finest pictorial images of all time."[56] And the figure of Adam (upper left in Figure 10-7) is considered to be the

very best. From his silent face to the breadth and nobility of his physique, Michelangelo's depiction of Adam has been described as "one of the most beautiful human
figures ever imagined."[57]

> A century of early Renaissance research into the nature and possibilities of
> human anatomy seems in retrospect only to lead up to the single, irrecaptur-
> able moment, in which all the pride of pagan antiquity in the glory of the
> physical, tangible body, all the yearning of Christianity for the "substance of
> things hoped for, the evidence of things unseen," seem at last to have reached
> a mysterious and perfect harmony. . . . Never again was he or anyone else to
> achieve such a figure.[58]

Holy Scripture tells us, *"The Lord God formed man out of the dust of the ground, and breathed
into his nostrils the breath of life; and man became a living soul"* (Gen. 2:7). Yet the biblical
version of creation is never illustrated in Renaissance art. Instead, in what is arguably
the most famous depiction of the creation of man (Figure 10-7), "the well-proportioned
figure of Adam, meant by Michelangelo to be a reflection of divine beauty, awaits the
divine spark."[59] Moreover, "Michelangelo's completely new image seems to symbolize a
still further idea—the instillation of divine power in humanity."[60]

The divinities of ancient Greece were thought to possess human form. In fact,
as far as many in that ancient land were concerned, their gods were immortal men,
and their men were mortal gods. "The athlete was religious, the god was athletic.
Both were intellectual."[61]

> Greek artists, free of limitations imposed by priest or by king, shaped their ideas
> to a prevailing philosophy of rationalism and humanism. Their art is distinc-
> tively clear, intellectual, and true to the seen object. Mystery is abhorred, the
> meaning of nature overlooked, the divinity of the gods minimized. All interest
> centers in man, his doings, his pleasure, his feats, the idealization of his outward
> aspects. If he still has spiritual vision, if he experiences intimations of a life
> more profound than can be explained by reason alone, they are forgotten. For
> the first time in the history of art, the thinking man controls.
> The key to the understanding of Greek civilization, as well as of Greek art, is in
> this matter of a thinking approach.[62]

Not surprisingly, then, the human and divine personalities in the works of the
Greek sculptors—as well as the Renaissance artists that followed—look virtually the
same. Michelangelo's portrayal of God (upper right in Figure 10-7), for example,
appears to have *"changed the glory of the incorruptible God into an image made like to corruptible
man"* (Rom. 1:23).

To be fair, however, the *Creation of Adam* does have symbolic revelation and historic
value for Christendom. Jesus Christ is the last Adam (cf. I Cor. 15:45), and Michelangelo's masterpiece is probably the first piece of Christian art to symbolically portray Him as
the fulfillment of Isaiah's prophecy regarding the advent of the promised Messiah. The
Old Testament prophet wrote:

> Who hath believed our report? And to whom is the arm of the Lord revealed?
> For he shall grow up before him as a tender plant, and as a root out of dry ground.
> Isa. 53:1-2A

The arm of the Lord is obviously revealed in the Creation of Adam in symbolic
fulfillment of the first part of Isaiah's messianic prophecy. The second part of the

Old Testament promise is symbolically effected by the scene below the recumbent Adam (see Figure 10-7). The young man, whose arm extends up into the picture from below, is holding a cornucopia of tender plants, and is about to touch Adam's thigh, suggesting the idea of growing up *as a tender plant, and as a root out of dry ground.* Whatever Biblical shortcomings Michelangelo's masterpiece may have in regards to the first Adam, it beautifully captures the significance of the incarnation of the last Adam.

> *The Lord hath made bare his holy arm in the eyes of all the nations; and all the ends of the earth shall see the salvation of our God.* Isa. 52:10

Raphael (1483-1520)

Another Renaissance artist, who was influenced by the classical Greeks, was Raphael. "Well-known for his frescoes in the Vatican Palace, Raphael was especially acclaimed for his numerous Madonna's, in which he attempted to achieve an ideal of beauty far surpassing human standards."[63] His *Alba Madonna* "reveals a world of balance, harmony, and order—basically, the underlying principles of the art of the classical world of Greece and Rome."[64]

From another one of Raphael's paintings, *The Madonna of the Chair* (Figure 10-8), we see evidence of the Renaissance shift in thought from glorifying God to exalting man. Whereas the art of an earlier period exalted the holiness of God, as seen in Fra Filippe Lippi's *Mary Kneeling before the Infant Jesus* (Figure 10-9), Renaissance art, as well as the literature and philosophy of the period, transferred the adoration from God to man. This shift gave birth to the doctrine of humanism, and incited men to depend upon their own powers of reason to discern truth.

> The humanists effected a deeply penetrating change in social manners. Through their influence as tutors, professors, orators, and courtiers, society was permeated by a fresh ideal of culture. To be a gentleman in Italy meant at this epoch to be a man acquainted with the rudiments at least of scholarship, refined in diction, capable of corresponding or of speaking in choice phrases, open to the beauty of the arts, intelligently interested in archaeology, taking for his models of conduct the great men of antiquity rather than the saints of the Church.[65]

The degree to which the man-centered culture of ancient Greece had penetrated the belief system of 16th century Christendom is seen in Raphael's magnificent and celebrated frescoes in the Vatican—the official residence of the popes, the nucleus of the city-state, and the spiritual center of the Roman Catholic Church.

At the same time that Michelangelo was painting in the Sistine Chapel, Raphael was laboring nearby in the Stanza, as series of private rooms in the Vatican Palace. The first room he frescoed, the Stanza della Signatura, has since become revered as "the Holy of Holies of the art of painting."[66] On entering "we experience that complete, over-powering impression of beauty, which excites our emotion even without the . . . understanding in interpretation."[67] This room, also known as the Papal Signature Room, is about 25 x 30 feet in size, and has a vaulted ceiling, which is divided into geometrical compartments. In the four largest, each circular in form, are splendid female personifications, which exalt the four Faculties (Disciplines) of Jurisprudence,

Poetry, Philosophy, and Theology. "On the walls are large frescoes with arch-shaped tops representing man's exercise of the faculties at their highest level. They are known, respectively, as *The Virtues, Parnassus, The School of Athens,* and *The Disputa.*"[68]

The first of these paintings completed by Raphael was *The Disputa* (Figure 10-10), in which "active groups of theologians on earth, coming from all parts of Christendom and from all ages and time, . . . vie in learned discussion on the nature of the sacrament."[69]

> The representatives of the Church assembled around the altar include all the several hierarchies: popes, cardinals, spiritual leaders of the laity and the monastic orders, sages, and artists. Immediately alongside the altar the place of honor is occupied by the four great Latin Fathers of the Church, at the left Pope Gregory and Jerome, at the right Ambrose and Augustine.[70]

The traditional name for this fresco, *Disputa del Sacramento* (The Disputation over the Sacraments), is somewhat misleading, however, "because nothing is being disputed here. . . . Heaven and earth are united in extolling the sacrament, which stands on an altar in the exact center of the composition with the horizon stretching behind it."[71]

Nevertheless, the essence of Roman Catholic Theology (as depicted in *The Disputa*) is countered on the opposite wall by *The School of Athens* (Figures 10-11 and 10-12) in which the pagan philosophy of ancient Greece is set forth. "The picture, universally recognized as the culmination of the High Renaissance ideal of formal and spatial harmony, was intended to confront *The Disputa's* theologians of Christianity drawn from all ages with an equally imposing group of philosophers of classical antiquity, likewise engaged in solemn discussion."[72]

> In the center stand Plato and Aristotle, the two greatest philosophers of antiquity. Plato holds the *Timaeus* in his left hand and points with his right to heaven, the realm whence his ideas radiate to their embodiment in earthly forms, while Aristotle holds the *Nichomachean Ethics* and points downward to the earth as his source for the observation of reality.[73]

The pagan Greek and medieval Christian concepts of truth and goodness, as depicted on opposite walls in the Stanza della Signatura, are synthesized in the scene on Mount Parnassus (Figure 10-13) that Raphael frescoed on the adjoining wall.

> In the *School of Athens* and the *Disputa,* pagan antiquity and Christendom are set up as antitheses. But the *Parnassus* shows those two worlds in happy union. Homer and Dante, Vergil and Petrarch join the company of Apollo and the nine Muses.[74]
>
> Thus, in this fresco where pagan and Christian poets keep company, the two different conceptions of the world, which are set forth on the two side walls, are reconciled.[75]

Raphael, like the other Renaissance artists who were influenced by Neoplatonism, believed in a basic agreement between Christianity and the philosophies of Plato and his followers.

> In Neoplatonic thought, all earthly forms of being derive ultimately from the cosmic world of pure forms. It was thus possible to reconcile Christianity with other modes of thought, since all were believed to have one common source. Consequently, the artist was freed to paint a classical theme as readily as a Christian one. Whereas the medieval mind had conceived of antiquity either

as a prefiguration of the Christian era or as an age of pagan wickedness, the Renaissance man was able to embrace the ideas of the classical age with an unabashed, almost romantic fervor.[76]

Synonyms for Perfection

The great masters of the High Renaissance in Italy—Leonardo da Vinci, Michelangelo, and Raphael—not only shared the ideals of their Greek predecessors, but "expressed them so completely that their names became synonyms for perfection."[77]

They represented the climax, the classical phase, of Renaissance art, just as Phidias seemed to have brought the art of ancient Greece to its highest point. . . .

In some fundamental respects . . . the High Renaissance was indeed the culmination of the Early Renaissance, while in others it represented a departure. Certainly the tendency to view the artist as a sovereign genius, rather than as a devoted craftsman, was never stronger than during the first half of the sixteenth century. Plato's concept of genius—the spirit entering into the poet that causes him to compose in a "divine frenzy"—had been broadened by . . . Neoplatonists to include the architect, the sculptor, and the painter. Men of genius were thought to be set apart from ordinary mortals by the divine inspiration guiding their efforts, and worthy of being called "divine" . . . and "creative" (before 1500, creating, as distinct from making, was the privilege of God alone). This cult of genius had a profound effect on the artists of the High Renaissance. It spurred them to vast and ambitious goals, and prompted their awed patrons to support such enterprises. But since these ambitions often went beyond the humanly possible, they were apt to be frustrated by external as well as internal difficulties, leaving the artist with a sense of having been defeated by a malevolent fate. At the same time, the artist's faith in the divine origin of inspiration led him to rely on subjective, rather than objective, standards of truth and beauty.[78]

The Renaissance Man

The ancient Greeks, like the Renaissance men that followed, searched for universal standards of beauty and truth, but sought them from a human, subjective point of view. This assertion of human individuality and self reliance was noted earlier in Raphael's great Vatican fresco, *The School of Athens* (Figures 10-11 and 10-12). We have seen that Plato—pointing upward—is emphasizing the search for universal ideals, but his follower Aristotle—pointing to the earth—shows where the source of those truths would be sought. Moreover, the artist's placement of these two great philosophers in the center of the picture reveals the Renaissance emphasis on a human-centered world. Furthermore, and even more noteworthy, is the fact that Raphael, who knew Leonardo da Vinci (Figure 10-14) has given Leonardo's face to the figure of Plato (left in Figure 10-12), who "is shown pointing to the heavens in a gesture that echoes figures in Leonardo's *Saint John the Baptist* . . . and *The Last Supper.*"[79] By placing this Renaissance man in *The School of Athens*, "Leonardo becomes the embodiment of classical philosophy, the wise man who inquires into the form and meaning of all things."[80]

The Italian Renaissance was the logical outgrowth and protracted fulfillment of classical Greek culture. Whereas Judaism produced the Pharisee, and Rome its Caesar, the Greek was parent to the Renaissance man.

The Renaissance man was a new ideal of man—one, like Leonardo da Vinci, "who displays his talents in all fields."[81] This was the kind of man the ancient Greeks were looking for. "The man on earth, with all the grandest power of thought and beauty of speech and action, was the highest man for the Greek, and nearest the place which he thought the gods ought to occupy."[82]

> From the time of Homer on, the religion of Greece had been a kind of artis-
> tic polytheism. The gods were conceived of as living in a lofty region of light
> and gladness. They had passions like men, they engaged in strife and deceit.
> But even when they were evil, they were beautiful. Greek religion, in its char-
> acteristic form, was aesthetic rather than moral; it was based upon the sense
> of beauty rather than upon the conscience. Its characteristics appear most
> clearly in the beautiful images of the gods—those unequalled masterpieces
> which are the wonder and delight of the civilized world. Beauty of form, but
> no satisfaction for the deepest needs of the soul.[83]

The Legacy of the Renaissance

Unfortunately, the Italian Renaissance fared no better in providing satisfaction for the deepest needs of the soul, than did the religion of ancient Greece. The awakened intelligence of the sixteenth century—instructed by humanism and polished by the fine arts—may have displayed a brilliant light on the stage of history, yet the drama had its darker side.

> Humanism, in its revolt against the Middle Ages, was, as we have seen already,
> mundane, pagan, irreligious, positive. The Renaissance can, after all, be re-
> garded only as a period of transition, in which much of the good of the past
> was sacrificed while some of the evil was retained, and neither the bad nor
> the good of the future was brought clearly into fact. Beneath the surface of
> brilliant social culture lurked gross appetites and savage passions, unrestrained
> by medieval piety, untutored by modern experience. Italian society exhibited
> an almost unexampled spectacle of literary, artistic, and courtly refinement
> crossed by brutalities of lust, treasons, poisonings, assassinations, violence. A
> succession of worldly pontiffs brought the Church into flagrant discord with
> the principles of Christianity. Steeped in pagan learning, emulous of imitat-
> ing the manners of the ancients, used to think and feel in harmony with Ovid
> and Theocritus, and at the same time rendered cynical by the corruption of
> papal Rome, the educated classes lost their grasp upon morality. Political hon-
> esty ceased almost to have a name in Italy. The Christian virtues were scorned
> by the foremost actors and the ablest thinkers of the time, while the antique
> virtues were themes for rhetoric rather than moving springs of conduct. This
> is apparent to all students of Machiavelli and Guicciardini, the profoundest
> analysts of their age, the bitterest satirists of its vices, but themselves infected
> with its incapacity for moral goodness.[84]

Neither the ancient Greeks nor the men of the Italian Renaissance were able to produce the ideal man. While a few may have escaped from a feeling of personal frustration and a life of unfulfilled aspirations, yet none could offer hope of a better life after one's soul would leave its earthly tenement. Their propensities were focused and their energies were expended on things that were earthly, temporal, and subjective. The Greeks, seeking after wisdom (cf. I Cor. 1:22) and *"professing themselves to be wise, . . . became fools"* (Rom. 1:22). For Scripture had warned that God would *"destroy the wisdom of the wise, and . . . bring to nothing the understanding of the prudent"* (I Cor. 1:19; cf. Isa. 29:14). The Renaissance men, in turn, repulsed by the religious inhibitions, papal corruption, and distorted Christianity of the Middle Ages, returned instead to the writings of classical antiquity, rather than the sacred Scriptures of Christianity, for their standards of truth and vision for humanity. Looking for the ideal man in the former, they neglected to find Him in the latter.

The Ideal Man

In his Gospel, Luke presents Jesus Christ as the ideal Man and Savior of the world. While there may never be unanimous agreement as to what features should be illustrated in a picture of human perfection or a story of an ideal life, yet the life of Jesus Christ is the one and only legitimate and suitable subject for such a study.

As to all the prime elements of perfect manhood, possibly no two persons may agree; yet none would deny that such was the manhood of Jesus, and none would question that there are two or three moral qualities which he exhibited in a superlative degree, qualities upon which Luke lays special stress. First of all Jesus manifested matchless courage. To some interpreters this fearlessness has formed the very essence of the "manliness of Christ." He was not a weak and nerveless preacher of righteousness, but a man of strength, of dauntless resolve, and of courageous action. The mob was eager to destroy him as he began his work in Nazareth, but his enemies quailed before his majestic presence, as "he passing through the midst of them went his way." He was advised to flee from the realm of Herod, but he flung defiance to the King, beginning his message with the words, "Go and say to that fox." The section of ten chapters in this Gospel which describes the last journeys of our Lord opens with a deeply significant phrase, "He steadfastly set his face to go to Jerusalem." Only five chapters devoted to his ministry precede, only five follow. During all the long period described in the chapters between, Jesus plainly foresaw his coming rejection and suffering and death, but fearlessly and with unfaltering steps he moved onward to the cross. All the heroisms of history are dwarfed to insignificance by this incomparable courage of Christ. More obvious still is the boundless and tender sympathy of this ideal man. He declared in his first address that he had come "to preach good tidings to the poor: . . . to proclaim release to the captives, and recovering of sight to the blind, to set at liberty them that are bruised"; and as we follow in his footsteps we see how his tender heart yearned over all who suffered and were distressed; he dried the tears of sorrow; he showed his pity for the outcast and the impure; he received sinners and was entertained by publicans; he praised Samaritans and comforted the dying thief. This world has no other picture of such perfect compassion, tenderness, and love; and these are essential to true manhood.

More mysterious, but none the less real, was his constant faith. His life was lived in continual fellowship with God. In his first recorded saying he declared, "I must be in my Father's house," and at the last he breathed out his spirit on the cross with the words, "Father, into they hands I commend my spirit." All the intervening days of his life and ministry were filled with cease-less prayer. . . . Such trust in God, such sympathy, such bravery, are surely prominent among the many elements which are blended in this impressive portrayal of the ideal Man.[85]

In order to effectively commend Jesus Christ to his readers, Luke needed to por-tray the Lord, in both private life and public ministry, as the ideal Man. "To the Greek these are the credentials of Jesus, no less essential than prophecy to the Jew, or power to the Roman. Without them there could not even be a reasonable hope of arresting his attention, much less of leading him to submit to Jesus as Savior."[86] Dr. Gregory wrote:

As the Messiah of the prophets, Jesus of Nazareth had an interest for the Jew; as the Son of God, the almighty worker and conqueror, he had an interest for the Roman; but in neither of these aspects would he interest the thinking Greek. A Gospel for the Greek must be shaped by the Greek idea; must pres-ent the character and career of Jesus of Nazareth from the Greek point of view, as answering to the conception of a perfect and divine humanity; must exhibit him as adapted, in his power and mercy, in his work and mission, to the wants of the Greek soul, and of humanity as represented in it. It must present Jesus as the perfect man, to meet the Greek ideal; as the divine man, to cure the wretchedness of the despairing Greek. It must bring God and the invisible world near, to meet the wants of the longing Greek soul, and elevate it above itself and into communion with God; must open the eyes of the blind Greek to see the sinfulness of sin and the desirableness of virtue and holiness. Reason and beauty, righteousness and truth, dignity and earnestness, must be exhibited as they meet in Jesus in their full splendor, and his divine tender-ness and compassion must have universal sweep. It must open the way to a mission grand enough for man here, and must bring to light an immortality beyond. In short, the Gospel must meet the true and correct the false in the Greek ideal.[87]

The Search for Truth

As early as the sixth century B.C., Greek philosophers had attempted to discern the truth and correct the false in the traditional religious beliefs of their day. Thales, Anaximander, Anaximenes, and others of the Ionian School, began to challenge the prevailing nature-myths and the reality of the fascinating array of gods, who suppos-edly lived on Mount Olympus, and had been immortalized in the poems of Homer. "They found it hard to believe that earthquakes were caused by the stamping of Posei-don or that lightning was a bolt from Zeus. They made the crucial intellectual leap from a primitive anthropomorphic view of nature to a rational, analytical view."[88]

One of the basic questions these pioneers of rational thought sought to answer, related to the composition of the physical universe. According to Thales of Miletus (in Asia Minor), who had accurately predicted the solar eclipse of 585 B.C., "the original principle of all things is water, from which everything proceeds and into which everything is again resolved."[89]

Though later philosophers rejected Thale's belief that everything can be reduced to water, they agreed he was on the right track. Some believed the prime substance to be air or fire; others concluded that there are four basic elements: earth, air, fire, and water. But during the fifth century B.C. Democritus of Abdera (in Thrace) developed the hypothesis that all physical things are formed by combinations of tiny particles, so small that they are both invisible and indivisible. He called them atoms. . . . They account, said Democritus, for everything that has been or even will be. Democritus offered no empirical evidence to prove the existence of atoms, but the fact that he could conceive this remarkable hypothesis demonstrates the far-reaching achievement of Greek rational thought.

By sheer logic another philosopher, Parmenides of Elea (in southern Italy), convinced himself that everything in the universe must be eternal and un-changeable. Change requires motion, he reasoned, and motion requires empty space. But empty space equals nonexistence, which by definition does not exist. Therefore, he concluded, motion and change are impossible. Parmenides readily admitted that some things appear to move and change; but this must be an illusion of the senses, he said, because it is contradicted by logic. And logic, thought the Greek philosophers, is the most reliable test of truth.[90]

The use of logic, however, did not prove to be very reliable, since it did not always lead philosophers to the same answers.

While Parmenides satisfied himself that matter was unchanging and perma-nent, another Greek reached the opposite conclusion. Heraclitus of Ephesus (in Asia Minor) insisted that the universe, instead of standing still, is in continu-ous motion. He declared that a man cannot step into the same river twice—in fact, the river is changing even as the man steps into it. This doctrine proved most disturbing, for if everything is constantly changing (including ourselves), how can we gain true knowledge of anything? By the time our mind has been informed, the object of our attention is no longer what it was!

Discomforting suggestions such as these led many Greeks to abandon the effort to find absolute or final truth. As philosophic inquiry began to center in Athens during the fifth century B.C., serious thinkers there turned away from baffling questions—about physical matter, permanence, and change—to the more immediate and engaging problems of human existence. A group of professional teachers, called Sophists because they claimed to make men wise (sophos), played a leading part in this shift. Most prominent among them was Protagoras, who lived and taught in Athens. He declared, "Man is the measure of all things, of what is and of what is not." Completely skeptical of general truths, even about the gods, he insisted that truth is different for each individual. What was true (or right) for a Spartan might well be false (or wrong) for an Athenian. Furthermore, as Heraclitus had suggested, our bodies and minds are changing every moment, and our perceptions and ideas change with them.

The Sophists concluded that it is pointless to look for absolute truth about nature or morals. Since truth is relative to each man, it is important only to know what one finds agreeable and useful, such as the arts of persuasion and how to succeed in life. As news of this teaching circulated in Athens and elsewhere in Greece, the more conservative citizens became shocked and alarmed. It smacked of blasphemy and threatened to subvert the laws and moral code of the state.[91]

Socrates' Approach

At this point one of the most famous—but ill-fated—men of all time made his debut in the cultural life of Athens. Wrongly identified with the Sophists, and accused of impiety and of corrupting the youth, he was ultimately condemned to death. Nevertheless, "his beauty of soul, his devotion to knowledge, and his largeness of spirit make him the greatest name in Greek history."[92]

> Socrates began the opposition to the Sophists; he directed the attention of men to the duties imposed on them as men and citizens, in the various relations of life, and thus led men from idle speculations about the origin of the universe, to consider the practical rules by which their conduct should be regulated, and thus laid the foundation of moral philosophy. He formed no connected system, because he made experience rather than theory his guide; and hence the systems devised by his followers differed from each other as widely as possible. The circumstances of his death not a little contributed to the strengthening of his influence over posterity, since he was generally venerated as a martyr in the cause of philosophy.[93]

Socrates' effect on philosophy was revolutionary, yet "it is impossible to say what it was in particular which made this Athenian a figure of such importance."[94] Nevertheless, the answer seems to be found "in the personality itself, rather than in any easily definable doctrine or logical method."[95]

> In him we are confronted with a character quite unlike any that had previously appeared. He is extra-ordinary through being ordinary, universal through being Athenian, religious through a method of skepticism, wise through a profession of ignorance. Yet in his character, his conduct and his opinions there are no contradictions. . . . His personality is always imposing and one feels that even so great an artist as Plato could not, even if he had wished to do so, have distorted it. It is a personality which has impressed itself on posterity as has the personality of no other philosopher.[96]

Socrates, unlike the Sophists, believed in the existence of a higher truth, although he did not claim to know this truth. He "spoke of himself only as a seeker after knowledge."[97] Furthermore, Socrates believed that this knowledge "must proceed from doubting, and he was forever posing questions and testing the answers people gave him."[98] As a result he made both friends and enemies. "Both in his own day and afterwards he has been represented as a saint and as a menace to society."[99] Nevertheless, he was convinced in the existence of an intellectual and moral order in the universe, and he was determined at all cost to discover it.

> It seems certain that Socrates himself considered that he had what we should call a "vocation" and even that, at a definite period of his life, towards the beginning of middle age, he had an experience which can be described almost as a "conversion." . . . Some time shortly before the outbreak of the Peloponnesian War, when he was approaching the age of forty, a friend of his inquired of the Delphic oracle who was the wisest man alive. The oracle replied that no one was wiser than Socrates. Why the oracle should have paid this compliment to an obscure Athenian who, up to this time, seems to have done nothing remarkable remains a complete mystery. It appears that Socrates himself was as astonished as anyone else by the god's reply. But he took the reply seriously and undoubtedly believed in his divine mission. He decided, with characteristic "irony," that his only claim to wisdom was that, unlike others, he was profoundly conscious of his own ignorance, and he regarded it as his duty to reveal to others, by means of his own particular method of cross-examination, exactly how ignorant they really were.[100]

Fifth-century Athens gave rise to the most numerous and greatest intellectual abilities of the ancient world, and witnessed some of the most notable and grandest achievements that have ever been displayed. In time, of course, the city's fortunes changed, its glory passed, and its monuments disintegrated. However, in spite of the fact that the Romans conquered Greece and the rest of the world by their arms, the Athenians continued to possess the world by their thought. As one author put it, "Though conquered by force of Roman arms, Greek mental advance was to conquer the conqueror,"[101] as it contributed largely to the culture of Rome, as well as that of future western civilizations. Nevertheless, in spite of securing permanent glory for their intellectual genius, the ancient Greeks were, unfortunately, truly ignorant of their own personal destiny. They sought for truth through rational inquiry, yet never realized it was available by divine revelation.

The Revelation of Truth for All People

Centuries before the Periclean Age, however, the prophet Isaiah had promised that *"the people that walked in darkness"* would see *"a great light,"* and they that dwelt *"in the land of the shadow of death,"* upon them would the light shine (cf. Isa. 9:2; Luke 1:79). The Old Testament prophet had also said:

> *Come now, and let us reason together, saith the Lord: though your sins be as scarlet, they shall be as white as snow; though they be red like crimson, they shall be as wool.* ISAIAH 1:18

In spite of all their intellectual achievements, the thinking Greeks had not reasoned that their sins, though they were as scarlet, could be as white as snow.

To remedy this situation, Luke addressed his Gospel to the Greeks, who were the representatives of universal humanity—of lost sinners—and of those who walked in darkness in the ancient world. To them he delivered a message of hope—of joy—and of light.

It was a message of hope, especially for Gentiles, as only Luke records that portion of Isaiah's prophecy, which promises: *"And all flesh shall see the salvation of God"* (Luke 2:30; cf. Isa. 40:3).

It was a message of joy, as only Luke recounts the angel's appearance to the shepherds, who were *"keeping watch over their flock by night"* (2:8).

> *And lo, the angel of the Lord came upon them, and the glory of the Lord shone round about them: and they were sore afraid. And the angel said unto them, Fear not: for, behold, I bring you good tidings of great joy, which shall be to all people. For unto you is born this day in the city of David a Savior, which is Christ the Lord.* 2:9-11

It was a message of light, as revealed in the song of Simeon, and recorded only by Luke.

> *Lord, now lettest thou they servant depart in peace, according to thy word:*
> *For mine eyes have seen thy salvation, Which thou hast prepared before the face of all people;*
> *A light to lighten the Gentiles, and the glory of thy people Israel.* 2:29-32

It was a message, the keynote of which is found in the opening chapter in the song of Zacharias: *"To give knowledge of salvation . . . by the remission of their sins"* (1:77). As Isaiah had prophesied centuries earlier, *"Though they be red like crimson, they shall be as wool"* (1:18b).

Writing with thoughtful eloquence and weaving together materials from various sources, Luke presents this knowledge of salvation to a meditative people, and commends Jesus Christ to them as the universal Savior of the world. And he does so in a style that would meet the Greek ideal—not only portraying Jesus as the perfect Man, but stressing the thoughts and perceptions of the Lord, as well as of the people who witnessed the life, death, and resurrection of this ideal Man.

After the virgin birth of her Son, and the visit of the shepherds, for example, Luke notes, *"But Mary kept all these things, and pondered them in her heart"* (2:19). The word "ponder" means "to weigh in the mind," and this is the only time it is used in the entire New Testament.

In the Temple, after the aged Simeon took the Christ child *"up in his arms, and blessed God"* (2:28ff.), Luke adds, *"And Joseph and his mother marveled at those things which were spoken of him"* (2:33). Then Simeon blessed them and said to Mary:

> *Behold, this child is set for the fall and rising again of many in Israel; and for a sign which shall be spoken against; (Yea, a sword shall pierce through thy own soul also,) that the thoughts of many hearts may be revealed.* 2:34-35

> In Simeon's song of praise, the strife and the suffering which lay ahead of Jesus were referred to for the first time in the Gospel. Jesus was to be, so he said, as it were, a stone over which many would stumble and fall and go to eternal doom, but which would cause others to rise and be eternally saved. Those who thought too highly of themselves and trusted in their own merits and strength would in the end come to a sad downfall, because their pride and arrogance prevented them from perceiving their lost and needy state and from taking refuge in Jesus. But the humble and lowly, bowing at His feet in confession of sin and believing in Him, would be raised up to life eternal by His mighty arm.[102]

Eventually, Joseph and Mary *"returned into Galilee, to their own city Nazareth"* (2:39). Then Luke relates: *"And the child grew, and waxed strong in spirit, filled with wisdom: and the grace of God was upon him"* (2:40).

> The intellectual, moral and spiritual development of the child Jesus was as real as His physical growth. He was completely subject to the ordinary laws of bodily and mental development, except that in His case there was no question

of sin and weakness exerting an evil influence on Him. Both in soul and body
He grew with a perfection unknown before or since. He was true man indeed,
but He was perfect man, even as a little child, and throughout the years of
growth and development, of increase in true wisdom and stature, the grace of
God and the love of God were His guide, His protection and His support.[103]

Some years later, Jesus accompanied His parents, who *"went to Jerusalem every year
for the feast of the Passover"* (2:41). Luke wrote:

> *And when he was twelve years old, they went up to Jerusalem after the custom of the feast.
> And when they had fulfilled the days, as they returned, the child Jesus tarried behind in
> Jerusalem; and Joseph and his mother knew not of it. But they, supposing him to have
> been in the company, went a day's journey; and they sought him among their kinsfolk and
> acquaintance. And when they found him not, they turned back again to Jerusalem, seeking
> him. And it came to pass, that after three days they found him in the temple, sitting in the
> midst of the doctors, both hearing them, and asking them questions. And all that heard him
> were astonished at his understanding and answers.* 2:42-47

Like Socrates, Jesus was *"in the midst of the doctors, both hearing them and asking them
questions"* (v. 46), and they in turn *"were astonished at his understanding and answers"* (v.47).
Luke continues:

> *And when they saw him, they were amazed: and his mother said unto him, Son, why hast
> thou thus dealt with us? Behold, thy father and I have sought thee sorrowing. And he said
> unto them, How is it that ye sought me? Wist ye not that I must be about my Father's
> business? And they understood not the saying which he spake unto them. And he went down
> with them, and came to Nazareth, and was subject unto them: but his mother kept all these
> sayings in her heart. And Jesus increased in wisdom and stature, and in favour with God
> and man.* 2:48-52

Just as Luke in 2:40 sums up in one pregnant sentence the life, growth and
development of Jesus from His birth to His twelfth year, so he gives in verse
52 an exquisite summary of the next eighteen (approximately) years of His
life, up to the time when He began His public ministry. He underwent a
process of development which was natural and yet absolutely perfect both
mentally ("increased in wisdom") and physically ("and in stature"). At each
stage of His life He was perfect, but between the perfection of a child and
that of a grown man there is a vast difference—the difference between perfect
innocence and perfect holiness. Therefore we are told that Jesus increased
in wisdom and stature and also in favor with God and man. There was thus
growth and development in His human nature and being, but in such a manner that His life and thought were constantly in full accord with the will of
God. For the first time, God's ideal at the creation was completely realized;
Jesus was Perfect Man in both soul and body. Adam and Eve had also been
perfect at creation, but their spiritual perfection before the Fall was the perfection of innocence. In order to attain to adult spiritual perfection, they should
have voluntarily and deliberately chosen good and rejected evil. Alas, this
they failed to do. But Jesus did not fail. Without external coercion, He chose
to serve the Father voluntarily and absolutely and to resist the wiles of the evil
one. That is why God could explicitly show Him favor and indicate that with
Him He was well-pleased.

Moreover, because He lived among the people of Nazareth and other parts of Palestine as an absolutely perfect human being both spiritually and physically, it was impossible for them (at least, for all such as were not completely degenerate) not to feel drawn towards Him. His body had never been marred by sin and was, in the best sense of the word, beautiful and attractive. His gaze was pure and lofty, the mirror of the untainted nobility of His soul. Because His whole being was without spot or blemish or weakness of any kind, He was Perfect Man and could not but be in favor with every right-thinking individual. This explains Luke's statement that He increased in favor with man also. In proportion as His mind and body developed into full, adult maturity, He was more and more loved and respected by all.

This state of affairs continued throughout the years before He began His public ministry. Then came the inevitable crises of which Simeon had spoken, for then the promised Messiah, the Son of God, publicly exposed the rottenness of the nation's spiritual life and began to fulfill His calling as Messiah and Savior in a way which could not be misinterpreted. The result was that people took sides, either for or against Him. Those who loved darkness better than light opposed Him and His divine claims. Consequently, He was no longer in favor with the people as a whole and soon the words of Isaiah 53 were to be fulfilled.[104]

The next event recorded by Luke takes place *"in the fifteenth year of the reign of Tiberius Caesar"* (3:1), and it involves the appearance of John the Baptist, who *"came into all the country about Jordan, preaching the baptism of repentance for the remission of sins"* (3:3). It is of interest to note that here, as in other incidents recorded by Luke, the universal aspect of the Gospel is stressed by linking the activities surrounding the life of Christ with secular events. "Luke alone gives the data which link the sacred story to the secular history of the world."[105] Of additional interest, however, is the response of the various peoples to whom John told, *"Bring forth therefore fruits worthy of repentance"* (3:8). Luke alone related:

> And the **people** asked him, saying, What shall we do then? . . . Then came also **publicans** to be baptized, and said unto him, Master, what shall we do? . . . And the **soldiers** likewise demanded of him, saying, And what shall we do? 3:10, 12, 14; EMPHASIS ADDED

Then the universal aspect of the third Gospel is stressed once more as Luke notes:

> Now when **all the people** were baptized, it came to pass, that Jesus also being baptized, and praying, the heaven was opened . . . 3:21; EMPHASIS ADDED

Immediately after His baptism Jesus *"was led by the Spirit into the wilderness"* (4:1). Luke's account of the temptation of the ideal Man, however, has a noteworthy difference to that recorded by Matthew—a variation that reveals the extent to which the Holy Spirit superintended the writings of the authors, in order to commend Jesus Christ to their respective audiences. First, look at Matthew's version, which reads:

> Then was Jesus led up of the spirit into the wilderness to be tempted of the devil. And when he had fasted forty days and forty nights, he was afterwards an hungred. And when the tempter came to him, he said, If thou be the Son of God, command that these stones be made bread. But he answered and said, It is written, Man shall not live by bread alone, but by every word that proceedeth out of the mouth of God. Then the devil taketh him up into the

holy city, and setteth him on a pinnacle of the temple, And saith unto him, If thou be the Son of God, cast thyself down: for it is written, He shall give his angels charge concerning thee: and in their hands they shall bear thee up, lest at any time thou dash thy foot against a stone. Jesus said unto him, It is written again, Thou shalt not tempt the Lord thy God. Again the devil taketh him up into an exceeding high mountain, and sheweth him all the kingdoms of the world, and the glory of them; And saith unto him, All these things will I give thee, if thou wilt fall down and worship me. Then saith Jesus unto him, Get thee hence, Satan: for it is written, Thou shalt worship the Lord thy God, and him only shalt thou serve. Then the devil leaveth him, and behold, angels came and ministered unto him. MATT. 4:1-11*

Now compare the above rendition with Luke's account, which reads:

And Jesus being full of the Holy Ghost returned from Jordan, and was led by the Spirit into the wilderness, Being forty days tempted of the devil. And in those days he did eat nothing: and when they were ended, he afterward hungered. And the devil said unto him, If thou be the Son of God, command this stone that it be made bread. And Jesus answered him, saying, It is written, That man shall not live by bread alone, but by every word of God. And the devil, taking him up into an high mountain, shewed unto him all the kingdoms of the world in a moment of time. And the devil said unto him, All this power will I give thee, and the glory of them: for that is delivered unto me; and to whomsoever I will I give it. If thou therefore wilt worship me, all shall be thine. And Jesus answered and said unto him, Get thee behind me, Satan: for it is written, Thou shalt worship the Lord thy God, and him only shalt thou serve. And he brought him to Jerusalem, and set him on a pinnacle of the temple, and said unto him, If thou be the Son of God, cast thyself down from hence: For it is written, He shall give his angels charge over thee, to keep thee: And in their hands they shall bear thee up, lest at any time thou dash thy foot against a stone. And Jesus answering said unto him, It is said, Thou shalt not tempt the Lord thy God. And when the devil had ended all the temptation, he departed from him for a season. LUKE 4:1-13*

The difference in the two narratives is found in the order of the temptations, the significance of which has been explained by the late Dr. Charles Erdman, Professor Emeritus of Practical Theology at Princeton Theological Seminary, in his excellent commentary, *The Gospel of Luke.* He wrote:

In both Matthew and Luke, three temptations are mentioned. They are probably intended to be symbolic and inclusive; and under one or the other of these enticements to evil can be grouped all the moral trials of mankind. It is to be noted, however, that the order of the temptations given by Luke differs from that of Matthew. In both accounts the first temptation is to make bread of stone; but Luke mentions as the second temptation that which is last in the account of Matthew, the temptation which offered Jesus all the kingdoms of the world. This was a fitting climax to the testing of the King. Luke, however, mentions last the temptation of Jesus to cast himself from the pinnacle of the Temple and thus to test God. It is the temptation in the sphere of intellectual desire and comes in the subtle form of presumptuous trust. It forms a true climax in the testing of the ideal Man.[106]

The greatest and final temptation in Matthew's text, which presents Christ as King and heir to a kingdom, "was in the sphere of earthly ambition. It consisted in an offer of unlimited human power."[107] By contrast, the greatest temptation in Luke's version, at least as far as the thinking Greek was concerned, "was in the sphere of intellectual curiosity. It suggested to Jesus that he should see for himself what would be the experience of one who should cast himself from a great height and then, by angel hands, be kept from harm."[108]

After His temptation, and at the very onset of His public ministry, Jesus went into the synagogue at Nazareth, where He had been brought up (cf. 4:16), and read a portion of Scripture from Isaiah chapter 61. After applying this prophecy to Himself, Luke says, *"And all bare him witness, and wondered at the gracious words which proceeded out of his mouth"* (4:22).

From the beginning to the end of His earthly ministry, Luke emphasizes the thoughts and perceptions of Jesus (cf. 5:22; 6:8; 7:9; 11:17; 20:23) as well as of those who came into His association (cf. 5:21, 26; 6:11; 7:39; 8:25, 56; 9:7, 43, 46; 11:38; 18:24; 19:48; 20:5, 19, 26, 40; 22:61; 24:4, 8, 11, 12, 15, 41). In fact, at the end of his Gospel, Luke makes this startling claim for the Lord's effectiveness in illuminating truth for His followers: *"Then opened he their understanding, that they might understand the scriptures"* (24:45). Neither the great Socrates nor the illustrious Plato was able to do that!

The Greeks prided themselves on their intellectual abilities and accomplishments, yet the essential truths they needed to know—but never discovered—would eventually be communicated in Greece in such as manner that even the weakest mind could comprehend them. Oliver Goldsmith noted:

> Christianity, the only light which can dispel "the shadows, clouds, and darkness" that rest upon futurity, and solve those doubts and difficulties which unassisted reason attempted in vain, was first preached in Greece by the apostle Paul. Its success was rapid, for the popular religion had sunk beneath the attacks of the philosophers, and no system had been substituted in its stead. The great mass of the people lived literally "without God in the world," for they saw that the faith of their fathers was absurd, but knew not as yet of any better creed. Victims indeed still bled in the temples, and sacrifices smoked on the altars, but these observances were continued more from habit than from any belief in their efficacy, the spirit and fervor of devotion no longer existed. With this practical infidelity a violent superstition was strangely mingled; new deities were introduced from Egypt, from Asia, and even from the barbarous tribes of Northern Europe; but they still felt a distrust in these objects of their worship, and erected altars TO THE UNKNOWN GOD. The preaching of Christianity produced a wonderful change; all that the wisest philosophers had proposed as the end of their speculations was here offered indiscriminately; the nature of man's dependence on his Creator, the design of his creation, the conditions of his future existence—questions which the schools had almost resigned in despair, were explained with a simplicity and clearness that the weakest mind could comprehend.[109]

In the Acts of the Apostles, which is the second part of Luke's two-volume work, we find that not only did converts became numerous as the result of the missionary activities of Paul and his companions, but "in the course of his brief career, the apostle founded several flourishing churches, in the very seats of luxurious idolatry and haughty philosophy."[110] In fulfillment of ancient prophecy, *"the people that walked in darkness have seen a great light"* (Isa. 9:2; cf. Luke 1:79), and that Light "brought God into a world that had been seeking, seeking very hard, to find God, but a world, as we have seen, that, in spite of all the seeking, was practically Godless."[111]

Then opened he their understanding, that they might understand the scriptures,
And said unto them, Thus it is written, and thus it behoved Christ to suffer, and to rise
from the dead the third day: And that repentance and remission of sins should be preached
in his name among all nations, beginning at Jerusalem. And ye are witnesses of these things.
LUKE 24:45-48

Chapter Ten Notes

[1] "Goldsmith, Oliver," *Encyclopaedia Britannica* (1903), X:763.

[2] *Ibid.*

[3] *Pinnock's Improved Edition of Dr. Goldsmith's History of Greece* (Philadelphia: F. W. Greenough, 1838), 13.

[4] *Ibid.*, 21-22.

[5] *Ibid.*, 33-37.

[6] Leonard Cottrell, *The Anvil of Civilization* (New York: The New American Library, Inc., 1957), 216.

[7] Jackson J. Spielvogel, *Western Civilization*, Vol. I: to 1715, 2nd ed. (Minneapolis/St. Paul: West Publishing Company, 1994), 77.

[8] C. M. Bowra, *et. al.*, *Classical Greece* (New York: Time, Inc., 1965), 70.

[9] Willis Mason West, *The Ancient World from the Earliest Times to 800 A.D.* (Boston: Allyn and Bacon, 1904), 138.

[10] *Pinnock's Goldsmith's Greece, op. cit.*, 104.

[11] *Ibid.*

[12] *Ibid.*, 105.

[13] *Ibid.*, 106-08.

[14] Spielvogel, *op. cit.*, 78.

[15] *Pinnock's Goldsmith's Greece, op. cit.*, 124-26.

[16] *Ibid.*, 131.

[17] *Ibid.*, 131-32.

[18] Spielvogel, *op. cit.*, 79.

[19] *Pinnock's Goldsmith's Greece, op. cit.*, 338.

[20] Cottrell, *op. cit.*, 220.

[21] Philip Van Ness Myers, *Ancient History* (Boston: Ginn & Company, 1904), 210.

[22] G. Campbell Morgan, *The Gospel According to Luke* (Westwood, N.J.: Fleming H. Revell Company, 1931), 10.

[23] West, *op. cit.*, 75.

[24] Cottrell, *op. cit.*, 218.

[25] *Ibid.*, 217-18.

[26] *Ibid.*, 219.

[27] D. S. Gregory, *Why Four Gospels? Or, the Gospel for All the World* (New York: Funk & Wagnalls, Publishers, 1890), 212.

[28] *Ibid.*, 211.

[29] William Smith, *A History of Greece from the Earliest Times to the Roman Conquest* (Boston:

Hickling, Swan, and Brown, 1855), iii.

[30] *Ibid.*, 132.

[31] Spielvogel, *op. cit.*, 88.

[32] F. B. Tarbell, *A History of Greek Art* (Meadville, Penn.: The Chautauqua-Century Press, 1896), 32-33.

[33] *Ibid.*, 204-06.

[34] Gregory, *op. cit.*, 211.

[35] "Apollo," *Funk and Wagnalls New Encyclopedia* (1990), 2:212.

[36] *Ibid.*

[37] Tarbell, *op. cit.*, 125.

[38] *Ibid.*

[39] "Greek Art and Architecture," *The American Peoples Encyclopedia* (1968), 9:192.

[40] *Ibid.*, 194.

[41] H. W. Janson, *History of Art: A Survey of the Major Visual Arts from the Dawn of History to the Present Day* (Englewood Cliffs, N.J.: Prentice-Hall, Inc., 1964), 104.

[42] Michael Grant, *The Founders of the Western World: A History of Greece And Rome* (New York: Charles Scribner's Sons, 1991), 103.

[43] Jerry H. Combee, *The History of the World in Christian Perspective, Vol. I* (Pensacola, Fla.: A Beka Book Publications, 1979), 475.

[44] Janson, *op. cit.*, 283-84.

[45] Jacob Burckhardt, *The Civilization of The Renaissance in Italy* (New York: Barnes & Noble, Inc., 1999), back cover.

[46] *Ibid.*

[47] "Burckhardt, Jakob," *Funk & Wagnalls New Encyclopedia* (1990), 5:41.

[48] Spielvogel, *op. cit.*, 407.

[49] *Ibid.*, 429.

[50] "Portrait Painting," *Encyclopaedia Britannica* (1970), 18:268.

[51] *Ibid.*

[52] Frank Rutter, *The Old Masters* (New York: George H. Doran Company, n.d.), 152-53.

[53] Helen Gardner, *Art Through the Ages*, 4th ed., Edited by Sumner McK. Crosby (New York: Harcourt, Brace & World, Inc., 1959), 329.

[54] Spielvogel, *op. cit.*, 430-31.

[55] "Michelangelo," *Funk & Wagnalls New Encyclopedia* (1990), 17:275.

[56] *Ibid.*

[57] Frederick Hartt, *Michelangelo* (New York: Harry N. Abrams, Inc., Publishers, 1984), 84.

[58] *Ibid.*

[59] Spielvogel, *op. cit.*, 431.

[60] Hartt, *op. cit.*, 82.

[61] Sheldon Cheney, *A New World History of Art* (New York: Holt, Rinehart and Winston, 1963), 95.

[62] *Ibid.*, 92.

[63] Spielvogel, *op. cit.*, 430.

[64] *Ibid.*

[65] "Renaisssance," *Encyclopaedia Britannica* (1903), XX:387.

[66] H. Knackfuss, *Raphael*, trans. by Campbell Dodgson (Leipzig: Velhagen & Klasing, 1899), 52.

[67] *Ibid.*

[68] *New International Illustrated Encyclopedia of Art*, Sir John Rothenstein, General Editorial Consultant (New York: The Greystone Press, 1970), 3497.

[69] Frederick Hartt, *History of Italian Renaissance Art* (New York: Harry N. Abrams, Inc., Publishers, 1969), 460-61.

[70] Harald Keller, *The Renaissance in Italy*, trans. by Robert E. Wolf (New York: Harry N. Abrams, Inc., Publishers, 1969), 286.

[71] *Ibid.*

[72] Hartt, *History of Italian Renaissance Art, op. cit.*, 462.

[73] *Ibid.*

[74] Keller, *op. cit.*, 288.

[75] *Ibid.*, 284-85.

[76] *New International Illustrated Encyclopedia of Art, op. cit.*, 3563.

[77] Janson, *op. cit.*, 348.

[78] *Ibid.*

[79] Alessandro Vezzosi, *Leonardo da Vinci: The Mind of the Renaissance* (New York: Harry N. Abrams, Inc., Publishers, 1997), 130.

[80] *Ibid.*

[81] Combee, *op. cit.*, 472.

[82] Gregory, *op. cit.*, 213.

[83] J. Gresham Machen, *The New Testament: An Introduction to Its Literature and History*, Edited by W. John Cook (Edinburgh: The Banner of Truth Trust, 1997), 29.

[84] "Renaissance," *Encyclopaedia Britannica* (1903), XX:387.

[85] Charles R. Erdman, *The Gospel of Luke* (Philadelphia: The Westminster Press, 1949), 9-11.

[86] Gregory, *op. cit.*, 218.

[87] *Ibid.*, 217-18.

[88] Thomas H. Greer, *A Brief History of Western Man* (New York: Harcourt, Brace & World, Inc., 1968), 25.

[89] "Thales," *Funk & Wagnalls New Encyclopedia* (1990), 25:288.

[90] Greer, *op. cit.*, 26.

[91] *Ibid.*, 26-27.

[92] West, *op. cit.*, 188.

[93] *Pinnock's Goldsmith's Greece, op. cit.*, 355-56.

[94] Rex Warner, *The Greek Philosophers* (New York: The New American Library of World Literature, Inc., 1962), 53.

[95] *Ibid.*, 54.

[96] *Ibid.*, 53.

[97] Greer, *op. cit.*, 27.

[98] *Ibid.*

[99] Warner, *op. cit.*, 53.

[100] *Ibid.*, 54.

[101] H. Framer Smith, *Why Four Gospel Accounts?* (Philadelphia: Westbrook Publishing Company, 1941), 18.

[102] J. Norval Geldenhuys, "Luke," *The Biblical Expositor,* ed. Carl F. H. Henry (Philadelphia: A. J. Holman Company, 1973), 895.

[103] *Ibid.*

[104] *Ibid.*, 896-97.

[105] Erdman, *op. cit.*, 9.

[106] *Ibid.*, 48.

[107] *Ibid.*, 49.

[108] *Ibid.*, 49-50.

[109] *Pinnock's Goldsmith's Greece, op. cit.*, 357-58.

[110] *Ibid.*, 358.

[111] Horace G. Hutchinson, *The Greatest Story in the World* (New York: D. Appleton and Company, 1923), 226.

Figure 10-1. Bas Relief of King Seti I (19th dynasty)

Figure 10-2. The Orpheus Relief

Figure 10-3.

Figure 10-4.

Figure 10-5. St. Francis of Assisi

Figure 10-6. Leonardo da Vinci: Mona Lisa

Figure 10-7. Detail of the Ceiling of the Sistine Chapel

Figure 10-8. Raphael: Madonna of the Chair

Figure 10-9. Fra Filippo Lippi: Mary Kneeling Before the Infant Jesus

Figure 10-10. Raphael: The Disputa

Figure 10-11. Raphael: The School of Athens

Figure 10-12. Detail from The School of Athens

Figure 10-13. Raphael: The Parnassus

Figure 10-14. Leonardo da Vinci: Self-Portrait

Chapter Eleven

The Son of Man: Sympathetic Priest

The ancient Greeks were the originators, and up until the time of Gibbon, the unequalled masters of Western historiography—the written record of significant events, usually including an explanation of their causes. "The standards and interests of the Greek historians dominated historical study and writing for centuries."[1] Unlike historians of a later era, however, Herodotus ("the father of history"), Thucydides (the greatest of the Greek historians), Xenophon, and other educated pagans, "considered speculation on human destiny and moral questions beyond those directly applicable to political life the proper work of philosophers, not historians."[2] Christianity, by contrast, as evidenced in the writings of Luke and the early Church fathers, "introduced new subjects and approaches to history."[3]

> As they contemplated the course of things, they perceived not merely blind chance or a ceaseless round of recurring events but God making his ways known to men; and for this reason they tend to speak in terms of purpose rather than of sequence—not so much "it next happened" as "that it might be fulfilled." The idea that history is, or displays, the fulfillment of a divine plan appears to harmonize with the actions and sayings of Jesus Himself. He made his claim to be the Lord's anointed in terms appropriate to the culture and education of the Hebrews among whom he lived; i.e., in accordance with the forecasts made in Scripture. So when Jesus entered Jerusalem "lowly and riding upon an ass," as Zechariah had foretold, or when he drove the money-changers from the court of the Gentiles in order to show that the days of the Son of Man had arrived when the Temple should be "a house of prayer for all the nations," it was natural enough for the simple folk of Palestine to acclaim him as Messiah.
>
> Similarly, when St. Luke composed the Acts of the Apostles, he related, as the first happening after the Ascension, the election of the twelfth man to replace the traitor Judas. In doing this the author put forward the claim that the Christian Church, the new Israel of God, based on twelve apostles, took the place of the twelve tribes of the old Israel. History is thus seen as a purposeful structure in which the earlier events offer indications of what is to come. It serves also as a schoolmaster drawing lessons from the past.[4]

History's Greatest Events

Historians, whether pagan or Christian, ancient or contemporary, never viewed all historical events with equal significance. Herodotus, for example, believed the conflict between the Greeks and the Persians was of such importance that he devoted nine volumes presenting the results of his enquiry and the causes of the hostilities, in order "to prevent the traces of human events from being erased by time, and to preserve the fame of the important and remarkable achievements produced by both Greeks and non-Greeks."[5]   The Apostle John, while admitting that "many other signs" did Jesus perform, selected only seven of the Lord's miracles for inclusion in his Gospel account. He noted: *"But these are written, that ye might believe that Jesus is the*

Christ, the Son of God; and that believing ye might have life through his name" (John 20:31).
While all historical events may be important, not all are of equal importance.

In 1954 Grosset and Dunlap of New York published a book entitled *History's 100
Greatest Events*, wherein the authors described and illustrated their selection of the
"most memorable and significant events from the dawn of civilization to the present
day."[6] The first sixteen events, which cover the period of time from the beginning of
recorded history to the fall of the Roman Empire in the West, are as follows:

1. Israelites Flee Egypt; Receive Commandments
2. Babylon Bows to Cyrus the Persian
3. Buddha's "Middle Way" Found under Bo Tree
4. Athens First with Democratic Government
5. Confucius Exiled from Lu
6. Greek Stand at Marathon Checks Persian Invasion
7. Alexander Stampedes Persians at Arbela, Starts World Conquest
8. Euclid Established Systematic Geometry
9. Carthage Leveled; Rome Becomes Supreme
10. First Jet Engine Alexandrian Toy
11. Aristotle's Writing Found in Basement
12. Caesar Assassinated
13. Jesus Crucified
14. Jerusalem Razed; Jews Condemned to Wander
15. Constantine Founds New Rome in East
16. Old Rome Falls to Barbarians[7]

Missing from the list covering this time period are events the Judeo-Christian
historians might consider very important, such as the creation of Adam and Eve,
their fall and subsequent eviction from the Garden of Eden, the world-wide flood,
or the confusion of tongues at the Tower of Babel. Yet another incident was to have
such far-reaching consequences that in time it, too, would be remembered as one of
history's greatest events. It is recorded in the second volume of Luke's two-volume
work, the Acts of the Apostles. Turning to the sixteenth chapter, we find the Apostle
Paul, accompanied by Silas, on his second missionary journey. After revisiting the
churches in Derbe, Lystra and Iconium, Luke noted:

> *Now when they had gone throughout Phrygia and the region of Galatia, and were forbidden
> of the Holy Ghost to preach the word in Asia, After they were come to Mysia, they assayed
> to go into Bithynia: but the Spirit suffered them not. And passing by Mysia came down to
> Troas. And a vision appeared to Paul in the night; There stood a man of Macedonia, and
> prayed him, saying, Come over into Macedonia, and help us. And after he had seen the vi-
> sion, immediately we endeavoured to go into Macedonia, assuredly gathering that the Lord
> had called us for to preach the gospel unto them.* ACTS 16:6-10

Paul's call to preach the Gospel in Europe—if it did not appear to be a momen-
tous occasion then—would have far-reaching and eternal consequences, and be the
source of blessing for mankind to the remotest generations. Eventually, the Gospel was
taken from Macedonia and proclaimed in lands that were unfamiliar and continents
that were unknown to the people of the first century. The good news of the saving

power of Jesus Christ was to be universal in its scope and influence, and its introduction into Europe was one of history's most significant events, and a surety that Christ's promise—and last words spoken on earth—would be fulfilled.

> *But ye shall receive power, after that the Holy Ghost is come upon you: and ye shall be witnesses unto me both in Jerusalem, and in all Judaea, and in Samaria, and unto the uttermost part of the earth.* ACTS 1:8

The Macedonian Call

Luke's account of the Macedonian call is of special interest and of some importance, if we are to appreciate the fact that "history has a purpose and humanity a destiny,"[8] as evidenced not only in the life of the Apostle Paul, but that of Luke as well. From this incident we can see that the Holy Spirit was not only leading and directing the former, but preparing the latter to write a Gospel to the Greeks, which would present Jesus Christ to them as the perfect Man and universal Savior of mankind. From the details Luke shares concerning the circumstances surrounding Paul's call to Europe, the following points are instructive:

(1). Luke personally enters into the account of the Acts of the Apostles and the acquaintance of Paul at the city of Troas, as noted by the writer's sudden change in the use of the pronoun from the third to the first person. The implications of this literary shift have been explained by the eminent nineteenth-century scholar, Sir William Mitchell Ramsay. He wrote:

> Every one recognizes here a distinct assertion that the author was present. Now the paragraph as a whole is carefully studied, and the sudden change from third to first person is a telling element in the total effect: if there is any passage in Acts which can be pressed close, it is this. It is almost universally recognized that the use of the first person in the sequel is intentional, marking that the author remained in Philippi when Paul went on, and that he rejoined the Apostle some years later on his return to Philippi. We must add that the precise point at which the first-personal form of narrative begins is also intentional; for, if Luke changes here at random from third to first person, it would be absurd to look for purpose in anything he says. The first person, when used in the narrative of XVI, XX, XXI, XXVII, XXVIII, marks the companionship of Luke and Paul; and, when we carry out this principle of interpretation consistently and minutely, it will prove an instructive guide. This is the nearest approach to personal reference that Luke permits himself; and he makes it subservient to his historical purpose by using it as a criterion of personal witness.
>
> Luke, therefore, entered into the drama of the Acts at Troas. Now it is clear that the coming of Paul to Troas was unforeseen and unforeseeable; the whole point of the paragraph is that Paul was driven on against his own judgment and intention to that city. The meeting, therefore, was not, as has sometimes been maintained, pre-arranged. Luke entered on the stage of this history at a point, where Paul found himself he knew not why. On the ordinary principles of interpreting literature, we must infer that this meeting, which is so skillfully and so pointedly represented as unforeseen, was between two strangers: Luke

became known to Paul here for the first time. Let us, then, scrutinize more closely the circumstances. The narrative pointedly brings together the dream and the introduction of the first-personal element, "when he saw the vision, straightway we sought to go"; and collocation is everywhere one of the most telling points in Luke's style.

When we examine the dream, we observe that in it "a certain man of Macedonia" was seen by Paul. Paul did not infer his Macedonian origin from his words, but recognized him as a Macedonian by sight. Now, there was nothing distinctive in the appearance or dress of a Macedonian to mark him out from the rest of the world. On the contrary, the Macedonians rather made a point of their claim to be Greeks; and undoubtedly they dressed in the customary Greek style of the Aegean cities. There was, therefore, only one way in which Paul could know the man by sight to be a Macedonian—the man in the dream was personally known to him; and, in fact, the Greek implies that it was a certain definite person who appeared. . . .

In the vision, then, a certain Macedonian, who was personally known to Paul, appeared, and called him over into Macedonia. Now, it has been generally recognized that Luke must have had some connection with Philippi; and we shall find reason to think that he had personal knowledge of the city. Further, Paul, whose life had been spent in the eastern countries, and who had come so far west only a few days past, was not likely to be personally acquainted with natives of Macedonia. The idea then suggests itself at once, that Luke himself was the man seen in the vision; and, when one reads the paragraph with that idea, it acquires new meaning and increased beauty.[9]

The providence of God and the leading of the Holy Spirit brought the foremost missionary to the Gentile world, the Apostle Paul, into close association with Luke, in order to involve and prepare him to write about the *"good tidings of great joy, which shall be to all people"* (Luke 2:10).

(2). The likelihood that Luke had resided for some time in Philippi—and was the *"man of Macedonia"* in Paul's vision—receives further credence from the author's affirmation that Philippi was *"the chief city of that part of Macedonia"* (Acts 16:12). While this may seem like an indifferent—if not irrelevant—statement to the casual reader today, it certainly was not so to the first-century Greek. Dr. Ramsay noted:

The description of the dignity and rank of Philippi is unique in Acts; nor can it be explained as strictly requisite for the historian's proper purpose. Here again the explanation lies in the character of the author, who was specially interested in Philippi, and had the true Greek pride in his own city. Perhaps he even exaggerates a little the dignity of Philippi, which was still only in process of growth, to become at a later date the great city of its division. Of old Amphipolis had been the chief city of the division, to which both belonged. Afterwards Philippi quite outstripped its rival; but it was at that time in such a position, that Amphipolis was ranked first by general consent, Philippi first by its own consent. These cases of rivalry between two or even three cities for the dignity and title of "First" are familiar to every student of the history of the Greek cities; and though no other evidence is known to show that Philippi had as yet began to claim the title, yet this single passage is conclusive. The descriptive phrase is like a lightning flash amid the darkness of local history, revealing in startling clearness the whole situation to those whose eyes are trained to catch the character of Greek city-history and city-jealousies.

It is an interesting fact that Luke, who hides himself so completely in his history, cannot hide his local feeling; and there every one who knows the Greek people recognizes the true Greek! There lies the strength, and also the weakness, of the Greek peoples; and that quality beyond all others has determined their history, has given them their strength against the foreigner, and their weakness as a united country.[10]

(3). The ancient city of Philippi stood about eight miles from the Aegean coast, and was on the great northern highway that connected the East and the West. It was named after Philip II, king of Macedonia and father of Alexander the Great, who established a colony there in 356 B.C. as a base for exploiting the gold and silver mines in the region. And it was here on the plains of Philippi in 42 B.C. that "the empire of the world had been determined when Augustus and Antony defeated Brutus and Cassius."[11]

Luke in this Macedonian city observed a glimpse of the destiny of the Christian missionary movement, "and in the persons who there met the apostles are mirrored the moral and spiritual needs of the ancient and modern world."[12] Together, the three people, who were converted under the ministry of the Apostle Paul, reveal the universal scope of the Gospel of Jesus Christ. Dr. Charles Erdman wrote:

> The first convert to be made in Philippi, and so the first in Europe, was Lydia. She was a woman of wealth, of intelligence, of wide experience, a seller of purple cloth, who had come from the city of Thyatira; moreover she was religious, godly, prayerful. Yet this woman needed salvation, she needed Christ. . . .
>
> The character of Lydia reminds the reader of the Ethiopian eunuch, of Saul of Tarsus, of Cornelius the centurion; all were good, upright, godly; yet they needed the salvation which comes from an intelligent faith in a crucified, risen, divine Christ; and these are typical converts in the history of the early Church.
>
> If Lydia suggests the need of that which the gospel messengers can bring, so her generous act, following her conversion, symbolizes the invaluable support given by women, in all the centuries, to the cause of Christian missions. Lydia the Jewess, however, is not the common type of womanhood in heathen lands; their condition is pictured rather by the poor slave girl . . . possessed by an evil spirit, whose distress was a source of gain to her masters. Such are either the toys or the tools of men. Their nameless agonies and anguish are the real "Macedonian cry" which the Church of Christian lands should heed. Nor is their deepest distress that of outward circumstances; they need to have the evil cast out of their hearts. . . .
>
> The woman of the Orient are not all like the slave girl; some are like Lydia; but millions are waiting for messengers who can speak to them with the confident faith felt by Paul in the omnipotent name of Christ.[13]

228 of the Future

If Lydia represented the upper class of society and the slave girl the lowest, then the Philippian jailor personified the middle class. Regarding his conversion, Dr. Erdman wrote:

> The earthquake which opened the prison, the strange charge against the apostles, the salvation of which they had spoken, his own fear and sense of need, resulted in the conversion of the jailor. He is a type of the debased, depressed, degraded manhood which always needs the gospel. Not all men are like Saul and Cornelius. The jailor's ready acceptance of the message, his subsequent conduct, his immediate confession of faith, all illustrate how clearly he understood the answer which Paul gave to his eager question as to the way of salvation: "Believe on the Lord Jesus, and thou shalt be saved, thou and thy house." Surely that message is adapted to the needs of men of every class and condition.[14]

These representative conversions, which Luke witnessed in Philippi, could not but impress upon him the universal scope of the plan of redemption and the extensive nature of the Kingdom of God. As expected, the Gospel that he wrote reveals the broad sympathies of its author and the wide sway of its message.

> He . . . wrote a gospel characterized by . . . universal interest. Here no narrow prejudice divides race from race; a despised Samaritan stands as the supreme example of a neighbor, the angels sing of peace among men, and the aged Simeon declares that Jesus is to be a "light for revelation to the Gentiles" as well as the glory of Israel. Luke alone gives the data which link the sacred story to the secular history of the world. His outlook is unlimited. He regards the good news concerning Christ as a message which is vital to the welfare and redemption of the entire human race.[15]

It was from Macedonia that Alexander the Great went forth "and for a brief space possessed one of the most splendid empires recorded in history."[16] And it was from there, also, that the Apostle Paul embarked on his European campaign to take the Gospel to the ends of the world, with results that would be even more remarkable!

(4). One of the prominent features in the account of the events leading up to Paul's arrival in Europe is the degree to which the Holy Spirit directed the movement of the Apostle. The Ultimate route of the missionary journey was not determined by coercion or physical restraint, but by Paul's sensitivity and response to the Spirit's leading.

> The natural development of Paul's work along the great central route of the Empire was forbidden, and the next alternative that rose in his mind was forbidden: he was led across Asia from the extreme south-east to the extreme north-west corner, and yet prevented from preaching in it; everything seemed dark and perplexing, until at last a vision in Troas explained the purpose of this strange journey. . . . The author was with Paul in Troas; and the intensity of this paragraph [Acts 16:6-10] is due to his recollection of the words in which Paul had recounted . . . and explained the whole Divine plan that had guided him through his perplexing wanderings. The words derive their vivid and striking character from Paul, and they remained indelibly imprinted on Luke's memory.[17]

The emphasis upon the work of the Holy Spirit that is noted in the Book of Acts is also to be found in the Gospel of Luke. In fact, the third Gospel has more references to the Holy Spirit than the other synoptic Gospels combined. All of the main characters in Luke's narrative are said to be empowered by the Holy Spirit, such as John the Baptist (1:15), Mary (1:35), Elizabeth (1:41), Zacharias (1:67), Simeon (2:25-26), and of course, the Lord, as observed throughout the entire account. Luke portrayed Jesus Christ as the ideal Man, and one of the proofs of this affirmation is that His whole life was under the control of God's Spirit, and by whose presence He was conceived (1:35), baptized (3:21-22), tested (4:1), empowered (4:14, 18), and encouraged (10:21). Furthermore, Luke notes that the Lord's work would continue in the future by His disciples, who would *"be endued with power"* (24:49) by the Holy Spirit on the day of Pentecost.

The prominence of the Holy Spirit in the lives of Jesus Christ and others in Luke's Gospel prefigures the indwelling of all believers in the Church age, and is another way—in addition to those points mentioned in previous chapters—in which his narrative was shaped by the needs of the future, when all those who have trusted in the Name of the Son must be guided by the Promise of the Father (cf. 24:49).

Tracing the Missionary Movement to Its Source

Frederic Louis Godet (1812-1900) was a Swiss clergyman, preceptor of the Crown Prince of Prussia, professor of exegetical and critical theology, and one of the most influential Protestant Reformed scholars of his day. In one of his best known works, *Studies in the New Testament*, he noted:

> If the first gospel may be considered as a treatise upon the messianic sovereignty of Jesus over Israel, the third is not less evidently that which sets forth the right of the Gentiles to share in the salvation marked out by Christ. A gospel such as this could only originate in the circle which surrounded St. Paul in his missionary life.[18]

The Holy Spirit brought Paul and Luke together, and the latter was greatly influenced by the former. From his association with Paul and his attention to the ministry in Macedonia, Luke—as evidenced in his writings—was convinced of two things regarding the Christian message:

1. The message is from God, and its divine origin was attested by manifest signs—works of power, visions and voices, marvelous changes in the minds and hearts of men.

2. It was intended for all men alike. What Luke derived from his master Paul was this spirit of universalism. He is always seeking to enforce the worldwide scope of the gospel, not because he writes for a Gentile public, but because he has fully grasped Paul's great principle that Christ came as the world's Savior. In the book of Acts, he was to trace out the expansion of the movement which began from Jerusalem, but his aim in the Gospel also is to show that Christianity, by its very nature, was universal. Even when Jesus was confining his ministry to Galilee, there was that in his teaching which involved the latter mission. We are shown how he rose superior to the Law, how he recognized faith in publicans and Samaritans, how Gentiles were drawn to him, how his sayings, addressed to his own countrymen, yet breathed the full-

est spirit of humanity. Paul sets himself to prove the universal sweep of the gospel, by arguments derived from scripture and theological reflection. Luke is content to assure us that it was inherent in the whole character and teaching of Jesus, even while he lived on earth.[19]

The points mentioned above are dramatically brought home by the manner and location whereby Luke begins the public ministry of Jesus Christ. He wrote:

> *And Jesus returned in the power of the Spirit into Galilee: and there went out a fame of him through all the region round about. And he taught in their synagogues, being glorified of all. And he came to Nazareth, where he had been brought up: and, as his custom was, he went into the synagogue on the Sabbath day, and stood up for to read. And there was delivered unto him the book of the prophet Esaias. And when he had opened the book, he found the place where it was written, The Spirit of the Lord is upon me, because he hath anointed me to preach the gospel to the poor; he hath sent me to heal the brokenhearted, to preach deliverance to the captives, and recovering of sight to the blind, to set at liberty them that are bruised, To preach the acceptable year of the Lord. And he closed the book, and he gave it again to the minister, and sat down. And the eyes of all them that were in the synagogue were fastened on him. And he began to say unto them, This day is this scripture fulfilled in your ears. 4:14-21*

Only in Luke's account do we find that Christ's first recorded sermon began with the reading of a portion of the Old Testament Scriptures. "Luke places this sermon at the very opening of his record of the public ministry of Jesus, probably because he regarded it as containing the program of that ministry, or as forming the proclamation of the saving work of our Lord.[20]

> It was a Sabbath Day. The place of worship was crowded with the relatives and friends and townsmen of Jesus. All were eager to hear one whom they knew so well, and who had attained so sudden a renown. Either at his request, or providentially, Jesus was handed the book of Isaiah to lead in the reading of the Scripture. He found the place in the prophecy where, in terms of the joy of Jubilee, the writer is describing the gladness of those who are to return from their long captivity in Babylon. When Jesus had finished the lesson he sat down, thereby taking the attitude of a public teacher. As all gazed upon him intently, he undertook to show that the prophecy was to be fulfilled by himself, claiming thereby to be the promised Messiah. The very phrase with which the prophecy begins, "The Spirit of the Lord is upon me," indicates, when applied to himself, that he had been anointed, not with oil as a prophet or a priest or a king, but with the Holy Spirit as the Anointed One, or the Christ of God. As such he was "to preach good tidings to the poor," that is, to those in spiritual as well as in physical poverty. He was to proclaim deliverance for those enslaved by sin and to establish those principles which will result in political freedom for mankind. He was "to set at liberty them that are bruised," that is, to remove the consequences and the cruelties of selfishness and of crime. He was to proclaim the era of universal blessedness which will result from his perfected reign. Thus in these words, which combine the figures of deliverance from captivity with those of the joy of jubilee, Jesus expressed the gracious and beneficent character of his ministry.[21]

Initially, His listeners were amazed, "and unable to resist the charm of his address or to deny the fascinating beauty of his words."[22] Luke noted, *"And all bare him witness, and wondered at the gracious words which proceeded out of his mouth"* (4:22a).

The accounts of this incident in the synagogue, as recorded by Matthew and Mark, are both similar to each other, but somewhat different from Luke's version. Matthew wrote:

> *And when he was come into his own country, he taught them in their synagogue, insomuch that they were astonished, and said, Whence hath this man this wisdom, and these mighty works? Is not this the carpenter's son? Is not his mother called Mary? And his brethren, James, and Joses, and Simon, and Judas? And his sisters, are they not all with us? Whence then hath this man all these things? And they were offended in him. But Jesus said unto them, A prophet is not without honour, save in his own country, and in his own house. And he did not many mighty works there because of their unbelief.* MATT. 13:54-58

In like manner, Mark noted:

> *And he went out from thence, and came into his own country; and his disciples follow him. And when the Sabbath day was come, he began to teach in the synagogue: and many hearing him were astonished, saying, From whence hath this man these things? And what wisdom is this which is given unto him, that even such mighty works are wrought by his hands? Is not this the carpenter, the son of Mary, the brother of James, and Joses, and of Juda, and Simon? And are not his sisters here with us? And they were offended at him. But Jesus said unto them, A prophet is not without honour, but in his own country, and among his own kin, and in his own house. And he could there do no mighty work, save that he laid his hands upon a few sick folk, and healed them. And he marveled because of their unbelief.* MARK 6:1-6A

The first two synoptic Gospels leave the impression that the Lord was rejected outright, and that His kinsfolk were immediately offended at Him, because *"a prophet is not without honour, save in his own country"* (Matt. 13:57; cf. Mark 6:4). And while this is true, it is not the whole story. Luke makes it clear that the unbelief of the people (cf. Matt. 13:58; Mark 6:6) was turned to overt hostility only when Christ revealed to His listeners the true scope of His ministry. Luke tells us:

> *And all bare him witness, and wondered at the gracious words which proceeded out of his mouth. And they said, Is not this Joseph's son? And he said unto them, Ye will surely say unto me this proverb, Physician, heal thyself: whatsoever we have heard done in Capernaum, do also here in thy country. And he said, Verily I say unto you, No prophet is accepted in his own country. But I tell you of a truth, many widows were in Israel in the days of Elias, when the heaven was shut up three years and six months, when great famine was throughout all the land; But unto none of them was Elias sent, save unto Sarepta, a city of Sidon, unto a woman that was a widow. And many lepers were in Israel in the time of Eliseus the prophet; and none of them was cleansed, saving Naaman the Syrian. And all they in the synagogue, when they heard these things, were filled with wrath, And rose up, and thrust him out of the city, and led him unto the brow of the hill whereon their city was built, that they might cast him down headlong. But he passing through the midst of them went his way.* 4:22-30

In Luke's account, the people's response, *"Is not this Joseph's son?"* (v. 22), seems to proceed more from surprise, rather than anger (cf. Mark 6:5). "But Jesus is finally rejected, not because he claims authority, but because he extends salvation to the wrong people."[23]

The unbelief of his auditors was turned to mad hatred as Jesus gave two examples from Old Testament history, both of which indicated that his townsmen, who knew him best, were less worthy of his saving ministry than even men of heathen nations. He even compared himself with Elijah and Elisha and indicated that as the former brought a great blessing to one who lived in Sidon and the latter to a prince in Syria, while the people in Israel were suffering for their unbelief, so the nations of the world would accept the blessed salvation of Christ while those who knew him best would suffer for their unbelief. So maddened were his hearers by this severe rebuke that they drove him from the city and tried to take his life, but he, with majestic calm and divine strength, "passing through the midst of them went his way."

It is still true that those who have enjoyed the best opportunities for knowing Christ often reject him; but, where faith is present, broken hearts are healed as by Elijah of old and lepers are cleansed as was Naaman by the word of Elisha. Thus in this scene in the synagogue of Nazareth, Jesus indicated not only the grace of his ministry but its universal power. He came to relieve all the needs of mankind and in all the world.[24]

An Interest in People

During a period of approximately 150 years—dated from the emergence of Athenian supremacy to the extinction of the empire after the time of Alexander the Great—the Greeks produced an incredible number of remarkable and distinguished individuals. Historians agree that the Greeks "looked upon themselves as having the mission of perfecting men."[25] They believed that man "was made to seek the true, to love the beautiful, to sympathize with human kind."[26] Yet they never fully achieved their goal. "Philosophy had strengthened the great minds of Greece, and the most accomplished intellects of Rome, but still had left an aching void in the heart."[27] To fill this void Luke penned a Gospel that would be of interest to the thinking Greek.

A Gospel for the Greek must present the character and career of Jesus of Nazareth from the Greek point of view, as answering to the conception of a perfect and divine humanity; must exhibit him as adapted, in his power and mercy, in his work and mission, to the wants of the Greek soul, and of humanity as represented in it.[28]

Sensitive to the Greek nature, which brought them "into sympathy with man as man,"[29] Luke introduced his readers to a fascinating array of memorable characters, both real and imagined (those in the parables), that would win the respectful attention of the most cultivated audience to which any book of the Bible was addressed. And while all the evangelists convey the compassion of Jesus Christ, Luke's approach is somewhat different. Comparing his style with that of Matthew, one commentator noted:

Because he believed in the universal power of the gospel, Luke focused attention upon its impact on the lives of various individuals. Jesus' three famous parables in chapter 15, unique to this gospel, stress His concern for individuals. Luke notes that Jesus was frequently surrounded by great crowds who were amazed at His words (5:26; 7:16-17; 11:14; 13:17; 14:25), but unlike Matthew (9:36; 15:32), Luke "does not speak of Jesus' compassion on the multitude. This is reserved for individuals."[30]

Luke's Character Sketches

The French savant, Joseph Ernest Renan (1823-1892), described the third Gospel as "the most beautiful book ever written" ("C'est le plus beau livre qu'il y ait").[31] It is universally recognized as the product of a writer of remarkable versatility and style, who wrote in a language more literary than that of his sources.

Not only Renan but many others have exhausted their copious vocabularies in praise of the large-heartedness and sweetness of this Gospel. This beauty of Luke's Gospel is in part because of its fine literary style, its scholarly presentation, and its freedom from involved statements. It is also beautiful because of the choice of material which Luke makes and because of the fact that he pictures Jesus in a most beautiful light in his relationship to humanity—men, women, and little children.[32]

Like other Greek artists, Luke "had an artist's soul. He loved the good and beautiful and true. . . . We know that he was an extraordinary man in many respects; and we know that if he never put any portraits on canvas, he has put them on his written page with such artistic excellence"[33] that the result is a masterpiece "which a competent critic declares to be the most beautiful book ever written."[34]

Luke's style is simple and dignified. He reveals a strong power of accurate observation, a vividness of description, and the ability to delineate a character or paint a scene with a few vigorous lines or words. "He possesses the art of composition. He knows not only how to tell a tale truthfully, but how to tell it with effect."[35]

Viewing Luke's work from another perspective, furthermore, it should be noted that his vivid word pictures of individual men and women have had such a great influence upon later Christian art, that "in a real sense he may be called the founder."[36]

Both medieval and modern artists have been specially fond of representing those scenes which are described by Luke alone: the annunciation, the visit of Mary to Elisabeth, the shepherds, the manger, the presentation in the temple, Simeon and Anna, Christ with the doctors, the woman at the supper of Simon the Pharisee, Christ weeping over Jerusalem, the walk to Emmaus, the good Samaritan, the prodigal son. Many other scenes which are favorites with painters might be added from the Acts.[37]

"He may not have been an artist with his brush, but we know that he was an artist with his pen."[38] "Luke's ability to draw word pictures is evident in his description of the godly priest Zacharias (1:5-23, 57-79), the extortionate tax collector Zacchaeus (19:1-10), and the mourning Cleopas and his companion on the Emmaus road (24:13-33)."[39] In fact,

His Gospel is everywhere a picture book, full of persons and scenes which stand out unforgettably. This side of his genius appears at its very best in his record of the parables. It may be that he is here indebted to his special source, but the manner in which he tells the parables is so much in keeping with his style in general that it must be his own. To the skill with which Luke has reported them, the parables owe much of the hold which they have taken on the world's imagination. Once more, Luke was endowed, in a rare degree, with tenderness and sympathy. It is he, more than any other of the evangelists, who helps us to understand the compassion of Jesus, his kindness to the weak and erring, the pathos and sorrow of his own life. Here again we need to remember that Luke had access to special sources, from which he borrowed such lovely stories as those of Martha and Mary, Zacchaeus, and the sinful woman who wept at the feet of Jesus. But he had a nature which could respond to such stories and preserve their beauty, where a single false touch would have spoiled them.[40]

Luke's illuminating descriptions of individual men, women, and children, as they unfold in the account of the life and ministry of Jesus Christ, help us to understand both the nature of His person and the significance of His mission.

We come back, however, to the chief purpose of the Gospel, which is to present an account of Jesus more adequate than those which had hitherto appeared. Luke is not content, like Mark, to deal simply with a few striking events of the ministry. His object is to write a biography, similar to those lives of famous men which were coming into vogue in the classical literature of the time. Like other popular biographers, he wishes by means of typical anecdotes to illustrate the character of Jesus and make him stand before us a human personality. In Mark the incidents are selected with a view to proving Jesus' messiahship. Luke wants to throw light on Jesus himself, and to make us realize how men felt towards him. This interest in character may be discerned also in Luke's record of the teaching. He wishes us to regard the sayings, not only as maxims for the conduct of the Christian life, but as revealing Jesus himself in his manner of thinking and his outlook on the world. If Luke was not a theologian, he had a keen eye for human life, and was susceptible in a peculiar degree to nobility and greatness wherever he found them. This is strikingly apparent in his portrait of Paul, and still more so in his picture of Jesus himself.[41]

The greatness of Jesus and the graciousness of His character are revealed in His response to the penitent thief, which was recorded only by Luke. We read:

> And there were also two other, malefactors, led with him to be put to death. And when they were come to the place, which is called Calvary, there they crucified him, and the malefactors, one on the right hand, and the other on the left. . . . And one of the malefactors which were hanged railed on him, saying, If thou be Christ, save thyself and us. But the other answering rebuked him, saying, Dost not thou fear God, seeing thou art in the same condemnation? And we indeed justly; for we receive the due reward of our deeds: but this man hath done nothing amiss. And he said unto Jesus, Lord, remember me when thou comest into thy kingdom. And Jesus said unto him, Verily I say unto thee, To day shalt thou be with me in paradise.
> 23:32-33, 39-43

How gracious he was to that dying thief! The malefactor was suffering his just deserts. He had been a robber, and in all probability a murderer, and he was receiving the penalty due for his crimes. His fellow malefactor prayed to Jesus for salvation, "Save thyself and us," but it was in words of mockery and not of devotion; and Jesus paid no heed to him. Possibly he was the only one who ever asked Jesus for salvation and found his cry for help unheeded. The other dying thief recognized the innocence of Jesus and rebuked his fellow sufferer for his failure in courtesy to such a character. He did not ask for salvation from the cross or from death. He asked Jesus only to remember him when the kingdom preached had come. It was the most sublime faith chronicled in our New Testament. He believed in the character of Jesus and in the coming of his kingdom, despite all contrary evidence. All of the disciples of Jesus had forsaken him and fled away. They had seen Jesus raise the dead and yet their faith had failed them in that hour. The thief upon the cross sees Jesus dying upon the cross at his side, and yet has faith in him![42]

The story of the penitent thief is one of the most significant narratives in the Gospels, "because it gives us such a picture of the unique person of Christ; here was a dying man who at the same time was a forgiving God."[43] Moreover, it provides "a picture of the transforming power of Christ who in an instant of time changed a robber into a saint."[44] The malefactor was by everyone's assessment a sinner, yet it was for such an individual that the Son of man came *"to seek and to save"* (Luke 19:10). Early in His ministry Jesus had said, *"I came not to call the righteous, but sinners to repentance"* (Luke 5:32).

This is the Gospel for the sinner. It brings out Christ's compassionate love in becoming man to save man.

In Luke we see God manifest in the flesh. Luke deals with the humanity of our Lord. He reveals the Savior as a man with all His sympathies, feelings and growing powers—a Savior suited to all. In this Gospel we see the God of glory coming down to our level, entering into our conditions, and being subject to our circumstances.[45]

Jesus Christ, The Son of Man

The Gospel of Luke contains information not elsewhere described, which vividly illustrates the true humanity of Jesus Christ. For example:

(1). He is introduced in Matthew by genealogy, in Mark by character, and in John as from eternity; but in Luke the Messiah is introduced by family surroundings. As man He "must be quite in touch with all human surroundings."[46]

The story opens with certain family portraits; His mother, her cousin Elisabeth and her husband Zacharias, the aged priest in the Temple. Then we find old Simeon and the aged prophetess Anna, and His own cousin John the Baptist. On almost the first page, you have an inn, sheep, shepherds, and angels, too. Heaven and earth mingling because some one from heaven has arrived on earth in a most interesting and human way.[47]

(2). Luke begins the second chapter of his Gospel by noting, *"And it came to pass in those days that there went out a decree from Caesar Augustus, that all the world should be taxed. . . . And all went to be taxed, every one into his own city"* (2:1, 3). Then he shares information we would never find in Matthew's Account: *"And Joseph also went up from Galilee, out of the city of Nazareth, into Judea, unto the city of David, which is called Bethlehem; . . . To be taxed with Mary his espoused wife"* (2:4-5). "Luke is not showing here One who has claims to rule, but One who is coming down to take the place man then occupied."[48] His detailed descriptions of the events surrounding the birth of Christ "make very real the true humanity of Jesus."[49]

(3). Jesus' parents were law-abiding people (cf. 2:39), who did for their Son what was required of them by the Law. Luke tells us that *"when eight days were accomplished"* (2:21) Jesus was circumcised according to the Law of Moses (cf. Lev. 12:3). When He was young, Christ's parents did *"for him after the custom of the law"* (2:27); but when He was of age, Jesus continued the customs under which He was brought up. At the very beginning of Christ's public ministry, Luke noted:

> *And he came to Nazareth, where he had been brought up: and, as his custom was, he went into the synagogue on the Sabbath day, and stood up for to read.* 4:16

Like any normal person, Jesus, too, had habits, and one of His was to attend synagogue services regularly on the Sabbath. Members participated in these services, and on this occasion the Lord was asked to read the Scripture and make a few comments. When Christ applied the prophecy of Isaiah 61 to Himself, the audience was astonished. They had known Jesus in His childhood and youth, and He did not appear to them as anyone other than what might be expected from someone of humble family working in the trade of carpenter.

(4). The one and only recorded event of Christ's boyhood is found in Luke 2:41-52. It "is the narrative of the first visit to the temple, to attend Passover, and the closing scene of it, when He was for three days lost to His mother."[50]

> The whole story is so human, so tender—the active mind of the boy, the keen interest in the wonderful surroundings, the anxious inquiries, the charm of such an intelligent seeker after truth amongst those teachers, the forgetfulness almost as to how time was going, the surprise in His voice and manner when He hears His mother has been seeking Him sorrowing, the unconscious position of the child, and yet the absorbing nature of the things which had so completely filled His vision, as His real relation to things around Him was evidently beginning to dawn upon Him in a new way—who He was, whence He came, and what was His mission in this world? Yet behind it all, there is the utter submission to the will of His parents so that, although He had in His mind chosen to undertake the business of teacher, to which He felt, in His inmost soul, God had called Him, He makes no further utterance about it, but goes back to Nazareth, there to be apprenticed to the business of carpenter, and give His first illustration of what He afterwards so frequently taught, that He had not come down to do His own will. This was the first step in that pathway which closed with the prayer in Gethsemane: *"Not as I will, but as Thou wilt."*[51]

(5). Only Matthew and Luke record the genealogy of Christ, yet there are differences in their versions, which are most significant. First of all, there is a difference in the order.

> The genealogy in Matthew follows the order of descent; Luke ascends the family line from son to father. The former is the order of an official record; individuals are registered only as they are born; the latter is that of a private document compiled from the public records with a view to fixing the attention upon the particular person whose name stands at the head of the list. This is quite in accord with the literary art of Luke, who desires at this point in the narrative to center the thought upon the supreme importance of Jesus, the Savior, of whose redeeming work he is now to write.[52]

Then again, there is in the two genealogical records a difference in the names.
    While the names given by Luke, from Abraham to David, correspond with those given by Matthew, the names from David to Jesus differ. Some have attempted to explain the differences on the ground that Matthew gives the genealogy of Joseph, while Luke gives that of Mary. . . .
    Then, too, the genealogy in Matthew begins with Abraham, while Luke traces the line back to Adam. The former proves Jesus to be a Jew, the true son of Abraham, in whom the covenant was fulfilled. The latter reminds us that Jesus belongs to the whole human race. It makes us look beyond all national lines and remember that this ideal Man on whom Luke is fixing our thoughts is the Savior of mankind.[53]

(6). Much more frequently than the other evangelists, Luke "pictures Jesus as entering into all the social relations of life."[54]
    In his gospel Jesus is portrayed as enjoying social fellowship in the homes of friends and followers: the meal in the house of Martha and Mary (10:38-42), His visit in the home of Zacchaeus (19:1-10), and the supper in the home of the two Emmaus disciples (24:29-31). Jesus readily associated with publicans and sinners at table, for which He was criticized (15:2). Luke alone recounts that on three separate occasions Jesus accepted an invitation to dine with a Pharisee (7:36; 11:37; 14:1). Jesus used the domestic setting to reach people regardless of their sex, background, or social status.[55]
    The domestic side of life is not confined to the personal activities of Christ, moreover, but is also revealed in the many parables that He used in His teaching ministry.
    In the parables peculiar to the third Gospel there are many glimpses of home life, showing how our Lord had been observant of many domestic experiences. The master of the house who rises up and shuts to the door and makes all safe for the night, the neighbor who comes knocking loudly at midnight and asking to borrow a few loaves of bread, the woman raising a great dust and upsetting the whole house until she finds the lost coin, the great banquet with music and dancing to celebrate the prodigal's return—all these things Luke lets us know that the Lord had seen and had made note of for use in his preaching. In the parable of the mustard seed Mark says that the seed was sown in the earth (Mark 4:31), and Matthew says in the field (Matt. 13:31), but Luke says the man sowed it in his own garden (Luke 13:19).[56]

(7). The physical side of Christ's Person is clearly revealed in Luke's account of Jesus' life and ministry. The references to His being wrapped in swaddling clothes and lying in a manger (2:12), the paps which He had sucked (11:27), that He increased in wisdom and stature (2:52), His tearful lament over Jerusalem (19:41), that He kneeled down to pray (22:41), and his sweat as it were great drops of blood falling down to the ground in the Garden of Gethsemane (22:44), are just a few of the many examples that could be given. Moreover, Christ's true humanity is not confined to His pre-resurrection life, but is evident even after His resurrection. "Only Luke informs us that Jesus verified the reality of His resurrection-body by inviting His followers to 'handle' Him, and ate a piece of 'broiled fish' before them (24:39-43)."[57]

By the time 40 days had elapsed since His resurrection, the Lord had on nine occasions "been visibly present to human eyes, and had been touched by human hands."[58] Nevertheless, the time eventually came when His earthly presence would be taken away. Yet even here the true humanity of Jesus is clearly revealed. After Christ met His disciples in Jerusalem, Luke noted:

> And he led them out as far as to Bethany, and he lifted up his hands, and blessed them. And it came to pass, while he blessed them, he was parted from them, and carried up into heaven. 24:50-51

Whereas Mark says, *"he was received up into heaven"* (Mark 16:19), Luke tells us that Jesus was *"carried up."* As a man, He was physically removed from earth and visibly parted from His disciples.

Today, Jesus Christ *"is set on the right hand of the throne of the majesty in the heavens"* (Heb. 8:1), where *"he ever liveth to make intercession for them,"* who have *"come unto God by him"* (Heb. 7:25). Yet the Messiah's ministry of intercession did not begin after His ascension, but much before it, as Luke makes very clear in his Gospel.

Christ's Ministry of Intercession

The term Messiah is a translation of a Hebrew word that means anointed one. This verbal noun is primarily applied to three types of individuals in the Old Testament, which symbolized the "three administrative offices established by God for His people Israel: the king, the priest, and the prophet."[59]

> The king ruled over Israel for God; the priest represented the people before God; and the prophet spoke to the people from God. Each was anointed with oil when he assumed his office either as king (1 Sam. 16:3), priest (Exod. 28:41), or prophet (1 Kings 19:16). Thus, each could be referred to as an "anointed one" or a "messiah" (*mashiah* in Hebrew) in the general sense of the term. While an individual could serve as both a priest and a prophet (e.g., Samuel), and one person might serve as both king and prophet (e.g., David), no single Israelite ever served in the dual roles of priest and king. Those who attempted to do so were judged by God (1 Sam. 13; 2 Chr. 26:16-21). Only the Messiah could serve as both priest and king (Zech. 6:12-13). The role of prophet also would belong to the Messiah, thus combining all three of these normally separate offices.[60]

Whereas the synoptic Gospels are alike in their presentation of Jesus Christ as the promised Messiah, they differ in their emphasis of the three-fold office He would assume. Matthew stresses the role of the King, and quickly brings the key personalities to Bethlehem, the city of David. Mark highlights the work of the Prophet, and begins in the wilderness, where some of the greatest prophets had lived (e.g., Elijah, John the Baptist). Luke emphasizes the office of the Priest, and begins in the Temple at Jerusalem, where we are introduced *"to a certain priest named Zacharias"* (1:5). The initial setting from which their stories unfold, is one indication of where the synoptic Gospels are going in their presentation of Jesus Christ, as One who was anointed of God for a special role. It is not without design, then, that Luke begins his story in the Temple at Jerusalem.

Alfred Edersheim in his classic work, *The Temple: Its Ministry and Services*, informs us that "direct choice and appointment by God were the conditions alike of the priesthood, of sacrifices, feasts, and of every detail of service."[61] He went on to say that "the fundamental ideas which underlay all and connected it into a harmonious whole, were reconciliation and mediation: the one expressed by typically atoning sacrifices, the other by a typically intervening priesthood."[62]

In His unique role as Priest, Jesus Christ would not only provide mediation, but reconciliation as well. The former was—and still is—carried out in life, but the latter was accomplished in death.

> For Christ is not entered into the holy places made with hands, which are the figures of the true; but into heaven itself, now to appear in the presence of God for us: Nor yet that he should offer himself often, as the high priest entereth into the holy place every year with blood of others; For then must he often have suffered since the foundation of the world: but now once in the end of the world hath he appeared to put away sin by the sacrifice of himself. And it is appointed unto men once to die, but after this the judgment: So Christ was once offered to bear the sins of many; and unto them that look for him shall he appear the second time without sin unto salvation. HEB. 9:24-28

"The Greek teachers had recognized the necessity for sacrifice in order to the realization of personal perfection, but that a perfect One should suffer for the imperfect was new, and this is the story of the last division of the Gospel."[63] Nevertheless, it is of interest to note that it is in a scene in the Temple, in the early part of Luke's narrative, that "the strife and suffering which lay ahead of Jesus were referred to for the first time in the Gospel."[64] Luke wrote:

> And, behold, there was a man in Jerusalem, whose name was Simeon; and the same man was just and devout, waiting for the consolation of Israel: and the Holy Ghost was upon him. And it was revealed unto him by the Holy Ghost, that he should not see death, before he had seen the Lord's Christ. And he came by the Spirit into the temple: and when the parents brought in the child Jesus, to do for him after the custom of the law, Then took he him up in his arms, and blessed God, and said, Lord, now lettest thou thy servant depart in peace, according to they word: For mine eyes have seen they salvation, Which thou hast prepared before the face of all people; A light to lighten the Gentiles, and the glory of thy people Israel. And Joseph and his mother marveled at those things which were spoken of him. And Simeon blessed them, and said unto Mary his mother, Behold, this child is set for the fall and rising again of many in Israel; and for a sign which shall be spoken against; (Yea, a sword shall pierce through thy own soul also,) that the thoughts of many hearts may be revealed. 2:25-35

The cross of the Son was to be a sword to the mother. Dr. Erdman noted:

> To the wondering mother, Simeon uttered a dark word of prophecy. The ministry of Jesus will be the occasion for the fall and rise of many. Their attitude toward him will be a revelation of character; some will reject him and thus condemn themselves; some will speak against him, even though he is the very token and instrument of divine salvation; this opposition will reach its climax at the cross, when bitter anguish like a sword will pierce the soul of Mary.[65]

The Old Testament reveals that thirty years was the legal age for one entering the priesthood (cf. Num. 4:3, 47). "It was also the age at which the scribes entered upon professional duty as teachers."[66] Because he stresses the high-priestly work of Christ, Luke begins the genealogy of the Son of man by saying, "And Jesus himself began to be about thirty years of age, being (as was supposed) the son of Joseph, which was the son of Heli . . ." (3:23).

Luke continues to trace Christ's family tree back not only to David or Abraham, but to *"Adam, which was the son of God"* (3:38). Because the Messiah would Himself become the atoning sacrifice for the sins of the whole world, the third Gospel links Christ to all mankind. Furthermore, it is most significant that Luke connects the Lord's genealogy (3:23-38) with His baptism (3:21-22), and not with His birth, as does Matthew. Whereas Matthew links the genealogy to the miracle of His birth, Luke ties it in with the symbolism of His death.

> In His life He had acted out the task assigned to the ideal man. In His death He fulfilled that of fallen man. Assuredly it was competent only to a man, a true man, to be in this way the representative before God of humanity in his guilt. An angel from heaven could not have fulfilled this mission. To bear the shame of a family, must one not be a member of it? In order that we may feel to the quick a great national crime, must we not ourselves belong to the guilty nation? Sympathy, carried to the extent of the miracle of actual solidarity and even self-substitution, presupposes complete community of life.[67]

"The fundamental idea of sacrifice in the Old Testament is that of substitution,"[68] and it is in His own baptism that Jesus identifies with those who received *"the baptism of repentance"* in order that he might assume the vicarious punishment for the remission of their sins (cf. Luke 3:3). Luke tells us:

> *Now when all the people were baptized, it came to pass, that Jesus also being baptized, and praying, the heaven was opened, And the Holy Ghost descended in a bodily shape like a dove upon him, and a voice came from heaven, which said, Thou art my beloved Son; in thee I am well pleased.* 3:21-22

From this passage a few points need to be recognized as they relate to the high-priestly work of Jesus Christ. First of all, only Luke tells us that *"when all the people were baptized,"* then Jesus also was baptized. Additionally, the voice from heaven declared that God was well pleased with His beloved Son. Together, these facts reveal the true nature of the Messiah's substitutionary work. The first discloses that Christ would be the atoning sacrifice for all people; the second, that He would be the perfect sacrifice.

> This substitution of Jesus for sinful humanity implies not only the reality, but also the perfect holiness, of His human nature. It was only in his vesture of fine white linen that the high priest could enter the holy of holies to intercede for the people. He was not permitted to sprinkle the blood of any but a victim without blemish upon the altar of propitiation. Accordingly, none but a perfectly holy man could expiate sin, and intercede for the sinner. In fact, only such an one could feel in his conscience the hateful character of the sin that had to be washed out, and estimate aright the greatness of the injury offered to the Divine majesty by this act of rebellion. Strange as it may seem, the moral compensation due to God for the sin of mankind could only be offered by a being who had not shared in it, and whose conscience had therefore remained free from the kind of pain which affects the man who has allowed himself to be led astray and blinded by sin. In order to be able to deplore and condemn sin in the way in which God judges and condemns it, one must be personally exempt from it. Man unfallen could alone offer the compensation due to God from man fallen.[69]

Finally, Luke's version of Christ's baptism suggests that His priesthood would not only involve reconciliation, but mediation as well. Only Luke tells us that Jesus was praying at the time of His baptism.

The third Gospel is unmistakably the Gospel of prayer. Ten times Luke calls attention to the prayers of Jesus (cf. 3:21; 5:16; 6:12; 9:18; 9:29; 11:1; 22:32; 22:41; 23:34; 23:46). Seven of these references are unique to this Gospel. Furthermore, the eleventh chapter contains what is commonly called the Lord's Prayer (vv. 2-4), as well as some instruction on prayer, as illustrated by the Importunate Friend (vv. 5-13). Elsewhere, we find two specially recorded parables on prayer; namely, the Widow and the Unjust Judge (18:1-8), and the Pharisee and the Publican (18:9-14).

Christ's priestly-work of mediation is clearly evident in two of His intercessory prayers, both of which are referenced to only in Luke. One is the Prayer of the Crucified for His enemies. From the cross Jesus said, *"Father, forgive them, for they know not what they do"* (23:34). The other is mentioned in the incident just prior to the arrival at Gethsemane, when Peter was foretold that he would three times deny the Lord (cf. 22:34). It was in this context that Luke "records Jesus' declaration to Peter that He had prayed for him that his faith would not fail (22:31-32)."[70]

Yet his faith did fail, and he and the other disciples distanced themselves from the Lord, the closer He came to the cross. This is especially noteworthy (and symbolic), since the high priest entered the Holy of Holies alone (cf. Heb. 9:7), when he offered the prescribed sacrifices on the Day of Atonement. No man could follow the high priest into the Holy of Holies, nor could any really accompany Christ, as He assumed the role of *"high priest of good things to come, by a greater and more perfect tabernacle"* (Heb. 9:11). G. Campbell Morgan noted:

> It is impossible to follow the Lord into the place of His mightiest work. Alone He entered and wrought. No man followed Him, nor could follow Him at all, in help, or in sympathy, or in understanding. Fallen man was degraded in will, emotion, and intelligence, and therefore was not able to help, or sympathize, or understand. From that inner mystery, therefore, man was excluded.
>
> Tracing the Lord through the three years in which He was constantly conscious of the Cross, it will be noticed how gradually and yet surely He moved out into the loneliness of the final fact of His work. While living in Nazareth He was a favorite. He "advanced in wisdom and stature, and in favour with God and men" (Luke 2:52). At the commencement of His public ministry both the rulers and the multitudes gathered round Him. The men of light and leading were at least interested in Him, and ready to listen to Him, and more than inclined to patronize Him. They were among the first to fall back from Him. As He, in the great progress of His teaching, uttered deeper and yet deeper truths, men who were merely curious became excluded, and only His own disciples remained in anything approaching close association with Him. Yet further on, the ranks of the disciples were thinned. After the discourse recorded in the sixth chapter of John, in which He declared He would give His flesh for the meat, and His blood for the drink, of the world, many went back and walked no more with Him. Without closely following the details, it will be seen that His approach to His Cross is marked by constant withdrawals, until at last the nearest flee, the story of their going being recorded in one tragic

sentence, "Then all the disciples left Him, and fled" (Matt. 26:56).

He passed into the actual place of His passion, the region of that mystery of pain through which He was about to solve these problems, in utter loneliness. No man could help, no man could sympathize, no man could understand. Let this always be borne in mind when His suffering is followed and contemplated.[71]

Although "men may gather reverently to the place of the passion,"[72] none can really comprehend the extent of Christ's sufferings or the depth of His love. Yet you can know most assuredly, that by the way of the cross, and by that way alone, Christ appeared one day *"to put away sin by the sacrifice of himself"* (Heb. 9:26).

> For on that day shall the priest make an atonement for you, to cleanse you, that ye may be clean from all your sins before the Lord. LEV. 16:30

Those who have been cleansed from all their sins should have a desire to *"worship in the Lord's house"* (Jer. 26:2); and it is a fitting conclusion to Luke's narrative that the last vision the disciples had of Christ (cf. 26:50) was "that of hands outstretched in priestly benediction as He left them, in consequence of which they returned to the Temple and to worship; thus, through His priesthood, fulfilling their own."[73]

Chapter Eleven Notes

[1] "History and Historiography," *Funk & Wagnalls New Encyclopedia* (1990), 13:127.

[2] *Ibid.*, 128.

[3] *Ibid.*

[4] "History," *Encyclopaedia Britannica* (1970), 11:531.

[5] Herodotus, *The Histories*, trans. by Robin Waterfield (New York: Oxford University Press, 1998), 3.

[6] William A. DeWitt, *History's Hundred Greatest Events: The Most Significant Events in the Record of Mankind from the Dawn of Civilization to the Present Day*, Illustrated by Samuel Nisenson (New York: Grosset & Dunlap, Publishers, 1954), ix.

[7] *Ibid.*, v.

[8] Paul Johnson, *A History of the Jews* (New York: Harper & Row, Publishers, 1987), 2.

[9] William M. Ramsay, *St. Paul the Traveller and the Roman Citizen* (New York: G. P. Putnam's Sons, 1904), 201-03.

[10] *Ibid.*, 206-07.

[11] Charles R. Erdman, *The Acts* (Philadelphia: The Westminster Press, n.d.), 118.

[12] *Ibid.*

[13] *Ibid.*, 118-19.

[14] *Ibid.*, 120.

[15] Charles R. Erdman, *The Gospel of Luke* (Philadelphia: The Westminster Press, 1949), 9.

[16] *Pinnock's Improved Edition of Dr. Goldsmith's History of Greece* (Philadelphia: F. W. Greenough, 1838), 261.

[17] Ramsay, *op. cit.*, 200.

[18] Frederic L. Godet, *Studies in the New Testament* (New York: E. P. Dutton & Co., 1895), 46.

[19] Ernest Findlay Scott, *The Literature of the New Testament* (New York: Columbia University Press, 1940), 86-87.

[20] Erdman, *Luke*, 52.

[21] *Ibid.*, 52-53.

[22] *Ibid.*, 53.

[23] Robert A. Spivey and D. Moody Smith, Jr., *Anatomy of the New Testament: A Guide to Its Structure and Meaning*, 2nd ed. (New York: Macmillan Publishing Co., Inc., 1974), 163.

[24] Erdman, *Luke*, 54.

[25] D. S. Gregory, *Why Four Gospels? Or, the Gospel for All the World* (New York: Funk & Wagnalls, Publishers, 1890), 211.

[26] *Ibid.*, 213.

[27] William Smith, *A History of Greece from the Earliest Times to the Roman Conquest* (Boston: Hickling, Swan, and Brown, 1855), 567.

[28] Gregory, *op. cit.*, 217.

[29] *Ibid.*, 213.

[30] D. Edmond Hiebert, *An Introduction to the New Testament, Volume 1: The Gospels and Acts* (Winona Lake, Ind.: BMH Books, 1993), 143.

[31] Ernest Renan, *Les Evangiles* (1877), 283.

[32] Earl L. Martin, *The Gospel of Luke: An Exposition* (Anderson, Ind.: Gospel Trumpet Company, 1944), 5.

[33] D. A. Hayes, *The Synoptic Gospels and the Book of Acts* (New York: The Methodist Book Concern, 1919), 191.

[34] *Ibid.*, 190-91.

[35] Hiebert, *op. cit.*, 146.

[36] Alfred Plummer, *The International Critical Commentary: A Critical and Exegetical Commentary on the Gospel According to St. Luke*, 4th ed. (Edinburgh: T. & T. Clark, 38 George Street, 1901), xxii.

[37] Hayes, *op. cit.*, 190.

[38] *Ibid.*

[39] Hiebert, *op. cit.*, 143.

[40] Scott, *op. cit.*, 84-85.

[41] *Ibid.*, 80-81.

[42] Hayes, *op. cit.*, 211.

[43] Erdman, *Luke*, 217.

[44] *Ibid.*

[45] Henrietta C. Mears, *What the Bible Is All About* (Glendale, Cal.: Regal Books Division, Gospel Light Publications, 1966), 391-92.

[46] George Soltau, *Four Portraits of the Lord Jesus Christ* (New York: Charles C. Cook, n.d.), 16.

[47] *Ibid.*, 16-17.

[48] Mears, *op. cit.*, 394.

[49] Hiebert, *op. cit.*, 141.

[50] Soltau, *op. cit.*, 110.

[51] *Ibid.*, 110-11.

[52] Erdman, *Luke*, 45.

[53] *Ibid.*, 45-46.

[54] Hayes, *op. cit.*, 259.

[55] Hiebert, *op. cit.*, 144.

[56] Hayes, *op. cit.*, 261.

[57] Hiebert, *op. cit.*, 142.

[58] Frederic W. Farrar, *The Life of Christ* (London: Cassel and Company, Limited, 1896), 650.

[59] Will Varner, "Messiah in the Law," *Israel My Glory* (Oct./Nov., 1992), 50:11.

[60] *Ibid.*

[61] Alfred Edersheim, *The Temple: Its Ministry and Services* (Peabody, Mass.: Hendrickson Publishers, Inc., 1994), 57.

[62] *Ibid.*

[63] G. Campbell Morgan, *The Analyzed Bible* (New York: Fleming H. Revell Company, 1908), 48-49.

[64] J. Norval Geldenhuys, "Luke," *The Biblical Expositor*, ed., Carl F. H. Henry (Philadelphia: A. J. Holman Company, 1973), 895.

[65] Erdman, *Luke*, 35.

[66] D. D. Whedon, *Commentary on the Gospels: Luke-John* (New York: Carlton and Porter, 1866), 53.

[67] Frederic L. Godet, *Studies in the New Testament* (New York: E. P. Dutton & Co., 1895), 116.

[68] Edersheim, *op. cit.*, 76.

[69] Godet, *op. cit.*, 117-18.

[70] Hiebert, *op. cit.*, 145.

[71] G. Campbell Morgan, *The Crises of the Christ* (Old Tappan, N.J.: Fleming H. Revell Company, 1936), 292-93.

[72] *Ibid.*, 293.

[73] Morgan, *Analyzed Bible*, 55.

PERSPECTIVE

God's Perfect Plan for the Perfect Man by G. Campbell Morgan

In Jesus of Nazareth, God gave to the world again a Man, perfect in His humanity, and therefore perfect in His revelation of the facts concerning Himself. In Jesus there was a fulfillment of all that was highest and best in the ideas of God, which had come to men by the revelations of the past. The continuous work of God from the moment when man fell from his high dignity, by the act of his rebellion, and so obscured his vision of God, was that of self-revelation. Through processes that were long and tedious, judged from the standpoint of human lives, God with infinite patience spoke in simple sentences, shone forth in gleams of light, and so kept enshrined within the heart of man, facts concerning Himself, which man was unable to discover for himself. So degraded was human intelligence, that speaking after the manner of men only, it may be said that it took whole centuries for God to enshrine in the consciousness of the race, some of the simple and most fundamental facts concerning Himself. Man's ruin was so terrible, and so profound, as witness the darkened intelligence, the deadened emotion, and the degraded will, that there was but one alternative open to the Eternal God. Either He must sweep out and destroy utterly the race, or else in infinite patience, and through long processes, lead it back to Himself. He chose the pathway of reconciliation in His infinite grace, at what cost the story of the Christ alone perfectly reveals.[1]

[1] G. Campbell Morgan, *The Crises of the Christ* (Old Tappan, N.J.: Fleming H. Revell Company, 1936), 87-88.

PART V

THE MYSTERIES OF THE ETERNAL

In that day shall the branch of the Lord
be beautiful and glorious,
and the fruit of the earth shall be excellent and comely
for them that are escaped of Israel.

ISAIAH 4:2

Nor was this all: many there were whom their deep searching of the human heart had taught to feel the want of a present God. These longed to see their ardent aspirations realized in the life of a Savior whom they had embraced, and to find their hopes confirmed and directed by His own words. For such a spiritual history was needed; and the Christian teachers had to exhibit our Lord in His eternal relations to the Father, alike manifested in the past, the present, and the future, as the Creator, the Redeemer, and the Judge. They had to connect Christianity with God.[1]

-Brooke Foss Westcott, *An Introduction to the Study of the Gospels*

St. Matthew had set forth the life of Jesus from the point of view of its relation with the sacred Israelitish past. St. Mark had described it simply as it appeared to the first eye-witnesses, without comparing the Christ with anything but Himself. St. Luke had seen opening before men, by means of it, a whole new future—the conquest of the pagan world by the Gospel.

All aspects of it seemed exhausted;—past, present, and future,—are not these all the possible dimensions of time? If there was to be a fourth gospel, and it was not to be, at least as to its fundamental idea, a repetition of one of those which preceded it, it must find its occasion and point of view in a sphere superior to time—in eternity. This is, in fact, the special characteristic of John's gospel.[2]

-Frederic L. Godet, *Studies in the New Testament*

St. John makes the denial of the incarnation of the Son of God the criterion of Antichrist, and consequently the belief in this truth the test of Christianity. The incarnation of the eternal Logos, and the divine glory shining through the veil of Christ's humanity, is the grand theme of his Gospel, which he wrote with the pen of an angel from the very heart of Christ, as his favourite disciple and bosom-friend.[3]

-Philip Schaff, *The Person of Christ*

---

[1] Brooke Foss Westcott, *An Introduction to the Study of the Gospels* (London: Macmillan & Co., 1875), 220.

[2] Frederic L. Godet, *Studies in the New Testament* (New York: E. P. Dutton & Co., 1895), 69-70.

[3] Philip Schaff, *The Person of Christ: The Perfection of His Humanity Viewed as a Proof of His Divinity*, 12th ed. (New York: American Tract Society, 1882), 5.

Figure V-1. Pierre Mignard: Christ and the Woman of Samaria

This seventeenth-century painting by Mignard (1610-1695) "is beautiful in the simplicity of its intention, yet dignified. As we look into the face of the Master, so intent in His desire to share truth with even this common woman of the Samaritan streets, . . ."[4] we, too, must decide how to respond to the words He said unto her:

> Whosoever drinketh of this water shall thirst again: But whosoever drinketh of the water that I shall give him shall never thirst; but the water that I shall give him shall be in him a well of water springing up into everlasting life. JOHN 4:13B-14

[4] Cynthia Pearl Maus, Christ and the Fine Arts (New York: Harper & Row, Publishers, 1959), 213.

Chapter Twelve

The Gospel of John: Revelation Through Signs

Until the time of the New Testament Church, the Book of Isaiah served "as a compendium of almost all the major doctrines revealed by God during the pre-Christian age, with extended treatment of the doctrine of God in His omnipotence, His omniscience, and His redemptive love."[1] Moreover, since the completion of the New Testament books and the final canonization of Scripture, this Old Testament book has been recognized as a condensation of the entire Bible in its subject and structure. For example, the former has 66 chapters; the latter, 66 books. Each has two major sections, with 39 divisions in the first part and 27 in the second.

The difference between the Old and New Testaments is as striking as the contrast between the two sections of the Book of Isaiah; some textual critics even suggesting a second, later author—the so-called "Deutero-Isaiah"—in order to account for the obvious dissimilarity. Nevertheless, we must conclude that the same author was responsible for the entire book. A passage in John's Gospel (12:38-40) has a quotation from each division of Isaiah (6:9-10 and 53:1) and attributes both to the prophet who saw the Lord's glory in his vision in the Temple (cf. John 12:41 and Isaiah 6:1).

On the other hand, the similarities between the Old Testament and the first 39 chapters of Isaiah are as striking as the parallelism between the New Testament and the last 27 chapters of Isaiah.

> The Old Testament opens with God's case against man because of his sin. Isaiah opens the same way (Isa. 1:18). The first section closes with the prophecy of the coming King of Righteousness and the redemption of Israel (34-35), just as the prophets close the Old Testament with the prediction of His coming Kingdom. The second part of Isaiah (chapter 40) opens with the voice of him that crieth in the wilderness (John the Baptist) and is concerned with the person and work of Jesus Christ. The New Testament opens in exact accord with this. John the Baptist, the forerunner of Jesus is announced (John 1:6, 23). Isaiah ends with the vision of new heavens and a new earth wherein dwelleth righteousness. The New Testament closes with this same view in Revelation. This striking similarity between Isaiah and the whole Bible is unforgettable when once mastered.[2]

As mentioned above, the New Testament opens with the ministry of John the Baptist, and all four Gospels record the fact that the forerunner of Jesus was *"the voice of one crying in the wilderness"* (cf. Matt. 3:3; Mark 1:3; Luke 3:4; John 1:23). Yet the nature of his message in the fourth Gospel is different from that recorded in the Synoptics.

The first three Gospels tell us that John the Baptist was *"preaching the baptism of repentance for the remission of sins"* (Luke 3:3; cf. Matt. 3:2; Mark 1:4). By contrast John says:

> *There was a man sent from God, whose name was John. The same came for a witness, to bear witness of the Light, that all men through him might believe. He was not that Light, but was sent to bear witness of that Light. That was the true Light, which lighteth every man that cometh into the world.* 1:6-9

"The appreciative reader is struck with the difference between John and the other Evangelists as soon as he reads the first sentence."[3] From a vast supply of facts (cf. John 20:30; 21:25) the beloved disciple and aged author selected his material and so molded it "by his literary and religious genius that his Gospel stands in splendid isolation from the others."[4]

> In recording the teaching of Jesus he omits the parables and short sayings and substitutes long discourses on recurring themes, all cast in an allegorizing style in which every phrase has a double meaning. The ministry expands to three years in this Gospel, most of it taking place in Jerusalem rather than Galilee. John knows nothing of the "Messianic secret." Here Jesus openly declares his Messiahship from the beginning, and others recognize him in this role. In a radical departure from the Synoptics, John places the Temple-cleansing at the beginning of the ministry and the Last Supper on the day before Passover. He omits four of the most important events in the life of Jesus, the baptism, the temptation, the transfiguration, and the agony in Gethsemane. There is no account of the Eucharist in the upper room. New characters, such as Nicodemus and the woman of Samaria, have long interviews with Jesus, and the astounding miracle of the raising of Lazarus is added and emphasized. In these and many other significant ways the Fourth Gospel differs from the other three.

> The main reason for these differences was noted as early as A.D. 200 by Clement of Alexandria who said, "After the other Evangelists had written down the facts of history, John wrote a spiritual Gospel." What he means is that John's intention is not to add another "historical" Gospel, but to interpret the career of Jesus in spiritual or theological terms. This explains his method of taking only a few events from the life of Jesus and elaborating upon their meaning, always relating them to Jesus in such a way as to show more clearly how he is "the Christ, the Son of God."[5]

Although John shares some important narrative with the Synoptics, no record is so conspicuous for its use of symbolism as the Gospel, which he wrote. Whether it is the events that are recorded or the individuals that are presented, "the whole Gospel from end to end is penetrated with the spirit of symbolic representation."[6] While this, perhaps, may be more apparent in the miracles or "signs" that John selected for inclusion in his account, yet the individual characters which he portrays are every bit as important for their symbolic intent. These people that move about the Lord exemplify both sides in the great conflict between light and darkness, as well as those who wavered between the two positions.

> On the one hand we have the mother of the Lord (2:3-5; 19:25-27), the beloved disciple and his master the Baptist (1:6-37; 3:23-36), St. Andrew and Mary of Bethany, all unfailing in their allegiance; St. Peter falling and rising again to deeper love (18:27; 21:17); St. Philip rising from eager to firm faith (14:8), St. Thomas from desponding and despairing love (11:16; 20:25) to faith, hope, and love (20:28). There is the sober but uninformed faith of Martha (11:21, 24, 27), the passionate affection of Mary Magdalene (20:1-18). Among conversions we have the instantaneous but deliberate conviction of Nathanael (1:49), the gradual but courageous progress in belief of the schismatical Samaritan wom-

an (see on 4:19) and of the uninstructed man born blind (see on 1:21), and in contrast with both the timid, hesitating confessions of Nicodemus, the learned Rabbi (3:1; 7:50; 19:39). On the other side we have the cowardly wavering of Pilate (18:38-39; 19:1-4, 8, 12, 16), the unscrupulous resoluteness of Caiaphas (11:49-50), and the blank treachery of Judas (13:27; 18:2-5). Among the minor characters there is the "ruler of the feast" (2:9-10), the "nobleman" (4:49), the man healed at Bethesda (5:7, 11, 14-15).

If these . . . individuals are creations of the imagination, it is no exaggeration to say that the author of the Fourth Gospel is a genius superior to Shakespeare.[7]

These individuals, however, are not creations of the imagination, but thoroughly real characters, which "offer typical representations of faith and unbelief in their traits and issues."[8]

The Symbolic Nature of the Fourth Gospel Illustrated by the First Epistle of John

The symbolism and emphasis upon principle in the fourth Gospel finds its counterpart in the First Epistle of John—the latter bearing much the same relationship to the former, as the Book of Isaiah does to the Scriptures as a whole. The shorter volumes provide a preview of the larger works. In the case of John's writings, his First Epistle illustrates the nature of his Gospel. One writer observed:

The connection is so close, in thought as well as in language, that the former may almost be called a summary of the latter. In the Epistle, even more clearly than in the Gospel, we see the author's habit of dealing rather with elements than with nations or individuals. With the exception of the illustration of "Cain," . . . he prefers to dispense with personal illustrations of principles. He does not, like Paul, speak of Abraham, or Hagar, or Sinai, or Isaac, or Melchisedec, or the Jews, or the Gentiles; but of the World and the flesh, the water, the blood, and the spirit, light and darkness, life and death. In the Epistle, as in the Gospel, we see the rejection of Christ explained, not as a casual outcome of individual caprice or wickedness, but as an inevitable result of the eternal antagonism between light and darkness. In the Epistle, as in the Gospel, the author insists that the new commandment of Christ to "love one another" is really an old commandment which men have had from the beginning: a commandment as old as the promptings of the Light which from the beginning has "lighted every man coming into the world—an old commandment only so far made new as it has been brought home to the hearts of men with quite new intensity by the manifestation of the incarnate Love of God. In the Epistle, as in the Gospel, it is recognized that the antagonism between the world and the spirit, between light and darkness, must go on without truce till one has prevailed; and each man must take one or other side, putting away all hope of compromise. There are two principles . . . contrary to and at variance with one another—the one represented by the God-loving Abel, the other by the self-loving Cain, which must needs be at variance when born, "for it is impossible for enemies to dwell for ever together." In precisely the same way does our author illustrate the same antagonism by the same personality: "Not as Cain, who was of that wicked one, and slew his brother. And wherefore slew he him? Because his own works were evil and his brother's righteous;" and then, relapsing from the unfamiliar method of personal illustration into his habitual language about principles or elements, he substitutes for Cain the "world," and for Abel the "children of God," and bids his readers "marvel not if the world hate you."

In this continuous strife between light and darkness the victory is to be gained by faith—but faith supported by witnesses; and we read in the Epistle that the object of our victorious faith is "He that came through water and blood, Jesus Christ.[9]

The Central Purpose of John's Gospel

Passing over the many differences of interpretation as to the meaning of the water and the blood, we come to the central purpose of John's Gospel. On this point we need not indulge in dubious conjecture, as the author expressly stated the objective of his work. John wrote:

> *And many other signs truly did Jesus in the presence of his disciples, which are not written in this book: But these are written, that ye might believe that Jesus is the Christ, the Son of God; and that believing ye might have life through his name.* 20:30-31

The record is therefore a selection from abundant materials at the command of the writer, made by him with a specific purpose, first to create a particular conviction in his readers, and then in virtue of that conviction to bring life to them. The conviction itself which the Evangelist aims at producing is twofold, as corresponding with the twofold relation of Christianity to the chosen people and to mankind. He makes it his purpose to show that Jesus, who is declared by that human name to be truly and historically man, is at once the Christ, in whom all types and prophecies were fulfilled, and also the Son of God, who is, in virtue of that divine being, equally near to all the children of God—His Father and their Father (20:17)—scattered throughout the world (11:52; comp. 1:49). The whole narrative must therefore be interpreted with a continuous reference to these two ruling truths, made clear by the experience of the first stage in the life of the Church; and also to the consequence which flows from them, that life is to be found in vital union with Him. . . . Each element in the fundamental conviction is set forth as of equal moment. The one (Jesus is the Christ) bears witness to the special preparation which God had made; the other (Jesus is the Son of God) bears witness to the inherent universality of Christ's mission. The one establishes the organic union of Christianity with Judaism; the other liberates Christianity from Jewish limitations.[10]

Every part of the fourth Gospel is designed to make clear that *"Jesus is the Christ, the Son of God"* (20:31). As such the miracles John selected for inclusion in his narrative point to some deeper truth concerning Christ, and are referred to not as wonders or mighty works, but as signs, for they are "a token and indication of the near presence and working of God."[11]

In this word the ethical end and purpose of the miracle comes out the most prominently, as in "wonder" the least. They are signs and pledges of something more than and beyond themselves (Isa. 7:11; 38:7); valuable, not so much for what they are, as for what they indicate of the grace and power of the doer, or of the connection in which he stands with a higher world. Oftentimes they are thus seals of power set to the person who accomplishes them ("the Lord confirming the word by signs following," Mark 16:20; Acts 14:3; Heb. 2:4); legitimating acts, by which He claims to be attended to as a messenger from God. We find the word continually used in senses such as these. Thus, "What sign showest thou?" (John 2:18) was the question which the Jews asked, when they wanted the Lord to justify the things which He was doing, by showing that He had especial authority to do them. Again they say, "We would see a sign from thee" (Matt. 12:1). St. Paul speaks of himself as having "the signs of an apostle" (2 Cor. 12:12); in other words, the tokens which should mark him out as such. Thus, too, in the Old Testament, when God sends Moses to deliver Israel He furnishes him with two "signs." He warns him that Pharaoh will require him to legitimate his mission, to produce his credentials that he is indeed God's ambassador, and equips him with the powers which shall justify him as such; which, in other words, shall be his "signs" (Exod. 7:9-10). He "gave a sign" to the prophet, whom He sent to protest against the will-worship of Jeroboam (1 Kings 13:3).

At the same time it may be convenient here to observe that the "sign" is not of necessity a miracle. . . . Many a common matter may be a "sign" or seal set to the truth of some word, the announcement of which goes along with it; so that when that "sign" comes true, it may be accepted as a pledge that the greater matter, which was, as it were, bound up with it, shall also come true in its time. Thus the angels give to the shepherds for "a sign" their finding of the Child wrapped in swaddling clothes in a manger (Luke 2:12; cf. Exod. 3:12). Samuel gives to Saul three "signs" that God has indeed appointed him king over Israel, and only the last of these is linked with aught supernatural (1 Sam. 10:1-9). The prophet gave Eli the death of his two sons as a "sign" that his threatening word should come true (1 Sam. 2:34; cf. Jer. 44:29, 38). God gave to Gideon a sign in the camp of the Midianites of the victory which he should win (Judg. 7:9-15), though it does not happen that the word occurs in that narration (cf. 2 Kings 7:2, 17-20). [12]

It is of interest to note that the word "signs," "which the synoptists almost always use in a bad sense—to denote the 'sign from heaven' demanded by the Pharisees, or the 'signs' which the false christs shall work to deceive, if it were possible, even the elect, Mark 13:22—is the very word selected by John to describe the miracles of Jesus,"[13] while the term mighty works, "which in the synoptists generally denotes the works of Jesus, is never used in the fourth Gospel."[14]

Partly, no doubt, the author may have felt that miracles were made cheap by excessive enumeration, and that the narrative created a stumbling-block rather than a help to philosophic and educated readers. Especially might this be felt in Ephesus, the home of wizards and wonders and "curious arts" (Acts 19:19), where even the last-called of the apostles had worked cures and exorcisms past numbering (19:1-12). Accordingly the author, though he makes mention of very many miracles, describes none but those which are obviously emblematic.[15]

It is a remarkable feature of John's narrative that while "the supernatural element is even more prominent in the fourth Gospel than in the Synoptists, . . . the miracles themselves are subordinated. Though frequent reference is made to the vast number of them (2:23; 3:2; 6:2; 7:31; 9:16; 11:47; 12:37; 20:30),"[16] he describes "not more than eight in all (including the post-resurrection miracle of the draught of fishes), and among these not a single case of exorcism. The element of mere wonder . . . is carefully subordinated to the symbolic element."[17]

As mentioned earlier, John noted that *"many other signs truly did Jesus in the presence of his disciples, which are not written in this book"* (20:30), yet he recorded eight of them, seven of which were miraculous in nature.

> *But these are written, that ye might believe that Jesus is the Christ, the Son of God; and that believing ye might have life through his name.* 20:31

The First Sign: The New Wine (2:1-11)

> *And the third day there was a marriage in Cana of Galilee; and the mother of Jesus was there: And both Jesus was called, and his disciples, to the marriage. And when they wanted wine, the mother of Jesus saith unto him, They have no wine. Jesus saith unto her, Woman, what have I to do with thee? Mine hour is not yet come. His mother saith unto the servants, Whatsoever he saith unto you, do it. And there were set there six waterpots of stone, after the manner of the purifying of the Jews, containing two or three firkins apiece. Jesus saith unto them, Fill the waterpots with water. And they filled them up to the brim. And he saith unto them, Draw out now, and bear unto the governor of the feast. And they bare it. When the ruler of the feast had tasted the water that was made wine, and knew not whence it was: (but the servants which drew the water knew;) the governor of the feast called the bridegroom, And saith unto him, Every man at the beginning doth set forth good wine; and when men have well drunk, then that which is worse; but thou hast kept the good wine until now. This beginning of miracles did Jesus in Cana of Galilee, and manifested forth his glory; and his disciples believed on him.* 2:1-11

This miracle, like the others recorded in John's Gospel, is a sign by which further revelation is made of the person and/or work of Jesus Christ. John's "purpose in writing is to present a religious interpretation of Jesus, a spiritual Gospel to supplement the historical Gospels that were already available."[18] This being said, there are some popular expositions of this passage, which are to be avoided:

> First, this is not a discourse on marriage. John is not stating that Jesus is here giving his official approval of human wedlock. That, God wrote into the roots of human nature at its creation. No such sanction from Jesus was needed. Second, . . . this is not data for a strictly temperance sermon. Neither John nor his listeners knew anything about local option, total abstinence, prohibition, nor an organized liquor traffic that corrupted politics and government. John would have rubbed his eyes in amazement at the modern explanation that that this water become wine was only unfermented grape juice. The only wine John knew was wine. With him wine-drinking was no more an issue than was slavery with Paul. Their scriptures had long warned that in excess "wine is a mocker, strong drink is raging."

No, John is not talking about the propriety of marriage, . . . nor the evils of liquor. John is talking about Jesus, and seeking to lead the reader to confess him as Lord and Master.[19]

The clue to the proper interpretation of *"this beginning of miracles"* is found in verse six, were we read, *"And there were set there six waterpots of stone, after the manner of the purifying of the Jews, containing two or three firkins apiece"* (2:6).

The meaning of this event at Cana, like most of the signs in John's Gospel, has a definite correlation with the Old Testament. John carefully observes that the waterpots used at the wedding feast in Cana were in accordance with the Hebrew rites of purification (2:6). That the six waterpots each contained "two or three firkins apiece," or a total of 120 to 180 gallons, reveals the extent of the ritual observances. When an embarrassing lack of wine occurs, Jesus requests that these waterpots be filled to the brim with water. He thereby dramatizes the inadequacy of the waterpots, long associated with the Old Testament ritual of cleansing, to meet the present need. In these waterpots, Jesus turns the water into wine, which elsewhere in Christian teaching symbolizes the blood of Christ. At the time, the disciples probably did not fully comprehend this symbolism. But John's comment is significant, namely, that in this first sign Jesus manifested "his glory" (v. 11; cf. 1:14).[20]

It is the blood of Jesus Christ, symbolized by the wine, that *"cleanseth us from all sin"* (1 John 1:7), and allows us through faith in His finished work to *"be partakers of the divine nature,"* whereby we may escape *"the corruption that is in the world through lust"* (2 Pet. 1:4). This new nature is very different from the old nature of *"the children of wrath,"* who have their conversation in the lusts of the flesh, *"fulfilling the desires of the flesh and of the mind"* (Eph. 2:3).

The miracle of the new birth, whereby believers are given a new nature, finds its source in the One, who *"manifested forth his glory"* (2:11) in Cana of Galilee.

By changing of the water into wine, Christ showed that He could change one substance into another. It was a sign that the Author of the world of nature was at work, and that He had the power to change the subjects of His own creation. That this has a bearing on the subject of regeneration described in St. John 3 we, who are now reading after the events, can plainly see. The great lesson, which it would impress on those who witnessed it, was that our Lord was the Master of the world of nature. They would see that Jesus of Nazareth was no ordinary man, but that He was One who had such power over inanimate nature that He could transform one substance into another. He could change a thing from one nature into another nature, which, from their point of view, was higher.

It was for this reason that the miracle was a "sign" which manifested forth our Lord's glory, with the result that "His disciples believed on Him."[21]

At Cana Jesus revealed His power; at Calvary He realized His purpose. By virtue of His divine power (as seen in the miracle) and his shed blood (symbolized by the wine) we can be assured that Christ can transform the very nature of all those, like His disciples, who *"believed on him"* (2:11).

The Second Sign: The New Temple (2:13-22)

And the Jews' Passover was at hand, and Jesus went up to Jerusalem, And found in the temple those that sold oxen and sheep and doves, and the changers of money sitting: And when he had made a scourge of small cords, he drove them all out of the temple, and the sheep, and the oxen; and poured out the changers' money, and overthrew the tables; And said unto them that sold doves, Take these things hence; make not my Father's house an house of merchandise. And his disciples remembered that it was written, The zeal of thine house hath eaten me up. Then answered the Jews and said unto him, What sign shewest thou unto us, seeing that thou doest these things? Jesus answered and said unto them, Destroy this temple, and in three days I will raise it up. Then said the Jews, Forty and six years was this temple in building, and wilt thou rear it up in three days? But he spake of the temple of his body. When therefore he was risen from the dead, his disciples remembered that he had said this unto them; and they believed the scripture, and the word which Jesus had said. 2:13-22

This second sign is a corollary to the first. At the wedding feast in Cana it was revealed that the Old Testament waterpots of purification were inadequate. The water was changed, indicating that "only the best wine, now available, can meet the need."[22] Here it is revealed that the Old Testament sacrifices are inadequate. The animals are driven out of the Temple, indicating that the "final conquest and judgment of sin are only in the flesh of the Messiah."[23]

Driving out the money-changers, sheep and oxen with a warning against commercializing the temple (vv. 15-16) was no miracle in the usual sense. The disciples, in view of the Old Testament, inferred from the event only a godly zeal for the integrity of the temple, as a house of worship and sacrifice (cf. Ps. 69). Jesus' sign meant far more, however. In answer to the Jews, Jesus fixed its specific meaning: "Destroy this temple, and in three days I will raise it up" (2:18-19). The evangelist indicates that Jesus referred not merely to the destruction of the temple, but to the resurrection of His body (vv. 20-21). His cleansing of the temple, therefore, dramatically signifies that Jesus' very body is the place where God is propitiated. Without this atonement, all the temple sacrifices become empty; with it, they become superfluous. As John notes, this truth was not apparent to the disciples until after Christ's resurrection. Once the resurrection had occurred, however, the relationship of the temple sacrifices to Christ's self-sacrifice shone from both the Old Testament and Christ's teaching (v. 22).[24]

The Relationship Between the First and Second Signs

The symbolic features of the first two signs in John's Gospel find their logical expression in the sacrament of the Lord's Supper. The shed blood (the new wine of the first sign) and the broken body (the new temple of the second sign) are the two elements which are remembered, as believers partake of the bread and the wine, and thereby *"shew the Lord's death till he come"* (1 Cor. 11:26).

The Third Sign: The Nobleman's Son Healed of Fever (4:46-54)

> *So Jesus came again into Cana of Galilee, where he made the water wine. And there was a certain nobleman, whose son was sick at Capernaum. When he heard that Jesus was come out of Judaea into Galilee, he went unto him, and besought him that he would come down, and heal his son: for he was at the point of death. Then said Jesus unto him, Except ye see signs and wonders, ye will not believe. The nobleman saith unto him, Sir, come down ere my child die. Jesus saith unto him, Go thy way; they son liveth. And the man believed the word that Jesus had spoken unto him, and he went his way. And as he was now going down, his servant met him, and told him, saying, Thy son liveth. Then enquired he of them the hour when he began to amend. And they said unto him, Yesterday at the seventh hour the fever left him. So the father knew that it was at the same hour, in the which Jesus said unto him, Thy son liveth: and himself believed, and his whole house. This is again the second miracle that Jesus did, when he was come out of Judaea into Galilee.* 4:46-54

The clue to understanding the sign of the healed son may be found in the rebuke to the anxious father: *"Except ye see signs and wonders, ye will not believe"* (v. 48).

The stated purpose of John's Gospel is to engender saving faith in Jesus Christ (cf. 20:31), yet it is clear from Jesus' own statement that the observation of His miraculous power is not the way such faith is produced. Saving faith is based, instead, on taking God at His Word.

> The desperate nobleman never saw Jesus work any miracle. He had to take Jesus' unsupported word. All he got was the quiet command, "Go thy way; thy son liveth." He had to accept that and that alone. It is a well-known fact that in the synoptics the motive for Jesus' miracles is compassion. It is often declared that in John the motive for miracles is to win followers. After a miraculous "sign" people "believe on him." This is a gross overstatement of John's meaning. For John, a wonder-seeking faith is a weak faith. For him faith in Christ is spiritual rebirth, not a surprised gasping at mighty marvels. With John, a miracle-seeking faith is no faith at all. The miracle is but the sign, or symbol, of God's deeper, inner work of grace. As in the synoptics, so in John, "no sign [miracle] shall be given." This will be reiterated in John's last, climactic story of Jesus' resurrection. "Blessed are they that have not seen, and yet have believed."[25]

Initially, the nobleman believed that Jesus needed to be physically present in order to heal his son, as evidenced by his plea, *"Sir, come down ere by child die"* (v. 49). Nevertheless, in response to Jesus' command, *"the man believed the word that Jesus had spoken unto him, and he went his way"* (v. 50). The extent of his faith, furthermore, is revealed in the fact that the doting father had not hurried right home to check on the condition of his dying son. Archbishop Trench noted:

> His confidence in Christ's word was so great that he proceeded leisurely homewards: it was not till the next day that he reached his house, though the distance between the two cities was not so great that the journey need have occupied many hours. Maldonatus quotes Isaiah 28:16, "He that believeth shall not make haste." It is worthy of note that his inquiry of the servants, who met him on his return with news of his child's recovery, and meaning probably to hinder the now unnecessary summons of the Lord, was when

the child "began to amend," to be a little better; for at the height of his faith, the father had looked only for a slow and gradual amendment. His servants answer, that at such an hour, the very hour when Jesus spake the word, the fever not merely began to abate, there was not merely a turning point in the disease, but it "left him," it suddenly forsook him. "So the father knew that it was at the same hour in the which Jesus said unto him, Thy son liveth, and himself believed, and his whole house." This he did for all benefits which the Lord had bestowed on him, he accepted another and the crowning benefit, even the cup of salvation; and not he alone, but, as so often happened, and this for the bringing us into a perception of the manner in which each smaller community, as well as the great community of mankind, a nation, or as in this case a family, is united and bound together under its federal head, his conversion drew after it that of all who belonged to him (cf. Acts 16:15, 34; 18:8).[26]

From another perspective the nobleman may be viewed as a representative of all true believers, for whom the Word of God can effect life-changing consequences, regardless of time or place. John may be "using this story as another 'sign' or symbol of spiritual truth."[27]

Here John pictures Jesus as possessing power to heal across the barrier of time and space. Space and time were no obstacle to him. But they were a sore problem to the gentile Christians. Galilee was far away. The crucifixion was long ago. How can the power of one who was far away and long ago be available now? It is the recurrent problem of all generations. Jesus could have helped and healed those about him, for he was there in the flesh. It is not so any longer. Time has gone—then decades of it, and now centuries of it. Jesus is gone from the flesh—then for years, and now for generations. He is no longer here in form, voice, and touch. How can he help now?

Here we meet another of John's glorious universalizations. This ancient nobleman at Capernaum is the symbol of all true believers. He believed, and across the barriers of time and space Jesus met his need without being physically present. This wonderful truth about the risen, spiritual Christ all sincere believers can verify in their own experience. In spite of continents of space and centuries of time, and without the supposed aid of startling miracles or of Jesus' physical presence, men can be convinced of and receive help from the Lord of life. Even Matthew, with all his insistence upon sweeping brilliancy of the second coming as a visible spectacle, undermines its literal fulfillment with his grand assertion about Jesus, "Lo, I am with you always." And John also insists, "I will not leave you desolate: I come unto you."

Herein is the supreme manifestation of Christ's glory that all he did were signs, suggesting to these with inner eyes to see, that before them stands the Word of God, who is New Wine, Fresh Water, New Birth, the True Temple, and for whom no obstacle of time and space is a hindrance to his immediate and empowering Presence.[28]

The Fourth Sign: Healing the Impotent Man on the Sabbath (5:1-16)

After this there was a feast of the Jews; and Jesus went up to Jerusalem. 5:1

John did not think it important to indicate what feast this was and we cannot certainly tell. It is remarkable that John in this case alone of all his allusions to

Jewish feasts should have failed to give its name. Dr. William Milligan, in the International Lesson Commentary, suggests the following explanation of this omission: "Why did John whose custom it is to mark clearly each festival of which he speaks (see 2:13, 23; 6:4; 7:2; 10:22; 11:55; 12:1; 13:1; 18:39; 19:14), write so indefinitely here? The only reply that it is possible is that the indefiniteness is the result of design. The evangelist omits the name of the feast, that the reader may not attach to it a significance that was not intended. To John—through clearness of insight, not from power of fancy—every action of his Master was fraught with deep significance; and no one who receives the Lord Jesus as he received him can hesitate to admit in all his words and deeds a fullness of meaning, a perfection of fitness, immeasurably beyond what can be attributed to the highest of human prophets. Our Lord's relation to the whole Jewish economy is never absent from John's thought. Jesus enters the Jewish temple (chapter 2:4). His words can be understood only by those who recognize that he is himself the true temple of God. The ordained feasts of the nation find their fulfillment in him. Never, we may say, is any festival named in this Gospel in connection with our Lord, without an intention on the author's part that we should see the truth which he saw, and behold in it a type of his Master or his work. If this be true, the indefiniteness of the language here is designed to prevent our resting upon the thought of this particular festival as fulfilled in Jesus, and lead to the concentration of our thought on the Sabbath shortly to be mentioned, which in this chapter has an importance altogether exceptional."[29]

Now there is at Jerusalem by the sheep market a pool, which is called in the Hebrew tongue Bethesda, having five porches. 5:2

Some of the early Church Fathers, who reveled in spiritualizing Scripture, saw in the five porches a type of the five books of Moses—the law. As Christ alone cured the needy, so grace alone can avail for the sinful. The law, in that it is weak, cannot deliver and save.[30]

In these lay a great multitude of impotent folk, of blind, halt, withered, waiting for the moving of the water. For an angel went down at a certain season into the pool, and troubled the water: whosoever then first after the troubling of the water stepped in was made whole of whatsoever disease he had. 5:3-4

Gathered near the ancient pool of Bethesda were four classes of sick people: (1) impotent folk, and those who were (2) blind, (3) halt, and (4) withered. Whereas we might use different terminology today to describe some of the medical problems to be found within that ancient population, these four categories were intended to encompass every possible condition. "The enumeration of four, when meant to be exhaustive, is frequent in Scripture (Ezekiel 14:21; Revelation 6:8; Matthew 15:31)."[31]

And a certain man was there, which had an infirmity thirty and eight years. 5:5

Among the sick who were lying there was one poor man who, for no less than thirty-eight years, had been lamed by paralysis. He had haunted the porticoes of this pool, but without effect; for as he was left there unaided, and as the motion of the water occurred at irregular times, others more fortunate and less feeble than himself managed time after time to struggle in before him, until the favorable moment had been lost.[32]

When Jesus saw him lie, and knew that he had been now a long time in that case, he saith unto him, Wilt thou be made whole? 5:6

From amongst the great horde of miserable people assembled near the pool, the Great Physician turned His attention to a single patient, and in one those rare situations recorded in Scripture, asked a question without first being addressed.

The impotent man answered him, Sir, I have no man, when the water is troubled, to put me into the pool: but while I am coming, another steppeth down before me. 5:7

At first the words hardly stirred the man's despondent lethargy; he scarcely seems even to have looked up. But thinking, perhaps, with a momentary gleam of hope, that this was some stranger who, out of kindness of heart, might help him into the water when it was again agitated, he narrated in reply the misery of his long frustration. Jesus had intended a speedier and more effectual aid.[33]

Jesus saith unto him, Rise, take up thy bed, and walk. 5:8

It was spoken in an accent that none could disobey. The manner of the Speaker, His voice, His mandate, thrilled like an electric spark through the withered limbs and the shattered constitution, enfeebled by a lifetime of suffering and sin.[34]

And immediately the man was made whole, and took up his bed, and walked: and on the same day was the Sabbath. 5:9

After thirty-eight years of prostration the man instantly rose, lifted up his pallet, and began to walk. In glad amazement he looked round to see and to thank his unknown benefactor; but the crowd was large, and Jesus, anxious to escape the unspiritual excitement which regarded Him as a thaumaturge alone, had quietly slipped away from observation.

In spite of this, many jealous eyes were soon upon the man. In proportion as the inner power of a religion is dead, in that proportion very often is an exaggerated import attached to its outer forms. Formalism and indifference, pedantic scrupulosity and absolute disbelief, are correlative, and ever flourish side by side. It was so with Judaism in the days of Christ. Its living enthusiasm was quenched; its lofty faith had died away; its prophets had ceased to sing; its priests were no longer clothed with righteousness; its saints were few. The axe was at the root of the barren tree, and its stem served only to nourish a fungous brood of ceremonials and traditions. . . . And thus it was that the observance of the Sabbath, which had been intended to secure for weary man a rest full of love and mercy had become a mere national fetish—a barren custom fenced in with frivolous and senseless restrictions. Well-nigh every great provision of the Mosaic law had now been degraded into a superfluity of meaningless minutiae, the delight of small natures, and the grievous incubus of all true piety.

Now, when a religion has thus decayed into a superstition without having lost its political power, it is always more than ever tyrannous and suspicious in its hunting for heresy. The healed paralytic was soon surrounded by a group of questioners. They looked at him with surprise and indignation.[35]

The Jews therefore said unto him that was cured, It is the Sabbath day: it is not lawful for thee to carry thy bed. He answered them, He that made me whole, the same said unto me, Take up thy bed, and walk. Then asked they him, What man is that which said unto thee,

Take up thy bed, and walk? And he that was healed wist not who it was: for Jesus had conveyed himself away, a multitude being in that place. Afterward Jesus findeth him in the temple, and said unto him, Behold, thou art made whole: sin no more, lest a worse thing come unto thee. The man departed, and told the Jews that it was Jesus, which had made him whole. And therefore did the Jews persecute Jesus, and sought to slay him, because he had done these things on the Sabbath day. 5:10-16

The hostility of the Jewish leaders was obviously aroused against Jesus because of His activities on the Sabbath. Yet the Lord chose that very day to heal that certain man in order to bring Himself face to face with His accusers. "He had determined to leave the leaders and rulers of the people without excuse, by revealing at once to their astonished ears the nature of His being."[36]

But Jesus answered them, My Father worketh hitherto, and I work. 5:17

More distinctly than this He could not have spoken. They had summoned Him before them to explain His breach of the Sabbath; so far from excusing the act itself, as He sometimes did in Galilee, by showing that the higher and moral law of love supersedes and annihilates the lower law of literal and ceremonial obedience—instead of showing that He had but acted in the spirit in which the greatest of saints had acted before Him, and the greatest of prophets had taught—He sets Himself wholly above the Sabbath, as its Lord, nay, even as the Son and Interpreter of Him who had made the Sabbath, and who in all the mighty course of Nature and of Providence was continuing to work thereon.[37]

Therefore the Jews sought the more to kill him, because he not only had broken the Sabbath, but said also that God was his Father, making himself equal with God. 5:18

Here, then, were two deadly charges ready at hand against this Prophet of Nazareth: He was a breaker of their Sabbath; He was a blasphemer of their God. The first crime was sufficient cause for opposition and persecution; the second, an ample justification of persistent endeavor to bring about His death.

But at present they could do nothing; they could only gnash with their teeth, and melt away. Whatever may have been the cause, as yet they dared not act. A power greater than their own restrained them. The hour of their triumph was not yet come; only, from this moment, there went forth against Him from the hearts of those priests and Pharisees the irrevocable sentence of violent death.[38]

At any rate, the truth of the matter, and the significance of this Sabbath miracle, is found in Jesus' words, *"My Father worketh hitherto, and I work"* (5:17). While it is true that in the unfallen world God did indeed rest on the Sabbath (cf. Gen. 2:2-3), the sin and rebellion of fallen man has since prevented Him from resting on this day. The Rev. Alfred Plummer, formerly Fellow and Tutor of Trinity College, Oxford, noted:

From the creation up to this moment God has been ceaselessly working for man's salvation. From such activity there is no rest, no Sabbath: for mere cessation from activity is not of the essence of the Sabbath; and to cease to do good is not to keep the Sabbath but to sin. Sabbaths have never hindered the Father's work; they must not hinder the Son's.[39]

The Son of God came to save man from the bondage of sin; and the intensity of

its stranglehold, as well as the extent of its consequences, is exemplified by the impotent man at Bethesda. Jesus' final words to the healed paralytic, *"Behold, thou art made
whole: sin no more, lest a worse thing come unto thee"* (5:17), clearly indicates that his miserable condition was the result of his own doing. Nevertheless, Jesus' warning to *"sin no
more"* reveals the power of sin over man's will. It is hard to imagine that a worse thing
could come unto the man, considering the fact that he had already spent the greater
part of man's allotted three-score and ten years in a wasted and pitiable state. Unfortunately, moral paralysis is a worse condition than physical paralysis; the latter is tragic,
but the former is fatal. Man, in spite of the awful consequences of sin, does not hate
sin. This is the realm where the real healing needs to take place.

> This John makes clear. "The Father loveth the Son, and showeth him all
> things that himself doeth." The great thing the Father does is to release men
> from their moral paralysis. "Greater works than these [the healing of the
> lame man] will he [God] show him [Christ]." "For as the Father raiseth the
> dead and giveth them life, even so the Son also giveth life." Jesus restores life
> unto those whom moral paralysis has rendered spiritually dead. In Jesus men
> not only walk again, they live again.[40]

The Relationship Between the Third and Fourth Signs

Together, the nobleman's son and the impotent man at the pool of Bethesda reveal
the divergent circumstances of those who need to come under the saving power of the
Lord Jesus Christ.

The impotent man was a Jew, and had spent many years near the center of Jewish
life, in the immediate vicinity of the second Temple. By contrast, the nobleman's son was
a Gentile, one of those *"strangers from the covenants of promise, having no hope, and without God
in the world"* (Eph. 2:12). Nevertheless, both Jew and Gentile were helpless without the
intervention of Christ.

The impotent man had spent many years in his miserable condition as a result of his
own sin. The nobleman's son was only a youth, yet his condition was every bit as serious,
as evidenced by his father's plea, *"Sir, come down ere my child die"* (4:49). Young and old alike
need the help that only Jesus Christ can give.

The impotent man was surrounded by people, yet he was friendless. He admitted
to the Lord, *"Sir, I have no man, when the water is troubled, to put me into the pool"* (5:7). The
nobleman's son, by contrast, had influential family and friends. He had a caring father
to plead his case, and servants to carry out his commands. Yet the son's situation was just
as desperate and hopeless as that of the impotent man. Only Christ can provide hope
for the hopeless.

The impotent man was healed in the physical presence of the Lord, and heard with
his own ears the actual command of Jesus, *"Rise, take up thy bed, and walk"* (5:8). The
nobleman's son, by contrast, represents all of us, who *"were afar off"* (Eph. 2:17), and
separated from the physical presence of the Lord by space and time. Yet his cure was
every bit as effective as that of the healed paralytic. Christ can save anyone who, like the
nobleman, *"believed the word that Jesus had spoken unto him"* (4:50).

Jew and Gentile, rich and poor, young and old, influential and insignificant, friend
and friendless, skilled and unskilled—all are incapable of saving themselves. None left to
their own devices can effect the true healing that is needed. As that nineteenth-century

hymn so beautifully confesses:

>   Not what my hands have done
>   Can save my guilty soul;
>   Not what my toiling flesh has borne
>   Can make my spirit whole.
>   Not what I feel or do
>   Can give me peace with God;
>   Not all my prayers and sighs and tears
>   Can bear my awful load.
>
>   Thy grace alone, O God,
>   To me can pardon speak;
>   Thy power alone, O Son of God,
>   Can this sore bondage break.
>   No other work save Thine,
>   No other blood will do;
>   No strength save that which is divine
>   Can bear me safely through.[41]

The Fifth Sign: Feeding the Five Thousand (6:1-15)

> *After these things Jesus went over the sea of Galilee, which is the sea of Tiberias. And a great multitude followed him, because they saw his miracles which he did on them that were diseased. And Jesus went up into a mountain, and there he sat with his disciples. And the Passover, a feast of the Jews, was nigh. When Jesus then lifted up his eyes, and saw a great company come unto him, he saith unto Philip, Whence shall we buy bread, that these may eat? And this he said to prove him: for he himself knew what he would do. Philip answered him, Two hundred pennyworth of bread is not sufficient for them, that every one of them may take a little.* 6:1-7

It was "to prove him," and what measure of faith he had in Him, whom he had himself already acknowledged the Messiah, as "Him of whom Moses in the Law and the prophets did write" (John 1:45). It was now to be seen whether Philip, remembering as he might the great things which Moses had done, who gave the people bread from heaven in the wilderness, and the notable miracle which Elisha, though on a smaller scale than that which now was needed, had performed (2 Kings 4:43-44), could so lift up his thoughts as to believe that He whom he had recognized as the Christ, greater therefore than Moses or the prophets, would be equal to the present need. Cyril sees a reason why to Philip, rather than to any other Apostle, this question should have been put, namely that his need of the teaching contained in it was the greatest; and refers to his later words, "Lord, shew us the Father" (John 14:8), in proof of the tardiness of his spiritual apprehension. But it does not need to fetch the reason from so far. They were now not far from Bethsaida, of which city Philip was (John 1:44); from his local knowledge he was likelier than another to answer this question. But whatever the motive which led to the addressing of him in particular, he does not abide the proof.

Long as he has been with Jesus, he has not yet seen the Father in the Son
(John 14:9); as yet he knows not that the Lord who has chosen him is even
the same who "openeth his hand and filleth all things living with plenteous-
ness," who feedeth and nourisheth all creatures, who has fed and nourished
them from the creation of the world, and who therefore can feed these few
thousands that are this day more peculiarly dependent on his bounty. He can
conceive of no other supplies save such as natural means could procure, and
at once names a sum, "two hundred pence," as barely sufficient to provide
what would be required—a sum much larger, no doubt, than any which they
had in their common purse at the moment.[42]

*One of his disciples, Andrew, Simon Peter's brother, saith unto him, There is a lad here,
which hath five barley loaves, and two small fishes: but what are they among so many? And
Jesus said, Make the men sit down. Now there was much grass in the place. So the men sat
down, in number about five thousand. And Jesus took the loaves; and when he had given
thanks, he distributed to the disciples, and the disciples to them that were set down; and
likewise of the fishes as much as they would.* 6:8-11

As God did for Moses and the people in the wilderness (cf. Exod. 16; Num. 11:31),
here, too, Jesus feeds a great multitude with bread from heaven and food from the sea.
This miracle, furthermore, answers the Psalmist's question, *"Can God furnish a table in
the wilderness?"* (Ps. 78:19), and also fulfills the prophecy of the One who said, *"I will
abundantly bless her provision: I will satisfy her poor with bread"* (Ps. 132:15). Just how the
Lord could have multiplied the boy's scant provision, however, will always be a subject
that defies elucidation. Archbishop Trench noted:

Here, too, even more remarkably than in the case of the water changed into
wine, when we seek to realize to ourselves the manner of the miracle, it evermore eludes our grasp. We seek in vain to follow it with our imaginations. . . .
But this is the wisdom of the sacred narrator, to leave the description of the
indescribable unattempted, his appeal is to the same faith which believes "that
the worlds were formed by the Word of God, so that things which are seen, were
not made of things which do appear" (Heb. 11:3).[43]

*When they were filled, he said unto his disciples, Gather up the fragments that remain,
that nothing be lost. Therefore they gathered them together, and filled twelve baskets with
the fragments of the five barley loaves, which remained over and above unto them that had
eaten. Then those men, when they had seen the miracle that Jesus did, said, This is of a
truth that prophet that should come into the world. When Jesus therefore perceived that they
would come and take him by force, to make him a king, he departed again into a mountain
himself alone.* 6:12-15

The people recognized that Jesus was the Prophet that should come (cf. Deut. 18:15),
and were eager to make Him their King, but they completely missed His significance as
Priest. Consequently, the Lord needed to send them away.

So in the gathering dusk He gradually succeeded in persuading the multitude
to leave Him, and when all but the most enthusiastic had streamed away to
their homes or caravans, He suddenly left the rest, and fled from them to the
hill-top alone to pray. He was conscious that a crisis of His day in earth was
come, and by communing with His heavenly Father He would nerve His soul
for the work of the morrow and the bitter conflict of many coming weeks.

Once before He had spent in the mountain solitudes a night of prayer, but then it was before the choice of His Apostles and the glad tidings of His earliest and happiest ministry. Far different were the feelings with which the Great High Priest now climbed the rocky stairs of that great mountain altar which in His temple of the night seemed to lift Him nearer to God.[44]

"This chapter, like the last, contains a discourse arising out of a miracle,"[45] and it is here that we learn the true significance of the Feeding of the Five Thousand. The day following this wonderful miracle—when the people *"had found him on the other side of the sea"* (6:25)—is the occasion for Jesus' message on the Bread of Life. John tells us:

Jesus answered them and said, Verily, verily, I say unto you, Ye seek me, not because ye saw the miracles, but because ye did eat of the loaves, and were filled. Labour not for the meat which perisheth, but for that meat which endureth unto everlasting life, which the Son of man shall give unto you: for him hath God the Father sealed. Then said they unto him, What shall we do, that we might work the works of God? Jesus answered and said unto them, This is the work of God, that ye believe on him whom he hath sent. They said therefore unto him, What sign shewest thou then, that we may see, and believe thee? What dost thou work? Our fathers did eat manna in the desert; as it is written, He gave them bread from heaven to eat. Then Jesus said unto them, Verily, verily, I say unto you, Moses gave you not that bread from heaven; but my Father giveth you the true bread from heaven. For the bread of God is he which cometh down from heaven, and giveth life unto the world. Then said they unto him, Lord, evermore give us this bread. And Jesus said unto them, I am the bread of life: he that cometh to me shall never hunger; and he that believeth on me shall never thirst. But I said unto you, That ye also have seen me, and believe not. All that the Father giveth me shall come to me; and him that cometh to me I will in no wise cast out. For I came down from heaven, not to do mine own will, but the will of him that sent me. And this is the Father's will which hath sent me, that of all which he hath given me I should lose nothing, but should raise it up again at the last day. And this is the will of him that sent me, that every one which seeth the Son, and believeth on him, may have everlasting life: and I will raise him up at the last day. The Jews then murmured at him, because he said, I am the bread which came down from heaven. And they said, Is not this Jesus, the son of Joseph, whose father and mother we know? How is it then that he saith, I came down from heaven? Jesus therefore answered and said unto them, Murmur not among yourselves. No man can come to me, except the Father which hath sent me draw him: and I will raise him up at the last day. It is written in the prophets, And they shall be all taught of God. Every man therefore that hath heard, and hath learned of the Father, cometh unto me. Not that any man hath seen the Father, save he which is of God, he hath seen the Father. Verily, verily, I say unto you, He that believeth on me hath everlasting life. I am that bread of life. Your fathers did eat manna in the wilderness, and are dead. This is the bread which cometh down from heaven, that a man may eat thereof, and not die. I am the living bread which came down from heaven: if any man eat of this bread, he shall live for ever: and the bread that I will give is my flesh, which I will give for the life of the world. The Jews therefore strove among themselves, saying, How can this man give us his flesh to eat? Then Jesus said unto them, Verily, verily, I say unto you, Except ye eat the flesh of the Son of man, and drink his blood, ye have no life in you. Whoso eateth my flesh, and drinketh my blood, hath eternal life; and I will raise him up at the last day. For my flesh is meat indeed, and my blood is drink indeed. He that eateth my flesh, and drinketh

my blood, dwelleth in me, and I in him. As the living Father hath sent me, and I live by the
Father: so he that eateth me, even he shall live by me. This is that bread which came down
from heaven: not as your fathers did eat manna, and are dead: he that eateth of this bread
shall live for ever. 6:26-58

Jesus clearly states that He is *"that bread of life"* (v. 48), and *"the true bread from heaven"*
(v. 32), which was symbolized in Moses' day by the manna. Furthermore, the people
are told, *"He that cometh to me shall never hunger; and he that believeth on me shall never thirst"*
(v. 35). "The character of this faith in Christ is expressed in the strongest imaginable
terms, as being a true eating of his flesh and a drinking of his blood, by which is meant
a complete identification with him, and an absolute dependence upon him, as a crucified, risen, living, divine Lord."[46]

It needs to be kept in mind that Jesus is identified with life-sustaining bread,
and not with delicious cake or other sumptuous food. Using the lad's "slender stock
of homeliest fare"[47] the Lord miraculously fed the multitude, and *"when they were*
filled, he said unto his disciples, Gather up the fragments that remain, that nothing be lost"
(6:12)—"the existence of these itself witnessing that there was enough and more
than enough for all (2 Kings 4:43-44; Ruth 2:14)."[48]

The people were filled, and were satisfied! They "were given the simplest food,
but they would have fainted without it. A Christian experience is not something which
may or may not be added to other blessings of life. Without Christ there is no real life,
here or hereafter."[49]

The Sixth Sign: Walking on the Water (6:16-21)

The miracle we are now about to consider followed shortly after the Feeding of
the Five Thousand, occurring on the evening of the same day. Of the interlude between these two events, John noted:

Then those men, when they had seen the miracle that Jesus did, said, This is of a truth
that prophet that should come into the world. When Jesus therefore perceived that they would
come and take him by force, to make him a king, he departed again into a mountain himself
alone. 6:14-15

The Feeding of the Five Thousand had convinced those men that Christ was
the long-expected Prophet, and they sought to proclaim Him King and establish His
government.

This miracle worked up to the highest pitch their enthusiasm in behalf of the
recognition of Jesus as the Messiah. Might not this, indeed, be taken as the
commencement of his reign? Hitherto his acts had been those of individual
beneficence. But here was a public act, performed in the sight of thousands,
and of which thousands had shared the benefit. Who so fit to be their King as
he who could banish want and labor from their borders, and revive the good
old times when their fathers were fed by bread from heaven? To escape their
well-meant efforts Jesus retired to a mountain alone. We learn from Mark that
he went to pray.[50]

And when even was now come, his disciples went down unto the sea 6:16

They went down unto the sea because they were told to do so. *"And straightway*

Jesus constrained his disciples to get into a ship, and to go before him unto the other side" (Matt. 14:22; cf. Mark 6:45). Meanwhile, Jesus *"sent the multitudes away"* (Matt. 14:22; cf. Mark 6:45). "The disciples were probably ready to join the people in an enterprise which would fulfill their remaining carnal expectations regarding the Messiahship of their Master. Hence our Lord dismissed them, sending them where they would feel the need of his presence."[51]

> *And [they] entered into a ship, and went over the sea toward Capernaum. And it was now dark, and Jesus was not come to them. And the sea arose by reason of a great wind that blew.* 6:17-18

To the disciples, no day had been so bright; now they must go before Him to the other side, and their bright day ended in a troubled night. They wanted to bask in the sun of the Master's popularity, but He knew that there was more danger in the favor of the crowd than from the fury of the storm. So Jesus sent them on, and the storm had the effect of saving them from wrong ambitions. They had to learn that the stormy night along with the bright day worked together for their good.[52]

> *So when they had rowed about five and twenty or thirty furlongs, they see Jesus walking on the sea, and drawing nigh unto the ship; and they were afraid.* 6:19

Out on the lake, the disciples were hard put, for one of the sudden furious storms common to the area gave the strong rowers hours of useless toil. Three hours after midnight they were still in the midst of the lake, about half way across, and, as the record says, "distressed in rowing" (Mark 6:48). What made the conquest with the storms more distressing was the fact that Jesus was not with them, as on the other sea-storm occasion. The disciples were tossed and tormented by the waves, for the winds were "contrary." These contrary winds are hard to face, yet when accepted in the right spirit, go to develop character and add to the joy of reaching the harbor.

What those weary, frustrated rowers did not know was that Jesus, in His prayer retreat on the mountain slope, saw them in the darkest hour of their extremity. In His solitude, the Eternal Being was watching the little specks of boats and was cognizant of the sore trouble of their toil. Buffeted by those contrary winds, the disciples were to learn of the Master's divine sympathy and of His willingness to enter the struggle. Thus it was that Jesus came to the distressed rowers in an unexpected way—walking on the sea, as if it had been a soft, smooth carpet. Here was a mode of progression unknown to the disciples. Every new experience of Jesus was an awe-filled surprise to them. He had seemed to neglect them, leaving them hour after hour wrestling with the storm, until they were almost exhausted. Once He calmed a storm for them, why not now? But the One who had been praying for them and watching them was now at hand, yet they knew Him not.[53]

> *But he saith unto them, It is I; be not afraid.* 6:20

Literally, I am. The same language used by Jesus in Jerusalem (John 8:58), for which the Pharisees would have stoned him, and in the Old Testament to designate Jehovah (Exodus 3:14). Here I should prefer to give it this meaning: Christ says not merely, "It is I, your friend and Master;" He says, at least implies, it is the "I AM," who is coming to you, the Almighty One who rules wind and waves, who made them, and whom they obey.[54]

Then they willingly received him into the ship: and immediately the ship was at the land whither they went. 6:21

"Better, whither they were going, or intending to go. The imperfect tense helps to bring out the contrast between the difficulty of the first half of the voyage, when they were alone, and the ease of the last half, when He was with them."[55]

We note, also, that *"immediately the ship was at the land."* "Unless the word 'immediately' has more latitude than is common with us, this implies another miracle."[56]

Many commentators have seen, furthermore, a symbolic parallel "between the picture of Jesus as he prays alone upon the mountain and then appears to rescue the disciples,"[57] and what was soon to take place; namely, that "Jesus at His ascension, going up to God to enter His present ministry of intercession, leaving His Church to face the billows of this stormy world during His absence."[58] Trench, for example, wrote:

> Nor ought we, I think, to fail to recognize the symbolic character which this whole transaction wears. As that bark was upon those stormy seas, such is oftentimes the Church. It seems as though it had not its Lord with it, such little way does it make; so baffled is it and tormented by the opposing storms of the world. But his eye is on it still; He is in the mountain apart praying; ever living, an ascended Savior, to make intercession for his people. And when at length the time of urgent need has arrived, He is suddenly with it, and that in marvelous ways past finding out; and then all that before was so laborious is easy, and the toiling rowers are anon at the haven where they would be.[59]

The Relationship Between the Fifth and Sixth Signs

A review of the events of chapter Six reveals that the sixth sign is a logical corollary and historic consequence of the fifth sign. The one is a symbol of Christ's ministry under the Old Dispensation at His first coming; the other a picture of the New Dispensation culminating in His bodily coming for the Church.

The Feeding of the Five Thousand anticipated that the body of Christ—symbolized by the bread from heaven (the manna in Moses' day)—would be broken for the multitudes in His sacrificial death. Yet while the people recognized Christ as Prophet, and wanted to make Him King, they did not understand His Priestly role. As a result, Jesus had to send the people away, after which He would go off alone to the mountain to pray.

The Jewish nation has been set aside for a time, the Lord has ascended into heaven, and the stage is now set for the miracle at sea—a place and term that is associated in Scripture with Gentile people (cf. Dan. 7:3; Matt. 13:1; Rev. 13:1). The Lord sends His few remaining followers out to face the storms of life, and the Church of Jesus Christ will be built, while He is watching, working, and interceding for them from above. Nevertheless, out on the storm-tossed sea the disciples in their own strength do not seem to be making much progress, and in spite of their inability to recognize Jesus in their time of trial and hardship, the Lord does come to their aid in a display of resurrection life. The weary disciples experienced some fearful times and inexplicable events, yet God's people eventually reach the happy destination to which they have been constrained to go, when the Lord suddenly appears for His own and miraculously takes them home!

I trust that each of us, in our own hour of trial or storm-tossed journey, can respond as did the songwriter, who wrote:

Should Thy mercy send me
Sorrow, toil and woe,
Or should pain attend me
On my path below,
Grant that I may never
Fail thy hand to see;
Grant that I may ever
Cast my care on Thee.[60]

The Seventh Sign: Healing the Man Born Blind (9:1-41)

The miracle to which we now turn our attention is one of the most important in the ministry of the Lord, if the amount of space John devotes to this sign and the events immediately surrounding it is any indication of this fact. All of the activities and discourses that are recorded in chapters Eight and Nine appear to have occurred on the same day.

In the morning after Jesus' confrontation with the scribes and Pharisees over *"a woman taken in adultery"* (8:3), John tells us:

> *Then spake Jesus again unto them, saying, I am the light of the world: he that followeth me shall not walk in darkness, but shall have the light of life.* 8:12

"That Jesus calls himself the light of the world . . . shows the close connection between the prologue and the Gospel proper."[61] In the first chapter we were told that John the Baptist came *"to bear witness of the Light"* (v. 7), and here, as well as in chapter Nine, Jesus clearly identifies Himself as that Light (cf. 9:5). The restoration of sight to the blind man verifies this claim, and the subsequent crisis it produced proved John's earlier statement, *"And the light shineth in darkness; and the darkness comprehended it not"* (1:5). Nevertheless, the story of the man born blind is introduced in a rather nondescript way, with a somewhat vague transition from the previous scene. John wrote:

> *Then said the Jews unto him, Thou art not yet fifty years old, and hast thou seen Abraham? Jesus said unto them, Verily, verily, I say unto you, Before Abraham was, I am. Then took they up stones to cast at him: but Jesus hid himself, and went out of the temple, going through the midst of them, and so passed by. And as Jesus passed by, he saw a man which was blind from his birth. And his disciples asked him, saying, Master, who did sin, this man, or his parents, that he was born blind?* 8:57-9:2

> All the Jews were trained to regard special suffering as the immediate consequence of special sin. Perhaps the disciples supposed that the words of our Lord to the paralytic whom He had healed at the Pool of Bethesda, as well as to the paralytic at Capernaum, might seem to sanction such an impression. They asked, therefore, how this man came to be born blind. Could it be in consequence of the sins of his parents? If not, was there any way of supposing that it could have been for his own? The supposition in the former case seemed hard; in the latter, impossible. They were therefore perplexed. [62]

Jesus answered, Neither hath this man sinned, nor his parents: but that the works of God should be made manifest in him. I must work the works of him that sent me, while it is day: the night cometh, when no man can work. As long as I am in the world, I am the light of the world. 9:3-5

Light shines at various times and in various degrees, whether the world chooses to be illuminated or not. . . . Here there is special reference to His giving light both to the man's eyes and to his soul.[63]

When he had thus spoken, he spat on the ground, and made clay of the spittle, and he anointed the eyes of the blind man with clay,

And said unto him, Go, wash in the pool of Siloam, (which is by interpretation, Sent.) He went his way therefore, and washed, and came seeing. 9:6-7

Jesus had continually declared that he himself had been sent of God, and he is now intimating that he alone could heal; that he fulfilled all the blessings which Siloam typified. Each day of the feast of tabernacles a libation had been brought from that pool, to suggest the gifts of God to his people. Jesus is now saying that as the waters of Siloam will wash the clay from the eyes of the blind man, so he, the true Siloam, the One sent of God, will take away his physical blindness, and also will restore spiritual sight to the world.[64]

The neighbours therefore, and they which before had seen him that he was blind, said, Is not this he that sat and begged? Some said, This is he: others said, He is like him: but he said, I am he. Therefore said they unto him, How were thine eyes opened? He answered and said, A man that is called Jesus made clay, and anointed mine eyes, and said unto me, Go to the pool of Siloam, and wash: and I went and washed, and I received sight. Then said they unto him, Where is he? He said, I know not. 9:8-12

What we do know is that the cure of the man born blind was one of the most scrutinized and best substantiated miracles that Jesus ever performed, for it resulted in an official, public hearing, wherein all the principal witnesses were formally interrogated. These proceedings, furthermore, provide one of the most interesting, if not entertaining, stories in all of Scripture. The religious leaders want to get to the bottom of things, as far as this alleged miracle and flagrant breach of Sabbath law is concerned, and they are not above using threats of excommunication and methods of intimidation in order to obtain the answers they want. They have their theories, so the facts are not really the main issue for them. Nevertheless, they are about to meet their match, when they come up against that miserable and sarcastic soul, whom they considered *"wast altogether born in sins"* (v. 34).

They brought to the Pharisees him that aforetime was blind. And it was the Sabbath day when Jesus made clay, and opened his eyes. Then again the Pharisees also asked him how he had received his sight. He said unto them, He put clay upon mine eyes, and I washed, and do see. Therefore said some of the Pharisees, This man is not of God, because he keepeth not the Sabbath day. Others said, How can a man that is a sinner do such miracles? And there was a division among them. They say unto the blind man again, What sayest thou of him, that he hath opened thine eyes? He said, He is a prophet. 9:13-17

They ask for each man's opinion and finally, in their perplexity and division, turned to the man healed. A little while before he had said that "a man called Jesus" healed him; now he declares that "he is a prophet;" a little later he is prepared to receive him as the Son of God. His convictions constantly deepened.[65]

But the Jews did not believe concerning him, that he had been blind, and received his sight, until they called the parents of him that had received his sight. 9:18

The dilemma of the Pharisees and their mode of reasoning are amusingly or pitifully reproduced today by many reputed wise men who attempt to prove that Jesus is not the divine Son of God. The Pharisees argued that the miracle had not been performed because it was the Sabbath, and God could not have healed a man on the Sabbath and by so working have broken the law of rest. That the Sabbath had been broken was merely their interpretation of a law; and they were thus opposing a theory to a fact, and on the ground of a speculation were denying a reality.[66]

And they asked them, saying, Is this your son, who ye say was born blind? How then doth he now see? His parents answered them and said, We know that this is our son, and that he was born blind: But by what means he now seeth, we know not; or who hath opened his eyes, we know not: he is of age; ask him: he shall speak for himself. These words spake his parents, because they feared the Jews: for the Jews had agreed already, that if any man did confess that he was Christ, he should be put out of the synagogue. Therefore said his parents, He is of age; ask him. Then again called they the man that was blind, and said unto him, Give God the praise: we know that this man is a sinner. 9:19-24

Their meaning is not "give God the praise for your cure," for the Jews were still trying to deny that there had been any cure. What they meant was "give glory to God by speaking the truth" (cf. Josh. 7:19; 1 Sam. 6:5; Ezra 10:11; and 2 Cor. 11:31).

He answered and said, Whether he be a sinner or no, I know not: one thing I know, that, whereas I was blind, now I see. 9:25

He does not mean that he has no opinion as to the character of Jesus; but he says that he is willing to leave the theological problems to their superior wisdom; he knows, however, what Jesus has done for him; and he intimates that they must form their opinion of Jesus in accordance with the fact of his cure.[67]

Then said they to him again, What did he to thee? How opened he thine eyes? He answered them, I have told you already, and ye did not hear: wherefore would ye hear it again? Will ye also be his disciples? 9:26-27

The poor man has had enough! Being weary of all this cross-examination, and aware of their dilemma, he boldly inquires, "*Will ye also be his disciples?*"(v. 27). "Clearly here was a man whose presumptuous honesty would neither be bullied into suppression nor corrupted into a lie."[68]

Then they reviled him, and said, Thou art his disciple; but we are Moses' disciples. 9:28

The Pharisees found the obstinate mendicant to be most uncooperative, for he would not admit that the whole affair had been a big hoax. "So, since authority, threats, blandishments had all failed, they broke into abuse."[69]

We know that God spake unto Moses: as for this fellow, we know not from whence he is. The man answered and said unto them, Why herein is a marvelous thing, that ye know not from whence he is, and yet he hath opened mine eyes. Now we know that God heareth not sinners: but if any man be a worshipper of God, and doeth his will, him he heareth. Since the world began was it not heard that any man opened the eyes of one that was born blind.

If this man were not of God, he could do nothing. 9:29-33

This is a remarkable statement in light of what he had earlier said, as recorded in verse 25.

They answered and said unto him, Thou wast altogether born in sins, and dost thou teach us? And they cast him out. 9:34

"Unable to control any longer their transport of indignation, they flung him out of the hall, and out of the synagogue."[70] In accordance to the decree, which had been agreed upon earlier (cf. v. 22), the poor man was now under those harsh spiritual censures, which they had threatened against any that would confess that Jesus was the Messiah. "The attempt to disprove the miracle was an utter failure and the court sought to discredit it by excommunicating the chief witness." [71]

Jesus heard that they had cast him out; and when he had found him, he said unto him, Dost thou believe on the Son of God? He answered and said, Who is he, Lord, that I might believe on him? And Jesus said unto him, Thou hast both seen him, and it is he that talketh with thee. 9:35-37

The eyes that have been opened are permitted to see him in the person of the great Healer and he that speaks at that moment is the Son of God. It is a striking fact that this declaration of himself, spontaneously, to the outcast from the synagogue, only has one parallel case, the revelation of Christ to the outcast woman of Samaria (John 4:26).[72]

And he said, Lord, I believe. And he worshipped him. 9:38

And now the end to which all that went before was but an introduction, has arrived: "He said, Lord, I believe; and he worshipped Him:" not that even now we need suppose him to have known all that was contained in that title, "Son of God"—or that, worshipping Him, he intended to render Him the adoration, which is indeed due to Christ, but only due to Him because He is one with the Father. For "God manifest in the flesh" is a fact far too transcendent for any man to receive at once: the minds even of Apostles themselves could only dilate little by little to receive it. There were, however, in him the preparations for that ultimate and crowning faith: the seed which should unfold into that perfect flower was safely laid in his heart; and he fell down at the feet of Jesus as of one more than man, with a deep religious reverence and fear and awe. And thus the faith of this poor man was accomplished; step by step he had advanced, following faithfully the light which was given him; undeterred by opposition which would have been fatal to a weaker faith, and must have been so to his, unless the good seed cast its root in a soil of more than ordinary depth. But because it was such a soil, therefore when persecution arose, as it soon did, for the word's sake, he was not offended (Matt. 13:21); but enduring still, to him at length that highest grace was vouchsafed, to know the only-begotten Son of God, however as yet he may not have seen all the glorious treasures that were contained in that knowledge.[73]

And Jesus said, For judgment I am come into this world, that they which see not might see; and that they which see might be made blind. 9:39

It was a wonderful day for the healed man for he experienced the saving power of the One who came "that they which see not might see." In one day he received both his physical and spiritual sight. Yet it was not without its negative consequences, since he had been excommunicated and ostracized from the religious society in which he had been born blind. While his social standing was now even more pitiable than before, he was, at any rate, freed from the shackles of a religious system that had gone to seed, and came to know the reality of those words Jesus spoke earlier in the day: *"And ye shall know the truth, and the truth shall make you free"* (8:32).

Nevertheless, the healing of the blind man was also a sign that Jesus came *"that they which see might be made blind."* "He came into the world to save it, but the effect of his coming is to reveal every man's true condition. The light reveals the stains that would otherwise be unseen, and Christ's presence reveals the presence and power of sin in the hearts of men."[74]

The scribes and Pharisees prided themselves on their insight and knowledge, yet their spiritual blindness was revealed, when they said of Christ, *"We know that this man is a sinner"* (v. 24). The Pharisees thought they saw, but they were blind.

There is a story of a mining explosion in West Virginia. The explosion plunged the trapped men into total darkness. When the rescue team managed to get a light through to them, one of the young men finally said, "Well, why don't they turn on the light?" They all looked at him in amazement, and then they realized that the explosion had blinded him. In the darkness, he did not know that he was blind. The light revealed to him and to them that he was blind.[75]

This illustrates what Jesus meant when he said, *"For judgment I am come into this world, . . . that they which see might be made blind."*

And some of the Pharisees which were with him heard these words, and said unto him, Are we blind also? Jesus said unto them, If ye were blind, ye should have no sin: but now ye say, We see; therefore your sin remaineth. 9:40-41

"It was a hopeless case. They rejected Him because they did not know the truth about Him; and they would never learn the truth because they were fully persuaded that they were in possession of it."[76] Consequently, to other sins was added the sin of rejecting the Light, and in a state of spiritual blindness the Pharisees would "pass from their fancied light into real darkness." [77]

Meanwhile, the earthly ministry of Jesus Christ was rapidly moving to its conclusion, and the words of the Lord spoken earlier would be marked by an even greater urgency. *"I must work the works of him that sent me, while it is day: the night cometh, when no man can work"* (9:4).

One more miracle was yet to be performed by the Lord Jesus Christ, and it would prefigure that which was to be His own experience.

The Eighth Sign: The Raising of Lazarus (11:1-44)

The miracles recorded in the fourth Gospel, while significantly fewer than in the synoptic accounts, are, nevertheless, more distinctive.

The sheerly miraculous element seems heightened in John, yet the acts themselves are no more sensational than in the other Gospels. After all, Jesus appears as quite a miracle worker in Mark. By and large John develops each story more fully by showing Jesus talking with bystanders and opponents about the implications of the miracle. This Johannine emphasis upon the explanatory discourses of Jesus reflects his concentration on the miracles as "signs"—pointers to the nature and mission of Jesus (see 6:26 ff. and cf. 20:30 f.).[78]

The discourses associated with the Feeding of the Five Thousand and the Healing of the Man Born Blind make very clear what the miracles were intended to signify. The same can be said for the miracle we are now about to consider. Jesus clearly stated, *"I am the resurrection, and the Life: he that believeth in me, though he were dead, yet shall he live"* (11:25).

The raising of Lazarus from the dead verifies Jesus' claim that *"as the Father raiseth up the dead, and quickeneth them; even so the Son quickeneth whom he will"* (5:21). "Thus, this miracle graphically portrays the character of his mission and work. Moreover, it leads directly to Jesus' own death, which, paradoxically, is the source of life to all who believe."[79]

At any rate, the eleventh chapter of John's Gospel brings us to "the culminating point of the miraculous activity of our Lord."[80] Although Jesus raises the dead in the Synoptics, one from her death bed (Mark 5:40-42) and another from the bier on which he was carried to burial (Luke 7:12-15), "there is nothing like the elaborate story of the raising of Lazarus anywhere else in the New Testament."[81] It begins:

> *Now a certain man was sick, named Lazarus, of Bethany, the town of Mary and her sister Martha. (It was that Mary which anointed the Lord with ointment, and wiped his feet with her hair, whose brother Lazarus was sick.) Therefore his sisters sent unto him, saying, Lord, behold, he whom thou lovest is sick.* 11:1-3

The sisters of Lazarus, finding his sickness was of a dangerous kind, thought proper to send an account of it to Jesus; being firmly persuaded that he who had cured so many strangers would readily come and give health to one whom he loved in so tender a manner. "Lord," said they, "behold, he whom thou lovest is sick." They did not add, Come down and heal him, make haste and save him from the grave: it was sufficient for them to relate their necessities to the Lord, who was both able and willing to help them from their distress.[82]

> *When Jesus heard that, he said, This sickness is not unto death, but for the glory of God, that the Son of God might be glorified thereby.* 11:4

> *Now Jesus loved Martha, and her sister, and Lazarus. When he had heard therefore that he was sick, he abode two days still in the same place where he was.* 11:5-6

To conceive any other reason for his tarrying where He was during those two days, than that He might have room to work that great miracle, is extremely unnatural. Sometimes it has been assumed that He had in hand some great work for the kingdom of God where He was, some work which would not endure to be left, and which therefore He could not quit for the most pressing calls of private friendship (see 10:41-42). But He could have healed with his word at a distance as easily as by his actual presence; and this tarrying was rather a part of the severe yet gracious discipline of divine love; He will let the need attain to the highest before He interferes. It is often thus. He comes in with mighty help, but not till every other help has failed, till even his own promise has seemed to the weak faith of men to have failed and come utterly to nothing.[83]

> *Then after that saith he to his disciples, Let us go into Judaea again. His disciples say unto him, Master, the Jews of late sought to stone thee; and goest thou thither again? Jesus answered, Are there not twelve hours in the day? If any man walk in the day, he stumbleth not, because he seeth the light of this world. But if a man walk in the night, he stumbleth, because there is no light in him. These things said he: and after that he saith unto them,*

Our friend Lazarus sleepeth; but I go, that I may awake him out of sleep. Then said his disciples, Lord, if he sleep, he shall do well. Howbeit Jesus spake of his death: but they thought that he had spoken of taking a rest in sleep. Then said Jesus unto them plainly, Lazarus is dead. And I am glad for your sakes that I was not there, to the intent ye may believe; nevertheless let us go unto him. Then said Thomas, which is called Didymus, unto his fellow disciples, Let us also go, that we may die with him. 11:7-16

We note here one of several parallels between the circumstances surrounding the death and resurrection of Lazarus, and that of Jesus Christ—the events of the former prefiguring those of the latter. The disciples—especially Thomas now and Peter later—seem most willing to die with their Master as He approaches the place of death (cf. Matt. 26:31-35; Mark 14:27-31; Luke 22:31-34; John 13:36-38), yet their lives are revealed to be a mixture of faith and unfaithfulness.

> In the words of Thomas to his fellow-disciples, "Let us also go, that we may die with him," there is a remarkable mixture of faith and unfaithfulness,—faith since he counted it better to die with the Lord, than to live forsaking Him,—unfaithfulness, since he conceived it possible that so long as his Lord had a work to accomplish, he or those in his company could be overtaken by any peril which should require them to die together. Thomas was, most probably, of a melancholic desponding character; most true to his Master, yet ever inclined to look at things on their darkest side, finding it most hard to raise himself to the high elevations of faith,—to believe other and more than he saw (John 14:5; 20:25), or to anticipate higher and more favorable issues than those which the earthly probabilities of an event promised. Men of all temperaments and all characters were within that first and nearest circle of disciples, that they might be the representatives and helpers of all that hereafter, through one difficulty and another, should attain at last to the full assurance of faith.[84]

Then when Jesus came, he found that he had lain in the grave four days already. Now Bethany was nigh unto Jerusalem, about fifteen furlongs off: And many of the Jews came to Martha and Mary, to comfort them concerning their brother. Then Martha, as soon as she heard that Jesus was coming, went and met him: but Mary sat still in the house. Then said Martha unto Jesus, Lord, if thou hadst been here, my brother had not died. 11:17-21

These words of Martha are repeated verbatim by Mary in verse 32. Both believed that Lazarus' death was preventable and totally unnecessary, and consequently rebuked the Lord for allowing it. Not many days hence, furthermore, Peter would exhibit the very same attitude and behavior as that of these other friends and followers of Jesus. When informed that Christ, too, would die, Peter *"rebuked him, saying, Be it far from thee, Lord: this shall not be unto thee"* (Matt. 16:22; cf. Mark 8:31-32). Nevertheless, Martha does say:

But I know, that even now, whatsoever thou wilt ask of God, God will give it thee. 11:22
Jesus saith unto her, Thy brother shall rise again. Martha saith unto him, I know that he shall rise again in the resurrection at the last day. 11:23-24

This conviction was probably in advance of average Jewish belief on the subject. The O.T. declarations as to a resurrection are so scanty and obscure, that the Sadducees could deny the doctrine, and the Pharisees had to resort to oral traditions to maintain it (see on Mark 12:18; Acts 23:8).[85]

Jesus said unto her, I am the resurrection, and the life: he that believeth in me, though he were dead, yet shall he live. 11:25

Christ makes the grand, striking declaration that he is the Resurrection and the Life, words that never could have fallen from the lips of a sane mortal. They mean that he is the power which opens every grave, gives life to the sleepers, and calls them forth to new existence; that the life that endows men with eternal being is in him and proceeds from him. In the light of his own resurrection they mean that when he burst open the tomb he did it for humanity and in him humanity has won the victory over death. His utterance was far above what mere man could utter; it proclaimed a divine being and power, but the resurrection of Lazarus, a few moments later, was the demonstration of the truth of his words.[86]

And whosoever liveth and believeth in me shall never die. Believest thou this? She said unto him, Yea, Lord: I believe that thou art the Christ, the Son of God, which should come into the world. And when she had so said, she went her way, and called Mary her sister secretly, saying, The Master is come, and calleth for thee. As soon as she heard that, she arose quickly, and came unto him. Now Jesus was not yet come into the town, but was in that place where Martha met him. The Jews then which were with her in the house, and comforted her, when they saw Mary, that she rose up hastily and went out, followed her, saying, She goeth unto the grave to weep there. Then when Mary was come where Jesus was, and saw him, she fell down at his feet, saying unto him, Lord, if thou hadst been here, my brother had not died. When Jesus therefore saw her weeping, and the Jews also weeping which came with her, he groaned in the spirit, and was troubled, And said, Where have ye laid him? They said unto him, Lord, come and see. Jesus wept. Then said the Jews, Behold how he loved him! And some of them said, Could not this man, which opened the eyes of the blind, have caused that even this man should not have died? 11:26-37

Some of the Jews believed that there was something quite contradictory in Jesus' conduct; He could presumably heal a blind man, but could do nothing for His friend Lazarus. This same perspective is revealed at the cross, when the chief priests and scribes mockingly proclaimed, *"He saved others; himself he cannot save"* (Matt. 27:42; cf. Mark 15:31; Luke 23:35).

Jesus therefore again groaning in himself cometh to the grave. It was a cave, and a stone lay upon it. 11:38

The sepulcher into which Lazarus was laid to rest is an indication of the social status of the family of the deceased brother. Archbishop Trench noted:

> The poor had not, and it lay not within their power to purchase in fee, portions of land to set apart for these purposes of family interment. The possession of such was a privilege of the wealthier orders; only such were thus laid in the sepulchers of their fathers. We have another indication of the same in the large concourse of mourners, and those of the higher ranks, which assembled from Jerusalem to console the sisters in their bereavement; for even in grief that word is too often true, that "wealth maketh many friends; but the poor is separated from his neighbour" (Prov. 19:4).[87]

The burial of Lazarus prefigured that of Jesus Christ (cf. Matt. 27:57-60; Mark 15:43, 46; Luke 23:50-53), of which was predicted: *"And he made his grave with the wicked, and with the rich in his death"* (Isa. 53:9).

Jesus said, Take ye away the stone. Martha, the sister of him that was dead, saith unto him,

Lord, by this time he stinketh: for he hath been dead four days. 11:39

Martha had little reason to suppose that decomposition had not already set in. And when Christ ordered the stone to be removed, it was no wonder that she objected—"partly from conviction that the soul had now utterly departed from the vicinity of the mouldering body, partly afraid in her natural delicacy of the shocking spectacle which the removal of that stone would reveal."[88] Nevertheless, while Martha's conclusion was a logical one, it was based neither on exposure to, nor observation of, her brother's remains. To what degree, if any, the corpse was deteriorated by decay has since been a subject for conjecture. Either scenario, however, suggests an interesting truth to be gleaned from this remarkable miracle.

If Lazarus' body was preserved from corruption, his resurrection foreshadowed that of Christ's, for it had been prophesied that He should not see corruption (cf. Psalm 16:10). On the other hand, if Lazarus' remains were already disfigured by corruption, his resurrection prefigures that of all deceased believers, whose bodies have long since returned to dust (cf. Gen. 3:19), and are waiting for that day when *"the Lord himself shall descend from heaven with a shout, . . . and the dead in Christ shall rise"* (1 Thes. 4:16; cf. John 5:28-29).

> *Jesus saith unto her, Said I not unto thee, that, if thou wouldest believe, thou shouldest see the glory of God? Then they took away the stone from the place where the dead was laid. And Jesus lifted up his eyes, and said, Father, I thank thee that thou hast heard me. And I knew that thou hearest me always: but because of the people which stand by I said it, that they may believe that thou hast sent me. And when he thus had spoken, he cried with a loud voice, Lazarus, come forth. And he that was dead came forth, bound hand and foot with graveclothes: and his face was bound about with a napkin. Jesus saith unto them, Loose him, and let him go.* 11:40-44
>
> *Then many of the Jews which came to Mary, and had seen the things which Jesus did, believed on him. But some of them went their ways to the Pharisees, and told them what things Jesus had done.* 11:45-46

Such an extraordinary power, displayed before the face of a multitude, and near to Jerusalem, even overcame the prejudices of some of the most obstinate among them. Many believed that Jesus could be no other than the great Messiah, so long promised: though others who still expected a temporal prince, and were therefore unwilling to acknowledge him for their Savior, were filled with indignation, particularly the chief-priests and elders. But this miracle, as well as all the rest he had wrought in confirmation of his mission, was too evident to be denied; and therefore, they pretended that his whole intention was to establish a new sect in religion, which would endanger both church and nation.[89]

> *Then gathered the chief priests and the Pharisees a council, and said, What do we? For this man doeth many miracles. If we let him thus alone, all men will believe on him: and the Romans shall come and take away both our place and nation. And one of them, named Caiaphas, being the high priest that same year, said unto them, Ye know nothing at all, Nor consider that it is expedient for us, that one man should die for the people, and that the whole nation perish not. And this spake he not of himself: but being high priest that year, he prophesied that Jesus should die for that nation; And not for that nation only, but that also he should gather together in one the children of God that were scattered abroad. Then from*

that day forth they took council together for to put him to death. 11:47-53

The Sanhedrin met in a spirit of hatred and perplexity. They could not deny the miracle; they would not believe on Him who had performed it. They could only dread His growing influence, and conjecture that it would be used to make Himself a king, and would cause Roman intervention and the annihilation of their political existence. And as they vainly raged in impotent counsels, Joseph Caiaphas arose to address them. He was the civil High Priest. . . . As such he was supposed to have that gift of prophecy which was still believed to linger faintly in the persons of the descendents of Aaron, after the total disappearance of dreams, Urim, omens, prophets, and Bath Kol, which, in descending degrees, had been the ordinary means of ascertaining the will of God. And thus when Caiaphas rose, and with shameless avowal of a flagitious policy, haughtily told the Sanhedrin that all their proposals were mere ignorance, and that the only thing to be done was to sacrifice one victim—innocent or guilty he did not stop to inquire—one victim for the whole people—ay, and, St. John adds, not for that nation only, but for all God's children scattered throughout the world—they accepted unhesitatingly that voice of unconscious prophecy. And by accepting it they filled to the brim the cup of their iniquity, and incurred the crime which drew upon their guilty heads the very catastrophe which it was committed to avert.[90]

Jesus therefore walked no more openly among the Jews; but went thence unto a country near to the wilderness, into a city called Ephraim, and there continued with his disciples. And the Jews' Passover was nigh at hand. . . . Now both the chief priests and the Pharisees had given a commandment, that, if any man knew where he were, he should shew it, that they might take him. 11:54-55A, 57

And so it was that the raising of Lazarus had such diverse results, as the conclusion of this chapter reveals. While some believed on Jesus Christ, most did not; and the plans of those who were the most hostile to His person and work, were soon carried out. Nevertheless, the ultimate purpose of God was not defeated, as Peter so boldly and eloquently explained it, *"when the day of Pentecost was fully come"* (Acts 2:1). Being filled with the Holy Spirit, he stood before a great crowd, and proclaimed:

Ye men of Israel, hear these words; Jesus of Nazareth, a man approved of God among you by miracles and wonders and signs, which God did by him in the midst of you, as ye yourselves also know: Him, being delivered by the determinate counsel and foreknowledge of God, ye have taken, and by wicked hands have crucified and slain: Whom God hath raised up, having loosed the pains of death: because it was not possible that he should be holden of it. For David speaketh concerning him, I foresaw the Lord always before my face, for he is on my right hand, that I should not be moved: Therefore did my heart rejoice, and my tongue was glad; moreover also my flesh shall rest in hope: Because thou wilt not leave my soul in hell, neither wilt thou suffer thine Holy One to see corruption. . . . This Jesus hath God raised up, whereof we all are witnesses. Therefore being by the right hand of God exalted, and having received of the Father the promise of the Holy Ghost, he hath shed forth this, which ye now see and hear. For David is not ascended into the heavens: but he saith himself, The Lord said unto my Lord, Sit thou on my right hand, Until I make thy foes thy footstool. Therefore let all the house of Israel know assuredly, that God hath made that same Jesus, whom ye have crucified, both Lord and Christ. Acts 2:22-27, 32-36

The Relationship Between the Seventh and Eighth Signs

The healing of the man born blind and the raising of Lazarus are "the most artfully constructed and theologically pregnant of the miracle stories"[91] recorded in the fourth Gospel. "In the one, Jesus restores the gift of sight (light), and in the other, life." [92]

Light and life are interrelated entities. The very act of living requires the presence of light. This fact, however, was not known in the scientific community until the 18th century, when the Dutch investigator, Jan Ingenhousz (1730-1799), discovered that photosynthesis couldn't occur without light. In 1779 he published a small book entitled *Experiments on Vegetables, Discovering Their Great Power of Purifying the Common Air in Sunshine, but Injuring It in the Shade or at Night*. He found "that this operation of plants diminishes towards the close of the day, and ceases entirely at sunset." [93]

Light is essential for life in the physical world. The plant kingdom needs it for photosynthesis, and the animal world would be deprived of oxygen and illumination without it. But light is also necessary for life in the spiritual realm. To experience eternal life, one needs to receive the true Light of the world—Jesus Christ. John said, *"In him was life, and the life was the light of men"* (1:4).

Light and *Life* are two words that are commonly used and closely associated in the fourth Gospel (cf. 8:12). For John, seeing the *Light* results in *Life*, whereas blindness brings judgment (cf. 9:39-41). Nevertheless, these two interrelated qualities (Light and Life) are not the only link that connects the seventh and eighth signs in this spiritual Gospel. A comparison of the ninth and eleventh chapters reveals two additional and unmistakable parallels.

The first of these two notable parallels between the man born blind and Lazarus, is that both the infirmity of the former and the death of the latter were not punishment for any particular sins, but foreordained in order to provide occasions for revealing the glory of God (cf. 9:3 with 11:4). "The point, however, is not that God deforms people in order to show his own power, but that in and through such misfortune the power of God vindicates itself (cf. Genesis 50:20)."[94]

> To apprehend fully the manner in which the miracles are presented in our Gospel, it must be considered that the true end of these acts went far beyond the consolation of the suffering being who was the object of them. If Jesus had only been moved with compassion for individual suffering, why, instead of restoring sight to some blind only, did He not banish blindness from the world? Why, instead of raising two or three dead, not abolish death itself? He did not do so, though His compassion would certainly have impelled Him so to do. The reason was because the suppression of suffering and death is only a blessing for humanity as a corollary from the destruction of sin. This must therefore precede that; and the miracles were signs intended to manifest Jesus as the deliverer by whom first sin, and then suffering and death, must one day be radically destroyed.[95]

The second parallel between the two miracle stories is revealed when we compare 9:4-5 with 11:8-10. In these passages "we are dealing with a subtle allusion to the coming death of Jesus. Already its inevitability has been indicated by passing references of the evangelist (2:22; 7:39) and by the attitude of the Jews in controversy with Jesus (5:18; 8:37, 40, 59). Now as the public ministry begins to draw toward a close, Jesus' last acts of healing are placed under the shadow of the cross."[96]

Be that as it may, for now there was an unconcluded day during any portion of which Christ could walk in safety, and His disciples would be safe in His company, as He performed the work given Him by the Father. In response to the concerns of His anxious disciples about returning to Judea to see Lazarus, since the Jews of late sought to stone Him (cf. 11:8), Jesus answered:

> *Are there not twelve hours in the day? If any man walk in the day, he stumbleth not, because he seeth the light of this world.* 11:9

Nevertheless, the Lord looked ahead to the time when the disciples would have to go on alone, and continue the work after His departure. Therefore, He added:

> *But if a man walk in the night, he stumbleth, because there is no light in him.* 11:10

> He . . . warns them that they never walk otherwise than as seeing Him who is the Light of men,—they never walk as in the night,—they undertake no task, they affront no danger, unless looking to Him, unless they can say, "The Lord is my Light;" for so to do were to involve themselves in sure peril and temptation. The final words which explain why such a walker in the night should stumble, "because there is no light in him," are a forsaking of the figure, which would have required something of this kind, "there is no light above him;" but in the spiritual world it is one and the same thing not to see the light above us, and not to have it in us: for having it here is only the consequence of seeing it there.[97]

> *Then spake Jesus again unto them, saying, I am the light of the world: he that followeth me shall not walk in darkness, but shall have the light of life.* 8:12

Chapter Twelve Notes

[1] Gleason L. Archer, "Isaiah," *The Biblical Expositor*, Ed. Carl F. H. Henry (Philadelphia: A. J. Holman Company, 1973), 543.

[2] Henrietta C. Mears, *What the Bible Is All About* (Glendale, Calif.: Regal Books Division, Gospel Light Publications, 1966), 211.

[3] B. W. Johnson, *The New Testament Commentary: Vol. III—John* (St. Louis: Christian Publishing Company, 1886), xviii.

[4] Edward W. Bauman, *An Introduction to the New Testament* (Philadelphia: The Westminster Press, 1961), 154.

[5] *Ibid.*

[6] Alfred Plummer, *The Gospel According to St. John* (Cambridge: The University Press, 1912), 40.

[7] *Ibid.*

[8] B. F. Westcott, *The Gospel According to St. John* (London: John Murray, Albemarle Street, 1908), lxxv.

[9] "Gospels," *Encyclopaedia Britannica* (1903), X:828-29.

[10] Westcott, *op. cit.*, xl-xli.

[11] Richard Chenevix Trench, *Notes on the Miracles of Our Lord*, 6th ed. (London: John W. Parker and Son, West Strand, 1858), 3.

[12] *Ibid.*, 3-5.

[13] "Gospels," *Encyclopaedia Britannica* (1903), X:825.

[14] *Ibid.*

[15] *Ibid.*

[16] *Ibid.*

[17] *Ibid.*

[18] Bauman, *op. cit.*, 158.

[19] Chester Warren Quimby, *John: The Universal Gospel* (New York: The Macmillan Company, 1947), 107-08.

[20] Carl F. H. Henry, "John," *The Biblical Expositor*, Ed. Carl F. H. Henry (Philadelphia: A. J. Holman Company, 1973), 946-47.

[21] T. W. Gilbert, *The Gospel According to St. John, Vol. I* (London: The Religious Tract Society, n.d.), 109.

[22] Henry, *op. cit.*, 948.

[23] *Ibid.*

[24] *Ibid.*, 947.

[25] Quimby, *op. cit.*, 122-23.

[26] Trench, *op. cit.*, 122-23.

[27] Quimby, *op. cit.*, 123.

[28] *Ibid.*, 123-24.

[29] Johnson, *op. cit.*, 85.

[30] Herbert Lockyer, *All the Miracles of the Bible* (Grand Rapids, Mich.: Zondervan Publishing House, 1965), 166.

[31] *Ibid.*

[32] Frederic W. Farrar, *The Life of Christ* (London: Cassel and Company, Limited, 1896), 264.

[33] *Ibid.*, 265.

[34] *Ibid.*

[35] *Ibid.*, 265-66.

[36] *Ibid.*, 270-71.

[37] *Ibid.*, 271.

[38] *Ibid.*

[39] Plummer, *op. cit.*, 127.

[40] Quimby, *op. cit.*, 128.

[41] Rev. Horatius Bonar, *Not What My Hands Have Done* (1864).

[42] Trench, *op. cit.*, 263-64.

[43] *Ibid.*, 267.

[44] Farrar, *op. cit.*, 286-87.

[45] Plummer, *op. cit.*, 137.

[46] Charles R. Erdman, *The Gospel of John* (Philadelphia: The Westminster Press, 1941), 64.

[47] Lockyer, *op. cit.*, 198.

[48] Trench, *op. cit.*, 270.

[49] Erdman, *op. cit.*, 65.

[50] Johnson, *op. cit.*, 99.

[51] *Ibid.*, 100.

[52] Lockyer, *op. cit.*, 200.

[53] *Ibid.*, 201.

[54] Johnson, *op. cit.*, 100-01.

[55] Plummer, *op. cit.*, 144.

[56] Johnson, *op. cit.*, 101.

[57] Erdman, *op. cit.*, 62.

[58] Lockyer, *op. cit.*, 201.

[59] Trench, *op. cit.*, 278.

[60] Rev. James Montgomery, *In the Hour of Trial* (1834).

[61] Robert A. Spivey, and D. Moody Smith, Jr., *Anatomy of the New Testament: A Guide to Its Structure and Meaning*, 2nd ed. (New York: Macmillan Publishing Co., Inc., 1974), 443-44.

[62] Farrar, *op. cit.*, 395.

[63] Plummer, *op. cit.*, 199.

[64] Erdman, *op. cit.*, 86.

[65] Johnson, *op. cit.*, 151.

[66] Erdman, *op. cit.*, 87.

[67] *Ibid.*

[68] Farrar, *op. cit.*, 398.

[69] *Ibid.*

[70] *Ibid.*

[71] Johnson, *op. cit.*, 155.

[72] *Ibid.*

[73] Trench, *op. cit.*, 309-10.

[74] Johnson, *op. cit.*, 155.

[75] J. Vernon McGee, *John:* Vol. I (Pasadena, Calif.: Thru the Bible Books, 1987), 141.

[76] Plummer, *op. cit.*, 209.

[77] *Ibid.*, 208.

[78] Spivey, *op. cit.*, 442.

[79] *Ibid.*, 443.

[80] Plummer, *op. cit.*, 226.

[81] Spivey, *op. cit.*, 443.

[82] John Fleetwood, *The Life of Our Lord and Savior Jesus Christ; Containing a Full, Accurate, and Universal History from His Taking Upon Himself Our Nature to His Crucifixion, Resurrection and Ascension: Together with the Lives, Transactions, and Sufferings of His Holy Evangelists, Apostles, Disciples, and Other Primitive Martyrs. To Which is Added the History of the Jews* (New Haven: Published by Nathan Whiting, 1831), 252.

[83] Trench, *op. cit.*, 394.

[84] *Ibid.*, 397-98.

[85] Plummer, op. cit., 235.

[86] Johnson, *op. cit.*, 175-76.

[87] Trench, *op. cit.*, 411-12.

[88] Farrar, *op. cit.*, 457.

[89] Fleetwood, *op. cit.*, 259.

[90] Farrar, *op. cit.*, 459-60.

[91] Spivey, *op. cit.*, 443.

[92] *Ibid.*

[93] Jeffery J. W. Baker and Garland E. Allen, *The Study of Biology* (Reading, Mass.: Addison-Wesley Publishing Company, 1967), 167.

[94] Spivey, *op. cit.*

[95] F. Godet, *Commentary on the Gospel of St. John*, Vol. I, 3rd ed., trans. by M. D. Cusin (Edinburgh: T. & T. Clark, 1887), 114.

[96] Spivey, *op. cit.*, 443.

[97] Trench, *op. cit.*, 395.

Chapter Thirteen

The World: Wealthy and Wretched

When Oxford University Press published J. M. Roberts' *A Concise History of the World* in 1994, it was immediately acclaimed as a classic. *The Christian Science Monitor* greeted it as a "landmark book . . . intelligently organized, insightful and balanced."[1] The *Sunday Telegraph* described the book as "a work of outstanding breadth of scholarship and penetrating judgments. There is nothing better of its kind."[2] A. J. P. Taylor, writing for *The Observer*, claimed that Roberts' *History of the World* was "a stupendous achievement. . . . The unrivaled world history of our day. . . . It is unbelievably accurate in its facts and almost incontestable in its judgments."[3]

From the first chapter of this work (entitled "Prehistory") in a section subtitled "At the Edge of History," we find a sample of that which many today would regard as "unbelievably accurate in its facts and almost incontestable in its judgments." The author—who until his retirement was Warden of Merton College at Oxford University and also General Editor of *The Short Oxford History of the Modern World*—wrote:

> By Neolithic times we are in a world full of human variety and potential. This variety was to increase. Some human communities were to progress rapidly; some would not. New forces would operate in human development as different peoples came into contact and learnt from one another, or reflected further on their own experience and plunged forward into new experiments. More and more, that is to say, human diversity could stem from mankind's ability to change things consciously as well as from the brute facts of environment. The result would be more untidy still; there have hardly ever been such possibilities of differences of human experience as exist in the world today. But, it was far from uniform in 5000 B.C. There is no clear line marking off the end of one human era from another, only a blurred, ragged-edged time zone, with some people forging ahead on their way to civilization and others still stuck firmly in the Stone Age where some of them were to remain for thousands of years yet. . . .
>
> The crucial reason why change had already speeded up a lot by 5000 B.C. is that by then the main source of innovation had moved from natural forces to human beings themselves. By the end of prehistory the human story is increasingly one of choice. Human beings are making more and more decisions to act and adapt in certain ways to meet their problems and to develop certain ways of doing things, to utilize certain materials or skills. This is why what we can reckon the most important change of all came about somewhere right at the beginning, though we cannot exactly know when or where, when some creature perhaps hardly recognizable to us as human first began to think of the world as a collection of separate objects distinct from himself. If we knew when it was, it might serve as the best definition of the beginning of the prehistory of man; it opened the way to using the world, and that is the story of the whole change from life shaped blindly by nature to one shaped by human culture and tradition.[4]

The author went on to say:

> One of the few good descriptions of Homo Sapiens is that he is, above all, a change-making animal. The evidence of that lies in what he has done—his history. Behind it lies all that has been only glanced at so far in this book, millions of years in which creatures were taking shape in ways which decided that among the primates, human beings alone were formed as creatures which could mould their own destinies. Even if for a long time they could only do so within narrow limits, the earliest evidence of the effect of that is very ancient.[5]

Conflicting Views of History

Although Robert's *History of the World* is interesting and well written, it does not agree with the Biblical account of either man's history or his destiny. Nevertheless, today it would be difficult, if not impossible, to find a recently released book (from a secular publisher) on the subject of world history that is not written from an evolutionary, man-centered perspective. Yet true history must begin, as Scripture affirms, with man's creation by the Word of God, and trace all subsequent history in light of his fallen nature. This God-centered view of history, unlike the thinking today, had been the consensus of earlier historians for centuries.

Charles Rollin (1661-1741), Late Principal of the University of Paris, Professor of Eloquence in the Royal College, and member of the Royal Academy of Inscriptions and Belles Lettres, had in the 1730's written a multi-volume work entitled *The Ancient History of the Egyptians, Carthaginians, Assyrians, Babylonians, Medes and Persians, Macedonians, and Grecians*. At the end of his once famous work, he wrote a conclusion, which—although in sharp contrast to modern thinking—represents the views of almost all the great historians from his day to the end of the nineteenth century. From an early American edition of his book, translated from the French and published by William Borradaile of New York in 1825, we read:

> We have seen hitherto, without speaking of the first and ancient kingdom of Egypt, and of some states separate, and in a manner entirely distinct from the rest, three great successive empires, founded on the ruin of each other, continue during a long series of ages, and at length entirely disappear; the empire of the Babylonians, the empire of the Medes and Persians, and the empire of the Macedonians and the Grecian princes, successors of Alexander the Great. A fourth empire arises, that of the Romans, which having already swallowed up most of those which have preceded it, will extend its conquests, and after having subjected all to its power by force of arms, be itself torn in a manner into different pieces, and by being so dismembered, make way for the establishment of almost all the kingdoms which now divide Europe, Asia, and Africa. We may here behold a picture of all ages; of the glory and power of all the empires of the world; in a word, of all that is splendid or admirable in human greatness! Every excellence is here presented, sublimity of genius, delicacy of taste, accompanied by solidity of judgment; the noblest efforts of eloquence, carried to the highest degree of perfection, without departing from nature and truth; the glory of arms, with that of arts and sciences; valour in

conquering, and ability in government. What a multitude of great men of every kind does it not present to our view! What powerful, what glorious kings! What great captains! What famous conquerors! What wise magistrates! What learned philosophers! What admirable legislators! We are transported with beholding in certain ages and countries, as if peculiar to themselves, an ardent zeal for justice, a passionate love of country, a noble disinterestedness, a generous contempt of riches, and an esteem for poverty, which astonish and amaze us, so much do they appear above human nature.

In this manner we think and judge. But while we are in admiration and ecstasy at the view of so many splendid virtues, the Supreme Judge, who alone can estimate all things, sees nothing in them but trifles, meanness, vanity, and pride; and while mankind are continually busied in perpetuating the power of their families, in founding kingdoms and eternizing themselves, if that were possible, God, from his throne on high, overthrows all their projects, and makes even their ambition the means of executing his purposes, infinitely superior to our understandings. He alone knows his operations and designs. All ages are present to him: "He seeth from everlasting to everlasting." He has assigned all empires their fate and duration. In all the different revolutions, we have seen that nothing has come to pass by chance. We know, that under the image of that statue which Nabuchodonosor saw, of an enormous height and terrible countenance, with the head of gold, the breasts and arms of silver, the belly and thighs of brass, and the legs of iron mixed with clay, God thought fit to represent the four great empires, uniting in them as we have seen in the course of . . . history, all that is glorious, grand, formidable and powerful. And what means does the Almighty use for overthrowing this immense Colossus? "A small stone was cut out without hands, which smote the image upon his feet that were of iron and clay, and brake them to pieces. Then was the iron, the clay, the brass, the silver, and the gold, broken together, and became like the chaff of the summer thrashing floors, and the wind carried them away, that no place was found for them; and the stone that smote the image became a great mountain, and filled the whole earth."

We see with our own eyes the accomplishment of this admirable prophecy of Daniel at least in part. Jesus Christ who descended to clothe himself with flesh and blood in the sacred womb of the blessed virgin, without the participation of man, is the small stone that came from the mountain without human aid. The prevailing characteristics of his person, of his relations, his appearance, his manner of teaching, his disciples, in a word, of every thing that relates to him, were simplicity, poverty, and humility; which were so extreme, that they concealed from the eyes of the proud Jews the divine lustre of his miracles, however effulgent, and from the sight of the devil himself, penetrating and attentive as he was, the evident proofs of his divinity.

Notwithstanding that seeming weakness, and even meanness, Jesus Christ will certainly conquer the whole universe. It is under this idea a prophet represents him to us: "He went forth conquering and to conquer." His work and mission are, "to set up a kingdom for his Father, which shall never be destroyed; and the kingdom which shall not be left to other people;" like those which we have seen in . . . history; "but it shall break in pieces, and consume all these kingdoms; and it shall stand for ever."

The power granted to Jesus Christ, the founder of this empire, is without bounds, measure, or end. The kings, who glory so much in their power, have nothing which approaches in the least to that of Jesus Christ. They do not reign over the will of man, which is real dominion. Their subjects can think as they please independently of them. There are an infinitude of particular actions done without their order, and which escape their knowledge as well as their power. Their designs often miscarry, and come to nothing even during their own lives. But with Jesus Christ it is quite otherwise. "All power is given unto him in heaven and in earth." He exercises it principally upon the hearts and minds of men. Nothing is done without his order or permission. Every thing is disposed by his wisdom and power. Every thing co-operates directly or indirectly to the accomplishment of his designs.

While all things are in motion and fluctuate upon earth; while states and empires pass away with incredible rapidity, and the human race, vainly employed in the external view of these things, are also drawn in by the same torrent, almost without perceiving it; there passes, in secret, an order and disposition of things unknown and invisible, which however determine our fate to all eternity. The duration of ages has no other end than the formation of the bodies of the elect, which augments, and tends daily toward perfection. When it shall receive its final accomplishment by the death of the last of the elect; "Then cometh the end, when he shall have delivered up the kingdom to God, even the Father; when he shall have put down all rule, and all authority, and power."[6]

Eventually, the Christ-centered views of world history, as expressed in such works as those of Charles Rollin, would all but disappear from our secular textbooks. In November of 1859 Charles Darwin's now classic work, *The Origin of Species by Means of Natural Selection*, was published, and "at once aroused a storm of controversy as no book of its kind has ever done."[7] Yet in the years to come, it was to have a profound effect, not only in the field of the natural sciences, but the social sciences as well. By the end of the nineteenth century, history books would relate as facts, those evolutionary features that stand in stark contrast to Scripture and the great historical works of the past. Typical of the textbooks of this period is Philip Van Ness Myers', *A General History for Colleges and High Schools* (1889, rev. 1903). The Introduction states:

We do not know when man first came into possession of the earth. We only know that, in ages vastly remote, when both the climate and the outline of Europe were very different from what they are at present, man lived on that continent with animals now extinct; and that as early as 4000 or 3000 B.C.— when the curtain first rises on the stage of history—in some favored regions, as in the valley of the Nile, there were nations and civilizations already venerable with age, and possessing languages, arts, and institutions that bear evidence of slow growth through long periods of time before history begins.[8]

By the time of the so-called "Scopes Monkey Trial" in 1925, our country was inundated with history books that contradicted the Scriptural record as well as all common sense. J. N. Larned's five-volume work, *Larned's History of the World or Seventy Centuries of the Life of Mankind* (Published in 1915), would have us believe the following:

The oldest traces of man, wherever found, show him in a state which corresponds to that of the lower savages of the present day. Through what still ruder stages of existence, prolonged through what stretches of time, he may have been passing before any durable traces of his life became marked on the earth, is a subject of speculation that will not be taken up here.[9]

Most of the historical works of the 20th century trace man's ancestors back to some savage creatures, who "creeping out of their first homes in forest and jungle, learned to stand upright," and managed "to fight the wild beasts which surrounded them, using weapons, rocks and clubs."[10] Such are the "facts," as evolutionary historians would have us to believe!

The truth is, the earliest evidence does not link man to prehistoric caves, but to an historic deluge—since all evidence of ancient civilizations from the time of Adam to Noah was destroyed in the worldwide Flood. And although the exact date may be difficult to ascertain with 100% certainty, civilization as we know it can only be traced back to the descendents of Noah and their dispersion from the continent of Asia. As one nineteenth-century historian noted:

> Asia was the cradle of the human race. The exact date of the Creation and Fall of man cannot be determined with any degree of certainty, neither can the interval between the Creation and the Deluge be ascertained. On these facts chronologists are absurdly at variance; but the difficulty of assigning the exact time of those events does not in any way diminish the evidence of their actual occurrence. It is supposed that the descendents of Shem, the eldest of Noah's sons, after the dispersion of mankind at Babel, went to the East, and populated Asia; those of Ham, with few exceptions, passing into Africa, and those of Japhet journeying to the West, where they occupied different parts of Europe.
>
> The oldest monarchies of which history gives us any account are those of Babylonia and Assyria in Asia, and Egypt and Ethiopia in Africa.[11]

The true history of mankind upon earth can only be understood in the context of the outworking of divine Providence.

> Since God is the author of history and He is carrying out His plan in the earth through history, any view of . . . history . . . that ignores God is not true history. He is sovereign over His creation and "His story" in the earth, and is at work in significant, and seemingly insignificant, events to accomplish His purposes for mankind. This is a providential view of history.[12]

A providential view of history is the only one that is consistent with the teachings of Scripture. As the Apostle Paul so eloquently told the men of Athens as he stood in the midst of Mars Hill:

> *God that made the world and all things therein, seeing that he is Lord of heaven and earth, dwelleth not in temples made with hands; Neither is worshipped with men's hands, as though he needed any thing, seeing he giveth to all life, and breath, and all things; And hath made of one blood all nations of men for to dwell on all the face of the earth, and hath determined the times before appointed, and the bounds of their habitation; That they should seek the Lord, if haply they might feel after him, and find him, though he be not far from every one of us.* ACTS 17:24-27

Geography Reflects the Principle of Design

Of interest to note is that God has not only determined the times of men and nations, but *"the bounds of their habitation."* By Divine Providence the nations of the world have been given "unique characteristics, such as their time of existence in history, their power, national spirit,"[13] and even their geographic location and boundaries, "in order that they can fulfill their divine purposes in history."[14]

Arnold Guyot (1807-1884), late Professor of Physical Geography and Geology at Princeton University, was an expert in the Providential view of geography. In his now classic book, *Physical Geography* (published in 1873), which was prepared for use in the public schools, he contrasted the Southern and Northern continents, and explained their differences in light of the purpose of God and the development of mankind. He wrote:

> The SOUTHERN CONTINENTS—lying mainly in the tropical zone, where all the conditions that stimulate physical life are most powerful, and where, with few exceptions, man has remained at the bottom of the social scale—may be designated the continents of nature. Each has its own especial character, wherein the influence of every distinguishing feature of the continent is seen.
>
> In South America—the tropical continent of the Western World, and especially the continent of plains—all the characteristics of the New World are exhibited in an exaggerated degree. It is preeminently the realm of vegetable life, where we find the largest, the most dense, and the most varied forests, and the greatest development of foliage on the face of the earth.
>
> Africa—the tropical continent of the Eastern World, and the continent of plateaus—has, in an extreme degree, the dry continental climate of the Old World. It is, above all, the realm of the nobler animals, of the mammalia—the highest division of the animal world—which, by their number, their variety, their size and strength, give the African fauna its distinctive character.
>
> Australia, the only sub-tropical continent, and the most isolated, the smallest, and the least varied of all, is the only one which preserves to a great extent the ancient forms of plants and animals. . . .
>
> The NORTHERN CONTINENTS, may properly be designated the continents of history. Less richly endowed with those elements which foster the life of nature, they possess all the conditions most favorable for the development and progress of the races inhabiting them; and each was apparently designed, from the beginning, for the performance of a peculiar part in the education of mankind.[15]

Professor Guyot went on to describe the unique characteristics and functions of Asia, Europe, and America—the three continents of history. He wrote:

> Asia . . . is the largest of the continents, the most central, the only one with which all the others are closely connected; and the one whose different physical regions show the strongest contrasts, and are separated by the greatest barriers.
>
> It has the loftiest mountains, the highest and most extended plateaus, the greatest plains, and the most numerous river systems; with all climates, from the hottest to the coldest, from the driest to the most moist. It has, also, a large

number of useful plants, and of animals capable of domestication; together with an abundance of both the useful and the precious metals. . . .

This great and strongly marked continent is the continent of origins. The human family, its races and civilizations, and the systems of religion which rule the most enlightened nations, all had their beginning here.

By the great diversity of its physical features and climate, and the strong barriers isolating them one from another, Asia was admirably fitted to promote the formation of a diversity of races; while its close connection with the other continents facilitated their dispersion throughout the earth.

Its alluvial plains, with their well-defined boundaries of mountains or deserts, and their rich soil—covered annually by overflowing rivers with a fruitful loam, and so easily tilled that a plough was scarcely needed—seem to have been especially adapted to foster the progress of a race still in its infancy.

The abundance of their resources, developed by agriculture, allowed the congregation of great numbers of men upon the same area, and thus favored the formation of organized governments; while the conflict with the overflowing rivers, the necessity of irrigation, and the alternation of the seasons, incited forethought, and gave birth to the useful arts and the sciences of observation. . . .

Europe . . . shows a diversity of structure even greater than that of Asia; but with smaller areas, more moderate forms of relief, less extreme contrasts of climate, a more generally fertile soil, and everywhere an abundance of the most useful minerals; while the relative extent of its coastline—its maritime zone—is greater than that of any other continent.

This continent is especially fitted, by its diversity, to foster the formation of distinct nationalities, each developing in an especial direction. Moreover, the proximity of these nations one to another, the greater facility of communication between them, and, above all, the common highway of the sea, nowhere very distant, facilitates mutual intercourse, the lack of which arrested the progress of the civilizations of Asia. . . .

Though not the continent of origins, Europe is emphatically the continent of development. The Indo-European race—the people of progress—find their fullest expansion and activity, not in their original seat in Iran, but in Europe, whence they are spreading over all quarters of the globe. The arts and learning of antiquity attained their highest development, not in western Asia and Egypt, the places of their origin, but in Greece and Rome.

Christianity, also, only germinated in western Asia. Transplanted to Europe, it gradually attained its fullest development, and became the foundation of which is reared the vast and noble edifice of modern civilization.

America . . . , different in position, structure, and climatic conditions, from both the other northern continents, seems destined to play a part in the history of mankind unlike that of Europe and Asia, though not less noble than either.

The structure of this continent . . . is characterized by a unity and simplicity as striking as is the diversity of Europe. . . .

In its climate, those contrasts in temperature which are so violent in Asia, and still prevail in Europe, are obliterated. . . .

The chief contrast of the continent is that of the coasts and the interior, the maritime and the continental climates; but even this is softened, the Great Gulf of Mexico carrying the maritime zone almost into the heart of the continent; while the warm equatorial wind spreads its wealth of vapors over the interior plains at the north and east. . . .

The difference in surface and climate, sufficient to create diversity in industries and in the products of the soil, are not, as in Asia, marked enough to give rise necessarily to entirely different modes of life among the inhabitants, and to create antagonistic interests. By fostering internal commerce, they unite rather than separate the people of the several regions.

Finally, the oceanic position of America secures its commercial prosperity, and prepares, at the same time, the means of its influence on the world. . . .

The most characteristic, as well as the most valuable, part of America, is the noble domain of the United States. Between the cold, semi-arctic northern slope, and the tropical climes of the south, it is situated wholly in temperate latitudes, with a climate the most favorable for the active life of civilized communities.

In the eastern half are fertile plains and valley, teeming with agricultural wealth, or covered with forests; in the west, pasture lands, or plateaus and mountains rich in silver and gold. On the north are corn lands, water-power, and inexhaustible mines of coal, copper, and iron; on the south, tobacco, cotton, rice, and cane.

This diversity of resources creates the necessity for constant intercourse, which is facilitated to the utmost by the vast river systems, the great length of coastline, and the absence to barrier between the different regions. Thus the unity of the entire people is promoted, and the formation of local nationalities is checked.

Again, the agricultural wealth of the eastern half, flowing naturally to the Atlantic ports, is essential to the overcrowded industrial nations of western Europe; and brings the youthful and vigorous American people into constant contact with European culture, acquired through long ages of progress. . . .

Nowhere do we find in America those local centers, each having a strongly marked individuality, which fostered the progress of the race in its infancy and its youth; but everywhere provision is made for mutual intercourse, a common life, and the blending of the entire population into one. Evidently this continent was not designed to give birth and development to a new civilization; but to receive one ready-made, and to furnish to the cultivated race of the Old World the scene most worthy of their activity.

Its vast plains, overflowing with natural wealth, are turned towards Europe, and its largest rivers discharge into the Atlantic, while its lofty mountains, and less fertile lands, are removed far toward its western shores. Thus it seems to invite the Indo-European race, the people of progress, to new fields of action; to encourage their expansion throughout its entire territory, and their fusion into one nation; while it opens for them a pathway to all the nations of the earth.

America, therefore, with her cultural and progressive people, and her social organization, founded upon the principle of the equality . . . of all mankind, seems destined to become the fountain of a new and higher life for all the races of men.

Conclusion. Each continent has, therefore, a well-defined individuality, which fits it for an especial function. The fullness of nature's life is typified by Africa, with its superabundant wealth and power of animal life; South America, with its exuberance of vegetation; and Australia, with its antiquated forms of plants and animals.

In the grand drama of man's life and development, Asia, Europe, and America play distinct parts, for which each seems to have been admirably prepared.

Truly no blind force gave our earth the forms so well adapted to perform these functions. The conclusion is irresistible—that the entire globe is a grand organism, every feature of which is the outgrowth of a definite plan of the all-wise Creator for the education of the human family, and the manifestation of his own glory.[16]

Providential Preparations for the Advent of Christ

A providential view of man's life on earth will, as Professor Guyot clearly pointed out, result in bringing glory to God. By contrast, an evolutionary view of history tries to divert that glory to man. The logical conclusion to an evolutionary world-view is that man, who has supposedly progressed from a very primitive state to his present exalted position, will eventually become a god in his own right. This perception of how the evolutionist views his world and lives his life is clearly seen in Jeremy Rifkin's book, *Algeny*, which was admittedly "a controversial reevaluation of Darwinism . . . and a critical examination of the way we view our relationship with nature."[17] In this 1983 publication the author claimed:

> Humanity is abandoning the idea that the universe operates by ironclad truths because it no longer feels the need to be constrained by such fetters. Nature is being made anew, this time by human beings. We no longer feel ourselves to be guests in someone else's home and therefore obliged to make our behavior conform with a set of pre-existing cosmic rules. It is our creation now. We make the rules. We establish the parameters of reality. We create the world, and because we do, we no longer have to justify our behavior, for we are now the architects of the universe. We are responsible to nothing outside ourselves, for we are the kingdom, the power, and the glory for ever and ever.[18]

Unfortunately, those who believe they are responsible to nothing outside themselves, will someday have to give account of their lives, when they appear *"before God, and the Lord Jesus Christ, who shall judge the quick and the dead at his appearing and his kingdom"* (2 Tim. 4:1). *"So then every one of us shall give account of himself to God"* (Rom. 14:12).

Moreover, those who believe they are architects of the universe need to review the lessons of history. The peoples of the great world empires of the past had each tried and failed in their attempts at perfecting mankind, and in so doing had providentially completed final preparations for the promised Messiah of the Old Testament Scriptures. "The entire world was thus evidently in an attitude of expectancy. The Oriental had despaired of his material magnificence, the Greek of his reason and philosophy, and the Roman was despairing of his universal empire. God must interpose or the world must perish."[19]

The providential preparations for the advent of the Messiah involved the mission of both Jew and Gentile. "In the case of the former, the work of preparation was carried on by means of revelation; in the case of the latter by means of free experience."[20] And it is especially in the free experience of the pagan nations that the utter failure of man to be the architects of his own universe becomes apparent. However, before we highlight the attempts of these ancient peoples to "establish the parameters of reality," let us briefly review the mission of the Jews, as it relates to the providential preparations of the heathen world for the reception of the Messiah, for whom they may not have looked, but desperately needed.

> It was the mission of the Jews to receive directly from God, and in due time, transmit to the whole human race the only religion of salvation, and therefore the only true world-religion. Everything connected with the history of the Jews had reference to the completion of this one religion for mankind. Each revelation and dispensation, all discipline and punishment, every promise and threatening, their constitution, laws, and worship, every political, civil, and religious institution (so far as they were legitimate and proper), tended toward this one goal. In the light of providential developments and later revelations, the divine plan as connected with the Jews may readily be traced, in its great outlines, from the calling of Abraham to the advent of Christ.
>
> The history of the chosen people has been providentially divided into two periods, the first of which ended with the captivity and the extinction of national independence, and the second, with the Advent. The first was, in general terms, a period of national unity and integrity, and of complete separation from the outside world. The second was a period of national disintegration, of dispersion throughout the whole world, and of most varied union with mankind.
>
> To the careless glance there seems a contradiction in the parts of this divine plan. Why first the policy of complete isolation, and then an abrupt change to the opposite? As always elsewhere, so here, to a closer inspection, the unity and consistency of the divine purpose clearly appear. The one purpose was twofold. The work of the period of isolation may be characterized as the revelation of the world-religion to the chosen people and the establishment of its sway over them. The work of the period of dispersion may be characterized as missionary in its nature, and as intended to impress the world-religion, in the form in which it had been revealed to the chosen people, upon the pagan races, in order to prepare them for the reception of the Divine Savior with his salvation.[21]

In the centuries immediately preceding the Advent of Jesus Christ, a majority of the Jewish people underwent a process of transformation that prepared and "enabled them to impress the world religion . . . upon the pagan races." Scripture refers to them as Grecians (cf. Acts 6:1; 9:29, 11:20), and of those who *"believed, and turned to the Lord"* (Acts 11:21), the best example was personified in Paul, the Apostle to the Gentiles.

> Following the Babylonian captivity and under the favoring influences of the Persian empire the Jew had been in a measure revolutionized. His character was not, however, thereby altered except in its external aspect. The revolution

had accomplished little else than to bring him into contact with the nations of the world. It broke up his habits of seclusion and rendered him content to live outside the narrow bounds of his own country. But he still continued to speak the same language, to adhere to the same exclusive regard for his own institutions, and to explain all things by the only philosophy with which he was acquainted—the tradition of his fathers. This was true of all Jews; there was but one class of them. We find, however, when we open the New Testament that two distinct classes are recognized. The first is known by the ancient name, "Jews;" the second are called "Grecians". We observe, also, that these Grecians comprise a large element, probably the majority, of the early Christian church. We discover, upon the first mention of them, that there is a certain amount of friction between them and their brethren who bear the ancient name. They are introduced to our attention in Acts 6:1, where we are told that "there arose a murmuring of the Grecians against the Hebrews, because their widows were neglected in the daily ministration." They are mentioned again in chapter 9:29, where we are told that Saul of Tarsus, when he returned from Damascus to Jerusalem, after his conversion "disputed against the Grecians; but they went about to slay him." In chapter 11:20, we read that certain believers who had come to Antioch "spake unto the Grecians, preaching the Lord Jesus." We should be disposed to conclude even from these simple statements, although we were ignorant of foregoing history, that some great providential movement had been in progress since the close of the Old Testament, in the course of which a people had been furnished out of the Jewish church itself, forming a connecting link between that church and the Gentile world. This conclusion would be a just one. It is a mistake to suppose—as the uninstructed reader of the New Testament is liable to do—that in the day wherein the hope of Israel was to be extended to all nations there was no mediator between the Jew and the Gentile. The very reverse was the case. The mediator had been provided, and his production is one of the most remarkable illustrations of divine providence, in its control of human history, which is anywhere afforded. The Gospel was not to depend for its agencies solely upon the Jew of Palestine, with his provincialism and prejudice. Under the omniscient leadership of God a fusion of races had been in progress, and there had been produced a new species, which intellectually realized what some ethnologists say is physically impossible, a true hybrid. That hybrid was the Grecian. He was a true Jew and a true Greek in the same person, but in him the stern and repulsive stiffness of Judaism had been softened by the elements of Hellenic culture. He adhered to the God of Israel and prayed toward the temple of Jerusalem; but he spake the language of Athens and lived in the atmosphere of the Acropolis. He was the ordained mediator of the new era. . . .

We must therefore find the true successor of the Hebrew not in the Jew of Palestine but in the Jew of the dispersion. The Jew of Palestine was occupying himself with the attempt the more jealously to preserve his inheritance from the profane presence of the stranger. He would wall the faith of his fathers round about up to heaven, and preserve it for his own benefit and for that of his children. The Grecian, on the other hand, would break down the wall upon every side, and admit all who would enter to the enjoyment of its privileges. The Jew of Palestine looked forward to the coming of a Messiah who should be their peculiar property, and who would lead them in a holy warfare, wherein all nations should be subjugated and brought under their yoke. The Grecian yearned for the coming of a great teacher who would lead, not only himself, but all with whom he was associated, both Jew and ·Gentile, to the knowledge of the truth. The Judaism of Palestine was ossified in its exclusiveness, its isolation and its pride. It was an old fig-tree withered at the roots. The Judaism of the dispersion was quickened into the promise of new life by its contact with the thought of the heathen world. It ws a cutting from the old tree, growing in new soil, putting forth fresh green leaves, and budding for a glorious fruitage. The multitude of the dispersion, rather than the minority of Palestine, were to become the missionaries of the world. Grecian thought and Grecian methods were to become the medium through which the kingdoms of the world were to be embraced in the kingdom of our Lord and of his Christ. Judaism shall be set aside; Grecianism in a measure adopted. The Jew shall experience a yet greater transformation; and having become a "new creature" shall extend the blessings of the new covenant to the whole wide world.[22]

Jesus told *"a woman of Samaria"* that *"salvation is of the Jews"* (John 4:7, 22), and their providential role in the advent of the Messiah must never be minimized. But at the same time the Gentiles also played a major part in preparing the world for Christ, even though they failed in their various attempts to satisfy the greatest needs of man.

A view of the preparation for the Messiah would be incomplete if confined to the Jews alone. Salvation has been seen to have come forth from Judaea, but to be adapted to the necessities of the world. Three great historic races, the Oriental, the Greek, and the Roman, successively entered, along with the Jew, into the work of preparing the world for the advent of Messiah and the spread of his divine salvation.

This was in accordance with the prophecies of Daniel, contained in the second and seventh chapters of his book. These great empires were to precede and prepare the way for the mightier kingdom of Messiah which the God of heaven should set up, and which should be an everlasting kingdom. Each will be found to have accomplished a twofold preparatory work.[23]

The Mission of the Oriental Peoples

The Oriental empires which entered into this work were the Babylonian, represented by the head of gold in the great image of prophecy, and the less magnificent Medo-Persian, represented by the arms and breast of silver. In the later prophecy, of the four beasts, the former is symbolized by the first beast, which was like a lion, and had eagle's wings, since it was a lion in strength and an eagle in swiftness; the latter is symbolized by the second beast, which was like a bear, since in the desire for conquest, it was all-voracious like the bear. . . .

These great Oriental races represented material riches, power, and grandeur. It was a subordinate part of their mission to prove the insufficiency of the greatest wealth, luxury, and splendor to satisfy and save man. It was the problem on which Solomon wrought, and whose solution he gives in Ecclesiastes when he brings back from his varied experience the conclusion: "Fear God and keep his commandments, for this is the whole of man"—the same problem, only on a vastly grandeur scale. The nations of the Orient came from its attempted solution wretched and perishing. But the more important part of their mission was to furnish the agencies and theatre for the Jewish dispersion, and for the early dissemination of the germs of the world-religion. For this they were eminently fitted. The Jew was their proper representative, belonging to their own race. He had come forth from the valley of the Euphrates, in Abraham the Chaldee. The captivity was but a return to the primitive home. Who was so entitled as the Jew to be called the representative Oriental?

The Oriental races could most easily come into sympathy with Judaism, and could most readily furnish the conditions requisite for the fuller development of the germs of the true religion. In the Oriental mind, therefore, the Jew was to place the grand truths of his religion first, and thus to open the way to reach, at a later date, the Greek and Roman. By their self-will and brute force the Oriental races were meantime to chastise the Jewish race and cure it of its idolatry.[24]

The Mission of the Greeks

The eastern empires fell successively under the sentence which the handwriting on the wall passed upon Belshazzar, and which history repeats against every despotism to the end of time: "Thou art weighed in the balance and found wanting"—wanting in fulfilling the true ends of states and governments, in securing the welfare of mankind and their union in the bonds of social life.

In the later period of its history, when in the height of power under Xerxes, the Medo-Persian empire came into direct and open conflict with the West as represented by Greece, the nation which was divinely appointed to work out another problem—whether man's free energy in poetry and art, in learning and philosophy, could perfect his social state, and thus accomplish that in which the East with its despotic power and wealth and magnificence had failed.

The Greek empire under Alexander was the third kingdom which was to rule over all the earth. Its strength is represented by the brass of the image of the vision, in Daniel, and the rapidity of its conquests and the insatiableness of its ambition, by the third beast, the leopard, with its four wings and four heads. . . .

In its career the Greek race tested the insufficiency of the human reason with the highest human culture to satisfy and save man; while in the conquests of Alexander it gave the world the highest human civilization of the ancient ages, and the most perfect of languages in which to embody the true religion. These are the main points of interest in the mission of the Greek. In fact, Greek wisdom exhausted its free energies upon the same problem which despotic Oriental power and magnificence had failed to solve.

For a millennium the Greek race directed its varied powers and consummate genius in vain to the work of perfecting humanity. It achieved the greatest results in thought ever permitted to unaided human effort. Its civilization was one of the grandest the world has ever seen—grand in its recognitions of humanity, in its poetry and philosophy, in its science and art. But its culture was purely intellectual, having no religious and moral ground of support capable of withstanding every shock and indestructible under all changes, and in the natural course of its development it could only degenerate into false civilization and end in social corruption. It had no light and life from God. "There was yet no salt to preserve the life of humanity from decomposing, or to restore it back again when passing to decomposition."

It is not too much to say that the Greek did everything toward the perfecting of man that could be done by a purely intellectual civilization. He demonstrated for all time what human reason, when situated most favorably and tasked to the utmost, could accomplish for the salvation of a race with endowments superior to the other races. The later ages showed it to be very little.

It became manifest that the glory of the Greek thought needed to be saved from its own corruption—saved for the good of mankind. This could only be accomplished by extending its sway over the Oriental empires, and bringing it in contact with the saving influences of the world-religion which was being diffused everywhere by the scattered and exiled seed of Abraham. . . .

When the Greek had voiced his wonderful thoughts of beauty and power in a language made for them and by them, and, therefore the most perfect of the languages of the ancient ages—the one most worthy to become the world-language—and before the blight and decay had fallen upon the race, Alexander of Macedon appeared to perform the needed office of Hellenizing the world. . . .

From Alexander to the Advent Judaism and Hellenism were in world-wide contact. The man of prophecy was elevating the view of the man of reason, while the man of reason was widening the vision of the man of prophecy. Even where the Greek contemptuously held himself aloof from the Jew, the Jewish religion was one of the most powerful influences in breaking down the old paganism. At the bar of reason, polytheism could not stand before the doctrine of one God. It was doomed from the hour when the Greek heard the first whispers concerning Jehovah. But the Greek did not everywhere hold himself aloof; the two modes of thought came into direct contact; the philosopher and the scribe met and became one. This occurred especially in the great centers. At Alexandria, the Septuagint, or Greek version of the Old Testament Scriptures, was made three centuries before the Advent, for the use of those employing the Greek language, and the old revelation of the world-religion was thus scattered abroad for the Greek-speaking communities. . . .

In this twofold manner, by despair of reason and hope from prophecy, the Greek was borne onward to the completion of his part in the work of preparation for the coming of the Messiah, until mankind was found in possession of the world-religion with its predictions of the coming Redeemer, written in the perfected world-language, and made capable of greater expansiveness by the Greek forms of thought.

The Greek mission was thus evidently essential in the preparation of the Messiah. It forced the thinking men of that age to feel and confess the insufficiency of human reason, even in its most perfect development, for the deliverance and perfection of mankind, and left them waiting and longing for one who could accomplish this work. . . . It made ready and living the better and broader forms of thought and speech in which the Gospel with its grander truths—too grand and living to be put into the narrow and dead Hebrew—should be proclaimed to all the world.[25]

The Mission of the Romans

Rome was already the rising power of the West when Alexander gave the Greek civilization to the East. The Roman Empire was the fourth kingdom of the prophecy of Daniel. Its strength is represented by the iron of the great image, since it was to be "strong as iron;" its terrible character, by the fourth beast, which had more than the power of the lion, more than the greed of the bear, and more than the swiftness and insatiable cruelty of the leopard, and to which no name could be given. . . .

The Roman was to try another solution of the problem on which the Oriental and the Greek had failed. He was to try whether human power, taking the form of law, regulated by political principles of which a regard for law and justice was most conspicuous, could perfect humanity by subordinating the individual to the state and making the state universal. . . .

In the old Roman race, the will, or that part of man which pushes to action and enables him to control and mould nature and mankind, was the predominant element, associated with conscience or the natural sense of justice. Its herculean tasks and its universal empire furnish the highest expression of the human soul as the repository of the energy for shaping the world to law and order. The Roman, as the man of power, was to attempt the solution of the same problem of perfecting man in which the man of prophecy and the man of reason and taste had already failed, and in his failure was to complete the preparation for the coming of him who could solve the hitherto insoluble problem. . . .

Before the time of the Advent, Rome had demonstrated the powerlessness of human power to save mankind. It had done its best, but its best was little— practically nothing. It needed the coming of Christ that itself might be saved. Imperialism was as helpless as Orientalism and Hellenism.

But the Roman performed a still more important part in preparing the world for the Messiah and the spread of the world-religion. It was Rome that cast up the highways along which the Jews plied their traffic and carried out to the ends of the earth the truth of God and the expectation of a coming Deliverer. It was Rome that made the influence of the divine religion free, rapid, and world wide.

But more than all, Rome did for the whole world that law-work without which man never feels the greatness of his need of the Gospel. In carrying out his mission of power the Roman was, as already hinted, the representative of natural justice in the world. . . . It was justice practically omnipotent and omnipresent, and so neither to be resisted nor escaped—justice which never dreamed of mercy until the work of conquest and consolidation was done. It made men long for mercy, because it demonstrated to them that there was no hope for them in righteous law.[26]

The Results of Providential History

So it came about that there was going up from all the world a wail for deliverance when the divine Deliverer appeared.

Says Neander: "The three great historical nations had to contribute, each in its own peculiar way, to prepare the soil for the planting of Christianity,—the Jews on the side of the religious element; the Greeks on the side of science and art; the Romans, as masters of the world, on the side of the political element. When the fullness of the time was arrived, and Christ appeared,—when the goal of history had thus been reached,—then it was, that through him, and by the power of the spirit that proceeded from him,—the might of Christianity,—all the threads, hitherto separated, of human development, were to be brought together and interwoven in one web."

Regarding the subject from another point of view, human nature had exhausted itself in the efforts of the Gentile world to solve the problem of man's elevation and salvation. The Oriental had given the freest rein to human desires, in the most favorable circumstances, and was perishing in magnificence and luxury. The Greek had given fullest scope to reason and taste, in circumstances equally favorable, and was perishing in the very glory of his creations of thought and beauty. The Roman had made all the other powers subordinate to his executive energy, and conscience, with its insatiate justice, was crushing him, and all the world with him, even by his universal empire. There were no other powers in human nature to bring to the task. The world over, on the great and all-absorbing question of man's salvation, the oracles of heathenism were dumb.[27]

Although the oracles of heathenism were dumb on the question of man's destiny, the Words of the Living God on the subject were both spoken and written. In fact, the fourth Gospel declares that the Word of God *"was made flesh and dwelt among us"* (1:14), and did so not *"to condemn the world; but that the world through him might be saved"* (3:17). In what has become the most well known verse in all of Holy Writ, John tells us:

> For God so loved the world, that he gave his only begotten Son, that whosoever believeth in him, should not perish, but have everlasting life. 3:16

The Fourth Gospel is the most familiar and the best loved book in the Bible.

It is probably the most important document in all the literature of the world. It has induced more persons to follow Christ, it has inspired more believers to loyal service, it has presented to scholars more difficult problems, than any other book that could be named.

The peculiar character of the book has been set forth by the single adjective "sublime;" for sublimity is said to result from the two factors of simplicity and profundity. The sea is sublime, because of its unbroken expanse and its measureless depths; and the cloudless sky is sublime because of its limitless vaults of blue. Such, too, is this little book; its stories are so simple that even a child will love them, but its statements are so profound that no philosopher can fathom them. . . .

The purpose of the author is indicated in the opening eighteen verses, commonly called the Prologue, and is definitely stated in the closing sentences of the twentieth chapter: "That ye may believe that Jesus is the Christ, the Son of God; and that believing ye may have life in his name." He wishes therefore to prove that Jesus is the "Messiah" who came in fulfillment of all the Old Testament types and prophecies; and further that he is a divine Being and is in this unique sense "the Son of God." The ultimate purpose, however, is to inspire in his readers such faith in Christ as will result in that eternal life which Christ alone can give.[28]

The Nature of Eternal Life

It needs to be stressed that the eternal life, which Christ alone can give, is not something that is synonymous with a future prospect. While eternal life definitely has its future aspect, it is not limited to that dimension of time. On this point John's Gospel differs somewhat from the synoptic accounts, as well as the Pauline epistles.

Paul, in accordance with the primitive Christian view, thought of life as the supreme blessing of the future. We have the sure promise of it, and can in some measure anticipate it by living even now "in the spirit;" but the actual possession is laid up for us in the world to come. John maintains that life in its full reality is communicated here and now. He speaks in several instances of "eternal life," but the epithet does not suggest that the life is still future. It only denotes the quality of the new life as having its origin in the higher, eternal world. Indeed, the primary aim of the evangelist is to affirm the claim of the believer in Christ to an actual and present possession of that life which had hitherto been associated with another state of existence. Christ had made Himself flesh in order that in this world of time, amidst the limitations of the earthly conditions, we might become partakers of the eternal life.

It follows that death, in the Fourth Gospel, no longer possesses the significance which was ascribed to it by Paul. The Old Testament idea of death as the chief evil, imposed on man as a penalty for sin, reappears in the Pauline theology, and determines in some important respects its whole character. To John, death is nothing but the natural close of the bodily existence. It marks the moment when the true life is finally set free, but does not alter in any way the essential nature of that life. The real change takes place in the act of the new birth, when the transition is effected, under the agency of the Spirit, from the lower to the higher world. From that time onward, through all the accidents of time, including death itself, the believer is in possession of eternal life. It is true that the antithesis of "life" and "death" is continually present in the Gospel, as it is in Paul, but it needs to be taken in a special, theological sense. As "life" is something different from the physical life, so death has nothing to do with the mere dissolution of the body. It denotes not so much a single event as the whole condition of exclusion from the higher life. The natural man, who has not participated in the change effected by the new birth, is in a state of "death." "He that believeth on Me is passed" (already in that very act) "from death unto life" (5:24).

At this point, however, we are met by one of those apparent contradictions which from time to time obscure the characteristic teaching of the Gospel. There are passages in which John might appear to depart deliberately from his view of life as present, and to fall back on a primitive eschatological view. "The hour is coming, when all that are in the graves shall hear His voice, and shall come forth; they that have done good, unto the resurrection of life; and they that have done evil, unto the resurrection of condemnation" (5:28-29). "This is the will of Him that sent Me, that every one which seeth the Son, and believeth on Him, may have everlasting life: and I will raise him up at the last day" (6:40; cf. 39, 44, 54). These passages are doubtless to be explained, like others that have already been noted, as reflecting a popular Christian dogma which was not wholly consonant with the writer's own thought, although he desired to allow due place to it. It has to be remarked that in all the passages the allusion to futurity is conjoined with emphatic reference to the present communication of the life. "The hour is coming, and now is." "That every one who believeth may [at this moment] have everlasting life." "Whoso eateth My flesh and drinketh My blood hath eternal life: and I will raise him up at the last day." The future resurrection is admitted; John is at one with popular Christianity in anticipating some fuller realization of life in the world to come. But he regards the "rising at the last day" as only the fulfillment and confirmation of something already effected, not as the real beginning of a new state of being.

This line of thought is developed most fully in the story of the raising of Lazarus, the culminating instance of Christ's work as Life-giver. The underlying idea of the whole narrative is contained in the great saying of Jesus, "I am the Resurrection, and the Life: he that believeth in Me, though he were dead, yet shall he live: and whosoever liveth and believeth in Me shall never die" (11:25-26). Martha has declared her faith—the traditional faith of the Church—that her brother "will rise in the resurrection of the last day." Jesus answers that the life imparted by Him is independent of physical life and death. Those who believe in Him have risen already; their death is only in seeming, and they carry with them, into the world beyond, the same life on which they entered here. Lazarus therefore had never died. Through faith in Christ he had possessed himself of the true life, and still continued in it, in spite of his apparent death. But this fact of his continuance in life is made manifest by his return at the call of Jesus to a bodily existence. The real miracle had been effected in him during his lifetime, in the act of his believing in Jesus; but his resurrection in the flesh gives a visible evidence and confirmation to the miracle.

Thus the effort of John, everywhere in the Gospel, is to apprehend the eternal life as something actual and present. He accepts the popular belief in a resurrection at the last day, but he empties it of the significance which had attached to it in earlier Christian thought. It is not the commencement, but simply the manifestation, of the new life. The true resurrection takes place in this present world, when a man believes in Christ and makes the great transition "from death unto life." The change is an inward, invisible one, but is none the less real and vital. All men could discern the wonder of Lazarus rising in his grave-clothes, and leaving the tomb where he had lain four days. But this was only the reflection in forms of sense of the real miracle which is ever repeated in Christian experience. "He that liveth and believeth in Me shall never die."[29]

The Character and Needs of the Christian

By the last decade of the first century the Apostle John was the lone survivor of the original twelve disciples chosen and called by Jesus Christ. The writings of this beloved disciple, including the Gospel that bears his name, were all completed during his waning years, late in the generation which followed the destruction of Jerusalem. Although John is undoubtedly the author of the fourth Gospel, there is insufficient evidence to fix the exact date of origin of this document. Nevertheless, the fact that this Gospel was written at a late date—at least in reference to the other New Testament Scriptures—and was therefore "intended for use of Churches which had already made some progress in the Christian life, and were well instructed in the events of our Lord's ministry, it is not difficult to prove."[30]

How came the narrator to speak of the Twelve, as he does in 6:70, as well-known persons, without having said a word of their election? How should he have left out between the return of Jesus into Galilee (4:43) and His sojourn in Judaea (5:1) two whole months; and again, between this sojourn and the miracle of the multiplying of the loaves (6:1), one whole month; and yet again, between this last event and the departure for Jerusalem (7:1), nearly eight months; and lastly, between this journey and the following one to the Feast of Dedication, an interval of more than two months—had he not supposed his readers to be well acquainted with all the events of the Galilean ministry with which the synoptic narratives are filled? How could he have described Bethany (11:1) as the town of Mary and her sister Martha, when he had never even mentioned these two persons? How should he describe Mary (11:2) as the woman which anointed the Lord with ointment, not having yet related that incident? We see from one end of the book to the other, indications that the author supposes his readers well acquainted with the history of Jesus, and that he wishes only to bring into notice certain events which had either been omitted by tradition, or not sufficiently comprehended.[31]

The Churches to which John's Gospel was addressed belonged to the Gentile world. "The universal note sounded in this Gospel (3:16; 10:16; 12:32) makes it evident that its intended scope should not be restricted to a narrow circle of readers. It was written to present the true nature of the supreme revelation in Christ as confessed by the Church, and to make an appeal to the world at large which was the object of God's redemptive love in Christ Jesus."[32]

"If, as has been seen, the fourth Gospel had its origin . . . after the missionary Gospels had been preached and the Church established throughout the world,"[33] then the character and needs of the Christian must be reflected in this document. "What manner of man was the Christian? What were his spiritual needs? The answer to these questions will cast light upon the Gospel prepared under the influence of the Holy Ghost for the Church."[34]

> The Christian is readily distinguished by marked characteristics from the natural man, whether Jew, Roman, or Greek. The Christian is the man who has heard the great facts of the Gospel, and who has accepted Jesus Christ as his Savior. He has attained, through faith in Christ, to a new life which is different in its origin, motives, and aims, from the earthly life. This life, originating in divine power, leads him to complete submission to Christ and to entire devotion to him in the cause of the Gospel. He lives this spiritual life of faith and obedience by fixing his eyes upon the central fact of the cross, and through guidance and help given in the Scriptures or by the Holy Ghost directly from above, which guidance and help he ever longs to receive in increased measure. He is reaching out toward that everlasting life of glory with Christ, of which this new life is the beginning.
>
> Out of these peculiar characteristics arose those spiritual needs of the Christian Church which were to be met by the Evangelist. By the aid of them must be sought the full understanding of the Gospel prepared by John.
>
> The Man of Faith. The starting point in the Christian life is found in the personal acceptance of Jesus Christ as the Savior from sin. This act involves the knowledge of God and the relation of man as a sinner to God, and of the incarnation, work, death, and resurrection of Jesus; the belief in his divine character and mission; and the practical resting of the soul on him for salvation. To this act the preaching of the Apostles and the promulgation of the first three Gospels brought that portion of the ancient world which at the close of the first century was found fully prepared for God's deliverer. By the grace of God the true Israelite accepted Jesus as his Savior, because he found in him the Messiah, the fulfiller of the Law and the Prophets, the Emmanuel who was promised for his salvation; the true Roman, because he found in him the Son of God, the almighty and universal conqueror, who was able to save him; the true Greek, because he met the Greek idea of the perfect and divine man, who longed for the salvation of the race, and who had the power to save it. Thus the true men of all races found in him the satisfaction of their spiritual wants; and in the very act of accepting him they were transformed in character and life.
>
> The Man of Christ. The Christian is the man who finds the aim of his life in Christ, and who can say with Paul "to me to live is Christ." If by his natural birth a Jew, he yet sees that the Jewish life of form and ceremony, is no

longer worthy of his soul, since in Christ's own example is the true ritual; if a Roman, he sees that the Roman life of earthly industry and conquest and supremacy is no longer worthy of him, since in Christ's gracious work, in his victory over sin, and in his kingdom are to be found the true work and conquest and empire; if a Greek, he sees that the Greek life of perfection sought through philosophy and art is no longer worthy of him, since through faith in Christ, whose reason is divine, and whose beauty is divine moral excellence, is to be realized the perfection of humanity. Whatever his earthly nativity he follows Christ, obeys him, aims to become like him, and devotes himself to him in the work of advancing the kingdom of God in the conquest of sinners. He finds the center of his system of faith and life, and the center of his Christ too, in the cross. The incarnate Son of God, crucified and raised from the dead, is the ground of all his hopes. He receives the remission of sin through the blood of Christ, and drinks of his shed blood, partakes of the boundless grace of God to sinners, and especially is made the recipient of the Holy Ghost, who is given to enlighten, renew, and sanctify the children of God.[35]

The Gospel for the Christian

If the character of the Christian is such as it has been explained, it will help us understand the Gospel intended for him. That Gospel must be suited to fit his needs and fashioned to stimulate his spiritual growth.

The Gospel for the Christian must present Jesus as the revelation of God—the word, the truth, the light, which the Christian needs in the new life. It must make plain all the great essential matters concerning the Christian course, so that in its light he may see clearly to avoid the danger, error, and death. It is obvious that the missionary Gospels do not deal largely with these subjects—do not deal with them at all, except as they have to do with leading men to the first acceptance of Christ and the beginning of the divine life in him. They leave the wants of this higher and peculiarly spiritual sphere for some later hand to supply. The fourth Gospel must in this sense be the supplement of the first three.

Most assuredly, if the Christian is to be in any high degree intelligent, he especially needs light concerning the divine life which, by the grace of God, he has undertaken to live—concerning its nature; its relations to God and Christ; its origin and beginnings; the modes of sustaining it to its full vigor; its mission in this world and its issues, after the death of the body, in the regions of immortality. These spiritual needs become the great ones with the Christian.

To the Christian these are the credentials of Jesus, no less essential than prophecy to the Jew, or power to the Roman, or the perfection of manhood to the Greek. Without them his most pressing needs would be left unsupplied. There could, therefore, be no Gospel for him in any production which should omit or pass slightly over these grand themes of the divine and immortal life of faith.[36]

It is apparent from the contents of this production, as well as the testimony of history, that the fourth Gospel was produced and published especially for Christian readers, regardless of their nativity or background. Moreover, it is not without design that "the Gospel's geographical origin is rightly attributed to—and symbolized by—the city of Ephesus."[37]

Other cities like Antioch and Rome might lay claim to its place of composition. Jerusalem could not. Even Alexandria might satisfy the demands of the Gospel's universalism. But the tradition that the author lived and wrote in Ephesus is sustained by the record's internal evidence. Ephesus was the rich and sumptuous mistress of the Aegean Sea. Its prestige as a center of commerce and culture was world-wide. It was a Roman imperial colony; it welcomed philosophers from Athens. But, at heart, it was Asiatic. Gnosticism, the Mystery Religions, Judaism, and Christianity alike were strongly represented there. Saint Paul had made it the base of his missionary activity in Asia Minor. Its cosmopolitanism, like its wealth, was unquestioned. So also was its deep-seated hunger for life and—and as we read in John 6—for the bread that satisfied the soul. In a word, Ephesus typified the world. In it men wandered blindly, searching, groping for the light. They were like lost sheep waiting for the good shepherd or trying to find the door to the sheepfold; they were like famished and thirsty men looking for a well of pure water.

To such among his readers in Asia, the Evangelist came with the treasured story of the gospel. It was essentially the same as that told by the three other Evangelists: the story of the earthly life of Jesus, culminating in the gospel of the Cross, and coming to a climax in the message of the risen Christ. This much was now world history, rooted in Old Testament prophecy and in Palestinian soil. But it was not all there was to record of divine history. . . . For the history of Christ did not end with his death and resurrection. Rather, in its world-wide outlook, it began there. For the ensuing generation of mankind it began anew in the life and activity of the risen and living Christ. That was, and is today, the message of the Fourth Gospel.[38]

This final Gospel has introduced countless souls to a saving knowledge of Jesus Christ, and lifted them to a spiritual firmament as if mounted on eagles' wings. Such is the power of the Living Word of God, and we trust that all who read these pages have experienced that transforming work of mercy and grace in their hearts. If so, we must agree with the songwriter, who wrote:

When we have exhausted our store of endurance,
When our strength has failed ere the day is half done,
When we reach the end of our hoarded resources,
Our Father's full giving is only begun.

His love has no limit; His grace has no measure;
His pow'r has no boundary known unto men.
For out of His infinite riches in Jesus,
He giveth, and giveth, and giveth again![39]

Chapter Thirteen Notes

[1] J. M. Roberts, *A Concise History of the World* (New York: Oxford University Press, 1995), book jacket.

[2] *Ibid.*

[3] *Ibid.*

[4] *Ibid.*, 32-33.

[5] *Ibid.*, 33.

[6] Charles Rollin, *The Ancient History of the Egyptians, Carthaginians, Assyrians, Babylonians, Medes and Persians, Grecians and Macedonians*, trans. from the French, in four volumes (New York: Published by William Borradaile, 1825), IV:410-11.

[7] "Darwin, Charles Robert," *Encyclopaedia Britannica* (1903), XXVI:358.

[8] P. V. N. Myers, *A General History for Colleges and High Schools* (Boston: Ginn & Company, 1903), 1-2.

[9] J. N. Larned, *Larned's History of the World or Seventy Centuries of the Life of Mankind*, vol. I (New York: World Syndicate Company, Inc., 1915) 3.

[10] Frederic Arnold Kummer, *The Earth's Story*, vol. 3 (New York: George H. Doran Company, 1925), 15.

[11] Nugent Robinson, *A History of the World with All Its Great Sensations together with Its Mighty and Decisive Battles and the Rise and Fall of Its Nations from the Earliest Times to the Present Day* (New York: P. F. Collier, Publisher, 1887), 5.

[12] Mark A. Beliles and Stephen K. McDowell, *America's Providential History* (Charlottesville, Va.: Providence Foundation, 1994), vii.

[13] *Ibid.*, 11.

[14] *Ibid.*

[15] Arnold Guyot, *Physical Geography* (New York: Charles Scribner's Sons, 1873), 119.

[16] *Ibid.*, 119-121.

[17] Jeremy Rifkin, *Algeny* (New York: The Viking Press, 1983), dust jacket.

[18] *Ibid.*, 244.

[19] D. S. Gregory, *Why Four Gospels? Or, the Gospel for All the World* (New York: Funk & Wagnalls, Publishers, 1890), 59-60.

[20] *Ibid.*, 30.

[21] *Ibid.*, 30-31.

[22] David R. Breed, *A History of the Preparation of the World for Christ* (Chicago: Young Men's Era Publishing Co., 1891), 215-17, 244-45.

[23] Gregory, *op. cit.*, 46-47.

[24] *Ibid.*, 47-48.

[25] *Ibid.*, 48-52.

[26] *Ibid.*, 52-54.

[27] *Ibid.*, 55.

[28] Charles R. Erdman, *The Gospel of John* (Philadelphia: The Westminster Press, 1944), 7-8.

[29] E. F. Scott, *The Fourth Gospel: Its Purpose and Theology* (Edinburgh: T. & T. Clark, 1920), 247-251.

[30] Frederic L. Godet, *Studies in the New Testament* (New York: E. P. Dutton & Co., 1895), 67.

[31] *Ibid.*, 67-68.

[32] D. Edmund Hiebert, *An Introduction to the New Testament*, Volume I: The Gospels and Acts

(Winona Lake, Ind.: BMH Books, 1993), 219.

[33] Gregory, *op. cit.*, 287.

[34] *Ibid.*, 288.

[35] *Ibid.*, 288-90.

[36] *Ibid.*, 291-92

[37] Henry M. Battenhouse, *Christ in the Gospels: An Introduction to His Life and Its Meaning* (New York: The Ronald Press Company, 1952), 112.

[38] *Ibid.*, 112-13.

[39] Annie Johnson Flint, *He Giveth More Grace* (1941).

Chapter Fourteen

The Son of God: Life-Giving Redeemer

There is, perhaps, not a more touching story in all the New Testament than the coming of Nicodemus to Jesus by night, seeking to understand the Kingdom of God about which Christ so frequently spoke. John tells us:

> There was a man of the Pharisees, named Nicodemus, a ruler of the Jews: The same came to Jesus by night, and said unto him, Rabbi, we know that thou art a teacher come from God: for no man can do these miracles that thou doest, except God be with him. Jesus answered and said unto him, Verily, verily, I say unto thee, Except a man be born again, he cannot see the kingdom of God. Nicodemus saith unto him, How can a man be born when he is old? Can he enter the second time into his mother's womb, and be born? Jesus answered, Verily, verily, I say unto thee, Except a man be born of water and of the Spirit, he cannot enter into the kingdom of God. That which is born of the flesh is flesh; and that which is born of the Spirit is spirit. Marvel not that I said unto thee, Ye must be born again. The wind bloweth where it listeth, and thou hearest the sound thereof, but canst not tell whence it cometh, and wither it goeth: so is every one that is born of the Spirit. Nicodemus answered and said unto him, How can these things be? Jesus answered and said unto him, Art thou a master of Israel, and knowest not these things? Verily, verily, I say unto thee, We speak that we do know, and testify that we have seen; and ye receive not our witness. If I have told you earthly things, and ye believe not, how shall ye believe, if I tell you of heavenly things? And no man hath ascended up to heaven, but he that came down from heaven, even the Son of man which is in heaven. And as Moses lifted up the serpent in the wilderness, even so must the Son of man be lifted up: That whosoever believeth in him should not perish, but have eternal life. For God so loved the world, that he gave his only begotten Son, that whosoever believeth in him should not perish but have everlasting life. For God sent not his Son into the world to condemn the world; but that the world through him might be saved. He that believeth on him is not condemned: but he that believeth not is condemned already, because he hath not believed in the name of the only begotten Son of God. And this is the condemnation, that light is come into the world, and men loved darkness rather than light, because their deeds were evil. For every one that doeth evil hateth the light, neither cometh to the light, lest his deeds should be reproved. But he that doeth truth cometh to the light, that his deeds may be made manifest, that they are wrought in God. 3:1-21

Why Nicodemus came to Jesus by night we do not know. "Perhaps it was because he was too much occupied as a Ruler among the Jews, during the day to see Him then. Or he may have felt that the seriousness of the questions that were troubling his mind about the Rabbi's teachings concerning the Kingdom of God could not be adequately discussed amid the multitudes that constantly crowded about Jesus."[1] Nevertheless, Nicodemus was certainly an admirer of Jesus, if not one of His open followers.

In the nineteenth-century painting, *Christus and Nicodemus* (Figure 14-1), the German artist, Fritz von Uhde, clearly depicts Nicodemus as an honest seeker after truth and righteousness. "And somehow as we look into the face of this man of years and wisdom, as von Uhde portrays him, we feel that it must be so."[2]

In von Uhde's painting the two are alone, "Christus and Nicodemus," probably in an upper room of some home in which Jesus may have been a guest while in Jerusalem. The room is simply furnished—a chair, a table, and perhaps a stool on which Nicodemus sits, an open book and some leaves of a parchment, which

Nicodemus may have brought with him when he came to confer with Jesus and try to square His teachings with the Jewish law, which as Ruler of the Jews he often had to propound.

We see but the profile of each man's face, yet that is sufficient to indicate the earnest effort which Nicodemus seems to be making to understand; and the eloquent upward pointing hand of the Master, when he says, "Verily, I say unto thee, Except one be born of water and the Spirit, he cannot enter the kingdom of God."[3]

The fourth Gospel, as typified and illustrated in this scene between Christ and Nicodemus, is primarily "a revelation of the eternal under the forms of time."[4] The Master's insistence upon a new birth revealed that Nicodemus needed more than private instruction; he needed personal regeneration! He had to be born again, which is only possible through spiritual union with a higher source of life. Nicodemus required more than a teacher. He came by night to see an enlightened Rabbi, but he met an eternal Savior. His interview in time was with none other than He who existed before time—the One who "was in the beginning with God" (1:2) and by whom "all things were made" (1:3).

The deity of Jesus Christ is a major emphasis of John's Gospel. Whereas Matthew pictures Jesus as One who would rule the people **for** God, and Mark presents Him as One sent **from** God, and Luke sees Him representing all men **before** God, John most clearly identifies Christ as One **with** God. In this book, more than anywhere else, the divine Sonship of Jesus is set forth.

> For God so loved the world, that he gave his only begotten Son, that whosoever believeth in him should not perish, but have everlasting life. . . . He that believeth on him is not condemned: but he that believeth not is condemned already, because he hath not believed in the name of the only begotten Son of God. 3:16, 18

Here, and elsewhere (1:34, 39; 9:35; etc.), Jesus referred to Himself as the Son of God, thereby claiming equality with the Father.

> That His great claim to be one with the Father is bound up with this title is evident from the impression its use made on the Jews, and from their charge of blasphemy preferred against Him on account of it (5:18; 10:30, 33). As Son, He declares Himself to be the object of the Father's highest love (3:35; 5:20). As Son, He discharges the same august offices as the Father (5:21-29). As Son, He reciprocates the Father's knowledge of Himself by an equivalent knowledge of the Father (10:14-15). As Son, He recognizes no essential distinction between Himself and the Father, except that which is inseparable from the relationship of the one to the other in the economy of redemption (10:30; 14:28). As Son, He needs no information about men, for He knows all men, and what is in man (2:24-25). He is most thoroughly acquainted with man, with his secret thoughts, motives, purposes, and history, as His words to Nicodemus, to the woman at the well, to the cripple at the pool, prove. Perfect knowledge of them and matchless wisdom in dealing with them belong to Him.[5]

In a word, although He nowhere calls himself God, He claims not to be esteemed less than God, and the only distinction between himself and Him whom He at the same time calls upon in prayer is, finally, that the one is the

Father and the other is the Son of His love, other than the Father, but yet of the same nature.[6]

Human and Divine Witnesses

In addition to the **Lord's** own statement, *"I am the Son of God"* (10:36), the Gospel of John records six different witnesses who avow and declare the deity of Jesus Christ. Note their testimonies:

John the Baptist said, *"And I saw, and bare record that this is the Son of God."* 1:34

Nathanael *"answered and saith unto him, Rabbi, thou art the Son of God; thou art the King of Israel."* 1:49

Simon Peter *"answered him, Lord, to whom shall we go? Thou hast the words of eternal life. And we believe and are sure that thou art the Christ, the Son of the living God."* 6:68-69

Martha *"saith unto him, Yea Lord: I believe that thou art the Christ, the Son of God, which should come into the world."* 11:27

Thomas *"answered and said unto him, My Lord and my God."* 20:28

John the Evangelist wrote: *"And many other signs truly did Jesus in the presence of his disciples, which are not written in this book: But these are written, that ye might believe that Jesus is the Christ, the Son of God; and that believing ye might have life through his name."* 20:30-31

Every attentive reader may see for himself, that one Leading Idea of this Gospel is founded upon the great historical principle of the validity of human testimony—the great safeguard against skepticism and fanaticism. "If we receive the testimony of men" to the effect that "Jesus is the Son of God"—writes St. John in his Epistle, with evident reference to his Gospel (1 John 5:9). The very form of the expression shows that we do assuredly receive such witness, not only as Christians, but as rational men, according to principles which recommend themselves naturally to the unsophisticated human intellect.

But again, as "the witness of God is greater," so this Gospel is full of Divine witness to Jesus. Hence the mention of the attesting voice from heaven—"I have both glorified it and will glorify it again" (12:28). Hence the intense conviction that the Scriptures are "they which testify of Him" (5:39-46); that "had they believed Moses, they would have believed Him." Hence the accumulated reference to type and prophecy in the narrative of the atoning death. To a mere human historian there might have seemed to be no more of deep purpose in the particular cruelties inflicted by the rude soldiery and the furious mob, than in the shape of the tangled knots of sea-weed flung by the spring-tide upon the beach. But every incident in the central event of the history of humanity is to his eye arranged "by the determinate counsel and foreknowledge of God." The lots upon the poor vestment that wrapped the wasted form were cast by a Divine hand. The vessel with vinegar, the sponge and hyssop, were not there by chance. The perfection and dignity of that body, which seemed so helpless, were guaranteed by the rubric of the Divine ritual in regard to the pascal lamb—"not a bone of him shall be broken." The thrust of the soldier's lance is in the dark background of Zechariah's prophecy, and written upon the very body that shall look on Him whom they pierced" (John 5:36-37; 19:24; Exodus 12:46; Psalm 22:18; 34:20; Zechariah 12:10). The evangelist's spirit sails over the deep of Scripture as over an Equatorial Ocean; on the far horizon of prophecy he sees its Southern Cross.[7]

Divine Words and Works

The deity of Jesus Christ is also asserted in the series of "I am" statements recorded in the fourth Gospel. In reference to Himself, the Lord declared:

> *I am the bread of life: he that cometh to me shall never hunger; and he that believeth on me shall never thirst.* 6:35
>
> *I am the light of the world: he that followeth me shall not walk in darkness, but shall have the light of life.* 8:12
>
> *I am the door: by me if any man enter in, he shall be saved, and shall go in and out, and find pasture.* 10:9
>
> *I am the good shepherd: the good shepherd giveth his life for the sheep.* 10:11
>
> *I am the resurrection, and the life: he that believeth in me, though he were dead, yet shall he live.* 11:25
>
> *I am the way, the truth, and the life: no man cometh unto the Father, but by me.* 14:6
>
> *I am the true vine, and my Father is the husbandman.* 15:1

These, and other similar statements (cf. 4:26; 8:24, 28, 58; 13:19), constitute some of the strongest claims to deity that Jesus could have made, as He identified Himself with the great *"I am"* or *"Yahweh"* of the Old Testament. This is the most important name for God, occurring over 6800 times.

Although the origin of the term *Yahweh* (usually translated *Lord* in English Bibles) is uncertain, "the meaning of the name most probably derives from the imperfect form of the Hebrew verb 'to be.'"[8] In the book of Exodus, for example, note God's response to Moses' question about His identity:

> *And Moses said unto God, Behold, when I come unto the children of Israel, and shall say unto them, The God of your fathers hath sent me unto you; and they shall say to me, What is his name? What shall I say unto them? And God said unto Moses, I AM THAT I AM: and he said, Thus shalt thou say unto the children of Israel, I AM hath sent me unto you.* EXOD. 3:13-14

Now compare this statement to Jesus' response to the Jews, who asked:

> *Art thou greater than our father Abraham, which is dead? And the prophets are dead; whom makest thou thyself? Jesus answered, If I honour myself, my honour is nothing: it is my Father that honoureth me; of whom ye say, that he is your God: Yet ye have not known him; but I know him: and if I should say, I know him not, I shall be a liar like unto you: but I know him, and keep his saying. Your father Abraham rejoiced to see my day: and he saw it, and was glad. Then said the Jews unto him, Thou art not yet fifty years old, and hast thou seen Abraham? Jesus said unto them, Verily, verily, I say unto you, Before Abraham was, I am.* JOHN 8:53-58

That the Jews understood Jesus' claim to be the *Yahweh* of the Old Testament is obvious from their reaction to His supposed blasphemy.

> *Then took they up stones to cast at him: but Jesus hid himself, and went out of the temple, going through the midst of them, and so passed by.* 8:59

Whereas the deity of Christ is asserted by the testimony of witnesses and the claims of Jesus Himself, it is confirmed by the working of miracles. Nicodemus, who came to Jesus by night, recognized this, when he said: *"Rabbi, we know that thou art a teacher come from God: for no man can do these miracles that thou doest, except God be with him"* (3:2).

The significance of the seven miracles recorded by John (not counting the post-resurrection miracle of the catch of fish) has been explained in Chapter Twelve, and will not be reiterated here. Nevertheless, a few generalizations might be in order.

First, while the whole of the fourth Gospel seems to breathe a supernatural atmosphere, the element of sheer wonder, which the Lord's miracles must have produced, is carefully subordinated to the symbolic element. John's primary interest in the miracles is to use them to highlight the divinity and heighten the dignity of Christ. Referring to Jesus as the Logos, one commentator noted:

> The Logos is never (as in Mark) "unable" to work miracles, never liable to "marvel," never "in an agony," never (with the single exception of the scene at the grave of Lazarus in . . . John 11:33) "sorrowful and very heavy;" . . . the Logos "knows what is in man," sees Nathaniel "under the fig-tree," discerns from the first that one of the twelve whom He had chosen is "a devil;" when He asks advice from His followers, it is a mere form, merely "to prove them, for He Himself knew what He would do;" there is not in the drama of the Fourth Gospel (as in Mark) any development of thought or plan in the chief actor; the development must be looked for in the drama taken as a whole, and including the creation, the fall, and all the preparation of the world for the coming of the Word as flesh; the life of Christ on earth is, in the Fourth Gospel, only one act as it were, in which the previous action of the drama is simply carried on and sustained; the whole of the future, His destined "lifting up," His death, His rising in three days, all lie mapped out before the Savior, so that He walks in a known country and in light, while all around, friends and foes alike, are stumbling or groping in the dark. In this sense, therefore, it is true that the supernatural element is even more prominent in the Fourth Gospel than in the synoptists. But the miracles themselves are subordinated. Though frequent reference is made to the vast number of them . . . , yet, not only are very few described, but even those few are described rather as "emblems" than as "mighty works." It is remarkable that the word . . . "signs," which the synoptists almost always use in a bad sense (to denote the "sign from heaven" demanded by the Pharisees, or the "signs," which the false Christs shall work to deceive, if it were possible, even the elect, Mark 13:22), is the very word selected by John to describe the miracles of Jesus; while the word . . . "mighty works," which in the synoptists generally denotes the works of Jesus, is never used in the Fourth Gospel. Partly, no doubt, the author may have felt that miracles were made cheap by excessive enumeration, and that the narrative of a multitude of miracles without apparent motive created a stumbling-block rather than a help to philosophic and educated readers. Especially might this be felt in Ephesus, the home of wizards and wonders and "curious arts" (Acts 19:19), where even the last-called of the apostles had worked cures and exorcisms past numbering (vs. 12). Accordingly the author,

though he makes mention of very many miracles, describes none but those which are obviously emblematic.[9]

Second, since the specific miracles recorded by John were intended as "signs," and often introduce or confirm Jesus' message, one would expect a direct correlation between His works and His words—and this is exactly what we find.

Against these seven signs, let us put the seven great I AM declarations.

First Sign. Water made wine. I AM THE TRUE VINE. He will always turn the ordinary of our life into the extraordinary of His life given to us. From the true vine, always the best wine.

Second Sign. The boy restored. I AM THE WAY, THE TRUTH, AND THE LIFE. He had said, "Go they WAY, they son LIVETH," and the father found it was the TRUTH that the Lord had spoken.

Third Sign. The impotent man had lain, for many years, in his helplessness, waiting for some one to put him into the pool of blessing, for He can say, I AM THE DOOR, by ME if any man enter in he shall be saved.

Fourth Sign. The five thousand fed is followed by the exposition of His own words, I AM THE BREAD OF LIFE, and he that eateth Me, he shall live by Me.

Fifth Sign. Stilling the tempest. It was dark and stormy, and the disciples were alone, for He had gone away up the mountain to spend the night in prayer. Has He forgotten them? Does He not know what is happening to them? Yes; for He says, I AM THE GOOD SHEPHERD, and know my sheep. The darkness and the light are both alike to Him. He is not far off, after all, but near enough to help and save.

Sixth Sign. Opening the blind eyes. In this case, He says, I AM THE LIGHT, and so the enlightened soul can follow Him and never again walk in darkness.

Seventh Sign. Raising Lazarus. I AM THE RESURRECTION AND THE LIFE.[10]

Third, the method by which Christ performs the specified miracles in the fourth Gospel tends to further accentuate His deity. Jesus was introduced by John as the Word that was with God in the beginning (cf. 1:1-2), and we should "note that these signs wrought by the Word are unaccompanied by the working of His hands, as so distinctly recorded in the group found in St. Mark's gospel."[11] In John's account we do not find Jesus touching either lepers or deceased persons (cf. Mark 1:40-42; 5:41-42), or putting his finger in the ears and on the tongues of deaf mutes (cf. Mark 7:32-35). Instead, with a single exception (cf. John 9:6), the sick are made whole by the spoken Word of the divine Logos!

Fourth, the Feeding of the Five Thousand is the only miracle recorded in all four Gospels; yet a brief analysis of John's version—noting his omissions and additions—reveals his "desire to heighten the Logos and to subordinate the disciples and the crowd."[12] Comparing Mark's account to John's, for example, one commentator observed:

Mark begins by saying that "Jesus had compassion on the multitude;" but the Logos, knowing beforehand "what He would do," determines His course at once as soon as He "lifts up His eyes" and discerns the multitude. In Mark, the disciples come to Jesus begging Him to send the multitudes away; in John, it is Jesus who first "proves" one of the disciples with the question, "Whence shall we buy bread that they may eat?" Then . . . Andrew, as well as Philip, and a servant-lad are introduced, the latter carrying the viaticum of the apostles. The loaves, a new circumstance not found in the synoptists, are of an inferior kind— "barley;" and Andrew bases an exposition on the smallness of the provision. After the command to "sit down," Mark says that they sat "down on the green grass," an epithet natural enough for a speaker perhaps, but inartistic, because too prominent, in a written narrative. John, on the other hand, turns a defect into an excellence, by judiciously connecting the "grass" with the command to sit down, so as to enhance the forethought of the wise Master of the feast, who made provision for the comfort of His guests in the minutest details: "Jesus said, Make the men sit down. Now there was much grass in the place." Lastly, in the synoptic narrative, the gathering of the fragments is the spontaneous act of the disciples; but in John, the feast ends as it began, with the display of the wisdom of the Master, even in the smallest matters—"Gather up the fragments that remain, that nothing may be lost." It is scarcely possible to deny that, in the symmetrical manner in which the story gathers itself around the Logos as its object and center, the narrative of the Fourth Gospel is far superior to that of the synoptists, and that many of the additional touches of the former are dictated by what has been happily described by Canon Westcott as "an instinctive perception of symmetry in thought and expression."[13]

Conversations and Discussions

Whereas the miracles of the fourth Gospel are usually associated with some formal, spiritual instruction, it should also be observed that informal conversation with both believers and unbelievers enters almost everywhere into the discourses of the Lord. This, too, is not without design, and a good example is found in the seventh chapter, wherein is described a scene during the last day of the Feast of Tabernacles. John wrote:

> In the last day, that great day of the feast, Jesus stood and cried, saying, If any man thirst, let him come unto me, and drink. He that believeth on me, as the scripture hath said, out of his belly shall flow rivers of living water. (But this spake he of the Spirit, which they that believe on him should receive: for the Holy Ghost was not yet given; because that Jesus was not yet glorified.) Many of the people therefore, when they heard this saying, said, Of a truth this is the Prophet. Others said, This is the Christ. But some said, Shall Christ come out of Galilee? Hath not the scripture said, That Christ cometh of the seed of David, and out of the town of Bethlehem, where David was? So there was a division among the people because of him. And some of them would have taken him; but no man laid hands on him. Then came the officers to the chief priests and Pharisees; and they said unto them, Why have ye not brought him? The officers answered, Never man spake like this man. Then answered them the Pharisees, Are ye also deceived? Have any of the rulers or of the Pharisees believed on him? But this people who knoweth not the law are cursed. Nicodemus saith unto them,

(he that came to Jesus by night, being one of them,) Doth our law judge any man, before it hear him, and know what he doeth? They answered and said unto him, Art thou also of Galilee? Search, and look: for out of Galilee ariseth no prophet. And every man went unto his own house. 7:37-53

The method of the author is admirably illustrated by the dialogue between the people (7:41-42): "Others said, this is the Christ, But some said, Shall Christ come out of Galilee? Hath not the scripture said that Christ cometh of the seed of David, and out of the town of Bethlehem where David was?" It is a curious instance of the degree to which the dramatic character of the Fourth Gospel has been ignored, that even an acute commentator has inferred from this passage that John "was not aware of the birth at Bethlehem." The fact is that the author uses these and similar errors and blind gropings of the people, the enemies, and even the disciples of the Lord, to enhance the majesty and insight of Him who walks above them all, high in the light of heaven, while they are creeping in the midst around His feet. He does not stop to correct these vulgar errors, for he presupposes that his readers are in the light, and able to see through them all; and it is with a frequency almost betokening en-joyment that he repeats this device over and over again, in every case holding up the error in silence to the contempt or pity of his readers, and delighting to exhibit human folly glorifying the wisdom of God. Instances of this device occur in this very chapter. "Who goeth about to kill thee?" says the ignorant multitude (7:20), at the very time when the arrest of Jesus is being planned by the Pharisees. "Out of Galilee ariseth no prophet," say the learned students of the law (7:52), so blinded by their malignity that they cannot even read the books that describe the birthplaces of Elijah and Jonah.[14]

Humility and Compassion

The prophecies of the Old Testament, as well as the synoptic Gospels, describe the Messiah as a person of remarkable humility and great compassion. The Gospel of John, by contrast, minimizes these traits, because it was designed to heighten the dignity of the divine Son of God.

In this Gospel Jesus has all the attributes of divinity. He has supernatural knowledge, supernatural power and supernatural calm. He walks upon the stage in the first scene of this Gospel clad in the full panoply of divinity and moves majestically and irresistibly through the program on which he and his divine Father have agreed. Humility is alien to the glory of this divine being, as is compassion. The scene of the Good Shepherd in early Christian art derived nothing but the name from the Fourth Gospel. The Good Shepherd of Luke and Matthew is one who cannot rest while even one sheep out of a hundred is lost; he seeks diligently till he finds it, and carries it home on his shoulders. The Good Shepherd of John is the one true leader of the flock; he lays down his life for the flock to take it up again, and the laying down of his life as well as its resumption is due to the command of the Father. . . .

Every action of Jesus in the Fourth Gospel is divinely motivated. Jesus works miracles of healing not because he sympathizes with the sick, but that he may manifest his glory. A man was born blind in order that Jesus by healing him might show himself to be the Light of the World. Jesus lets Lazarus die and stays away from the sisters for four days so that the resurrection may demonstrate that Jesus is the Resurrection and the Life. All Jesus' actions and all his words are manifestations of the divine glory which the Father bestowed upon him before Abraham's day. . . . Not here can he say, I am meek and lowly. What he says in the scenes of his Gospel are the words he heard in heaven; all the words of Jesus in John are proud words. The Jesus of John is slapped on one check, but there is not humiliation in the retort with which he rebukes the smiter. John and Matthew are the only Gospels that quote Zechariah 9:9 in the triumphal entry, but John differs from Zechariah and Matthew in that he omits the word "lowly." Not abasement but exaltation is the keynote of Jesus' teaching. In the Synoptics he teaches his followers that the Son of man must suffer many things; in John, that he must be exalted.[15]

Betrayal and Arrest

When Jesus had spoken these words, he went forth with his disciples over the brook Cedron, where was a garden, into the which he entered, and his disciples. 18:1

The synoptic Gospels tell us that the place was called Gethsemane, and it was there that Jesus *"fell on his face, and prayed, saying, O my Father, if it were possible, let this cup pass from me: nevertheless, not as I will, but as thou wilt"* (Matt. 26:34). This important part of the Gethsemane story, however, is not generally recognized in the fourth Gospel, "since John has transferred it to a place immediately before the last meal (12:27-30). Jesus is momentarily troubled in his heart as he announces that the time of his death has come."[16]

Now is my soul troubled; and what shall I say? Father, save me from this hour: but for this cause came I unto this hour. Father, glorify thy name. Then came there a voice from heaven, saying, I have both glorified it, and will glorify it again. The people therefore, that stood by, and heard it, said that it thundered: others said, An angel spake to him. Jesus answered and said, This voice came not because of me, but for your sakes. 12:27-30

An interesting detail . . . is the comment of the crowd on the voice. Some displayed the gross misunderstanding which characterizes all the audiences of this Gospel, and heard nothing but thunder. But others claimed that it was an angel speaking to him. . . . But even those who regarded the voice as angelic were, of course, wrong. It was the Father who spoke. No angels come between Jesus and God in this book, nor does Jesus have any weakness or sense of separation from God which would require angelic ministration. . . .

In the scene described in the twelfth chapter of John, it is the bystanders who experience Gethsemane, not Jesus.[17]

As a consequence of Jesus' foreknowledge and his complete control of all situations, there is in John no sense of stress, none of the elements of tragedy so familiar in the earlier Gospels. . . . For him there can be no sorrow or defeat in a betrayal, since that was part of God's plan.[18]

"In John, Jesus goes into a garden to be arrested, not to strive with God in prayer."[19] We read:

And Judas also, which betrayed him, knew the place: for Jesus oftimes resorted thither with his disciples. Judas then, having received a band of men and officers from the chief priests and Pharisees, cometh thither with lanterns and torches and weapons. Jesus therefore, knowing all things that should come upon him, went forth, and said unto them, Whom seek ye? They answered him, Jesus of Nazareth. Jesus saith unto them, I am he. And Judas also, which betrayed him, stood with them. As soon then as he had said unto them, I am he, they went backward, and fell to the ground. Then asked he them again, Whom seek ye? And they said, Jesus of Nazareth. Jesus answered, I have told you that I am he: if therefore ye seek me, let these go their way: That the saying might be fulfilled, which he spake, Of them which thou gavest me have I lost none. 18:2-9

The betrayal in the Fourth Gospel is purely a matter of form. It was planned by God before the incarnation. . . . "For Jesus knew from the first who would not believe and who was going to betray him" (6:64). Jesus of course carries out the Father's will in this respect, and so do the disciples! The most striking example of the . . . relation of Jesus to his disciples in this Gospel is shown in their acquiescence in his betrayal. He tells them after the feeding of the five thousand that one of them is a devil (i.e., as the evangelist explains, a traitor). This announcement is repeated at the Last Supper, and the traitor is pointed out to Peter and the disciple whom Jesus especially loved (13:21-28). The disciples do nothing to prevent the betrayal. To interfere would have been to go against both Jesus and his Father. Jesus himself tells Judas to proceed with the betrayal (13:27-30). This may seem incredible in the story of a man and his friends, but it is very plausible in the relations of a divine being with those mortals whom he has chosen. It is part of the elevation of the betrayal to cosmic significance that we note in the omission of the price paid to Judas. Judas made no bargain with Jesus' enemies; nothing so mundane as a handful of silver motivates the betrayal. Judas acted in accordance with the divine plan. Every criticism of Jesus as a God that was raised by the earlier betrayal stories is answered by the Johannine narrative of the betrayal.

One of the best known features of the Judas story is omitted by John to answer criticisms of the arrest of Jesus: Judas does not betray Jesus with a kiss. This is because John, like the cultured critics of Christianity in the second century, could not conceive of a god as arrested and forcibly carried off to stand trial. In the earlier gospels, the kiss of Judas was a signal by which Judas identified Jesus so that the posse might seize him and hurry him away. But in John, when the appointed hour comes Jesus identifies himself and allows the military to carry him off for trial. But not before the hour agreed on by God and Jesus. Before that moment, attempts to arrest him are numerous but vain (7:30, 32, 44-46; 8:20; 10:39). Nor is Jesus surprised and overpowered. He tells his followers before they enter the garden that the arresting party will soon arrive (14:30-31). When they approach, Jesus goes out to meet them in full knowledge of what they are planning to do. He takes charge of his own arrest, as a god should. He asks them whom they are looking for, states his identity, and manifests that divine power which in Matthew is merely mentioned. He who can knock a detachment of troops to the ground with a word has no need of legions of angels. But this exercise of divine power was not intended as an attempt at defense; it merely proved that Jesus had the power to defend himself and was not, therefore, overpowered. The disciples who in earlier accounts took to their heels are here dismissed with dignity after Jesus has secured immunity for them from the authorities. This happened to fulfill his own prediction (18:8-9; cf. also 17:12). The whole story of the arrest has become the story of a divine being acting as divinity should act in what otherwise might be an awkward or trying situation.[20]

> Then Simon Peter having a sword drew it, and smote the high priest's servant, and cut off his right ear. The servant's name was Malchus. Then said Jesus unto Peter, Put up they sword into the sheath: the cup which my Father hath given me, shall I not drink it? 18:10-11

An important part of the Gethsemane story is John's account of the cutting off of Malchus' ear. One commentator noted:

> In Mark there is no comment on this; in Luke it is the occasion for a miracle; in Matthew there is more consciousness of the ludicrous futility of that blow—the disciple is rebuked by the quotation of a proverb, by a reference to the angelic host who could defend Jesus, and by an appeal to the necessary fulfillment of Scripture. In John, Peter strikes the blow and is rebuked by Jesus for suggesting by such an action that Jesus was not ready to drink the cup which his Father had offered him (18:10-11). The reference to the legion of angels is replaced by a demonstration of Jesus' (supernatural) power to defend himself (18:4-6). But this is only a demonstration of power, not a serious attempt to use it. It was one of Jesus' followers, not Jesus himself, who revolted at the thought of the imminent catastrophe.
>
> For Jesus is here portrayed as calmly and confidently following a program which he had accepted in its entirety long before. He sees the end from the beginning, sees it clearly and sees it constantly. He predicted his death in his first public action at Jerusalem (2:19-20). He explained the necessity of his death to Nicodemus (3:14). The "hour" of his death was fixed before the ministry began, and both Jesus and the evangelist were constantly aware of it.[21]

In such a situation the account of Christ's agony in the Garden of Gethsemane could serve no useful function, and so John omits it from his account.

> In the Fourth Gospel the divine Jesus whom Paul knew only after the resurrection appears on every page and in every scene. The evangelist intends his reader to follow the words and deeds of this divine Jesus to a faith like that of Thomas who hails him as "My Lord and my God!" But there is no contrast in quality here between the earthly and the risen Lord; they are equally divine, and equally of cosmic significance.[22]

Trial and Crucifixion

> Then the band and the captain and officers of the Jews took Jesus, and bound him, And led him away to Annas first; for he was father in law to Caiaphas, which was the high priest that same year. Now Caiaphas was he, which gave counsel to the Jews, that it was expedient that one man should die for the people. 18-12-14

From the presence of Annas Jesus was eventually taken, and subsequently brought before one official after another during that awful night of trial (cf. 18:12-19:16), until

Pilate eventually gave in to the demands of the Jews, who cried: *"Away with him, away with him, crucify him"* (v. 15). Nevertheless, the dignity and majesty of the Lord is seen throughout these reprehensible proceedings in spite of the cruel and humiliating treatment to which He was subjected.

> In the trial, as at the arrest, Jesus is more powerful than his enemies, but he acquiesces in their actions because he knows that what they are doing is in accord with the divine plan. He tells Pilate plainly, "You would have no power at all over me if it were not given to you from above" (19:11). Pilate could not avoid crucifying Jesus (however much he might want to) because the divine Jesus had predicted his own death by crucifixion, and the words of a deity must be fulfilled (18:32). In John, the trial of Jesus is the trial of a god. The only disturbance of its dignity is the mistreatment of Jesus by the Jews before the High Priest (18:19-23). Even this is turned by Jesus into a demonstration of his innocence, since the Jews are unable to justify the mistreatment.[23]

Yet in spite of His innocence, the Son of God was condemned to death by means of crucifixion. John wrote:

> *And he bearing his cross went forth into a place called the place of a skull, which is called in the Hebrew Golgatha: Where they crucified him, and two other with him, on either side one, and Jesus in the midst. And Pilate wrote a title, and put it on the cross. And the writing was, JESUS OF NAZARETH THE KING OF THE JEWS. This title then read many of the Jews: for the place where Jesus was crucified was nigh to the city: and it was written in Hebrew, and Greek, and Latin. Then said the chief priests of the Jews to Pilate, Write not, The King of the Jews; but that he said, I am King of the Jews. Pilate answered, What I have written I have written. Then the soldiers, when they had crucified Jesus, took his garments and made four parts, to every soldier a part; and also his coat: now the coat was without seam, woven from the top throughout. They said therefore among themselves, Let us not rend it, but cast lots for it, whose it shall be: that the scripture might be fulfilled, which saith, They parted my raiment among them, and for my vesture they did cast lots. These things therefore the soldiers did. Now there stood by the cross of Jesus his mother, and his mother's sister, Mary the wife of Cleopas, and Mary Magdalene. When Jesus therefore saw his mother, and the disciple standing by, whom he loved, he saith unto his mother, Woman, behold thy son! Then saith he to the disciple, Behold thy mother! And from that hour that disciple took her unto his own home. After this, Jesus knowing that all things were now accomplished, that the scripture might be fulfilled, saith, I thirst. Now there was set a vessel full of vinegar: and they filled a spunge with vinegar, and put it upon hyssop, and put it to his mouth. When Jesus therefore had received the vinegar, he said, It is finished: and he bowed his head, and gave up the ghost. The Jews therefore, because it was the preparation, that the bodies should not remain upon the cross on the Sabbath day, (for that Sabbath day was an high day,) besought Pilate that their legs might be broken, and that they might be taken away. Then came the soldiers, and brake the legs of the first, and of the other which was crucified with him. But when they came to Jesus, and saw that he was dead already, they brake not his legs: But one of the soldiers with a spear pierced his side, and forthwith came there out blood and water. And he that saw it bare record, and his record is true: and he knoweth that he saith true, that ye might believe. For these things were done, that the scripture should be fulfilled, A bone of him shall not be broken. And again another scripture saith, They shall look on him whom they pierced.* 19:17-37

There are many distinctive details of the Passion story in John that combine to make the story of the death of Jesus more dignified, . . . more triumphant. The taunting and jeering at the crucified find no place in John's account. The theme of the taunts reported by the earlier evangelists was that Jesus claimed to be a Savior of others, but could not even save himself. Such a charge presupposes that Jesus did not want to be crucified. John has so clearly shown that Jesus came to earth for the purpose of being crucified that he is consistent when he omits this charge from the story of the death.

The omission of the taunt scene was easy for him also in that it made the death scene more dignified. That John was interested in increasing the dignity of Jesus' departure is shown by his failure to label the two who were crucified with Jesus as "criminals" or "robbers." . . .

There are a number of details in the Johannine Passion that remove the story altogether from the category of tragedy. As John interprets the death of Jesus, it was triumph and exaltation for Jesus. The concomitants of misery and tragedy are, therefore, absent from his narrative. He shows us a Jesus who, having already conquered the cosmos, now completes his mission and begins his exaltation by being crucified. He has no despairing cry from the forsaken Jesus, reproaching the Father for abandoning him. In the earlier accounts, the result of his cry was that a bystander ran to get Jesus a drink. . . . Why, then, did the bystander offer Jesus a drink? Because Jesus had called out, "I am thirsty." Not that he just happened to be thirsty—but rather because Jesus, aware that the last detail of the plan was finished, said this that the Scripture might be fulfilled. Nor was there any loud cry from Jesus at the moment of his death, as Matthew and Mark report. On the contrary, Jesus in the leading role in the drama of redemption closes the scene with the pronouncement, "It is finished."

The interpretation of the crucifixion as triumph rather than tragedy leads John to omit such miracles as the Synoptics report to have accompanied the death of Jesus. There is in John's story no eclipse, no supernatural tearing of the temple veil, no earthquake or resurrection of the dead when Jesus dies. Such portents are signs of gloom and dread disaster; nature mourns in sympathy with the suffering and death of Jesus. In the Fourth Gospel there is no excuse for mourning; Jesus experiences crucifixion as a triumph.

Entirely consistent with this is the story of Jesus' assigning his mother to the care of the beloved disciple. Whatever may be intended as the symbolic message of the incident, it definitely suggests that the crucified Jesus was still the Leader and Director. He calmly gives directions for the future care of his mother within a few moments of his own death. The placidity of the incident helps to establish the dominant tone of the Johannine Passion as one of dignity. That Jesus was the most important person of the three executed that day had been suggested by earlier accounts which located his cross in the middle. John retains this tradition; and, in the account of the breaking of the legs, he reports that the soldiers broke the legs of the first man, that they then walked past Jesus to the other, and finally came to Jesus. This reservation of Jesus to the last is one more minor detail to suggest the importance of Jesus in the story.[24]

Burial and Resurrection

> *And after this Joseph of Arimathaea, being a disciple of Jesus, but secretly for fear of the*
> *Jews, besought Pilate that he might take away the body of Jesus: and Pilate gave him leave.*
> *He came therefore, and took the body of Jesus. And there came also Nicodemus, which at the*
> *first came to Jesus by night, and brought a mixture of myrrh and aloes, about an hundred*
> *pound weight. Then took they the body of Jesus, and wound it in linen clothes with the*
> *spices, as the manner of the Jews is to bury. Now in the place where he was crucified there*
> *was a garden; and in the garden a new sepulcher, wherein was never man yet laid. There*
> *laid they Jesus therefore because of the Jews' preparation day; for the sepulcher was nigh at*
> *hand.* 19:38-42

The same suggestion of importance is given in the burial story. There is in
John no suggestion of hurried, incomplete and temporary burial. . . . Two
of the leading men of the Jewish nation bury Jesus in royal, or perhaps
divine, fashion. Nicodemus supplies a hundred pounds of myrrh and aloes
for the burial, a munificent contribution. It must be remembered that Christian accounts of the burial of Jesus would be measured by the pagan popu-
lace against the presentation of the burial of various deities in mystery cult
practice. That such presentations were magnificent spectacles is suggested by
the promise made to a follower of magic that his body would be buried in a
manner "fitting for a god."[25]

Unlike the followers of the pagan mystery religions, however, the grave could
not long hold the body of the Lord Jesus Christ, as the twentieth chapter of John's
Gospel reveals. As we view the four scenes described in this chapter, we should note
"the nature of the evidence to the fact of the resurrection which each presents."[26]
Furthermore, it may be pointed out that the resurrection appearances recorded here
"meet with much less incredulity from the disciples than in the earlier gospels. The
beloved disciple believes; Mary's message is not disbelieved; the ten believe gladly, and
the doubts of Thomas supply the opportunity for a strong encomium of those who
believe without seeing."[27]

Whereas the unbelief of the disciples may have found its consummation in the
cross of Christ, the first scene in this chapter reveals that the faith of one disciple, at
least, reached "its climax at the sight of the empty tomb."[28] John wrote:

> *The first day of the week cometh Mary Magdalene early, when it was yet dark, unto the*
> *sepulcher, and seeth the stone taken away from the sepulcher. Then she runneth, and cometh*
> *to Simon Peter, and to the other disciple, whom Jesus loved, and saith unto them, They*
> *have taken away the Lord out of the sepulcher, and we know not where they have laid him.*
> *Peter therefore went forth, and that other disciple, and came to the sepulcher. So they ran*
> *both together: and the other disciple did outrun Peter, and came first to the Sepulcher. And he*
> *stooping down, and looking in, saw the linen clothes lying; yet went he not in. Then cometh*
> *Simon Peter following him, and went into the sepulcher, and seeth the linen clothes lie, And*
> *the napkin, that was about his head, not lying with the linen clothes, but wrapped together*
> *in a place by itself. Then went in also that other disciple, which came first to the sepulcher,*
> *and he saw, and believed.* 20:1-8

What was it, however, that John believed? That Jesus had risen? Surely this,
but further that, as he had risen, he was therefore the divine Son of God. The
conviction then produced was the origin of this Gospel, the source of a life

of loving devotion for the Apostle John. Such, too, in the mind of the writer, is the only possible conclusion to draw from the fact of the resurrection; Jesus must be divine, and deserving of our devotion and our love.[29]

The second scene in this chapter describes the encounter between Christ and Mary Magdalene, the first person to whom the risen Lord appeared. John noted:

But Mary stood without at the sepulcher weeping: and as she wept, she stooped down, and looked into the sepulcher, And seeth two angels in white sitting, the one at the head, and the other at the feet, where the body of Jesus had lain. And they say unto her, Woman, why weepest thou? She saith unto them, Because they have taken away my Lord, and I know not where they have laid him. And when she had thus said, she turned herself back, and saw Jesus standing, and knew not that it was Jesus. Jesus saith unto her, Woman, why weepest thou? She, supposing him to be the gardener, saith unto him, Sir, if thou have borne him hence, tell me where thou hast laid him, and I will take him away. Jesus saith unto her, Mary. She turned herself, and saith unto him, Rabboni; which is to say, Master. Jesus saith unto her, Touch me not; for I am not yet ascended to my Father: but go to my brethren, and say unto them, I ascend unto my Father, and your Father; and to my God, and your God. Mary Magdalene came and told the disciples that she had seen the Lord, and that he had spoken these things unto her. 20:11-18

She had come to the tomb to weep, and to pay homage to the body of the dead; she was surprised by a vision of angels, and was convinced of the resurrection by a single spoken word. She saw Jesus but did not recognize him until her own name fell from his lips. . . . It is the mourner who stands weeping at the grave of buried hopes who, perhaps first of all, needs the vision of a risen Christ; and sometimes he speaks, to the very heart, a message which inspires as true a faith as that which comes to John as he reasons from the fact of an empty tomb.

What is the message to Mary; what the content of her faith? That Jesus is a divine Being, who stands in an absolutely unique relation to the Father, as the Son of God. Jesus bids her tell the disciples that he is about to ascend, not to our Father, but "unto my Father and your Father, and my God and your God."[30]

The third scene finds the risen Lord suddenly in the midst of the ten disciples; Thomas on this occasion being absent. John wrote:

Then the same day at evening, being the first day of the week, when the doors were shut where the disciples were assembled for fear of the Jews, came Jesus and stood in the midst, and saith unto them, Peace be unto you. And when he had so said, he shewed unto them his hands and his side. Then were the disciples glad, when they saw the Lord. Then said Jesus to them again, Peace be unto you: as my Father hath sent me, even so send I you. And when he had said this, he breathed on them, and saith unto them, Receive ye the Holy Ghost: Whose soever sins ye remit, they are remitted unto them; and whose soever sins ye retain, they are retained. But Thomas, one of the twelve, called Didymus, was not with them when Jesus came. The other disciples therefore said unto him, We have seen the Lord. But he said unto them, Except I shall see in his hands the print of the nails, and put my finger into the print of the nails, and thrust my hand into his side, I will not believe. 20:19-25

The first appearance to the disciples occurred the same day, in the evening, when, fearing the Jews, they had withdrawn for safety to an upper room. They believed the fact of the resurrection, not when reported to them by credible witnesses, but on the evidence of a physical demonstration: "Jesus . . . stood in the midst . . . and . . . he showed unto them his hands and his side." Such proof was needed then, but not now. Other kinds of evidence should suffice for us. We should know the blessedness of those who "have not seen, and yet have believed." Their faith was now in one who was unquestionably divine, one who could give peace to the soul, one who could impart the Spirit of God, one who was indeed the Son of God.[31]

The final scene in this chapter finds the disciples together again, one week later, with the doubting Thomas present. When he had initially heard the report of the others about seeing the risen Christ, Thomas "demanded practically the same proof that had been given them. He should, however, have accepted their testimony."[32] John noted:

> And after eight days again his disciples were within, and Thomas with them: then came Jesus, the doors being shut, and stood in the midst, and said, Peace be unto you. Then saith he to Thomas, Reach hither thy finger, and behold my hands; and reach hither thy hand, and thrust it into my side: and be not faithless, but believing. And Thomas answered and said unto him, My Lord and my God. Jesus saith unto him, Thomas, because thou hast seen me, thou hast believed: blessed are they that have not seen, and yet have believed. And many other signs truly did Jesus in the presence of his disciples, which are not written in this book: But these are written, that ye might believe that Jesus is the Christ, the Son of God; and that believing ye might have life through his name. 20:26-31

Conviction came to Thomas as the Lord appeared and offered to give the kind of evidence desired. Then Thomas believed, but without demanding the proof he had before required. He was convinced by the love and mercy and knowledge of his Lord, not only his resurrection, but of his divine nature. He cried out in adoring wonder: "My Lord and my God." This confession is not only the culmination of belief: it is also the climax of the Gospel. John at once adds that his purpose in writing has been to bring his readers to just such faith in Christ. If one naturally so skeptical as Thomas was convinced that Jesus rose from the dead, we have no excuse for doubt. If Jesus did so rise, then we should argue, as did Thomas, that he is divine. If Jesus allowed Thomas to worship him as God, we should yield ourselves to him in adoration and love as to a divine Master, who has been proved to be by his resurrection from the dead, "very God, of very God."[33]

Summary and Conclusion

And so it came to pass that when John completed his Gospel, the fourth and final portrait of Jesus Christ was also finished.

Four portraits of Himself—this is the whole of the legacy left by Jesus to His family on earth. But they are sufficient for its needs, because by the contemplation of these the Church receives into herself, through the communications of the Spirit, the life of Him whose characteristic features they set forth.

These four pictures originated spontaneously, and (the three first, at all events,) independently of each other. They arose, accidentally in a manner, from the four principal regions of the earth comprehended by the Church in the first century—Palestine, Asia Minor, Greece, Italy.

The characteristics of these four regions have not failed to exercise a certain influence upon the manner in which the Christ has been presented in the pictures intended for the use of each. In Palestine, Matthew proclaimed Jesus as Him who put the finishing stroke to the establishment of that holy kingdom of God which had been fore-announced by the prophets, and of which the foundations had been laid in Israel. In Rome, Mark presented Him as the irresistible conqueror who founded His Divine right to the possession of the world upon His miraculous power. Amongst the generous and affable Hellenic races, Luke described Him as the Divine philanthropist, commissioned to carry out the work of Divine grace and compassion towards the worst of sinners. In Asia Minor, that ancient cradle of theosophy, John pictured Him as the Word made flesh, the eternal life and light, who had descended into the world of Time. Thus it was under the influence of a profound sympathy with those about Him that each evangelist brought into relief that aspect of Christ which answered most nearly to the ideal of his readers.[34]

From the four principal regions of the earth in the first century, then, the evangelists have given the world an accurate four-fold portrait and a perfect account of the Gospel of God for all time. The four Gospels are the consummate record of the life and ministry of the divine Son of God, even though, as John admits:

> And there are also many other things which Jesus did, the which, if they should be written every one, I suppose that even the world itself could not contain the books that should be written. 21:25

Figure 14-1. Fritz Von Uhde: Christus and Nicodemus

Chapter Fourteen Notes

1 Cynthia Pearl Maus, *Christ and the Fine Arts* (New York: Harper & Row, Publishers, 1959),166.

2 *Ibid.*

3 *Ibid.*, 166-67.

4 B. F. Westcott, *The Gospel According to St. John* (London: John Murray, Albemarle Street, 1908), lxxv.

5 William Moorehead, *Studies in the Four Gospels* (Philadelphia: The Westminster Press, 1900), 200-01.

6 J. J. Van Oosterzee, *The Theology of the New Testament: A Handbook for Bible Students*, trans. by Maurice J. Evans (New York: Dodd & Mead, Publishers, 1875), 148.

7 William Alexander, *The Leading Ideas of the Gospels* (London: Macmillan and Co., 1892), 224-26.

8 "Names of God in the Old Testament," *Harper's Bible Dictionary* (1985), 685.

9 "Gospels," *Encyclopaedia Britannica* (1903), X:825.

10 George Soltau, *Four Portraits of the Lord Jesus Christ* (New York: Charles C. Cook, n.d.), 158-59.

11 *Ibid.*, 153-54.

[12] "Gospels," *Encyclopaedia Britannica* (1903), X:826.

[13] *Ibid.*

[14] *Ibid.*, 835-36.

[15] Ernest Cadman Colwell and Eric Lane Titus, *The Gospel of the Spirit: A Study in the Fourth Gospel* (New York: Harper & Brothers Publishers, 1953), 72-75.

[16] *Ibid.*, 78.

[17] *Ibid.*, 79-80.

[18] *Ibid.*, 76.

[19] *Ibid.*, 80.

[20] *Ibid.*, 82-85.

[21] *Ibid.*, 80-81.

[22] *Ibid.*, 76.

[23] *Ibid.*, 87-88.

[24] *Ibid.*, 103-05.

[25] *Ibid.*, 105-06.

[26] Charles R. Erdman, *The Gospel of John* (Philadelphia: The Westminster Press, 1944), 165.

[27] Colwell, *op. cit.*, 106.

[28] Erdman, *op. cit.*

[29] *Ibid.*, 167.

[30] *Ibid.*, 167-68.

[31] *Ibid.*, 168-69.

[32] *Ibid.*, 170.

[33] *Ibid.*

[34] Frederic L. Godet, *Studies in the New Testament* (New York: E. P. Dutton & Co., 1895), 79-80.

PERSPECTIVE

A Proof of Christ's Divinity by William Nast

Instead of basing the truth of Gospel history and the Divinity of Christ upon the miracles recorded by the Evangelists, we may prove the historic verity of the miracles and the Divinity of Christ by the unparalleled perfectness of the moral and intellectual character of the man Jesus of Nazareth, as he is presented to us by the plain and honest fishermen of Galilee. "Demanding nothing more," says Mr. Young, in his Christ of History, "than the simple humanity of Jesus of Nazareth, we shall venture from this platform to assert and expound his true Divinity. Dismissing all preconceptions, however fondly cherished, and however long adopted into the faith of the Churches, assuming nothing which is not virtually and even formally admitted by enemies as well as friends, we hope to show that the manhood of Christ, as it appealed to the senses and the minds of the men of his own times, supplies and sustains the proof of his Godhood. Behold only the man Jesus—he shall indicate and demonstrate his union with absolute Godhead. Such a humanity as his is utterly inexplicable except on the ground of true Divinity."

From this stand-point it is our object to show that the character and life of Jesus could not possibly have been the natural product of the times and country in which the Gospel Records incontestably originated—nor, indeed, of any other age or country; that the moral and intellectual perfectness of the character of Jesus, and the wonderful harmony and consistency of his doctrines and works, could not possibly have been conceived and delineated by the Evangelists, unless they had been actually witnessed by them; that the moral and intellectual perfectness of Jesus imparts to the testimony he gives of himself, as well as to the miracles which the Evangelists ascribe to him, a verity absolutely unassailable; and, finally, that the unparalleled human perfection of Jesus—which by almost universal consent, even of unbelievers, rises far above every human greatness known before or since—can not be rationally explained, except on the ground of such an essential union with the Godhead as he claimed himself, and as the Evangelists ascribed to him. Thus, as the eye of a traveler at the foot of a mountain may slowly travel up the majestic slope till it is lost in the clouds or dazzling glories of the summit, so the mind may contemplate Christ from his lowliest and most human traits, where he is one with the humblest human being, up beyond the highest reach and limit of humanity, "far above all principalities, and powers, and every name that is named," to that dazzling summit of glory where he is one with God.[1]

---

[1] William Nast, *The Gospel Records: Their Genuineness, Authenticity, Historic Verity, and Inspiration, with Some Preliminary Remarks on the Gospel History* (Cincinnati: Cranston and Stowe, 1866), 231-34.

PART VI

THE MESSAGE FOR ALL TIME

He will swallow up death in victory;
And the Lord God will wipe away tears from off all faces;
and the rebuke of his people shall he take away from off all the earth:
for the Lord hath spoken it.

Isaiah 25:8

[The] variety in the forms of the Apostolic preaching, which was directed to meet the hope of the Jew and the energy of the Roman, to satisfy the cravings of our moral nature and the wants of our speculative reason, could not fail to influence the form in which the facts of the life of Christ were apprehended and grouped. These facts were the groundwork of all Christian teaching, and in virtue of their infinite bearings admitted of being variously combined. In this way the common evangelic narrative was modified in the special labors of the different apostles, and that which was designed to meet the requirements of one period was fitted to meet the requirements of all. For it is not enough to acknowledge the marvelous adaptation of the Gospel to the apostolic age. It was equally destined for all times.[1]

-Brooke Foss Westcott, *An Introduction to the Study of the Gospels*

What is this common witness? Not His birth, not His age, not His baptism, fasting, or transfiguration; but the cross and resurrection, the death of the flesh, the life of the spirit; the sufferings of Christ, and the glory which should follow. Out of the countless acts and words of Jesus, death and resurrection is chosen to be the great subject for the common testimony.[2]

-Andrew Jukes, *The Characteristic Differences of the Four Gospels*

There stands the mysterious cross—a rock against which the very waves of the curse break. He who so mercifully engaged to direct this judgment against Himself hangs yonder in profound darkness. Still He remains the Morning Star, announcing an eternal Sabbath to the world. Though rejected by heaven and earth, yet He forms the connecting link between them both, and the Mediator of their eternal and renewed amity. Ah see! His bleeding arms are extended wide; He stretches them out to every sinner. His hands point to the east and west; for He shall gather His children from the ends of the earth. The top of the cross is directed toward the sky; far above the world will its effects extend. Its foot is fixed in the earth; the cross becomes a wondrous tree, from which we reap the fruit of an eternal reconciliation. O, nothing more is requisite, than that God should grant us penitential tears, and then, by means of the Holy Spirit, show us the Savior suffering on the cross. We then escape from all earthly care and sorrow, and rejoice in hope of the glory of God.[3]

-F. W. Krummacher, *The Suffering Savior*

1   Brooke Foss Westcott, *An Introduction to the Study of the Gospels* (London: Macmillan & Co., 1875), 221.
2   Andrew Jukes, *The Characteristic Differences of the Four Gospels* (New York: Fleming H. Revell Company, n.d.), 144.
3   F. W. Krummacher, *The Suffering Savior: Meditations on the Last Days of Christ* (Chicago: Moody Press, 1948), 332.

Figure VI-1. Peter Paul Rubens: Descent from the Cross

Peter Paul Rubens (1577-1640) was the most important Flemish painter of the 17th century, and one of he greatest artists of all time. Today his paintings are found in all the principal galleries of Europe, and this one is considered technically superb.

"The body of Christ is a piece of masterly work. There is no doubt about Christ's being dead. . . .The body has slid into the arms of John. . . . Among the three Marys it is easy to distinguish the Virgin because of her greater dignity and sorrow. She does not touch the body but follows its every movement with a quick sympathy. Mary Magdalene receives the feet. . . . In this way the artists picture her passionate sorrow and her sense of unworthiness because of past sins."[4]

Every devout Christian, like Mary Magdalene and the disciples of old, can be thankful that the story of Christ did not end with the scene depicted in this magnificent painting. There is yet another chapter in the story of the life of Christ, which "was opened on that first Easter morn—a chapter that was to send these beaten and defeated followers of the lowly Nazarene out with deathless courage to finish, under the guiding Spirit of their Lord, that Kingdom of Love for which He lived and wrought and prayed and died."[5]

[4] Albert Edward Bailey, *The Gospel in Art* (Boston: The Pilgrim Press, 1946), 371-72.

[5] Cynthia Pearl Maus, *Christ and the Fine Arts* (New York: Harper & Row, Publishers, 1959), 393.

Chapter Fifteen

The Four Gospels: The Common Testimony

As noted in the previous sections of our study, the typical Jew, Roman, Greek, and Christian of the first century each had a different perspective and outlook on life; and to these people the Gospel narratives were respectively addressed. But yet, the Gospel reader today should not view this former audience merely as randomly-selected individuals, nor politically-separate peoples, "but true types of the various classes into which the Roman world was divided in its religious aspect. The characteristic feelings which they embodied express the cardinal tendencies of men, and mark the great divisions of the apostolic work."[1]

Down the corridors of time and across the pages of history, the world has always been divided in its religious aspect according to the same four attitudes and tendencies, each with a unique focus on life from the standpoint of time. In *An Introduction to the Study of the Gospels*, published in London in 1875, Dr. Brooke Foss Westcott explained this phenomenon and made the following application:

There are many whose thoughts still linger in the past, and who delight to trace with a vain regret "the glories which have passed away from the earth." To them St. Matthew speaks, as he did to the Jew of old, while he teaches that all which was great and good in former days was contained in the spirit, and not in the outward shape, and exhibits the working of Providence in the course of national history. There are many, again, whose sympathies are entirely with the present, who delight in the activity and warmth of daily life, who are occupied with things around them, without looking far beyond their own age and circle. To them St. Mark addresses a brief and pregnant narrative of the ministry of Christ, unconnected with any special recital of His birth and preparation for His work, and unconnected, at least in its present shape, with the mysterious history of the Ascension. Many, also, there must be in every age who dwell with peculiar affection on the Gospel of St. Luke, who delight to recognize the universality of our faith, whose thoughts anticipate the time when all shall hear the message of Christianity, who know no difference of class and acknowledge no claims of self-righteousness, but admit the bonds of a common humanity, and feel the necessity of a common Savior. And, lastly, are there not those, even in an era of restless excitement, who love to retire from the busy scenes of action to dwell on the eternal mysteries which St. John opened for silent contemplation: men of divine eloquence and mighty in the understanding of the word, who water the churches which others have planted? No period of life, no variety of temperament, is left without its Gospel. The zealous and the pensive, the active and the thoughtful, may draw their peculiar support from the different Evangelists, and find in them their proper end and road.[2]

Centuries before the Messiah would appear, the prophet Isaiah looked forward to that time of blessing, when he said: *"The people that walked in darkness have seen a great light: they that dwell in the land of the shadow of death, upon them hath the light shined"* (Isa. 9:2).

Jesus Christ is *"the light of the world"* (John 8:12), and the Gospels bear witness to that Light. The narratives of the four evangelists were divinely fashioned so the light of the

Gospel could break through spiritual barriers, and diffuse the darkness that surrounded their respective audiences, both then and now. Unfortunately, we live in a day and age in which many—even in the Church with ample access to the Light—live as if they were still in darkness.

> Many in the Church today consider the Gospel merely to be a historic record rather than a personal resource. They read the Bible for information rather than inspiration. They attend classes or services as a routine expecting simply to hear about God rather than to encounter God.
>
> What the Church needs is a revival of expectation. We are serving almighty God, who dramatically interrupted the routines of the citizens of Jerusalem on the Day of Pentecost two thousand years ago. He is perfectly capable of interrupting our routines as well. . . .
>
> What sort of expectations do you have of the Gospel? The present time is replete with extraordinary opportunities for the Gospel. Spiritual darkness abounds, and the challenge for the Christian messenger is great. But the power of the Gospel dispels that darkness, and the Gospel's Author promises to be with His servants to meet the challenges involved in confronting the spiritual darkness of this world.[3]

The cardinal truths with which the world needs to be confronted are found in those facts that provide the common testimony of the four evangelists. Nineteenth-century writer, Dr. Daniel Seeley Gregory, explains:

> There is a central mass of fact and truth around which Matthew, Mark, Luke, and John alike group their other material. This is the essential, fundamental element which must make the productions of the Evangelists Gospels, good news, to man the sinner wherever and whenever they come to his hearing. These chief facts and truths may be summed up in four particulars.
>
> The first is found in the incarnation of the Son of God. The four Evangelists set it forth in such a way as to make it patent to every candid reader. With Matthew, Jesus is Emmanuel, God with us, in fulfillment of prophecy; with Mark, he is the Son of God in human form exercising his almighty power; with Luke, he is the descendant of Adam and the child of the virgin, yet the Son of the Highest; with John, he is the eternal Word made flesh.
>
> The second is found in the life of the Son of God on earth in human form and subject to human conditions and laws. This makes up the central portion of each of the Gospels. With Matthew, it is the life of Messiah; with Mark, of the almighty worker and victor; with Luke, of the divine and universal man; with John, of the incarnate Word.
>
> The third of these common particulars is found in the death upon the cross. As this is the all-essential fact, all the Gospels devote large space to it, delineating also the events centering in it. In short, here is the ground which all the Evangelists traverse most fully and carefully. They all give the triumphal entry into the Holy City, which was the public claim of Jesus to be the Messiah, the Saviour of the world; the Passover supper, which was his act of putting himself voluntarily in the place of the Pascal Lamb, as the one whose sacrifice alone could deliver from the destruction of sin; the agony and betrayal in Gethsemane, which marked his voluntary submission to drink the cup of

his Father for the salvation of the lost; the trial and condemnation, which were at once the public vindication of the innocence of the Redeemer, and his public rejection by the ancient Jewish and Gentile world; the death by crucifixion, which was his actual sacrifice for the sins of the world; and his burial, which signalized his subjection to death for a season. All these are the constituent parts of the great fact of the cross, or of Christ's sacrifice for the sins of mankind.

The fourth and last of these common features is found in the rising of Jesus from the dead on the third day, in his subsequent intercourse with his disciples, in his giving to the Apostles their great commission to preach the Gospel to all the world, and in his ascension to heaven, at once establishing his claim to be the Savior of mankind and organizing and beginning his saving work.

All these—the incarnation, the life, the death, the resurrection—are the essential facts and truths of the Gospel, those which at the first made it good news to men. Without any one of them all it would cease to be good news; for, without the incarnation, the Son of God would have no part in our human nature; without the life on earth he could neither be our righteousness nor our example; without the death he could not be our sacrifice for sin; and without the resurrection and ascension his claims would be proved baseless and the world would be left to perish without a Saviour. The Son of God became incarnate, lived, died, rose from the dead, for the redemption of the lost—this cannot grow old but must be glad tidings for man, the sinner, till the end of time.[4]

That the death and resurrection of Jesus Christ should be pre-eminent in any account of His life, the four evangelists are in full agreement. Collectively, there are 89 chapters in the Gospels, of which only four chapters cover the first 30+ years of Christ's life. The bulk of the narratives detail the Lord's earthly ministry during His last three years on earth, with over one-third of these 85 chapters highlighting the events beginning eight to ten days prior to His crucifixion. Furthermore, each of the Gospels stresses the fact that from the very beginning of His earthly ministry, Jesus Christ "was perfectly conscious of the Cross. Through the three years of preaching, of working of miracles, of conflict, and of training His own, He moved with quiet dignity, and set determination, towards the Cross of His passion."[5]

Anticipation of His Cross

If we examine some of the Lord's own statements in the early phase of His ministry, we find that "many of the things He said, which while not revealing the fact of the Cross to the men of His age, clearly prove His consciousness of it, in the light of subsequent events. Behind all the teaching and activity of the Master there is evidently a sub-consciousness of the Cross."[6]

In the first place then an examination of words of His, which while not immediately revealing the fact of the Cross, do yet conclusively prove that it was present to His mind, in the midst of all the ceaseless activity of three years of public ministry.

There is a notable silence concerning it as to open declaration until the moment when His Messiahship was confessed by Peter. He then began to speak plainly of the Cross, but yet during all that period of preaching and teaching, it was present to His mind, and is the only explanation of certain things He did, and words He uttered.[7]

From each of the Gospels, then, an examination of some of these things He did and words He uttered will now be considered. "In such a study as this, the principal factor is that of careful attention to the Master's own words. Comments upon them are of minor importance, and will only be made in an attempt to indicate their true meaning."[8]

Matthew records that the disciples of John the Baptist came to Jesus and asked, *"Why do we and the Pharisees fast oft, but thy disciples fast not?"* (9:14). Christ responded by saying, *"Can the children of the bride chamber mourn, as long as the bridegroom is with them? But the days will come, when the bridegroom shall be taken from them, and then shall they fast"* (9:15).

> In astonishment at the absence of fasting in the lives of His disciples, men contrasted this fact with the fasting of the disciples of the Baptist, and asked His explanation. In answer He declared that while He was with them, there was no room for mourning, and then there is evident His consciousness of the coming Cross, as He declared that when the bridegroom should be taken away, the sons of the bride-chamber would mourn.[9]

In his Gospel, Mark emphasizes the miracles of Jesus. The following account is not only interesting, but also most informative:

> *And again he entered into Capernaum after some days; and it was noised that he was in the house. And straightway many were gathered together, insomuch that there was no room to receive them, no, not so much as about the door: and he preached the word unto them. And they come unto him, bringing one sick of the palsy, which was borne of four. And when they could not come nigh unto him for the press, they uncovered the roof where he was: and when they had broken it up, they let down the bed wherein the sick of the palsy lay. When Jesus saw their faith, he said unto the sick of the palsy, Son, they sins be forgiven thee. But there were certain of the scribes sitting there, and reasoning in their hearts, Why doth this man thus speak blasphemies? Who can forgive sins but God only? And immediately when Jesus perceived in his spirit that they so reasoned within themselves, he said unto them, Why reason ye these things in your hearts? Whether is it easier to say to the sick of the palsy, Thy sins be forgiven thee; or to say, Arise, and take up thy bed, and walk? But that ye may know that the Son of man hath power on earth to forgive sins, (he saith to the sick of the palsy,) I say unto thee, Arise, and take up thy bed, and go thy way into thine house. And immediately he arose, took up the bed, and went forth before them all; insomuch that they were all amazed, and glorified God, saying, We never saw it on this fashion.* 2:1-12

> Here by a miracle of healing, He demonstrated to His critics His power to forgive sins, while His very claim to be able to do this, proves His consciousness of the fact that "His own self bare our sins in His body upon the tree" (1 Pet. 2:24), for by this bearing of sin alone has He power to forgive.[10]

In his Gospel, Luke reports the very first words of Christ that are recorded in the New Testament. They were addressed to His earthly parents when He was still an adolescent. The incident is found in Chapter Two, where we read:

> *Now his parents went to Jerusalem every year at the feast of the Passover. And when he was twelve years old, they went up to Jerusalem after the custom of the feast. And when they had*

fulfilled the days, as they returned, the child Jesus tarried behind in Jerusalem; and Joseph and his mother knew not of it. But they, supposing him to have been in the company, went a day's journey; and they sought him among their kinsfolk and acquaintance. And when they found him not, they turned back again to Jerusalem, seeking him. And it came to pass, that after three days they found him in the temple, sitting in the midst of the doctors, both hearing them, and asking them questions. And all that heard him were astonished at his understanding and answers. And when they saw him, they were amazed: and his mother said unto him, Son, why hast thou thus dealt with us? Behold, thy father and I have sought thee sorrowing. And he said unto them, How is it that ye sought me? Wist ye not that I must be about my Father's business? And they understood not the saying which he spake unto them. 2:41-50

There is considerable divergence of opinion as to whether Jesus was conscious of the full meaning of His mission during the days of His boyhood and young manhood. A full discussion of this subject is not here attempted. Neither recorded word of His, nor clear statement of scripture, give any decisive declaration on the point. Believing in the perfection of His unfallen human nature, it would seem as though all the probability were in favour of the opinion that He saw the Cross, and knew through all the quiet processes of preparation, that therein lay the final fact of His wondrous work.

His communion with His Father was perfect, and in unclouded intelligence He would understand the meaning of the sacred writings of His people. It is unthinkable that He shared their blindness as to that portion of the prophetic writings, which had reference to the suffering of the Messiah. His first utterance declares His consciousness of relation to His Father, and understanding of the fact. This in itself would seem to warrant belief that He realized the fact of His Messiahship. If this be so, then there can be no doubt that He also knew that the pathway of the Messiah to the throne was the pathway of suffering and the Cross.

This position is strengthened by His accurate apprehension of the meaning of the symbolism of the Hebrew worship. All the types and shadows of the ceremonial law were luminous to Him. The very calendar of the feasts must have spoken to His heart its true message.[11]

In his Gospel, John alone records the miracle of the water being turned into wine. We are told: *"This beginning of miracles did Jesus in Cana of Galilee, and manifested forth his glory; and his disciples believed on him"* (2:11). Nevertheless, the conversation between Jesus and His mother, which preceded this very first miracle of the Lord, is most instructive. We read:

And the third day there was a marriage in Cana of Galilee; and the mother of Jesus was there: And both Jesus was called, and his disciples, to the marriage. And when they wanted wine, the mother of Jesus saith unto him, They have no wine. Jesus saith unto her, Woman, what have I to do with thee? Mine hour is not yet come. 2:1-4

This is the first of a series of references in the Gospel of John to an hour yet to come. A comparison of them will show that they all refer to the Cross. His mother evidently thought that now at the commencement of public ministry, He would demonstrate His divine calling, and accomplish His work, and in the first fact she was correct, but her understanding was limited. He wrought the miracle she suggested and it was His first sign, but His words prove His understanding of the fact that His mightiest work could only be accomplished by the way of the Cross.[12]

Some time later, John tells us of an incident involving Jesus and his brethren. He wrote:

> *Now the Jews' feast of tabernacles was at hand. His brethren therefore said unto him, Depart hence, and go into Judaea, that thy disciples also may see the works that thou doest. For there is no man that doeth any thing in secret, and he himself seeketh to be known openly. If thou do these things, shew thyself to the world. For neither did his brethren believe in him. Then Jesus said unto them, My time is not yet come: but your time is always ready. The world cannot hate you; but me it hateth, because I testify of it, that the works thereof are evil. Go ye up unto this feast: I go not up yet unto this feast; for my time is not yet full come.* 7:2-8

Here is another reference to the hour that had not yet come, this time spoken to His brethren, as at the first it was addressed to His mother. They were urging Him to manifest Himself, and accomplish something. He declared that the supreme moment had not yet arrived, knowing perfectly that between Him and any manifestation of real power, there lay the Cross.[13]

In Chapter Nine, John records the discussion between Jesus and His disciples, upon seeing *"a man which was blind from his birth"* (9:1). We read:

> *And his disciples asked him, saying, Master, who did sin, this man, or his parents, that he was born blind? Jesus answered, Neither hath this man sinned, nor his parents: but that the works of God should be made manifest in him. I must work the works of him that sent me, while it is day: the night cometh, when no man can work.* 9:2-4

This declaration of Christ has very often been taken out of its setting and its relation, and has been made to teach that which is undoubtedly true, but what is not here declared. Through John, as has been seen, there is a reference to an hour which was coming. It was to be an hour of darkness, of night; and here He said to His disciples in connection with the healing of the man born blind, "We must work," and then declared that presently the night was coming in which no man could work. His mind was almost certainly fixed upon that deep, dense, dark night, in which man should be excluded, and God alone should accomplish the redemption of the lost race.[14]

From these few references in the Gospels, we have seen "that from the moment when His public ministry began, there was present to His mind its consummation in the Cross."[15] As far as the Lord Jesus Christ was concerned, "the pathway of the three years was a pathway ever resolutely trodden towards the Cross. And while the consciousness of its pain was ever upon Him, so was also the sense of its value, for upon the triumph there to be won, He based His authority for all the wonders which He wrought, and the blessings which He scattered were in his view made possible thereby."[16]

Efficacy of His Death and Resurrection

The apostle Paul told the Church at Corinth, *"For I determined not to know any thing among you, save Jesus Christ, and him crucified"* (1 Cor. 2:2). When from the cross Jesus said, *"It is finished"* (John 19:30), "sin was finished as to its power to work the final ruin of any man. In the mystery of the passion of Jesus, sin which had mastered men, and held them in slavery, was in turn mastered and robbed of its force."[17] Nevertheless, if the story of Christ ended at Calvary, there would be no value in preaching *"Jesus Christ, and him crucified."* Dr. G. Campbell Morgan wrote:

> It was his resurrection from among the dead that demonstrated the infinite value of the mystery of His death. When the apostle declared to the Christians in Corinth that he was determined not to know anything among them, save Jesus Christ and Him crucified, the reason lay in the fact of their carnality. All kinds of disorders had crept into the church, and the tone of the life of the members was carnal and not spiritual. It was necessary to hold their thinking in the realm of the Cross, for they had not learned this first lesson, and could not therefore be led into the deeper and fuller truth.[18]

At the end of his letter to Corinth, however, Paul did have his readers consider the consequences, had the resurrection not occurred. He wrote:

> *And if Christ be not risen, then is our preaching vain, and your faith is also vain. Yea, and we are found false witnesses of God; because we have testified of God that he raised up Christ: whom he raised not up, if so be that the dead rise not. For if the dead rise not, then is not Christ raised: And if Christ be not raised, your faith is vain; ye are yet in your sins. Then they also which are fallen asleep in Christ are perished. If in this life only we have hope in Christ, we are of all men most miserable.* 1 COR. 15:14-19

The bodily resurrection of Christ, however, was so widely acknowledged, and His post-resurrection appearances so extensively witnessed, that even those who questioned His virgin birth were forced to admit, *"that he was buried, and that he rose again the third day"* (I Corinthians 15:4).

> It is not an exaggeration—it is only putting in words the impression left by the facts—to say that the conviction among Christians that Christ was really raised, dates from the very morrow of the Resurrection itself. It was not a growth spread over a long period and receiving gradual accretions of strength; but it sprang suddenly into existence, and it swept irresistibly over the whole body of disciples. Of the force and universality of the belief there can be no doubt, but when we come to details it would seem that from the first there was a certain amount of confusion, which was never wholly cleared up. We have records of a number of appearances, not all contained in a single authority, but scattered over several distinct authorities; and it is probable enough that even when all the recorded appearances are put together they would not exhaust all those that were experienced.[19]

Considering the supreme importance of the death and subsequent resurrection of Jesus Christ, it is not surprising to discover that John devotes almost as much space in his Gospel to the last 48 hours of Christ's life, as he does on all the rest of His time on earth. And this is the emphasis of all the evangelists. Such is the common testimony.

In the book of Revelation, John describes the four living creatures—which many see as symbolic to the four-fold manner in which Christ is presented in the Gospels—and observes them around the throne of God, where *"they rest not day and night, saying, Holy, holy, holy, Lord God Almighty, which was, and is, and is to come"* (Rev. 4:8). "The four living creatures, speaking out of the depths of God's sanctuary, here speak but one language. For the veil whereupon they are wrought is rent from the top throughout; and, in its rending, their forms must needs be rent also."[20]

Such is the common witness. In all the Gospels, Christ is betrayed by one disciple and denied by another. In all He is judged by the religious rulers and condemned by Pontius Pilate. In all Barabbas, who was imprisoned for insurrection and murder, is preferred before Him. In all He is stripped of His garments, which are parted amongst His executioners. In all He is crucified and numbered with transgressors. In all He dies and is buried in a borrowed tomb. In all He arises, and as risen speaks with His followers.

Before Christ's crucifixion, the disciples were frightened, confused, and scattered. After His resurrection, they were gathered, encouraged, and comforted. As a result of the resurrection, the disciples *"were all with one accord in one place"* (Acts 2:1), and eagerly awaiting *"the promise of the Father"* (Acts 1:4). Just before His ascension, the Lord had told the disciples:

> But ye shall receive power, after that the Holy Ghost is come upon you: and ye shall be witnesses unto me both in Jerusalem, and in all Judaea, and in Samaria, and unto the uttermost part of the earth. ACTS 1:8

The resurrection of Jesus Christ gave meaning to all the preceding events in His life, and the Church was born as its consequence. And in spite of any weakness and worldliness that may characterize the body of believers in this present hour, *"the gates of hell shall not prevail against it"* (Matt. 16:18), and the Church of Jesus Christ stands as the supreme confirmation of His resurrection, and of the Gospel narratives that bear record of it.

> Turning from this subject of resurrection with the great glad exultant cry, Christ is risen, there is in the cry the affirmation of His perfect victory, the declaration of the Divine seal set upon that victory, and the proclamation of a sure anchorage for the faith of men. The living risen Christ is the center of the Church's creed, the Creator of her character, and the Inspiration of her conduct. His resurrection is the clearest note in her battle-song. It is the sweetest, strongest music amid all her sorrows. It speaks of personal salvation. It promises the life that has no ending, it declares to all bereaved souls that "them also that are fallen asleep in Jesus will God bring with Him" (1 Thes. 4:14), and therefore the light of His resurrection falls in radiant beauty upon the graves where rest the dust of the holy dead. [21]

Chapter Fifteen Notes

[1] Brooke Foss Westcott, *An Introduction to the Study of the Gospels* (London: Macmillan & Co., 1875), 219.

[2] *Ibid.*, 221-22.

[3] Alan G. Ahlgrim, "A Gospel for All Time," *Standard Lesson Commentary: 1995-96*, James I. Fehl, ed. (Cincinnati: The Standard Publishing Company, 1995), 5.

[4] D. S. Gregory, *Why Four Gospels? Or, the Gospel for All the World* (New York: Funk & Wagnalls, Publishers, 1890), 344-45.

[5] G. Campbell Morgan, *The Crises of the Christ* (Old Tappan, N.J.: Fleming H. Revell Company, 1936), 276.

[6] *Ibid.*

[7] *Ibid.*, 276-77.

[8] *Ibid.*, 277.

[9] *Ibid.*, 279.

[10] *Ibid.*, 278-79.

[11] *Ibid.*, 275-76

[12] *Ibid.*, 277.

[13] *Ibid.*, 282.

[14] *Ibid.*, 283.

[15] *Ibid.*, 287.

[16] *Ibid.*, 287-88.

[17] *Ibid.*, 314.

[18] *Ibid.*, 372.

[19] William Sanday, *Outlines of the Life of Christ* (New York: Charles Scribner's Sons, 1905), 176.

[20] Andrew Jukes, *The Characteristic Differences of the Four Gospels* (New York: Fleming H. Revell Company, n.d.), 150.

[21] Morgan, *op. cit.*, 383-84.

PERSPECTIVE

The Crucifixion of Christ by Frederic W. Farrar

The sun was westering as the darkness rolled away from the completed sacrifice. They who had not thought it a pollution to inaugurate their feast by the murder of their Messiah were seriously alarmed lest the sanctity of the following day—which began at sunset—should be compromised by the hanging of the corpses on the cross. And, horrible to relate, the crucified often lived for many hours—nay, even for two or three days—in their torture. The Jews therefore begged Pilate that their legs might be broken, and their bodies taken down. This *crurifragium*, as it was called, consisted in striking the legs of the sufferers with a heavy mallet, a violence which seemed always to have hastened, if it did not instantly cause, their death. Nor would the Jews be the only persons who would be anxious to hasten the end by giving the deadly blow. Until life was extinct, the soldiers appointed to guard the execution dared not leave the ground. The wish, therefore, was readily granted. The soldiers broke the legs of the two malefactors first, and then, coming to Jesus, found that the great cry had been indeed His last, and that He was dead already. They did not, therefore, break His legs, and thus unwittingly preserved the symbolism of that Paschal lamb, of which He was the antitype, and of which it had been commanded that "a bone of it shall not be broken." And yet, as He might be only in a syncope—as instances had been known in which men apparently dead had been taken down from the cross and resuscitated, and as the lives of the soldiers would have had to answer for any irregularity—one of them, in order to make death certain, drove the broad head of his *hasta* into His side. The wound, as it was meant to do, pierced the region of the heart, and "forthwith," says St. John, with an emphatic appeal to the truthfulness of his eye-witness—an appeal which would be singularly blasphemous if his narrative were the forgery which so much elaborate modern criticism has wholly failed to prove that it is—"forthwith came there out blood and water." Whether the water was due to some abnormal pathological conditions caused by the dreadful complication of the Savior's sufferings—or whether it rather means that the pericardium had been rent by the spear-point, and that those who took down the body observed some drops of its serum mingled with the blood—in either case that lance-thrust was sufficient to hush all the heretical assertions that Jesus had only seemed to die: and as it assured the soldiers, so should it assure all who have doubted, that He, who on the third day rose again, had in truth been crucified, dead, and buried, and that His soul had passed into the unseen world.[1]

---

[1] Frederic W. Farrar, *The Life of Christ* (London: Cassell and Company, Limited, 1896), 633-34.

CONCLUSION
THE GLORY IN THE END

The spirit of the Lord God is upon me; because the Lord hath anointed me to preach good
tidings unto the meek;
he hath sent me to bind up the brokenhearted,
to proclaim liberty to the captives,
and the opening of the prison to them that are bound;
To proclaim the acceptable year of the Lord,
and the day of vengeance of our God; to comfort all that mourn;
To appoint unto them that mourn in Zion,
to give unto them beauty for ashes, the oil of joy for mourning,
the garment of praise for the spirit of heaviness;
that they might be called trees of righteousness, the planting of the Lord,
that he might be glorified.

ISAIAH 61:1-3

The Atonement will appear honorable and glorious, even in the destruction of those who reject it. The apostles' ministry was to God a sweet savor of Christ, even in them that perish; and so is the atonement itself. Its great and distinguished ends will have been answered, in the glory and the harmony of the divine perfections, in the eternal condemnation of sin, in the honor and safety of the divine government, in the "many crowns" of the Mediator, and in the salvation of countless millions of the human race. All holy and blessed intelligences will own, and approve, the justice of the condemnation of all the despisers of the way of salvation; and their punishment will be forever, to the universe, an awful monument, and example, of the evil of sinning against God. In the fixing of the eternal state of the universe, all holy intelligences are represented as singing, " AMEN, ALLELUA, WORTHY IS THE LAMB."[1]

-Thomas W. Jenkyn, *The Extent of the Atonement*

Having fully revealed Himself to His apostles as the Messiah promised, the time had now come for offering another testimony, in addition to the miracles performed, to the complete substantiation of His claims, in which God Himself was to be the witness. Therefore, while Jesus was praying on the mountain peak, somewhere near Caesarea Philippi, the proof of His divinity suddenly blazed up in a cloud of glory, to dazzle, bewilder and to awe the three disciples. "And as he prayed, He was transfigured before them; the fashion of His countenance was altered, and His face did shine as the sun, and His raiment was as white as the light, glistening and shining exceeding white as snow; so as no fuller on earth can white them. And behold, there talked with Him two men, which were Moses and Elias: who appeared in glory, and spoke of His decease which He should accomplish at Jerusalem. But Peter and they that were with him were heavy with sleep; and when they were awake, they saw His glory, and the two men that stood with Him."

Oh, what wondrous, sublime, ecstatic spectacle! Behold this glorious vision! Jesus had heretofore appeared to His disciples and the multitudes as only a servant, a man so merciful that His heart was always bursting with sympathy; so kind that His eyes spoke benedictions upon all who came to claim His help; so generous, that He gave up everything and worked unceasingly that the suffering might be able to share all His bounty. They had seen Him pale and faint from protracted exertion in His mission of immeasurable mercy; His feet blistered from hard travel over dusty highways, and rugged steeps and rocky valleys; they had seen Him reviled, traduced, persecuted by mendacious Pharisees, who sowed His paths with slander, and set crowds against Him by the vilest of all possible misrepresentations. But now behold the everlasting testimony of that great Trinity of which God Himself stood at the head. See how His benign face shines like a blazing sun, and how His worn raiment scintillates with ineffable light radiating from His precious body. Glory on His head, and at His feet, and holding Him in the sublimation of Messianic splendor, and the super-exaltation of transfiguration.[2]

-T. DeWitt Talmage, *From Manger to Throne*

---

[1] Thomas W. Jenkyn, *The Extent of the Atonement in Its Relation to God and the Universe* (Boston: Gould and Lincoln, 1859), 368.

[2] T. DeWitt Talmage, *From Manger to Throne* (Philadelphia: Historical Publishing Company, 1889), 413.

Figure C-1. Raphael: The Transfiguration

This painting is really two pictures in one: The Transfiguration (upper half) and the Healing of the Epileptic Boy (lower half). This masterpiece is not only "a supreme work of character-interpretation, but an expression of the deepest truth of life. And what is that truth? That man needs a Savior; and that to save us God in his love has given us Christ, a realization of transfigured and redeemed humanity."[3]

At His crucifixion there would be assembled beneath the cross of Christ a wide spectrum of human need and depravity, much like that represented in the scene so wonderfully portrayed by Raphael in the lower portion of The Transfiguration. It was for these people, which represent all mankind in every age—for you and me—that the Scriptures declared: *"And the Lord hath laid on him the iniquity of us all"* (Isaiah 53:6b). By placing our faith in the finished work of Christ, we can have our share in that glorified state, which His Transfiguration prefigured, and give thanks to the Father, *"Who hath delivered us from the power of darkness, and hath translated us into the Kingdom of his dear Son"* (Col. 1:13).

---

[3] Albert Edward Bailey, *The Gospel in Art* (Boston: The Pilgrim Press, 1946), 245.

Chapter Sixteen

The Representative Crowd and the Redeemed Church

In the letter to the Hebrews, the unknown but gifted author reminded his Jewish readers that God *"at sundry times and in diverse manners spake in time past unto the fathers by the prophets"* (Heb. 1:1). And yet, while the Old Testament prophets predicted both the suffering and the glory of the Messiah, they did not clearly understand those things about which they spoke. To the strangers scattered throughout Asia Minor, the Apostle Peter wrote:

> *Of which salvation the prophets have enquired and searched diligently, who prophesied of the grace that should come unto you: Searching what, or what manner of time the Spirit of Christ which was in them did signify, when it testified beforehand the sufferings of Christ, and the glory that should follow. Unto whom it was revealed, that not unto themselves, but unto us they did minister the things, which are now reported unto you by them that have preached the gospel unto you with the Holy Ghost sent down from heaven: which things the angels desired to look into.* 1 Pet. 1:10-12

Returning to where we left off in the letter to the Hebrews, we read that God *"hath in these last days spoken unto us by his Son"* (Heb. 1:2). And from the many profound and poignant statements that could be cited, our attention is drawn to the words addressed to certain Greeks *"that came up to worship at the feast"* (John 12:20). Just prior to the Passover and His own sacrificial death, Jesus declared:

> *Now is the judgment of this world: now shall the prince of this world be cast out. And I, if I be lifted up from the earth, will draw all men unto me.* John 12:31-32

When Jesus was hanging on the cross, deserted of men and seemingly of God, the crowd cried out, "He trusted in God; let him deliver him now, if he desireth him." If God should deliver him, it would be a proof that he was good and pleasing to God; but if not, then it was sure proof that God did not desire him. So they thought. God did not deliver him. But he did something better.[1]

As a result of His being lifted up on the cross, the ultimate victory over Satan was assured, as well as the judgment upon all those who reject Christ's substitutionary death. However, His saving grace was also made available not only to all those of true faith who witnessed His death, but to people of every type and character in every age, which are represented by those who were assembled beneath the cross.

> Standing back and gazing out upon that mixed multitude, we notice the women, the soldiers, the malefactors, the centurion, the chief priests, the members of the Sanhedrin, the group of His own disciples, and in addition to these, the vast multitudes of people from the whole surrounding country. All sorts and conditions of men are gathered to the Cross, representative crowds, the whole scene being a picture and a prophecy of how, through all the centuries, every sort and condition would be gathered to the uplifted Cross of the Son of man.[2]

All four of the Gospel writers indicate that a superscription was placed on the cross, which read, *"THIS IS JESUS, THE KING OF THE JEWS"* (Matt. 27:37). Furthermore, this was written in the three great languages of that day, so that the entire world could be confronted with the reality of the situation in their own tongue.

At the time of Christ's life and death, the three great world forces were all represented in that land of Palestine, and it is not without deep significance that over His Cross these words were written in letters of Hebrew, and Latin, and Greek, the national language, the official language, the common language; the language of religion, the language of government, and the language of culture. The attitude of all the forces represented by these things was antagonistic to Christ. Out of the religion of the time, the Hebrew, arose the inspiration of the crucifixion, while the power of the time, the Roman, was the agent for its execution, and the culture of the time, the Greek, was scornfully indifferent to Him and His claims. Sinful religion rejected Him, sinful power murdered Him, sinful culture neglected Him. He was cast out.[3]

But yet, *"the stone which the builders rejected, the same is become the head of the corner"* (Matt. 21:42), and the Church was built upon it. The Apostle Peter wrote:

> *Wherefore also it is contained in the scripture, Behold, I lay in Sion a chief corner stone, elect, precious: and he that believeth on him shall not be confounded. Unto you therefore which believe he is precious: but unto them which be disobedient, the stone which the builders disallowed, the same is made the head of the corner, And a stone of stumbling, and a rock of offence, even to them which stumble at the word, being disobedient: whereunto also they were appointed. But ye are a chosen generation, a royal priesthood, an holy nation, a peculiar people; that ye should shew forth the praises of him who hath called you out of darkness into his marvelous light.* 1 PET. 2:6-9

The four Gospels were written to commend Jesus to a world engulfed in darkness, in order to bring them into His marvelous light. As such, they constitute the perfect and perpetual witness "for the world of the ages subsequent to the apostolic."[4] Dr. Gregory wrote:

> Not only is it ever true that man is a sinner and needs the good news of Christ's incarnation, life, death, and resurrection; but it remains equally true that the world of mankind is always divided into the same great classes and always exhibits the same generic phases of thought. In all ages the Jewish, Roman, and Greek natures reappear among men, and, in fact, make up the world of natural men; while the Christian nature and wants likewise remain essentially identical. From age to age the four Gospels appeal to the classes who, in temperament, mental constitution, training, and modes of thought, are like those for whom of old, in obedience to the inspiring breath of God, they were prepared. Thus it is that these brief but all-important productions have had power to captivate men by a perpetual fitness and a perennial freshness.
>
> For the man with nature inclined to bow to authority, to appreciate divine religious forms, to exalt the peculiar position of the people of God, and to trace the marvelous plan of God in the preparation for the Messiah and in the progress of his kingdom, the Gospel which Matthew wrote for the Jew must possess a permanent absorbing interest.
>
> For the man of power, reverencing law, given to action, fitted to be an actor or leader in pushing forward the conquest of the world for Christ, the Gospel which Mark wrote for the Roman must retain its old significance and an ever-potent inspiration as the battle-call of the Almighty Conqueror.

For the man of reason and taste, of philosophic and aesthetic culture, the man longing for the perfect manhood, cherishing a world-wide sympathy with mankind, delighting to contemplate the universal reach of the grace of God the Father to sinners, the Gospel which Luke wrote for the Greek must maintain an increasing reasonableness and an undying influence as the voicing of the infinite Reason of the one Divine Man.

For the man of faith saved by the incarnation and atonement of the Son of God, the man of the new and divine life of obedience and devotion to Christ, the man enlightened, guided, and helped by the Holy Ghost, the Gospel which John wrote for the Christian Church cannot fail to retain an immortal fascination and to furnish a supreme satisfaction as the utterance of God's eternal Word to the believing soul.

It is on this wise that the one Gospel of God in four-fold form, which was exactly fitted to commend Jesus of Nazareth to the ancient world, and which could not then have been put in other shape without a radical change in the races and history of the apostolic age, is still so perfectly adapted to meet the wants of the modern world, that it would require a revolution in the mental structure and experience of man, before any other number of Gospels or any different ones from the four in the New Testament could meet the necessities of ruined and redeemed humanity. God appears, therefore, in his Word no less that in his world, as a God of order. The same perfect, divine plan which science is finding in the latter, a rational and reverential study finds in the former. The Gospels are the perfect thought of God for the restoration of a lost world.[5]

The death of Jesus Christ has become "the pathway of deliverance for those who at the Cross turn from the things the Cross condemns, to put their trust in Him."[6] My prayer is that you, dear reader, have made your way to the Cross, and can say with the hymn-writer:

Beneath the cross of Jesus I fain would take my stand,
The shadow of a mighty Rock within a weary land,
A home within the wilderness, a rest upon the way,
From the burning of the noontide heat, and the burdens of the day.

Upon that cross of Jesus mine eye at times can see
The very dying form of One who suffered there for me;
And from my smitten heart with tears, two wonders I confess:
The wonders of His glorious love and my unworthiness.

I take, O cross, thy shadow for my abiding place;
I ask no other sunshine that the sunshine of His face;
Content to let the world go by, to know no gain nor loss,
My sinful self my only shame, my glory all, the cross![7]

346 Conclusion: The Glory in the End

Chapter Sixteen Notes

[1] E. Stanley Jones, *Christ and Human Suffering* (New York: The Abingdom Press, 1933), 20.

[2] G. Campbell Morgan, *The Crises of the Christ* (Old Tappan, N.J.: Fleming H. Revell Company, 1936), 332.

[3] *Ibid.*, 306-07.

[4] D. S. Gregory, *Why Four Gospels? Or, the Gospel for All the World* (New York: Funk & Wagnalls, Publishers, 1890), 346.

[5] *Ibid.*, 346-48.

[6] Morgan, *op. cit.* 343-44.

[7] Elizabeth C. Clephane, *Beneath the Cross of Jesus* (1868).

POSTSCRIPT

The Scene at the Cross by Frederic W. Farrar

It was now noon, and at the Holy City the sunshine should have been burning over that scene of horror with a power such as it has in the zenith of an English summer-time. But instead of this, the face of the heavens was black, and the noonday sun was "turned into darkness," on "this great and terrible day of the Lord." It could have been no darkness of any natural eclipse, for the Paschal moon was at the full; but it was one of those "signs from heaven" for which, during the ministry of Jesus, the Pharisees had so often clamoured in vain. . . . But whatever it was, it clearly filled the minds of all who beheld it with yet deeper misgiving. The taunts and jeers of the Jewish priests and the heathen soldiers were evidently confined to the earlier part of the crucifixion. Its later stages seem to have thrilled alike the guilty and the innocent with emotions of dread and horror. Of the incidents of those last hours we are told nothing, and that awful obscuration of the noonday sun may well have overawed every heart into an inaction respecting which there was nothing to relate. What Jesus suffered then for us men and our salvation we cannot know, for during those hours He hung upon His cross in silence and darkness; or, if He spoke, there were none there to record His words. But towards the close of that time His anguish culminated, and—emptied to the very uttermost of that glory which He had since the world began—drinking to the deepest dregs the cup of humiliation and bitterness—enduring, not only to have taken upon Him the form of a servant, but also to suffer the last infamy which human hatred could impose on perfect helplessness—He uttered that mysterious cry, of which the full significance will never be fathomed by man—

"ELI, ELI, LAMA SABACHTHANI? ("My God, my God, why hast Thou forsaken Me?")

In those words, quoting the Psalm in which the early Fathers rightly saw a far-off prophecy of the whole passion of Christ, He borrowed from David's utter agony the expression of His own. In that hour He was alone. He was sinking from depth to depth of unfathomable suffering, until, at the close approach to a death which—because He was God, and yet had been made man—was more awful to Him than it could ever be to any of the sons of men, it seemed as if even His Divine Humanity could endure no more.

Doubtless the voice of the Sufferer—though uttered loudly in that paroxysm of an emotion which, in another, would almost have touched the verge of despair—was yet rendered more uncertain and indistinct from the condition of exhaustion in which He hung; and so, amid the darkness, and confused noise, and dull footsteps of the moving multitude, there were some who did not hear what He had said. They had caught only the first syllable, and said to one another that He had called on the name of Elijah. The readiness with which they seized this false impression is another proof of the excitement and terror—the involuntary dread of something unforeseen, and terrible—to which they had been reduced from their former savage insolence. For Elijah, the great prophet of the Old Covenant, was inextricably mingled with all the Jewish expectations of a Messiah, and these expectations were full of wrath. The coming of Elijah would be the coming of a day of fire, in which the sun should be turned into blackness and the moon into blood, and the powers of heaven should be shaken. Already the noonday sun was shrouded in unnatural eclipse: might not some awful form at any moment rend the heavens and come down, touch the mountains and they should smoke? The vague anticipation of conscious guilt was unfulfilled. Not such as yet was to be the method of God's workings. His messages to man for many ages more were not to be in the thunder and earthquake, not in rushing wind or roaring flame, but in the "still small voice" speaking always amid the apparent silences of Time in whispers intelligible to man's heart, but in which there is neither speech nor language, though the voice is heard.[1]

[1] Frederic W. Farrar, *The Life of Christ* (London: Cassell and Company, Limited, 1896), 627-29.

Appendix A

SUMMARY CHART OF THE CHARACTERISTIC DIFFERENCES OF THE FOUR GOSPELS				
	MATTHEW	MARK	LUKE	JOHN
PORTRAIT OF CHRIST	SON OF DAVID	SERVANT OF GOD	SON OF MAN	SON OF GOD
ROLE OF CHRIST	KING	PROPHET	PRIEST	REDEEMER
HOW CHRIST INTRODUCED	BY GENEALOGY	BY CHARACTER	BY FAMILY SURROUNDINGS	AS FROM ETERNITY
OPENING SCENE IN GOSPEL	BETHLEHEM	WILDERNESS	TEMPLE	WITH GOD BEFORE TIME
FOR WHOM WRITTEN	JEWS	ROMANS	GREEKS	CHRISTIANS
FOCUS OF AUDIENCE	PAST	PRESENT	FUTURE	ETERNAL
DISPOSITION OF AUDIENCE	RELIGIOUS	PRACTICAL	INTELLECTUAL	SPIRITUAL
LITERARY CHARACTERISTIC	DIDACTIC	DESCRIPTIVE	HISTORICAL	SYMBOLIC
MAJOR THEME	RIGHTEOUSNESS	POWER	UNIVERSAL WITNESS	BELIEF
KEY VERSE	5:20	10:45	2:10	20:31

Appendix B

A Case Study of The Characteristic Differences of the Gospels: A Look at the Four Accounts of Christ's Resurrection and Subsequent Appearances

An Examination of Matthew's Account

> *In the end of the Sabbath, as it began to dawn toward the first day of the week, came Mary Magdalene and the other Mary to see the sepulcher. And, behold, there was a great earthquake: for the angel of the Lord descended from heaven, and came and rolled back the stone from the door, and sat upon it.* 28:1-2

In Matthew's account of Christ's birth, we find that the angel of the Lord had on several occasions appeared to Joseph (cf. 1:20, 24; 2:13, 19). The angel of the Lord would have special interest for the Jews, who were looking for signs of the promised Messiah. Here at the resurrection, only Matthew tells us that the stone was rolled away by the angel of the Lord. The other three accounts just inform us that the stone was rolled away (cf. Mark 16:4; Luke 24:2; John 20:1).

Additionally, only Matthew tells us that there was a great earthquake. This again would catch the attention of the Jews, who were always requiring a sign (cf. 1 Cor. 1:22).

> *His countenance was like lightning, and his raiment white as snow.*
> *And for fear of him the keepers did shake, and became as dead men.*
> 28:3-4

The description of the angel is more elaborate than in the other accounts, and resembles what Daniel saw in his visions (cf. Dan. 7:9; 10:6). A face that had *the appearance of lightning*, and clothing that was *white as snow*, would be familiar expressions to those versed in the Old Testament Scriptures.

> *And the angel answered and said unto the women, Fear not ye: for I know that ye seek Jesus, which was crucified. He is not here: for he is risen, as he said. Come, see the place where the Lord lay.* 28:5-6

Notice here the emphasis the angel places on what the Lord had said: He is risen, as he said. What a King says is very important!

> *And go quickly, and tell his disciples that he is risen from the dead; and, behold, he goeth before you into Galilee; there shall ye see him: lo, I have told you.* 28:7

The phrase *goeth before you* could be translated "leadeth you." Another important characteristic of a King is his ability to lead his people.

> *And they departed quickly from the sepulcher with fear and great joy; and did run to bring his disciples word. And as they went to tell his disciples, behold Jesus met them, saying, All hail. And they came and held him by the feet, and worshipped him.* 28:8-9

They fell at Jesus' feet, and worshipped him. Only Matthew relates the homage and prostration of these women in the presence of their King. Matthew uses the word "worship" about 20 times in his Gospel, whereas the other synoptic accounts only use it a couple of times. This emphasis on worship is to be expected in a narrative of the King.

> *Then said Jesus unto them, Be not afraid: go tell my brethren that they go into Galilee, and there shall they see me.* 28:10

This verse is peculiar to Matthew's account, and is another example of the King giving a command.

> Now when they were going, behold, some of the watch came into the city, and shewed unto the chief priests all the things that were done. And when they were assembled with the elders, and had taken counsel, they gave large money unto the soldiers, Saying, Say ye, His disciples came by night, and stole him away while we slept. And if this come to the governor's ear, we will persuade him, and secure you. So they took the money, and did as they were taught: and this saying is commonly reported among the Jews until this day. 28:11-15

This interesting portion of narrative, about the report of the guards, the conspiracy, the bribery of large sums of money, etc., is unique to Matthew's Gospel. It is no surprise to find this plot recorded here, because conspiracy against a King is not something that is unusual or unexpected. There are always conspiracies against a King.

> Then the eleven disciples went away into Galilee, into a mountain where Jesus had appointed them. And when they saw him, they worshipped him: but some doubted. 28:16-17

These verses are unique to Matthew's account, and show that the disciples obeyed the command of their King, and also worshipped Him, as did the women in verse 9.

> And Jesus came and spake unto them, saying, All power is given unto me in heaven and in earth. Go ye therefore, and teach all nations, baptizing them in the name of the Father, and of the Son, and of the Holy Ghost: Teaching them to observe all things whatsoever I have commanded you: and, lo, I am with you alway, even unto the end of the world. 28:18-20

This, of course, is the Great Commission, which is the King's instructions to his followers to *observe all things whatsoever I have commanded you*. Note also that the King claimed that *All power is given me in heaven and in earth*. A King with no power would not be a very effective King. But this is not the case here. The Lord even told the disciples that He would be with them always, *even unto the end of the world*. We note here, then, a royal command, a royal claim, and a royal promise. Jesus Christ is King, as clearly revealed in Matthew's account.

An Examination of Mark's Account

> And when the Sabbath was past, Mary Magdalene, and Mary the mother of James, and Salome, had brought sweet spices, that they might come and anoint him. 16:1

Mark addressed his account to the Romans, who were a very practical people. Here he tells his readers why the women came to the tomb. Matthew just said they came to see the sepulcher.

> And very early in the morning the first day of the week, they came unto the sepulcher at the rising of the sun. And they said among themselves, Who shall roll us away the stone from the door of the sepulcher? 16:2-3

Mark here explains the problem the women were concerned about—how to get into the tomb. Again, the Romans were a practical people, and would be interested in these kinds of things.

> And when they looked, they saw that the stone was rolled away: for it was very great. And entering into the sepulcher, they saw a young man sitting on the right side, clothed in a long white garment; and they were affrighted. 16:4-5

Compare this description of the angel to that of Matthew's account. Mark merely says that he was a young man. The Romans did not have the same attitude towards angels as did the Jews.

And he saith unto them, Be not affrighted: Ye seek Jesus of Nazareth, which was crucified: he is risen; he is not here: behold the place where they laid him. 16:6

Mark notes that the angel said Christ was risen, but does not add the words *"as he said."* Mark does not portray Christ as King, but presents Him as the Servant of God.

But go your way, tell his disciples and Peter that he goeth before you into Galilee: there shall ye see him, as he said unto you. And they went out quickly, and fled from the sepulcher; for they trembled and were amazed: neither said they any thing to any man for they were afraid. Now when Jesus was risen early the first day of the week, he appeared first to Mary Magdalene, out of whom he had cast seven devils. 16:7-9

A servant is noted for the things he is able to do. This is the emphasis in Mark's Gospel of the Servant. We see here what Jesus did for Mary Magdalene. It was she *out of whom he cast seven devils.*

And she went and told them that had been with him, as they mourned and wept. And they, when they had heard that he was alive, and had been seen of her, believed not. After that he appeared in another form unto two of them, as they walked, and went into the country. And they went and told it unto the residue: neither believed they them. Afterward he appeared unto the eleven as they sat at meat, and upbraided them with their unbelief and hardness of heart, because they believed not them which had seen him after he was risen. 16:10-14

The emphasis in Mark's Gospel is what Jesus as the Servant of God does, rather than what He says. Note what Jesus is doing in these verses. He appeared first to Mary Magdalene in verse 9, then He appeared in another form unto two of them in verse 12, and then afterward he appeared unto the eleven in verse 14. The emphasis, even after Christ's resurrection, is still on what He is doing.

And he said unto them, Go ye into all the world, and preach the gospel to every creature. He that believeth and is baptized shall be saved; but he that believeth not shall be damned. And these signs shall follow them that believe; In my name shall they cast out devils; they shall speak with new tongues; They shall take up serpents; and if they drink any deadly thing, it shall not hurt them; they shall lay hands on the sick, and they shall recover. 16:15-18

Here we see what those who continue the work of the Servant of God will be able to do and accomplish after the Lord's departure. Nevertheless, note what Mark tells us in conclusion:

So then after the Lord had spoken unto them, he was received up into heaven, and sat on the right hand of God. And they went forth, and preached every where, the Lord working with them, and confirming the word with signs following. 16:19-20

After the Lord's ascension, we see that He *sat on the right hand of God.* The emphasis is still on what the Servant is doing. At the same time, however, as the disciples went forth and preached, we find that the Servant of God was still working with them. Mark portrays the faithful Servant, and His credentials are His abilities to work, and to *confirm the word with signs following.*

An Examination of Luke's Account

Now upon the first day of the week, very early in the morning, they came unto the sepulcher, bringing the spices which they had prepared, and certain others with them. And they found the stone rolled away from the sepulcher. And they entered in, and found not the body of the Lord Jesus. 24:1-3

Luke emphasizes the humanity of the Lord, and it is of interest to note here that the women *found not the body*. Luke was a physician, and only he uses this word in this context.

> *And it came to pass, as they were much perplexed thereabout, behold, two men stood by them in shining garments:* 24:4

Luke addressed his Gospel to the Greeks, who represented the thinking man of the ancient world. Note here and elsewhere Luke's emphasis on the thought processes of the people: *they were much perplexed*. Like Mark, Luke refers to the angels as men, rather then angels.

> *And as they were afraid, and bowed down their faces to the earth, they said unto them, Why seek ye the living among the dead?* 24:5

Because Luke is writing to the thinking Greek, he records the question the angels asked the women: *Why seek ye the living among the dead?* Questions, as Socrates knew and employed so well, were designed to stimulate thought.

> *He is not here, but is risen: remember how he spake unto you when he was yet in Galilee, Saying, The Son of man must be delivered into the hands of sinful men, and be crucified, and the third day rise again. And they remembered his words, And returned from the sepulcher, and told all these things unto the eleven, and to all the rest.* 24:6-9

More emphasis on the thought processes of man is to be noted here: *Remember how he spake unto you. . . . And they remembered his words.*

These followers of Christ may have also remembered—or at least been familiar with—the words He spoke as recorded in Luke chapter 3: *That God is able of these stones to raise up children unto Abraham* (v. 8). The Greeks could raise up some pretty amazing structures out of stone, but they could never make them live. God could not only raise the dead, but raise people up from stones if needs be.

> *It was Mary Magdalene, and Joanna, and Mary the mother of James, and other women that were with them, which told these things unto the apostles.* 24:10

Luke's narrative places a special emphasis on women, as noted here and throughout his Gospel.

> *And their words seemed to them as idle tales, and they believed them not. Then arose Peter, and ran unto the sepulcher; and stooping down, he beheld the linen clothes laid by themselves, and departed, wondering in himself at that which was come to pass.* 24:11-12

Luke is the Gospel of humanity, and we see here glimpses of true human behavior. Unlike Matthew and Mark, Luke tells us that Peter *ran unto the sepulcher*, and when he departed, we are told that he was *wondering in himself at that which was come to pass*.

> *And, behold, two of them went that same day to a village called Emmaus, which was from Jerusalem about threescore furlongs. And they talked together of all these things which had happened. And it came to pass, that, while they communed together and reasoned, Jesus himself drew near, and went with them. But their eyes were holden that they should not know him. And he said unto them, What manner of communications are these that ye have one to another, as ye walk, and are sad? And one of them, whose name was Cleopas, answering said unto him, Art thou only a stranger in Jerusalem, and hast not known the things which are come to pass there in these days? And he said unto them, What things? And they said unto him, Concerning Jesus of Nazareth, which was a prophet mighty in deed and word before God and all the people: And how the chief priests and our rulers delivered him to be condemned to death, and have crucified him. But we trusted that it had been he which should*

*have redeemed Israel: and beside all this, to day is the third day since these things were done.
Yea, and certain women also of our company made us astonished, which were early at the
sepulcher; And when they found not his body, they came, saying that they had also seen a
vision of angels, which said that he was alive. And certain of them which were with us went
to the sepulcher, and found it even so as the women had said: but him they saw not. Then he
said unto them, O fools, and slow of heart to believe all that the prophets have spoken:
Ought not Christ to have suffered these things, and to enter into his glory?* 24:13-26

This section begins that great portion of Scripture that is unique to Luke's Gospel—Jesus' appearance to two disciples on the road to Emmaus. This wonderful episode would be of special interest to the Greeks. Note the references to their interac-
tions and contemplations: *they talked together of all these things* (v. 14); *they communed together
and reasoned* (v. 15); *their eyes were holden that they should not know him* (v. 16); *we trusted that
it had been he* (v. 21); and *certain women . . . made us astonished* (v.22), *who had also seen a
vision of angels* (v. 23). Note also the many questions that were asked one to another:
What manner of communications are these that ye have one to another, as ye walk, and are sad?
(v.17); *Art thou only a stranger in Jerusalem, and hast not known the things which are come to pass
there in these days?* (v.18); *What things?* (v. 19); and *Ought not Christ to have suffered these things,
and to enter into his glory?* (v. 26).

*And beginning at Moses and all the prophets, he expounded unto them in all the scriptures
the things concerning himself. And they drew nigh unto the village, whither they went: and he
made as though he would have gone further. But they constrained him, saying, Abide with us:
for it is toward evening, and the day is far spent. And he went in to tarry with them. And it
came to pass, as he sat at meat with them, he took bread, and blessed it, and brake, and gave
to them. And their eyes were opened, and they knew him; and he vanished out of their sight.
And they said one to another, Did not our heart burn within us, while he talked with us by
the way, and while he opened to us the scriptures? And they rose up the same hour, and returned to Jerusalem, and found the eleven gathered together, and them that were with them,
Saying, The Lord is risen indeed, and hath appeared to Simon. And they told what things
were done in the way, and how he was known of them in breaking of bread.* 24:27-35

This section concludes that wonderful episode that begun on the road to Emmaus.
Here we find that the Lord takes time to clarify things for these two disciples. *And beginning at Moses and all the prophets, he expounded unto them in all the scriptures the things concerning
himself* (v. 27). Nevertheless, it wasn't until Christ *sat at meat with them* (v. 30) that *their eyes
were opened* (v.31), and they really knew who He was. It is a most human and touching
story, as the two disciples reviewed the events of the day, and *said one to another, Did not
our heart burn within us, while he talked with us by the way, and while he opened to us the scriptures?* (v. 32). Of interest to note is that the Lord was finally revealed to these disciples
in a most human way—*he was known of them in breaking of bread* (v. 35).

*And as they thus spake, Jesus himself stood in the midst of them, and saith unto them, Peace
be unto you. But they were terrified and affrighted, and supposed that they had seen a spirit.
And he said unto them, Why are ye troubled? And why do thoughts arise in your hearts?
Behold my hands and my feet, that it is I myself: handle me, and see; for a spirit hath not
flesh and bones, as ye see me have. And when he had thus spoken, he shewed them his hands
and his feet. And while they yet believed not for joy, and wondered, he said unto them, Have
ye here any meat? And they gave him a piece of a broiled fish, and of an honeycomb. And he
took it, and did eat before them.* 24:36-43

Jesus stood in the midst of the disciples, and after posing a few questions to them in verse 38, He says: *"Behold my hands and my feet, that it is I myself: handle me, and see; for a spirit hath not flesh and bones, as ye see me have"* (v.39). Jesus also demonstrated the reality of His resurrected humanity by eating a piece of broiled fish before them (vv. 42-43).

> *And he said unto them, These are the words which I spake unto you, while I was yet with you, that all things must be fulfilled, which were written in the law of Moses, and in the prophets, and in the psalms, concerning me. Then opened he their understanding, that they might understand the scriptures.* 24:44-45

Socrates, Plato, and Aristotle were trying to open the understanding of their listeners, but they never communicated to their audiences those things that enabled them to understand the Scriptures. Jesus Christ, on the other hand, was able to do for His disciples what the Greek philosophers were never able to accomplish—*then opened he their understanding, that they might understand the scriptures.* An understanding of the Holy Scriptures is what the thinking Greeks needed to focus their attentions on.

> *And said unto them, Thus it is written, and thus it behoved Christ to suffer, and to rise from the dead the third day: And that repentance and remission of sins should be preached in his name among all nations, beginning at Jerusalem. And ye are witnesses of these things.* 24:46-48

An Examination of John's Account

> *The first day of the week cometh Mary Magdalene early, when it was yet dark, unto the sepulcher, and seeth the stone taken away from the sepulcher.*
> *Then she runneth, and cometh to Simon Peter, and to the other disciple, whom Jesus loved, and saith unto them, They have taken away the Lord out of the sepulcher, and we know not where they have laid him.* 20:1-2

John's Gospel is different from the first three narratives, which have much material in common to each other. Note first of all that the stone is matter-of-factly rolled away, with no explanation as to how this came about. Furthermore, John records Mary's words at finding the tomb empty as: *"They have taken away the **Lord** out of the sepulcher."* In Matthew's account, the angel told Mary Magdalene: *"Fear not ye: for I know that ye seek **Jesus**, which was crucified"* (Matt. 28:5). In Mark's account, Mary Magdalene came to the tomb in order to anoint **him** (Mark 16:1); and the angel said: *"Ye seek **Jesus** of Nazareth, which was crucified"* (v. 6). In Luke's account the *women entered the tomb and found not the* **body** (Luke 24:3). John's Gospel emphasizes the deity of Jesus Christ, and refers to Him as **Lord**.

> *Peter therefore went forth, and that other disciple, and came to the sepulcher. So they ran both together: and the other disciple did outrun Peter, and came first to the sepulcher. And he stooping down, and looking in, saw the linen clothes lying; yet went he not in. Then cometh Simon Peter following him, and went into the sepulcher, and seeth the linen clothes lie, And the napkin, that was about his head, not lying with the linen clothes, but wrapped together in a place by itself. Then went in also that other disciple, which came first to the sepulcher, and he saw, and believed. For as yet they knew not the scripture, that he must rise again from the dead. Then the disciples went away again unto their own home.* 20:3-10

In this passage John makes no mention of any angels in the tomb. John wants to instill in his readers belief in Jesus as Lord and Savior, and it was enough for the disciples to be convinced of the resurrection by virtue of the empty tomb and the careful arrangement of the grave clothes that remained. As far as John himself was concerned, *he saw, and believed* (v.8). What did he believe? Not only that Christ was arisen, but that He was the divine Son of God. Nothing more than what John saw in the empty tomb was required for him to reach these conclusions.

> *But Mary stood without at the sepulcher weeping: and as she wept, she stooped down, and looked into the sepulcher, And seeth two angels in white sitting, the one at the head, and the other at the feet, where the body of Jesus had lain. And they say unto her, Woman, why weepest thou? She saith unto them, Because they have taken away my Lord, and I know not where they have laid him. And when she had thus said, she turned herself back, and saw Jesus standing, and knew not that it was Jesus. Jesus saith unto her, Woman, why weepest thou? Whom seekest thou? She, supposing him to be the gardner, saith unto him, Sir, if thou have borne him hence, tell me where thou hast laid him, and I will take him away. Jesus saith unto her, Mary. She turned herself, and saith unto him, Rabboni; which is to say, Master. Jesus saith unto her, Touch me not; for I am not yet ascended to my Father: but go to my brethren, and say unto them, I ascend unto my Father, and your Father; and to my God, and your God. Mary Magdalene came and told the disciples that she had seen the Lord, and that he had spoken these things unto her.* 20:11-18

Whereas John reasoned his way to the conclusion that Jesus was raised, and truly God, Mary Magdalene was convinced of these facts by the single spoken word of her name. The Lord now stands in a unique relationship to these followers of His, and He tells Mary Magdalene to say to the others: *"I ascend unto my Father, and your Father; and to my God, and your God"* (v.17). She is no longer to have the same earthly relationship she once had, for He told her, *"Touch me not; for I am not yet ascended to my Father."*

Later in the same chapter John records that Jesus showed Himself to the other disciples, Thomas absent, but subsequently to him also. After granting Thomas the evidence he demanded, which was given to the other disciples eight days earlier, Thomas, too, believed on the risen Savior, and declared: *"My Lord and my God"* (20:28).

> *Jesus saith unto him, Thomas, because thou hast seen me, thou hast believed: blessed are they that have not seen, and yet have believed. And many other signs truly did Jesus in the presence of his disciples, which are not written in this book: But these are written, that ye might believe that Jesus is the Christ, the Son of God; and that believing ye might have life through his name.* 20:29-31

Appendix C: Test Your Knowledge of the Gospels

Part 1: Multiple-Choice Questions Regarding Specific Verses

Directions: Identify from which Gospel the following passages are found. A. Matthew; B. Mark; C. Luke; D. John. Place the letter (A, B, C, or D) on the line to the left of the verse. The correct answers are found at the end of the examination, together with references to parallel passages, if and when they exist. Many of the verses in this test, however, are unique to a particular Gospel.

Hint: These passages reveal either a major emphasis of the Gospel from which they are found, or an aspect of how Christ is therein portrayed. You may want to review the Summary Chart of the Characteristic Differences (Appendix A), as well as the case study of these differences (Appendix B) before you start.

Score: There are 150 verses in this test. Give yourself two (2) points for each correct answer, and divide this total by three (3). The result is your score as a percentage of 100. If you elect to take only a portion of the test, calculate your percentage score accordingly. For example, if you do only 50 verses, give yourself two (2) points for each correct answer. If you attempt 75 verses, your percentage is found by giving four (4) points for each correct response, and dividing the product by three (3).

Verses:

_____1.   The men of Ninevah shall rise in judgment with this generation, and shall condemn it: because they repented at the preaching of Jonas; and, behold, a greater than Jonas is here.

_____2.   For the kingdom of heaven is as a man traveling into a far country, who called his own servants, and delivered unto them his goods.

_____3.   And he commanded them to make all sit down by companies upon the green grass. And they sat down in ranks, by hundreds, and by fifties.

_____4.   And he withdrew himself into the wilderness, and prayed.

_____5.   And Jesus answered and said unto her, Martha, Martha, thou art careful and troubled about many things: But one thing is needful: and Mary hath chosen that good part, which shall not be taken away from her.

_____6.   Then shall the king say unto them on his right hand, Come, ye blessed of my Father, inherit the kingdom prepared for you from the foundation of the world.

_____7.   The queen of the south shall rise up in the judgment with this generation, and shall condemn it: for she came from the uttermost parts of the earth to hear the wisdom of Solomon; and, behold, a greater than Solomon is here.

_____8.   This beginning of miracles did Jesus in Cana of Galilee, and manifested forth his glory; and his disciples believed on him.

_____9.   Then said Pilate to the chief priests and to the people, I find no fault in this man.

_____10.   And he said unto him, If they hear not Moses and the prophets, neither will they be persuaded, though one rose from the dead.

_____11.   And Mary said, My soul doth magnify the Lord.

_____12.   And he came to Nazareth, where he had been brought up: and, as his custom was, he went into the synagogue on the Sabbath day, and stood up for to read.

_____13.   Blessed are the peacemakers: for they shall be called the children of God.

_____14.   And it came to pass, that, while they communed together and reasoned, Jesus himself drew near, and went with them.

_____15.   No man hath seen God at any time; the only begotten Son, which is in the bosom of the Father, he hath declared him.

_____16.   What man of you, having an hundred sheep, if he lose one of them, doth not leave the ninety and nine in the wilderness, and go after that which is lost, until he find it?

_____17.   But all this was done, that the scriptures of the prophets might be fulfilled. Then all the disciples forsook him, and fled.

_____18.   Marvel not that I said unto thee, Ye must be born again.

_____19.   Let your light so shine before men, that they may see your good works, and glorify your Father which is in heaven.

_____20.   Master, which is the great commandment in the law?

_____21.   And when they could not come nigh unto him for the press, they uncovered the roof where he was: and when they had broken it up, they let down the bed wherein in the sick of the palsy lay.

_____22.   And they remembered his words.

_____23.   And Jesus said unto him, Verily I say unto thee, To day shalt thou be with me in paradise.

_____24.   And his father Zacharias was filled with the Holy Ghost, and prophesied, saying, Blessed be the Lord God of Israel; for he hath visited and redeemed his people.

_____25.   Then said Jesus unto the twelve, Will ye also go away? Then Simon Peter answered him, Lord, to whom shall we go? Thou hast the words of eternal life.

_____26.   Then shall the kingdom of heaven be likened unto ten virgins, which took their lamps, and went forth to meet the bridegroom.

_____27.   And Jesus came and spake unto them, saying, All power is given unto me in heaven and in earth.

_____28.   And all the people were amazed, and said, Is not this the son of David?

_____29.   Then Jesus said unto them, Verily, verily, I say unto you, Moses gave you not that bread from heaven; but my Father giveth you the true bread from heaven.

_____30.   And he said unto them, Come ye yourselves apart into a desert place, and rest a while: for there were many coming and going, and they had no leisure so much as to eat.

_____31.   And Jesse begat David the king; and David the king begat Solomon of her that had been the wife of Urias.

_____32.   And they departed, and went through the towns, preaching the gospel, and healing everywhere.

_____33.   And when he rose up from prayer, and was come to his disciples, he found them sleeping for sorrow.

_____34.   And there were set there six waterpots of stone, after the manner of the purifying of the Jews, containing two or three firkins apiece.

_____35.   And in the sixth month the angel Gabriel was sent from God unto a city of Galilee, named Nazareth, to a virgin espoused to a man whose name was Joseph, of the house of David; and the virgin's name was Mary.

_____36.   Now when all the people were baptized, it came to pass, that Jesus also being baptized, and praying, the heaven was opened.

_____37.   And he said, Lord, I believe. And he worshipped him.

_____38.   Then came together unto him the Pharisees, and certain of the scribes, which came from Jerusalem. And when they saw some of his disciples eat bread with defiled, that is to say, with unwashen, hands, they found fault. For the Pharisees, and all the Jews, except they wash their hands oft, eat not, holding the tradition of the elders.

_____39.   This is he of whom I said, After me cometh a man which is preferred before me: for he was before me.

_____40.   Then arose Peter, and ran unto the sepulcher; and stooping down, he beheld the linen clothes laid by themselves, and departed, wondering in himself at that which was come to pass.

_____41.   Then said Jesus unto them again, Verily, verily, I say unto you, I am the door of the sheep.

_____42.   And the Word was made flesh, and dwelt among us, (and we beheld his glory as of the only begotten of the Father,) full of grace and truth.

_____43.   When any one heareth the word of the kingdom, and understandeth it not, then cometh the wicked one, and catcheth away that which was sown in his heart. This is he which received seed by the way side.

_____44.   Either what woman having ten pieces of silver, if she lose one piece, doth not light a candle, and sweep the house, and seek diligently till she find it?

_____45.   And call no man your father upon the earth: for one is your Father, which is in heaven.

_____46.   Now the disciples had forgotten to take bread, neither had they in the ship with them more than one loaf. And he charged them, saying, Take heed, beware of the leaven of the Pharisees, and of the leaven of Herod.

_____47.   The same day went Jesus out of the house, and sat by the sea side.

_____48.   And they entered in, and found not the body of the Lord Jesus.

_____49.   And it came to pass in those days, that there went out a decree from Caesar Augustus, that all the world should be taxed.

_____50.   And many of the people believed on him, and said, When Christ cometh, will he do more miracles than these which this man hath done?

_____51.   When Jesus lifted up his eyes, and saw a great company come unto him, he saith unto Philip, Whence shall we buy bread, that these may eat? And this he said to prove him: for he himself knew what he would do.

_____52.   Now I tell you before it come, that, when it is come to pass, ye may believe that I am he.

_____53.   Come unto me, all ye that labour and are heavy laden, and I will give you rest. Take my yoke upon you, and learn of me; for I am meek and lowly in heart: and ye shall find rest unto your souls. For my yoke is easy, and my burden is light.

_____54.   Search the scriptures; for in them ye think ye have eternal life: and they are they which testify of me.

_____55.   And many other signs truly did Jesus in the presence of his disciples, which are not written in this book.

_____56.   And, behold, there was a great earthquake: for the angel of the Lord descended from heaven, and came and rolled back the stone from the door, and sat upon it.

_____57.   When Jesus therefore had received the vinegar, he said, It is finished: and he bowed his head, and gave up the ghost.

_____58.   After these things the Lord appointed other seventy also, and sent them two and two before his face into every city and place, wither he himself would come.

_____59.   But woe unto you, scribes and Pharisees, hypocrites! For ye shut up the kingdom of heaven against men: for ye neither go in yourselves, neither suffer ye them that are entering to go in.

_____60.   Enter ye in at the strait gate: for wide is the gate, and broad is the way, that leadeth to destruction, and many there be which go in thereat.

_____61.   Nathanael saith unto him, Whence knowest thou me? Jesus answered and said unto him, Before that Philip called thee, when thou wast under the fig tree, I saw thee.

_____62.   Another parable spake he unto them; The kingdom of heaven is like unto leaven, which a woman took, and hid in three measures of meal, till the whole was leavened.

_____63.   Then Joseph her husband, being a just man, and not willing to make her a publick example, was minded to put her away privily.

_____64.   There was in the days of Herod, the king of Judaea, a certain priest named Zacharias, of the course of Abia: and his wife was of the daughters of Aaron, and her name was Elisabeth.

_____65. Marvel not at this: for the hour is coming, in the which all that are in the graves shall hear his voice.

_____66. And he went forth, and preached every where, the Lord working with them, and confirming the word with signs following.

_____67. Then was fulfilled that which was spoken by Jeremy the prophet, saying, And they took the thirty pieces of silver, the price of him that was valued, whom they of the children of Israel did value; and gave them for the potter's field, as the Lord appointed me.

_____68. Think not that I am come to destroy the law, or the prophets: I am not come to destroy, but to fulfil.

_____69. He that believeth on the Son hath everlasting life: and he that believeth not the Son shall not see life; but the wrath of God abideth on him.

_____70. For many are called, but few are chosen.

_____71. And he spake a parable unto them to this end, that men ought always to pray, and not to faint.

_____72. And straightway he called them: and they left their father Zebedee in the ship with the hired servants, and went after him.

_____73. And he ordained twelve, that they should be with him, and that he might send them forth to preach.

_____74. Then said they unto him, Where is thy Father? Jesus answered, Ye neither know me, nor my Father: if ye had known me, ye should have known my Father also.

_____75. And it came to pass, while he blessed them, he was parted from them, and carried up into heaven.

_____76. But as the days of Noe were, so shall also the coming of the Son of man be.

_____77. He that loveth his life shall lose it; and he that hateth his life in this world shall keep it unto life eternal.

_____78. Behold, your house is left unto you desolate.

_____79. He that hateth me hateth my Father also.

_____80. And he looked round about to see her that had done this thing.

_____81. Jesus answered them, Do ye now believe?

_____82. That upon you may come all the righteous blood shed upon the earth, from the blood of righteous Abel unto the blood of Zacharias son of Barachias, whom ye slew between the temple and the altar.

_____83. Behold, a virgin shall be with child, and shall bring forth a son, and they shall call his name Emmanuel, which being interpreted is, God with us.

_____84. But he answered and said, I am not sent but unto the lost sheep of the house of Israel.

_____85. And he sat down, and called the twelve, and saith unto them, If any man desire to be first, the same shall be last of all, and servant of all.

_____86. And I say unto you, That many shall come from the east and west, and shall sit down with Abraham, and Isaac, and Jacob, in the kingdom of heaven. But the children of the kingdom shall be cast out into outer darkness: there shall be weeping and gnashing of teeth.

_____87. Now it came to pass, as they went, that he entered into a certain village: and a certain woman named Martha received him into her house.

_____88. Therefore the Jews sought the more to kill him, because he not only had broken the Sabbath, but said also that God was his Father, making himself equal with God.

_____89. And as the people were in expectation, . . . all men mused in their hearts of John, whether he were the Christ, or not.

_____90. For I say unto you, That except your righteousness shall exceed the righteousness of the scribes and Pharisees, ye shall in no case enter into the kingdom of heaven.

_____91. And he was there in the wilderness forty days, tempted of Satan; and was with the wild beasts; and the angels ministered unto him.

_____92. Then opened he their understanding, that they might understand the scriptures.

_____93. And it came to pass, that as he was praying in a certain place, when he ceased, one of his disciples said unto him, Lord, teach us to pray, as John also taught his disciples.

_____94. There was a certain rich man, which was clothed in purple and fine linen, and fared sumptuously every day: and there was a certain beggar named Lazarus, which was laid at his gate, full of sores.

_____95. For the kingdom of heaven is like unto a man that is an householder, which went out early in the morning to hire labourers into his vineyard.

_____96. The thief cometh not, but for to steal, and to kill, and to destroy: I am come that they might have life, and that they might have it more abundantly.

_____97. And when Jesus came to the place, he looked up, and saw him, and said unto him, Zacchaeus, make haste, and come down; for to day I must abide at thy house.

_____98. And when his friends heard of it, they went out to lay hold on him: for they said, He is beside himself.

_____99. And he said unto them, Verily I say unto you, That there be some of them that stand here, which shall not taste of death, till they have seen the kingdom of God come with power.

_____100. And the angel said unto them, Fear not: for, behold, I bring you good tidings of great joy, which shall be to all people.

_____101. I am the vine, ye are the branches: He that abideth in me, and I in him, the same bringeth forth much fruit: for without me ye can do nothing.

_____102. Notwithstanding, lest we should offend them, go thou to the sea, and cast an hook, and take up the fish that first cometh up; and when thou hast opened his mouth, thou shalt find a piece of money: that take, and give unto them for me and thee.

_____103. These words spake Jesus, and lifted up his eyes to heaven, and said, Father, the hour is come; glorify they Son, that thy Son also may glorify thee.

_____104. And when he had gathered all the chief priests and scribes of the people together, he demanded of them where Christ should be born.

_____105. A wicked and adulterous generation seeketh after a sign; and there shall no sign be given unto it, but the sign of the prophet Jonas. And he left them and departed.

_____106. And he said unto them, Thus it is written, and thus it behoved Christ to suffer, and to rise from the dead the third day: and that repentance and remission of sins should be preached in his name among all nations, beginning at Jerusalem.

_____107. But go rather to the lost sheep of the house of Israel.

_____108. And the graves were opened; and many bodies of the saints which slept arose, and came out of the graves after his resurrection, and went into the holy city, and appeared unto many.

_____109. And many of the Samaritans of that city believed on him for the saying of the woman, which testified, He told me all that ever I did.

_____110. When the even was come, they brought unto him many that were possessed with devils: and he cast out the spirits with his word, and healed all that were sick: that it might be fulfilled which was spoken by Esaias the prophet, saying, Himself took our infirmities, and bare our sicknesses.

_____111. And very early in the morning the first day of the week, they came unto the sepulcher at the rising of the sun. And they said among themselves, Who shall roll us away the stone from the door of the sepulcher?

_____112. As long as I am in the world, I am the light of the world.

_____113. Be ye therefore perfect, even as your Father which is in heaven is perfect.

_____114. Jesus saith unto her, I that speak unto thee am he.

_____115. Jesus answered and said unto him, If a man love me, he will keep my words: and my Father will love him, and we will come unto him, and make our abode with him.

_____116. And because I tell you the truth, ye believe me not.

_____117. Then answered all the people, and said, His blood be on us, and on our children.

_____118.   But the hour cometh, and now is, when the true worshippers shall worship the Father in spirit and in truth: for the Father seeketh such to worship him.

_____119.   And he said unto them, Go ye, and tell that fox, Behold, I cast out devils, and I do cures to day and to morrow, and the third day I shall be perfected.

_____120.   Therefore is the kingdom of heaven likened unto a certain king, which would take account of his servants.

_____121.   And he looked round about on them which sat about him, and said, Behold my mother and my brethren!

_____122.   But Mary kept all these things, and pondered them in her heart.

_____123.   For the Son of man is come to seek and to save that which was lost.

_____124.   And he said unto them, Ye are from beneath; I am from above: ye are of this world; I am not of this world.

_____125.   All things were made by him; and without him was not any thing made that was made.

_____126.   Then Jesus six days before the Passover came to Bethany, where Lazarus was which had been dead, whom he raised from the dead.

_____127.   I am come a light into the world, that whosoever believeth on me should not abide in darkness.

_____128.   But I say unto you, It shall be more tolerable for Tyre and Sidon at the day of judgment, than for you.

_____129.   Let not your heart be troubled: ye believe in God, believe also in me.

_____130.   And it came to pass, when Jesus had made an end of commanding his twelve disciples, he departed thence to teach and to preach in their cities.

_____131.   And he was in the hinder part of the ship, asleep on a pillow: and they awake him, and say unto him, Master, carest thou not that we perish?

_____132.   Martha saith unto him, I know that he shall rise again in the resurrection at the last day.

_____133.   And going on from thence, he saw other two brethren, James the son of Zebedee, and John his brother, in a ship with Zebedee their father, mending their nets; and he called them.

_____134.   And being in an agony he prayed more earnestly: and his sweat was as it were great drops of blood falling down to the ground.

_____135.   And when they had sent away the multitude, they took him even as he was in the ship. And there were also with him other little ships.

_____136.   And these signs shall follow them that believe; In my name shall they cast out devils; they shall speak with new tongues; they shall take up serpents; and if they drink any deadly thing, it shall not hurt them; they shall lay hands on the sick, and they shall recover.

_____137.   And they crucified him, and parted his garments, casting lots: that it might be fulfilled which was spoken by the prophet, They parted my garments among them, and upon my vesture did they cast lots.

_____138. But seek ye first the kingdom of God, and his righteousness; and all these things shall be added unto you.

_____139. Verily, verily, I say unto you, He that heareth my word, and believeth on him that sent me, hath everlasting life, and shall not come into condemnation; but is passed from death unto life.

_____140. At the same time came the disciples unto Jesus, saying, Who is the greatest in the kingdom of heaven?

_____141. And Jesus increased in wisdom and stature, and in favour with God and man.

_____142. So then after the Lord had spoken unto them, he was received up into heaven, and sat on the right hand of God.

_____143. But when thou makest a feast, call the poor, the maimed, the lame, the blind.

_____144. Behold my hands and my feet, that it is I myself: handle me, and see; for a spirit hath not flesh and bones, as ye see me have.

_____145. Then came Peter to him, and said, Lord, how oft shall my brother sin against me, and I forgive him? Till seven times? Jesus saith unto him, I say not unto thee, Until seven times: but, Until seventy times seven.

_____146. So Jesus came again into Cana of Galilee, where he made the water wine. And there was a certain nobleman, whose son was sick at Capernaum.

_____147. And it came to pass, that after three days they found him in the temple, sitting in the midst of the doctors, both hearing them, and asking them questions.

_____148. And when he was come near, he beheld the city, and wept over it.

_____149. So they went, and made the sepulcher sure, sealing the stone, and setting a watch.

_____150. And they worshipped him, and returned to Jerusalem with great joy: and were continually in the temple, praising and blessing God. Amen.

Part 1: Answers

		Reference	**Parallel Passages**
1.	A.	Matt. 12:41	none
2.	A.	Matt. 25:14	none
3.	B.	Mark 6:39-40	Matt. 14:19; Luke 9:14-15; John 6:10
4.	C.	Luke 5:16	Mark 1:45
5.	C.	Luke 10:41-42	none
6.	A.	Matt. 25:34	none
7.	A.	Matt. 12:42	none
8.	D.	John 2:11	none
9.	C.	Luke 23:4	John 18:38
10.	C.	Luke 16:31	none
11.	C.	Luke 1:46	none
12.	C.	Luke 4:16	none
13.	A.	Matt. 5:9	none
14.	C.	Luke 24:15	none
15.	D.	John 1:18	none
16.	C.	Luke 15:4	none
17.	A.	Matt. 26:56	Mark 14:49-50
18.	D.	John 3:7	none
19.	A.	Matt. 5:16	none
20.	A.	Matt. 22:36	Mark 12:28
21.	B.	Mark 2:4	Luke 5:19
22.	C.	Luke 24:8	none
23.	C.	Luke 23:43	none
24.	C.	Luke 1:67-68	none
25.	D.	John 6:67-68	none
26.	A.	Matt. 25:1	none
27.	A.	Matt. 28:18	none
28.	A.	Matt. 12:23	Mark 3:22-24
29.	D.	John 6:32	none
30.	B.	Mark 6:31	none
31.	A.	Matt. 1:6	none
32.	C.	Luke 9:6	Matt. 11:1; Mark 6:12-13
33.	C.	Luke 22:45	Matt. 26:40; Mark 14:37
34.	D.	John 2:6	none
35.	C.	Luke 1:26-27	none
36.	C.	Luke 3:21	Matt. 3:16; Mark 1:10
37.	D.	John 9:38	none
38.	B.	Mark 7:1-3	Matt. 15:1-3
39.	D.	John 1:30	none
40.	C.	Luke 24:12	John 20:3-10
41.	D.	John 10:7	none
42.	D.	John 1:14	none

43.	A.	Matt. 13:19	Luke 8:12
44.	C.	Luke 15:8	none
45.	A.	Matt. 23:9	none
46.	B.	Mark 8:14-15	Matt. 16:5-6
47.	A.	Matt. 13:1	Mark 4:1
48.	C.	Luke 24:3	none
49.	C.	Luke 2:1	none
50.	D.	John 7:30	none
51.	D.	John 6:5-6	Matt. 14:15-16; Mark 6:35-37; Luke 9:12-13
52.	D.	John 13:19	none
53.	A.	Matt. 11:28-30	none
54.	D.	John 5:39	none
55.	D.	John 20:30	none
56.	A.	Matt. 28:2	none
57.	D.	John 19:30	Matt. 27:50; Mark 15:37; Luke 23:46
58.	C.	Luke 10:1	none
59.	A.	Matt. 23:13	none
60.	A.	Matt. 7:13	none
61.	D.	John 1:48	none
62.	A.	Matt. 13:33	none
63.	A.	Matt. 1:19	none
64.	C.	Luke 1:5	none
65.	D.	John 5:28	none
66.	B.	Mark 16:20	none
67.	A.	Matt. 27:9-10	none
68.	A.	Matt. 5:17	none
69.	D.	John 3:36	none
70.	A.	Matt. 22:14	none
71.	C.	Luke 18:1	none
72.	B.	Mark 1:20	Matt. 4:22
73.	B.	Mark 3:14	Matt. 10:5, 11:1; Luke 6:13
74.	D.	John 8:19	none
75.	C.	Luke 24:51	Mark 16:19
76.	A.	Matt. 24:37	none
77.	D.	John 12:25	none
78.	A.	Matt. 23:38	none
79.	D.	John 15:23	none
80.	B.	Mark 5:32	Luke 8:46
81.	D.	John 16:31	none
82.	A.	Matt. 23:35	none
83.	A.	Matt. 1:23	none
84.	A.	Matt. 15:24	none
85.	B.	Mark 9:35	none
86.	A.	Matt. 8:11-12	none
87.	C.	Luke 10:38	none
88.	D.	John 5:18	none

89.	C.	Luke 3:15	none
90.	A.	Matt. 5:20	none
91.	B.	Mark 1:13	Matt. 4:1; Luke 4:1
92.	C.	Luke 24:45	none
93.	C.	Luke 11:1	none
94.	C.	Luke 16:19-20	none
95.	A.	Matt. 20:1	none
96.	D.	John 10:10	none
97.	C.	Luke 19:5	none
98.	B.	Mark 3:21	none
99.	B.	Mark 9:1	Matt. 16:28; Luke 9:27
100.	C.	Luke 2:10	none
101.	D.	John 15:5	none
102.	A.	Matt. 17:27	none
103.	D.	John 17:1	none
104.	A.	Matt. 2:4	none
105.	A.	Matt. 16:4	Mark 8:12
106.	C.	Luke 24:46-47	none
107.	A.	Matt. 10:6	none
108.	A.	Matt. 27:52-53	none
109.	D.	John 4:39	none
110.	A.	Matt. 8:16-17	Mark 1:32-34; Luke 4:40-41
111.	B.	Mark 16:2-3	Luke 24:1-2; John 20:1
112.	D.	John 9:5	none
113.	A.	Matt. 5:48	Luke 6:36
114.	D.	John 4:26	none
115.	D.	John 14:23	none
116.	D.	John 8:45	none
117.	A.	Matt. 27:25	none
118.	D.	John 4:23	none
119.	C.	Luke 13:32	none
120.	A.	Matt. 18:23	none
121.	B.	Mark 3:34	Matt. 12:49
122.	C.	Luke 2:19	none
123.	C.	Luke 19:10	none
124.	D.	John 8:23	none
125.	D.	John 1:3	none
126.	D.	John 12:1	none
127.	D.	John 12:46	none
128.	A.	Matt. 11:22	none
129.	D.	John 14:1	none
130.	A.	Matt. 11:1	Mark 6:12-13; Luke 9:6
131.	B.	Mark 4:38	Matt. 18:25; Luke 8:24
132.	D.	John 11:24	none
133.	A.	Matt. 4:21	Mark 1:19-20
134.	C.	Luke 22:44	none

135.	B.	Mark 4:36	Matt. 8:23; Luke 8:22
136.	B.	Mark 16:17-18	none
137.	A.	Matt. 27:35	Mark 15:24; Luke 23:33; John 19:18
138.	A.	Matt. 6:33	none
139.	D.	John 5:24	none
140.	A.	Matt. 18:1	Mark 9:33-34; Luke 9:46
141.	C.	Luke 2:52	none
142.	B.	Mark 16:19	Luke 24:51
143.	C.	Luke 14:13	none
144.	C.	Luke 24:39	John 20:20
145.	A.	Matt. 18:21-22	none
146.	D.	John 4:46	none
147.	C.	Luke 2:46	none
148.	C.	Luke 19:41	none
149.	A.	Matt. 27:66	none
150.	C.	Luke 24:52-53	none

Part 2: Thought Questions Regarding Specific Gospels

Directions: There are twenty (20) questions in this part of the examination. The answers are found at the end of the test. Give yourself a maximum of five (5) points for each question answered correctly. The total number represents your score as a percentage of 100.

Questions:

1. If Matthew addressed his Gospel to the Jewish people, why does he omit mention of Jewish customs (cf. Mark 7:2-5), Jewish topography (cf. Luke 24:13), and certain Jewish feast (cf. John 6:4), which the other Gospel writers included in their narratives?

2. Some of the differences in the Gospel accounts seem rather trivial, if not contradictory, yet they do, nevertheless, reflect the author's purpose. For example, in recording the Lord's Prayer, Luke says, *"Forgive us our sins"* (11:4), instead of *"Forgive us our debts,"* as found in Matthew 6:12. What is the reason or significance of this difference?

3. Why does Mark describe Jesus as *"the carpenter"* (6:3), whereas Matthew calls Him *"the carpenter's son"* (13:55)?

4. Luke emphasizes the humanity of Jesus Christ. Is there anything in his preface (1:1-4) that would indicate such an emphasis?

5. Why does Matthew—written for the Jew—omit the Judean ministry of Christ—as found in the Gospel of John—together with the discourses that would be understood by the true Israel?

6. Mark contains only four parables, yet the one about the seed growing secretly is unique to this Gospel. What is its significance?

7. Why is the order of Christ's temptations in Matthew (4:1-11) different from that recorded in Luke (4:1-13)?

8. Why does only Mark tell us that Christ was with the wild beasts at the time of His temptation (cf. 1:12-13)?

9. Why does Matthew tell us in narrating the temptation that Jesus was specifically *"led up of the spirit into the wilderness"* for the express purpose of being *"tempted of the devil"* (4:1)?

10. Why is Matthew the only Gospel to introduce the Church?

11. Mark records two miracles which are peculiar to his Gospel; namely, healing the

deaf mute in Decapolis (7:31-37) and the blind man at Bethsaida (8:22-26). How does Jesus' actions in both of these situations reveal the heart of a servant?

12. Another incident in Mark, which reveals the heart of a servant, is Jesus' encounter with the rich young ruler (10:17-27)—a scene common to the other synoptics (cf. Matt. 19:16-26 and Luke 18:18-27). Yet what is different and instructive in Mark's account?

13. Numbers are frequently used in Scripture with symbolic meaning. Three is the number of deity, and as such we might expect John's Gospel to be constructed around this number, in view of the fact that the deity of Christ is a major emphasis. Can you cite two examples where John arranges his material around the number three?

14. The number seven is considered to represent perfection or completed action, whereas the number eight is the figure of the resurrection, or new birth. How does John construct his Gospel around these numbers?

15. All three of the synoptic Gospels record the calling of Peter (Matt. 4:18-22; Mark 1:16-20; Luke 5:1-11). Yet how is Luke's version different, and how does this emphasize his purpose?

16. What is significant about the fact that only Luke records the miraculous catch of fish in the context of the call of Peter?

17. All three of the synoptic Gospels also record Christ's teaching regarding *"new wine"* and *"old bottles"* (cf. Matt. 9:16-17; Mark 2:21-22; Luke 5:36-39). Again, how is Luke's version different, and how does this emphasize his purpose?

18. Why in John's Gospel is not a word said about Jesus' apprehensions of the Cross, as in the other Gospels?

19. There is the principle of adaptation that explains most of the so-called discrepancies among the Gospels. One of the most obvious of these, is the cursing of the fig tree, as found in Matthew 21:18-22 and Mark 11:12-14, 20-25. How does the apparent difference in the time the tree withered suit the specific purpose of these two Gospels?

20. In which Gospel(s) would you expect to find more references to demons—evil or unclean spirits, devils, etc.—and why?

21. Bonus question: A single verse in the Gospel of John provides the only clue in all of Scripture that sheds light on the physical size of Jesus Christ. Where is it found and what does the passage suggest?

Part 2: Answers

1. The other Gospel writers added this material to explain what the reader may not have known or understood. The Jews did not need to be informed of those things that were to them common knowledge.

2. "Trifling as the difference may appear, the instructed eye will see how perfectly it accords with the distinctive character of the respective Gospels. 'Debts' being the thought as connected with a kingdom, where righteousness is the rule; 'sins,' where men generally are regarded, who without law are yet sinners."[1]

3. Because Mark emphasizes Jesus' role as Servant, it is important to relate what Jesus can do, even with His hands. As such, Mark identifies Jesus as a carpenter. Matthew presents Jesus as King, and so identifies Him as the carpenter's son.

4. Luke addressed his Gospel to a man—his friend Theophilus. "Human affection is thus displayed here. A man is to be described, and the writer will draw his friend to the subject 'by the bands of a man.' Then this Evangelist—and this one alone—refers to his own personal knowledge of his subject, 'having had perfect understanding of all things from the very first'; thus bringing something human into his task, which this Gospel presents to us. As another has observed, 'the writer himself appears, as having the faculties and affections of a man exercised about the things which were engaging him.'"[2]

5. "Those preeminently spiritual discourses which constitute the greater part of the fourth Gospel . . . [were] . . . fitted . . . for the Christian, the man already united to Christ by a living faith. One might at first suppose that these teachings were exactly suited to the wants of the Jewish race, since they were addressed directly to those who belonged to that race. But more careful consideration will make it plain that, as they were in the main addressed to that small class of Jews who held the advanced ground on the doctrine of the Messiah, and were possessed of more or less of the true spiritual insight, so they could have proved to the mass of the Jews only a stumbling-block, and were therefore fitted to form a part of that Gospel only which was prepared by John distinctively for the Christian."[3]

6. This parable, found only in Mark, is "an encouragement to servants to sow in faith, and leave the results to Him who only can give increase."[4]

7. You may want to re-read Chapter Ten if you do not know the answer to this question. The reason for the difference in the order of Christ's temptations is explained in the section entitled "The Revelation of Truth for All People."

8. Only Mark tells us that Jesus was with the wild beasts at the time of His temptation. "This is a true mark of him who can serve, that, like David of old, he has, in the wilderness and alone, overcome the lion and the bear before in public he fights against Goliath. Let such as would serve lay this to heart, if called to service, they may expect for a season to be among the wild beasts. Alone with God, let us overcome such. Then we may go forth and fight for, and serve, Israel."[5]

9. Matthew stresses that the Spirit led Jesus into the wilderness for the express purpose of being tempted by the devil. The reason is "the Jew alone felt it to be a necessity that the second Adam, in his work of fulfilling the law and restoring man, should meet and overcome the tempter by whom the first Adam fell."[6]

10. Matthew's Gospel portrays a King and a Kingdom. As such, the Church "is the

body of Christ's followers, called out from the unspiritual world, from the kingdom of darkness, and brought into spiritual obedience to him as their head. Matthew represents Jesus as identifying the Church with the kingdom of heaven, and giving it his divine authority: 'And I say also unto thee, that thou art Peter, and upon this rock will I build my church, and the gates of hell shall not prevail against it. And I will give unto thee the keys of the kingdom of heaven; and whatsoever thou shalt bind on earth shall be bound in heaven; and whatsoever thou shalt loose on earth shall be loosed in heaven' (16:18-20)."[7]

11. Mark "records two miracles, which, as they are peculiar to this Gospel, are also very characteristic of what befits true ministry. The one is the case of 'him who was deaf' (7:32-37); the other, of the blind man at Bethsaida (8:22-26). In both I find not only in word, but in act, the Lord manifesting a desire to throw a veil of secrecy over these gracious actions. And surely this is one unfailing mark of service according to God, 'alms in secret,' 'the right hand ignorant of what the left hand doeth.' This comes out brightly here. We read, 'He took him aside, and charged them that they should tell no man;' again, 'He took the blind man by the hand, and led him out of the town, and said, Neither go into the town, nor tell it to any in the town.' Words like these requiring secrecy, though not so frequently repeated, may be found elsewhere: but acts in which the Servant so remarkably strives to hide Himself, are peculiar to this Gospel. So in the case to the woman of Canaan, here only it is added, 'He entered into a house, and would have no man know it.' For this is perfection in service—to serve unseen, unthanked."[8]

12. "Another secret comes out in those references to the exercises of our Lord's soul, which are quite peculiar to this Gospel. Thus, here only do we read, when the leper came, that 'Jesus was moved with compassion.' The act of healing is mentioned in St. Matthew and St. Luke; but St. Mark alone gives a glimpse of the exercise of heart in our Lord which accompanied the outward service. So in the feeding of the multitude, here again the heart is laid bare: we read that 'When He came out, and saw much people, He was moved with compassion toward them, and began to teach them many things.' So again, when the young ruler comes—a scene common to the other Gospels—here only is it recorded that 'Jesus beholding him, loved him.' This exercise of soul, the secret of all service, comes out in this Gospel, and only here. As a key to service, here it is quite perfect, teaching a lesson many need to learn, that without love the most costly service will be unlike the Lord's, and all barren."[9]

13. John is the Gospel of symbolism, "and mystic numbers prevail even throughout the arrangement of the topics. . . . The arrangement of the book is throughout constructed with direct references to the sacred numbers three and seven. Almost all the sub-sections run in triplets. 'Jesus is thrice in Galilee, thrice in Judea, twice three feasts take place during His ministry, and particularly three Passover feasts—in the beginning, the middle, the end—which either foretell or procure His death. He works three miracles in Galilee and three in Jerusalem. Twice three days is He in the neighborhood of John; three days are covered by the narrative of Lazarus, and six by the fatal Passover. He utters three sayings on the Cross, and appears thrice after His Resurrection.' The grouping round three Passovers is part of St. John's original plan (2:13; 6:4; 11:55).[10]

14. John records seven miracles of Christ's earthly ministry, whereas the eighth and final miracle in his Gospel is the post-resurrection miracle of the draught of fish.

15. Luke addressed his Gospel to the thinking Greek, and emphasized the humanity of Jesus Christ. "Closely allied with this special regard for man as such, is the fact that throughout this Gospel in passages peculiar to St. Luke, man as he is in his thoughts and ways, is searched and manifested in a truly wondrous manner. Take, for example, the particulars of the call of Peter, as recorded here. This call is very briefly mentioned in the other Gospels; but here only are we shown the feelings of a man, when for the first time he feels that God and His power are really brought near to him. He has been unsuccessful in fishing. The Lord bids him let down the net. A great multitude of fish is at once caught, insomuch that the net broke. Then Peter is astonished, and falls down, and says, 'Depart from me, for I am a sinful man, O Lord." Many secrets of the heart are here. A little matter, a draught of fishes, some providential occurrence, and it may be very slight, at times flashes in upon a man whom the Lord is leading, making him feel that God is very near him. When this is the case, man at once discovers that he is sinful, and as such would have the glory, which shows him his littleness, to depart from him. All this, as it is peculiar here, is quite in keeping, as showing man as he is."[11]

16. Fish in the sea is symbolic of the universal extent of the Gospel, which is a key element in Luke's narrative (cf. 2:10).

17. "The scene generally, and the conversation touching 'new wine and old bottles,' is in three of the Gospels; but here only are we carefully told the effect produced by drinking the old wine. In this another secret of human nature is disclosed, as to the power of habit and association to affect and bind the soul of man. If we indulge ourselves with the old wine, the excitements of the flesh, the new wine of the kingdom will not be relished by us. He that drinks the old will not desire the new; indeed, while the savor of the old remains, though the new far surpasses the old, he will yet say, 'The old is better.' St. Luke, and it is perfect here where man is the object before the mind of the Spirit, gives us, in what is peculiar to his Gospel, many fine touches of this nature. . . ."[12]

18. John says not a word about Jesus' apprehensions of the Cross, because he emphasizes the deity of Christ. "Here He stands as it were above His sorrows. In St. Luke (18:32), He may speak of being 'delivered to the Gentiles, and mocked, and spitefully entreated, and spitted on.' All this is entirely omitted here. Instead of speaking of His griefs, the Son of the Father, . . . is occupied in pouring comfort into His disciples' hearts. . . . Throughout He is the incarnate Word. 'Jesus, knowing all things that should come upon Him, went forth, and said unto them, Whom seek ye? They answered, Jesus of Nazareth. Jesus saith unto them, I am He. As soon as He had said unto them, I am He, they went backward, and fell to the ground.' Here, instead of weakness and agony, is power appalling His adversaries. Then again, instead of seeking sympathy from His disciples, here He is seen as possessing and exercising the power to protect them: 'Jesus saith, I have told you that I am He. If therefore ye seek me, let these go their way; that the saying might be fulfilled which He spake, Of them which Thou gavest me I have lost none.' Surely here is both the peace, and the power, of heaven, even in the bitter cross. He stands as One from whom no one can take His life, unless He please to lay it down."[13]

19. In Mark's Gospel the story is told for its prophetic significance. "Note that between the cursing and the withering Jesus pronounces a similar judgment on Judaism by His cleansing of the temple. However, the story of the fig tree had great meaning for the early church also because of the lesson on faith that concludes it. In Matthew's Gospel the lesson on faith is the sole interest of the story, so he relates the cursing and the withering together in order to emphasize this point."[14]

20. One would expect to find more references to demons in Mark and Luke, rather than Matthew or John, but you can check this out for yourself. In Mark Jesus is presented as the miracle-working prophet of God, whose ministry was summarized with the words, "And he preached in their synagogues throughout all Galilee, and cast out devils" (1:39). In the Gospel of Luke, addressed to the Greeks, one would also expect numerous references to demons. The Greeks were looking for the perfect man physically—as seen in their art and sculpture—as well as intellectually—as evidenced in their literature and philosophy—and demons would be of special interest to them, because of their superhuman strength (cf. Luke 8:29) and knowledge. "Plato's etymology of daimon from an adjective meaning 'knowledge' or 'intelligent' (Cratylus I, 39) points to intelligence or knowledge as the basic characteristic of demonic nature."[15] The Greeks, remember, represent the thinking man of antiquity.

21. The verse is John 19:39. The common burial practice was to use one-half the body weight in spices, suggesting that the Lord weighed about 200 pounds.

[1] Andrew Jukes, *Four Views of Christ*, edited by James Shiffer Kiefer (Grand Rapids, Mich.: Kregel Publications, 1982), 82-83.

[2] *Ibid.*, 73.

[3] D. S. Gregory, *Why Four Gospels? Or, the Gospel for All the World* (New York: Funk & Wagnalls, Publishers, 1890), 132.

[4] Jukes, *op. cit.*, 56.

[5] *Ibid.*, 61.

[6] Gregory, *op. cit.*, 144.

[7] *Ibid.*, 146-47.

[8] Jukes, *op. cit.*, 66.

[9] *Ibid.*, 67.

[10] F. W. Farrar, *The Messages of the Books Being Discourses and Notes on the Books of the New Testament* (New York: E. P. Dutton & Co., 1885), 112-13.

[11] Jukes, *op. cit.*, 80-81.

[12] *Ibid.*, 81.

[13] *Ibid.*, 104-06.

[14] Gordon D. Fee and Douglas Stuart, *How to Read the Bible for All Its Worth: A Guide to Understanding the Bible* (Grand Rapids, Mich.: Zondervan Publishing House, 1982), 115-16.

[15] "Demons," *The Living Bible Encyclopedia in Story and Pictures* (1968), 4:547.

Bibliography

Alexander, Joseph Addison. *The Gospel According to Mark*. London: The Banner of Truth Trust, 1960.

Alexander, William. *The Leading Ideas of the Gospels*. London: Macmillan and Co., 1892.

Anderson, Bernhard. *Rediscovering the Bible*. New York: Haddam House, 1954.

Bailey, Albert Edward. *The Gospel in Art*. Boston: The Pilgrim Press, 1946.

Baker, Jeffrey J. W., and Garland E. Allen. *The Study of Biology*. Reading, Mass.: Addison-Wesley Publishing Company, 1967.

Barclay, William. *The Letter to the Hebrews*, rev. ed. Philadelphia: The Westminster Press, 1977.

Barnett, Albert E. *The New Testament: Its Making and Meaning*. New York: Abingdon Press, 1946.

Barrow, R. H. *The Romans*. Baltimore: Penguin Books, 1961.

Battenhouse, Henry M. *Christ in the Gospels: An Introduction to His Life and Its Meaning*. New York: The Ronald Press Company, 1952.

Bauman, Edward A. *An Introduction to the New Testament*. Philadelphia: The Westminster Press, 1961.

Beliles, Mark A., and Stephen K. McDowell. *America's Providential History*. Charlottesville, Va.: Providence Foundation, 1994.

Bowra, C. M. et. al. *Classical Greece*. New York: Time, Inc., 1965.

Breed, David R. *A History of the Preparation of the World for Christ*. Chicago: Young Men's Era Publishing Co., 1891.

Burchkhardt, Jacob. *The Civilization of the Renaissance in Italy*. New York: Barnes & Noble, Inc., 1999.

Cheney, Sheldon. *A New World History of Art*. New York: Holt, Rinehart and Winston, 1963.

Clarke, William Newton. *An Outline of Christian Theology*. New York: Charles Scribner's Sons, 1898.

Clarke, William Newton. *The Ideal of Jesus*. New York: Charles Scribner's Sons, 1911.

Colwell, Ernest Cadman, and Eric Lane Titus. *The Gospel of the Spirit: A Study in the Fourth Gospel*. New York: Harper & Brothers Publishers, 1953.

Combee, Jerry H. *The History of the World in Christian Perspective, Vol. I*. Pensacola, Fla.: A Beka Book Publications, 1979.

Copeland, Lewis, editor. *The World's Great Speeches*. New York: The Book League of America, 1942.

Cottrell, Leonard. *The Anvil of Civilization*. New York: The New American Library, Inc., 1957.

Daniel-Rops, Henri. *Daily Life in the Time of Jesus*. Patrick O'Brian, translator. New York: Hawthorne Books, Inc., 1962.

Deane, Anthony C. *How to Understand the Gospels*. New York: Harper & Brothers Publishers, 1929.

DeWitt, William A. *History's Hundred Greatest Events in the Record of Mankind from the Dawn of Civilization to the Present Day*. New York: Grosset & Dunlap, Publishers, 1954.

Durant, Will, and Ariel Durant. *The Lessons of History*. New York: Simon and Schuster, 1968.

Edersheim, Alfred. *The Temple: Its Ministry and Services*. Peabody, Mass.: Hendrickson Publishers, Inc., 1994.

Ellicott, C. J. *Historical Lectures on the Life of Our Lord Jesus Christ, Being the Hulsean Lectures for the Year 1859*. With Notes, Critical, Historical, and Explanatory. Boston: Gould and Lincoln, 1867.

Ellicott, Charles John, ed. *The Gospel According to St. Matthew*, with commentary by E. H. Plumptre. London: Cassell & Company, Limited, n.d.

English, E. Schuyler. *Studies in the Gospel According to Matthew*. New York: Our Hope, 1943.

Enslin, Morton Scott. *Christian Beginnings: Parts I and II*. New York: Harper & Row, Publishers, 1956.

Enslin, Morton Scott. *The Literature of the Christian Movement*. New York: Harper & Brothers, 1956.

Erdman, Charles R. *The Acts*. Philadelphia: The Westminster Press, n.d.

Erdman, Charles R. *The Gospel of John*. Philadelphia: The Westminster Press, 1944.

Erdman, Charles R. *The Gospel of Luke*. Philadelphia: The Westminster Press, 1949.

Erdman, Charles R. *The Gospel of Mark*. Philadelphia: The Westminster Press, 1945.

Erdman, Charles R. *The Gospel of Matthew*. Philadelphia: The Westminster Press, 1948.

Farrar, F. W. *The Messages of the Books Being Discourses and Notes on the Books of the New Testament*. New York: E. P. Dutton & Co., 1885.

Farrar, Frederic W. *The Life of Christ*. London: Cassell and Company, Limited, 1896.

Fee, Gordon D., and Douglas Stuart. *How to Read the Bible for All Its Worth: A Guide to Understanding the Bible*. Grand Rapids, Mich.: Zondervan Publishing House, 1982.

Fleetwood, John. *The Life of Our Blessed Lord and Savior Jesus Christ: and the Lives and Sufferings of His Holy Evangelists and Apostles*. Philadelphia: J. W. Bradley, 48 North Fourth St., 1858.

Fleetwood, John. *The Life of Our Lord and Savior Jesus Christ; Containing a Full, Accurate, and Universal History from His Taking Upon Himself Our Nature to His Crucifixion, Resurrection and Ascension: Together with the Lives, Transactions, and Sufferings of His Holy Evangelists, Apostles, Disciples, and Other Primitive Martyrs. To Which Is Added the History of the Jews*. New Haven: Published by Nathan Whiting, 1831.

Gardner, Helen. *Art Through the Ages*, 4th ed. Sumner McK. Crosby, ed. New York: Harcourt, Brace & World, Inc., 1959.

Gibbon, Edward. *The History of the Decline and Fall of the Roman Empire*, 3 vols. David Womersley, ed. London: Penguin Books, Ltd., 1995.

Gibson, George M. *A History of New Testament Times*. Nashville, Tenn.: Cokesbury Press, 1926.

Gilbert, T. W. *The Gospel According to St. John*, 2 vols. London: The Religious Tract Society, n.d.

Gisborne, Thomas. *A Familiar Survey of the Christian Religion, and of History As Connected with the Introduction of Christianity, and with Its Progress to the Present Time*, 6th ed. London: Printed for T. Cadell and W. Davies, in the Strand, 1816.

Godet, F. *Commentary on the Gospel of St. John*, 3rd ed. M. D. Cusin, translator. Edinburgh: T. & T. Clark, 1887.

Godet, Frederic L. *Studies in the New Testament*. New York: E. P. Dutton & Co., 1895.

Grace, Perce C. *Outlines of History*. New York: Edward Dunigan and Brother, 1851.

Grant, Michael. *The Founders of the Western World: A History of Greece and Rome*. New York: Charles Scribner's Sons, 1991.

Gray, James M. *Christian Workers' Commentary on the Whole Bible*. Old Tappan, N.J.: Fleming H. Revell Company, 1973.

Greer, Thomas H. *A Brief History of Western Man*. New York: Harcourt, Brace & World, Inc., 1968.

Gregory, D. S. *Why Four Gospels? Or, the Gospel for All the World*. New York: Funk & Wagnalls, Publishers, 1890.

Guyot, Arnold. *Physical Geography*. New York: Charles Scribner's Sons, 1873.

Hadas, Moses, and the editors of Time-Life Books. *Imperial Rome*. New York: Time Incorporated, 1965.

Halley, Henry H. *Halley's Bible Handbook*, 24th ed. Grand Rapids, Mich.: Zondervan Publishing House, 1965.

Hartt, Frederick. *History of Italian Renaissance Art*. New York: Harry N. Abrams, Inc., Publishers, 1969.

Hartt, Frederick. *Michelangelo*. New York: Harry N. Abrams, Inc., Publishers, 1984.

Hayes, D. A. *The Synoptic Gospels and the Book of Acts*. New York: The Methodist Book Concern, 1919.

Henry, Carl F. H. ed. *The Biblical Expositor*. Philadelphia: A. J. Holman Company, 1973.

Henry, Matthew. *Commentary on the Whole Bible*, One Volume Edition. Dr. Leslie F. Church, ed. Grand Rapids, Mich.: Zondervan Publishing House, 1961.

Herodotus. *The Histories*. George Rawlinson, translator, with Introduction by Rosalind Thomas. New York: Alfred A. Knopf, Inc., 1997.

Herodotus. *The Histories*. Robin Waterfield, translator, with Introduction and Notes by Carolyn DeWard. New York: Oxford University Press, Inc., 1998.

Hiebert, D. Edmond. *An Introduction to the New Testament Volume 1: The Gospels and Acts*. Winona Lake, Ind.: BMH Books, 1993.

Hoag, Edwin. *The Roads of Man*. New York: G. P. Putnam's Sons, 1967.

Hutchinson, Horace G. *The Greatest Story in the World*. New York: D. Appleton and Company, 1923.

Hutchison, William G., translator. *Renan's Life of Jesus*. London: Walter Scott Publishing Co., Ltd., n.d.

Ice, Thomas, and Randall Price. *Ready to Rebuild: The Imminent Plan to Rebuild the Last Days Temple*. Eugene, Ore.: Harvest House Publishers, 1992.

Ironside, H. A. *Mark*, rev. ed. Neptune, N.J.: Loizeaux Brothers, Inc., 1994.

Janson, H. W. *History of Art: A Survey of the Major Visual Arts from the Dawn of History to the Present Day*. Englewood Cliffs, N.J.: Prentice-Hall, Inc., 1964.

Jenkyn, Thomas W. *The Extent of the Atonement in Its Relation to God and the Universe*. Boston: Gould and Lincoln, 1859.

Johnson, B. W. *The New Testament Commentary: Volume III-John*. St. Louis: Christian Publishing Company, 1886.

Johnson, Paul. *A History of the Jews*. New York: Harper & Row, Publishers, 1987.

Jones, E. Stanley. *Christ and Human Suffering*. New York: The Abingdon Press, 1933.

Jukes, Andrew. *Four Views of Christ*. James Shiffer Kiefer, ed. Grand Rapids, Mich.: Kregel Publications, 1982.

Jukes, Andrew. *The Characteristic Differences of the Four Gospels*. New York: Fleming H. Revell Company, n.d.

Keller, Harald. *The Renaissance in Italy*. Robert E. Wolf, translator. New York: Harry N. Abrams, Inc., Publishers, 1969.

Keller, Werner. *The Bible as History*, 2nd rev. ed. William Neil, translator. New York: Bantam Books, 1980.

Kennett, Basil. *The Antiquities of Rome*. Dublin: Printed for J. Exshaw, and H. Bradley, in Dame-Street, 1767.

Knackfuss, H. *Raphael*. Campbell Dodgson, translator. Leipzig: Velhagen & Klasing, 1899.

Krummacher, F. W. *The Suffering Savior: Meditations on the Last Days of Christ*. Chicago: Moody Press, 1948.

Kummer, Frederic Arnold. *The Earth's Story*, 3 vols. New York: George H. Doran Company, 1925.

Larned, J. N. *Larned's History of the World or Seventy Centuries of the Life of Mankind*. 5 vols. New York: World Syndicate Company, Inc., 1915.

Lasor, William Sanford. *Great Personalities of the New Testament: Their Lives and Times*. Westwood, N.J.: Fleming H. Revell Company, 1961.

Lawson, George. *The Life of Joseph*. 1807; reprint, Southampton, Great Britain: The Camelot Press, 1988.

Lockyer, Herbert. *All the Miracles of the Bible*. Grand Rapids, Mich.: Zondervan Publishing House, 1965.

MacArthur, John, Jr. *God: Coming Face to Face with His Majesty*. Wheaton, Ill.: Victor Books, 1993.

Machen, J. Gresham. *The New Testament: An Introduction to Its Literature and History*. W. John Cook, ed. Edinburgh: The Banner of Truth Trust, 1997.

Major, H. D. A., et. al. *The Mission and Message of Jesus*. New York: E. P. Dutton and Co., Inc., 1951.

Martin, Earl L. *The Gospel of Luke: An Exposition*. Anderson, Ind.: Gospel Trumpet Company, 1944.

Maus, Cynthia Pearl. *Christ and the Fine Arts*. New York: Harper & Row, Publishers, 1959.

McGee, J. Vernon. *John*, 2 vols. Pasadena, Calif.: Thru the Bible Books, 1987.

McGee, J. Vernon. *Matthew*, 2 vols. Pasadena, Calif.: Thru the Bible Books, 1980.

Mears, Henrietta C. *What the Bible Is All About*. Glendale, Calif.: Regal Books Division, Gospel Light Publications, 1966.

Milman, H. H., ed. *Introduction and Notes to The History of the Decline and Fall of the Roman Empire* by Edward Gibbon, 6 vols. Boston: Phillips, Sampson, and Company, 1856.

Milman, H. H. *The History of the Jews from the Earliest Period to the Present Time*, 3 vols. New York: Harper & Brothers, Cliff St., 1837.

Moorehead, William. *Studies in the Four Gospels*. Philadelphia: The Westminster Press, 1900.

Morgan, G. Campbell. *The Analyzed Bible*. New York: Fleming H. Revell Company,

1908.

Morgan, G. Campbell. *The Crises of the Christ*. Old Tappan, N.J.: Fleming H. Revell Company, 1936.

Morgan, G. Campbell. *The Gospel According to Luke*. Westwood, N.J.: Fleming H. Revell Company, 1931.

Moulton, Richard G., ed. *The Modern Reader's Bible: St. Matthew and St. Mark and the General Epistles*. New York: The Macmillan Company, 1898.

Myers, P. V. N. *A General History for Colleges and High Schools*. Boston: Ginn & Company, 1903.

Myers, Philip Van Ness. *Ancient History*. Boston: Ginn & Company, 1904.

Nast, William. *The Gospel Records: Their Genuineness, Authenticity, Historic Verity, and Inspiration, with Some Preliminary Remarks on the Gospel History*. Cincinnati: Cranston and Stowe, 1866.

National Geographic Society. *Greece and Rome: Builders of Our World*. Washington, D.C.: National Geographic Society, 1968.

Painter, F. V. N. *A History of Education*. New York: D. Appleton and Co., 1886.

Pentecost, J. Dwight. *Things to Come: A Study in Biblical Eschatology*. Grand Rapids, Mich.: Zondervan Publishing House, 1964.

Pink, Arthur W. *Why Four Gospels?* Swengel, Penn.: Bible Truth Depot, 1921.

Pinnock's Improved Edition of Dr. Goldsmith's History of Greece. Philadelphia: F. W. Greenough, 1838.

Plummer, Alfred. *The Gospel According to St. John*. Cambridge: The University Press, 1912.

Plummer, Alfred. *The International Critical Commentary: A Critical and Exegetical Commentary on the Gospel According to St. Luke*, 4th ed. Edinburgh: T. & T. Clark, 38 George Street, 1901.

Quimby, Chester Warren. *John: The Universal Gospel*. New York: The Macmillan Company, 1947.

Ramsay, Sir William. *The Bearing of Recent Discoveries on the Truthfulness of the New Testament*, 4th ed. London: Hodder & Stoughton, Ltd., 1920.

Ramsay, William M. *St. Paul the Traveller and the Roman Citizen*. New York: G. P. Putnam's Sons, 1904.

Reader's Digest Family Guide to the Bible: A Concordance and Reference Companion to the King James Version. Pleasantville, N.Y.: The Reader's Digest Association, Inc., 1984..

Renan, Joseph Ernest. *Les Evangiles et la Seconde Generation Chretienne*. 1877.

Rifkin, Jeremy. *Algeny*. New York: The Viking Press, 1983.

Robbins, Royal. *The World Displayed, in Its History and Geography; Embracing A History of the World, from the Creation to the Present Day*. New York: Published by H. Savage, 1833.

Roberts, J. M. *A Concise History of the World*. New York: Oxford University Press, 1995.

Robinson, Nugent. *A History of the World with All Its Great Sensations together with Its Mighty and Decisive Battles and the Rise and Fall of Its Nations from the Earliest Times to the Present Day*. New York: P. F. Collier, Publisher, 1887.

Rollin, Charles. *The Ancient History of the Egyptians, Carthaginians, Assyrians, Babylonians, Medes and Persians, Macedonians and Grecians*, 4 vols. Translated from the

French. New York: Published by William Borradaile, 1825.

Russell, D. S. *Between the Testaments*. Philadelphia: Fortress Press, 1975.

Rutter, Frank. *The Old Masters*. New York: George H. Doran Company, n.d.

Sanday, W. *Outlines of the Life of Christ*. New York: Charles Scribner's Sons, 1905.

Schaff, Philip. *The Person of Christ: The Perfection of His Humanity Viewed as a Proof of His Divinity*, 12th ed. New York: American Tract Society, 1882.

Scott, E. F. *The Fourth Gospel: Its Purpose and Theology*. Edinburgh: T. & T. Clark, 1920.

Scott, Ernest Findlay. *The Literature of the New Testament*. New York: Columbia University Press, 1940.

Severy, Merle, ed. *Greece and Rome: Builders of Our World*. Washington, D.C.: The National Geographic Society, 1971.

Smith, H. Framer. *Why Four Gospel Accounts?* Philadelphia: Westbrook Publishing Company, 1941.

Smith, Huston. *The Religions of Man*. New York: Harper & Row, Publishers, 1989.

Smith, William. *A History of Greece from the Earliest Times to the Roman Conquest*. Boston: Hickling, Swan, and Brown, 1855.

Soltau, George. *Four Portraits of the Lord Jesus Christ*. New York: Charles C. Cook, n.d.

Spielvogel, Jackson J. *Western Civilization. Volume I: To 1715*, 2nd ed. Minneapolis/St. Paul: West Publishing Company, 1994.

Spivey, Robert A., and D. Moody Smith, Jr. *Anatomy of the New Testament: A Guide to Its Structure and Meaning*, 2nd ed. New York: Macmillan Publishing Co., Inc., 1974.

Stebbing, Rev. H. *Introduction to The Life and Works of Flavius Josephus*. William Whiston, translator. Philadelphia: The John C. Winston Company, n.d.

Stob, Henry. *Ethical Reflections: Essays on Moral Themes*. Grand Rapids, Mich.: William B. Eerdmans Publishing Company, 1978.

Stob, Ralph. *Christianity and Classical Civilization*. Grand Rapids, Mich.: William B. Eerdmans Publishing Company, 1950.

Suetonius. *The Twelve Caesars*. Robert Graves, translator. Harmondsworth, Middlesex, England: Penguin Books, Ltd., 1978.

Talmage, T. DeWitt. *From Manger to Throne*. Philadelphia: Historical Publishing Company, 1889.

Tarbell, F. B. *A History of Greek Art*. Meadville, Penn.: The Chautauqua-Century Press, 1896.

Thomson, Edward A. *The Four Evangelists; with the Distinctive Characteristics of Their Gospels*. Edinburgh: T. & T. Clark, 38 George Street, 1868.

Tozer, A. W. *The Pursuit of God*. Wheaton, Ill.: Tyndale House Publishers, n.d.

Trench, Richard Chenevix. *Notes on the Miracles of Our Lord*, 6th ed. London: John W. Parker and Son, West Strand, 1858.

Trevor-Roper, Hugh R. *Introduction to The Decline and Fall of the Roman Empire* by Edward Gibbon. New York: Twayne Publishers, Inc., 1963.

Van Oosterzee, J. J. *The Theology of the New Testament: A Handbook for Bible Students*. Maurice J. Evans, translator. New York: Dodd & Mead, Publishers, 1875.

Vezzosi, Alessandro. *Leonardo da Vinci: The Mind of the Renaissance*. New York: Harry N. Abrams, Inc., Publishers, 1997.

Walvoord, John F. *Israel in Prophecy*. Grand Rapids, Mich.: Zondervan Publishing

House, 1980.

Warner, Rex. *The Greek Philosophers.* New York: The New American Library of World Literature, Inc., 1962.

Wells, H. G. *The Outline of History,* 4th ed. in 4 vols. New York: P. F. Collier & Son Company, 1925.

West, Willis Mason. *The Ancient World from the Earliest Times to 800 A.D.* Boston: Allyn and Bacon, 1904.

Westcott, B. F. *The Gospel According to St. John.* London: John Murray, Albemarle Street, 1908.

Westcott, Brooke Foss. *An Introduction to the Study of the Gospels.* London: Macmillan & Co., 1875.

Westcott, Brooke Foss. *Christus Consummator: Some Aspects of the Work and Person of Christ in Relation to Modern Thought.* London: Macmillan and Co., 1890.

Whedon, D. D. *Commentary on the Gospels: Luke-John.* New York: Carlton and Porter, 1866.

Whiston, William, translator. *The Life and Works of Flavius Josephus.* Philadelphia: The John C. Winston Company, n.d.

Willard, Emma. *Universal History in Perspective: Divided into Three Parts, Ancient, Middle, and Modern,* rev. ed. New York: A. S. Barnes & Company, 1855.

Williams, Rosemary, ed. *Gibbon's Decline and Fall of the Roman Empire,* abridged and illustrated. Chicago: Rand McNally & Company, 1979.